Pauline Elizabeth Hopkins

Pauline Elizabeth Hopkins

Black Daughter *of the* Revolution

L O I S   B R O W N

The University of

North Carolina Press

Chapel Hill

THIS VOLUME WAS PUBLISHED WITH THE
ASSISTANCE OF THE GREENSBORO WOMEN'S FUND OF
THE UNIVERSITY OF NORTH CAROLINA PRESS.
*Founding Contributors: Linda Arnold Carlisle, Sally Schindel
Cone, Anne Faircloth, Bonnie McElveen Hunter, Linda Bullard
Jennings, Janice J. Kerley (in honor of Margaret Supplee Smith),
Nancy Rouzer May, and Betty Hughes Nichols.*

Manufactured in the United States of America
Designed by Eric M. Brooks
Set in Sabon and Bernhard Modern by
Tseng Information Systems, Inc.

The paper in this book meets the guidelines for permanence
and durability of the Committee on Production Guidelines for
Book Longevity of the Council on Library Resources.

Library of Congress Cataloging-in-Publication Data
Brown, Lois, 1966–
Pauline Elizabeth Hopkins : Black daughter of the revolution /
Lois Brown.
p. cm. — (Gender and American culture)
Includes bibliographical references and index.
ISBN 978-0-8078-3166-3 (alk. paper)
1. Hopkins, Pauline E. (Pauline Elizabeth) 2. Authors, American—
19th century—Biography. 3. Authors, American—20th century—
Biography. 4. African American women authors—Biography.
5. African American journalists—Biography. 6. African American
women—Intellectual life. 7. African Americans in literature.
8. African Americans—History—1877-1964. 9. Racism—
United States—History—20th century. 10. United States—Race
relations—History—20th century. I. Title.
PS1999.H4226Z58 2008
818'.409—dc22 2007048985
[B]

12 11 10 09 08 5 4 3 2 1

for

Pauline Elizabeth Hopkins

and her family and ancestors

whose lives, ambitions, resilience, & actions

made this story possible

and offered with much love to

my cherished family

Contents

Illustrations

Acknowledgments

This biography is a testament to the ways in which family, friends, librarians, and genuinely interested folk make all the difference in one's writing life. Many individuals in and beyond New England have shaped this book and its author in subtle and dramatic ways. I offer heartfelt thanks to all who have engaged with me fully and sincerely as this book came to fruition.

This project began in graduate school, and my dissertation adviser, Chris Wilson, and doctoral program adviser, Robin Lydenberg, offered early and instrumental mentoring and perspectives on the possibilities and demands of scholarship, research, and writing. They and my graduate school professors Anne Ferry, Henry Blackwell, Paul Doherty, Carol Hurd Green, Dayton Haskin, Laura Tanner, Jim Wallace, and Judith Wilt encouraged critical engagement at many stages of learning and writing. Graduate school deans Donald White and Pat DeLeeuw offered memorable welcomes to Chestnut Hill and grants that enabled some of the earliest research for this project. Cornell University colleagues Dorothy Mermin, Joan Jacobs Brumberg, and Margaret Washington have inspired, exhorted, and accompanied me at critical moments in my professional life and in the life of this evolving work of literary history and biography. Their friendship and their faith in the power and delight of the word have been invaluable. Jonathan Culler and Dominick LaCapra provided helpful support during my time at Cornell and in my year as a faculty fellow at the A. D. White Center for the Humanities. At Mount Holyoke College, Rochelle Calhoun, Carolyn Collette, Edwina Cruise, Amber Douglas, Harold Garrett-Goodyear, Leah Glasser, John Grayson, Amy Martin, Jillian McLeod, Bonnie Miller, Lynda Morgan, Karen Remmler, Lauret Savoy, Sally Sutherland, and Lucas Wilson make even richer the time spent in the history-laden ivory tower that we share. President Joanne Creighton and my colleagues in the Department of English and the African and African American Studies Program have provided invaluable support. Former and current deans of the faculty Peter Berek and Donal O'Shea, respectively, have provided steady mentoring, hearty collegial inspiration, and much-appreciated research funds. John Gruesser gave me the first opportunity to present my work on Pauline Hopkins, and he has been a most inspiring and generous colleague.

Beverly Morgan-Welch, executive director of the Museum of African-

American History in Boston, invited me to spend time in the place where the Boston story of Pauline Hopkins began. For the chance to dwell in the sanctuary that is the African Meeting House and contribute to the museum's illuminating exhibitions and programs that honor our nation's substantial African American histories, I thank her. Museum staff and colleagues Chandra Harrington and L'Merchie Frazier are true stewards of the past and present, and for their friendship, professionalism, and creative example, I thank them.

For the gifts of time, succor, sanctuary, and food that enabled more thoughts, friendship, and encouragement, I offer truly heartfelt thanks to Dacia Gentillella, Catherine John, Barbara Sicherman, Maryemma Graham, Cynthia King, Eleanor Shattuck, Alexandra Kallenbach, Peggy Ramirez, Elizabeth Stordeur-Pryor, Sara Wolper, Amy Daudelin, Martha Hopkins, Wolfsong, Patrice Scott, Alycia Smith-Howard, Kathy Washburn, Kay Washburn, Rachel and Leslie Cooke, Jill Watts, and Robin Lydenberg. For their gracious and energizing friendship, I thank Mark Welch, Alexandra Morgan-Welch, Margaret Rakas, Bret Jackson, Janiece Leach, Kate Rindy, Elizabeth Savage, Pat Scigliano, Janet Lansberry, Maryanne Alos, Patricia Ware, and Sarah Somé. Missed deeply, always treasured, and I hope pleased by this moment of publication is Richard Newman, a friend with whom the nineteenth century came alive and the present became more and absolutely real.

Faculty, research, and visiting fellowships at the Society for the Humanities at Cornell University, the W. E. B. Du Bois Center for African and African American Research at Harvard University, the American Antiquarian Society, and the Massachusetts Historical Society provided time for full immersion in the project and vital archival research. A Ford Foundation postdoctoral fellowship was instrumental to the completion of this manuscript. A Mount Holyoke Faculty Fellowship also provided key support. This book has also been made possible by grants from the Humanities Council of the Society for the Humanities and the President's Council for Cornell Women at Cornell University.

Librarians, archivists, and staff at the following institutions contributed to the foundational research for this volume: American Antiquarian Society; Boston Public Library; Historic New England; Massachusetts State Archives; Suffolk County Courthouse; Museum of African American History; Exeter Historical Society; New Hampshire Historical Society; Olin Library at Cornell University; Franklin Library Special Collections at Fisk University; Brown University Special Collections; Schomburg Center for Research in Black Culture, The New York Public Library; Maine State Archives; Maine Historical Society; Portland Room of the Portland Public Library, Maine;

Library of Congress; Moorland-Spingarn Research Center at Howard University; National Archives; National Portrait Gallery; Sisters of the Holy Family Archives; Archdiocesan Archives of New Orleans; Dillard University Library; North Carolina State Archives; New Bern Historical Society; and New Bern Public Library. The Sisters of the Holy Family in New Orleans, especially Mother Mary de Chantal, Sr. Sylvia Thibodeaux, and Sr. Eva Regina, were inspiring and gracious hosts who so warmly shared the order's history and hopes. Nancy Merrill of the Exeter Historical Society honored my early interest in the world of Caesar Nero Paul, and her enthusiasm and openness laid a sure foundation for this project. Sally Farnham, Stacy Pringle, Nancy Carter Moore, Richard Foster, and Diane Lee provided helpful editorial support and research, and their attention to details and organization contributed to this project.

For their assistance with images and permission to publish illustrations included in this volume, I thank the Franklin Library Special Collections at Fisk University, former archives librarian Anne Allen Shockley and chief archivist Beth Howse; National Portrait Gallery, Washington, D.C.; Photographs and Prints Division, Schomburg Center for Research in Black Culture, The New York Public Library, Astor, Lenox and Tilden Foundations; U.S. Naval Historical Center; Department of Prints and Photographs, Moorland-Spingarn Research Center, librarian Donna Wells; Historic New England, librarians Lorna Condon, Jeanne Gamble, and Emily Gustainis; and Amherst College librarian Tracy Sutherland.

It has been a privilege and a blessing to work with Sian Hunter of the University of North Carolina Press. She is a patient, attentive, and gracious editor, whose professional generosity has enabled me to grow as a writer and literary historian. Her unfailing commitment to this project, affirmations of the writing process, optimism, and encouragement at all stages of preparation have contributed immeasurably and so deeply to the evolution and completion of this work. Sincere thanks to Sian and to the editorial staff at the University of North Carolina Press, who have made this Duke University alumna truly appreciate Chapel Hill.

It is with deep gratitude and much love that I thank my family. My parents, Jean and Edgar, have been extraordinary teachers in and beyond our home. Their loving friendship, wholehearted investment in this project, and mighty faith have carried this book on angel's wings for all the years it has taken to complete it. My sister, Anna, and her husband, Michael, have cheered me on, and I thank them for their questions about this work I do and their sincere interest in all the answers. Conversations—local and transatlantic—with Eva and John Monson have added to this enterprise.

My husband, Peter, who has come to know Pauline so very well, has helped to make possible the writing life that I love, want, and need. For the bolstering gifts of time, confidence, perspective, and cheer, I thank him. His love and our darling Emily, who delights in words, music, and dance, make all the difference.

Introduction

Pauline Elizabeth Hopkins regarded herself as a true daughter of New England, and her rich family history granted her a place in the history of the region as well as the nation. Hopkins was born into an antebellum world populated by gracious and uncompromising racial activists, accomplished artists and performers, dedicated scholars, and enterprising professionals and entrepreneurs. She absorbed the substantial African American histories that documented the efforts by people of color in the North to acquire political representation, educational opportunity, and civil rights. She also took careful note of the inspiring traditions of moving public performances, which ranged from classical concerts to juvenile recitations, all evidence of the thriving intellectual and cultural environment in which her ancestors had played a defining role. All of Hopkins's works—from her earnest prizewinning high school essay on the virtues of a temperate life to her engaging anthropological evaluations of populations she referred to as "the dark races" of the modern age—confirmed her deep sense of cultural entitlement, political authority, and racial pride.

Born in Portland, Maine, in 1859 to free parents of color, Pauline Hopkins relocated to Boston at a young age and lived in Massachusetts for almost her entire life. She grew up in a loving and large extended family that linked her to freedom in the colonial North and to bondage in the antebellum South. Her first mentors were drawn from her family; these influential figures recognized and nurtured her creative genius and flair for performance. By the early 1870s, Hopkins was breaking new ground as an African American playwright, and by her early twenties, she had become the first woman of color to write and star in her own dramatic work. Her public performance life was rooted in both secular and religious New England traditions. She collaborated with leading entertainment figures such as Sam Lucas, Anna Madah Hyers, and Emma Louise Hyers and with them enjoyed national success and acclaim. In Boston, Hopkins consolidated her family ties and with her parents established a concert company that offered traditional and religious songs.

Pauline Hopkins's transition from a performance career to a writing life was inextricably linked to her participation in antilynching debates and protests of the 1890s. When she became a leading literary figure and cultural critic in Boston in the early twentieth century, she did so by confronting the unpalatable and often unspeakable histories of concubinage, enslavement, and lynching. In 1900, at the age of forty, she published her first novel, *Contending Forces: A Romance Illustrative of Negro Life North and South*, a work imprinted by her own evasive and unsettling maternal family history, which linked her to the Atlantic slave trade, the West Indies, and the American South. Hopkins's turn toward the profession of authorship was financed by the Colored Co-operative Publishing Company, an enterprising black-owned, Boston-based organization founded by Virginians Walter Wallace, Harper Fortune, Walter Johnson, and Jesse Watkins. Hopkins, who had strong ties to Virginia through her stepfather William, allied herself with these four ambitious young men, who promptly invited her to join the staff of their new venture, the *Colored American Magazine*, America's first black literary periodical. The only woman on the staff when the magazine began, Hopkins eventually became literary editor and then editor in chief. Hopkins was the most prolific contributor to the monthly magazine, which provided engaging articles by and about African Americans on topics including professional endeavors, literary works and traditions, art and photography, cultural outreach, political activism and contemporary issues, military matters, and social movements.

The professional partnership that Hopkins established with Wallace, Fortune, Johnson, and Watkins launched her career as a race writer, clubwoman, and public intellectual. She began to craft a new public role for herself as a spirited cultural critic, clubwoman, and writer of both fiction and nonfiction, and her work gained her entry into some of Boston's most elite social and literary groups. Ultimately, Hopkins's "bursts of righteous heat," as poet Gwendolyn Brooks referred to them, her forthright evaluations of contemporary race issues, her pan-Africanist sentiments, and her resistance to Booker T. Washington's accommodationist policies led to her demise.[1] Within five years of Hopkins's joining the *Colored American Magazine*, her promising career as one of the most eloquent, versatile, and insightful cultural critics and writers of the age was undone. Washington, the man who came to represent the antithesis of Hopkins's politics and convictions, was the architect of her demise. Despite repeated denials of involvement with the journal, Washington infiltrated the *Colored American Magazine*. He assumed financial control, seized its property, including copies of Hopkins's pioneering novel *Contend-*

ing Forces, relocated the magazine to New York City, and effectively banished Hopkins and her colleagues from the world of periodical publishing.

The resilience that Pauline Hopkins displayed in the years following her ouster from the *Colored American Magazine* testifies to the strong networks and alliances on which she came to depend. Her professional triumphs at the *Colored American Magazine* facilitated her connections with debonair journalists such as William Monroe Trotter and J. Max Barber, individuals known for their bold and unceasing resistance to accommodationist politics and what they and others regarded as its fruits: problematic white privilege and deadly, entrenched racism. Hopkins's affiliations with prominent African Americans sustained her at a critical point in her professional life; with public support from her community, she defied Washington's stranglehold on the African American press. In 1915, Hopkins rallied former colleagues and longtime family associates and launched the *New Era Magazine*, a promising journal that pledged itself to advancing the race, documenting its history, and illuminating its potential.

Pauline Hopkins has existed for many scholars in the context of her professional life, which began in 1900 with the publication of *Contending Forces*. Despite the intensity and enduring relevance of Hopkins's writings—which include, in addition to *Contending Forces*, over thirty articles, three serialized novels, one monograph, and several public speeches—Hopkins slipped into complete obscurity. Her connections to the women's club movement, the Baptist church, and the Grand Army of the Republic were not enough to keep her at the forefront of discussions of American women's writing or the African American literary tradition. Scholars Ann Allen Shockley, Mary Helen Washington, and Claudia Tate have made important efforts to reclaim Hopkins for contemporary readers, and in 1988, their efforts were complemented by the inclusion of Hopkins's novels and short fiction in the multivolume Oxford University Press and Schomburg Library series on nineteenth-century African American writers edited by Henry Louis Gates Jr. The re-publication of Hopkins's work in this series generated long-overdue critical attention to Hopkins, and she has been hailed consistently for works that dispense insightful political critiques, demonstrate innovative applications of nineteenth-century race theory, and document racial violence. The scholarship on Hopkins has been steady and ambitious and has done much to secure her place in discussions of canonical African American literature. Yet there still has been room to provide detailed information about her origins, the evolution of her writing career, her intellectual development, and her political sensibilities.

This critical study of Pauline Hopkins builds on the scholarly and historical profiles of Pauline Hopkins and the members of her family who gained prominence as activists, ministers, poets, lawyers, performers, scholars, and educators in the nineteenth century. It also is enriched greatly by comprehensive studies of New England history and African Americans in the North and the continued scholarship on African American women's work and literary production. The foundation of this work lies in the detailed accounts of the ancestral past that shaped Hopkins's identity as a New England woman of color, performer, writer, and public figure. Offered here for the first time is a comprehensive reconstruction of the maternal and paternal lines of Pauline Hopkins, a writer who invoked her past in strategic and often nuanced ways and whose veiled references to her family often have created more questions than they have answered. Central to this biography is the newly presented account of the earliest known Hopkins maternal family ancestor in North America, Caesar Nero Paul, who lived as an enslaved and then free man in New Hampshire. The maternal Paul family history provides rich context for Hopkins's considerations of bondage and freedom, as well as her proud declarations in which she linked herself to the spirited history of American abolition. Throughout her career, Hopkins incorporated her family history into her own works of fiction and nonfiction; the themes of loss, triumph, family bonds, and social activism echo profoundly in her works and reinforce the biography delineated in this study.

The paternal history of Pauline Hopkins has been one of the most provocative untold stories in the scholarship about the writer and her works. Offered here for the first time is an account of Hopkins's biological father and his well-known and politically active Providence, Rhode Island, family. The early family history of Pauline Hopkins and the tumultuous marital experience of her mother Sarah had a complicated but enduring impact on Pauline Hopkins. The information about the extended Northup family and the abolitionist and racial-uplift networks in which they moved provides a new lens through which to consider Hopkins's own political legacies and the ways in which she honored the long-unacknowledged family of her biological father. In addition, this study provides new details about the richly textured relationship that Pauline and her mother forged with William Hopkins, her devoted stepfather and one of her earliest mentors.

This volume also explores the close-knit, resilient, enterprising, and sophisticated Beacon Hill community where the Massachusetts story of Pauline Hopkins lives on most dramatically today in the African Meeting House, the oldest extant African American church building in America and the sanctuary over which her maternal ancestor Thomas Paul presided as minister. Pauline Hopkins honors repeatedly and with great reverence her long-standing connections to Beacon Hill and its vivid abolitionist history and traditions of intellectual, social, and moral uplift. Her activities as a twentieth-century clubwoman are linked to the activist work of her ancestors Susan Paul and Ann Paul Smith, for example, and her career as a promising playwright and singer, which began in the 1870s, extended the celebrated African American classical and concert traditions of the early antebellum period. This analysis confirms Hopkins's close study of nineteenth-century African American social, intellectual, and political histories and the ways in which she was determined to value those histories in her own writings and activism.

This biography of Pauline Hopkins focuses on distinct periods of her creative and political development. Chapters 1–3 focus on her maternal and paternal genealogies and provide illuminating details about the families' connections to the French and Indian War and the American Civil War, the abolitionist and emigrationist movements, and African American literary and cultural traditions in New England. These chapters also outline the Northern and Southern genealogies that blended in both personal and political ways for Hopkins, as the families of her biological father and stepfather worked alongside each other to secure civil rights and social justice for people of color. Chapters 4–6 chronicle Hopkins's earliest forays into postbellum performance culture. They provide new information about Hopkins's earliest writings and the community performances that gave her invaluable perspectives on African American agency, political history, and racial solidarity. These chapters discuss the relationships Hopkins enjoyed with her first mentors, her socialization as a freeborn child of color in the North during Reconstruction, and the triumphs on the American stage and in African American musical circles that linked her to celebrated artists such as Sam Lucas and the Hyers Sisters. Also presented here are accounts of how Hopkins worked to defend herself as an African American performer on the public stage and how she successfully preserved the integrity of her artistic vision in the face of destructive and demoralizing forms such as blackface minstrelsy.

Hopkins's connection to the *Colored American Magazine*, her evolution as a race writer and efforts to support emerging writers of color, and her published work in the magazine are the primary focus of chapters 7–14. Presented here are accounts of her associations with uncompromising community groups such as the Colored National League and assessments of her important affiliation with Grand Army of the Republic posts, whose members were part of the historic African American Civil War regiments. These chapters confirm the depth of Hopkins's ties to Boston's empowered and assertive community of color and propose that her move away from a conventional life in civil service employment was bolstered, if not inspired, by her close ties to eloquent activists determined to obtain political equality and protection, as well as social and educational opportunities, for all people of color in the United States.

Chapters 15–20 document Hopkins's increasingly tumultuous tenure at the *Colored American Magazine* and her new professional alliances with provocative and bold journalists, intellectuals, and activists such as J. Max Barber, editor of the *Voice of the Negro*, and William Monroe Trotter, editor of the Boston-based *Guardian*. These chapters also shed new light on her ideological and literal battles with Booker T. Washington during the early 1900s, her overtures to W. E. B. Du Bois, her affiliation with outspoken black Boston liberals, and her long-obscured contributions to diverse race-related campaigns in Boston's black communities. The chapters reflect, too, on Hopkins's friendships, her connections to Baptist circles in and beyond New England, and her participation in the African American women's club movement. Finally, they document her efforts to establish her own publishing house and provide a critique of the promising but short-lived journal, the *New Era Magazine*, for which she served as editor in chief.

In December 1905, Pauline Hopkins declared at Boston's Faneuil Hall that she was an unacknowledged "black daughter of the revolution." This biography is informed by the bold call to action that Hopkins delivered on that day, as well as the impassioned writings that testify to her unwavering belief in democracy, honor, and justice.

1

Black Daughter, Black History

Is it not true that the fate of the Negro
is the romance of American history?
PAULINE HOPKINS
September 1902

On 5 December 1905, in the wake of a winter snowstorm that blanketed Boston, Pauline Elizabeth Hopkins traveled from her Cambridge, Massachusetts, home to Faneuil Hall, located in the heart of Boston. She was part of a much-touted "galaxy of orators" scheduled to speak on the third and final day of the city's centennial celebration of William Lloyd Garrison, the forthright New England abolitionist and editor of the *Liberator* newspaper. Hopkins was no stranger to Faneuil Hall, the two-story brick market house and "noble structure" that Peter Faneuil, the enterprising scion of a successful French Huguenot family, had offered to the city in the 1740s. Although financed by a Faneuil family fortune derived from substantial investments in the Atlantic slave trade and Caribbean markets where enslaved Africans were traded for molasses and sugar bound for Massachusetts and the colonies, the Boston building, since its construction, had hosted many significant abolitionist and African American events.[1] Hopkins's ancestors frequented Faneuil Hall and often had leading roles at gatherings that ranged from public religious meetings to community antislavery rallies.

When she spoke at the Garrison Centennial, Hopkins ensured the continuation of her impressive family tradition of public advocacy and uplift. She did so in the company of legendary activists and leading public figures of the day. Alongside her was Garrison family descendant Oswald Villard, editor of the *New York Evening Post*; Frank Sanborn, the celebrated Concord, Massachusetts, teacher, abolitionist, and former ally of John Brown; Alice Stone Blackwell, longtime *Woman's Journal* editor and daughter of the indefatigable feminist Lucy Stone; and William Monroe Trotter, a Phi Beta Kappa gradu-

Pauline Hopkins. *Courtesy of the Moorland-Spingarn
Research Center, Howard University.*

ate of Harvard College and the uncompromising founding editor of Boston's
feisty weekly newspaper, *The Guardian*. Hopkins earned great praise for her
spirited account of Garrison's origins and his storied thirty-four-year career
as *Liberator* editor. Trotter's *Guardian*, which provided detailed coverage of
the citywide celebration, insisted that her "stirring" words not only helped to
make her speech the day's "Chief Address" but also captivated the hundreds
who gathered there for the ceremonies. Hopkins prefaced her remarks about
Garrison with a moving account of how she prepared herself to "stand in this
historic hall and say one word for the liberties of [her] race." She also threatened—in the name of her forefathers, their patriotism, and their blood sacrifice—to acquire the long-denied honor of full citizenship and equality due to
her, to her race in general, and to her African American sisters in particular:

Yesterday I sat in the old Joy street church and you can imagine my emotions as I remembered my great grandfather begged in England the money that helped the Negro cause, that my grandfather on my father's side, signed the papers with Garrison at Philadelphia. I remembered that at Bunker Hill my ancestors on my maternal side poured out their blood. I am a daughter of the Revolution, you do not acknowledge black daughters of the Revolution but we are going to take that right.[2]

Hopkins's speech was especially memorable because by expounding on her ancestral links to him she claimed Garrison for her family and her race. She noted the history of the New England Anti-Slavery Society and most likely introduced some members of her audience for the first time to the history of that organization's intimate connection to, and dependence upon, the African Baptist Church on Beacon Hill, the oldest black Baptist sanctuary in the North. Garrison had assembled his fellow abolitionists there at the invitation of the Reverend Thomas Paul, the church's first pastor and Hopkins's maternal great-granduncle. The founding in 1832 of the New England Anti-Slavery Society, the nation's first organization committed to immediate abolition and emancipation, was facilitated by Paul's politics and faith, as well as by his willingness to allow Garrison and his white colleagues to use the African American sanctuary for their political meeting.[3] Garrison also supported the enterprising abolitionist and publishing campaign of Thomas Paul's daughter and Hopkins's distant cousin, Susan Paul, and he was a watchful mentor and friend to Hopkins's orphaned granduncle, Elijah, and his siblings during the 1840s.[4] Hopkins was fully aware of how Garrison's philanthropy and political zeal were intricately bound up in her own family's rich Boston history. It was inevitable, then, on this winter day when she had an unprecedented opportunity to acknowledge his contributions to and reliance on her family, that she would do so in a manner that both honored him and paid tribute to her ancestors.

The events that Pauline Hopkins recalled in her 1905 Faneuil Hall address transported her audience to the antebellum world of Beacon Hill. The "old Joy street church" to which Hopkins referred was the First African Baptist Church, a stately two-story brick sanctuary located at the end of Smith Court, a short cobblestoned road on the north slope of Beacon Hill. Smith Court was accessible from Joy Street, a road formerly known as Belknap Street and renamed in honor of Dr. John Joy, a local apothecary. Some of black Beacon Hill's most enterprising activist families and learned individuals resided on this well-known road—including David Walker, author of *Walker's Appeal*, the provocative 1829 antislavery manifesto; and the family of printer and equal school rights advocate Benjamin Roberts, who filed the 1849 school desegregation suit in the name of his daughter Sarah that led to the integration in 1855 of Boston public schools.[5] Hopkins also used her speech to conjure up for her audience the momentous times in the 1830s when Garrison launched *The Liberator*, founded the New England Anti-Slavery Society in the basement schoolrooms of the African Baptist Church, and forged deep and formative connections to Boston's African American community. Hopkins used her speech to reconstruct powerful examples of early African American support for white ventures and to demonstrate the lasting legacy for all Bostonians of cooperative interracial efforts that shaped the antebellum era. Garrison was rebuffed several times by white minister colleagues who refused to accommodate a gathering of antislavery men; ultimately, Thomas Paul offered his sanctuary to Garrison and his peers and the group of twelve flocked to it, despite inclement weather, to formalize their commitment to abolition and social justice. Unlike some of his white contemporaries, Paul did not regard abolition as a challenge to religious practice. According to the tenets of his Freewill Baptist training and his own particular Baptist practice, fighting slavery was a mandate of his faith. Pauline Hopkins's invocation of the First African Baptist Church, a church that still stands today, resurrected the era of enterprising African American political activity and bold interracial ventures under the auspices of organizations such as the New England Anti-Slavery Society. It also provided her with an opportunity to detail an often unacknowledged and emphatically Afrocentric history built on religious principles and emancipatory politics.

Central to Hopkins's reconstitution of her family history was Thomas Paul, a "dignified, urbane, and attractive man" beloved for "colloquial powers" that were "exuberant and vigorous" and for "eloquence that charmed the ear . . . and piety [that] commended itself to its bearers."[6] He was one of at least six children born free in Exeter, New Hampshire, to a native of Africa named Caesar Nero Paul and his white New Hampshire–born wife, Lovey, née Rollins, Paul.[7] His brothers Benjamin and Nathaniel also were Baptist ministers and served congregations in New York City and Albany, New York, respectively. Thomas made his way south to Massachusetts in the late 1780s, and he launched his religious career when, as a sixteen-year-old, he became as "an exhorter of scripture passages" at segregated religious meetings at Faneuil Hall. He also organized and hosted religious meetings on Beacon Hill and enjoyed the regular attendance of a modest number of worshippers.[8]

Paul, who was educated in New Hampshire's Freewill Baptist schools, was installed in December 1806 as the first minister of Boston's First African Baptist Church. He cherished his pastorate at the sanctuary that came to be

Portrait by Thomas Badger of the Reverend Thomas Paul,
first minister of the African Baptist Church in Boston and
great-granduncle of Hopkins. *Courtesy of National
Portrait Gallery, Smithsonian Institution.*

known as the "colored People's Faneuil Hall and where he was "wont to proclaim Christ and him crucified to crowded audiences."⁹ He presided for more
than two decades over Boston's first black church and the first Baptist congregation in the North that met in the building built entirely by African American labor. In 1823, Paul's congregation endorsed his temporary relocation to
New York City, where he and a group of disenfranchised African American
churchgoers there founded the Abyssinian Baptist Church, a church that still
thrives today. When he returned to Boston, Paul resumed his ministry at the
African Church and renewed his ties with the Prince Hall Masonic Lodge,
where he served as chaplain alongside its accomplished founder, Prince Hall.
Paul preached regularly in other churches, including several prominent ones
with white congregations, and he earned a reputation as a persuasive and
enlightened preacher. He cultivated his political powers and allied himself
with ambitious African American educators, ministers, and writers, such as
Samuel Cornish and John Russwurm, editors of *Freedom's Journal*, the first
African American newspaper, and David Walker, author of the 1829 *Appeal*

The African Baptist Church, Smith Court, Boston, ca. 1885.
Courtesy of Historic New England.

to the Coloured Citizens of the World. Paul also was a successful missionary, whose travels to Haiti resulted in numerous conversions to Christianity and included several audiences with the Haitian president and government officers. The American Baptist administration touted his visit as an example of professionalism and true faith.

Hopkins could take great pride in her ancestor's key support for Garrison's political endeavors. This partnership, though largely undocumented in histories of Garrison or the city of Boston, was founded on deep mutual respect and a shared desire for African American freedom. William Cooper Nell, one of the city's most eloquent historians and an exemplary graduate of the Abiel Smith School that stood adjacent to the African Baptist Church, provided one of the rare accounts of a meeting between Paul and Garrison. Apparently, in 1830, there was "earnest hand-shaking" between the two men after one of Garrison's antislavery lectures. In addition, Paul and his colleague, the Reverend Samuel Snowden, who also was in attendance and dispensing "hearty amen[s]" during Garrison's remarks, "vowed . . . devotion to the cause," and according to Nell, "to [this] pledge, their life was remarkably consistent."[10] The commitment to Garrisonian politics extended to Thomas's brother Nathaniel, who traveled to England in the 1830s with Garrison, raised funds for Negro settlements in Canada, addressed members of Parliament about American antislavery work, and completed a successful lecture tour in the United Kingdom that took him from London to Glasgow and many points in between.

In a manner reminiscent of Thomas Paul's own "great solemnity of manner" and Nathaniel Paul's polished oratory, Pauline Hopkins used her Garrison Centennial speech in 1905 to assert her ancestral legacy and her family's long-established campaign for freedom, democracy, and racial equality in America.[11] Hopkins's reference to the "old Joy street church" in the opening lines of her address was a pointed reminder about the city's oldest African American historic site and an effort to supplement the long-established city histories with information about the Paul family. The Pauls had been one of the city's most prominent and active antebellum African American families. Their name was synonymous not only with the Baptist Church but also with campaigns to improve African American education, to promote cultural expression, and to abolish slavery.[12] The family record of achievement was substantial: Thomas and Catherine Paul's son Thomas Jr. was one of the first African Americans to graduate from Dartmouth College. Their daughter Susan was a pioneering abolitionist who was one of the first women and the first woman of color to join the New England Anti-Slavery Society and also the woman who integrated the Boston Female Anti-Slavery Society. In addition to these public accomplishments, Susan became the family's first published author and was the first African American woman to publish a biography, the first to chronicle the life of a freeborn child of color, and the first African American woman to produce a published work of evangelical juvenilia. In addition, Paul grandchildren, the third generation of freeborn descendants of Caesar and Lovey Paul, were at the heart of the divisive battle to end segregated education in the city during the 1840s. Members of this early African American dynasty were active in the early literary and music societies in the 1820s and 1830s, transformed local antislavery debates into riveting critiques by African American schoolchildren of the slave trade, colonization, and insidious social oppression, and worked diligently on temperance reform and racial uplift.

The African Baptist Church was an enduring touchstone for Hopkins, and it provided her with an unassailable connection to the tumultuous antebellum world of her ancestors. This building accommodated much more than religious services. There, the African American community educated its children, drafted plans for social uplift, organized protests, attended lectures and concerts, and enlisted men for the first African American Civil War regiments. The community celebrated political triumphs, such as the abolition of slavery in the British colonies, enactment of the Emancipation Proclamation, and passage of the Civil War Amendments that ended slavery, granted citizenship to people of color, and provided African American men the right to vote. Yet the Joy Street church of which Hopkins spoke in December was not a site solely of importance for African Americans. It also provided her, a twentieth-century race activist, writer, and journalist, with a direct link to, and even a rightful claim to, William Lloyd Garrison, the nation's most famous white antislavery activist. Hopkins took this precious opportunity to insist on the great degree to which Garrison depended upon and benefited from the unwavering support and leadership of African Americans in the city.

In December 1905, Hopkins insisted that her audience at Faneuil Hall consider Garrison's achievements in the context of her family's representative African American history of patriotic service and sacrifice, international antislavery campaigns, and American abolitionist efforts.[13] On the occasion of what she described earnestly as "the greatest honor that will ever come to me," Pauline Hopkins cloaked herself in the impressive history of her family and her race and delivered a most memorable protest of the nation's penchant for generating exclusionary histories. She decried in eloquent terms the national tendency to underestimate the substantial roles that African Americans had played in the struggles for freedom and equality. When she delivered her unapologetic indictment of America's racially biased, and thus incomplete, history, Hopkins had been highly visible in Boston's cultural and political circles for some thirty years. During the 1870s and 1880s, she had enjoyed careers as a celebrated vocalist and dynamic playwright. During the 1890s and early 1900s, she became a prolific novelist, talented journalist, inspiring public speaker, and an active member of the regional branch of the National Association of Colored Women. In 1905, at age forty-six, Hopkins's professional careers and roles in public life had been shaped by her unswerving commitment to represent and to celebrate the inspiring, diverse, and complex history of African Americans.

Pauline Hopkins certainly had a rightful place in the Paul family dynasty of which she spoke that day. Yet, during this moment of greatest public visibility that she had experienced since her days on the stage, Hopkins manipulated her genealogy for dramatic effect. She merged her maternal family lines, blurred her actual relationship to the forefathers that she mentioned, and presented herself as a direct descendant of the abolitionist Baptist minister and her maternal great-granduncle, the Reverend Nathaniel Paul, when she was in fact the descendant of his sister Dorothy (Dolly) Paul Whitfield. It may have been the thrill and excitement of the moment or the unprecedented opportunity to appear before so many New Englanders that made her reinvent herself. However, it was not the first time that she had made calculated revisions of her genealogy and disseminated in a public forum a new biography.

When she appeared at the Garrison Centennial, it had been just over a year since Pauline Hopkins had been ousted rather unceremoniously from her position as editor in chief of the *Colored American Magazine*, the nation's first African American literary journal. During her five-year tenure with the pioneering monthly, she had established herself as a prolific and compelling writer, as a gifted historian of her race, and as an ardent advocate of Pan-African unity. The audience she addressed in Faneuil Hall included men and women who knew of her ambition and of her mistreatment at the hands of Booker T. Washington, founder of Tuskegee University and a Southern power broker, who masterminded the magazine's takeover and relocation to New York City. William Monroe Trotter, organizer of the Garrison Centennial and editor of Boston's stridently anti-Washington *Guardian*, was one who knew much about Hopkins's recent struggle. As he watched and listened to her at Faneuil Hall during the Garrison Centennial, Trotter may well have thought that Hopkins was exhorting herself to persevere in the face of Washington's manipulation. Her new biography, so succinct and uncompromising, stood as compelling evidence that although she had been denied access to the *Colored American Magazine*, her political mouthpiece, her political enemies had not silenced her. Hopkins's sentiments suggested that she thought of herself as a casualty in a larger struggle, as a person outnumbered but determined to work for African American suffrage and civil liberties. As she herself acknowledged in her speech that day, the "battle for the abolition of slavery" had been "[g]reat indeed," but "the battle for manhood rights" would be "greater by far."[14] In order to retain her place in this conflict, Pauline Hopkins presented herself as a legitimate and capable soldier, a person whose ancestry conferred upon her a precious legacy of valor and victory and the responsibility to fight.

Pauline Hopkins began to assiduously cultivate the public image of herself as the product of a steady, respectable, middle-class family as the twentieth century began. At Faneuil Hall in December 1905, Hopkins's discussion of origins and the need for unyielding personal conviction revealed her fascination with destiny and self-creation, principles and parentage. She had explored these issues in much of her writing, and the circumstances of her own birth and her evolution from stage performer to public intellectual tapped into these same subjects and anxieties. But it was not only her political objectives that compelled her to rewrite her own beginnings. It appears that she did so in order to emancipate herself further from social stigmas and class prejudices that were reinforced by the educational, social, and economic privileges of New England's African American elite.

Pauline Elizabeth Hopkins was a fifth-generation New England writer, feminist, and public intellectual whose family history was shaped by freedom and enslavement, colonial warfare and American patriotism, keen religious vocation, and secular class politics. A purposeful woman with a keen awareness of place, she used her writings to facilitate both private and public agendas. Her novels, prose writings, and other works often used her own family history, as she educated her American readers about the substantial, though often disregarded, contributions of people of color in and beyond the United States. Reared in the North, Hopkins had strong familial and political ties to the American South, the West Indies, England, and Africa. The histories of global dominance, subjugation, emancipation, and colonization that defined these regions became historical meta-narratives that motivated Hopkins to write and compelled her to produce absorbing critiques of public history, nationalism, and political activism.

Hopkins's maternal and paternal histories are built upon some of the earliest examples of African American industry, fortitude, and self-preservation. Although it is possible to reconstruct her life and ancestral histories in an organized manner, Hopkins's biographical narrative does not lend itself to a straightforward account. It, like so many other life stories, reveals startling facts suppressed, major events reinterpreted, and primary relationships redefined. In some cases, the alterations produce more desirable and uplifting scripts; in others, they continue to obscure key truths about her kin, social circles, professional alliances, and central life experiences. Ultimately, however, the life and past of Pauline Hopkins constitute an absorbing story of African American family life that spans three centuries.

The most formal account of Pauline Hopkins's origins appeared in 1901. The biographical profile was published in the city's recently established *Colored American Magazine*, the journal that promoted *Contending Forces*, Hopkins's first novel. Hopkins introduced herself to the journal's readers as the only female member of the editorial staff. Yet the introduction also was a vital step in her deliberate professional transition from the working-class entertainment world to that of the intellectual and writerly American elite. The biographical information, for all intents and purposes, constitutes Hopkins's only published professional résumé. As such, it functions as the most formal document that she ever created in order to authorize her full participation in the elite world of African American letters and the dynamic multifaceted sphere of American feminist, intellectual, and political debate. The *Colored American Magazine* profile, which Hopkins probably wrote herself, was one of several staff biographies published in the issue. It appeared to offer a straightforward genealogy:

> Pauline E. Hopkins of North Cambridge, Mass. was born in Portland, Me., but came to Boston when an infant; subsequently she was raised a Boston girl, educated in the Boston public schools, and finally graduated from the famous Girls' High School of that city.
>
> Her father, William A. Hopkins, a G.A.R. veteran of the Civil War, is a native of Alexandria, Va. He is a nephew of the late John T. Waugh of Providence, R.I., and a first cousin of the late Mrs. Anna Warrick Jarvis of Washington, D.C.
>
> By her mother Miss Hopkins is a direct descendant of the famous Paul brothers, all black men, educated abroad for the Baptist ministry, the best known of whom was Thomas Paul, who founded St. Paul Baptist Church, Joy Street, Boston, Mass.[,] the first colored church in this section of the United States. Susan Paul, a niece of these brothers, was

a famous colored woman, long and intimately associated with William Lloyd Garrison in the anti-slavery movement. Miss Hopkins is also a grandniece of the late James Whitfield, the California poet, who was associated with Frederick Douglass in politics and literature.[15]

The seemingly straightforward biographical profile established Hopkins's regional credentials, confirmed her links to the founders of Boston's early black community, and suggested her potential for upward mobility. But embedded in the orderly profile was a powerful and alternative autobiography.

The identity that Hopkins claimed for herself in the *Colored American Magazine* purposely sidestepped some two decades of artistic innovation and public political outreach. That unruly counternarrative could complicate, and even threaten to undo, her claim on the respectability that could enhance the highly visible and professional persona that she hoped to cultivate at the beginning of the twentieth century. The details of her years as an innovative playwright, accomplished singer, and patriotic performer in the late nineteenth century contributed much to the woman that she was as the twentieth century began. Yet Hopkins studiously eliminated these successes and any potential sensationalism that they produced as she carefully redefined the parameters of her professional life and outlined her objectives as a determined race woman of the new century.

As her public life in the early 1900s evolved, it would become clear that the lack of increasingly bourgeois social and educational credentials impeded Hopkins's access to high respectability. She invested proudly in her status as an alumna of Girls' High School, a venerable Boston institution founded in the early 1850s that, despite considerable opposition from families and even family physicians who "strongly advised" against certain advanced courses of studies for the girls, placed graduates in leading American colleges such as Radcliffe. In addition, Girls' High had an especially strong science curriculum and is credited as the first American high school to offer chemistry with laboratory instruction.[16] In addition to Hopkins, accomplished Girls' High School graduates included Marcella O'Grady Boveri, who in 1885 was the first woman to graduate from the Massachusetts Institute of Technology with a degree concentration in biology.[17] Hopkins also honored in her *Colored American Magazine* writings fellow Girls' High students like Joan Imogen Howard, the first African American student from Boston's grammar schools to graduate from the institution, who, after receiving honors from Girls' High School, went on to earn her Master of Pedagogy from New York University and serve on the Board of Women Managers for the Columbian Exposition, and Jane E. Sharp, of the class of 1873, who emigrated to Liberia and with her husband established a school at Mt. Coffee.[18]

It was ironic that Hopkins's past, which included celebrated public stints as a public performer, competed with her efforts to craft a more reserved, though no less outspoken, reputation of intellectual and political awareness. Yet, as the last three decades of her life reveal, her colorful early years, combined with her liberal politics, appear to have brought about social snubs. The social exclusion that she suffered at the hands of Boston's and New England's emerging intellectual and social elite, for example, translated into Hopkins's disenfranchisement within the women's club movement and her relegation to the periphery of the larger civil and equal rights movement. In response to the harsh realities of African American social elitism and class privilege, Hopkins financed her second professional debut with intellectual capital rather than social pedigree. She justified her claim to high social respectability even as she ventured once again into the public sphere. This time, however, she endeavored to position herself as a public intellectual, an insightful and savvy peer of individuals such as William Monroe Trotter, Ida B. Wells-Barnett, Frances Harper, and W. E. B. Du Bois, all of whom wielded the written word to great effect as a tool for political and social critique. In this professional reincarnation, Hopkins also sought to become part of the forceful black feminist activist tradition defined by the deeds, public platforms, and advocacy work of women such as Harper, Wells-Barnett, Mary Church Terrell, and Anna Julia Cooper.

Hopkins's emphasis in the *Colored American Magazine* profile on her place in the Paul family genealogy belies an anxiety about her political viability. It also reflects her effort to locate female ambition squarely within a larger and more conventional tradition of black masculinity. Hopkins was a direct descendant of a lone and relatively obscure Paul sister and not of the "famous Paul brothers, all black men, educated abroad for the Baptist ministry." The legacy of Hopkins's Paul foremother, Dorothy (Dolly) Paul Whitfield, was one of unsung and insular domesticity, rather than a celebrated ministry of global dimensions. Nonetheless, the family connection allowed Hopkins to invoke unabashedly and to the fullest her Paul family affiliation. When she invested in the patriarchal successes of the Paul family, Hopkins cloaked herself in an undisputed and rich tradition of antebellum racial uplift and activism. By so doing, she appropriated a powerful social rhetoric and presented herself as an extension of an accomplished African American history that had transformed Boston, the nation, and even the world. The move itself reveals much about Hopkins's conceptions of domesticity and the degree to which she manipulated patriarchal history to create a modern matri-focal agenda that she could deploy in the often-unyielding world of black Boston and white America. Hopkins's appropriation of the larger Paul family patriarchal record and her emphasis on the Reverend Thomas Paul underscored her unremitting quest for social and political legitimacy in the charged black public sphere. Hopkins overcame the threat of marginalization within the larger local and global hierarchical social and political circles by being overly insistent about her claims of inclusion in the Paul family.

The earliest known details about the Paul family's American history are rooted in the eighteenth-century colonial world of New Hampshire. Pauline Hopkins was one of eight great-great-grandchildren descended from Caesar Nero Paul (1741–1823), a "little, exceedingly dark complexioned man," who was her family's oldest known patriarch of African descent in America.[19] Caesar Paul's life in the New World began in the British colony that became New Hampshire, the ninth state admitted to the Union. Colonial records do not include information about the circumstances that brought him to the town of Exeter, nor do the town histories reveal much about the local trade in slaves that led to Caesar Paul's purchase by one of Exeter's leading families. Although some significant details have been lost, it is possible to construct much about Caesar Paul's early life in the New World. His was a memorable evolution, one borne of conflict and contest. He lived as a slave and as a free man, as a colonial soldier fighting for the British crown and as an American patriot celebrating his sons and their substantial achievements in the newly established republic. Caesar Paul also lived deliberately in the colonial New World as an African and as the father of biracial children who became recognized members of the pantheon of African American men intent on ensuring the survival and the success of the race in and beyond America.

During the 1740s and 1750s, the years in which Caesar Paul would have arrived in New Hampshire, the American slave market was catering increasingly to owners who wanted to replace their white indentured servants with Africans and to those who believed that "[f]or this market they must be young, the younger the better if not quite children."[20] New Englanders interested in acquiring servants, as they often were called, frequently lodged purchase orders with the captains of departing ships. Whether captains had such requests or not, however, children like the boy who became Caesar Nero Paul were frequently part of the coffles that appeared in colonial ports. In 1756, for example, the *Exeter* docked in New Hampshire's Portsmouth harbor with sixty-one Africans aboard. Seventeen of them were boys and girls.[21] In addition, Paul was part of the new insidious phase of American slave importation that saw a dramatic increase in the number of males, and more specifically boys, in the market.

Caesar Paul's death records suggest that he was born in 1741. He arrived in Exeter some time before he had reached his fourteenth birthday in the year 1755, which was when he accompanied Major John Gilman, the man who acquired him as a slave, into one of the battles of the French and Indian War. Caesar was brought to a town established by white British settlers in the late 1630s who negotiated with Sagamore Indian chiefs for extensive acreage along the banks of the Piscataqua River. He was enslaved to Major Gilman, a descendant of early town founders hailed as "men of property and energy." The Gilman family sawmills and acquisition of choice land use grants made them wealthy and increased their stature locally and across the colony. It is likely that Caesar Paul lived in a "fine specimen of colonial architecture" with a gambrel roof that John Gilman built on the corner of Park and Summer Streets in 1737. The home, which ultimately sheltered Gilman's large family of twelve children, still stands today.[22] Like several other Africans in Exeter, Caesar worked as a house servant, and his domestic position was shaped profoundly by his owner's high social station. He was part of an impressive African cohort in Exeter, one dominated by men who had been enslaved as children and who, like Caesar, had come of age in the colonial New World. His peers included Corydon, an Exeter centenarian and the longtime "man-servant" of Dr. John Phillips, founder of Phillips Exeter Academy; Prince Light, a short, thickset servant of a seasoned military man, who became one of New Hampshire's Continental Army soldiers in 1780 and was Exeter's only Revolutionary War veteran to witness the execution of Major John André, Benedict Arnold's coconspirator;[23] and Charles Tash, whose enslavement included a term of service to John C. Long, a midshipman on the USS *Constitution*, who became the commodore of the Pacific squadron whose flagship was the *Merrimac*. Tash was the "private servant" to Long on one of his cruises and was praised for being "the ideal man in that position."[24]

Paul, whose forenames of Caesar and Nero reflect the antebellum tradition of giving classical Roman names to enslaved Africans, arrived in a colony whose slave population was growing steadily. This increase was occurring even as official government offices denied that the sale, purchase, and maintenance of slaves were state-sanctioned practices. In 1721, some thirty-four years before Caesar Paul officially emerged in Exeter history accounts, there were 150 slaves in New Hampshire. By 1767, the state census reported 633, an increase of over 400 percent.[25] Despite the significant increase in Africans in New England and in New Hampshire, Caesar was relatively isolated from other people of color. The earliest Exeter town census reveals that in 1775—some twenty-five years after Paul's earliest documented residence in Exeter—of the total population of 1,703, there were only 38 "Negroes and slaves for life."[26] This number included other people of African descent held by Gilman family members, such as "a Negro boy nam'd Bob," valued, in 1779, at fifteen pounds, who was owned by Nicholas Gilman, a shipbuilder and the first treasurer of New Hampshire.[27]

Exeter was the only other town besides Portsmouth in which there was "an appreciable number of Negroes at the outbreak of the Revolutionary War."[28] Yet, until after the Revolutionary War, Caesar Nero Paul appears to have lived without the broad supportive racial networks that existed in a larger slave community like that in Portsmouth, a town located some sixteen miles to the north. In Exeter, slaves were part of most leading households, and owners had between one and three slaves. Since neither the region's climate nor its landscape was suited to large-scale farming operations, most slaves worked in all levels of community life: in homes and local businesses, in lumber and shipyards, and on the fishing and trade ships that docked in the sea and river ports. Caesar Paul lived in a colony that was part of the fur trade and also a thoroughfare for the "first streams of trappers and pioneers [who] began to pour throughout the Appalachian passes into the unbroken forests of the West."[29] This traffic resulted in more frequent contact with the Indian populations of the region—contact that often resulted in invasion of Indian hunting lands and challenges to their control of the fur trade. Increasingly hostile relations between the English forces and the French forces meant that colonial outposts like Exeter were embroiled in conflicts with Indian tribes sympathetic to and armed by the French. By 1755, these tensions affected Caesar Nero Paul directly. He would soon be swept up into the heart of the conflict and find himself an armed soldier fighting for his life, in defense of Exeter, and on behalf of the British crown.

Caesar Paul was enslaved to John Gilman, a man whose family had served on the front lines of Exeter's defense since its arrival in the colonial outpost. The majority of the family's military appointments assigned them to defend Exeter and New Hampshire from the Wampanoags and French Mohawks. Exeter historian Charles Bell reports that Exeter "escaped actual hostilities" with its Native American neighbors until 1690. The townspeople enjoyed "pacific and friendly" relations with the Squamscot, Piscataqua, and Pennacook tribes. Nonetheless, the settlers "maintained [their] watchhouse and some show of an organized militia" because the law required both. By 1710, the climate had changed significantly. Like the nearby towns Dover and Portsmouth, which had suffered devastating invasions in the 1690s, Exeter began to suffer what it deemed "irreparable loss[es]."[30] Colonel John Gilman, the father of Caesar's owner, led a sizeable company of ninety-one Exeter men and "pursued the enemy" following an ambush that left seventeen Exeter men dead.[31] In 1756, Captain John Gilman, the thirty-one-year-old grandson of town founder Councilor John Gilman and son of the colonel, took his place in the family's tradition of military service. As a result, Caesar Nero Paul also became poised to take up arms to defend himself in this new country.

In March 1757, sixteen-year-old Caesar Nero prepared himself and his master for war. His own personal supplies were simple and amounted only to a "Gun and Cloathing." He was responsible, however, for packing and maintaining the substantial wardrobe and supplies that Gilman, now promoted to the rank of major and responsible for larger regiments and assignments designed to support British troops, deemed necessary for the expedition. The "Great Coat" of drab kersey valued at fifteen pounds, worsted caps and stockings, lined jackets of "Green Silk Camblet Trimmed with Silver Twist on Vellum," cut velvet and scarlet broadcloth, laced hats and gloves, new breeches of fine blue broadcloth and deerskin, a half dozen tea cups, a punch bowl, pump nails, a chest lock, a tablecloth, a pepper box, six pounds of soap, a volume on military discipline, a sword with silver hilt, and an impressive array of other items were Paul's responsibility to pack and to maintain.[32] Ultimately, Gilman would return from this doomed expedition without his wardrobe, his stash of domestic comforts, or his slave.

Gilman and Caesar Paul were bound for Fort William Henry, the northernmost fort of the three established on Lake George, a place that lay at the centerpiece of James Fenimore Cooper's gripping 1826 novel, *The Last of the Mohicans: A Narrative of 1757*. They arrived in spring 1757 and found a relatively new, imposing, and well-equipped garrison defended by "twenty-nine cannons, three mortars, a howitzer," and some twenty other pieces of artillery. By mid-1757, there were more than 2,000 people within its walls of "timber cribbing filled with earth and gravel and faced off with logs," and the tensions between the French and English had reached fever pitch.[33] By July 1757, Caesar Nero Paul and the occupants of Fort William Henry were outnumbered four to one by French and Indian forces. Leading the French forces and their Indian allies was the legendary general Louis-Joseph de Montcalm, a man who had spent more than half his life in the military. On the eve of his assault on Fort William Henry, Montcalm had won victories at the British forts at Oswego with a combination of stealth, massive artillery, and 3,000 men. When the British there surrendered, Montcalm boasted that he had become "master of three forts of [Oswego], of 1600 prisoners, five flags, one hundred guns, three military chests, victuals for two years, six armed sloops, two hundred bateaux, and an astonishing booty." Montcalm's victory was the death knell for Fort William Henry.

Montcalm's 8,000 regulars and 2,000 Indians at Ticonderoga now were preparing to lay siege to Fort William Henry's 750 enlisted men and 1,200 volunteers and the 250 women and children also encamped there. The battle proper lasted nine days. He managed to escape injury in the face of unceasing enemy fire, but Caesar Paul watched the garrison sink into a frightening state. More than 300 were dead and wounded, smallpox erupted, infections spread, and the casemates overflowed with the sick. Military health was no better. As Montcalm's forces prepared to unleash the power of some thirty-one cannons and fifteen mortars and howitzers, those inside Fort William Henry were grappling with the loss of all of their cannons and the fact that fewer than ten small pieces of artillery still were operable.[34] On 9 August, a white flag was hoisted into sight, and a wounded lieutenant colonel made his way to the enemy camp to discuss the terms of surrender. Less than twenty-four hours later, the able-bodied British and colonial forces began what was supposed to be an escorted march to Fort Edward, their sister fort some six miles away. They left about seventy sick and wounded behind, having negotiated for French military surgeons to care for them. That was to be one of several unfulfilled and deadly agreements. Seventeen of the infirm were dragged from their beds and, in front of the French surgeon responsible for them, killed by aggrieved Indians. That brazen display of murderous strength and intent by the attacking forces escalated into what the novelist Cooper described as a "bloody and inhuman scene" that "deepened the stain . . . upon the reputation of the French commander [Montcalm]," a man who "was deficient in that moral courage without which no man can be truly great."[35] Caesar Nero was one of the "blacks and mulattos among the English soldiers and camp followers . . . hauled away" to be divided up as loot. Ironically, Caesar Nero's life was spared that day because the Indians believed that blacks were property.

Once Caesar Nero and the other men of color were removed from the group, the remaining Fort William Henry occupants were lined up in columns and readied for their march to Fort Edward. Separated from the fort's regiments, Paul and the other men of color were spared the sights of the carnage. They could not, however, escape the terrible sounds of the massacre that was about to unfold. Hundreds of Indians descended on the lines of white British colonials as they prepared to march. Historical accounts of the period report that they encircled the "panic-stricken British, jostling [them], demanding more rum, which they were given out of the soldier's canteens, and snatching at their guns, clothing and personal belongings." Screams and war whoops soon filled the air as the Indians fell upon the defenseless survivors. According to one of the few eyewitness accounts, "[English soldiers] were stript by the Indians of everything they had . . . the Women and children drag'd from among them and most inhumanly butchered before their faces." The "voracious Bloodhounds" tore "Children from their Mother's Bosoms and their mothers from their Husbands, then Singling out the men . . . Carr[ied] them in the woods and kill[ed] a great many."[36] The "Savages were let loose upon us," recalled Colonel Frye in his diary; "drove [us] into Disorder Rendered it impossible to Rally, the French Guards we were promised shou'd Escort us to Fort Edward Could or would not protect us."[37] Caesar Nero's master, John Gilman, and just over 900 others survived the bloody daylong attack; 600 "took to their Heels and fled . . . and arrived soon after at Fort Edward, giving out, that they supposed all who did not escape as they did, were either massacre'd, or carried off by the Indians."[38] Gilman made one of the most dramatic escapes. According to Charles Bell's history of Exeter, local lore maintained that "to avoid the Savages [Gilman] was obliged to swim the Hudson River three times."[39] Gilman's elaborate wardrobe and property were lost, taken as booty by the attackers or destroyed by the fire that razed the fort. Nine months later, however, Gilman applied for full reimbursement for his losses.

Caesar Nero Paul was one of five slave-soldiers snatched from the Fort William Henry ranks of survivors. Like him, the four other men, Jock Linn, Caesar, Jacob Lindse, and Canada Cuggo, were also New Englanders. Of them, only Caesar Paul, Linn, and Caesar returned to their Massachusetts homes. Jacob Lindse, the mulatto slave of Jacob Bigelow, and Canada Cuggo failed to return home to the New England colonies even after the 1760 conquest of Montreal that resulted in Caesar Nero's emancipation. The scanty records pertaining to Caesar Paul's Canadian abduction from Fort William Henry and his subsequent Canadian bondage reveal only that he was gone for three years and that John Gilman sought compensation for his slave's labor in the amount of eighty British pounds.

In August 1757, just one month after the Fort William Henry defeat, Captain John Gilman itemized his losses and was reimbursed by the province. The final entry of that detailed list reads: "To my Negro boy's Gun & Cloathing he being taken & carryd to Canada." The value Gilman attached to that property was 30 pounds.[40] In May 1761, ten months after Caesar Paul returned to Exeter, Gilman submitted another reimbursement request to the state legislature. It read, in part, "I pray the consideration of the legislature in making [me] some allowance—[I] had a slave in the year 1757 who was taken captive at the surrender of Fort William Henry and Returned in Captivity till the

Reduction of Canada &c."[41] His petition for eighty pounds was granted in full.

Caesar Paul returned to Exeter without fanfare, it seems, in July 1760. In Canada, he had been living in a settlement that, by 1760, was populated by some 10,250 inhabitants, 900 of whom were slaves and some 600 of whom were British subjects taken as prisoners during the recent wars.[42] Where had he been? What was the nature of his servitude during those three years? What kind of trauma had he survived? What were his impressions of New France, a place that was teeming with military forces that represented almost one-third of the settlement's 10,000 inhabitants?[43] To what degree had Caesar Nero been in contact with enslaved Indians, many of whom were from the Pawnee tribe? Neither Caesar Paul's Canadian slave narrative nor his account of the Fort William Henry siege and massacre were incorporated into the numerous contemporary histories of the French and Indian War, into Exeter's local histories, or into the thick volumes of Indian captivity stories. His saga of self-defense, camp life, captivity, and possible attempted escapes surfaces only fleetingly in the concise phrases of John Gilman's applications to the legislature for compensation for the loss of work and access to his enslaved servant.[44]

Caesar Paul achieved a striking level of domesticity once he returned from the French and Indian War to New England. Between 1761 and 1773, Paul obtained his freedom, married, began using the surname Paul, and became an autonomous head of his own household when he moved three miles from Exeter to Stratham, New Hampshire. He and his wife, Lovey Rollins, a white woman from an Exeter family, had several children, including Thomas, Nathaniel, Benjamin, Anne, and Dorothy. By 1790, fifty-two-year-old Caesar Paul was a free head of household living eight miles from the seacoast in Stratham with his wife and three of their children.[45] Paul, identified in the 1790 New Hampshire census as "C'sar Paul," and Lovey continued to live in New Hampshire and appear to have resided there until at least 1811. As late as January of that year, the Exeter *Constitutionalist* regularly listed the name "Cesar Paul" in its roster of "Persons for Whom Letters Remaining in the Post Office." Caesar and Lovey Paul relocated to Boston when they became elderly and lived with their son Thomas, daughter-in-law Catherine, and three grandchildren, Anne, Susan, and Thomas Jr. Caesar passed away from old age in Boston on 15 January 1823. The family, who enlisted the undertaker Samuel Winslow, buried Caesar, the family patriarch, in the historic Copp's Hill Cemetery, an "ancient cemetery" on the "highest hill in North Boston," and located not far from the Old North Church from which lanterns hung in 1775 to signal the British march on Lexington.[46] Caesar Paul's final resting place also was the burial site of famous New England Mathers—Increase, Cotton, and Samuel—as well as the final resting place for two other members of the Paul family. Caesar's son Thomas, who succumbed to tuberculosis in 1831, and his wife Lovey, who at sixty-four years of age died as a result of breast cancer, were laid to rest there, in April 1831 and April 1832, respectively.[47]

The silence about Caesar Paul's bondage foreshadows Hopkins's later elisions of her family's New England slavery past and other general biographical reconstructions. However, it is possible to document Caesar Paul's rapid social and cultural metamorphoses despite this missing history. His evolution from slave to accidental colonial soldier and emancipated man embodied the republican ideals of the emerging nation. That social and political trajectory enabled his sons, as first-generation free people, and Hopkins as a proud fifth-generation descendant in an American family of color, to make persuasive claims as they advanced their own purposeful campaigns for professional development and racial equality. In the space of forty years, Paul's socioeconomic and cultural transformations included living as a free African, an enslaved colonial subject, a slave-soldier in the French and Indian War, a prisoner of war, and finally as an independent man of color whose sons achieved impressive and steady gains as educated men and political representatives in the New World. The Paul family triumph—their invalidation of the dehumanizing claims that justified African enslavement and institutionalized disenfranchisement in America—was embodied first by Caesar Paul and then reinforced by his sons, as they garnered formal educational and social pedigrees as ministers, ambassadors, and international activists. This distinguished record of achievement made it possible for Paul family members and descendants to insist that emancipation, rather than enslavement, was the family's primary foundation. This substantial ancestral history emboldened descendants like Pauline Hopkins and bolstered their forthright explications of honorable democracy and race rights.

Hopkins's emphasis in public speeches and in her published writings on ancestral freedom and her deeply sentimental claim on an emancipatory black New England genealogy was justified further by the fact that New Hampshire both accommodated and invalidated slavery. The state constitution of 1776/1784 declared that "all men are born equally free and independent."[48] Indeed, state historian Isaac Hammond confidently asserted, "Negro slavery was never established in New Hampshire by any law of the province, or state; nor was it ever abolished by an legislative enactment."[49] Some historians note that New Hampshire "at no time boasted of many slaves" and that its people "disliked bondage of any kind." Others concede that slavery existed in the Granite State. Such admissions, however, are routinely qualified by assurances that although "[i]t is true that in Portsmouth, prior to the Revolution, there had been slavery," the practice of bondage amounted to "slavery with a difference": the enslaved Africans were "household retainers with a certain place in the community and an organization of their own."[50] This domestic autonomy and set of qualified definitions of enslavement aside, it was not until 1857, two years before Pauline Hopkins was born, that the New Hampshire state legislature dealt squarely with the shifting state history of enslavement and "specifically bann[ed] slavery and declar[ed] all Negroes to be full citizens of the state."[51]

Pauline Hopkins never explicitly invoked the name of Caesar Paul, nor did she articulate publicly or in writing her connection to colonial New England and to the African slave trade that brought her earliest known African ancestor to the New World. She would compensate for that silence about Caesar Nero, though, in her proud invocations of his family's early nineteenth-century claim on domesticity, piety, and education. The Paul family story seems, for her, to have begun in freedom and was embodied best by Caesar and Lovey's freeborn sons who were ordained in the Baptist faith and became influential ministers, educators, and antislavery activists of international reputation. Caesar and Lovey must have reveled in this glorious evolution from bondage to freedom as they witnessed, and enjoyed firsthand in Boston, the professional lives of their sons. It was this righteous and mobilizing Paul family activism that Hopkins invoked in 1901 when she laid claim to the accomplishments of her maternal forefathers.

Caesar Nero Paul's life and legacy was an implicit subtext in all the works of African American life and history that his great-great-granddaughter Pauline composed. That undocumented African and colonial history of his, while certainly a factor in the public careers of his sons and male descendants, also manifested itself very quickly, albeit with more public reserve, in the lives and accomplishments of his female descendants. Pauline Hopkins's tacit embrace of Caesar Paul's history allowed her to celebrate still unacknowledged women's histories and African American feminist legacies. She reconstructed with great tenderness, for example, the humble Exeter, New Hampshire, home of Dorothy Paul, one of Caesar and Lovey's daughters and her own great-grandmother, in her first novel, *Contending Forces*. She also took part in the distinct Paul family tradition of feminist activism. Her invocation of Susan Paul, Caesar's granddaughter and the daughter of Thomas and Catherine Paul, allowed her to reintroduce her public to the substantial tradition of African American women's enterprise, political activism, and effective interracial and mixed-gender collaborations of old.

The most compelling ancestral foremother that Pauline Hopkins could claim was Susan Paul (1809–41). Paul bequeathed to her distant cousin an invaluable legacy of high aesthetic sensibilities, a history of sophisticated private and public musicianship, inspired educational leadership, and trail-blazing literary enterprise. Susan was the second of three children and was born in Boston shortly after her father, Thomas, began his pastorate at the African Baptist Church. Susan was early on exposed to the impassioned and calculated efforts of her father and community as they developed the nation's most well-known antislavery campaigns. The immediacy of Caesar Nero's New England enslavement, coupled with the Protestant revivalist doctrines to which Thomas Paul ascribed, underscored for the Paul children and the community in which they came of age that slavery was a sin and that "opposition to slavery," then, was "a sign of holiness and a Christian duty."[52] A life of true faith, as Susan Paul understood it then, did not rely solely on quiet communion with God; it was a state that justified a deployment of one's beliefs and it required public work.

Susan Paul became the first woman in the Paul family to actively develop a public persona and to become a visible and accomplished activist. Her blend of piety and activism, education and mentoring, modeled for Hopkins the ways in which she might preserve her dignity while addressing some of the most complex and volatile issues of the day. Paul confronted the antebellum evils of enslavement and colonization; Hopkins would grapple with the post-Reconstruction realities of disenfranchisement, lynching, and segregation. Taken together, their efforts constitute a powerful bridge from one era to another and reinforce the substantial feminist record of activism that reveals the degree to which the Paul and Hopkins family histories contributed to the advancement of the race, of women, and of the nation.

The first documented public political campaign that Susan Paul undertook honored the principles and politics for which her father was so respected. She successfully sidestepped the vitriolic protests of women's activities in the public sphere and seems to have thoroughly deflected the often "hostile speculation[s]" that usually accompanied reviews of women's abolitionist speeches and activities.[53] Paul's activities, begun as the cult of true womanhood began to take hold, challenged many to confront the implications of unexpected true black womanhood and the tenets of such an emancipatory principle. In 1833, two years after her father's passing, twenty-four-year-old Susan formed a children's choir whose concerts advanced the message of abolition and raised public awareness about the inhumanity of slavery. The children's choir was made up entirely of students from her African American primary school, Boston Primary School, Number 6. Her goal, as *The Liberator* later reported, was "not to make money" but to "awaken an interest in behalf of an oppressed and persecuted race, and to abate the malignity of prejudice, by exhibiting some fifty or sixty colored pupils under circumstances eminently calculated to surprise and delight beholders."[54] The "circumstances" to which *The Liberator* referred were gorgeously choreographed, well-publicized, and well-attended antislavery meetings of the New England Anti-Slavery Society, the organization that William Lloyd Garrison had established in 1832 in the African Baptist Church.

Susan Paul and her abolitionist choir performed at least eight times from 1833 through mid-1835. The children offered at least two independent community concerts and six performances at formal New England Anti-Slavery Society conventions and meetings. The predominantly male membership of the New England Anti-Slavery Society provided Susan Paul with invaluable social and political protection, and she used this patronage to secure the safety and deploy into the highly charged abolitionist and antiabolitionist world the powerful voices of the impressionable children in her charge. Susan, however, was not simply a beneficiary of white institutional power; she was part of the organization. In August 1833, just one month before she and her choir made their debut at a New England Anti-Slavery Society meeting, Susan Paul became the first African American woman and one of the first female members to join the society. The society was perfectly suited to her moral and political prerogatives, and she had the foresight to recognize the public and private power available to her through affiliation. The organization, led by William Lloyd Garrison until its heated reorganization in 1840, was committed to immediate abolition, vigorously challenged the procolonization platform, and promoted radical abolitionism as the best means by which to end slavery.[55] The group also granted membership and voting privileges to women, although it was arguments about the role and rights of women that ultimately contributed to its 1840 schism. The society also considered its mission as one of cultural and moral intervention. Its primary objective was to emancipate all American slaves, but it also aimed to "achieve a noble work of beneficence, in regard to the free people of color . . . to encourage and assist them in all laudable efforts for their moral and intellectual improvement, to provide schools from the lowest to the highest grade, for their education; and to exterminate those prejudices which now reign with such tyrannous sway against them."[56]

Susan Paul was able to take her place on the public political stage because, for all intents and purposes, she never said a word. She did not co-opt the concerts and make speeches, and during her tenure as choir director, she published no controversial critiques nor did she issue any assessments of pro-slavery forces or legislation that could be deemed inappropriate to her gender, class position, or race. Yet, despite maintaining what might seem to be great political restraint, Paul orchestrated a most eloquent and vocal argument for the immediate abolition of slavery and for the overhaul of American society. Certainly her family's reputation, to a degree, elevated and protected her, but Paul successfully avoided drawing the invectives directed toward other women of her day by adhering to her position as a teacher, a "public" role that was suitable for an unmarried nineteenth-century woman.

In 1835, Paul intensified her political activity by using her position as a teacher to document the spiritual, racial, and political evolution of a free child of color. Her book, *Memoir of James Jackson, the Attentive and Obedient Scholar, Who Died in Boston, October 31, 1833, Aged Six Years and Eleven Months by his Teacher, Miss Susan Paul*, was an impressive accomplishment. In addition to being the first published work by a member of the Paul family, it also was the earliest known published prose narrative and biography by a black woman in the United States and the first work to document the life of a free African American child. Paul intended originally to publish the book under the auspices of a religious organization such as the American Sabbath School Union, but the very mention of slavery in the text prompted the organization to reject the manuscript in order to accommodate its pro-slavery Southern affiliates. Frustrated but undeterred, Paul sold the copyright to James Loring, a local publisher with abolitionist sympathies. Garrison and others quickly rallied around Paul and heralded the book for its persuasive humanistic message. Garrison in particular used the publication to publicly embrace Susan Paul as a promising ally in the abolitionist cause, and she responded purposefully. Not only did she become the first woman of color to take out a life membership in the New England Anti-Slavery Society, but she also partnered with Garrison as he strategized about how best to confront nagging racism and elitism within Boston's antislavery community in general, and within the ranks of its female societies in particular. With his support, Paul integrated the Boston Female Anti-Slavery Society, the sister society to the New England Anti-Slavery Society. In addition, she continued to train her public school and Sabbath school students to perform pointed political and religious songs at public antislavery meetings and secular community concerts. Her demonstrated record of achievement as a biographer and aspiring public historian increasingly reflected the forceful perspective of her father and extended family on slavery and freedom. Paul modeled for Pauline

Hopkins the power of carefully politicized African American domesticity and the necessity for astute public testimony about African American lives and deaths. In 1905, some seventy years after the publication of the *Memoir of James Jackson* and the heyday of the children's choir performances, Pauline Hopkins reflected publicly at the Garrison Centennial celebration about the power of family, political conviction, and the still-unrealized agenda of African American women. She was able to do so, in part, because she was both challenged and encouraged by the deliberate example of Susan Paul. Pauline Hopkins could embrace and learn from her distant cousin's commitment to securing full freedoms for African Americans, to initiating necessary social reforms, and to promoting intellectual and professional opportunities for people of color. The New England history that Hopkins inherited from Caesar, Thomas, Susan Paul, and their relations gave her a rightful claim to colonial America. Her access to and inheritance of history that celebrated white national history and consistently overlooked the African experience compelled her to deputize herself in the ongoing struggle to tell the rich story of African American origins and history and to work diligently on behalf of the race for full citizenship rights.

2

Patriarchal Facts and Fictions

A child should always say what's true
And speak when he is spoken to . . .
At least as far as he is able.
ROBERT LOUIS STEVENSON
"The Whole Duty of Children"

The Garrison Centennial celebration in 1905 provided Pauline Hopkins with her greatest opportunity for public articulation of her political sensibilities and celebration of her family history. As she declared herself a "black daughter of the revolution," she cloaked herself not only in the powerful legacy of African American patriarchs but also in the unsung history of her familial, literary, and political foremothers. Hopkins was a woman consumed by the rhetoric and power of genealogy; indeed, she frequently spoke of lineage as a perpetually vexed, sometimes hobbling, and possibly emancipatory construct. Such inclinations, however, were not solely the cultivated hallmarks of a professional writer or tactics used to enhance the melodramatic plots of her serialized stories. There was a set of genuine and deep personal facts, fictions, and mysteries that shaped her views of bloodlines and inheritance.

Hopkins seems never to have had during her lifetime the opportunity to luxuriate in being the subject of a biography. Indeed, as the most complete published biographical profiles such as the *Colored American Magazine* account confirm, she not only was responsible for generating her own life story but also was charged with crafting such narratives by adopting an objective third-party voice and perspective as she related the details. Such tasks, possibly onerous at times, provided her with great license at other times, and sometimes freed her from historical accountability. Her purposeful appropriation of history and genealogy is hidden in plain view in the 1901 *Colored American Magazine* biography that appeared in 1901. That article has stood since that time as the foundational account of her life story.

The *Colored American Magazine* biography that Pauline Hopkins used to introduce herself to twentieth-century readers effectively obscures one of the most important and traumatic aspects of her genealogy. Her paternal history is neither as concise nor as straightforward as the *Colored American Magazine* profile suggests. Until now, Hopkins's accepted biography has suggested relative stability and uneventful domesticity. Based on the magazine profile and the cryptic details included in her death certificate, the majority of scholarly accounts of Hopkins report that she was the daughter of Sarah and Northup Hopkins, before going on to recite the familiar details of her birth in Portland, Maine, arrival in Massachusetts, and emergence as a writer and lady editor of the *Colored American Magazine*. This record of her early life, however, is deeply misleading and strikingly incomplete.

Pauline Elizabeth Hopkins was the daughter of Benjamin Northup, a member of one of the most politically active and established African American families in Providence, Rhode Island. She was born in 1859 to Sarah and Benjamin, two years after their June 1857 marriage in Boston. She was not, as has been suggested, the daughter of a man named Northup Hopkins—no such person in her life existed.[1] William Hopkins was the man that Pauline came to regard and refer to as her father. While adoption papers do not seem ever to have been filed, she took the surname of Hopkins when a teenager, and did so at a moment that coincided with an auspicious development in her public writing life. Although Pauline appears to have had no documented contact with her biological father after his marriage to her mother, Sarah, dissolved in the early 1860s, her identity as a Northup significantly broadens the scholarly understanding of her forthright claim to a professional life as a public intellectual. It sheds additional light on her understanding of enslavement and of the ways in which her immediate and extended family actively negotiated freedom in the North. Her father's family was visible and influential in the early nineteenth-century African American community of Providence, Rhode Island. The Northups lodged eloquent and effective challenges to segregated education and the practice of taxation without representation for the people of color in the state during the antebellum period. This significant genealogical revelation completes and thoroughly enriches Hopkins's long-accepted life story, an already intriguing narrative that she herself reshaped and edited liberally.

The long-obscured genealogical truths about Hopkins's patrimony also reveal a compelling set of connections that linked the families of her mother, Sarah, father, Benjamin, and stepfather, William. Benjamin Northup and William Hopkins, the two men who played primary roles in Pauline Hopkins's life, moved in similar community circles, and members of their extended families knew each other very well. Both men were related to individuals who achieved prominence in local and regional African American circles, identified with staunch Garrisonian abolitionist principles, and rejected squarely colonizationist ideologies.[2] As a Northup descendant, Pauline Hopkins was part of a New England family that, like the Pauls with whom they were contemporaries, waged campaigns to achieve intellectual and political equality for people of African descent. The revelation of Pauline Hopkins's true paternity truly clarifies and enriches her emphatic 1905 claim that she was a "black daughter of the revolution."

Benjamin Northup, the son of a well-established free New England family of color, was twenty-three years old when he took Sarah Allen of Boston as his wife on 16 June 1857. At the time of the marriage, he was earning his living as a waiter, one of the few steady professions open to men of color. The fourth of eight children, Benjamin was born in Providence in 1832, the same year in which the city of Providence was incorporated. He was one of five sons and three girls born to Cato (1802–60) and Alice Northup (1808–65). He and his siblings were born into circumstances that promised few material comforts and no easy access to vital basic rights such as education. They would be strengthened in the face of such extensive disenfranchisement, however, by the example of their elders, individuals like their father and uncle who were committed to defending the rights of African Americans, to acquiring racial equality, and to cultivating racial uplift. The Northup family history of demonstrated political outreach complemented the tireless efforts of Pauline Hopkins's maternal Paul family ancestors. Ichabod Northup, Benjamin's uncle and Pauline's granduncle, became one of the region's most outspoken advocates for African American rights. In addition, he lobbied fervently for fair housing, protested the hypocritical practice of African American taxation without representation, and was a passionate advocate in the fight to acquire equal educational opportunities for children of color. Benjamin and his siblings benefited directly, and by association, from the strategic political interventions that their elders in particular made on behalf of the race and the future generations of freeborn African Americans.

Benjamin Northup's parents, both of whom were identified as mulattos in the 1850 Rhode Island census, were natives of the state.[3] Although his father and mother were, technically, born free, both may well have been quite literally shackled by slavery. Rhode Island, in 1784, had passed a Gradual Emancipation Act, but it was legislation that indulged slave owners and provided people of color with only limited relief from bondage. The act, advanced by the wealthy white antislavery proponents Moses Brown, Samuel

Hopkins, and James Manning, was narrow in its scope because of the enormous influence that powerful slave trading families such as the DeWolfes were able to exert. Early federal census records do not confirm conclusively Cato Northup's status as enslaved or free at the time of his birth. Indeed, he may have been one of the state's free population, which in 1790 numbered 4,370, or one of the nearly 1,000 enslaved people documented by the state census. Although, by 1807, most African Americans in Rhode Island were free, if Cato Northup was born to an enslaved woman, he would have been subject to the act's pernicious clause that allowed his mother's owner to be "compensated for the loss of 'property' by binding [him] out to service and taking [his] wages until [he] reached the age of twenty-one."[4] Evidence of the region's disregard for African American freedoms was, for some, illustrated most pointedly and tragically by the fact that it was not until 1859 that the last slave in Rhode Island was freed and that the emancipation of this individual was only achieved by death.

Neither the 1774 nor the 1782 Rhode Island censuses include Providence households headed by white or Negro individuals named Northup. However, there are several white Northup families that also included people of color in the returns for North Kingstown, Rhode Island, a coastal town located then in the large county of Narragansett, a Rhode Island region that was home to the state's large plantations and the majority of the slaves held in the state. The scanty information of the early censuses reveals potential details about the origins of Pauline's paternal grandfather, Cato Northup, but does not allow conclusive claims about his origins. The 1782 Rhode Island census, for example, includes twenty-four heads of household with the surname Northup. Of these, four include individuals of color in their households. The census, which only listed the name of the head of household and did not include the names or precise ages of other individuals, includes Stephen Northup, living with a white woman, who like him was older than fifty years, and three mulattos: Margery Northup, who presided over a household of six whites and four mulattos; Immanuel Northup, in whose home were four white boys under fifteen, two white females, one Indian, and four mulattos; and Henry Northup, whose household included one mulatto and four whites.

Pauline Hopkins's paternal ancestors appeared for the first time in the federal census in the 1830 Rhode Island returns. Ten years later, in 1840, when they were residents of the fourth ward of Providence, the census provided the first official glimpse of the family. By 1840, the Northups had seven children, but it was not until 1850 that the census provided the names, ages, and specific racial identity of all inhabitants of the Northup home. The family emerged as fully as it ever had in this year. Cato was listed as a forty-eight-year-old mulatto; his wife, Alice, was a forty-two-year-old mulatto; and their seven children, all of whom also were listed as mulattos, were listed by name: Edward, Mary, James, Benjamin, Charles, Mary J., and David.

During his lifetime, Cato Northup, who would pass away in 1860 at the age of fifty-eight, provided for his growing family by working as a laborer. It was one of the occupations most frequently filled by men of color in the state—individuals who because of their race were denied possibilities of full professional development. Northup and other men of color, if free from racial prejudice and its severe economic constraints, likely would have sought employment in the numerous textile mills or arranged apprenticeships as mechanics. Virulent racism effectively suppressed the growth of an African American professional class in cities such as Providence. Yet individuals such as Cato Northup and his enterprising younger brother, Ichabod, who also worked for years as a laborer, were able to achieve high status, domestic stability, and political agency.[5] In addition, members of the Northups' African American community seized the opportunities to work in the service sector as caterers, gardeners, hostlers, waiters, and porters. Many proved to be extremely resourceful and were able to amass sizeable real estate holdings that valued in the thousands of dollars. By 1860, for example, Ichabod Northup II, Benjamin's uncle, was one of thirty-one African Americans who had acquired real estate valued at more than five hundred dollars. Ichabod's holdings of $3,200 placed him in the top 20 percent of that group, alongside individuals such as Manuel Fenner, a farrier whose real estate was valued at $5,000, James M. Cheves, whose property was worth $3,900, George Henry, a gardener whose holdings totaled $3,500, and George Head, a grocer whose real estate was appraised at $3,000.[6]

Like the Paul family and the large contingent of black Bostonians who lived on Beacon Hill near the State House during the antebellum period, Cato Northup and his family lived in the shadow of the Rhode Island state capitol. As Providence residents, they were part of the statewide African American population that in 1840 numbered 3,238, less than 3 percent of the state's total population. In Providence, which in 1840 had a total population of 23,000, the Northups were among the 1,500 African Americans in Rhode Island who lived in the capital city.[7] Between 1832, the year of Benjamin's birth, and 1841, the year after his youngest son was born, Cato Northup and his family moved at least three times.[8] The Providence city directory reveals that in 1836, the family was living on Planet Street, a road best known as the location of the historic Sabin Tavern from which a group of white men led by the slave trader John Brown, brother to Moses, the Brown University founder and eventual antislavery proponent, set forth in 1772 to burn the British ship

Gaspee in order to protest continued British taxation.[9] In 1838, the Northups were residing on Federal Hill, and in 1841, they were living near Westminster Street, which would become, by the late 1870s, one of the city's main streets and business thoroughfares.[10]

Benjamin Northup was born into a Northern state that, like Massachusetts, was immune neither to destructive racial violence nor to the spirited antislavery campaigns in which Pauline Hopkins's Paul family ancestors immersed themselves. Just one year before Benjamin's birth, the Northups and the city's larger African American community weathered a destructive racist attack by Irish mobs. The aggressive invasion and destruction of the neighborhoods began shortly after news from the South of the deadly Nat Turner Revolt in Southampton, Virginia, filtered into the city press and became the chief story for several days. Events such as the Hardscrabble Riot in 1824 and subsequent upheavals such as the Olney Lane and Snow Town riots of 1831 prompted young and earnest men like Cato Northup to mobilize on behalf of their beleaguered families. While a young man in his twenties, Cato Northup combined his race pride with his fierce desire to protect his community, and he joined the African Greys, a militia company that several young men of color established in 1821 because white authorities had failed to protect African Americans when they were besieged by bloodthirsty mobs.[11]

As a member of the African Greys, Cato Northup contributed to a calculated campaign designed not only to protect the community, but also to embody the respectability and cohesion of the local community of color.[12] The African Greys were a recognized militia and participated in militia parades that drew groups from other states as well as in ceremonial civilian events. In 1822, they played a key supporting role in the services held to dedicate Providence's African Baptist Church and School. Militia members "wore black belts and carried muskets," and the officers, of whom Cato Northup was one, carried sidearms on these occasions. On at least one occasion, Northup, who in 1822 had achieved the rank of corporal, was instrumental in preserving the integrity of a significant African American community event. On this particular occasion, Cato Northup's intervention preserved the integrity of the formal dedication of the African Baptist Church, a new sanctuary for people of color that was large enough to accommodate 500 worshipers and the schoolroom attached to the church that could hold between 150 and 200 students. According to William J. Brown, a longtime resident of the city and one of its early African American local historians, one of the African Greys was "tapped on the shoulder, and a bill was presented to him by an officer, charging him five dollars for a pair of boots." Brown, who recorded the tense event some sixty years later in his 1883 memoir, recalled that "Corporal Cato G. Northup drew out his pocket-book, took out a five dollar bill, and passed it to the officer," an act that derailed "the trick which [the bystanders] thought would create such beautiful fun" and enabled the African Greys "to resum[e] their march as if nothing had happened."[13] The incident, which calls attention to Cato Northup's vigilance and decisive action, is notable also because it reveals that he did not hesitate to use precious resources—whether the money was his own or from a fund maintained by the militia—to prevent the baiting of his fellow militia members.

The Northups were part of an embattled interracial minority determined to support the eradication of slavery in the United States and to promote the uplift of free African Americans in the North. Unfortunately, they could not avoid the dramatic and outspoken proslavery sentiments that continued to erupt in their city. In 1835, when Benjamin Northup was barely three years old and his parents were young parents with a growing family, town leaders in five Rhode Island cities, including Providence, rallied residents to participate in anti-antislavery meetings. White citizens responded promptly to the schedule of antiabolitionist public meetings. On these occasions, they visited "silence and utter contempt" upon "the unholy efforts and projects of those 'reckless fanatics,' whom they regarded as an undisciplined and careless group whose actions would 'let slip the dogs of civil war.'"[14]

The African American community, however, was already mobilizing itself against fearmongers and proslavery institutional organizations in the years before the anti-antislavery forces succeeded in drumming up support for these exclusionary ideologies. African American initiatives reflected the multifaceted nature of their lives and experiences and were not limited solely to slavery-related issues. As early as 1830, Benjamin's uncle Ichabod was encouraging the city's people of color to "plead the cause of black suffrage." The organizing committee, of which small-business owner Ichabod Northup was a member, held an important meeting in the African Union Meeting House to discuss the issues. The gathering was advertised as an opportunity "to discuss the issue of taxation in the absence of representation."[15] Empowered by their community, the committee, made up of men who worked as traders, laborers, farmers, and independent small businessmen, filed their complaint with the Rhode Island General Assembly. Such action represented the kind of self-assertion that William Lloyd Garrison hoped to see. During his strategic visits to Providence, the *Liberator* editor was pleased to absorb the details about the political initiative of the city's African Americans and of Ichabod Northup, whom Garrison came to know because Northup served as treasurer of the Mutual Relief Society, an organization that raised funds to support Garrison's work. Writing to his brother-in-law Henry Benson about the colonizationist platform that was gaining momentum, Garrison admitted plainly that he hoped the African American community would act "fearlessly, firmly, understandingly."[16]

The Northups played a significant role in Providence's antislavery efforts. Ichabod Northup II, Pauline Hopkins's paternal granduncle, was the family member who was most visible in the public campaign to end slavery and eradicate its attendant evils such as segregation and mob violence. Yet Ichabod Northup's success as an energetic antislavery and civil rights activist was made possible, in large part, by the steady support of his extended family and larger community. The collaborative nature of the early antebellum African American activism is made especially clear by events such as those that occurred in the spring of 1833 when William Lloyd Garrison journeyed to Providence and addressed the people of color there. In early April, Garrison met with the people of color, and he described the experience to his *Liberator* coeditor, Isaac Knapp. "According to appointment," he wrote,

> I addressed our colored friends in Providence, on Friday evening last and although they had but short notice, they gave me a large audience. At the close of the address, they voluntarily made a collection of my mission, which, with the contributions of some white friends, amounted to the handsome sum of *thirty dollars*. In addition to this, the colored "Mutual Relief Society" gave $15, at the hands of their Treasurer, Ichabod Northup. The colored "Female Literary Society" also presented me $6, and the colored "Female Tract Society" $4[.]oo making in all $55.00.

The generosity and unhesitating self-sacrifice that Garrison witnessed on that Friday evening was not all that impressed him. As Garrison related to Harriet Minot (1815–88), a fellow New England abolitionist, his audience that night "felt and exhibited" the "highest and most intense feeling." "They wept freely," he recalled; "they clustered round me in throngs, each one eager to receive the pressure of my hand and implore Heaven's choicest blessings upon my head." "You cannot imagine the scene," he told Minot as he assured her that "my pen is wholly inadequate to describe it."[17]

During Benjamin's childhood, William Lloyd Garrison frequently praised and exhorted Benjamin's Providence neighbors. In 1832, he declared that "[t]here is probably no other place in which our [antislavery] cause has more hearty, indefatigable, estimable advocates, than in Providence."[18] Benjamin's daughter Pauline prided herself on the close relation that Garrison had with her Paul ancestors. It appears now, however, that her ancestral ties to Garri-

Patriarchal Facts and Fictions

son were not limited to her maternal relatives. Her father, his family, and their extended community developed close ties to the great antislavery editor as well. After making his several trips to Providence in the 1830s, Garrison admitted to having deep feelings for the community there. Both whites and African Americans demonstrated their commitment to the antislavery cause by organizing societies that attended larger regional and national meetings, celebrated the abolition of slavery in the West Indies, and generally pursued social and civic equality for African Americans. The Northup legacy that Pauline Hopkins could claim as her own was one of impressive public action, fearless civic ambition, and strong community consciousness.

Details about how Benjamin Northup and Sarah Allen met, the nature of their courtship, and their early years as newlyweds remain unknown. The two were members of enterprising and highly regarded New England activist families and may have met during one of the various regional meetings that often brought families such as theirs together. Ichabod Northup and John T. Waugh, another Providence resident and a future step-relation of Pauline's, for example, both traveled to Boston for political meetings hosted by leaders of New England's African American and abolitionist communities. As attendees, they would have been hosted by the city's African American community in general and by the wives and female kin of the men involved. All would rally to provide lodging and sustenance for the conventiongoers during their stays.

What is known about the Allen-Northup marriage comes from the official legal records that confirm the marriage and that mark its end. Boston marriage records reveal that both Northup and Allen were living in Boston in 1857. The record does not name the church or site where the couple wed. It, however, does confirm that Sarah and Benjamin turned to Sebastian Streeter, a well-known seventy-four-year-old Mason and Universalist minister, and asked him to preside at their ceremony.[19] The marriage represented a promising merger of New England families who for generations had worked to abolish slavery, to desegregate public schools, and to gain fair and consistent political representation for the race.

Benjamin and Sarah Northup disappeared from public records such as the census or city directories after their wedding. They do not appear in the 1860 census returns for Rhode Island, Massachusetts, or Maine, the three states in which they lived during their six years of marriage.[20] They also do not appear in city directories of Portland, Maine, published during the years of their marriage. The birth of their daughter Pauline provided an opportunity for the Northups to document their location. However, only a minority of Maine residents filed birth certificates during the antebellum period, and the Northups were not among those who did so. Northup, like many men of color who were his age, may have attempted to join a Civil War regiment. To date, there is inconclusive evidence that he indeed did so.[21] Information about their domestic arrangements, employment, and moves throughout New England emerges only as a result of the narrative that Sarah Allen Northup provided as she tried to dissolve the union.

On 31 October 1863, three months after the battle at Gettysburg, Sarah Allen Northup initiated divorce proceedings against her husband, Benjamin. The narrative that she provided about her private life as a wife reveals that she had been waging her own civil wars as a wife and mother. Represented by Boston attorney Paul Willard, Sarah Northup filed a petition for divorce from Benjamin Northup.[22] The document was required by law and was submitted to the Supreme Judicial Court representing Suffolk County and the state of Massachusetts. It provided a haunting account of Sarah Northup's trials and testifies to her great resolve as she attempted to reconstruct her life in the wake of betrayal and irreconcilable differences. The petition reveals that, like so many African Americans, the Northups moved frequently. After the wedding, they lived in Boston and Roxbury, Massachusetts, in Portland, Maine, and in Providence, Rhode Island. Their last place of residence was Roxbury, where they were living until March 1862. It appears that at this point, the marriage began to unravel. Sarah could and did claim that "she has ever been faithful to her marriage obligations," but she could not assert the same for her husband. "[T]he said Benjamin," cited the petition, "being wholly regardless of [his marriage obligations] has committed adultery with various lewd women, whose names are to your Libellant unknown."[23] Northup's infidelity, portrayed as both highly disrespectful of and intensely repulsive to his wife, was the cornerstone of Sarah Northup's case against him.

Sarah Allen Northup brought her suit for divorce at a time when women far exceeded men as divorce petitioners and when divorce rates in the United States were climbing, in part because of the great stresses brought on by the Civil War.[24] Sarah Northup, although part of a growing national trend, was in the minority when it came to African American marital patterns. Since colonial times, people of African descent in New England had been minimally represented in the courts. Since 1745, when one of the earliest African American divorce cases came before a Massachusetts court, many people of color sought the rulings of their churches rather than of the courts.[25] This trend also was much more a part of Southern culture, since enslaved and formerly enslaved peoples were denied access to the judicial spheres and rulings that would have recognized their humanity and right to domestic order. Sarah Northup's initiative to have her case arbitrated in the public legal sphere certainly reveals her deep desire to ensure the dissolution of her marriage. Yet the move to engage counsel and use legal channels also suggests that she may have wanted to maximize the possibility that she would receive alimony to support herself and her young child. Finally, her course of action was a decidedly middle-class gesture, one that affirmed publicly her intolerance of a situation that would compromise her claims on true womanhood and upstanding domesticity. Sarah Northup's actions represented the kind of bold social self-assertion that prompted Auguste Carlier, a Frenchman and author of *Marriage in the United States*, to remark that it was "[t]o the honor of American women . . . that the majority of the divorces are granted at their request, and not against them."[26]

In addition to filing for divorce, Sarah Allen Northup instructed her attorney to file for her full custody of "Pauline Elizabeth Northup, minor child of herself and her said husband." She also requested that "suitable alimony may be decreed to be paid to her . . . at said times and in such manner as to the court shall seem proper" and that she be granted permission to "resume her maiden name of Sarah Allen."[27] Although her husband's whereabouts were unknown, the court would not rule on her petition before it granted Benjamin Northup the opportunity to contest the petition against him. The Superior Judicial Court, in the interest of providing Northup with the chance to "show cause why the prayer of said libel should not be granted," instructed Sarah's attorney to post the divorce petition and their ruling "once a week, three weeks successively, in the *Boston Daily Courier*."[28]

Benjamin Northup was living at 150 Russell Street on Beacon Hill in 1864. He was accessible enough to George Ruffin, who included Northup's name in the historic survey he undertook to assess all local men of color eligible to vote.[29] However, there currently is no evidence to suggest that Northup appeared to challenge his wife's claims against him or her suit for divorce. As a result, the spring 1864 docket for the Suffolk County Court included case number 384. On Thursday, 7 April, Sarah attended a court session that granted her a final judgment of her petition. Supporting Sarah and serving as her legal witnesses on that day were her mother, Elizabeth Allen, and also Henry Cummings, a fifty-one-year-old African American physician who lived in Boston.[30] Sarah Northup received a "divorce from the bonds of matrimony, on the grounds of adultery." In addition, Judge Willard awarded her alimony in the amount of 200 dollars, legal costs, custody of her minor child, and the

The Reverend Leonard Grimes, minister of the Twelfth Street
Baptist Church in Boston, who officiated at the marriage
ceremony of Sarah Allen and William Hopkins on
25 December 1864. *Courtesy of Moorland-Spingarn
Research Center, Howard University.*

legal right to resume the use of her maiden name.[31] The court's judgment provided Sarah Allen with the opportunity to move beyond what, by her account, became a tumultuous and distressing marriage.

1864 may have begun on a difficult note for Sarah Allen and her five-year-old daughter, Pauline Elizabeth. Despite their travails, though, the year would close in a most splendid and celebratory manner. On 25 December, Sarah Allen wed William A. Hopkins, a five-foot-four-inch-tall, brown-eyed Civil War veteran and the man with whom she happily would spend the next forty-one years of her life. The couple chose the Reverend Leonard Andrew Grimes, the minister of the extremely well-attended Twelfth Street Baptist Church on Phillips Street where Pauline's maternal cousin and mentor, Elijah Smith, and his family were members "for many happy years," to officiate at their Christmas Day ceremony.[32] Sarah and William likely knew of the church's early ties to the African Baptist Church on Beacon Hill and the controversies that had led to the formation of the Twelfth Street Baptist Church. The Twelfth Street church was formed in the 1830s, shortly after the death of the Reverend Thomas Paul, when friction drove a group of African Baptist Church parishioners to secede from the original congregation. Such unfortunate acrimony was displaced by the subsequent history of community solidarity, and it was this rich and uplifting tradition that informed the celebratory proceedings. William Hopkins, whose family had been enslaved in Virginia, may have had an independent connection with Grimes, a fearless antislavery man who had worked so closely with the Underground Railroad during the antebellum years that his church came to be known as the Fugitives' Church.

The rich antebellum history of Grimes's outreach to the Boston community was complemented by the steady efforts that so many in his church made to secure African American rights to domestic bliss and the pursuit of happiness. The wedding ceremony, with its links to Grimes and the undeniable history of the Twelfth Street church, represented much more than a new love relationship for Sarah and the establishment of a new primary family arrangement for Pauline. Indeed, Sarah Allen and William Hopkins chose to begin their life together in a church that was known as "the home of the oppressed [and] the vantage ground of the champions of human freedom," a place in which the "fugitive was never refused its shelter and protection" and "from which slavery was assailed most grandly and fearlessly."[33] The marriage of Sarah Allen and William Hopkins, and the reconstitution of a family for Pauline, thus became part of the longstanding effort by Boston African Americans to create and to preserve an empowered, increasingly cohesive, and politically active middle class.

3

The Creation of a Boston Family

If [any] spot on this planetary system be sacred
to the goddess of liberty—to the rights of man—
that spot should be our capital.

Freedom's Journal,
16 November 1827

The early life of Pauline Hopkins was colored by the marital distress of her parents, Sarah and Benjamin Northup, and the upheaval wrought by their divorce. Her childhood regained stability when her mother married William Hopkins, a kindly man who was protective and indulgent of both Sarah and her daughter, Pauline. The bond between Pauline and William was rooted in their love of the arts. His active participation in some of the city's most enterprising amateur arts groups gave him considerable cachet with her and the extended Allen family. William cultivated Pauline's own love of the theater and did so steadily and with considerable professionalism. He witnessed her performance debut as a vocalist and was a key supporter when she made her stage debut. William set his sights on marshaling the creative interests of his new family into pioneering and potentially lucrative arts ventures. It took some time before Pauline adopted the surname of Hopkins. It was an entirely private decision, one not apparently mandated by formal adoption proceedings. Indeed, as later census records would show, the decision would complement the family's erasure of Sarah's previous marriage and also would obscure the identity of Benjamin Northup, Pauline's biological father.

William Hopkins was a steady and innovative provider, a man who blended practical work pursuits that maintained the family with creative artistic and performance ventures that enriched their lives and contributed much to the community. He was a man whose life experiences, military service, ambition, and entrepreneurial spirit far exceeded his slight frame. A longtime sailor, Civil War veteran, barber, amateur actor, and active race man, Hopkins played an increasingly supportive role in the life of his stepdaughter, Pauline.

His tours of duty in the United States Navy, his family links to Virginia and the District of Columbia, and his proud participation in nationally recognized veterans' organizations constituted a rich resource for her. Indeed, her earliest writings and evolution as a singer, actress, and dramatist reflect not only William Hopkins's enthusiastic and purposeful support of her talents, but suggest also the influence of his perspectives on such diverse subjects as the American South, African American patriotism, black masculinity, and public service.

The son of Virginians Peter Hopkins and Catherine Waugh Hopkins, William was born in Alexandria, Virginia, in 1835.[1] When William was twelve years old, his father, Peter, became a free man. Slave owner James Dempsey initiated proceedings to legalize Peter Hopkins's emancipation, and on 16 March 1847, the legal contract was enacted before two witnesses, William Yeaton and Cassius F. Lee. Although not designated as such in the contract, Lee was serving at the time as District Court clerk for the District of Columbia. There are intriguing hints about the possible links between Lee, the first cousin of the Confederate general Robert E. Lee, and the family of William Hopkins. It is possible that a family link through slavery and estates may have contributed to Lee's serving as witness to the emancipation of Peter Hopkins, a man who may have had connections to Lee's in-laws, a white slave-owning Virginia family with ancestral ties to King Edward I of England.[2]

William grew up in Alexandria, Virginia, a city that lay less than ten miles north of the historic Mount Vernon estate and plantation of George Washington, the first president of the United States. Incorporated in 1779, Alexandria lies in Fairfax County on the west bank of the Potomac River and, during the antebellum period, was known for its "bustling harbor" that "teemed with brigs, schooners, and ships of the line, which traversed the high seas and engaged in international and coast-wise trade."[3] As Washington supervised plans for the creation of the capital, he claimed the city of Alexandria and additional portions of Fairfax County in the late 1790s. Although the seat of government was located squarely in the federal city, Alexandria enjoyed the regular presence of the nation's first president. He not only kept a home there but also maintained ties to one of the local churches and to a Masonic Lodge that was based in the city.[4]

Alexandria, which was reincorporated into the state of Virginia in 1847, was one of the most prosperous trading centers on the East Coast. That prosperity, however, was not reaped from honest commerce in material goods but was inextricably bound up in the slave trade.[5] The city made a gradual transformation from a pastoral locale into a bustling Southern proslavery environment. Indeed, the city's white residents for whom the slave trade became a livelihood saw the opportunities that contemporary federal legislation might provide them. Once federal laws of 1808 outlawed the importation of Africans, the capital's internal trade in enslaved people began to flourish.[6] Within four years, slavery had taken root in the capital and been allowed, if not encouraged, to do so when the federal government allowed traders to use its jails and resources to support the trade.[7] As a result of its connections to the trade, the city contributed much to the "ill-fame" of the District of Columbia as a whole. This thriving society that grew up alongside what the writer Thomas Moore once described as "the proud Powtowmac's streams" became "a natural outlet" for and "the very seat and center of the domestic slave traffic" that catered to the "coastwise slave ships and the overland coffles" that arrived there.[8]

The District of Columbia compensated for its inability to participate in "slave rearing" by serving instead as "depot for the purchases of interstate traders who combed Maryland and northern Virginia for slaves."[9] At the core of such commercial enterprise were businesses such as the "pretentious estate of Armfield and Franklin" and the Bruin "Negro Jail," both located on Duke Street. John Armfield and Isaac Franklin, who established their company in 1828, presided over an extremely profitable enterprise that became a formidable leader in the slave trading business. During the early years of William Hopkins's childhood in the mid- to late 1830s, the enterprise of Armfield and Franklin was responsible for almost 50 percent of the "sea trade in slaves between Virginia and Maryland and New Orleans" and was "sending more than a thousand slaves a year to the South west."[10] Its slave pens, which housed the men, women, and children who were on the verge of being sold, were "large walled areas" surrounded by high brick walls that blocked public views of the interior and the regular displays of the captives. Joseph Bruin, who established his business in 1843 and quickly became the city's "dominant slave dealer" in the city, gained much publicity in 1848 when seventy-seven enslaved people, captured before they could achieve their escape aboard the schooner *Pearl*, were sold to Bruin, who held them in his jail before negotiating additional sales and transfers that sent enslaved people, such as fifteen- and thirteen-year-old sisters Emily and Mary Edmondson, further into the deep South.[11] When Joshua Leavitt, the abolitionist editor of the *New York Evangelist*, went to the capital to see firsthand the conditions under which captive people of color were being held, he recalled the scene vividly for his readers. Leavitt witnessed a symbolic and deadly resurrection of men who emerged from the cellars below the building and recalled that when fifty to sixty women and children appeared, he imagined that he could see in the "faces of these mothers some indication of irrepressible feeling. It seemed to me," Leavitt stated mournfully, "that they hugged their little ones more closely, and that a cold perspiration stood on their foreheads."[12] The captives who appeared before Leavitt on that day were part of the estimated 6,000 slaves who were sold in the District of Columbia and transported to the Commonwealth of Virginia.[13]

The anguish, the inhumanity, and the apparent hypocrisy that the trade represented even prompted slave owners to protest the very system upon which their livelihoods depended. John Randolph, one of the region's most well-known slave owners, was moved to strident protest because of the trade and the devastating mockery that it made of American principles. "In no part of the earth," Randolph intoned, "even excepting the Coast of Africa, was there so great, so infamous a slave market, as in the metropolis, in the seat of government of this nation which prides itself on freedom."[14] Slavery in the capital also elicited sharp critique from the fledgling African American press. In 1838, the *Weekly Advocate*, the precursor of the *Colored American*, roundly castigated those who bartered in human lives. "We regard these slave dealers as Cannibals," declared the editors, and "we mention them with the same feelings as we would a gang of thieves or counterfeiters. . . . Washington, the seat of government of a free people, is disgraced by slavery."[15]

William Hopkins came of age in a region that symbolized both the noble promise and the devastating flaws of America. The capital and by extension the city of Alexandria were sandwiched between the slave states of Virginia and Maryland. These two states were home to over 50 percent of all people of African descent in the United States in 1790. In sharp contrast to the disenfranchised masses of color was the powerful white minority that included the slaveholding president of the United States and other representatives of the new American democracy who were highly visible figures in the region. The fixtures of the slave trade—its pens, auction markets, and ships—also were an insistent part of the landscape. The inconsistency of American democratic rhetoric was embodied in the "familiar" sight of "manacled slaves, like a butcher's drove of hobbled cattle, passing along the east front of the . . . Capitol."[16] The opportunity to behold the distance between the rhetoric of freedom and the reality of enslavement in the capital would persist for decades after the Civil War and the abolition of slavery. W. E. B. Du Bois, the eminent Harvard University scholar, would remark in 1936, "The District of Columbia is of especial interest because it is the seat of the United States government. The status of slavery there not only was of intrinsic importance, but the nation and the world actually saw slavery in Washington and judged the whole system largely from what they saw."[17]

What William Hopkins saw in the city was a nation divided. Washington,

D.C., and the proslavery culture that it sustained both upheld and invalidated the founding principles and beliefs that many fought to preserve and still held dear. Like so many people of color, William Hopkins was exposed early to the complexity of African American life and the perennially shifting concepts of freedom. His immediate and extended family living in the area were part of a dynamic world, one in which enslaved people defied the mythologies that rendered them dependent and willfully imagined them as threatening and incapable of deep feeling and intellectual hunger. He and his family were part of a world in which people in bondage, despite the overwhelming odds against them and the persistent unpredictability of their lives, were industrious, ambitious, loving, and wholly committed to preserving themselves and their kin in the face of slavery's invasive reach.

In 1836, just one year after William Hopkins was born, the U.S. Congress took draconian measures to impose an artificial peace on the topic of slavery. The very inconsistencies that provoked an enlightened former slave owner like Randolph to outrage also moved lawmakers to action. Yet the measures they took enforced the proslavery status quo, protected white supremacy, and quelled what they deemed to be potentially divisive debate. Elected representatives ensured that the very topic of slavery would not reach the floor of the House by voting to uphold a gag rule on the topic. Their repressive action followed the strategies used by numerous other organizations with broad national constituencies that desired to sidestep the issue and to cater to the proslavery interests of their Southern affiliates. Pauline Hopkins's literary foremother, Susan Paul, ran afoul of such conservatism when the American Sunday School Union, which insisted that none of its materials take up the issue of slavery, refused to publish her 1835 *Memoir of James Jackson* because she referred to it, however briefly, in the text. It was not until 1850, during heated discussions about the Fugitive Slave Act, that the issue of slavery in the District of Columbia was revisited formally. Even then, however, the issue continued to reflect the willful social binaries that shaped the lives of people of African descent. In the course of debate about what became known as the Compromise of 1850, the House and Senate ultimately agreed that slave trading in the capital region was prohibited. The bill did not, however, abolish slavery in the District of Columbia, and it granted Congress a conspicuous immunity from the raging moral and economic debate when it also used the Compromise of 1850 to insist that Congress was not bound to weigh in on the interstate slave trade.[18]

Slavery in the District of Columbia was abolished in April 1862 following the passage of legislation brought by Massachusetts Republican senator Henry Wilson. Once passed, the city became a veritable "mecca for free

The Creation of a Boston Family

blacks," and in the ten years immediately following the passage of the bill, the African American population is estimated to have increased by 200 percent.[19] The orator statesman Frederick Douglass later described the move to abolish slavery in the District as "a staggering blow to slavery throughout the country" and, given its passage as the battles of the Civil War raged, as "a killing blow to the rebellion."[20] Until that time, however, people of color in the city and their white allies had to contend with the city's highly visible accommodation of slavery.

Free and enslaved people of African descent in the District of Columbia had to grapple with stringent laws aimed at undermining their community bonds, eroding their personal liberty, undercutting their intellectual potential, and limiting their economic advancement. Unfazed by the ways in which white society sought to rein them in, however, people of color mobilized themselves and kept abreast of the political issues in which they had a major stake. For example, they positioned themselves as witnesses in the gallery of the Congress during the 1827 debates about Missouri and the terms of its admission into the Union. White officials immediately sought to stifle any potential show of further political strength and promptly enacted some of the most restrictive Black Laws ever introduced in the nation.

Black codes, as they were known, constituted de facto local legislation by whites that not only asserted white political control but also reinforced the racial hierarchies of the period. These rules even transformed lengthy African American church meetings into illegal gatherings. City officials in Washington, D.C., and in Alexandria sought to contain potential outbreaks of African American dissatisfaction with social conditions or inspired by catalytic events such as the Nat Turner insurrection in Southampton.[21] The revolt claimed first the lives of whites and, in the bloody aftermath, saw reprisals against people of color and the murders of African Americans. The revolt generated a host of repressive political, social, educational, and religious actions against African Americans throughout the nation. In Georgetown, the insurrection prompted city officials to enact, for the first time, a set of black codes. African Americans, free and enslaved, were forced to comply with rules that governed their movements in and around the city, as well as their social interactions and intellectual pursuits.

The Black Laws in the District of Columbia did much more than restrict political gatherings. They struck hard at the very heart of African American potential and autonomy. By the mid-1830s, during the first years of William Hopkins's life, mulattos and free people of African descent, for example, could only receive licenses to operate "cards, drays, hackney carriages or wagons," and were ineligible for licenses for any other kind of business enterprise.

In addition, city councils monitored the mails, and any free person of color or mulatto could be jailed if found to be "a subscriber to or receive through the post office or any other medium" or to "have in his possession, or to circulate any paper or book [that would] excite insurrection or insubordination among the slaves or colored people."[22] Historians note that this particular law was meant to target the Boston-based *Liberator*, but that once passed, it was used liberally to refer to any controversial, or proemancipatory, material.

Yet even as slavery prevailed in the District, free people of color in the city refused to relinquish their own American dreams. Although they did not benefit from periods of domestic stability such as the "era of good feeling" associated with the two-term presidency of President Monroe, African Americans in the capital region demonstrated their dogged determination to succeed. They proved to be extremely resilient even in the face of political and social mandates that denied their equality and threatened their livelihood and basic economic stability. In addition, African Americans found ways to circumvent the local laws that would deny them a foothold in American society. Like their counterparts in Boston and Providence, people of color in the region were committed to educating themselves and their children. As early as 1807, just one year after the Pauls and their Boston congregation established the African Meeting House and the school housed in the building, three African American men established one of the earliest documented schools for children of color in Washington, D.C. Their triumph was intensified and made that much more secure because they built the school on land that one of the three men owned.[23] Men in the community worked primarily as barbers, porters, and waiters. Women, like so many of their counterparts in urban centers, earned their livelihoods in domestic trades and worked as dressmakers, domestic servants, and laundresses.

Despite being born into slavery in the shadows of Virginia, the region regarded as the birthplace of American slavery, William Hopkins viewed African American life as being inextricably linked to freedom and to self-determination. Like the ambitious free communities of color to the North, African Americans in Washington, D.C., made concerted efforts to provide for their own edification and progress despite the lack of widespread social support or funding. Despite the pervasive bans on education for African Americans, free people of color in the capital made impressive gains in education as early as the 1800s. These efforts, spurred on by similar campaigns in cities such as Boston, resulted in impressive ventures. Between 1807 and 1811, four modest schools for African American children were established in Washington, D.C. This welcome phase of educational opportunity that began in 1807 coincided with the efforts of Pauline Hopkins's Paul family ancestors, who, in 1807, were welcoming students from the African School into brand-new schoolrooms in the African Baptist Church. These efforts preceded by almost a decade the collective effort of the Colored Resolute Beneficial Society in 1818 to open a private school for African Americans.[24]

The bonds between the free and enslaved people of color in the district were strengthened through a variety of entrepreneurial ventures, many of which enabled individuals to purchase their own freedom as well as that of their kin. Enslaved people in the capital were permitted to hire themselves out to work, and labor arrangements such as these translated into mobility within and beyond the African American community.[25] Many in the world into which William Hopkins was born insisted that people of African descent were destined only for bondage, but he learned otherwise. He could witness and learn from indefatigable people of color such as Sophia Browning Bell, an enslaved woman who for many years sold produce in Market Square, the same location in which slaves were sold. Bell's profits accumulated steadily, and in 1801 she purchased her husband, George Bell, from his master and promptly freed him. In 1807, less than a decade later, George Bell was one of three men of color to found the first Washington, D.C., school for African American children.[26]

William Hopkins's awareness of alternatives to bondage were derived from several contexts. Some gave him a keen appreciation of local African American history and others underscored for him the agency and determination of his own family. The insistent practice of slavery in the capital and the accommodationist political platforms of the government, for example, could not prevent the organization of antislavery societies or the activities of the Underground Railroad network. Indeed, the Underground Railroad did not skirt the capital but had numerous way stations within it that were vital stops on the journey to freedom. The network of safe houses and resources that stretched from the Deep South to Canada helped thousands of enslaved people as they fled slavery and sought freedom beyond the American South. In addition, people of color in the capital also relied heavily on the network. The records of Mount Zion United Methodist Church, one of the oldest African American congregations in the capital, reveal that the District of Columbia community was especially vigilant. Membership logs with notes about parishioners "gone away" confirm the persistent threats to African American individuals and their families.[27]

In the District of Columbia, the Underground Railroad was instigated and maintained by a resistant, even subversive, community that worked assiduously to combat kidnapping, slave sales, and the commerce that allowed slavery to exist in the capital.[28] This community, or "underground network of uncommon courage and design," successfully aided thousands of people enslaved in Virginia and in Maryland. The city of Alexandria, located squarely on the "Washington Line" of the Underground Railroad, played a key role in the antislavery network that spanned the Southern states and had routes that led to the North and beyond into Canada.[29] Citizens such as Henry Hallowell, a Quaker who lived in the famous Lloyd House in Alexandria, worked closely with free and enslaved people of color, white Quakers, and Northern sympathizers. In addition to the surreptitious and essentially invisible Underground Railroad network, the city of Alexandria was home to abolitionist societies that attempted to foster support for the eradication of slavery. Yet groups such as the Society for the Abolition of Slavery, organized in 1827, for example, also suffered from their public profiles. In the wake of the Nat Turner revolt, whites and proslavery advocates targeted this organization because they regarded it as a resource for those interested in sustaining African American resistance or solidarity.[30]

One of the most influential figures in the world of William Hopkins was his energetic maternal uncle, John T. Waugh, a man who seized his own freedom and went on to become one of the most earnest civil rights advocates in New England. Born in Alexandria in 1820 to William and Mary Waugh, John T. was just sixteen years older than his nephew William. He was an inspiring example to the family and was known for his eloquent speeches and letters on matters ranging from the evils of colonization to the value of education. Waugh's activism also placed him in close proximity to William Lloyd Garrison; the two men shared the stage at political meetings, and the *Liberator* editor's perspectives on Providence were enriched by the activism and goals of men like Waugh. The energy with which John T. Waugh conducted his activities hints at the kind of impatience that he might have had with slavery. Waugh married Mary Brooks, a native Virginian, before he was twenty-one years of age. Before he was twenty-five, Waugh "attempted his freedom." It is unclear whether or not he and Mary escaped to the North at the same time, but the couple did successfully become self-emancipated people before the end of the 1840s.

The Waughs established themselves in Providence and there became closely allied with the Northup family and paternal ancestors of Pauline Hopkins. The Waughs interacted frequently with Cato Northup and his brother, the abolitionist activist Ichabod Northup, and were active in the circles of other enterprising men and women in the Providence community of color. The Waughs' first child, John A., was born into freedom in Providence in Febru-

The Creation of a Boston Family

ary 1849 but died tragically six months later of cholera infantum.[31] Four years later, the couple was blessed with a second son, Daniel J.[32] John T. Waugh was an industrious man, one whose occupation as a janitor in the last years of his life paled in comparison to his years of political endeavor, community uplift, and entrepreneurial ability. In 1859, he was one of the most financially secure men in Providence, owning some $1,500 worth of real estate. He was a forceful advocate for equal school rights; his perspectives may well have been shaped by the school desegregation efforts in Boston and the ongoing debates there about the fate of the Abiel Smith School, the nation's first public primary school for African Americans, and the decisive *Roberts v. Boston School Board* case that led to the first desegregation of Boston schools.[33] In 1863, Waugh was present at Camp Dexter, the Providence training grounds for the state's first African American Civil War regiment. Waugh, identified as a "colored native of Virginia," was there as an emissary for the "colored ladies of Providence" who had sewn "a handsome silk flag, bearing appropriate emblems" for the first battalion of the Fourteenth Regiment, Rhode Island Heavy Artillery, to take with them into battle.[34]

Once they relocated to the North, members of the Waugh and Hopkins families became extremely eloquent opponents of slavery, colonization, and school segregation. By 1859, the year of Pauline Hopkins's birth, John T. Waugh, her step-granduncle, was emerging as one of the leading men of color in the race reform movement. He traveled from Providence to Boston often and established there a reputation as an uncompromising and eloquent race activist. In August 1859, at the Boston Convention of Colored Citizens, Waugh held forth on the illegality of segregated schools in Rhode Island. Before the "large delegations" that hailed from the Massachusetts cities of New Bedford and Worcester, as well as from the states of Illinois, New Jersey, and Pennsylvania and from Canada, Waugh declared forcefully that "when he was a slave in the South and attempted his freedom—he had no idea of living to see his only son excluded from a Rhode Island School."[35] Waugh was disgusted by colonization and like many regarded it as a maneuver to deprive African Americans of their livelihoods, their homes, and their families. John Waugh vowed to fight the colonizationists to the end. The man whom many regarded as "one of the right hand men in Rhode Island in behalf of equal schools" declared without equivocation that he would "leave his bones in this land." In his speech at the August 1859 Boston Convention of Colored Citizens that, according to the *Liberator* correspondent present, "told well on the audience," which included Lewis Hayden, the city's leading Underground Railroad conductor, William Wells Brown, the well-known writer and abolitionist, and Charles Lenox Remond, the Salem abolitionist orator, Waugh insisted that "if he could not live in one section of the country, he would go to another."[36] John Waugh's studied dismay when confronted with racial intolerance and his forceful critiques of deliberate social and political inequities made him one of the most spirited members of the cohesive New England network of race men. It is not surprising, then, that he should have some seemingly uncanny links to the families of Benjamin Northup and to William Hopkins, the two men who figured so prominently in the life of Sarah Allen and her daughter, Pauline. Waugh, whom his step-grandniece Pauline mentioned in her 1901 *Colored American Magazine* autobiographical profile, worked closely with Benjamin's uncle Ichabod Northup. Their peers often mentioned both men in the same breath and praised them for their inspiring effectiveness as race activists. New Haven minister Abiel Beman described Waugh and Northup as two of the "most earnest and devoted men" of the race, individuals who "constitute the glory of any city."[37]

Waugh's active role in regional politics and his frequent trips to Boston placed him in regular and intense contact with some of the most important members in the city's African American community. As a result, he could promote his nephew William Hopkins's standing in the city and links to the African American community of Boston and to his future wife, Sarah Allen. One of the most important men with whom Waugh was in contact was Mark De Mortie, a Boston boot maker from Virginia whose wife, Cordelia, was the daughter of the Newport, Rhode Island, abolitionist, activist, and entrepreneur George T. Downing. De Mortie would one day describe his friendship with Waugh's nephew William Hopkins as a "continuous soulmate acquaintance." De Mortie met Hopkins in the mid-1850s, and the two men enjoyed a friendship that lasted for half a century.[38]

One of the earliest indications that William Hopkins was living in Boston comes from his participation in the Histrionic Club, one of the city's most creative amateur arts companies. Founded in 1857, the club began as a "literary association" and complemented other organizations such as the Adelphic Union, the Afric-American Female Intelligence Society, and the Philomathean Society, which the city's community of color founded in order to satisfy and advance their own arts and intellectual interests.[39] William Wells Brown described the pioneering African American dramatic society as one established by "a few of the most enterprising colored men and women" of Boston "for their own improvement and elevation."[40] The organization benefited from the vision and influence of three of the city's most prominent families of color. In addition to having William Cooper Nell, son of Revolutionary War hero

Mark De Mortie, Underground Railroad conductor, Boston civil rights and labor activist, sutler for the Massachusetts Fifty-fourth Regiment under Col. Robert Gould Shaw, and for at least fifty years the "continuous soulmate" of William Hopkins. *Courtesy of Moorland-Spingarn Research Center, Howard University.*

Peter Nell, as its manager, the club was shaped by members of the Bannister and Greener families.[41]

The Histrionic Club was one of the earliest mixed gender groups in the city, and it did not relegate women to a lesser role. Indeed, at the weekly meetings, "both ladies and gentlemen var[ied] the exercises with readings, essays, and discussions," and the interactions quickly proved to be extremely beneficial for all. As one supportive observer would note about the Histrionic Club members, "thus far their efforts have proved very encouraging to themselves and others."[42] The collegiality of the group contributed to its steady evolution, and soon its private meetings, in which members read aloud their own "original compositions or choice selections from the best authors," gave way to noteworthy public performances. The private weekly gatherings of the Histrionic Club indicate the intensity of intellectual engagement of which William Hopkins became a part when he moved to Boston. Meetings often included "readings, essays, and discussions," and members developed lectures and wrote poems that they also shared with the public.[43] Its members included William Cooper Nell, who was serving as president in 1858, and George Ruffin, the first African American graduate of Harvard Law School and the husband of Josephine St. Pierre Ruffin, the women's club leader with whom Pauline Hopkins would work in the early 1900s.[44] William Hopkins was part of the group as early as 1858, the year in which his name appeared on one of the club's programs.

In April 1858, Hopkins and his fellow Histrionic Club members presented a "very interesting and successful" show at Chapman Hall, a Boston facility that not only accommodated African American groups such as the Histrionic Club but also provided Bostonians with the opportunity to engage in meaningful debate about pertinent issues and racial matters. Just before the group appeared in April 1858, Dr. John Rock, one of Boston's most beloved figures and "a worthy man" known for his "striving to elevate himself and the race," delivered the second of two lectures organized on his behalf. The advertisements for Rock's lecture, listed just below the 2 April 1858 *Liberator* notices about the upcoming Histrionic Club performance, announced that Rock would be lecturing on "The Unity of the Races" at the Joy Street Church. Rock appeared at Chapman Hall the next evening to deliver a talk entitled simply "Slavery." Chapman Hall maintained a year-round schedule that supported African American ventures and lectures as well as larger debates that had significant bearing on people of color in and beyond New England. At year's end, in December 1858, the public could journey to Chapman Hall to witness a debate sparked by the question "Is the American slave better off in his present condition than he would be by a speedy emancipation?"[45]

The Histrionic Club show revealed the depth and range of its members' artistic talent: "Many of the scenes were designed and painted by members of the Club—which, with the whole paraphernalia, reflected much credit on [the members'] artistic and mechanical genius."[46] In addition, "[t]he details of appropriate costuming, stage business, and general rendering of the characters, elicited high commendations from the large and intelligent circle present." According to the eyewitness who provided a vivid commentary on the events to *The Liberator*, the club performed a riveting program of several works, including "[a] sketch prepared for the occasion by a member, entitled *The Indian's Visit*; Tobin's elegant comedy of the *Honey Moon*, with scenes from the *Hunchback*, *Four Sisters*, *Perfection*, and *Raising the Wind*."[47]

The April 1858 repertoire of the Histrionic Club signaled the members' awareness of current popular trends in the theater. They chose works by popular European playwrights, ones that other theater groups throughout the Northeast and the South were adapting as well, and the Histrionic Club members organized an evening of romantic drama, farce, and comedy for their audiences. In the spring of 1858, members appeared in *Honey Moon* (1804), a blank verse romantic drama by John Tobin, a British playwright and friend of the Romantic poets Samuel Coleridge and William Wordsworth.[48] *Honey Moon* was Tobin's fourteenth play and the first one to be accepted for production at London's famed Drury Lane. Unfortunately, Tobin, who died while en route to the West Indies for health reasons, did not live long enough to see his work finally accepted in high British drama circles. In addition to *Honey Moon*, the Histrionic Club presented *Raising the Wind* (1803), a popular farce by James Kenney (1780–1849), an eccentric Irish poet and playwright whose son was a longtime friend of Irish-born actor and dramatist Dion Boucicault but whose work prompted the poet Byron to lament that Kenney's wit "[t]ires the sad gallery [and] lulls the listless pit."[49] William Hopkins had major roles in two of the dramatic pieces performed at Chapman Hall in the spring of 1858. He played the role of "Jacques, the Mock Duke" in *Honey Moon*, and his fellow cast members included George L. Ruffin as "Duke Aranza," Edward Bannister as "Montalban," and Mrs. Anne Gray in the role of "Zamora."[50] The scene taken from *Raising the Wind* featured five men from the Histrionic Club, Nell, Ruffin, Greener, Ira Nell Gray, and William Hopkins. Hopkins played the role of Sam to Nell's "Jeremy Diddler" and Ruffin's "Failwould."[51]

The immersion that William Hopkins experienced in this vibrant New England arts circle foreshadowed the early dramatic ventures of Pauline, his future stepdaughter, and would prove to be of great value to her. William maintained his love of the theater and shared it so richly with Pauline that she declared it to be her first love. Hopkins's experience in the Histrionic Club prepared him to mentor Pauline and to serve as a primary influence who spurred her to begin writing plays during her high school years. William Hopkins's participation in the Histrionic Club also enabled him to forge connections to his wife's maternal family history. His late antebellum dramatics in Boston surely grew out of the city's impressive legacy of early nineteenth-century African American entertainment. In addition to emerging as a symbolic extension of early abolitionist enterprises such as Susan Paul's Juvenile Choir of the 1830s, William Hopkins and the Histrionic Club paid tribute to the secular musical enterprises of other Bostonians of color. These included the Amateur Society of the 1830s, a group that included Susan Paul's brother-in-law Elijah Smith, whose son and namesake Elijah Jr. would become the city's African American poet laureate. The group also included Tobias Cutler, a descendant of the family with whom Pauline's maternal grandfather, Jesse Allen, would seek sanctuary in New Hampshire, and other beloved members of the Boston community such as the Lew family and the Hiltons. The Amateur Society was an especially inspiring precursor of the Histrionic Club since it not only demonstrated the range of musical talents and productions that could be staged by and for people of color but also succeeded as a community-based arts initiative. In April 1833, twenty-five years before William Hopkins appeared with the Histrionic Club, the Amateur Society announced proudly through *The Liberator* that the society would present a "'Sacred Concert' with orchestra under direction of Mr. George Hamlet and Vocal Conductor, Mr. Elijah Smith." Tickets, available at the *Liberator* office, at the door, and at the Cambridge Street shop of Peter Howard, one of the community's most active musicians, would grant the holder access to the Butolph Street Mission House and an evening of "[v]ocal and instrumental music."[52] As Tobias Cutler noted in his review of the performance, the "audience was highly respectable, and appeared to appreciate fully the rich treat which was afforded them by the great combination of musical talent and skill belonging to this society. . . . They all did themselves ample credit in their several performances. It was a rare treat for the lovers of sweet sounds, for they never sang better on any former occasion." Cutler, who noted the memorable trombone performances of Elijah Smith Sr., also singled out Susan Paul, congratulating her for making "an impression which her warmest admirers could hardly have anticipated."[53]

William Hopkins, the Southerner, immersed himself in the arts when he arrived in Boston and merged with this distinctive Northern history and arts tradition. It was one of the most invaluable connections that he could make; the African American arts world gave him access to the ambitious literary and social circles on Beacon Hill. It also allowed him to cultivate a meaningful alliance with the extended family of his wife and stepdaughter. That the alliance was forged in the years before his marriage to Sarah Allen also was in his favor. Pauline, if she was at all hesitant about being adopted by William Hopkins, may have come to see his participation in the antebellum Beacon Hill arts movement as a trustworthy and intriguing effort. As a result, it may

The Creation of a Boston Family

have made it possible for William Hopkins to endear himself that much more easily to the child whom he embraced as his own. Indeed, as her singing and theatrical debuts would prove, William Hopkins's arts ventures contributed much to the valuable foundation upon which Pauline built her first and highly successful career as a pioneering dramatist, actor, and vocalist.

In Boston, William Hopkins took advantage of the Beacon Hill boarding-house culture that catered primarily to new arrivals and seamen. In 1859, he was living in rented quarters at 189 Grove Street; the next year, he was residing in the Beacon Hill home of Mrs. Ewana Grey on Southac Street. At the time, he was working as a hairdresser and barber and also engaged in trade, what he described as "[c]oastwise service."[54] In 1860, he left Boston for New York City where, on 16 May, he traveled to Brooklyn and joined the United States Navy.[55] Hopkins was no stranger to the sea and was one of thousands of African American men whose history as mariners dated back to the Colonial era. When he joined the navy, Hopkins could claim experience gained from "[o]ne cruise in Yorktown as [a] boy" and at least one tour that took him to the coast of Africa.[56] He was assigned first to the USS *North Carolina* and then to the USS *Niagara*, one of the fastest ships in the navy fleet and a vessel that by war's end would be armed with ten formidable 150-pounder Parrott rifles.[57] Despite his early experiences, Hopkins was enlisted as a landsman, a rank accorded to inexperienced civilian recruits.

He joined the navy on the very day that the Republican Party, meeting at its convention in Chicago, nominated Abraham Lincoln of Illinois for president. Though his enlistment occurred before the Civil War began, Hopkins joined the military as the nation moved deliberately toward what would become a deadly and costly internecine conflict. Boston's politically astute community of color would have been well apprised of the increasingly volatile sectional tensions. That year, Jefferson Davis, who would become the president of the Confederacy, was advancing the agenda of proslavery Southern extremists. In the Senate, Davis successfully presented a set of resolutions that insisted on states' rights and fiercely upheld slavery. Eight days after William Hopkins joined the navy, the Senate ratified the Davis resolutions, which included assertions that "any attack on slavery within the slave states was a violation of the Constitution" and that "neither Congress nor a territorial legislature was in any way empowered to impair the right to hold slaves in the territories and the federal government should extend all needful protection . . . to slavery in the territories" and that "all state legislation interfering with the recovery of fugitive slaves was inimical to the constitutional compact."[58] Hopkins became part of an impressive cohort of African American navy men, one of the estimated 10,000 men of color who served in the U.S. Navy during the Civil

The USS *Niagara* docked in Boston in 1863. The ship is shown here
as it was at the time William Hopkins ended his Civil War service in the
U.S. Navy. *Courtesy of U.S. Naval Historical Center.*

War and who made up 25 percent of all who served in the Union forces.[59] Before his three-year enlistment period concluded, Hopkins had been promoted
from landsman on the *North Carolina* to officer steward aboard the *Niagara*,
the ship on which he would gain his most intense firsthand experience of the
Civil War.[60]

William Hopkins may have joined the navy because he wanted to be among
the first to be on hand for Civil War skirmishes. His early enlistment meant
that he would be among the first African Americans to go to war, because,
unlike the U.S. Army, this branch of the military had been integrated since
its inception. Thus, Hopkins avoided the contentious debates about African
American contributions that delayed the enlistment of willing African American volunteers. Indeed, the navy in 1861 instituted a new policy that allowed
for the recruitment of formerly enslaved men. Had he stayed in Boston, by
1863 he would have had ample opportunity to heed the call of Frederick
Douglass and others who encouraged men of color "to arms!" once President
Lincoln approved the use of African American soldiers. Hopkins would have
been poised to join one of the companies of the historic Massachusetts Fifty-
fourth, the first African American regiment raised in the North.

When he joined the crew of the *Niagara*, Hopkins became part of an impressive ship. A "5540-ton (displacement) steam screw frigate" that was "lightly
armed," the *Niagara* had been commissioned in April 1857 following its con-

struction in the New York Navy Yard.[61] At that time, the *Niagara* was one of the newest vessels in the navy fleet, and it was the largest of the six frigates that made up the first class of screw-propelled navy ships.[62] It was designed by the Devonshire-born George Steers, a gifted naval architect and designer of yachts and schooners, whose previous impressive designs included the yacht *America*.[63] The *Niagara* testified to Steers's fascination with speed and the navy's desire to have a lean fighting ship. It had "sharp clipper hull lines" and a "commodious gundeck," upon which were "twelve 11-inch Dahlgrens, all on pivot rails." In addition, the *Niagara* "proved to be fast—10 to 11 knots under steam—and was known to exceed 16 knots under sail."[64] Over the course of its first four years of service, the *Niagara* responded to a diverse set of missions. It played a key role in the effort to lay the first transatlantic telegraph cable. In the fall of 1858, two years after Steers died at age thirty-seven from injuries suffered in an accident, the *Niagara* sailed to Liberia with about 200 African passengers who, having been rescued from a slave ship off the coast of Cuba, were being relocated to Monrovia, Liberia.[65] Bostonians also may have been familiar with the vessel, since it docked at least twice there.

In May 1861, just over a year before William Hopkins left the navy, the USS *Niagara* joined the Civil War effort when it undertook its first assignment of the war: to blockade Southern ports on the Atlantic and Gulf coasts. The ship joined the West Gulf Blockade Squadron, and on 10 May, the *Niagara* "initiated" the blockade of Charleston. Two days later, on 12 May, the ship, under the command of Admiral William W. McKean, captured the *General Parkhill*, a ship from Liverpool that was attempting to run the blockade and to reach the city of Charleston.[66] Hopkins was part of the crew when, shortly thereafter, McKean received an urgent dispatch from Gideon Welles, secretary of the navy under President Lincoln, instructing McKean and the *Niagara* to depart for the Gulf of Mexico in order to establish a blockade of New Orleans and Mobile. In no time, McKean was disseminating Welles's mandate, writing to other Union navy captains and urging them to "use all diligence to capture vessels with arms and munitions . . . [and] any privateer or vessel [they] may meet on the high seas or in our waters depredating on our commerce or making hostile demonstrations toward the United States or any of its citizens."[67] The ship and its crew committed themselves wholeheartedly to the mission that Welles assigned them. In June 1861, the *Niagara* and its crew were in the waters off Mobile, Alabama, embroiled in a "cutting out expedition" that ended in the capture of the *Aid*, a Confederate schooner. The ship was active in the Gulf of Mexico for several months in 1861 and, while there, "served for some of that time as flagship of the East Gulf Blockading Squadron."[68] McKean, the *Niagara* commander, became the second of four squadron commanders in October 1861.[69] One month later, McKean led Hopkins and the crew "in a bombardment of Confederate fortifications at Pensacola, Florida."[70]

The end of William Hopkins's term of enlistment coincided with the *Niagara*'s withdrawal from Civil War conflict during the summer of 1862. He sailed with his ship to Boston and the Charlestown Navy Yard in June, where it was scheduled for repairs and refurbishing designed to "enhance her battery of heavy guns."[71] On 20 June, William Hopkins left the *Niagara* and was formally discharged from the U.S. Navy. He walked out of the Charlestown Navy Yard as a Civil War veteran with an honorable record of performance.

William Hopkins had been discharged from the U.S. Navy for just over two years when he married Sarah Allen, on Christmas Day in 1864. He began to settle into life as a civilian at a time when Boston was "ripe for invasion," not by Confederate forces but rather by the thousands of migrants. Their arrival in the city contributed to Boston's dramatic transformation from a "small-scale walking city character" to what it would become by the 1900s, a "sprawling, volatile metropolis of the twentieth century."[72] Following his navy discharge, Hopkins resumed his former trade as a barber and began what appears to have been a smooth assimilation into the Boston community of which he had been a part during the late 1850s. The newly established Hopkins family enjoyed a significant amount of domestic stability in the first years of their lives together. Unlike many of their neighbors, they had resources that enabled them to avoid the domestic upheaval of frequently moving from house to house, a situation that many African Americans in Boston endured, due to economic hardships and illness.

The first Hopkins family home was at 67 Joy Street, an almost mythic residence that lay in the very heart of black Beacon Hill. In the 1850s, 67 Joy Street had been the primary residence of Coffin Pitts, a clothier, African Baptist church deacon, and staunch abolitionist. Just ten years prior to the Hopkinses' residency there, in 1854, it had been the Boston home of fugitive Anthony Burns, who initially had worked for Pitts and had lived with him before his contested capture and return to bondage in Virginia.[73] In 1866, the Hopkins family moved to 1 Allen Place, a side street abutting the east-west major thoroughfare of Allen Street, on which the Massachusetts General Hospital, which occupied one half of the city block, was located in the mid-1850s. The Hopkinses lived at Allen Street for twelve years, until they relocated in 1875 to rooms in a commercial building located at 15 State Street.

The Creation of a Boston Family

The building in which they lived was directly adjacent to the Old State House and commanded a spectacular view of downtown Boston.

The family relied primarily on William's earnings as a barber, a profession that provided them with both financial security and social capital. As a barber, Hopkins not only became one of the most visible workers in the community, but he had the opportunity to cultivate a rich set of relationships with the men of his diverse and evolving Beacon Hill and Boston community. His fellow barbers included Peter Howard, who moved in the music circles that Hopkins enjoyed in the early 1850s and had shops located on Cambridge Street, and J. J. Smith, who in 1846 had his hairdressing shop located at the intersection of Staniford and Green Streets.[74] Like Howard and Smith, Hopkins presided over a shop that also functioned as a vital community site, one in which men debated and shared political views and other information relevant to the race.[75] In addition to being often "the only form of political education available to barely literate members of the black community," as historian James Horton notes, barbershops also fostered collective action among African Americans and served as invaluable resources for white abolitionists and civil rights advocates.[76] As Horton reveals in his detailed study of free people of color in the North, at least one man "was convinced to join the Fifty-fourth Colored Infantry from Massachusetts" as a result of his "discussions" with others in the "colored shops," and "a group of . . . regulars" who frequented another shop "enlisted together then dropped by the shop to say goodbye."[77] Charles Sumner, the legendary white senator and attorney who collaborated with Bostonian Robert Morris on the 1849 Boston school desegregation suit, for example, was "often found engaged in earnest debate" at the barbershop that J. J. Smith maintained.

William Hopkins set up shop at 1 Cambridge Street, near the intersection of Bowdoin and Green Streets in the downtown area. This main thoroughfare in the West End led, in one direction, to the West Boston Bridge across the Charles River and into Cambridge. Its opposite route cut through the heart of black Boston, until it ended in Temple and Mount Vernon Streets, two roads that one could travel south toward the Boston Common only a few blocks away. He was an enterprising man who seized opportunities to diversify his business. By 1868, Hopkins had a business partner, J. West, with whom he maintained the barbershop.[78] In addition to relying on William's earnings, the Hopkins family also secured their stability by providing accommodations to boarders. In 1870, Sarah Hopkins was able to list her occupation as "Keeping House," and at the time she was presiding over a home in which three young women of color were living with the family. Fourteen-year-old Pauline had the company of Lizzie Riddes and Elizabeth Dawsey, twenty-one-year-old and nineteen-year-old shop clerks from New York, and Georgeana Mingall, a twenty-four-year-old dressmaker from Nova Scotia.[79] Over the course of the next three decades, William Hopkins did his best to maintain his small family and to earn enough to fund their increasingly bold and much acclaimed family arts ventures.[80]

By 1871, Hopkins had transformed himself into a dermatologist and relocated to Hanover Street. He appears to have weathered the devastating Great Fire of Boston that destroyed almost 800 buildings in the city and razed an extensive area located between Washington Street and the Boston harbor.[81] He maintained his dermatological venture at 120 Hanover Street through 1875, the year in which Pauline made her performance debut as a member of The Progressive Musical Union, yet another sophisticated musical society whose membership reflected the consistently impressive range of talent of black Bostonians. The following year, in 1876, he took a job on State Street in the city's financial district. On this side of Beacon Hill, Hopkins was moving among the city's "business barons" and working as a janitor in one of the stately buildings that were "badges of their prosperity."[82] The State Street job may have represented a rather dramatic relocation from the predominantly African American sphere in which he had worked since 1862, but William's new employment provided him with housing, a significant benefit that he accepted. The Hopkins family moved into rooms at 15 State Street, a building that was directly adjacent to the Old State House, the oldest building in Boston. Fifteen-year-old Pauline now had a bird's-eye view of the building in which the Declaration of Independence first was read to citizens in July 1776 and that had served as headquarters for John Hancock, the state's first governor.[83] In 1880 and 1881, William Hopkins supplemented his State Street job by going into business with David Walker. The two men opened a clothes-cleaning business, the same venture that William's closest friend Mark R. De Mortie would also pursue in Boston in the early 1890s. Hopkins and Walker established their shop at 61½ Bromfield Street, a busy street not far from the Boston Common. William held his State Street janitorial job until 1882 and left, it appears, only after the family moved into a home at 164 Chambers Street and had time to establish themselves there. In 1881, he returned again to barbering and by 1882 had set himself up in business at 136 Broad Street. In 1889, he moved his business a few doors down to 122 Broad Street and maintained this location until 1891, the year in which the *Boston City Directory* included the entry noting that he had "removed to Cambridge."[84] In Cambridge, he began working as a tailor, and he worked in this profession until his death in 1906.

The Hopkins family registered officially for the first time as a family in the 1865 Massachusetts State Census, which was compiled just less than one year after Sarah and William's 1864 Christmas Day wedding. The concise profile of the family that emerges in the census confirmed that the family of three was living in the city of Boston in Suffolk County. William Hopkins was identified as a twenty-nine-year-old mulatto and Virginia-born barber; his wife, Sarah, was a thirty-year-old mulatto woman born in New Hampshire who had no occupation listed; their daughter, Pauline, was profiled as an eight-year-old mulatto girl whose birthplace was Maine. By the time they were polled for the 1870 Massachusetts census, six years after the marriage of William and Sarah, the family had blossomed into a thriving household whose industrious inhabitants were in full pursuit of a steady middle-class existence. Both William and Sarah were listed as being thirty-three years of age. William's occupation was that of "barber." The occupation for Sarah, whose age had been cropped by two years, was listed, like many wives in their Boston neighborhood, as "keeping house." Their daughter, Pauline E., now a fourteen-year-old, whose place of birth once again was listed as Maine, was "at school."

The adolescent Pauline, who was documented in this first post–Civil War census, was identified correctly as a child born well before the marriage of William and Sarah Hopkins. It appears, however, that the 1865 Massachusetts State Census and the 1870 Massachusetts Federal Census returns are the only two census reports that appear to contain the unmanipulated date of birth for Pauline Hopkins. Her age of fourteen, which clearly precedes the 1864 marriage date of Sarah Allen and William Hopkins, reconfirms her birth year of 1859. After the summer of 1870, when the Federal Census report was filed, however, Hopkins's birth date was subject to major manipulation for several decades and not corrected until her death in 1930, when the documents certifying her death included her original birth date. In 1900, thirty years after the census of 1870, the Hopkins family essentially emerged anew. In the scanty information gleaned from the 1880 Federal Census, which contained only a brief and slightly inaccurate profile of William Hopkins, and the missing data of the vital 1890 census that was destroyed by floods, it is impossible to confirm all steps in the evolution of this family's presentation. In 1900, however, the Hopkinses make insistent inroads on the public record and manipulate their claims on the domestic.

The 1900 Massachusetts Census calls the most attention to the issues that may have prompted the Hopkins family in general and Pauline in particular to deliberately revise their own family history and to do so in a way that raises issues about respectability and family cohesion. In the 1900 Federal Census for Massachusetts, Pauline Hopkins is transformed: she no longer is a forty-one-year-old spinster born in 1859, but a thirty-four-year-old woman born in 1866, two years after her mother's marriage to William A. Hopkins, on Christmas Day in 1864. In addition, the age of Sarah Allen is drastically revised so that it suggests that she was twenty-one years old, rather than almost thirty years of age, when she wed William Hopkins. Had there been only one date changed in this census, it would suggest an unwitting aberration, one that might have resulted during the exchange with the census taker, for example. That there are calculated changes made to the birth dates of mother and daughter, however, completely erases the possibility of an accidental inaccurate transcription. The birth dates for Pauline and her mother, Sarah, suggest premeditated changes that effect a dramatic transformation of Pauline into the legitimate daughter of William and Sarah. The revised birth dates that insist on Sarah's youth and, by extension, her ability to bear children also allowed the family to protect the apparently valuable impression of their familial unity and their daughter's true origins. These premeditated and complementary changes appear to have been done in order to lay an apparently irrefutable claim to respectability and legitimacy. If this is so, then it signals the deep and pervasive anxieties about public image and perhaps Sarah's distaste for her own marital past that plagued the Hopkins family and that prompted them to discuss and then implement a doctored record.

The 1900 census evidence based on the changed birth years and the revised ages of the principals involved reveal deliberate efforts to create a palatable, revisionary genealogy. That this project coincides with Pauline's professional renaissance is not a coincidence. She was essentially rising like a phoenix, from a career that the city's elite may well have regarded as untoward and one that at first glance might have suggested a tawdry past rather than one that represented impressive cultural achievement. Certainly, their family relations and especially Sarah Allen's extended family who lived in Boston and in nearby Charlestown would have known their sister's true history. So it appears that the manipulations were done as part of another campaign, one that might be implemented as Pauline prepared to take her place in the public eye. Claims on legitimacy such as these would have bolstered her self-confidence as she came into contact more regularly with the more celebrated public genealogies that the African American elite was not shy about discussing.

There is no doubt that the Sarah Allen who wed Benjamin Northup in 1857 and the woman who married William Hopkins on Christmas Day in 1864 is the same person. In addition, the divorce records clearly confirm that

Sarah and her first husband had a child together. The child of that union, Pauline, appears to have been the only child that Sarah bore during her lifetime. In addition, the fact that Pauline Hopkins signed herself and was promoted as Pauline Allen as she embarked on highly reputable public endeavors strengthens the theory that she was the child of her mother's first marriage. It also suggests that Sarah Allen Northup reverted to her maiden name shortly after Pauline's birth but maintained the title of "Mrs." when she did so. Sarah bestowed her maiden name upon her child when she returned from Portland, Maine, to Boston in the years preceding the dissolution of her first marriage. Pauline Allen Hopkins maintained her identity as Pauline Allen until 1875, when she began a series of musical and theatrical collaborations with her mother and stepfather. In 1875, it was beneficial for her to adopt the surname "Hopkins"; she and her parents promptly became the Hopkins Family Troubadours, and William, who had become Pauline's agent, began to represent himself as the manager of his stepdaughter's budding stage career.

The Pauline Hopkins who emerged in the late 1870s and asserted herself officially in the 1900 census claimed a new paternal narrative for herself. She became the child of a Union navy veteran and a recognized military leader in one of Boston's African American Grand Army of the Republic posts. As she stood on the threshold of her careers as an actress and playwright, novelist and magazine writer, Hopkins invoked William Hopkins's personal history, one that resurrected the era of heroic African American self-help and emancipation during the Civil War. This was the legacy that may have facilitated her exploration of her family's history of enslavement; as a Paul, she was the descendant of free blacks. As a Hopkins, she was able to link her mother's murky family history of slavery to her stepfather's documented Civil War service, to African American emancipation, and to racial uplift. This blended genealogy made her an heir to substantial traditions of uncompromising race pride, political resistance, educational excellence, and literary innovation. Hopkins's complex and at times misleading genealogy does not invalidate the facts established by her early public performance record. Nor does her partially elusive family history obscure the fact that from a very early age she was aware of her long-standing maternal and paternal traditions of community uplift and activism. Ultimately, these were the defining family histories that established her as a "black daughter" in white America.

4

Progressive Arts and the Public Sphere

Progressive: ay, we hope to climb,
With patient steps fair Music's height
And at her altar's sacred flame
Our care-extinguished torches light.
ELIJAH WILLIAM SMITH JR.
Boston, 1875

The story of the Negro musician is fraught
with intense interest for us. Wherever God dwells he
leaves a token of His presence, and he steeped the
American serf to the lips in divine harmony.
PAULINE HOPKINS
"Phenomenal Vocalists,"
Colored American Magazine,
November 1901

The artistic life of Pauline Hopkins began in 1875 in the protective world of Boston's black Beacon Hill, an environment rich in traditions of black activism, community philanthropy, and racial uplift that dated back to the late 1700s. Those who sought to claim the public sphere for artistic or political expression did so first before members of their supportive and engaged African American community and whites who were committed to exploring with them racial justice and social reform. On the evening of Tuesday, 9 March 1875, Pauline Elizabeth Allen, as Hopkins was known at this time, appeared at the North Russell Street Methodist Church with the city's newest African American choral group, the Progressive Musical Union, and made her debut as a musical performer. With this performance, she was formally initiated into her maternal family's long-standing tradition of high art performance and public activism.

The founder of the Progressive Musical Union was Elijah William Smith Jr.

Elijah William Smith Jr., grandson of the Reverend Thomas
and Catherine Paul and founder of the Progressive Musical
Union, with which Hopkins made her performance debut.
Smith was regarded by many as Boston's African American
poet laureate. *From* Colored American Magazine, *1902.*

(1830–95), Allen's forty-five-year-old cousin, a maternal grandson of the African Baptist Church founding pastor, the Reverend Thomas Paul, and a lifelong Bostonian who during his youth had worked as a printer's apprentice
to William Lloyd Garrison in the *Liberator* offices.[1] Smith's organization featured artists who had forged modest records of individual and small group
performances in Boston during the 1870s. Pauline Allen's membership in this
musical society connected her directly, and for the first time publicly, to her
Paul ancestors. At this proud moment, Pauline appeared as a promising ex-

tension of the Paul family's tradition of using the arts to promote racial uplift and raise political awareness. Her appearance on this night most honored Susan Paul, her beloved and enterprising great-grandaunt, who some forty years earlier had mastered the politics of art, as it were, when she used music to facilitate her entry into the nation's most influential abolitionist circles and to initiate unprecedented intergenerational and interracial antislavery collaborations between white Americans and African American children.[2]

The poise that Pauline Allen exhibited at the Progressive Musical Union concert certainly resulted from the supportive rehearsals that her cousin Elijah led. But a key element of her preparation for this momentous night had occurred some three years earlier when she witnessed firsthand moments of stirring professionalism and musical talent. In 1872, when Pauline was thirteen years of age, she had had the opportunity to witness an epic musical event and African American performance history when two child prodigies, Anna Madah and Emma Louise Hyers of California, took the East Coast by storm. The sisters and their parents forged important connections to Pauline and her Boston community of color, ties that would introduce Pauline Allen to the nation as one of its most promising playwrights and earnest actresses.

The Hyers Sisters came to Boston in 1872 as part of the "colossal show" that was the World Peace Jubilee, an enormous performance venture created by Patrick S. Gilmore, a legendary white band leader, which was slated to occur that year in Boston. The Jubilee featured internationally renowned performers, an orchestra of 2,000 musicians directed by Johann Strauss the Younger, and a vocal chorus of some 20,000 singers. Of particular significance for Pauline and her extended performance family in Boston was the inclusion of African Americans and, in particular, the prominent presentation of two African American groups, the Fisk Jubilee Singers and the Hyers Sisters, two young musical prodigies from Sacramento, California. The Hyers parents cultivated assiduously the talents of their children. Sam Hyers, a barber, and Annie, his wife and a skilled artisan known for her "embroidery, leather work, and wax work," cultivated assiduously their children's talents. They trained the girls for some years before they enlisted the professional musicians Professor Hugo Sank and Madame Josephine D'Ormy as teachers for their gifted daughters. The Hyers Sisters studied the piano and vocalization and received instruction in French and German, subjects that further refined their gifts and enabled them to master a formidable array of European works. After their debut at ages ten and twelve, they embarked on a successful and demanding tour of the East and Midwest and arrived some three years later in Boston. Patrick Gilmore was on hand for their first performance in the city, a private audition with a group of self-proclaimed "musical connoisseurs" and

ANNA MADAH HYERS.

EMMA LOUISE HYERS.

The Hyers Sisters, celebrated prodigies with whom Hopkins worked closely during the 1870s and 1880s. *Courtesy Manuscripts, Archives and Rare Books Division, Schomburg Center for Research in Black Culture, The New York Public Library, Astor, Lenox and Tilden Foundations.*

others of "the highest musical ability," who intended to evaluate the sisters "by the same standards as Nilsson or Kellogg," two popular performers of the day. The historical backdrop for that Boston interview was the illuminating colonial moment when the African-born poet Phillis Wheatley was grilled by leading men of Boston before being accepted as the true and sole author of her exquisitely sophisticated 1773 volume of poems. According to James Monroe Trotter, who records the Hyers incident in his 1886 history of African American music, Mr. Hyers "readily assented" to the screening that "proved that his confidence [in his daughters] was well founded": "[A]ll became satisfied, after

Progressive Arts and the Public Sphere   73

hearing them sing, that these young ladies had not been too highly praised by the press of other cities. Said Mr. Gilmore, 'These ladies promise much that is great.'"[3] Having won admission to Boston's musical circles, the Hyers family took up residence in Boston. Given the cohesive black community and its documented investments in the arts, it is highly likely that Pauline Allen and the Hyers family forged a bond through music and their love of the stage well before the sisters literally took the world by storm at the 1872 World Peace Jubilee.

The World Peace Jubilee appearance by the Hyers Sisters and the Fisk Jubilee Singers represented the first time in American history that African Americans were included and so prominently showcased in a monumental production and formal celebration of music. Gilmore enthusiastically promoted the historic integration. Advertisements for the Jubilee encouraged the public to come and witness the "[f]irst appearance of the Coloured Chorus of 150 voices, including the celebrated Hyers Sisters and the Jubilee Singers from Nashville." Henry G. Parker, press secretary for the Jubilee, even went so far as to predict that the African American appearances would be the "Best Programme of the Week." Although the major Boston newspaper reports about the festivities do not mention the racial composition of the World Peace Jubilee audiences, they do offer detailed eyewitness accounts of the African American performances. According to the *Boston Globe*, the rendition of "Mine Eyes Have Seen the Glory of the Lord" by the African American chorus was "received in a manner that ended in a perfect ovation." The encore "produced a repetition of the outburst of enthusiasm that followed [the song's] performance the first time."[4] The Fisk Jubilee Singers, appearing alone on Sunday, 23 June, performed "Swing Low, Sweet Chariot" with "great pathos and sentiment." The crowd "loudly applauded and a general enthusiasm pervaded the entire audience." After two encores, the group was still being "rapturously applauded," and these "outbursts" soon exceeded all other responses given to the distinguished performers who appeared that weekend. The crowd did its best to "have them sing again," but the efforts were "in vain." The level and intensity of the applause and the multiple encores that followed these African American performances were unmatched by any other of the orchestras, choruses, or soloists that performed that weekend. The success that the Fisk Jubilee Singers enjoyed at Gilmore's World Peace Jubilee contributed mightily to their fame. Indeed, the overwhelmingly enthusiastic response that they received in 1872 appeared to be entirely genuine, and the singers enjoyed similar receptions in the city in the years to come.

The Jubilee Singers and the Hyers Sisters became regular acts on Boston's theater calendar from 1872, the year of the World Peace Jubilee, through 1879, the year in which Pauline Allen completed her third play. These two groups offered audiences interested in seeing African American performers a high quality alternative to blackface minstrelsy, the Tom shows, or plays such as Dion Boucicault's *The Octoroon* and others about slavery and miscegenation. In 1875, the Fisk Singers appeared at least four times at the historic Tremont Temple, a site made sacred because of its religious history and because of its centrality in key moments of Boston's cultural history. In addition to being the site where the Hyers Sisters made their Boston debut, the Tremont Temple was where Pauline's great-grandaunt Susan Paul had appeared at New England Anti-Slavery Society meetings in the 1830s with her African American Juvenile Choir. Charlotte Cushman made her stage debut in the hall that also hosted Fanny Kemble's first Boston appearance and the first operas to be produced in the city, and this was where Charles Dickens gave his last readings in America.[5] The success of the Fisk Jubilee Singers and the Hyers Sisters in Boston signaled to the city's African American amateur and aspiring professional artists like Pauline Allen that performers of color could secure critical legitimacy and respectability. Following their Boston debut, the Hyers Sisters lived in New England for several years and enjoyed the celebrity that intensified following their participation at the World Peace Jubilee. According to Trotter, they were "loath to leave [the city's] congenial art-circles, and to leave behind its many facilities for improvement in their profession." Here they made "many warm personal friends" and apparently "received from many of its most cultured people very flattering attentions."[6] Anna Madah and Emma Louise performed to much acclaim in New England. They appeared in some of Boston's grandest venues, including the Boston Theatre, which had a seating capacity of over 3,000 and in which patrons en route to their seats passed beneath a breathtaking chandelier of "great cut-glass" that shimmered like a "great glowing jewel" when lit.[7]

These were part of the dazzling realities that Pauline Allen could consider as she began to imagine her own scripts and the sets that would showcase them. She could consider herself part of a rising generation of talented and dynamic young African American women, groomed to perform with both artistic elegance and racial awareness. Yet even as she could see the status and privilege that talented performers enjoyed, Pauline also realized that the larger postbellum world invested and regularly celebrated European and American white theater productions much more than it did those organized by African Americans. What constituted successful white Boston theater, in terms of scripts, productions, and venues, could therefore mean something entirely different for an African American playwright and theater company. Although Boston had a strong abolitionist history, that did not translate into an equal and open society. This was, after all, the city that James Monroe Trotter, in his groundbreaking 1886 history of African American music, referred to as the "modern Athens," the "acknowledged centre of musical and general aesthetic culture . . . whose critical audiences ever receive coldly, at first, all newcomers, and who, guided by their own judgments, and having their own standard of merit, never yield praise because it has been accorded in other sections."[8] The initial screening of the Hyers Sisters proved Trotter's point completely.

As a descendant of one of the city's most influential black families, Pauline Allen knew only too well that African Americans faced overwhelming opposition and entrenched prejudice in their fights for equal education and employment and civic and political rights. Therefore, as Pauline Allen considered making her livelihood in the arts, she realized that she too could face resistance, especially if her work had political overtones and threatened the racial status quo of the day. The professionalism and artistic resilience that she displayed so early on in her career, though, was undoubtedly linked to the inspirational and romantic history of Annie Pauline Pindell, her cherished aunt and a celebrated American prima donna of color.

One of five Allen daughters born in New Hampshire, Annie Pauline had since childhood been fascinated by music. "When an infant," recalled Hopkins in her 1901 biographical profile of her aunt, "the sound of a musical instrument would cause the most intense excitement in [her], and as she grew older it was discovered that she possessed a remarkable organ in height, depth and sweetness."[9] In 1853, when she was nineteen years old, Annie married Joseph J. Pendell, a native of Baltimore, who then was working as a hairdresser in Boston.[10] Pendell, who according to Pauline Hopkins, was "a brother of the Baltimore Pindells [*sic*], so well-known in that city, and later in Boston," was enthusiastic about his wife's talents. The combination of her husband's support of her formal voice study and the knowledge of her maternal family's inspiring and formative role in Boston's African American arts tradition, further motivated Annie Pindell in her pursuit of excellence. Already "[i]ndefatigable in her desire to acquire knowledge and improve in her art," she pursued diverse training with a variety of teachers, including the Marshall brothers of Boston and an unnamed but "celebrated German professor."[11] Pindell studied elocution with Wyzeman Marshall, an actor whose credits included performances at the Bowery Theatre in New York City and who, by 1875, was the manager and proprietor of the Howard Athenaeum, a popular Boston venue where figures like Adah Isaacs Menken appeared to much fanfare.[12] Pindell, who became known as the "Black Nightingale," in part because her voice spanned some "twenty seven notes, from G in bass clef to E in treble clef," also "delighted in original composition." By November

Annie Pauline Pindell, maternal aunt of Hopkins, a composer
and celebrated prima donna whose memorable performances
included a presentation before Queen Emma of Hawaii.
From Colored American Magazine, *1901.*

1859, Annie Pauline Pindell had become the first member of the Paul family line to embark upon a professional career as a vocalist.

Just over one hundred years after the Paul family patriarch, Caesar Paul, had returned from the grueling horrors of the French and Indian War and time spent in Canadian captivity, his granddaughter Annie Pauline Pindell was enjoying a freedom of expression in America that he could only have imagined. Her stage identity as the "Black Nightingale" placed her squarely within the elite antebellum group of African American women performers that included the legendary Hyers Sisters, Elizabeth Greenfield, and Madame Marie Selika, who was known as "The Queen of Staccato." Indeed, when writing as a social historian in 1901, Hopkins would insist that these women were neither anomalies nor fleeting talents. Their performance in the secular sphere did not, according to her, jeopardize the veritable sanctity of their mission. "The great artist belongs to God," she declared emphatically, "and is imperishable." Hopkins's theories of art as sanctified outreach were informed by principles similar to those that transformed for Susan Paul the work of abolition into the work of God. Hopkins proposed that "[t]he existence of music is coeval with the creation of man" and that any study of "the music of all nations, civilized or uncivilized," would reveal that "they bear a great resemblance to each other," since they all are "founded on an original law of nature."[13] The intensity of such humanist principles signaled to readers that the first and subsequent installments of "Famous Women of the Negro Race" would be righteous testimony that used the diverse accomplishments of African Americans to assert the humanity of the race. Indeed, it was a substantial first salvo in what would become Hopkins's fight against public policies that depended on an obscured African American history and a demoralizing isolation of the race. Although she never mentioned in her *Colored American Magazine* writings her own history as a singer and performer in Boston, Hopkins's tribute to her recently deceased aunt provided invaluable insights into her own philosophies. "Music is one of the very elements of the soul and voice," she insisted, "implanted by an all-wise Creator, part of our God-given nature—sign—manual of the universal kinship of all races."[14]

Hopkins's appreciation of the political nature of art was part of her ongoing campaign to protest the "popular fad" of the day that "regard[ed] the Negro as hopelessly incompetent and immoral, doomed to years of self-abasement and apprenticeship before he will be worthy to be classed among the men of civilization."[15] The race was already in animated conversation with high civilization, insisted Hopkins. Bolstering her bold assertion was evidence, such as the fact that young women born into or just beyond the reach of slavery graciously conducted themselves in audiences with British monarchs and Hawaiian queens. This was in fact the case when Elizabeth Greenfield performed at Buckingham Palace before Queen Victoria in 1854 and when Annie Pindell traveled to Hawaii, sang for Queen Emma, and "was presented with a diamond necklace worth fifteen hundred dollars."[16] Such notable professional triumphs were compelling evidence that denigrating stereotypes and cultural mythologies were indeed social fictions, ones that might be essentially invalidated by women like Pindell, Greenfield, and the Hyers Sisters.

The professional triumphs of Annie Pauline Pindell would shape indelibly Pauline Hopkins's perspectives on art and women's public performance. Annie Pauline Pindell was a tireless performer who shuttled back and forth between engagements in a host of California cities such as Sacramento, Stockton, and San Francisco. In California, where she lived for some three decades until her death in 1901, there were regular notices about her in the state's newspapers. The *Sacramento Daily Union*, for example, heralded her "first appearance before citizens of Sacramento on November 28, 1850." Her appearance came on the heels of extremely well-received concerts in San Francisco, which the *Daily Union* characterized as having a "success [that] has been unprecedented." In the West, it appears, no woman of color before her had achieved such triumphs as a public performer. Pindell was part of an organized musical ensemble that traveled with her. In California, she often was "assisted by Messrs. De Courcy, Johnson, Hodge, and de Gromes."[17] De Courcy, a second tenor, and de Gromes, a first tenor, who were referred to in subsequent press notices as Coursey and Grooms, had been members of the Philadelphia-based band of Frank Johnson. Even her collaboration with them underscored the connections within organized African American music circles; Annie Pindell's mother, Elizabeth, was related by marriage to Elijah Smith Sr., who traveled with Frank Johnson's band during the 1830s and 1840s and was with them when they performed for Queen Victoria. Annie Pauline Pindell's professional effort at times was an interracial enterprise. According to contemporary accounts of her concerts, she on occasion had white pianists and orchestra members accompanying her when she performed. In the course of the year, Annie Pindell's opera troupe also would include Mr. Hobbs, "a young man from Cincinnati, with considerable reputation [in California] as a bass-violinist," and Mr. Johnson, "formerly comic vocalist to a company of serenaders" who had been performing in a number of California towns and cities.[18]

The career of Annie Pauline Pindell was a tangible inheritance and inspirational model for her niece and namesake Pauline Allen Hopkins. Hopkins seized the first professional opportunity that she had to make plain the depth of her respect for her aunt and to preserve for posterity Annie Pauline Pindell's achievements. In 1901, the inaugural installment in Hopkins's "Famous Women of the Negro Race," a groundbreaking historical biographical series in the *Colored American Magazine*, was devoted to "Phenomenal Vocalists." Published five months after the death of Annie Pauline on 1 May in Los Angeles, the profile, enriched by Hopkins's moving remarks about music and its role in American slave culture, focused on five accomplished vocalists, women whom Hopkins lauded on behalf of her race as "beacon lights along the shore in the days of darkest history."[19] Pindell and her celebrated female contemporaries of color built on the lesser-known but foundational legacies of vocalists such as Susan Paul. In so doing, Pindell, and women like her, according to

Pauline Hopkins, succeeded in accomplishing "work . . . more sacred than the exquisite subtleness of their art, for to them it was given to help create a manhood for their despised race."[20]

If art was an embodiment of the spiritual, then it was for Hopkins capable of transforming and redeeming its agents and its audiences. Her respectful *Colored American Magazine* tribute to her Aunt Annie, Elizabeth Greenfield, the Hyers Sisters, and Marie Selika Williams mined this empowering juxtaposition of the private woman and public figure, deliberate artist and nuanced activist. In addition to being able to draw on private family accounts of her aunt's achievements, Hopkins also had access to published contemporary reports from leading African American newspapers that documented Annie Pauline Pindell's experiences. "Tall Son of PA," an anonymous contributor who was the paper's San Francisco correspondent, for example, regularly updated readers of the New York City–based *Anglo-African* about Pindell's California enterprises. In his 3 December 1859 missive, "Tall Son of PA" provided illuminating details about a recent Pindell concert in San Francisco. The droll tone notwithstanding, he noted that "[o]ur new prima donna, Mrs. Anne Pendell, formerly of Boston, it is said, announced a concert, which was given on the first [of this month]." The concert, which showcased Pindell in a substantial number of solos and in at least one duet, with music provided by an orchestra that included Erastus Briscoe and Samuel Grooms, was "a decided success." Included in his list of the "selections of music" performed were a host of arias from recently debuted operas that reflected Pindell's wide range, her capacity for dramatic interpretation, and her classical training. The program featured "Ask Me Not Why" from the Donizetti comic opera *La Fille du Régiment* (*The Daughter of the Regiment*), the song "Where Are Now the Hopes I Cherished," from *Norma*, an opera by Bellini that according to contemporary music critic Peter McCallum features "many false gods: abandoned vows, craven sacrifice and treacherous love" and requires its protagonist, Norma, to be "the high priestess of the vocal arabesque, and the protectoress of lingering pathos and rising excitement."[21] Additional works included ballads such as "Far Away" and Louis Henry Lavenu's "My Dreams Are Now No More of Thee," "O, Whisper What Thou Feelest" from the popular 1841 opera *Crown Diamonds* by the prolific composer Daniel-Francois-Esprit Auber, "Ah! I Have Sighed To Rest [Me]" from *Il Trovatore*, the 1853 four-act opera by Giuseppe Verdi.[22]

Annie Pindell, whom contemporary reviewers compared to the celebrated nineteenth-century Italian contralto Madame Alboni, became part of a pioneering new wave in American performance. In the age of Jenny Lind, Pindell and other female vocalists of color captured audience attention and became powerful cultural figures that deployed their grace, refinement, femininity, and classical talent to great effect.[23] They helped to maintain the historic link that artists of African descent, such as the talented tragedian Ira Aldridge, forged with foreign audiences. They also sought out new territories, as was confirmed by Annie Pindell's bold contemplation of an Australian tour. Such a possibility, which Pindell began considering shortly after she arrived in California, reflected her confidence, but her plans apparently exceeded the expectations of some onlookers. It appears that Pindell never did reach Australia, and sobering family news unexpectedly disrupted her career plans. Once again, the "Tall Son of PA" was the one to provide readers with an update on her activities. The watchful "Tall Son of PA" announced to *Anglo-African* readers with a hint of melodramatic flair in his 26 February 1860 column that "Mrs. Anne Pindell, the prima donna . . . having received news of the death of her sister, has abandoned all engagements for the present."[24] The career that paved the way for Pauline Allen's entry into the performing arts ended when family tragedy struck. Yet, despite the sudden close to Annie Pindell's accomplished career, Pauline Allen Hopkins was steadied by the example of her sophisticated and ambitious foremother. Indeed, it appears that Hopkins was catalyzed by the national accomplishments of her sophisticated arts foremother, with whom Pauline shared not only a name but a powerful, lyrical voice.

Three years after the World Peace Jubilee transfixed and awed Bostonians, Pauline Allen and the members of the Progressive Musical Union confirmed that a powerful postbellum African American high concert tradition was thriving. The first Progressive Musical Union concert was a well-choreographed show that included two violin and piano instrumentals and twelve songs that ranged from classical romantic ballads to rousing military pieces. Advertisements of the show appeared in the *Boston Evening Transcript*, and the *Boston Globe* published an enthusiastic review the day following the performance in which it declared enthusiastically that all of the pieces "gave delight" and assured Pauline and her fellow Union members that they could "hope for a high place among [the city's] resident musical societies."[25] Listed on the program as "Miss Allen," Pauline's first performance was a duet arrangement of "On Mossy Banks" with Miss E. M. Pinkney, one of the three other women who were part of the Union.[26] She next appeared accompanied by the newly established Auber Quartet, an all-male group that her cousin Elijah also had founded and named in honor of the recently deceased French composer Daniel-François-Esprit Auber. By the time of the Union's debut concert, the Auber Quartet already had "attracted much attention by their very pleasing rendering of some of the best popular music of the day."[27] Pauline and the quartet performed Gustav Reichardt's "The Image of the Rose," and their presentation concluded the first portion of the concert program.[28]

Elijah Smith had great confidence in his cousin's talent, and he provided Pauline with ample opportunity to showcase her gifts. During the second half of the program, she appeared onstage with David T. Oswell, a close friend of Smith's from Worcester, Massachusetts. Oswell's appearance that evening was a particular high point for all those in attendance and further confirmed the sophisticated nature of the performance. Well known as an "artistic violinist," Oswell consistently was hailed as one who "perform[ed] in a finished style the most classical and difficult music for the violin."[29] He accompanied Mrs. D. Wilson and Pauline Allen in a rendition of "Waiting," a popular song by Harrison Millard, a former Bostonian and member of the city's Handel and Haydn Society chorus.[30] Pauline's final appearance came at the end of the program when she and the entire company were accompanied by organ and piano in a piece entitled "Angel of Peace."[31] The *Globe* declared the concert "agreeably diversified" and noted that all pieces were performed "creditably."[32] Pauline Allen had allied herself with a performance company that was believed to have "several of the qualities which bring success."[33]

Elijah Smith coordinated the March debut of the Progressive Musical Union with a much anticipated and broadly advertised Tremont Temple concert by the Fisk Jubilee Singers, the first in America following an extended and extremely successful tour of England.[34] The *Boston Globe* anticipated in its rapt musings about the event that "thousands of persons will welcome the troupe of Jubilee Singers." They will, "no doubt, be greeted by a very large audience and ticket sales will be brisk," the paper proclaimed, and that prediction was fulfilled. The group, which generated enormous pride for people of color and inspired all who came to see and hear them, was so well received that two additional concerts had to be scheduled.

The Union concert preceded the Fisk performance by just one night, and so the group, for all intents and purposes, served as a highly suitable opening act for the celebrated African American gospel troupe. There does not appear to have been a formal arrangement between the two troupes, but the Union positioned itself to capitalize on the confluence of events and also smartly prevented any overshadowing of its own debut by the Fisk Jubilee event. It is highly likely that Union members and Jubilee singers attended each other's concerts, especially if the latter group arrived in Boston the day before their concert. The immediate benefits of the Fisk concert to the impressionable Pauline Allen and her ambitious cousin, Elijah Smith, exceeded simple aesthetic pleasure and inspiration. The Union's debut, coupled with the great success of the Jubilee troupe, reinforced the reality of an African American high concert tradition and the potential for national and international acclaim. Such realities emboldened Smith and his protégé to envision future and increasingly sophisticated concerts, performances that would clarify further the divide between their high cultural reality and the low fantastic tradition of blackface minstrelsy, for example, which both depended upon and fueled divisive racial fictions bolstered by racial prejudice and acrimony.

The Progressive Musical Union was part of the long-standing effort to establish empowering intellectual and social forums for African Americans that began in Boston as early as 1832. Literary societies such as the Afric-American Female Intelligence Society, founded in 1832, and the Adelphic Union for the Promotion of Literature and Science, organized by some of the city's most promising African American young men in 1836, were among the first to institutionalize cultural and artistic ventures in the city.[35] Members, whose church affiliations, occupations, and origins reflected Boston's diverse black constituency, used these societies to showcase their talents, to explore their diverse intellectual interests, and to exhort their community in the face of demeaning prejudice and systemic disenfranchisement. Like her relatives Susan and Thomas Paul Jr., Pauline Allen would benefit socially from her participation in a black Boston community arts venture. More importantly, however, she, like them, would experience firsthand the political potential of the arts and appreciate the vital connections between community uplift, political activism, and African American aesthetics.

Pauline Allen undoubtedly was aware of the great symbolism of her Union debut. With Elijah Smith Jr. as her attentive mentor, she had ready access to her maternal family's histories and record of recognized accomplishments in arts, education, and abolition. The life of Pauline's ancestral and literary foremother Susan Paul especially informed the new collaboration between Elijah and Pauline because it was Paul who fostered Elijah's own musical growth and racial awareness. Following the tragic early death of his mother, Anne Catherine, in 1835 due to complications from childbirth, Elijah and his siblings became the responsibility of Susan, and they "passed much of their younger days . . . under the instruction of their accomplished Aunt." It was this "excellent teacher . . . who guided [Elijah's] infantile steps in literature."[36] Paul's formative influence upon her nephew, and by extension, upon Pauline, her great-grandniece, was facilitated by her guardianship of Smith and his siblings. As a gifted teacher, highly successful children's choir director, and antislavery activist, Paul demonstrated the political power of the arts and education, and it was this legacy that enriched the life and arts career of Elijah Smith.

A talented vocalist, performer, and musical enthusiast herself, Susan Paul consolidated—during her lifetime, for Elijah, and in memory, for Pauline—the link between the arts and African American activism. The performances by her children's choir began in 1833, under the auspices of the New England Anti-Slavery Society. The presentations evolved quickly into independent community concerts in Boston. Paul and her students offered compelling evidence of the intellectual and artistic talents of African American children just as Boston debated the merits of abolition and the integration of its public schools. As one of the Reverend Thomas Paul's only two grandsons and as a student at the Abiel Smith School, Elijah Smith surely was part of the children's concerts organized by his guardian aunt and her fellow teachers.[37]

Elijah's interest in the performing arts was also piqued by the exciting career of his father. Elijah Smith Sr. was a composer and a trumpet player in the Frank Johnson Band. Made up entirely of African American men, the band enjoyed an international reputation for its innovative compositions and stylish presentations. In his account of the group, James Monroe Trotter, a dedicated music historian and the father of future *Guardian* editor William Monroe Trotter, noted that "the novelty formed by such an organization,—all colored men,—its excellent playing, and the boldness of the enterprise, all combined to create a decided sensation wherever these sable troubadours appeared."[38] During an English tour, the band played for Queen Victoria and her court with much success. He may have been deeply influenced by his father's career, but unlike his father, Elijah Jr. pursued a life in music that bonded him to, rather than separated him from, his family. His work as a musician in his community also allowed him, as it had his Aunt Susan, to minister directly to his peers and neighbors.[39] Through his efforts, numerous members of Boston's black community developed their musical talents and a variety of forums in which to display them.

Elijah Smith was an accomplished and nationally recognized poet when he organized the Progressive Musical Union. He had noteworthy advocates such as William Wells Brown who delighted in Smith's work and positioned Smith's majestic poem, "Welcome to 'The Rising Son,'" as the first text in his 1874 *The Rising Son; or, The Antecedents and Advancement of the Colored Race*. Brown praised Smith publicly for "the evenness of his numbers . . . the polish of his diction, the rich melody of his musically embodied thoughts, and the variety of his information," all gifts that Brown believed proved that "Nature was not sparing in showering her gifts upon him."[40] Smith's reputation for masterminding uplifting cultural collaborations was reinforced by his dynamic poetry and public use of art for the advancement of the race. Like many in his community, he believed that the arts were of vital importance to their uplift and that African Americans could ensure their intellectual and social advancement. The poem that he wrote especially for the Union group and then published on the cover of the evening's program reaffirmed this sentiment and articulated clearly the mission to which Pauline Allen had begun to contribute:

> Progressive: ay, we hope to climb,
> With patient steps fair Music's height
> And at her altar's sacred flame
> Our care-extinguished torches light;
> And, while their soft and cheering rays
> Life's rugged path with joys illume,
> May Harmony's enchanted wand
> Bring sunshine where before was gloom.
>
> And though we may not walk apace
> With Mendelssohn or Haydn grand,
> Nor view with undimmed eyes the mount
> Where Mozart's shining angels stand;
> Yet in the outer courts we wait
> Till Knowledge shall the curtain draw,
> And to our wondering eyes disclose
> The mysteries the masters saw.[41]

Smith used classical images of mythological goddesses of the arts, "sacred flames," and "care-extinguished torches" to redefine racial segregation and prejudice. He suggested that African Americans could bear the injustice that they suffered if they considered this oppressive world as part of heaven's "outer courts." Convinced that music had restorative powers, Smith represented suffering as a state that could not persist in the face of harmony. Music, he proposed, could "bring sunshine where before there was gloom" and enable "undimmed" and "wondering" eyes to see "the mysteries" revealed to musical "masters" such as Felix Mendelssohn, Franz Joseph Haydn, and Wolfgang Amadeus Mozart. Although the references to hardship and the effort to move upward suggest daily life struggles, Smith's allusions here are also suggestive of racial uplift and self-determination. He advocates persistence in the face of exhaustion, proposing that ultimately even the less fortunate and unschooled will have the opportunity to gain clarity and knowledge. Smith's vision of music and the arts, as expressed in the dedicatory poem, evolves into an insistent political allegory that solidifies the link between public performance, race pride, and the continued revitalization of the African American community.

Elijah Smith Jr. was an inspiring mentor for the teenaged Pauline, but not solely because of his close family connection to the Pauls. By 1875, Smith had established himself as a talented poet, enterprising arts coordinator, and incisive social historian. His skills as a writer and historian of his race developed during his apprenticeship at *The Liberator* where he "learned the printer's trade under Mr. Garrison's supervision."[42] There he became "an expert typesetter, and afterwards a proofreader in that office." Pauline Allen would later propose that it was the years that Elijah Smith spent working alongside William Lloyd Garrison, helping to document the tumultuous events of the day, that developed "the genius of poetry for which he became so celebrated."[43] Throughout the 1870s, Elijah Smith had been writing poems that documented political events and milestones that were of particular relevance to African Americans. The majority of Smith's poems were rousing anthems that rallied the African American community or somber odes that honored the sacrifices made by blacks and whites in the fight for civil rights. The man whose elegant works prompted many to regard him as the city's African American poet laureate cheered the leadership of stalwart antislavery activists like Charles Sumner, meditated on the importance of the reelection of Ulysses S. Grant in 1872, contemplated the sacrifices of the state's African American Civil War soldiers, and expounded on the value of African American suffrage. Some of these published pieces even were performed. "Freedom's Jubilee" (1870), a poem that marked the passage of the Fifteenth Amendment and that Pauline Hopkins later extolled as a "beautiful and soul-stirring poem," was read at a Ratification Meeting in the city.[44] Smith's works consistently reflected his Republican affiliation and advanced the call for racial uplift in all aspects of African American life. He published these vivid and spirited pieces in local dailies such as *The Liberator*, the *Boston Daily Traveler*, the *Saturday Evening Express*, and the *New National Era*.

The specificity and vigor of Smith's political poetry suggest that he was a keen reader and that he followed closely a wide range of national and regional political issues. His works confirm, for example, that he was well informed about anti–Ku Klux Klan legislation being debated in the Congress, as well as attuned to local issues such as the fight to integrate Boston schools. The African American community looked to Smith to memorialize the events that they deemed important and to honor those who dedicated themselves to racial progress. He was an avid reader, and his extensive personal library that was "well stored with useful works" included a "large collection of works by colored men," busts, and portraits of the abolitionist leaders with whom he was familiar.[45] The opportunities that Smith had to witness and to interact with antislavery activists and writers in the *Liberator* offices fueled his "fond" feelings for the "old antislavery leaders," such as William Lloyd Garrison, Charles Sumner, Wendell Phillips, and Gerrit Smith, whom he memorialized in his poems.[46] Some six years after his death, Pauline included a lengthy tribute to Elijah Smith Jr. in her *Colored American Magazine* series, "Famous Men of the Negro Race." There she described him as one who "wrote on various themes" but noted that "the highest inspiration came to him through the wrongs of his race and the efforts of his friends to right these wrongs. His greatest enthusiasm," she declared, "was aroused by those great men,— Garrison, Sumner, Phillips, Douglass, Nell and other leaders, and his poetic tributes to their valiant leadership have never been surpassed by poet of any race."[47]

There was ample opportunity for Elijah Smith to follow in the footsteps of family members like his granduncle, the Reverend Nathaniel Paul, and take his place on the political stage. He chose, instead, to appear in public as a politically astute performer and creative artist. His poems and the concerts presented by his Auber Quartet and the Progressive Musical Union contributed to the African American fight for equality and catered to the intellectual and social aspirations of Boston's African American community. It was invaluable for Pauline Hopkins to have such close ties to Smith, a man who came of age in antebellum and Civil War Boston. The details she learned from him about Boston's explosive and inspiring past were coupled with intimate details about her influential ancestors, vivid recollections of the heyday of *The Liberator*, musings about the challenges and successes of his segregated school days at the Abiel Smith School, and proud delineations of the triumphant moments of black community activism. These historic elements constituted an invaluable primer for Hopkins, and the details that she absorbed shaped her future recollections and reconstructions of African American life and history.

In 1876, Pauline Allen moved with her parents from 1 Allen Place, where they had lived since William and Sarah's marriage in 1864, to rooms at 15 State Street, a commercial building in downtown Boston where William now was working as a janitor. The building, which was flanked by machine shops, banks, and printing offices, stood opposite the Old State House, a three-story red brick structure located in the middle of State Street that divided the road there just above Washington Street. The Hopkins family may have had regrets about having to move their daughter to a less residential neighborhood, but there were distinct advantages to their new location. There may have been some financial improvement for them if William's work required him to live on site, and they were not isolated from relatives on Beacon Hill.[48] Pauline's increasingly close relationship with her cousin, Elijah Smith, may have been enhanced because of the family's increased proximity to him. He worked as the steward and headwaiter at Young's Hotel, two blocks away from State Street, on the narrow stretch of Court Street just off Cornhill Court. In addition, their central downtown residence deepened Pauline's fascination with Boston's history and gave her easy access to the absorbing world of nineteenth-century entertainment. The Hopkins's apartment at 15 State Street was literally around the corner from 46 Washington Street, the building that had housed William Lloyd Garrison's *Liberator* printing offices until the end of the Civil War. After leaving her home and walking past four storefronts, Pauline simply had to turn left and walk up Washington Street to the former *Liberator* office building. She was following, quite literally, in the footsteps of her great-grandaunt Susan Paul, who had during the 1830s and early 1840s, staged Juvenile Choir concerts in the lecture room adjacent to the *Liberator* office.[49] Pauline now was traveling the streets patrolled by what abolitionist Mary Weston Chapman had referred to as an angry mob of "Boston gentlemen," a group that descended in October 1835 on Susan Paul and her fellow Boston Female Anti-Slavery Society members and then turned their proslavery fervor against William Lloyd Garrison, chased him into the streets, and nearly lynched him.[50]

From her State Street home, Pauline was moments away from streets papered with bills announcing upcoming grand productions at the opera houses, notices that expanded on the colorful listings in the "Dramatics" columns in the *Boston Herald* that noted times and ticket prices for events ranging from sacred concerts by the Fisk Jubilee Singers to riotous blackface minstrelsy routines and classical European dramas. Shakespearean productions, especially of *The Merchant of Venice*, *Othello*, *Romeo and Juliet*, and *Macbeth*, were staples in the Boston theaters. In addition to these, city theaters offered stagings of *Uncle Tom's Cabin*, special appearances by the Reverend Josiah Henson, who was known as the "Original Uncle Tom," and charity concerts sponsored by groups such as the Alexander Dumas Society when they sought to raise funds for a "temporary home for destitute colored children."[51]

Boston's vibrant political history and Paul family memories permeated the air of the Hopkins family's new neighborhood. Pauline began to dream about a life in the theater, as well as follow closely the careers of some of the most celebrated actors of the day. It was during this formative time of her life that she became infatuated with Edwin Wilkes Booth, and she signaled her deep interest in him by carefully gluing a full-page published sketch of Booth on one of the first pages of the scrapbook that would soon contain carefully pasted copies of the programs for her own shows. The portrait emphasized his soulful dark eyes and showed him costumed as if for a Shakespearean play.[52] Audiences in Boston and other major cities celebrated this renowned actor for his performances as Hamlet. Booth, brother of Lincoln's assassin, appeared frequently in Boston venues during the late 1870s, and Pauline's fascination with the actor was fueled by her proximity to the world that he inhabited. It may have pleased her deeply that her March 1875 debut with the Progressive Musical Union coincided with Booth's appearances as Othello and as Richelieu at the Boston Theatre.[53]

By 1877, eighteen-year-old Pauline Allen had come of age in a close-knit family and a supportive community. She was about to pursue new avenues in the arts that would intensify her passion for theater and showcase further the voice that would soon earn her a reputation as "Boston's favorite colored soprano." Once again, she would collaborate with Smith and benefit substantially from his ambitious artistic endeavors and his capacity for infusing performed art with nuanced and unwavering political critique. This second documented public collaboration with Smith catapulted Pauline Allen beyond the safe spheres of black Beacon Hill. Through song and dramatic performance, she became part of a bold portrayal of African American heroism, social inequality, disenfranchisement, and racial uplift to a diverse Boston audience.

On 28 March 1877, two years after her debut as a concert singer with the Progressive Musical Union, Pauline Allen appeared as the lead actress in a production of *Pauline; or, The Belle of Saratoga, a Cantata in Two Acts*. Billed as the finale of "The Grand Musical Festival of the Season," her theatrical debut occurred in Parker Memorial Hall on Berkeley and Appleton Streets in downtown Boston. Smith's reputation for organizing sophisticated, African American troupes and producing high-art productions meant that *The Belle of Saratoga* became part of an ambitious, politicized African American Boston arts agenda. At first glance, the 1873 play, written by George Cooper with score by Hart Pease Danks, appears to be a comical romance in which two thwarted lovers are united in spite of the opposition that they face from family and friends. The play's invocation of the Mexican War, however, when staged by an African American company, transformed *The Belle of Saratoga* into a charged political critique. The musical became a daring commentary on social and political disenfranchisement, an unmistakable meditation on

Program for the 1877 production of *Pauline; or, The Belle of Saratoga* at Boston's Parker Memorial Hall. Elijah Smith and William Hopkins were two of the primary organizers of this show, which featured Pauline Allen in her stage debut. *Courtesy of Fisk University, Franklin Library Special Collections.*

the racial implications of American expansionism, and an emphatic rebuttal of white blackface minstrelsy.[54]

The Committee of Arrangements for Smith's production of *The Belle of Saratoga* was made up of four men, two of whom were relatives of Pauline Allen. Working with Elijah Smith and William Hopkins were James T. Henry, who sang in Smith's Auber Quartet, and Horace Grey. Together, the four men booked a venue for the play, managed publicity and production-related details, and oversaw sales of the fifty-cent tickets and the refreshments. They chose Parker Memorial Hall, a site used primarily for small classical concerts by groups such as the Boston Quintette Club and for literary readings by such well-known writers as Wilkie Collins. Just days before the *Belle of Saratoga* production, Bostonians thronged to the hall for "a delightful evening" of song by a diverse group of classically trained soloists and oration by Samuel R. Kelley, "the popular elocutionist," who was making his first appearance of the season at Parker Hall.[55]

In an effort to appeal to regular Parker Memorial patrons, the committee emphasized the formal musical aspects of *The Belle of Saratoga* when it advertised the upcoming performance. The "Notes and Announcements" column of the *Boston Courier* included a decidedly reserved description: "On Wednesday evening next, in the Parker Memorial, will be given *Pauline, or the Belle of Saratoga* a cantata, by five soloists and a chorus of twenty-five."[56] This notice, noticeably devoid of any performers' names, is in stark contrast to the celebratory tone and detailed description of the play distributed in the actual theater programs. In these, *The Belle of Saratoga* was characterized as a "brilliant and charming Cantata" that included "elaborate costumes and full scenic effects." It "will be judged by all who attend," claimed the play's promoters, "as the most *amusing* and *interesting* entertainment of the season."[57]

The cast was made up of black Bostonians, many of whom lived in close proximity to Smith in the heart of Beacon Hill. James Henry, a forty-five-year-old laborer from Virginia, played the role of Captain Western.[58] Pauline, in the leading female role, played opposite William Walker, a twenty-three-year-old clerk who lived with his family near Elijah Smith's home and who was cast as George Ardent, the play's romantic male lead.[59] Appearing as Sir Charles Grandiswell was Parker Bailey, the twenty-one-year-old son of a successful boxing teacher with substantial Boston property holdings.[60] Mrs. Celia Boston, the accompanist, was a much-celebrated performer herself, known for her "clever abilities as organist, pianist, and contralto-vocalist."[61] Members of the play's twenty-five-person chorus also functioned as "hotel guests" and were drawn most likely from Smith's church choir and local musical network.[62]

The Belle of Saratoga is set in Saratoga, New York, where two of the principal characters, Captain Western, a widowed veteran, and Pauline, his daughter, are in residence for the season. The captain arranges for his daughter to marry Sir Charles Grandiswell, a decidedly foppish and unreliable British tourist whose surname underscores the play's critique of colonial interests, aristocratic pretensions, and class prejudice. Pauline Western's true love, however, is George Ardent, a Yale University student whose intellectual pursuits contribute to his poverty. Her father rejects Ardent because of his lower-class status and because he equates the young man's advanced schooling with an unsettling lack of moral conviction. Yet George does become an acceptable match for Pauline after he becomes a colonel during the Mexican War and is able to boast to his future father-in-law about the "very hard service" he endured with his regiment.[63] Pauline Western and George Ardent, the overly sincere and passionate couple of the play, are juxtaposed against Clara Rivers and Sir Charles Grandiswell, indecisive, comical, and sometimes duplicitous individuals, who end up together. Captain Western functions as an intermediary figure; the attention he pays to the two couples determines their social worth and romantic potential. Although the romantic machinations that Western engineers ultimately fail, his emphasis on conventional notions of manhood and female subordination both justifies and challenges the aspirations of the play's protagonists.

The role of Pauline Western required an actress to portray a moody, sentimental young woman. Indeed, the songs in Pauline Allen's scenes with the character George Ardent, "the poor student," enabled her to wax rhapsodic about the power and the pains of love. These stereotypical gendered affectations, however, did not completely obscure the autonomous and self-confident young woman who emerged by play's end. Clara Rivers, the supporting female character, refers to Pauline Western as "that artful flirt, who thinks herself so irresistible." Pauline's opening soliloquy reveals, however, that she is actually "wearied to death with [the] continued round of excitement" in Saratoga and is exasperated by the "shallow-brained fops who follow . . . and come . . . and go at [her] beck."[64] Throughout act I, Pauline Western suffers from a melodramatic social ambivalence that she never is able to set aside. This is most evident when her sentimental confessions are punctuated with sobering thoughts about her role as a dutiful daughter and potential wife. During her first scene, Pauline, lingering over a letter from George, announces that "there is no happiness in life for me, unless we can share it together. Morning, noon and night he is in my thoughts. Is it undutiful of me to go contrary to the foolish whim of a parent? It is now too late to think of this. Once loved—is loved forever."[65] Her reference to "a parent" rather than to her father, the only living relative that she has, indicates her capacity for extreme objectivity. Her ability to dismiss matters—however important—that would overshadow her love relationship makes Pauline the most steady and deliberate character in this otherwise farcical production.

Pauline Western's willfulness actually drives the play to its triumphant end. Although embroiled in the frenetic social world of Saratoga, she remains devoted to George during the "[one] long weary year" in which he is away. She survives by going "mechanically thro' the dance," and when she is "surrounded by a dozen admirers, each one vying with the other to win a smile" from her, "her thoughts are far away! Far away with the man [she] love[s]!"[66] She refuses to honor the advances of the persistent Sir Charles and drives him to distraction. "I weally think I have made a confounded noodle of myself!" he admits as act II begins. "It's very plain that Miss Western is anything but stwicken with me. I've made love to her for a long time, and in the most approved manner; but, as they say in these parts—she did'nt see it."[67] Soon thereafter, Pauline Western confesses to her father that she has never accepted the English aristocrat as her future husband. Captain Western attempts to persuade her to comply with his wishes: "Come now, Pauline, please your old father in this affair," he says, before "patting her cheek" as he asks her to "[l]et [him] issue cards for your wedding this very week. There, that's a darling little daughter." In response, Pauline replies, first with an aside to the audience, and then to her father: "Let me end this persecution at once and forever. Father, I have told you again and again that I could never be the wife of Sir Charles! I consented to his addresses only under protest, and to please you. If Sir Charles imagines that I have led him to think that he is of the least consequence to my happiness, he deceives and flatters himself!" It is her father's infantilization of her, in addition to his insistence that she wed another man, that provokes Pauline Western to finally shed her ambivalence about dutiful submission to her father. The captain, "petrified with astonishment" in the face of Pauline's frank opposition, attempts to bully her into compliance: "If you won't marry Sir Charles, you sha'nt marry anyone else! I'll lock you up in your room for a disobedient, ungrateful child! There! See if I won't!"[68] Pauline does disappear to her room, but only because that is where she can pore over her love letters from George Ardent and try not to "die of ennui" brought on by the "hateful monotony" of her empty days.

Pauline Western's second soliloquy, like the first speech that she delivers in act I, is interrupted by the man she loves. Halfway through her meditation on love, she retrieves the note that he tosses through her window. George then clambers into her room and the two prepare to elope. The arrival of Captain Western, the feckless Sir Charles, and the unpredictable Clara prevents their getaway. After Pauline is accused of being an "ungrateful girl" and a "schemer," George attempts to defend her honor. His explanations are, however, postponed and even deemed unnecessary once the captain takes note of his uniform. George's "honorable distinction in our army" and his promotion to colonel transform him altogether. When asked for his name, the former self-confessed "poor and unknown" Yale student answers, "Colonel George Ardent." His use of rank both to defend and to rename himself makes it difficult for the captain, who is now his military subordinate, to reject him. The final sanction for the unions of George and Pauline and Sir Charles and Clara comes when Captain Western interrupts the civilian banter about love and reunion with a final order. "Hold on!" he shouts. "One thing more! Present arms! Salute partners! [*They kiss.*] As you were!"[69]

The Boston 1877 African American production of *The Belle of Saratoga* opened just days after the Republican presidential candidate, Rutherford B. Hayes, was declared the winner of the much-disputed 1876 election. The decision to recognize Hayes as the nineteenth president of the United States was based in large part on Republican concessions to the South. Federal troops stationed in Southern states and charged with facilitating post–Civil War transitions were directed to withdraw. The Hayes administration also agreed to appoint at least one Southerner to the cabinet and to invest in Southern interests. Pauline Allen and her troupe were in rehearsals as federal troops prepared to leave the South and as Southern blacks prepared for the imminent backlash of racial violence and disenfranchisement that signaled the end of Reconstruction.[70]

This production of *The Belle of Saratoga* also coincided with the thirty-first anniversary of the declaration of war on Mexico. Initially, it seems inconceivable that an autonomous African American troupe would choose to stage a play that glorified this particular war. During the 1840s, New Englanders and many African Americans protested the conflict because they considered it to be a conspiracy to expand Southern slavery. Henry Highland Garnet, a Presbyterian minister who attended the ill-fated integrated Noyes Academy in Canaan, New Hampshire, with Pauline Allen's granduncle, Thomas Paul Jr., was among those who actively criticized the war effort. He characterized it as the project of the "propagators of American slavery" who were "spending their blood and treasure that they may plant the black flag in the heart of Mexico and riot in the halls of the Montezumas."[71] *The Belle of Saratoga*, while clearly equating the Mexican War with heroism and the perpetuation of domesticity, celebrated white American goals that were ultimately achieved at the expense of African Americans and Native Americans. In this play, the white leading character has limited heroic potential when he is a civilian and intellectual. He is transformed into an acceptable American and patriot once he rejects the scholarly life for one that requires and honors offensive aggressive action. Such terms for white manhood and white citizenship were problematic in general. Given the increasingly militarized realities of the day, these ideals were extremely menacing to African Americans in particular.

The Belle of Saratoga, in which an eastern boy successfully courts a "western" girl, also promotes the joy of romantic and symbolic national union. The prominence of the Westerns and the fact that their destiny is the driving issue of the play reinforce the doctrine of Manifest Destiny and the reality of American expansion. George's ability to "claim" Pauline Western eventually makes the play an extended political allegory that references America's conquest of Mexico and its acquisition of the western territories. Ultimately, *The Belle of Saratoga* situates romance, social politics, and class privilege within what Northerners, and especially African Americans in the North, would have regarded as an antiblack expansionist ideology.

The Mexican War was not a campaign in which African Americans, particularly those in Boston, tended to believe or had the official opportunity to join.[72] During the 1820s, U.S. Army policy banned African Americans from military service, despite their documented and heroic service in the Revolutionary War and the War of 1812. State laws of the 1820s also prohibited African American enrollment in militias. Soldiers of African descent who accompanied the American regiments into Mexican War service did so as part of the retinues of servants assigned to white officers. Ulysses S. Grant's letters, for instance, contain references to the "black boy" who spoke English, French, and Spanish whom he planned to "take along as [his] servant." Other officers enlisted the aid of their families as they sought to purchase or acquire African American men or boys to attend to them.[73] Generous military reimbursement policies encouraged officers to assemble large attachments of servants, a fact that explains how African Americans were involved in the conflict from its beginnings. On occasion, these servants, many of whom were enslaved, defended themselves from enemy fire or made heroic sacrifices on the battlefield to protect the lives of their masters.[74]

The African American leadership in the North protested the war that conscripted African Americans in the South into domestic service and also threatened to compromise further their own freedom. Abolitionists published formal protests and rallied Northerners to protest the war and the machinations that sparked it. In 1847, *The Liberator*, for which Elijah Smith at the time was working as a typesetter, published a copy of the letter from the integrated Massachusetts Anti-Slavery Society delivered to President James K. Polk during his late July visit to Boston. The letter began with a straightforward declaration: "We address you simply as the friends of liberty and equality, in no partisan state of mind, and for no political object." Its tone soon changed, however, as the society excoriated Polk for being a slaveholder: "The fact that you occupy a high station is no proof of your worthiness, but only demonstrates the gross wickedness which prevails in the land. Truly, it may be affirmed at this day, as of old—'The rulers of the people cause them to err, and they that are led of them are destroyed.'"[75] Boston poet James Russell Lowell stoked the fires of opposition as well, charging,

> They just want this Califormy,
> So's to lug new slave-states in
> To abuse ye, an' to scorn ye,
> An' to plunder ye like sin.[76]

Benjamin Lundy, editor of the *Genius of Universal Emancipation* based in New York City, strove to inform his readers about the origins and political significance of the war. He published a series of indictments of the government and consistently exhorted his readers to "AROUSE FROM THEIR LETHARGY, and nip the monstrous attempt [to further extend the war] in the bud."[77] Whether or not Polk, a Tennessee slaveholder, was a continentalist interested in western expansion to America's "natural" border at the Pacific Ocean or a Southern sectionalist dedicated to protecting slavery, his interactions with the Mexican Republic ultimately resulted in proslavery legislation and heightened sectional tensions. Historians have proposed direct links between the American annexation of Texas and the Compromise of 1850, the *Dred Scott* decision that denied citizenship to African Americans, John Brown's raid on Harper's Ferry, and the American Civil War.[78]

Contemporary analyses of the conflict suggested that the war with Mexico was in fact the result of a carefully planned Southern campaign. Newspaper reports portrayed Mexico as a "FREE STATE": "It must be borne in mind, that the system of slavery *has been abolished in Texas*, by the Mexican government," declared one fervent antiexpansionist in the *Genius of Universal Emancipation*. The article continued, reminding readers that in Mexico

> nearly all the colonists in Texas were from our slave holding states, and either slave holders themselves, or friendly to the re-establishment and perpetuation of the system of slavery there. The plan thenceforth pursued was, to misrepresent the Mexican laws and colonial regulations, rela-

Progressive Arts and the Public Sphere

tive to slavery, and induce the emigration of persons favourable to their views, until their numerical and physical strength should enable them to take advantage of some critical conjuncture, and subject the country, at least to their legislative control.[79]

On principle alone, the Mexican War was one that African Americans in the North could not support; it threatened their already fragile claims to freedom and an American homeland.

During the Mexican War years, Northerners actively petitioned for policies that would curtail the expansion of slavery into the newly acquired Mexican territories. Southerners advocated that slavery be allowed in these lands. There were official denials that proslavery politicians were instigating the Mexican War in order to advance their own interests. Yet the only way to circumvent the limits on slavery's expansion established in the 1820 Missouri Compromise was to acquire the northern Mexican lands south of the 36°30′.[80] Antebellum opponents of the war and slavery recognized the direct connection between the Missouri Compromise and what they regarded as American aggression. In August 1836, as American settlers in Texas began to agitate, a lengthy article in the *Genius of Universal Emancipation* declared,

> It is susceptible of the clearest demonstration that the immediate cause and the leading object of this contest originated in a settled design, among the slaveholders of this country, (with land-speculators and slave-traders) to wrest the large and valuable territory of Texas from the Mexican Republic in order to re-establish the SYSTEM OF SLAVERY; to open a vast and profitable SLAVE-MARKET therein; and, ultimately, to annex it to the United States.[81]

The Massachusetts Legislature believed that the Mexican War was being fought for "the triple object of extending slavery, of strengthening the slave power, and of obtaining control of the free states" and declared it unconstitutional.[82]

The Belle of Saratoga was part of a larger arts initiative that resulted in the publication of a myriad of anecdotes, tributes, and histories of the war. Beginning in the late 1840s, there were contemporary works like the "Jim Crow Polka," arranged by E. P. Christy and performed by the highly popular Christy Minstrels as early as 1847, and volumes like the one-hundred-plus-page collection entitled "National Songs, Ballads, and Other Patriotic Poetry, Chiefly Relating to the War of 1846," compiled by William M'Carty. In addition to the documents disseminated by such groups as the Veterans of the Mexican War, there were memoirs, editions of collected letters, novels, plays, and patriotic and minstrel songs that recalled diverse experiences associated with the war effort. There also were formal commissioned pieces, many of them poems like "Episodes of the Mexican War" by Lieutenant Colonel George W. Patten, which was performed in 1878 at the Lexington Avenue Opera House in New York City on the thirty-first anniversary of the taking of Mexico City.[83] Plays like *The Belle of Saratoga*, written and performed long after the war's end, reveal that the conflict was still very much a part of American cultural imagination throughout and after Reconstruction. Its pertinence to the post-bellum nation—as an affirmation of American military might or as a reminder of African American disenfranchisement, for instance—was emphasized by and through the arts.

The African American production of *The Belle of Saratoga* sheds light on the politicization of African American aesthetics and the nature of African American political propaganda during the post–Civil War era. At first glance, Elijah Smith, an accomplished artist and champion of African American honor, seems to have lent his support to a production that honored an aggressive white campaign that resulted in the expansion of Southern slavery. Why would a man with a well-known family history such as his commit not only himself but also his young niece to such a venture? In this Boston venue, performers risked social and political censure if they offered such an uncomplicated and pro-Southern reminiscence about the war. In fact, the staging of *The Belle of Saratoga* in Boston by an African American troupe represented an emphatic appropriation of white agency. Elijah Smith and the African American arts community in which he moved, in the years immediately prior, had successfully adapted classical European musical works. At first glance, then, this venture seemed to be no different. However, by turning to drama, Smith and his amateur acting company confronted one of the most pervasive and racially essentialist entertainments of the day: blackface minstrelsy. This production, staged outside the environs of black Beacon Hill and in a secular performance space frequented more often by whites than blacks, represented a new artistic landscape altogether.

The Belle of Saratoga was an ideal vehicle through which to challenge the flawed representations of African American life and character that now were de rigueur throughout the city and much of the nation. *The Belle of Saratoga*, as Pauline Allen and her colleagues deployed it, easily would accommodate both nuanced and overt messages about segregation, social disenfranchisement, and African American class aspirations. This African American adaptation of *The Belle of Saratoga* succeeded precisely because it staged a series of alternative realities. First, African American actors appeared in a white-authored piece written about a specific white military and social experience.

Exclusionary military prohibitions on the basis of race meant that African American men never could have occupied the roles dramatized by George Ardent, the aspiring soldier, and Captain Western, the obstreperous paternal veteran. Second, although social circumstances were improving for African Americans in the North, there were few occasions for African American girls in the North to enjoy Pauline Western's privilege or social capital. Thus, the play's material circumstances took on an aspect of domestic fantasy when performed in an African American context. The play evolved further into a piercing social critique as it challenged blackface minstrelsy, one of the most pervasive cultural realities of the day, and its insistent messages about "real" African American life, character, and priorities.

When they appeared in *The Belle of Saratoga*, Pauline Allen and her African American cast members essentially masked themselves in whiteness and donned the identity of privileged white Americans. The script, its historical context, and its overall message were transformed into an extended African American caricature of "real" white American behaviors, priorities, and private social goals. Once the play was adapted by an African American troupe, its script, which depended on flowery metaphors and melodramatic statements for its humor, became a kind of "unnatural" Anglo-dialect. This linguistic transformation went to the heart of an African American rebuttal of the white blackface tradition. Dialect, which historian Nathan Huggins has described as "coarse, clumsy, ignorant . . . [and] at the opposite pole from the soft tones and grace of what was considered cultivated speech," was one of the chief elements of blackface entertainment.[84] It was language that asserted racial difference—linguistic and cultural—and often financed problematic racial objectification. By transforming the script into comical hyper-Anglicized speech, Pauline Allen and her African American company objectified white life and character. Their appropriation of the linguistic heart of blackface minstrelsy reversed the oppressive symbolic messages and now implied that whites, not blacks, had failed to assimilate successfully into American culture. This culture, of course, now became one established on African American terms. Since African American perspectives were the defining standards against which "privileged" white Americans were to be judged, these white characters were portrayed as being essentially alienated from a black "majority" perspective. *The Belle of Saratoga* had, in its own words, quite literally, become a startling whiteface production.

In this African American production of *The Belle of Saratoga*, the play's five characters—all of whom were coded but not specified as white in Cooper's prefatory descriptions—devolved into caricatures of recognizable white American types. Yet the Boston cast was not presenting a flagrant re-racialization of the minstrel script or mimicking standard minstrel stereotypes such as the coon or jezebel. Pauline Allen and the amateur dramatics company offered instead a most decorous whiteface satire, one devoid of grotesque characterization and that deftly highlighted the sexual impropriety, gender anxieties, and class tensions so frequently portrayed on the minstrel stage. The sexual rivalry between the play's two leading female characters prevented them from establishing any potentially helpful sisterhood. Unlike the intraracial solidarity that defined the relationships in Pauline Allen's female world, the white female characters of the play repeatedly compromised themselves in their highly patriarchal social arena. The three male characters, all of whom remain unattached for most of the play, were more excessive in their buffoonery than the female characters. The men's seeming inability to succeed in love, their laughable interactions with women, and their fear of revealing their true feelings or identities marked them as objects of ridicule. In this way, they, more than the women, embodied the evasive, morally challenged, and often male figures depicted on the blackface stage.

The upper class milieu and pretensions of *The Belle of Saratoga* allowed Allen and her African American troupe to signify upon—or reference and revise—the pervasive and extremely popular blackface minstrel tradition without compromising their respectability or artistic ambitions. The representation of white American life that emerged in this African American production was a simultaneously objective "real" portrait and a racially biased fiction. With its unapologetic glorification of the war's ability to unite, rather than destroy, an American family, this African American production of which Pauline Allen was a part evolved into a whiteface romance and calculated political satire of privilege and appropriation. On the one hand, this tremendous theatrical coup provided evidence of the aesthetic schizophrenia with which African American actors in nineteenth-century America had to contend. It revealed the cultural schizophrenia resulting from what scholars have discussed as "the necessity of living in two worlds and utilizing the mask as a survival mechanism."[85] Yet this version of *The Belle of Saratoga* was not hampered by the "unreconciled strivings" and "warring ideals" that W. E. B. Du Bois would one day describe as the condition of the American Negro. Instead, it demonstrated African American mastery borne of substantial political acumen and collective self-confidence.

Boston played a central role in the dissemination of blackface minstrelsy and its problematic racial ideologies and caricatures. During the late 1870s, blackface minstrelsy was in its heyday, and white Bostonians enthusiastically welcomed leading troupes of the day. Consistently large audiences for these shows contributed to the form's popularity and to its entrenchment in American popular culture.[86] M. B. Leavitt, an actor and theatrical manager in the city for more than fifty years, maintained that Boston was in fact "the place of origin of more burnt cork shows than the rest of the country combined."[87] The city has been characterized since as a "minstrel rendezvous," one in which "[n]umerous juvenile minstrel companies . . . were launched in Boston as a new experiment in burnt cork attractions."[88] Boston audiences were exposed frequently to blackface minstrelsy, and the local notes about the performances suggest that the blackface troupes received unqualified enthusiastic reception in the city. Given this known reality of intense and visible racial performance, then, the city was an extremely appropriate place in which to signify on blackface minstrelsy and to offer a carefully staged rebuttal to the form's denigrating depictions of African Americans.

Pauline Allen developed as a performer in the vexed shadow cast by blackface minstrelsy. Indeed, her concerts and dramatic appearances frequently coincided with highly touted, widely advertised minstrel tours. Her 1875 debut with the Progressive Musical Union, for instance, coincided with the Fisk Jubilee Singers concert and also with a lengthy Boston run by the Georgia Minstrels, the first all–African American minstrel group that Charles Hicks, a legendary African American former minstrel, organized in 1865. The Georgia Minstrels, which enjoyed a particularly strong following in Boston throughout the years in which Allen was honing her dramatic skills, was one of numerous minstrel groups that appeared in major Boston venues such as the Tremont Temple—the same site that was filled to overflowing on other occasions for concerts by the Fisk Jubilee Singers. Shortly after Pauline debuted with the Progressive Musical Union, the *Boston Herald* announced that the Minstrels, who were in their third week of shows, were meeting "with much success at Beethoven Hall, Boston," and that "[t]he rush to see them is unparalleled in the history of minstrelsy, and such audiences have never been seen at a minstrel performance, and they comprise the very best people of Boston."[89] The Northern press lauded this group in particular for its racial authenticity. "These are real 'nigs,'" pronounced *The Clipper*, the New York City–based entertainment weekly, before noting that the group is "not only reported as being first rate, but . . . doing a good business."[90]

The African American production of *The Belle of Saratoga* was part of the murky racialized performance milieu that emerged from blackface minstrelsy, and it is no surprise that it, like so many productions of the time, adopted a racial mask. In this case, though, the *Belle of Saratoga* troupe appeared to envelop itself in a pronationalist romantic fantasy, but one that functioned as a racialized critique of white social and nationalistic anxieties and did not indulge in problematic racist caricature. The African American performance of *The Belle of Saratoga* differentiated itself from the minstrel tradition that historians have cited for its aggressive indictments of class and ethnicity, uncensored political criticisms, and risqué sexual elements.[91] The Parker Memorial Hall staging of *The Belle of Saratoga*, by virtue of its actors, was a white-face production, but one that refused to incorporate highly misleading, or, to borrow from scholar Mel Watkins, "fraudulent image[s]" of a race's behavior.[92] In fact, this play, with its white-authored validation of the Mexican War and metaphoric social and property contracts, enabled Pauline Allen and the African American troupe to offer an extended and ironic assessment of whiteness. They appropriated it as a vehicle through which to revisit white antebellum political agendas, the legacies of social and military segregation, and the implications that the agendas of the white American South had on African American development and uplift. Originally, the white playwright George Cooper may have believed that he had created an uncomplicated salute to Manifest Destiny. Adapted by an African American troupe, however, *The Belle of Saratoga* became an innovative explication of oppressive white democratic ideals just as the Democratic Party was privileging white Southern interests and sacrificing the domestic stability of African Americans in the name of a supposed nonracially differentiated "national" unity.

Throughout, *The Belle of Saratoga* suggests that national unity can be threatened by a crisis of masculinity, and that assertive action, best exemplified by successful military service, most reliably staves off such domestic upheaval. Thus, a play with African American actors voluntarily committing to and supporting a military crusade was not so far-fetched just a few years after the heroic service of African American Civil War regiments, and especially by the three pioneering Massachusetts units, the Fifty-fourth and Fifty-fifth Regiments and the Fifth Cavalry. In Boston, the Civil War stood in sharp contrast to the goals of the Mexican War, and this theatrical adaptation reinforced the honorable aspects of African American participation in the War between the States, and by extension, the honorable goals of that conflict. The record of heroism demonstrated by Massachusetts' own Fifty-fourth Regiment, the first black fighting unit raised in the North, stood in sharp relief against the legally sanctioned exclusion of men of color from the Mexican War regiments. In addition, the premise and results of that 1840s conflict that made it anathema to African Americans intensified their understandable glorification of the Civil War as a means to demonstrate African American manhood and advance the race's claim for full citizenship rights. The New

England audience that attended Smith's adaptation of *The Belle of Saratoga*, familiar with the documented successes and heart-wrenching sacrifices of its own African American Civil War regiments, would have appreciated the unmistakable irony of the African Americanized *Belle of Saratoga*. That shared and recent history would have enhanced, if not hastened, their willingness not only to revisit the controversial Mexican War, but also to stand in solidarity with the city's black community and its Civil War veterans and to decry the institutional prejudice that permeated so many aspects of their lives.

The first scene between Pauline Western and George Ardent confirms just how evocative *The Belle of Saratoga* was in relation to pride in African American military service and patriotic feeling. At first glance, the couple appears to be discussing their imminent separation and their longing for each other:

GEORGE: O, Pauline, I am so glad to see you once more! I have thrown away my musty books for a little while, my sweet, and I am going to Mexico with our army.

PAULINE: Then you have only come, after our long separation, to bid me good-bye? How cruel of you, George! How very cruel!

GEORGE: Darling, I have obtained a position as Lieutenant in a regiment that hails from my native State, and I shall win my way to distinction; that is, if a brave heart can aid me. Only a little while I shall be away, and then I shall come to claim the hand of my adored one. Her heart is mine already. We exchanged those long, long ago, I mean our hearts; did we not Pauline?

Pauline, realizing the futility of her pleas to George, then proposes another solution, one that would take her to the front and enable the young lovers to avoid a lengthy and worrisome separation. In response to her question, "Will nothing that I can say keep you here?" George replies, "I must go, darling. My word is pledged. Why I shall only be away a year. Think of that! May be not so long. When I return full of honors, and with a Colonel's commission, perhaps your father will consent to our marriage." Pauline's response reveals her desire for both romantic companionship and heroic actions. "I would it were possible for me to go with you. To tend to all your wants. To shield you from all dangers," she says, before declaring nobly, "That woman is no woman who is unwilling to share every hardship with the man she loves!" Her musings elicit indulgent praise from George, who refers to her now as "a little hero!"[93] Although these lines appear to be conventional and relatively serious, they in fact may have provoked sardonic laughter from a predominantly African American or mixed Northern audience. In the first instance,

George imagines that in this war he can "win his way to distinction" and achieve honors that a university degree apparently cannot confer upon him. Northern opinions about the men who volunteered, as George Ardent does, however, were emphatically different.

George Cooper's script suggests that his student volunteer is a fearless and sincere man. At the war's onset, however, Boston reviled "the patriots of 1847, the 'volunteer' defenders of the honor of the country," upon whom Cooper based the character of George Ardent. They were regarded as "rash, inconsiderate, penniless young men."[94] Although the latter holds true for Cooper's aspiring soldier, *The Liberator* went so far as to suggest that no man associated with the war effort could be honorable. In response to a report on the Massachusetts volunteers, the outspoken *Liberator* editor Garrison announced that

> none but unprincipled adventurers, cormorant office-seekers, the watchdogs of southern slavery, recreant and degenerate sons of Puritan and Revolutionary sires, the base betrayers of the people, and traitors to the cause of human liberty, who have the hardihood and audacity to declare it to be the duty of the citizens of this Commonwealth to engage in a war for the invigoration of the foreign and domestic slave trade, and the re-establishment of slavery on a free and independent soil.[95]

To support its claims, the newspaper cited a recent statement by H. K. Oliver, the adjutant general: "It must be borne in mind that men offering for this service are *generally* of that class in community, *least successful in providing for themselves*." These men, according to *The Liberator*, had "no shirts to their backs, not a solitary 'red' cent in their pockets, no means of comfortable subsistence—alias LOAFERS and VAGABONDS!"[96] *The Belle of Saratoga* did not shrink from such devastating characterizations. Rather than compromise the heroic potential of its young American man, Cooper develops a new fall guy.

The evasive and ambivalent man of the Mexican War era is not an ordinary American but a British aristocrat. Sir Charles is especially prone to muddled soliloquies in which he tries to figure out how best to extricate himself from problematic social and nationalist scenarios. His self-indulgent ruminations suggest that an ambivalent, possibly pacifist, masculinity can endanger society. As a result, the character of Sir Charles justifies the argument that military heroism and manly conquests—of land and women—are vital for a stable society. Following Pauline Western's rejection of him and her frank admission that she never intended to follow her father's instructions to marry the count, Sir Charles admits his disdain for mortal combat:

I don't exactly fancy old Western for a father-in-law, after all. He spoke of me going to Mexico to fight. I haven't the least idea of doing anything so absurd. What! I go to Mexico to be eaten by bears and poisoned by snakes! not to speak of being peppered by bullets! I respectfully decline to leave these twanquil scenes awound me! Besides, I don't think I've got exactly the figure for the soldier. I was born for more peaceful conquests than those of the battlefield. I should think so.[97]

Grandiswell's confessions help to delineate the terms on which George Ardent will be deemed an exemplary American. However, Cooper sees it as important to preserve Sir Charles's capacity for conquest. Although this character refers to these devastating social accomplishments in military terms that maintain the aura of hyper-military masculinity, he systematically undermines the manliness and honorable dimensions of such ventures.

Pauline Allen ultimately was showcased in a play in which the war on female virtue and family stability emerged as a competing allegory of American expansionist ideology. As Sir Charles, representative of the resisting colonizing empire, elaborates on his strategies for "more peaceful conquests," he solidifies the colonial imperative that was threatening American interests at the same time that the offensive was being waged against Mexico. Again, it is the African American appropriation of this piece that transposes these lines into an extended assessment of white supremacy and dilettante-like approach to already-occupied foreign lands. In a song entitled "To Please the Girls," Sir Charles becomes the sexually irresponsible figure often essential to blackface minstrelsy scripts:

> I make love here,
> I make love there,
> And then I leave the pretty dears!
> I make their papas kick an[d] tear
> Just like that "horse" with monstrous ears!
> Ha! ha! ha! ha!
> To please the girls is my delight,
> My figure, too, is all the rage!
> I follow them by day and night,
> Just like some little dandy page![98]

The social conquests of which Sir Charles sings so proudly promote white patriarchal distress and quite literally diminish female worth. As the character who essentially represents European colonial interests and the British dominion over the northwestern territory of Oregon in the 1840s, Sir Charles, and by extension, England, become wholly undesirable partners in land appropriation. Thus, in the context of American social harmony, it is no tragedy when Pauline Western, the embodiment of these disputed territories, forcefully rejects an alliance with this man.

Immediately following Sir Charles's shocking revelations about his social campaigns, Pauline Western appears to confirm the chronicle of the successes of George Ardent, the man whose surname now attests to his commitment to the American expansionist cause. She complains about the "impertinent solicitations of such fops as Sir Charles, and a few others of his ilk," and pines openly for the man who has "won an honorable distinction in *our* army."[99] Pauline's assertions here, coupled with her use of the possessive "our," validate the terms on which white American manhood is attained. Her discernible pride and celebration foregrounds the nationalist contexts that permeate this play. Indeed, Pauline's final words offer the final domestic fantasy: "Having succumbed at last to my pleasant destiny," she declares on the eve of her marriage to George, "I lay down my sceptre, and descending my throne, I shall no longer queen it as the belle of Saratoga."[100] Her surrender of Saratoga, which is presented as a monarchical abdication, is a pointed reminder of Britain's surrender there during the Revolutionary War. Ultimately Pauline Western's union with her ardent suitor—all puns intended—is couched in self-congratulatory patriotic rhetoric. This language glorifies the colonial and antebellum campaigns that consolidated American independence and increased dramatically white American holdings of both land and slaves.

The Belle of Saratoga becomes a stirring exposé of racist Democratic policies and white nationalist mythologies when considered in the context of antebellum African American history and Reconstruction. The play also illuminates the insidious aspects of a national romance in which military might—or overwhelming masculine force—secures domestic "happiness." Given that *The Belle of Saratoga* was staged during a period of intense political instability and African American disenfranchisement, Pauline Allen easily could have been criticized for appearing in a work deemed a form of literary political revolt, a kind of black trespass on hallowed white historical ground. Instead, Elijah Smith's steady and politically astute vision enabled Pauline Allen to participate in a calculated and productive reconsideration of exclusionary American history. The participants in this collective black arts enterprise skillfully insinuated themselves and their African American perspectives into a dominant, and increasingly intolerant, pro-white American cultural mythology. Pauline Allen played a central role in *The Belle of Saratoga* and its racialized critique of American domesticity and exclusionary social politics. This formative experience enabled her to participate in a systematic African American effort, one that generated an alternative racial discourse and displayed an empowered black presence on the American stage. She and this Boston cast contested contemporary notions of blackness, generated new versions of exaggerated racial performance, and reinforced African American theater as a viable defense against racism.

The large full-page sketch of Edwin Wilkes Booth that is carefully glued into the adolescent scrapbook that Pauline Allen kept testifies forcefully to her passion for the theater. This deep feeling not only intensified in the days following her appearance in *The Belle of Saratoga*, but began to take on a most promising professional aspect. She dedicated the rest of the spring of 1877 to fulfilling the "greatest desire" of her childhood. On 16 August 1877, just five months after her theatrical debut at Parker Memorial, she filed a copyright for *Aristocracy—A Musical Drama in 3 Acts*. Echoes of *The Belle of Saratoga* resound in the title of this still unrecovered play that she later retitled *Colored Aristocracy*.[101] The black aesthetic that informed Hopkins's scripts, like it had in *The Belle of Saratoga*, would reaffirm black autonomy even as it illuminated the history of black disenfranchisement. Although extant copies of her first dramatic works have yet to be found, the early dramatic works that are available confirm her sincere efforts to honor collective black resistance and reveal an inherited talent for creating powerful political critique.

5

Dramatic Freedom

The Slaves' Escape; or,
The Underground Railroad

On the stage the Negro has naturally
had a most difficult chance to be recognized.
W. E. B. DU BOIS
"Negro Art and Literature,"
1924

In the months following her 1877 dramatic debut in *The Belle of Saratoga*, Pauline Hopkins applied herself with zeal to realizing her professional dream of becoming a playwright. Her focus and determination were made manifest in the formal applications that she made to the federal copyright office in Washington, D.C. Her effort to claim ownership of her first plays, *Aristocracy* and *Winona*, signals just how quickly this pioneering playwright made her first forays into the world of public theater. Hopkins's applications, the first of which she lodged when only eighteen years old, indicated that playwriting was neither a private childish indulgence nor a casual pursuit. She clearly expected her work to become part of a highly visible public sphere, one that would anticipate and challenge seminal early-twentieth-century debates about the cultural integrity and political responsibilities of African American theater. The copyright information for *Aristocracy*, which lists "P. E. Hopkins" as author, is the first official extant source to identify her officially and for the first time as Pauline Hopkins. By adopting the surname of her stepfather, Pauline not only signaled her acceptance of William, the only man with whom she had lived since she was five years old, but also enacted a symbolic break with the emotionally fraught past that she shared with her mother.[1] This deliberate act of renaming, implemented at the threshold of a professional career, transformed Pauline and her history. No longer was she the child of a youthful union that came to be plagued by infidelity or the daughter of a divorced single mother. As Pauline Hopkins, she became the only child of devoted parents whose marriage accommodated a lively professional working relationship, and a daughter whose parents would wholly support and vigorously protect her professional dreams.

Barely a decade after the Civil War had ended, the fledgling playwright was anticipating and enacting incisive philosophies that W. E. B. Du Bois, one of the nation's mightiest intellectual powers, would articulate nearly fifty years later. In 1926, Du Bois published in the *Crisis* his manifesto on the true principles of African American theater. His essay included no references to Hopkins; indeed her name would appear only in the journal of the National Association for the Advancement of Colored People for the first and last time in a brief obituary notice. In his oft-cited 1926 summer essay on African American drama and aesthetic imperatives, Du Bois intoned that "a real Negro theatre" would be "About us, By us, For us, and Near us." Yet, where Du Bois would call for a twentieth-century segregated racialized theater experience, the young playwright Pauline Hopkins responded fearlessly to the challenges and realities of nineteenth-century, postbellum multiracial audiences. In the course of the lengthy and storied two-year national tour of *The Slaves' Escape; or, The Underground Railroad*, the play for which she would become best known, however, she demonstrated also the fearsome protection of Negro art that was needed precisely because of its performance in America and its consumption by predominantly white audiences. Her pioneering journey, which Du Bois would overlook entirely in his grand overviews of African American performance histories, would begin in the company of her parents and of performers whose talents and artistic flair made them major nineteenth-century stage phenomena.

Peculiar Sam; or, The Underground Railroad, a Musical Drama in Four Acts, the third and what appears, to date, to be Hopkins's last play, catapulted her to the forefront of nineteenth-century African American theater culture. Hopkins used the play to examine African American life in three competing nineteenth-century worlds: the antebellum plantation South, the Underground Railroad network, and Canada some six years after the end of the American Civil War. The play implements an impressive array of social critiques and systematically explicates the myths and realities of enslavement, the nature of black domesticity, and the enduring value of the black female body in and beyond the slaveholding South. The play offers a steady critique of ownership, an issue that Hopkins links persistently to the objectivity of the black female body. The work's focus on emancipation is both real and symbolic; Hopkins ultimately invites audiences to consider if it is possible to free oneself from home, no matter how contested a site it is, or from cultural traditions that place value on a woman's honor and desirability.

The title of Hopkins's 1879 work changed several times over the course of its performance life. The original copyrighted title was *The Slaves' Escape; or, The Underground Railroad*. During 1879, it was billed consistently as *The Underground Railroad*; later performances advertised the play as *Peculiar Sam*, a title that referred to the leading role played by Sam Lucas, or as *Escape from Slavery*. In addition, it was promoted as a musical comedy or as a musical and moral drama. In spite of these changes, however, the play always retained the phrase "Underground Railroad." By presenting this subtitle, Hopkins invoked collective rather than individual resistance to enslavement, and in the small but visible canon of American slavery plays, this was the first work to use that term. The prominence that Hopkins gave to the Underground Railroad, a mythic construct and a substantial network that successfully transported as many as 300,000 slaves to freedom before the Civil War began, was significant. Her invocation of the antislavery network countered the hysteria prompted by images of the solitary and determined slave—as seen in Dion Boucicault's extremely popular *The Octoroon* and J. T. Trowbridge's *Neighbor Jackwood*. The Underground Railroad replaced the autonomous and unpredictable slave with a strategic collective resistance. This new emphasis on the subversive slave support network, a mobilized and yet amorphous institution, resulted in a riveting re-presentation of Southern slaves. The play's empowering emphases on inclusivity, family cohesion, and community insisted that Hopkins's multiracial and ethnic audiences reconsider the story of slavery. The title, *The Slaves' Escape*, with its use of the possessive, not only suggested the slaves' ownership of their emancipation but also issued a triumphant statement of their achievement and defiance: the slaves escape!

The Slaves' Escape focuses on the metamorphoses that an enslaved family undergoes once it runs away from the plantation in southeastern Mississippi. The family's decision to flee slavery comes when a young field slave named Sam learns that his master has arranged the marriage of his sweetheart, Jinny, who labors in the plantation great house, to Jim, a brutish Negro overseer on the plantation. The bulk of the play focuses on the adventures, trials, and threatening encounters that the sweethearts and Sam's family face en route to Canada. Hopkins sets the final scene in 1870s Canada, but despite the fact that the American Civil War and slavery have officially ended, African Americans are still denied full freedom. The lingering antebellum atmosphere curtails the emotional rather than physical freedom of the play's romantic leads, Jinny and Sam. When Sam appears, he is a newly elected Ohio senator.

That Sam is still unable to wed the woman he loves distracts attention from his meteoric rise in American politics and seeming prosperity. Jinny insists she is still legally married to the overseer, Jim, and that he is the only person who can annul her marriage to him. The play closes soon after Jim, now a successful Massachusetts attorney, appears and does just that.

Almost as soon as Hopkins copyrighted *Peculiar Sam*, the play was prepared for a regional and national tour that featured three of the most accomplished stars of the minstrel and concert stage. Starring as Peculiar Sam was Sam Lucas, the veteran minstrel performer and the man who would become the first African American to play the role of Uncle Tom in film.[2] Anna Madah Hyers, and her sister, Emma Louise Hyers, were at the helm of the group billed as "Colored Dramatic, Vocal and Specialty Artists of Rare Excellence."[3] The *Peculiar Sam* company that joined Lucas and the Hyers Sisters consisted of eight other performers. In addition to the pianist Miss Lillie Williams, there were three female singers: Inez Fernandez, a "prima donna" soprano with a "clear and musical voice,"[4] Alice Mink, a contralto who was "possessed of a voice of almost phenomenal power and purity,"[5] and Jennie Smith. The cast also included J. H. Crawford, a tenor, Fred Fernandez, a second tenor, Charles C. Cary, a baritone, and Edward Johnson, a basso described as one "who sings exceedingly well."[6] By the time the cast reached Minneapolis, the play's stage manager, Charles Z. Sprague, also had "secured" José Brindis de Salas, "the wonderful native violinist . . . whose mastery of the violin was the theme of praise by the musical critics of Havana." Sprague regarded the eighty-year-old musician, whose full name was Claudio José Domingo Brindis de Salas and whose mother was African, as "the greatest colored violinist in the world." He believed "that [de Salas's] great powers would prove an attraction to the music loving public of America, who are ever ready to recognize talent regardless of birth or color." He contracted with the elderly but still vigorous de Salas, known to nineteenth-century audiences in Cuba and Europe as "El rey de las octavas," to perform during the *Peculiar Sam* performances and then featured him in specially arranged moments immediately following the play that were billed as "miscellaneous concert programme[s]."[7]

A mere seven days after Hopkins filed her copyright application, *Peculiar Sam* was being performed in Milwaukee and earning "liberal expressions of approval" from audiences. Despite longtime scholarly assertions that the play was performed just once in Boston, as a favor to Hopkins, the record clearly shows that this was not the case.[8] *Peculiar Sam* was performed in Boston numerous times throughout 1879 and 1880, and it enjoyed a successful national tour and played repeatedly in major cities of the Northeast and Midwest such as Boston, Buffalo, Chicago, Minneapolis, Milwaukee, and St. Paul. In addi-

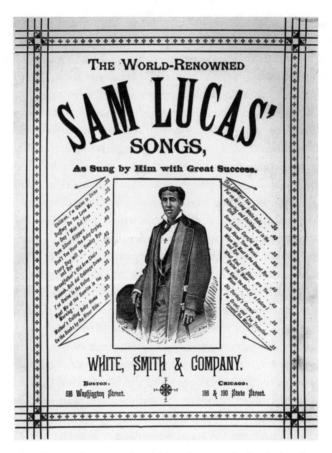

Sam Lucas, the most celebrated performer of color during the
nineteenth century and the actor who starred in Hopkins's
1879 play, *Peculiar Sam. Courtesy of Brown University Library.*

tion, the company "combed the midwest exhaustively, moving through New
York, Illinois, Minnesota, Wisconsin, Michigan, Iowa, Kansas, and Missouri,
playing one- and two-night stands in any place that offered accommodations,
and returning by request for repeat performances to St. Paul, Chicago, and
some of the larger towns."[9]

The 1879 national tour of *Peculiar Sam* was extensive and transformative,
and the company seized all opportunities to build on the excitement about
its production. Within weeks, the play was renamed *Underground Railroad*,
and advertisements and theater reviews were hailing the arrival of the new
production, for which Lucas always was billed as the "chief attraction."[10]
The group's westward route and southern trek through Iowa, Kansas, and

Missouri, facilitated by the rapidly expanding railroad system, made them part of an increasingly mobilized world of American stock theater companies. Indeed, the grueling performance itinerary of the *Underground Railroad* troupe on the one hand was made possible by the expansion of the American railway system. Yet this new development and growth of touring companies now contributed to the marked drop in permanent stock companies affiliated with large city theaters, from fifty to seven between 1870 and 1880.[11]

The speed with which *Underground Railroad* was showcased suggests that Hopkins was commissioned to write the piece and that arrangements were being made for its national tour even as she was completing the work. Advertisements for the play confirm that she was in fact selected to create this musical drama. According to early prepublicity notices published in April issues of the *Minneapolis Tribune*, Sam Lucas was to appear in a "Brilliant Musical and Dramatic Episode" that was "[w]ritten expressly for him by Miss Pauline E. Hopkins."[12] She may have been writing "expressly" for Sam Lucas, but Pauline Hopkins also developed a script that was heavily influenced by the recent theatrical successes of the Hyers Sisters. By 1879, the sisters had established themselves as the Hyers Sisters Combination, a "company of colored performers known the country over," and were one of the "numerous companies under the control and management of the Redpath Lyceum Bureau."[13]

The prominence of the leading performers in the *Underground Railroad* tour and the Hyers Sisters' affiliation with the Redpath Lyceum Bureau, the organization founded in 1868 by James Redpath and whose substantial client list included best-selling writer Mark Twain, resulted in an efficient tour and substantial publicity before and during the shows.[14] The company was booked into reputable and sizeable venues, including the Opera House in Milwaukee and the Academy of Music in Minneapolis. The newly renovated Academy of Music, which became the city's primary theater venue, had a third-floor auditorium that could seat 1,300 people on plush upholstered seats "with elevating bottoms to allow free passages."[15] Ticket prices were comparable to those set for the operas and large shows of the day and ranged from twenty-five cents to seventy-five cents. Advertisements noted that there was "no extra charge for reserved seats."[16] On 31 March 1879, *Underground Railroad* debuted at the Grand Opera House in Milwaukee, a town dominated by "adventurous, intelligent, independent, dignified, socially progressive" German immigrants who were credited with establishing "the tone of the city's early civic life."[17] When Hopkins's *Underground Railroad* production arrived in Milwaukee, the town was enjoying a post–Civil War renaissance in its theater culture and actively supported its Grand Opera House, Academy of Music, Milwaukee Theater, and Metropolitan Theater on South Water Street, which was managed by Marsh Adams, "the well known minstrel,"[18] and was the site that regularly had the lowest admission price of all the city's performance venues.

In Milwaukee in the spring of 1879, *Underground Railroad* was part of the Grand Opera's theater calendar, which included the "inimitable" *Lotta* and the "farcical conceit" *La Cigale*. The Grand Opera's patrons were not new to images of African Americans on stage. Minstrel companies had been arriving with much fanfare since the beginning of the year. In January, it was "Benedict & Cotton's Grand Troubadour Minstrel Scene," complete with the "Child Wonder, Little Idalene Cotton" starring in a Saturday matinee and weekday show. That was followed in late February by an even more involved production "Comprising fifty-five First Class Artists" in a "Grand Parlor Minstrel Scene with Sixty People."[19] In addition, *Underground Railroad* was appearing in the Opera House just over two months after *Uncle Tom's Cabin*, a "well-worn drama" for which "interest . . . was as fresh as ever" and that prompted "tears, laughter and applause" from its audiences. In Minneapolis, the piece was staged "every night during the week" before a "house . . . well filled in the upper circles."[20]

Milwaukee reviewers, struck by the innovative and sustained drama of Hopkins's *Underground Railroad*, deemed it an "interesting entertainment" and a "musical novelty." The final review of the play, published on 21 April 1879 in the city's leading newspaper, asserted that "[t]he musical part of the performance is excellent" and encouraged ticket holders to attend the "Grand Parlor Concert" that followed each performance. The entire company, whose singers were praised for having "[s]ome of the finest voices that have been known among colored people," appeared to sing ballads that were "new and taking," or appealing.[21] One Milwaukee journalist praised the supplementary performance, which offered different programs and "new sketches" each night, as "altogether good."[22] The postperformance show allowed the group to be "seen to good advantage" and to interact more directly with their audiences. The Cuban violinist de Salas enthralled audiences during these sessions, which, because of their success, became a permanent feature of the road show. "He is indeed a wonder," intoned the *Sentinel*'s awed drama critic, who recounted vividly the talented musician's renditions of De Bériot's Fifth and Sixth Airs before the "enthusiastic audience" that so enjoyed the play. De Salas played with "rare precision and feeling," and "at the close of his performance there was one moment of almost painful silence; then came such an encore as perhaps no other company ever had in the opera house. To say they were pleased, is to say the least—they were delighted."[23]

Following its enthusiastic reception in Milwaukee, the troupe, which now had been on the road for seven weeks, traveled to Minneapolis for a one-day show. The company arrived in Minneapolis on the afternoon of 22 April and prepared for its evening performance at the Academy of Music located on Washington and Hennepin Avenues. By the time the cast arrived in this heavily Scandinavian city, *Underground Railroad* had metamorphosed from the "novel and pleasing entertainment" it had been in Milwaukee into a "musical and dramatic extravaganza." The show, which now included a full-fledged concert by Brindes de Salas, generated much excitement in the press. "The conductors of the new line will run a train into Minneapolis to-morrow, and give a single entertainment at the Academy of Music," declared the writer of the *Minneapolis Tribune* "Amusements" column. He touted the excellent voices, Sam Lucas's ability to "caus[e] the audience to explode with laughter," and the "excellent" performance that the cast had delivered during their stint in Milwaukee as reasons for turning out to see the play.

In the days leading up to the *Underground Railroad* show, the *Minneapolis Tribune* published articles that praised the show and cited favorable reviews published in other major newspapers, including the *Buffalo Courier*. Yet there were voices of dissent. Some theater critics apparently had low expectations for the drama scheduled for shows in their cities. In Minneapolis, days before *Underground Railroad* was to arrive, the *Tribune* described it as a "shred of plot on which is hung more or less of music and a portrayal of the slave life similar to that in *Out of Bondage*."[24] The *Tribune*'s regularly featured "Melange" column went on to note that *Underground Railroad* had been "written to afford Sam Lucas, formerly the chief attraction with the Hyers Sisters combination, an opportunity to display his comicalities. The piece is said to resemble very much the Hyers Sisters' *Out of Bondage*."[25] Although this writer was of the opinion that Hopkins's script was a thinly veiled version of the play, which the Hyers Sisters had used to their advantage, he was impressed by the appearance of Brindes de Salas, who "plays the most difficult and complicated operatic music at sight with accuracy."[26] De Salas's performance of De Bériot's Seventh Air in Minneapolis was deemed a "thoroughly artistic performance, such as has not been heard in this city for some time."[27] The winning combination of a dynamic show and highbrow musical event translated into financial gains and increased publicity for the cast. The one-day show in Minneapolis turned into a return engagement, and this was not the only city in which the cast piqued the interest of theatergoers and was booked for additional performances. Diverse audiences were turning out in sizeable numbers to witness the sensational African American dramatic success of the year.

The first Minneapolis reviews of *Underground Railroad* were less enthusiastic than those published in Buffalo and Milwaukee, and critics noted that the show was still evolving. The *Minneapolis Tribune* "Amusements" column featured a lengthy assessment of the production and noted that "[t]he Sprague Underground Company performed to a fair audience at the Academy of Music last evening, and gave a great deal of enjoyment to a large part of their audience." Apparently, however, this critic was not one of those who were pleased. He concluded that the "entertainment was a success," but it was "flimsy in construction, as is the drama," and that "[t]he action was not of great merit." Only two members of the cast merited praise: Sam Lucas and Mr. J. H. Crawford. The article then bordered on racial essentialism as its author noted that "the company sang the old plantation songs as only the colored people can."[28]

Pauline Hopkins, who does not appear to have traveled with the Lucas-Hyers company, observed from afar the ways in which trends in cultural consumption and white public desire shaped the evolution of public works. The shift in title and the new focus on the legendary and mythic multiracial American antislavery network, as well as the racial subtexts of this Minneapolis reception and in other reviews of the *Underground Railroad* cast, confirm that the company occupied a delicate and sometimes tenuous place in the theatrical marketplace. From the invocation of a resistant political network such as the Underground Railroad to the reappropriation of Lucas from minstrelsy to a sophisticated musical, these African American performers were upsetting the traditional over-determined assumptions about why and how they would occupy public and performative space. *Underground Railroad*, both in cast and content, created a dynamic liminal realm, one that existed between the familiar, self-deprecating black minstrelsy farces and the high sacred cultural performances best exemplified by the Fisk Jubilee Singers.

The cast, in an effort to showcase its talents and to capitalize on its bookings, created supplementary shows that catered to audience desire for "authentic" racial performances and that built on Hopkins's focus on the earnest black family. In addition to an innovative musical analysis of slavery, the *Underground Railroad* company performed "old plantation songs" and offered formal sacred concerts. During return engagements in Minneapolis, for example, the company starred in a separate sacred concert at the Academy of Music. Although the members of the company made an effort to distinguish between the play and the formal postperformance religious presentations, their reviewers and audiences always linked the two. "The sacred concert given last evening by Sam Lucas and the underground railroad party was well attended," announced a *Minneapolis Tribune* writer, who went on to declare that "[t]he concert was excellent in character."[29]

The 1879 production of Pauline Hopkins's *Underground Railroad* provided American audiences with the first staged reenactments of slavery that were not offered through the lens of the white imagination. Hopkins's script, the first wholly racialized rendition of slavery and freedom, was a masterpiece because it was written for and performed by an all-black cast. Indeed, this very history imposes an altogether emancipatory history on black performance, one that Du Bois quietly notes when he suggests that there was no black theater that was not minstrelsy. In 1924, he alludes to the ways in which African American artists "began to develop and uplift the art" of minstrelsy and that it "took a long time" before celebrated figures such as Bob Cole, George Walker, and Bert Williams appeared. The oversight by Du Bois and other early twentieth-century race writers of Hopkins's work and the pioneering parallel and predominantly female tradition of high concert performances is unfortunate, since her efforts and those of Annie Pauline Pindell, the Hyers Sisters, and Sam Lucas, to name a few, represent the kind of early foundations for the black performance tradition that enable vigorous refutations of problematic canonical histories.

The African American dramatic tradition of which Hopkins became a part featured the pioneering work of William Wells Brown, a fellow Massachusetts resident and the polymath who early celebrated the writing and poise of the future Pauline Hopkins. Hopkins's play was in direct conversations with Brown's 1858 *The Escape*, a colorful drama set in the antebellum South. Echoes of *The Escape* permeated Hopkins's work and it was tempting to compare the work of the two New England writers and performers. However, the work with which hers was most frequently compared was Joseph Bradford's *Out of Bondage*, which showcased the Hyers Sisters and brought them much attention. The works by Bradford and Hopkins essentially were written for the same performers and shared similar settings and character types. The plots of both pieces were based on the evolution of a family from enslavement to a life in freedom. *Out of Bondage*, one of the early staples in the Hyers Sisters' repertoire, was a rollicking plantation comedy that white Bostonian Joseph Bradford wrote expressly for them. With this play, the Hyers Sisters and Sam Lucas, who played the roles of "modified Topsies" and a "wild plantation negro," respectively, had "achieved marked success in all the large cities."[30] Reviewers regarded it as "full of incident and interest," but they also noted that it was "a skeleton sketch, barely more than a title itself," a "peg upon which is hung the acting and musical efforts of the several performers."[31] A comparison of the two works suggests that Hopkins may have wanted to model her own work on Bradford's demonstrated, albeit thinly plotted, dramatic success. She accomplished more African American character development, though, and incorporated a significant historical context while also exploring more fully the dilemmas of enslaved African American women and mothers.

Bradford and Hopkins did triumph in their creations of substantial portrayals of the African American home. On the nineteenth-century stage and even in later twentieth-century treatments of enslavement, writers consistently diverted action away from slave homes. Conflicts involving the slaves were often played out in rooms of the main house such as the kitchen, in wooded areas nearby, or in various Northern locales, resulting in critical, dehumanizing, and disorienting displacement of African American characters. This avoidance literally displaced slave characters. It seriously compromised their ability to assert domestic sensibilities of their own, and, by extension, denied their humanity and autonomy. *Out of Bondage* and *Underground Railroad* remain the only two extant nineteenth-century plays that attempted this revisionist staging. The most noticeable difference between *Out of Bondage* and *Underground Railroad*, however, lay in the writers' conception of African American identity. Bradford's heavy-handed stereotyping of black life and language prevented any true explorations of African American domesticity, masculinity, or social relations. *Out of Bondage* was set in a slave cabin in which "[c]oon skins and possum skins stretched upon the walls" and where "[s]trings of onions and Stitches of bacon &c, &c [were] hanging from the rafters." There the characters gather to discuss their plans to become fugitives over a dinner of possum. Instead of generating a probing analysis of their options, however, the cast engages in a thoroughly unappealing dissection of the dinner entrée. The play devolves quickly into a grotesque farce and hardly resembles the "moral and musical drama" that it was advertised to be.

Underground Railroad revisited key elements of Bradford's script, but Hopkins used her play to reconfigure two primary symbolic sites of enslavement, the plantation manor house and the slave quarters. Prepublicity advertisements of Hopkins's work may have likened it to Bradford's play, but audiences, in fact, were to be treated to Hopkins's more enlightened and humanizing portrait of antebellum African American life. Like the family in *Out of Bondage*, the primary characters in *Underground Railroad* inhabit a cabin in the slave quarters located on a Southern plantation. Yet in Hopkins's play this modest dwelling becomes a refined signifier of the domesticity and humanity that the slaves possess in spite of their enslavement. The "old cabin" that the hero Sam occupies with his family does not resemble the ramshackle smokehouse of *Out of Bondage*; it is filled with the "usual furniture" and literally accommodates serious discussions about self-emancipation, marriage, and family unity.

Hopkins's embrace of black domesticity in *Peculiar Sam* enabled her to confront blackface minstrelsy, a form that insinuated itself into her play because Sam Lucas was a well-known minstrel performer and minstrelsy was such a pervasive entertainment. One of the richest elements of the script emerges because Hopkins flirts with the cultural expectations of African American entertainment, by providing Sam Lucas with ample opportunities to sing and to dance and by placing such actions in the play's foreground. She tames the grotesque physicality of blackface and does so emphatically by placing in the foreground melodic and serious song and dance. These are the play's racial performances, and Hopkins deploys them in her critique of African American marriage rights, autonomy, and preservation of the black family.

The play's opening lines establish the sparse world of the slave quarters as a communal space and as one in which pleasure is possible. The first scene features Sam gathering with other male field slaves in the cabin he shares with Mammy, his mother, and Juno, his sister. "Come on boys," he shouts, "we'll hab a right smart time hyar, all to ourselves. Mammy and Juno is gone out an' de coast am clar."[32] The young men's practice of the latest dance steps, at first glance, might seem to reinforce the popular stereotype that slaves are lighthearted and unconcerned with their condition. Yet, in the context of a play on black domesticity, this scene allows two innovative rereadings. First, men of color are not identified as enslaved individuals and, second, their first performed actions are done unself-consciously and beyond the scrutiny of whites. Rather than adhere to the prevailing white notion of the home as a space synonymous with female activity and domestic priorities, Hopkins represents this space first as a communal space in which young black men, free of both black matriarchal and white patriarchal governance, can take pleasure in themselves and in each other. Hopkins's radical regendering of the Southern slave home countered the images of countless Tom shows that were being staged at this same time. Those productions and the work that inspired them, Harriet Beecher Stowe's 1852 novel *Uncle Tom's Cabin; or Life among the Lowly*, depicted black men as forced to relinquish their own homes and families as a result of white men's inability to maintain and stabilize their own domesticity.

Pauline Hopkins used the play that quickly became known as *Underground Railroad* to introduce a new African American archetype to the American public, which flocked to music halls, opera houses, and theaters to see the play during summer and fall 1879. For the first time in a staged American play, an African American actor was playing the role of a romantic hero. Sam Lucas, a former minstrel star long regaled for his versatility and winning charm, had the rare opportunity to cultivate and shape this new character type. The groundbreaking character of Peculiar Sam, as played by Lucas, both inspired and cultivated romance in this drama about slavery and self-emancipation. Not only did Hopkins suggest that African American manliness could be achieved in bondage and maintained in a world that still accommodated slavery, but she also proposed that the wholly dehumanizing system of slavery could be rendered powerless by love and devotion. Hopkins used Peculiar Sam to invalidate and replace the destructive image of the powerful and uncontrollable black man that so terrified her fellow Boston playwright J. T. Trowbridge. Hopkins's creation of Peculiar Sam constituted a most insistent act of cultural revisionism; the move to depict and reclaim African American manhood, and to do so in response to his social and physical desire for a wife, took direct aim at the persistent myths about African American licentiousness, amorality, and honor.

Hopkins's use of song as the first tool with which Peculiar Sam begins to build a new foundation for African American family life demonstrated her unabashed engagement with black face minstrelsy. The opening song complements the first dance routines of the young men gathered in Sam's family cabin, establishes Sam's romantic nature, and demonstrates his capacity for aggressive assertions of his masculinity. This first solo also foreshadows the degree to which imagination and dreams, rather than being oppressive and restrictive realities of enslavement, drive the play. Its lyrics confirm that Sam's heroic development is not prompted by threats from the white patriarchy, which could easily render him powerless and mute. Sam's primary challenges—imaginary and real—emerge within the enslaved black community. After congregating in Sam's cabin, the slaves decide to move their revelry to another location in the slave quarters. Sam tells them he will come shortly, after he "sposes ob some tickler bisness . . . on han'."[33] This prompts one of the men to warn him about Jim, the overseer, who has "got young Marse mighty sweet" and who may well use his favor to acquire Jinny, a mulatto house slave and Sam's sweetheart, as his wife. In the script, Sam "[a]nswers Pete with solo," and he launches into the following song:

> One night as the moon was beamin'
> I lay fas' asleep a dreamin';
> That the sun was shinin' bright,
> In the middle of the night
> And the darkies had assembled to have a little fight.

Dramatic Freedom

> I woke an' the banjo was soundin'
> An' the bones through the air was boundin';
> How happy I did seem, I was married in a dream
> In an ole Virginie mudscow floating down stream.

Immediately following the chorus offered by a male quartet, Sam justifies and clarifies his actions:

> Din I warn all de niggers not to love her
> Ef they do it'll cause them to blubber;
> Now git out of my way an' member what I say
> I'm gwine to marry her myself some very fine day.

Sam's dream contains peculiar pairings: moonlight and sunlight, seductive dreams and alienating reality, public violence and private domestic harmony, blissful marriage and movement "down river." Although Sam's musings conjure up notions of a romantic sail, they also easily call to mind the increasingly harsh slavery conditions that existed in the Deep South and the trepidation that slaves had about being sold "down river." Hopkins co-opts this loaded term and transforms the river, a site complicit in the internal American slave trade and synonymous with the intensely sexualized bondage of women and an intimidating physical violence to all who were sold "down river," into an indicator of high romance.

Throughout *Underground Railroad*, Hopkins illuminates the challenges that made it difficult for enslaved people to imagine, much less maintain, social order within the unpredictable antebellum world that they inhabited. Almost immediately, the opening scene underscores the upheaval and invalidation that compromise black domesticity. Sam's mother, identified only as Mammy, appears and conveys the news of his sweetheart's marriage to Jim, the African American overseer. Mammy, "breathing hard" and distressed, declares, "For de Lor's sake boy do you kno' what dey's gone and done up to de big house? Dey's gone an married dat dear chile, dat lamb ob a Jinny to dat rascal ob an oberseer Jim." In disbelief, Sam "grasps her arm" and urges her to repeat the news. "Mammy, tell me agin!" he says, "You don't mean it! Tell me dey haint done dat!" Mammy seems taken aback, both by Sam's disbelief and the strength of his grip on her arm as he demands more details. "He yar, boy, lef' be my arm. You mean to scrunch me to a jelly?," she says before confirming, "Yes, deys bring dat gal up like a lady; she neber done nuthin' but jes wait on Marse fambly an' now ole Marser's dead dey's gone an' married her, their way to Jim and de gal can't bar de sight ob him. It's de meanes thing I eber seed."[34] The interaction between Sam and his mother was astonishing for its intimacy and an emphatic example of how Hopkins's play went beyond the jocular script that was Bradford's *Out of Bondage*. The close bond between Mammy and Sam, rooted in their shared disbelief at the actions committed by the white slave owners and residents of the main house, also accomplishes another key reversal of stature. The exchange, marked for its five references to "dey"—the plural dialect term for "they"—transforms the powerful white characters into an undifferentiated and thus potentially disarmed mass.

Once Hopkins establishes the rationale for heroic intervention, she focuses intently on the often unspeakable legacy of antebellum sexual oppression. She hints at both the powerlessness of the primary victim and the ways in which concubinage is a rallying cry for community solidarity by introducing several reports of Jinny's plight. Details of the forced union of Jinny and the overseer are described three times in quick succession, first by Mammy, then by Jinny, and finally by the spirited Juno, Sam's sister. When Jinny appears, she refrains from offering vivid details about the event. Significantly, she addresses Mammy directly, and in so doing, reinforces Hopkins's new model of empowered black maternity. The unwilling bride then explains her plans to fight the undesirable union. "Yes, Mammy and Sam, I have come to say goodbye." She follows this announcement with the following practical assessment: "It's hard to leave the place where I was born, but it is better to do this, than to remain here, and become what they wish me to be. To fulfill this so-called marriage."[35] Immediately following this stilted but moving pronouncement, Sam's sister Juno delivers a spirited account of the debacle. She offers this verbatim account to Mammy, the most respected slave on stage at the moment and the figure who would best understand the plight of young defenseless slave women. Juno's chief complaint, however, is that Jinny, who represents a type of young woman to which Juno herself aspires, has been denied romance. As she tells her mother, "Yes, Mammy, onlies thing they done in de worl' was, Marse he say, 'Jim you want to marry Jinny?' Jim he say yes, course Jim say yes. Marse he say, 'Jinny, you want to marry Jim?' Jinny, her say *no*, like to kno' what Jinny want of ignorant ole Jim. Marse say 'You man an' wife, an Lor' hab mussy on you soul.' Dat no kin ob weddin'."[36] The first and third versions of Jinny's marriage are offered by Mammy and Juno, characters whose language, occupations, and residence in the slave quarters mark them as dark-skinned slaves. Their accounts, conveyed in black dialect, frame the restrained and conventional speech that the light-skinned Jinny delivers in prim tones and cultivated language. In the retelling of Jinny's plight, Hopkins frames the tragic mulatto speech with stirring black female folk commentary, a discursive strategy that suggests how a racially inclusive antebellum black female agency will protest this sexual appropriation and symbolic silencing of women of color. The linguistic void in Jinny's account testifies to her trauma, but Hopkins's supplementary interpretations of Jinny's trials insert a comprehensive black analysis, one that is consistently missing in the white-authored slavery plays of the day.

The vivid reportage of the advocates, Mammy and Juno, that frames the reserved declaration of the victimized Jinny increasingly justifies heroic intervention and a romantic corrective. Hopkins intensifies this imbroglio by allowing the character Juno to deliver the symbolic "last word" and most emphatic assessment of the situation. Hopkins's choice of the name Juno, modeled after the white American tradition for ascribing mythological names to enslaved people, also relies on irony here, since Juno, Hera in Roman tradition, was the wife and sister of Jupiter or the Roman Zeus, was revered as the protector of women, and was a formidable individual who repeatedly defended her own honor in the face of her husband's infidelities. Hopkins signals that her romance plot will not concentrate solely on the sympathetic tragic mulatto figure; indeed, the romance plot will depend on the defense of marriage by all women, and the ultimate recuperation of the tragic mulatto will depend in no small part on the effectiveness of her impassioned black female folk advocates.

Underground Railroad matched the new romantic black male hero with a newly constructed romantic female lead. Many of Hopkins's audiences had become familiar with the mulatta through popular plays such as Boucicault's *The Octoroon* and Thomas Aiken's adaptation of Stowe's *Uncle Tom's Cabin*. Boucicault's tragic heroine, Zoe, is cherished by the mistress whose adulterous slave-owning husband has fathered the young slave woman. Eventually, Zoe is faced with overwhelming sexual compromise that is directly related to her newly established identity as a woman of color. Isolated from the African American community and unfamiliar with the slave quarters, Zoe is overwhelmed by the shocking revelations of her true slave origins and dies tragically, unclaimed by members of either race. Aiken's Eliza, also an inhabitant of the big house, is isolated from her enslaved husband and from the field slaves of the plantation. When faced with the sale of her child, Eliza engineers her own salvation. The octoroon plot, as it came to be called, was a white creation designed to "win sympathy for the antislavery cause by displaying a cultivated 'white' sensibility threatened by, and responding to, a 'black situation.'"[37] In late antebellum and early post–Civil War dramas, the plight of the besieged mixed-race heroine was the most compelling cultural signifier of American slavery. Hopkins took direct aim at this tradition and worked to redirect the public gaze toward the larger black family of which the tragic mulatta was a part.

In *Underground Railroad*, Hopkins altered significantly the octoroon plot by reclaiming for the race this mixed-race figure and evaluating her plight from a black perspective. Hopkins's tragic mulatta became a woman whose virtues were representative of upstanding black morality and not the result of her claims on white ancestry. Once the sexual crisis is unveiled in *Underground Railroad*, the heroine is absorbed into an articulate and mobilized black milieu, one located in the slave quarters and, as such, part of a community undeniably identified as a segregated black world. Hopkins's slavery drama introduced thoroughly new suspense precisely because, once threatened by white power and immorality, the tragic mulatta could only see her honor and morality restored as a result of collective black resistance. This daring social and symbolic revisionism had multiple implications, the most powerful of which culminates in the elevation of the black folk, the necessary animation of black masculinity, and the consolidation of a multiracial community.

The refashioned antebellum black domesticity that Hopkins explored in *Underground Railroad* strengthened the play's unprecedented racial dynamics. The principal agent here was Mammy, a character whose vital intervention challenges her traditional role as a "centerpiece in the ante-bellum Southerner's perception of the perfectly organized society."[38] Central to Hopkins's refutation of white Southern cultural mythology was her creation of a figure whose primary domestic allegiance was to her own biological and extended family and not to the family of her white owners.

Hopkins relies on linguistic cues such as dialect and the term "Mammy" to locate the play's only matriarch squarely within the world of Southern slavery. The play also relies on traditional material markers of the Southern Mammy. The costume directions, for example, call for Sam and Juno's mother to make her entrance wearing a "[p]lain plaid house dress and yellow turban." Once the slaves begin their escape from slavery, however, Mammy replaces her turban with an "immense bonnet."[39] This apparel change introduces a light comedic note, but Hopkins uses it to underscore effectively that the pursuit of gentility also is fueling the black slave family's exodus to the North. Despite these traditional markers, however, Hopkins systematically challenges the domestic iconography and proscriptive cultural politics applied to the character that were antithetical to notions of femininity, desirability, or womanhood.[40] Mammy's desire for freedom is never complicated by her allegiance to the white family she serves. Her primary allegiance to her children and their happiness obscures the typically romanticized slavery relationship between a mammy and the family of her white owners. Once again, the power of Hopkins's play lay in its assertive celebration of the family. Her revisionist slavery drama did not feature a black mammy but instead introduced audiences to an African American mother, one whose priorities emanated from her republican desires to facilitate her children's acquisition of citizenship and domestic stability.

Pauline Hopkins used African American domesticity in *Underground Railroad* as the primary lens through which to revisit American slavery. This discourse also enabled her to honor the African American nationalist agendas articulated so eloquently by her ancestors, the Reverend Nathaniel Paul and the poet James Monroe Whitfield. The defense of domesticity was the primary catalyst for the self-emancipation that culminates in the slaves' escape, a feat celebrated when Hopkins incorporated the very phrase "slaves' escape" into one of the play's revised titles. In *Underground Railroad*, domesticity in general, and African American domesticity in particular, was under siege by a willful white patriarchy and a complicit African American male contingent. Hopkins suggested that self-emancipation was not only necessary for slaves who wanted to wrest control of their bodies away from their masters, but for all those who sought to determine their own domestic and familial agendas. In many respects, Hopkins's play reinforced the persuasive argument that Harriet Beecher Stowe embedded in *Uncle Tom's Cabin* that the greatest crime of American slavery was the damage that it did to American families.

Unlike Stowe, however, Hopkins imagined an African American hero whose triumphs were rooted not in his religiosity but in his secularity. Sam's metamorphosis into "Peculiar" Sam succeeds because he capitalizes on prevailing images of race and conceptions of traditional black folk culture. Sam's ability to signify on the iconic American, Uncle Sam, a figure whom Nathaniel Paul discussed before British audiences in the early 1830s, is part of his systematic appropriation of key elements of white culture, and it is through these acts of cultural acquisition that Hopkins's leading man secures his transformation into a new, and unassailable, American hero.

Underground Railroad, one of the first postbellum American plays to focus so squarely on race matters, was intricately connected to powerful antebellum meditations on bondage and African American survival. Indeed, Hopkins's theatrical projects evolved in the wake of rich examples, chief among them the groundbreaking work of William Wells Brown, the earliest known African American playwright and a longtime member of Pauline's Boston community. The early title of Hopkins's play, *The Slaves' Escape; or, The Underground Railroad*, directly acknowledges Brown's drama, entitled *The Escape; or, A Leap for Freedom*. The last subtitle that Hopkins used, "A Flight for Freedom," reasserted the connection between the two pieces and her respect for Brown.

Indeed, Brown's work, an 1858 drama that was read widely but never fully staged, was the only African American dramaturgical example that Hopkins had at her disposal. Brown's play, which he often performed as a solo artist, featured twenty-seven principal characters and a number of unnamed actors in secondary support roles. *The Escape* chronicled the plight of a mulatto slave couple whose marriage was threatened by a lascivious master and malicious overseer. Brown depended on sentimental conventions such as flowery language and soliloquies to underscore the tragic circumstances of his enslaved heroine and her frustrated husband.

It was not just the subtitle of Hopkins's play, which suggested a covert rather than public acquisition of freedom, that signaled the key differences between the two earliest known African American authored representations of black life on the American stage. Brown emphasized the individuality of his leading actors and frequently sequestered them in bowers where they delivered earnest speeches and indulged in intense self-scrutiny. Hopkins consistently staged social crises within the collective black space of the slave quarters. Her hero was a man of his people; his success was a microcosm of the triumphs that the race could achieve. The play's emphasis on a unified African American effort to secure emancipation and future stability continued throughout her manuscript.

Throughout the play, Hopkins alternates between Southern black dialect and stilted English prose. In addition to these linguistic shifts, Hopkins also juxtaposes folk superstition and mainstream realism and the emasculated blackness of the minstrel shows against the high manliness embodied in classical Anglo-European drama. Like Brown's leading male character, Peculiar Sam was a figure whose heroic development could be followed by watching his interpretive strategies and linguistic feats. Sam's initial foray into heroic language presented two tantalizing and possible outcomes. Hopkins's use of dialect in Sam's speeches emphasized the black folk dimensions of his character. His linguistic patterns also registered his character development along clearly demarcated and racialized lines. In addition, however, the alternating use of dialect and high English prose, not just standard conversational language, suggested a linguistic hybridity. This new and shifting state was an appropriate symbol of the unprecedented racialized masculinity of an African American character.

Evidence of the double-sided heroic sensibility in the *Underground Railroad* appears in the first act. Even before his sister Juno and sweetheart Jinny appear and corroborate the story that his mother has shared, Sam lapses into song. Over the course of the original four-stanza composition by Pauline Hopkins, Sam transports himself away from the Southern landscape of slavery. Within the bucolic world that he conjures up, Sam explores his complaint about the unnatural nature of his circumstances. The song begins by proving Sam's ability to redefine the Southern landscape over which he should have no control. His first revisions are applied to the big house where Jinny works as a house slave and has been married against her will. Instead of acknowledging the overwhelming and symbolic aspects of that quintessential antebellum space, Sam reduces the plantation home to "the gate." He then imagines Jinny, like the Ethiopian-born Andromeda of Greek mythology, chained to this disembodied structure and in desperate need of rescue. After "sorrowfully" uttering, "Po' Jinny, po' little gal," Sam launches into song:

> Ah! Jinny is a simple chile,
> Wif pretty shinin' curls,
> An' white folks love her best, of all
> The young mulatto girls;
> Tell her to wait a little while,
> Tell her in hope to wait,
> For I will surely break the chain,
> That binds her to the gate.[41]

This solitary structure, used to regulate entries and departures, suggests Jinny's isolation and inability to reach the world beyond. Yet it also places Jinny on the threshold of freedom. Hopkins's repeated references to the gate also empower Sam, who is now tackling an isolated structure rather than a fortified—literally and symbolically—Southern structure. His heroic objectives increasingly become acts of repossession. At first his primary objective is to "break the chain / That binds her to the gate." As the song proceeds, however, he vows to "take po' Jinny from de gate" and to "set [his] darling Jinny free / And take her from the gate." By the last stanza, his conviction has heightened considerably: "Tell her in hope to wait," he declares to his audience, "For I am he, shall make her free / And take her from the gate."[42] This slave hero subjects the discourse of enslavement to a purposeful, racially coded rhetoric of emancipatory romance.

The fact that the character Sam is enslaved in Mississippi, a state with a history of debilitating bondage and oppressive plantation systems, should signal the overwhelming odds against his success as a heroic lover. In the account of his enslavement, Sam makes several references to "Ole Marser," "Mississippi state," his family's "old cabin," and his recent sale. "Ole Marser's dead an' I am sold / From Mississippi state," he laments in stanza two. Undaunted by his precarious position, however, he refuses to accept that his impending removal from the plantation strips him of power. He also refuses to acknowledge the power of his antebellum Southern reality. He reasons:

> T'would be wrong for me to leave her 'lone,
> In Mississippi state . . .
> Pray heaven I'm not too late;
> To set my darling Jinny free.[43]

This man, undaunted by the reality of his situation, is impervious to the constraints on his behavior and the imposed restrictions that deny romantic agency to him and to all other slaves.

Underground Railroad, a play driven by critiques of ownership, proposed that symbolic or imaginative possession of the landscape was key to creating a viable African American hero. Indeed, the play's willful hero is fueled by his ability to reimagine, and thus repossess, the nineteenth-century world in which he lives. Sam takes control of his future by redefining, quite literally, the landscape of Southern slavery and the nature of Jinny's sexual distress. The quarters, a site of potential collective resistance and a place that the opening scenes associated with a cohesive African American brotherhood, becomes "our old cabin," a sentimentalized place that now stands "upon the stream." The offstage mixed quartet that punctuates Sam's song with a four-line chorus emphasizes this image, one that exudes universal domestic appeal rather than slaves' deprivation. The Mississippi River was, of course, a well-known body of water that came to symbolize the horrors of enslavement. It was the principal river corridor that facilitated internal American slave traffic and commercial trade of Southern goods. Here, in this antebellum, and antislavery, romance, however, the enslaved protagonist strips the Mississippi River of its cultural power. In this song, Sam's home "stands upon the stream." The repeated references to this modest body of water deflect power from the natural elements—such as the master's home and the Mississippi River—that were, and still remain, mighty symbols of slavery and the power that American slave owners wielded over their human property.

Classical heroic rhetoric and romantic language define the opening scenes of *Underground Railroad*. It is important to notice, however, that Sam's vigorous heroic development along these lines occurs in Jinny's absence. Until she appears, he is able to imagine her as the object of a classic chivalric enterprise. She becomes his "darling Jinny," a "girl with patient eyes" who "weeps" about their "cruel fate." Her concubinage and sexual exploitation are subsumed by the courtly language in which Sam indulges. Is it possible to sustain this anglicized identity in the face of black American antebellum reality, however?

Hopkins invites her audience to consider the possibility. When Sam's love interest appears for the first time, for example, she does so as "Virginia." Hopkins's deliberate rejection of the diminutive and Southern folk version of her name certainly suggests the young woman's preference for formality and conservatism. Jinny's alienation from the field slave community is confirmed further when she uses clipped tones to deliver a concise statement about her plans to run away. It is clear that she does not consider Sam or the community as resources to which she might turn. The heroic identity that Sam has begun to shape seems well matched to Virginia's personality. Yet, at the very moment when the two might forge an elite alliance, Sam abandons that role all together. "Jinny," he says, "you isn't 'fraid to trust ol' peculiar Sam, I know, kase you see Ise allers willin' to die fer you." The young slave's dizzying shift from high anglicized heroic rhetoric to excessively staged dialect continues: "You needn't bid any on us good-bye, kase dis night I 'tends to tote you and Mammy and Juno 'way from hyar. Yas, an' I'll neber drop ye till Ise toted you safe inter Canidy."[44] The man who aspired to "break the chain" that held his sweetheart now declares himself "willin' to die." Hopkins invites her audience to account for Sam's striking new articulation of his heroic intentions.

Hopkins's use of classic heroic rhetoric functions as a lens of whiteness through which her audience can "see" Sam. He stands before them not as a poorly clad field slave but as a man who embodies the courtly heroic tradition. Dialect becomes the language of action and slave resistance in this pivotal scene with Jinny. Characterized as a "stage language" that is the absolute opposite of "the soft tones and grace of what was considered cultivated speech," it is a dependable and familiar linguistic weapon that Hopkins's African American hero will use to defend and to emancipate himself and those he loves.[45] In 1879, twenty-year-old Pauline Hopkins knew dialect as a literal stage language, as the unequivocal mark of blackness and race on the American stage. Minstrel acts frequently featured men in blackface making a mockery of blacks who aspired to positions above their stations. Their tortured rendition of standard English signaled their effort to adopt airs and exposed them to ridicule and social censure. In *Underground Railroad*, Hopkins links dialect to Sam's slavery origins. Yet she quickly asserts this character's facility for language and his capacity to articulate his desires in high English, the anglicized dialect of courtly romance. As a result, Hopkins reminds her audiences that both of these linguistic forms are unreliable racial signifiers. Hopkins's appropriation of standard English is deliberately staged. So, too, is her application of dialect. Her turn to it reveals that she is rewriting the minstrel script and crafting an alternative black stage language. The key to Hopkins's rebuttal of American blackface minstrelsy lies not in her rejection of burnt cork and face paint but in her characters' masterful deployment of language.

Dialect speech constitutes a mask of blackness, or even more specifically, a mask of blackface. This overt application of racial linguistic characteristics, accompanied by Sam's turn to subterfuge, dissemblance, and crafty acts of self-defense, approaches a "visible" appropriation of "black practices."[46] Through Sam, Hopkins extricates the primary stock figure of blackface minstrelsy and redirects his traditional behaviors toward his emancipation. Sam's performance, which was in fact done by Sam Lucas, one of minstrelsy's best African American practitioners, is highly suggestive of blackface. Over the course of the play, however, Hopkins systematically endows her central black hero with an emphatic masculinity and an increasingly inspiring race-consciousness. In effect, then, at a time when blackface minstrelsy was the primary vehicle through which blackness was imagined on the American stage, Hopkins engineers a humanizing minstrelization and performs a keen double-edged satire.

In *Underground Railroad*, blackface and dialect are the forms that best accommodate Sam's heroism and showcase his race pride and commitment to family. Hopkins reveals Sam's unrefined blackness, and she uses language to acknowledge the gulf that exists between him and the woman he loves. Linguistic difference between the two reinforces the hierarchies and social divide that historians have long discussed as part of intraracial slave communities. Hopkins also uses other linguistic signs to assert Sam's resistance and application of aspects of blackness in his quest for emancipation. In his first onstage encounter with Jinny, Sam introduces himself as "ol [P]eculiar Sam."[47] The self-deprecating manner that he uses at this moment belies his unwavering heroic aspirations. The irony of this situation cannot be missed, however: slavery, a system known as "the peculiar institution," has met its match. Over the course of the play, characters use the phrase "Peculiar Sam" nine times. Of all the characters, including the members of his family, only Sam pronounces the word "peculiar" correctly. The various pronunciations, which include "pecoolar," "peccoliar," "culiar" and "cular," throw Sam's own articulation into sharp relief. That Sam maintains a sharp enunciation, even while in the throes of dialect, signals his resistant heroic identity and self-conscious use of standard English to underscore the nature of the unprecedented role that he is playing. This African American heroic identity, he insists, is compatible with dominant white discourse. It is also confirmation of his symbolic and literal distance from slavery and of his unwavering romantic aspirations.

Many American slaves prayed for and sustained a belief in a messianic savior who would end their suffering. Hopkins honors this enduring cultural hope and links Sam's transformation from slave to slave emancipator to his mother's lifelong belief in a Moses figure who will lead slaves to freedom. Moments after Sam concludes his romantic song and just before he encounters Jinny, he and his mother reflect on the need for a slave hero. A "dejected" Sam, whom the stage directions instruct to "cove[r] face with arm and tur[n] away," asks his mother about "dat time comin' dat you's tol me 'bout eber sence I was knee high to a cricket, when am Moses gwine to lead us po' forsook niggers fro' de Red Sea?" In response, Mammy encourages her "[p]oor boy! Poor Sammy!" not to gib up nor lose your spirits, for de Lord am comin' on his mighty chariot, drawn by his big white horse, an' de white folks hyar, am a gwine to tremble. Son Ise been waitin' dese twenty-five year, an I ain't guv up yet.[48] Hopkins's references to Moses here revisit the persistent African American antebellum trope that defined American slavery in relation to the Old Testament plight of the Israelites. Slavery was like their Egyptian bondage, and the Northern states and Canada figured as the Promised Land. Like Moses, the biblical figure whose marriage to Zipporah, an Ethiopian woman, was challenged by members of his family, Sam does not initially recognize himself as the hero of his people. Immediately after Jinny confirms her situation, however, Sam claims a new identity for himself, invokes the name "Peculiar Sam" for the first time, and prepares his family for their Southern exodus.

Once he declares himself to be "Peculiar Sam," the character flirts most intensely with the blackface minstrel routine. His dialect speech becomes increasingly labored and exaggerated, racial references become more explicit, and his actions are more aggressive and even violent. He also turns more frequently to mischief and play in the face of great danger. As she intensifies this unruly element in *Underground Railroad*, Hopkins takes care to prevent it from corrupting the family's social ascent and acquisition of gentility and middle-class stability, which their flight from slavery increasingly symbolizes. Through her strategic use of dialect as a signifier of blackface minstrelsy, Hopkins increasingly identifies it as an oppressive linguistic tool used to perpetuate racial oppression and to stunt African American social development.

Hopkins essentially encapsulates Sam's minstrel performance by limiting it to encounters with Sam's chief rival, Jim the overseer. Hopkins strikes a delicate balance as she plays to the audiences who may well have expected to see Sam Lucas, the veteran of blackface minstrelsy, reprise his former roles in *Underground Railroad*. She managed to satisfy audience expectations and capitalize on Lucas's celebrated talents by designing an oral and aural descent into blackface, one defined by sharp repartee, malapropisms, and other lexical deviations. One of the most compelling scenes between the two men occurs just before Sam and his family escape from the plantation. Jinny's new husband storms the slave quarters in search of "Miss Airy," his wife. His demands and violent threats threaten the cohesive African American domestic scene so carefully established in earlier scenes:

> JIM: I 'spected I'd fin you hyar Miss Airy, but you's my wife now, an' you's got to do as I says. Dars dat hoe cake ain't bake fer my supper, an' dars my ol' pants want mendin', an' you's got it to do. (*V. shrinks from him. Jim follows her. Sam follows him.*) You's full o' airs, dats what you is, but I'll bring em out o' you, eff I has to tie you up an' gib you a dozen lashes. (*Seizes V. by her arm, Sam seizes him by collar, jerks him to c., then releases him.*)
>
> SAM: (*Stutters with anger.*) See hyar, Ise seed you swellin' round hyar consid'able, but when you talks 'bout strucking Jinny, Ise got suthin' to say.
>
> JIM: You's anoder sassy nigger. But you's fixed long wif de res ob your 'culiar coons. Marse gwine to sell you all down Red riber tomorrer, den I reckon Miss Jinny will 'have herself. An mean time I don't want eney ob your sass. (*Women huddle to-gether.*)
>
> MAMMY: (*Rocking herself to & fro.*) Ef ole Marse had libed he'd neber 'low it. O Lor', O Lor!⁴⁹

The tension continues to escalate and becomes increasingly violent. Sam challenges Jim's claim to Jinny and is rebuffed by the overseer who "[c]racks his whip at Sam" as he taunts him. In response, Sam "[l]eaps upon him, seizes the whip" and acts the part of the thwarted lover. "You's a liar sar, dats what you is! You crack your whip at me!" Sam declares as he "[f]lourishes whip around Jim, then takes it by butt end as if to strike him down with it," and then resumes his tirade. "You say Jinny's your wife again an' I' mash you all up, you mean ol' yank nigger," he shouts while chasing his adversary around the room with a whip.⁵⁰ The confrontation between the two men is marked by rough language, unrestrained physicality, and threats. The characters' spirited dialogue about class status, indicated by their use of racial epithets and airs, recalls a staple aspect of blackface minstrel scripts. Hopkins's stage directions alleviate the tension produced during Sam and Jim's verbal repartee. While she encourages the men to "spar," Hopkins emphasizes that they are to make their "set to as comical as possible."⁵¹ As a result, the scene becomes slapstick comedy. Yet, in the comical mayhem of this revisionary blackface scene, Sam's defense of Jinny remains a fight to assert his own manhood. He is determined to invalidate, rather than to justify, the casually applied but effectively binding law of the dominant white patriarchal culture.

Hopkins's next application of the minstrelsy script begins early in act II. The scene occurs in the woods after Sam sends his family on with Caesar, the Underground Railroad conductor and a former slave whom Mammy has thought was "dead an' gone dese ten year!"[52] Determined to confuse their pursuers, Sam takes on the identity of an old uncle and resorts to cunning and intraracial deception, two more primary elements of the traditional minstrelsy script. Sam now intensifies his linguistic mask and relishes the exaggerated dialect performance that will confuse Jim, their pursuer, and amuse audiences. When he appears on the scene, Jim fails to recognize Sam as the "sassy" Negro he fought or as one of his fugitive "nigs." "I doesn't mean no defense uncle, but you sees some ob my nigs is runned away, an' I wants to kno' has you hyard ob dem eny whar?" says Jim. With a "scolding voice," Sam asks, "What you doin' lettin' your slaves run 'way? What kin' obseer is you losing nigs, an den runnin all ober creation an ebry whar else looking for em. No I hain't seed 'em, I jes haint."[53] Hopkins's mastery of dialect is evident here as she uses it to both assert Sam's slave identity at the beginning of the play and to completely obscure it later. The wilderness scene between the disguised Sam and the desperate overseer also uses minstrelsy's primary tools of racial comicality to reassert the heroic potential of Hopkins's slave hero.[54] The scene succeeds—not only as a spoof of minstrelsy but also because it maintains the overall story line through its dramatic mimesis. Having staged a physical battle over the young mulatto house slave, the two men now engage in a rhetorical battle of wits. During the comical, but nonetheless tense, interaction, Jim, whose master has given him one hundred dollars to finance his pursuit, pays for each word of information about the runaways:

JIM: See hyar uncle, if you'll tell me anythin' 'bout dem fellars, I'll gib you, (*Thoughtfully.*) I'll gib you fifty cents.

SAM: Wha's fifty cents side ob a hundred dollars? No, I don't 'member nuthin'.

JIM: Ef you'll 'member anythin' 'bout dem pussons uncle, I'll gib you, yas I'll gib you dollar.

SAM: 'Pears like dar was a tall coon wif de crowd I seed, but I isn't sho.

JIM: Yas! Yas! dem's em, dem's em! An' a singin' gal, say dar war a singin' gal, an' I gib you, (*Pauses.*) I'll gib you two *whole* dollars.

SAM: Lor' chile 'tain't no use axing on me, kase I jes don' know weafer I 'member dat tickler gal or not.

JIM: Ef you'll jes say she war dar, kase I know'd you seed her, I'll gib you *free* dollars, dat's all de change Ise got.

SAM: Lay de money onter de do' sill dar, den I'll see ef I can 'member any mo'. (*Jim lays money down.*) I reckon de singing gal war wif dem fellars, reckon you'll fin' her sho nuff, when you kotch 'em.[55]

The overseer's bids and payments amount to a metaphorical slave auction. The irony and the triumph here, of course, is that, despite the transaction, this slaveholder's representative fails to acquire actual slaves. In contrast, Sam, the fugitive and leader of the Underground Railroad expedition, has successfully financed the first stage of his family's emancipation from the slaveholding South.

Hopkins's penultimate disciplining of blackface occurs in the final act and is contained within a fully evolved African American domestic context that has both political and familial dimensions. The scene opens in Canada, six years after the American Civil War, in "an old fashioned kitchen." Once again, Hopkins's stage directions call for evidence of domesticity and family order. In this place where a fire crackles in the fireplace and a clock sits on the mantel above, Mammy "sits at table knitting. Caesar, her husband now, sits before fire in arm chair." Once again, Hopkins enlists familiar material objects to affirm domesticity and to contextualize realistic discussions of African American enslavement and freedom. This portion of the play opens as Caesar declares to Mammy that "de Lor' has blessed us all" and itemizes the family's successes. "Hyar's you an' me married," he notes, "Jinny a singist, Juno a school marm; an las' but not leas' dat boy, dat pecoolar Sam, eddicated an' gwine to de United States Congress."[56] Mammy agrees and suggests that she and Caesar are in fact "setting hyar like kings an' queens, waitin' fer dat blessed boy o ours to come home to us."[57] While these successes constitute an inspiring emancipation romance, Hopkins insists that African American emancipation, even in the wake of a successful Underground Railroad escape or the end of the Civil War, may still be invalidated. The subtlety of this potential loss is revealed when Jinny begins to sing the plaintive strains of Stephen Foster's "Suwanee River," a popular antebellum plantation melody. The song, evocative of white proslavery sentiment, also generates emotional longing in the hearts of former slaves. Mammy declares that although she is "total 'tented hyar," such "ol' songs . . . carries me way back to dem good ol' times dat'll neber return." In the catalog of her cherished long-ago memories are the "ol' plantation, an mi an' ol' Marser, an de dear little lily chillern." Mammy is transfixed by the Southern landscape that now looms before her, and she marvels that she "kin seem to see de fiels ob cotton, an' . . . kin seem

Dramatic Freedom

to smell de orange blossoms dat growed on de trees down de carriage drive." Her powerful recollections reduce Caesar to tears, threaten to undo the high Northern romance that he enjoys in Canada, and loosen his hold on his hard-won individuality. As he wipes his eyes, he lapses into the third person, a linguistic shift that suggests an alarming loss of ownership of self, and tells Mammy, "[E]f de ol' man dies firs', bury me at ol' Marser's feet, under de 'Nolia tree."[58] The elders' speedy sentimental return to the antebellum South threatens the closure that they seemed to achieve just before fleeing the Southern plantation. At that earlier moment of transition, a weeping Mammy bade goodbye to her "ole home, de place whar [her] chillern war born, an' [her] ole man am buried." "Ise ole now," she declared, "I may neber see you 'gin, but my chillern's gwine an' I'm boun' to go. So good-bye ole home."[59] The terms that dictate, and legitimize, her abandonment of the personified home are rooted in the desire to preserve her family and the next generation of the race.

The Underground Railroad journey on which Hopkins's *Underground Railroad* characters embarked spanned the entire length of the Northeast, from the far Southern reaches of Mississippi, through the free Northern states, and on into Canada. Mammy's sentimental longing for home now, then, could be regarded as an outdated Southern sentimentalism, feelings that, literally, are misplaced. However, in the wake of such uncomplicated longing and deep emotional response, Hopkins asks pointedly, what constitutes a slave's escape? In *Underground Railroad*, the slaves' escape is not secured by their physical self-emancipation nor their geographic relocation. Hopkins suggests that bondage—moral and psychological—persists because of the pervasive and invasive nature of antebellum enslavement. Some years later, the poet Paul Laurence Dunbar revisited this very quandary when he mused about a plantation abandoned to "de swallers." Dunbar's speaker, like Hopkins's character named Caesar, cannot help but admit that the Southern site "hol's in me a lover till de las'; / Fu' I fin' hyeah in de memory dat follers / All dat loved me an' dat I loved in de pas'."[60] The Southern plantation is a vexed site indeed, one whose inhabitants experience complicated returns as they attempt to reclaim the fractured, but still cherished, symbols of its domesticity.

Underground Railroad proved itself as a contemporary drama when its conclusion invoked Reconstruction-era politics and the historic election of African Americans to federal political office. Hopkins's political, and thus more broadly defined "domestic," solution does not compromise her proposal that slavery persists as a still-unresolved national and local issue, one that severely circumscribes those who were enslaved and whose lives were so circumscribed by the peculiar institution. The private sentimental longing of the elders is set aside decisively by the public assertions of the figure who represents the next generation of self-emancipated free people. Moments after he arrives in his mother's home, Sam is surrounded by his family and friends. "Jest tell us one thing cap'n, 'for you goes eny farther," they demand. "[I]s you 'lected?" It is important to note how Sam responds: "I think you may safely congratulate me on a successful election," he declares. "My friends in Cincinnati have stood by me nobly."[61] Sam responds with the language and demeanor of a high romantic black hero who appears to have shed all marks of slavery. The anxiety about racial and regional authenticity that persists throughout the play emerges again as Caesar, in response to Sam's declaration, approaches his stepson. "Lef' me look at you," he says; "I wants to see ef you's changed eny," he says. After shaking his head "solemnly," the old man declares, "No, you's all dar jes de same."[62] Despite his proclamation, Caesar's query invites questions about which Sam is "all dar." In the scenes that follow, Hopkins once again attends to the anxieties that prompt Caesar to examine Sam in this manner.

Underground Railroad is a work in which the primary critical imperative calls for characters, and even more specifically slaves, to see—to ascertain and to then confront the facts and fictions that govern their lives. Repeatedly, the slaves' success is linked to their determination to look elsewhere, to see themselves in ways that challenge the ways in which they are seen by the dominant, or domineering, classes above them. The final reunion is a case in point. Shortly after Sam appears, there is a knock at the door. Sam opens it, and when a man "rushes past him into [the] room," he asks, "Whom do you wish to see sir? I think you have made a mistake." Caesar mutters, 'Pears like I knows dat fellar," before Jim "[l]ooks smilingly around" and responds to all present, "Don't you know one? Well I don't reckon you do, bein's Ise changed so," and presents to Sam an oversized business card that identifies him as "Mr. James Peters, Esq., D.D., attorney at law, at the Massachusetts bar, and declined overseer of the Magnolia plantation." As Virginia "shrinks behind Mammy" and the rest of the group barely contain their astonishment, Jim "bows profoundly" and says simply, "Dat's me. Declined overseer ob de 'Nolia plantation."[63] This is the first and only time in the play that Sam shows a complete lack of discernment. When he reads from Jim's oversized calling card, which recalls the enormous bonnet that Mammy dons as she flees the plantation, Sam confirms Jim's identity for the others. Yet the identity and role that Jim claims are not that of his highly successful postslavery life. He echoes Sam's last words and describes himself only as the "declined overseer ob de 'Nolia plantation." That this former occupation is on his postbellum calling card achieves at least two things. First, it locates Jim, and by extension, the family he is now visiting, undeniably in slavery. Second, it resurrects slavery and establishes it as the operative context in which these survivors will interact.

The unusual reunion that Hopkins stages here represents Sam's ongoing struggle to free himself from slavery and to enjoy the full benefits of liberty. This freedom, of course, would be realized by his marriage to Jinny. Unfortunately, she continues to believe herself married to the overseer Jim and refuses to accept Sam's proposal until she obtains an annulment. As a result, the Canadian backdrop in this closing scene underscores Sam's powerlessness; this newly elected American lawmaker is unable to legislate the terms of his social emancipation. The man who can effect change here, however, is not a Northern lawyer of the postbellum era, but instead a man commissioned to uphold the laws of the antebellum South. A "declined overseer," a figure supposedly rendered obsolete by the Civil War, is the only man capable of effecting the true freedom of these former slaves. In the scene that follows, Hopkins stages the overtures needed to bring closure for Sam and Virginia. Hopkins grapples with the evidence of Sam's still-thwarted masculinity, a state made evident by his inability to claim the woman he loves. Yet she refuses to let this diminish Sam's claim on nobility and romantic principles. He and Jinny use high standard English to express themselves, even as everyone else around them lapses into excited dialect prose:

> SAM: If you have come here to create a disturbance sir, I warn you to go out the way you came in, or I'll *throw* you out.
> JUNO: (*Re-enters on a run, with pistol; rushes at Jim.*) Did you wink, did you dare to wink?
> JIM: (*Frightened, stumbles over two or three chairs. Groans.*) O Lord no! (*To Company.*) Don't let her shoot me, Ise oly called hyar to stantiate myself an' be frien's long wif you.
> (*Juno lays pistol aside[,] laughing.*)
> JIM: Virginie, you needn't be fraid on me, kase I isn't hyar to mislest you. Chile, I kno's dat warnt no weddin, de law wouldn't 'low it nohow. (*To all.*) An' den you see, I has no free dislution ob mysel' at all, kase Ise got a truly wife, an' Ise got twins, a boy an' gal; one's nam'd Jinny an' de tother one Sam. (*Laughter.*)
> SAM: Mr. Peters, I congratulate you, you have certainly made the most of your freedom.[64]

This scene certainly provides closure to the family saga. But what implications emerge now that slavery has been resurrected and that African Americans have recalled it in order to obtain their "true" freedom? Hopkins, perhaps anticipating that very question, makes a startling move.

The cast, in response to Jim's peaceful overtures and details about his life, clears the kitchen for a rousing dance, "an ol' Virginie" reel that Juno believes to be "the only safe exit for surplus steam."[65] As the cast hurries about, Sam "rushes to the footlights" and makes the following declaration: "Ladies and gentlemen, I hope you will excuse me for laying aside the dignity of an elected M.C., and allow me to appear before you once more as peculiar Sam of the old underground railroad."[66] Sam's transformation, prefaced by his suspension of theatrical reality as he addresses the audience, raises several questions. Has Hopkins surrendered to a minstrel script, the kind that only attains resolution as it conjures up a frisky, nonthreatening black male figure? In returning to a role created on the Magnolia plantation, one could suggest even that Sam is an unsuccessful fugitive. Yet, ultimately, that is the role that confirmed his autonomy from the system and signaled what now appears to be his lifelong mastery of the system. In the role of Peculiar Sam, rather than that of the elected congressman, Sam emerges once again as a masterful black folk hero. It is also important to note that Sam's return to slavery days does not result in his adoption of dialect. By sidestepping this racial linguistic marker, Sam finally succeeds in making a place in the postbellum world for a figure like Peculiar Sam. The play's final comment, then, seems to be that it is entirely appropriate, if not plainly strategic, to wield those tools that were hallmarks not only of slavery days but also an integral part of an earnest and rich life during the antebellum era. In an effort to grapple with and even interpret the uneasy tension between their Southern past and Northern present, Hopkins's characters revive dialect as a signifier of racial intimacy and segregation and as a powerful and evocative performed medium.

Hopkins accommodates recollections of Southern scenes and emotional ties that her African American characters cherish. At the play's conclusion, however, such lapses are used to signal the conquest of the antebellum Southern social scripts and American theatrical scripts used to define and constrain African American identity in the ante- and early postbellum years. Throughout *Underground Railroad*, Hopkins illustrates the pervasive qualities of blackface minstrelsy but systematically appropriates it as a defensive racial mechanism. She deprives it of its offensive strengths—both in terms of its capacity to offend listeners and its deployment as a tactical element in minstrel scripts. In this play, dialect and contrived blackness are tools used to secure domestic stability and protect personal choice at a time when neither was necessarily possible for people of color in America. Hopkins's use of sentimentalism, dialect, and folk culture in *Underground Railroad* secured not only her own dramatic freedom but that of generations of new Americans in the postbellum age.

6

Spectacular Matters

"Boston's Favorite Colored Soprano" and Entertainment Culture in New England

Miss Pauline E. Hopkins, the Soprano, has a
sweet voice and is a favorite wherever she sings.

JAMES H. ROBERTS

1882

And O, how few have seen the bud
Of youthful hope unfold
Into the perfect flower of joy,
With leaves of burnished gold!
How few have heard the chorus grand
Whose first notes caught their ear
Amid the clashing of the chain,
The sigh, the groan, the tear!

ELIJAH W. SMITH

1883

Pauline Hopkins was the first African American dramatist to emerge in the post–Civil War era and the first American playwright to write and star in her own play on American slavery. The power of *Slaves' Escape; or, The Underground Railroad* (1879), her most successful and widely performed play, lay in part in its transformation of fugitive slaves into aspiring American patriots. In her deliberate reconstruction of antebellum experiences, Hopkins redefined desperate flights from bondage as early African American migrations, as relocations prompted by the wholly American desire to realize one's dreams and invest successfully in one's future. The play's powerful messages about the preservation of the family, the value of noble masculinity, and African American humanity all contributed to its enduring success and marketability as the era of Reconstruction ended and the Gilded Age began.

Indeed, the political commentary embedded in the work that was performed under names such as *Slaves' Escape; or, The Underground Railroad* and *The Flight for Freedom* resonated and departed from influential American stories of the time such as Mark Twain's 1873 novel, *The Gilded Age.* Twain and his coauthor, Charles Dudley Warner, announced that their work focused on "an entirely ideal state of society" and that "the chief embarrassment of the writers in this realm of the imagination has been the want of illustrative examples."[1] The story, which focused on the dizzying nature of social and emotional devolution, named the age that was to be synonymous with rapacious greed, excessive materialism, and American expansionism. It was in the shadow of this literary critique of a world plagued by the "fever of speculation . . . [that] inflamed desire for sudden wealth,"[2] to borrow from Twain and Warner's unapologetic preface, that Pauline Hopkins scrutinized the commodification of blackness, the increasingly institutionalized poverty of African Americans, and the constriction, rather than expansion, of territories hospitable to African Americans and their families.

Pauline Hopkins also experienced the Gilded Age as an era that quite literally financed her work and transformed her from a local to a nationally recognized dramatist. She lived vicariously through the plethora of dramatic successes and challenges associated with the 1879 *Underground Railroad* national tour that featured Sam Lucas, the Hyers Sisters, and Brindes de Salas. She monitored closely the play's success from afar and in her scrapbook carefully placed newspaper clippings about the troupe and its successes. In the summer of 1880, Hopkins finally reunited with the cast with whom she had traveled in spirit to the American heartland and urban industrial centers of the Midwest. Once the company returned to Boston, plans were quickly made to produce the play there, and twenty-one-year-old Pauline Hopkins, who was poised to star in this New England run of *Slaves' Escape*, now was on the threshold of becoming the first American woman to perform publicly in her own play. One of the company's most significant 1880 Boston bookings was at the Oakland Garden, Boston's leading summer theater and located on a sprawling estate in Roxbury, just north of the city proper. Oakland Garden welcomed thousands of visitors each summer to its shows, exhibitions, and picnic grounds. An engagement there had the potential to transform Pauline Hopkins into a local phenomenon and invigorate her fledgling career as a playwright and actress. However, as the history of the Oakland Garden experience reveals, this important booking did anything but ensure the troupe's professional autonomy as African American artists. The occasion actually threatened to compromise Hopkins's perspectives on American history and African American advancement in the post–Civil War years.

The 1880 Boston productions of *Underground Railroad*, which began with its name change and marketing as *Slaves' Escape*, enabled Hopkins to continue doing the public history work that she had begun three years earlier when she worked with her cousin Elijah Smith Jr. on *The Belle of Saratoga*. In 1877, Hopkins's leading role in the musical drama contributed to a sophisticated assessment by her African American community of American expansion and African American disenfranchisement. Smith and Hopkins facilitated the artistic political critique during the transition from the presidency of Civil War hero Ulysses S. Grant to the controversial tenure of Rutherford B. Hayes, the "Dark Horse president," whose authorization of the federal troop withdrawal from the Southern states brought on a tumultuous period that Hopkins characterized as the beginning of the "Negro's political troubles."[3]

The dramatization of enslavement, emancipation, and migration in *Slaves' Escape* contributed significantly to the postbellum African American debate about American culture, patriotism, and race pride. It linked Hopkins to the increasingly public efforts to make visible African American memories of slavery and freedom. *Slaves' Escape* directly challenged flawed mythologies about slavery that fueled racial intolerance in post-Reconstruction America. Hopkins had directed her vision of the South and the North directly at those who would deny the reality of African American postslavery trauma, discount the upheaval associated with migration or displacement, and suppress, often violently, black political agitation. The work was designed to entertain and to heighten public awareness about African American political sensibilities and collective motivations for racial uplift.[4] However, as the history of the play's production in Boston and New England reveals, Hopkins and her newsworthy drama were subject to intense and potentially hobbling racial and cultural politics.

The circumstances in which Pauline Hopkins made American theater history as a pioneering American playwright-actress were anything but modest. The events transpired on 4 July 1880 during a highly publicized and vibrant Independence Day celebration in Boston. Hopkins's appearance at the popular Oakland Garden propelled her to the forefront of public entertainment in the city. The Oakland Garden, accessible by the Highland Street Railway, was an extraordinary place that sought to offer its patrons unusual sights and scenarios.[5] By 1883, for instance, this seasonal performance site was home to

"Swings, Horses, [and] a Menagerie of Wild Beasts."[6] Hopkins's most note-worthy play was incorporated fully into the Garden's unpredictable entertainment milieu. According to an especially eye-catching and decorative *Boston Herald* advertisement, Hopkins was slated to appear in the "popular musical drama 'Escaped from Slavery,'" and she and her supporting cast would "introduc[e] some remarkably realistic scenes and effects, characteristic songs and choruses, etc., presenting a perfect picture of life in the South in slavery days."[7]

During the first extended Boston run of *Slaves' Escape* since the close of the play's extensive 1879 national tour, Pauline Hopkins played the role of Virginia or Jinny, the mixed-race house slave buffeted by male desire and her efforts to preserve a modicum of virtue. Sarah and William Hopkins joined their daughter on stage in supporting roles. The *Slaves' Escape* company was slated initially to present seven evening performances at 8:15 PM during the week of 4 July. The success of the play's Independence Day performance, however, resulted in the immediate addition of a 3 o'clock matinee to accommodate the crowds that thronged to the Oakland Garden. Performances lasted two hours, and evening shows were followed by a "grand display of fireworks" and "Cotton Plantation Scene" reenactments orchestrated by Charles Hicks, the well-known former minstrel and entertainment manager.[8] These panoramas featured Sam Lucas and "the entire company" of *Slaves' Escape*, and advertisements announced with great enthusiasm that "[a]fter the evening performance will be presented the COTTON PLANTATION SCENE on the lawn, with Sam Lucas in his specialities, and the entire company in a GRAND PLANTATION FESTIVAL, with a working representation of the boats Robert E. Lee and the Natchez, on the Mississippi River."[9]

At the Oakland Garden in July, Hopkins was participating in a celebration of American independence and freedom, one that placed America's history of slavery in the foreground. At first glance, it would seem that slavery was to be the lens through which Bostonians and other Northerners could appreciate the nation's autonomy. Certainly, the characters' struggles to gain their freedom could be construed as an altogether representative American story. The realities of African American life, disenfranchisement, and suffering from mob rule and the terrors of lynching suggested otherwise, however. Even though the white South was proclaiming by the late 1870s that its land and identity were "fully redeemed," the news reports of racial violence, agricultural tensions, and economic tyranny proved that there were new civil wars being waged.[10] At the heart of this embedded national conflict was a struggle over which histories of American slavery would be institutionalized and how African American civil, social, and political rights might best be defended.

Spectacular Matters

Slaves' Escape became enmeshed in Northern politics and Southern romance in the unrelenting cultural war on African American agency.

The politics of the Oakland Garden quickly confirmed that *Slaves' Escape* was being co-opted. New details about the terms of her engagement at the Garden and the contexts in which *Slaves' Escape* would be presented reveal that the play was used for purposes that were markedly different from those that Hopkins, an aspiring public historian and deliberate custodian of African American history, might have intended. At the Oakland Garden, Hopkins's play was used to finance an alternative American romance, a problematic cultural mythology about white freedoms that depended, eerily enough, on the perpetual bondage of black people. Ironically, it was in New England and not in cities beyond the "free North," that the play was appropriated as a tool to promote white nostalgia for the antebellum era. The play's accessibility and engaging historical meditation on the multifaceted nature of bondage and racial oppression now contributed to its potential undoing.

Performances at this former estate tended to be "of the variety order or light English opera."[11] Although Hopkins's play did fit the criteria of a variety show, the racial dimensions of the play made it susceptible to co-optation as a version of minstrelsy. As such, it reflected the kind of new genres that Oakland Garden managers wanted to offer to their patrons. Since her earliest public performance in 1875, Hopkins had studiously avoided any association with blackface minstrelsy. However, her move into the world of professional or, even more specifically, for-profit performance made it impossible for her to escape its reach any longer. Charles Hicks, the entrepreneurial manager and an established leader in black minstrelsy circles, drew up her contract at the Oakland Garden. Hicks, a light-skinned formerly enslaved man, was no stranger to black entertainment. He is credited in the historical record for bringing African Americans into mainstream American show business, and, at first glance, it appears that Hicks was ideally positioned to help Hopkins. In 1880, she was making a critical transition from the predominantly African American world of musical uplift and politicized art into the white-dominated public sphere of entertainment and leisure. The record shows, however, that Hopkins's involvement with Hicks quickly threatened the family arts tradition to which she had been true.

When Pauline Hopkins met Charles Hicks in 1880, he was attempting to stage at the Oakland Garden an event "never before attempted by any other management."[12] Some fifteen years after the end of the Civil War, Hicks wanted to portray slavery for Northern audiences and do so in a city where he had organized lucrative blackface minstrelsy concerts a decade earlier. Hopkins was not unfamiliar with Hicks; in 1875, her public performance debut with the Progressive Musical Union competed against the Georgia Minstrels, the African American blackface minstrelsy group that Hicks founded and managed. Now, five years later, Hicks was envisioning panoramas of antebellum Southern life that would provide New Englanders with "A True and Living Picture of the DAYS OF SLAVERY" and was incorporating Pauline Hopkins and her work into that endeavor. The productions that Hicks envisioned included presentations of "[t]he Planter's Home, the Mounted Overseers, the Slaves at Work in the Field, [and] the Bloodhounds."[13] This was to be no idle or short-lived venture, and these antebellum reality shows quickly became a fixture in Boston summer theaters. During the summer of 1882, audiences could seat themselves on the lawns of the Oakland Garden and participate in "Cotton Culture and Plantation Pastimes" by watching "Genuine Negroes Picking Real Cotton in a Vast Cottonfield."[14] The former slaves whom Hicks supposedly had hired for "De Ole Plantation" scenes were characterized in advertisements as "Blacks, Brunettes, and Pickanninnies" whose "Curious Choruses and Happy Dancing" would provide a "Vivid Illustration of Slavery Days."[15] Pauline Hopkins, the aspiring dramatist and descendant of freeborn pioneering Baptist ministers, faced this alarming and racially scripted world when she attempted to establish her professional career as a dramatist and actress.

The Oakland Garden engagement placed Pauline Hopkins in the spotlight alongside the celebrated Sam Lucas and the Hyers Sisters, Anna Madah and Emma Louise. She also stood to profit—financially and professionally—as a New England writer generating scripts for New England audiences. Yet this opportunity was clearly full of compromise. The reenactment scenes that Charles Hicks imposed on the work as Hopkins joined the production were antithetical to her political and writerly ethics. In the absence of extant documents that might shed light on the contract arranged by Hopkins and Hicks, it is not possible to determine to what degree she was aware of Hicks's plans. Certainly, the subject matter of *Slaves' Escape* initially seems complementary to the plantation scenes on the Garden's lawns, and, indeed, it was positioned as the theatrical draw for Hicks's 1880 summer slavery show. In this prominent billing, though, *Slaves' Escape* contributed to an innovative but dangerous re-presentation of American history. Hicks may have generated these scenes in response to Northern interest in the antebellum Southern system that sparked the War between the States. Yet his efforts also accommodated and promoted an apolitical voyeurism. To render slavery as a spectacular event encouraged a host of misreadings. The flawed interpretations of the system, though, were essentially legitimized by Hicks's emphasis on his participants. At best, slavery panoramas would emerge as a supplement or a postscript to the play's effectively conveyed critiques of enslavement, female oppression, emancipation, and minstrelsy. At worst, the play's message would be obliterated by the fanfare and purported "realism" of the staged scenes that followed.

The Oakland Garden insisted throughout the summer of 1880 that it could offer authentic presentations of early black life. Bills for the reenactments declared that Hicks had recruited "Real Negroes" to pick "Genuine Cotton" during these shows.[16] Hopkins's play was promoted that summer for its "remarkably realistic scenes" and presentation of a "perfect picture of life in the South in slavery days." It was at this juncture that Hopkins could hope that the content of her work would prevail, since *Slaves' Escape* was about fugitives rather than field hands, about sexual predation rather than "[h]appy [d]ancing," and about the value of freedom rather than the value of slaves. Her play incorporated popular Negro music and lively dialect that reinforced Hicks's entertainment agenda, but her work also was informed by historical realism that repudiated proslavery myths about African American identities. It was both ironic and fitting, then, that *Slaves' Escape* became the primary vehicle through which New Englanders would suspend the postbellum reality of Northern life and immerse themselves in the antebellum Southern past.

During the summer of 1880, the Oakland Garden management was determined to do more than reenact antebellum events. It promised to reanimate and sustain a Southern pre–Civil War slaveholding milieu. Hicks and his associates may have been pandering to a national nostalgia, one linked most explicitly to white longing for times past. However, if these reenactment performances were generated, however deliberately or not, by contemporary realities, then the Oakland Garden enterprise testifies to a discernible white public desire or nagging appetite to return once again to more than two and a half centuries of inflexible racial hierarchies, skewed social science, and economic greed. In this Northern context, reenactments also were linked at this time to a sobering public gesture of recognition, one that honored the courageous sacrifice of Northern Civil War soldiers. However, the commercialization of antebellum Southern bondage seemed to veer toward more insidious justifications of continued segregation, white privilege, and divisive racialized theories of intellectual and moral superiority.

The Oakland Garden stressed its ability to provide historical authenticity and to provide Northern audiences with access to Southern "reality." To offer such cultural truths, however, the Garden's stage had to be imagined as a neutral space, one impermeable to Northern historical reality and unchanged by an entirely different documented African American history. The suspension of postbellum time obscured the potentially emancipatory facts of Boston's racial past. That history included the accomplishments of its vocal and historically free black communities and demonstrations of interracial collaboration in an array of abolitionist and Civil War endeavors. At the Oakland Garden, white perspectives were privileged and rendered ahistorical, and its audiences were not challenged by a social conscience or the demonstrated needs and sobering racial realities of their post–Civil War age. The African American perspective was lost; the community and its experiences were emphatically depoliticized and dehistoricized, and the powerful African American abolitionist discourse and history of activism and resistance to slavery was muted.

The highly publicized participation of Pauline Hopkins, a freeborn, educated, Paul family descendant, reveals the degree to which the play's political integrity was under siege. Yet it is precisely that history that enabled Hopkins to resist the cultural co-optation of her work. One of the most compelling motivations for resistance lay in the accessible history of her devoted stepfather, William, a veteran of the U.S. Navy and descendant of enslaved Virginians. She decided that she would neither surrender her first nationally recognized work to the cultural marketplace nor corrupt her artistic agenda for fleeting popular trends. In collaboration with her parents and inspired by the cultural interventions deployed by the Hyers Sisters to great financial and professional success, Hopkins developed a strategy that would safeguard her professional integrity, political legacy, and personal respectability. The Hopkins family established the Hopkins Colored Troubadours, a professional African American arts group, and added sacred concerts to Oakland Garden performances of *Slaves' Escape*. As a founding member of this high arts company, Pauline Hopkins entered the gates of the Oakland Garden not as a vulnerable aspiring playwright, but as a sophisticated classical performer linked to an impressive Boston tradition of African American music and culture.

The Hopkins Colored Troubadours was a dynamic family enterprise and enterprising collective black arts group. Pauline used this organization to achieve a vital racial and cultural intervention. Her Beacon Hill apprenticeship under the watchful eye of Elijah Smith had impressed upon her the importance of politically responsible African American art. A foray into the capitalistic sphere of Boston theater required that she act quickly to defend the integrity of her political sensibilities and racial uplift work. That the Hopkins family was prepared to counter the market strategies of Charles Hicks was evident immediately from the dignified name that they chose for their choral group. The title, Hopkins Colored Troubadours, highlighted their respectability as a family, invoked Arthurian and courtly musical traditions, and placed in the foreground the racial identity of the performers. The family signaled its own commodification of blackness and its readiness to participate in the intense and overtly racialized performance world of nineteenth-century America. Indeed, the Oakland Garden program that Hopkins preserved in her personal scrapbook testifies to the demands of the post-Reconstruction entertainment marketplace. The largest capital letters in the advertisement were used for the phrases "Colored Troubadours" and "Escape from Slavery." The presentation, then, was consistent with Hicks's conviction that minstrelsy and black burlesque rather than a "Great Musical Drama" would draw audiences.

Slaves' Escape had evolved significantly since Hopkins had completed it for Sam Lucas and the Hyers Sisters in the spring of 1879. "The Great Musical Drama" now touted by the local Boston press included a sixty-person chorus. Specialty performances by other groups were scheduled for the intermissions between each of the acts. It was an exhilarating, albeit exhausting, experience for Pauline Hopkins, and one that was certainly gratifying. It was clear by the end of the very first show that she was part of an undeniable and highly respectable triumph. The *Boston Herald*'s "Local Intelligence" column, positioned prominently on the newspaper's front page, declared that "[t]he Hopkins Colored Troubadours are very successful in entertaining thousands of people every evening," and encouraged Bostonians to "[a]pply for seats early."[17] William Hopkins estimated that the Hopkins Colored Troubadours and their supporting cast members performed for 30,000 patrons during the weeklong engagement.[18] During her one-week stint at the Oakland Garden, Pauline was celebrated as the author of *Slaves' Escape* and recognized as a member of the Hopkins Colored Troubadours. The overwhelming appeal of the play and its cast prompted *Boston Herald* reporters covering the summer entertainment scene to say more about the dramatic phenomenon who had emerged at the Garden. At the end of the week, the paper noted that "[t]he author of 'Escaped from Slavery; or the Underground Railroad' the realistic and sensational play, which has been so successful at Oakland Garden during the past week is Miss Pauline E. Hopkins, a young colored lady of this city, who has written several other dramatic pieces of merit, and who has orders for a number more that will be produced the coming season."[19]

The Oakland Garden would have been one of the logical places to commission Pauline to write and produce the shows alluded to in the Boston press. Yet Pauline Hopkins and the Hopkins Colored Troubadours never again performed her plays at the Oakland Garden. This fact, which draws attention to the forum itself, also illuminates how Hopkins negotiated her earliest documented engagement with minstrelsy and the racialized appropriations of her creative works. The details about the Garden suggest that any relationship between the Hopkins family and Hicks would have had to preserve the integrity of Pauline's works and safeguard the professional reputations of the Hopkins family members. This indicates the family's resourcefulness and enterprising savoir faire. In addition to developing their own independent productions of the play in New England, they used Charles Hicks's marketing to their advantage. They contracted with Hicks to use the Garden for concerts and choral extravaganzas in which they would receive top billing. The family first tested its new plan on the last night of its one-week engagement in July 1880.

On 11 July 1880, the day after their last *Slaves' Escape* show at the Garden, the group appeared with the Hyers Sisters in a "Grand Sacred Jubilee Concert."[20] The Hopkins troupe, billed as the main attraction and listed before the Hyers Sisters in the publicity materials, was to be "[a]ssisted" by Sam Lucas and Fred Lyons, a musician known as "The Big Mouth Banjoist."[21] The scheduling of this concert, the first of several that the Hopkins Colored Troubadours would stage, suggests that the Hopkinses sought to leave the Oakland Garden and its audiences on their own terms and with a particular impression. They staged a "[s]acred" concert, and the event was in sharp contrast to the secular shows in which they had been participating all week long. The Hopkins Colored Troubadours used the concert to demonstrate their diverse talents and to dissociate themselves from the problematic creative contexts in which Hicks had placed them.

The Hopkins Colored Troubadours performed four times in Sacred Jubilee Concerts at the Oakland Garden between 11 July and 10 September, when the venue's summer season ended. William Hopkins spearheaded the family's efforts to capitalize on the success that Pauline, and by extension the Hopkins Colored Troubadours, had achieved. "Hopkins Colored Troubadours in their great Musical Comedy, 'The Escape From Slavery,' by Miss P. E. Hopkins, is no experiment, but an established success," he announced proudly in a 25 July 1880 *Herald* classified advertisement. "30,000 people witnessed and speak in praise of this performance at Oakland Garden during the week of July 5, 1880. This company embraces a jubilee chorus and a fine quartet for lyceum entertainments and Sunday concerts." He encouraged "[m]anagers, lecture associations, or private speculators wishing to secure this company for one or more nights, or for season of 1880–81," to contact him. William Hopkins, still working as a janitor in downtown Boston, listed his State Street work address in his contact information. It was a good marketing strategy move since it suggested not only that the company had formal offices but that it was conducting its business in an upscale space.

Although the Hopkins Colored Troubadours had good prospects for regular engagements, the group appears to have functioned as a supplement to

Spectacular Matters

everyday employment. William Hopkins kept his primary jobs. In 1880, these included co-ownership of a clothes cleaning business at 61½ Bromfield Street and work as a janitor at 15 State Street.[22] Just one year of performances improved the Hopkinses' financial situation so much that they could afford their own residence. In 1881, they moved to 164 Chambers Street, a Beacon Hill home that they would occupy for the next nine years. Their entrepreneurial arts initiatives had brought them precious domestic stability and were further strengthening Pauline's ties to her African American community.

William Hopkins's advertising strategies paid off quickly. The family began to succeed on its own terms, without outside local management or sponsorship by a nationally recognized management agency like the Redpath Bureau. Like the Hyers Sisters and Sam Lucas, who were calling New England home for the time being, the Hopkins family began to receive invitations to appear at other nearby New England summer spots. On Sunday, 1 August 1880, the anniversary of British abolition of slavery in its colonies, the Hopkins family and Sam Lucas appeared in two shows.[23] A few days later, Pauline and the Hopkins Colored Troubadours "entertain[ed] the good people at Manchester-by-the-Sea," a scenic coastal town not far from Boston.[24] A rare original copy of the concert program that twenty-one-year-old Hopkins included in her scrapbook sheds light on the group and its early evolution. For the Manchester concert at Town Hall, the Troubadours billed themselves as the Hopkins Colored Troubadour Quartette "under the direction of Mr. C. W. Payne."[25] Pauline, the soprano in the group, was the only Hopkins family member included on this occasion. Accompanying her were three other Bostonians: Cora Howard, contralto, Charles W. Payne, "the favorite [t]enor" and director, and W. H. Hogan, bass.[26] The group followed this performance with one at the Revere Beach Theatre. The Hopkins family sought out private and civic forums in which to perform once the 1880 summer season at the Oakland Garden officially ended. During the fall of 1880, William, Sarah, and Pauline concentrated on building their reputation as a choral group and developing a regional client base. Although it seems that they never again staged a play at the Oakland Garden, they did agree to appear there for several concerts during the next five years.

In 1881, well after the hype and splendor of the Oakland Garden experience had subsided, Pauline Hopkins reclaimed *Slaves' Escape* for her African American community. With her parents and the additional imprimatur of the Hopkins Colored Troubadour reputation for stately performances, the play enjoyed a profitable, ennobling renaissance. Hopkins and her performing company forged a connection with Massachusetts Union veterans groups, specifically with some of the thirteen state posts in the Grand Army of the Republic (GAR) organization. Formed in 1866, the GAR was a patriotic and "secret semi-military organization composed exclusively of honorably discharged soldiers and sailors who served in the Civil War," and men like William Hopkins prided themselves on membership.[27] The Hopkins family worked most closely with the John A. Andrew Post 15, a GAR branch named after the Massachusetts Civil War–era governor who endorsed the formation of the first all-black regiments in the state and in the Union. The Fifty-fourth Massachusetts Regiment, the nation's first African American regiment, the Fifty-fifth, and the Fifth Colored Calvary were organized during the governor's tenure.[28] The Hopkins Colored Troubadours were also recruited by groups west of Boston, such as the Ayer, Massachusetts, Post 48 and its female auxiliary, the Women's Relief Corps Post 49.

In late September 1880, the Hopkins Colored Troubadours reconvened the cast of *Slaves' Escape* and prepared to appear in the first of many performances to benefit GAR veterans' groups. At this moment of departure from the public entertainment sphere and return to autonomous community productions, Hopkins made yet another major revision to the play. She set aside the name *Slaves' Escape* and retitled the play *Flight for Freedom*. This new title referenced the political, historical, and social race politics that informed the play. The new title was implicitly deferential toward the GAR audiences that were predominantly made up of Union veterans and their families. As *Flight for Freedom*, the play downplayed the message conveyed by earlier titles that the slaves' emancipation was the result of their own agency. Keenly aware of the sacrifices that many African American Civil War veterans and their families had made, Hopkins offered them a renewed sense of justification for their military service and suffering. Even now that it was being staged beyond the frenetic world of Oakland Garden, the play was still "demonstrating" slavery for audiences of whites and of free and formerly enslaved blacks. The patriotic African American spheres in which the play was now being performed motivated Hopkins to reassert the historicity of her play. Her reclamation of the work reaffirmed the importance of long-denied freedom and featured a fundamental message that Southern slavery endangered African American families and that freedom was a complicated experience that never could be unyoked from that invasive peculiar institution. *Flight for Freedom* suggested that people of color could experience elements of a romanticized American dream. Yet the power of its closing scenes lay in its demonstration of the perpetual nightmare that formerly enslaved people experienced as their families, homes, and communities remained vulnerable to white aggression. Hopkins delivered a most compelling call to post–Civil War audiences when she demonstrated the extent to which psychological and emotional bondage could impede African American success in marriage, political life, and professional ventures. Yet here Hopkins made a subtle call for tolerance, fair social practice, and interracial cooperation and underscored the ongoing national recovery from slavery and the Civil War.

The relationship that the Hopkins family developed with Massachusetts veterans' groups made Pauline's work part of high patriotic tradition and honorable cultural discourse. Her decision to rename the play revealed a professional autonomy that also enabled her to reject problematic cultural expectations for performers of color. The new title, *Flight for Freedom*, also emphatically distanced Hopkins and her play from Charles Hicks and the Oakland Garden's negative marketing strategies. From 1880 through 1885, Pauline Hopkins and various configurations of the Hopkins Colored Troubadours performed *Flight for Freedom* for GAR groups. They used the work to support fund-raising efforts and on several occasions to support the John A. Andrew Post. On 29 September 1880, Hopkins staged her show at the Boston Music Hall "[i]n aid of the Charity Fund" of the John A. Andrew Post 15. The troupe's first 1881 appearance was at a post benefit, scheduled for 23 September at the Boston Music Hall. It was postponed when President Garfield died from injuries sustained during an attempted assassination some three months earlier. Announcements in several Boston papers proclaimed that local theaters were closed and that the Hopkins show was postponed, "On Account of the Death of Our Late Comrade, President Garfield."[29] The show was rescheduled for 29 September. The entire Hopkins family participated in this production: Pauline was Virginia; her stepfather, William, was the overseer, Jim; and her mother, Sarah, played the role of Mammy. Frank Nelson, a new cast member, starred as Peculiar Sam; George Deamus appeared as the elderly Uncle Caesar; and T. Scotron performed as the "educated colored Quaker." George Simonds played the role of Augustus; and S. Williams appeared as Juno, the sister of Peculiar Sam.[30] Carrie Alden, a musician whose affiliation with the Troubadours began in 1880, "was an efficient pianist."[31] An orchestra led by Frederick E. Lewis, a Bostonian who would later collaborate with the Hyers Sisters and Sam Lucas, "furnished music" for the occasion.[32]

Reporters from the *Boston Herald* and *Boston Globe* were on hand for the Hopkins Colored Troubadours' first post–Oakland Garden theater performance. The *Herald* noted that the show "was fairly well attended," that it was "thoroughly enjoyed by those present," and that "the characters were generally sustained in a praiseworthy manner."[33] In its only specific comment about the Troubadour singers, the writer noted that "the Hopkins quartet gave several vocal numbers in a very acceptable manner."[34] The *Globe* reporter offered a much more detailed and enthusiastic report. The "most enjoyable occasion" was fueled by the play, a "running narrative of the escape of a band of refugees in 'de days befo' de wah' interspersed with musical selections, both vocal and instrumental."[35] The production was energized by the "saucy and pert" antics of S. Williams in the part of Juno and the "jolly rollicking" behavior of George Simond.

The musical components of the play were particularly strong. Adding to the piano and orchestra accompaniments were individual presentations by individual actors. The "banjo specialities" of George Simonds were "thoroughly appreciated" and prompted the *Globe* reporter to write that Simonds's "fine execution and sympathetic interpretation deserve more than a passing notice." Hopkins appears to have borrowed a strategy from Hicks and the Oakland Garden version of the play. Where "speciality" musicians had appeared between each act in the *Slaves' Escape*, Hopkins inserted the Hopkins Colored Troubadours. The quartet, which included Pauline, Adah Hector, William S. Copeland, and an unidentified fourth singer, made "several appearances during the evening" and won "well-merited applause." In addition to her quartet appearances, Pauline, in the role of the lovelorn Virginia, delivered solos that were "fine and won her a deserved recall."[36]

It was highly fitting that Pauline's first dramatic success, the 1879 play originally entitled *Slaves' Escape; or, The Underground Railroad*, ended its two-year run in her home city of Boston and in the Music Hall, one of the state's most prestigious entertainment venues. In the process of realizing her "greatest desire," Hopkins demonstrated her creative genius and grappled with significant cultural and social issues that shaped the world in which she lived. Her forays into the public entertainment world required fortitude and ingenuity, and, as she made her way to the footlights, she successfully defended her family name, diversified the Paul family performance tradition, and consistently adapted her art so that it would best represent and advance her political commitment to racial uplift and advancement.

The Hopkins family continued to build their repertoire in the years following the Oakland Garden debut. On 29 July 1882, William, Sarah, and Pauline traveled out to "the most beautiful and interesting, as well as the most convenient to reach of all the Charming Sea-Side Resorts Now Becoming so popular along the Revere and Winthrop shore."[37] Sam Lucas had appeared here in 1880 as the long-suffering and noble slave Uncle Tom in a stage adaptation of Harriet Beecher Stowe's *Uncle Tom's Cabin*.[38] Advertisements for the Hopkins's show suggested that the Troubadours were in fact contributing to the ambience of the resort to which "thousands are flocking" and where "[t]housands more can be entertained." Publicity notices encouraged the public to "Come and enjoy the delightful SEA BREEZES, the ever Musical Ocean Surf, and the Hopkins Jubilee Singers. All Free! All Free!! All Free!!"[39] The venues in which Pauline and her family now appeared were free of the troubling racial agendas that they had encountered at Oakland Garden. They still were performing in places that offered respite to hardworking New Englanders but now were better able to control the degree to which they occupied that place as representatives of the race, as polished performers, and as a dynamic entrepreneurial American family.

The Hopkins Colored Troubadours lived up to the name of their group from 1881 through 1885. They traveled constantly and performed in diverse venues such as town halls in Malden, Massachusetts; enormous tent-covered spaces set up opposite the Providence, Rhode Island, train depot; and small Massachusetts cultural centers like the Arcanum Hall in Allston and Page's Hall in Ayer. On 17 March 1885, the Women's Relief Corp Number 49 based in Ayer, Massachusetts, booked the group for a GAR fund-raiser. On this occasion, Pauline Hopkins and her family, reconstituted as the Boston Colored Concert Company, appeared at Page's Hall in the small town west of Boston. The program for the event included colorful descriptions of the performers. Pauline was billed as the "Well-known and Cultivated Solo Soprano," and her mother, Sarah, was described as a "Specialty Artist." The advertisement promised that William Hopkins, "Guitar Player and Character Artist," would deliver "his very laughable and Instructive Sketch of Southern Life, entitled 'Uncle Pete's Cabin.'"[40]

The Hopkins family continued to prove itself as versatile self-promoters and adaptable performers. Cultural trends revealed that audiences were especially interested in African American groups that performed pieces most closely associated with black life and suffering. In response to this interest, they generated programs that mixed high sacred hymns, spirituals, and popular pieces. They went even further, though, and refashioned themselves to promote the racially specific repertoire that appealed to audiences of the day. By 1882, they were advertising as the "Hopkins' Colored Troubadours, Guitar Players and Southern Jubilee Singers."[41] One year later, when they performed in Providence, Rhode Island, in May 1883, they temporarily set aside their identity as the Hopkins Colored Troubadours and instead claimed to be the "Original Savannah Jubilee Singers."[42] In 1884 and 1885, they became the Hopkins Colored Vocalists and the Boston Colored Concert Company, respectively. These name changes suggested the performers' formal training rather than their expertise in authentic race songs. They also suggest the efforts of the Hopkins family to defend itself against those who would make pejorative

HOPKINS'
COLORED TROUBADOURS

Guitar Players and Southern Jubilee Singers,

Will give one of their Pleasing Entertainments, consisting of Jubilee Singing, the
sweetest ever heard,

UNDER THE AUSPICES OF THE ROYAL ARCANUM,

At ARCANUM HALL, ALLSTON,
Friday Evening, Nov. 24, 1882.

Miss PAULINE E. HOPKINS, Boston's Favorite Colored Soprano.
Miss ANNIE PARKS, Washington City Favorite Contralto.
Mr. JAMES FREEMAN, Tenor.
Mr. JAMES HENRY, Bass.
Assisted by Mr. GEORGE TOLLIVER, Camp Meeting Songster.
Mr. W. A. HOPKINS, Guitarist and Vocalist.
Miss CARRIE ALDEN, Pianist and Vocalist.

Despite the unfavorable weather the Hopkins Colored Troubadours had a very good audience
at the City Hall, last Sunday evening. The programme was an appropriate one, and excellent in
all respects, consisting of solos, duets, piano and guitar renderings, and chorus singing by the
entire company. The company has left behind a very good impression, and will be heartily welcomed whenever they choose to visit our city again.—*Malden Press*, Jan. 28, 1882.

BOSTON, AUGUST 19, 1882.
Having employed the Hopkins' Jubilee Singers several times, I take pleasure in recommending them to societies, especially temperance organizations. No meeting of this kind is complete
without good music. Miss Pauline E. Hopkins, the Soprano, has a sweet voice, and is a favorite
wherever she sings. JAMES H. ROBERTS.

PROGRAMME.

PART I.

1. OVERTURE, Piano, ... Miss Carrie Alden
2. " We are all hyar," .... Jubilee Singers
3. SONG AND CHORUS, "Sunny Home," .... Miss Hopkins and Quartette
4. " Blow Gabriel," .... Mr. Freeman and Jubilee Company
5. " I 'll be dar," .... Mr. Tolliver and Jubilee Company
6. SOLO, Selected, ... Miss Hopkins
7. " Yellow Rose of Texas," .... Mr. Freeman and Jubilee Company
8. DUET, " Whispering Hope," .... Misses Hopkins and Alden
9. " Moses," .... Mr. Tolliver and Company
10. " Water chilly and cold," .... Company

PART II.

1. " Live Humble," old fashioned Camp Meeting Hymn, Mr. Tolliver and Com'y
2. " Magnolia," .... Mr. Freeman
3. " Children I 'm gwine to shine," .... Mr. Freeman and Company
4. " Sweet Chiming Bells," .... Quartette
5. SPECIALTY, Exedus, ... Mr. Tolliver
6. " Ship of Zion," .... Mr. Tolliver and Company
The whole to conclude with a SKETCH OF SOUTHERN LIFE.

Tickets, - - - - - - 25 and 35 Cents.

Reserved Seats sold by any member of Society.   Doors open at 7.15.   Commence at 8 o'clock.

Program for the November 1882 concert by the Hopkins Colored
Troubadours at Arcanum Hall in Allston, Massachusetts, in
which Hopkins is listed as "Boston's Favorite Colored Soprano."
Hopkins pasted the program into her personal scrapbook.
Courtesy of Fisk University, Franklin Library Special Collections.

racist assumptions about its repertoire based on the family's race. Concert programs reveal, however, that although the family members adopted these formal titles, they still were incorporating Southern sketches, black folk songs, and Negro spirituals into their performances.

The Hopkinses were extremely well received during their five-year singing career. Pauline Hopkins's scrapbook contains precious copies of programs from some of her concerts. Some of these items shed light on how the Troubadours marketed themselves and attempted to embody middle-class mores such as temperance and piety. In November 1882, the singers appeared "Under the Auspices of the Royal Arcanum—At Arcanum Hall," in Allston, Massachusetts. The program for that occasion, a copy of which Hopkins pasted into her scrapbook, included a highly complimentary and personalized accolade on its cover. James A. Roberts, identified as a man who had "employed the . . . Jubilee Singers several times," made the following sincere declaration: "I take pleasure in recommending [the Troubadours] to societies, especially temperance organizations. . . . Miss Pauline E. Hopkins, the Soprano, has a sweet voice and is a favorite wherever she sings."[43] It was on the occasion of this performance in Allston, Massachusetts, that Pauline was identified as "Boston's Favorite Colored Soprano."[44] While the original source of her nickname is unclear, the phrase underscores her uncontested place at the forefront of Boston's African American musical circles.

The local New England press provides the most sustained set of details about Pauline Hopkins, her group, its concerts, and its reception. In January 1882, the Hopkins Colored Troubadours appeared at the Malden City Hall on a stormy Sunday evening. "Despite the unfavorable weather," wrote the reporter in attendance, the group "had a very good audience." The program, described as "appropriate" and "excellent in all respects," consisted of "solos, duets, piano and guitar renderings, and chorus singing by the entire company." Having "left behind a very good impression," the Troubadours earned an open invitation to return. They "will be heartily welcome whenever they choose to visit our city again," declared this enthusiastic new fan.[45]

As the 1880s progressed, the solid reputation of the Hopkins family enabled them to reach a broader New England audience. In late spring 1883, when they were billing themselves as the Original Savannah Jubilee Singers, they journeyed to Providence, Rhode Island. There, at the Park Garden, underneath a "Circus Tent" erected opposite the Providence Railway Depot, they delivered another grand sacred concert. Rare details about the concert, program, and performance roster included in a *Boston Herald* advertisement reveal that the concert, for which tickets were priced at fifteen cents, was divided into two parts, both of which included eight selections that included piano overtures, saxophone solos, and horn duets. In addition, an Australian band was scheduled to "render some choice selections" during the evening's performance. The Hopkinses took with them to Providence a fresh company. The only person with whom they had performed in the past was the pianist and vocalist Carrie Alden.[46] Pauline, the only female soloist that evening, performed a "Waltz Solo" entitled "Come Buy My Flowers." She was prominently featured in two arrangements. The first was with the all-male quartet in a rendition of "Chiming Bells," and the second, with Carrie Alden in an unnamed duet, closed the first act. The company alternated between spirituals and Negro folk songs like "Exodus," "Blow, Gabriel," "Jonah," "I'll Meet You Dar," and "Water Chilly and Cold," to songs like "Magnolia of Tennessee" that evoked a romanticized South. The saxophone solo of George Morris and his duet with a cornetist identified only as Tinsley rounded out the program. The show brought in enough patrons to warrant a second concert one week later on 3 June.[47]

The Hopkins family developed a signature musical style and reputation for refined concerts that appealed to socially conscious, middle-class Northern audiences. Although the majority of their engagements were organized by and for predominantly white audiences, the Hopkinses maintained strong ties to the African American performance world. Pauline's early commission to write for Lucas and the Hyers Sisters facilitated later collaborations with members of the diverse African American local and national musical community. The family's continued affiliations and concert appearances with the Hyers Sisters and Sam Lucas boosted their popularity. Yet even as they cultivated ties throughout and beyond New England, the Hopkins family continued to nurture its connection to the Beacon Hill community. The group's local partnerships within the neighborhood reinforced respectability at a time when class lines and social hierarchies in Boston's black community were reinforced, as families like the Trotters and Ruffins increasingly became members of the certified intellectual and social elite. Black Brahmin Boston families steadily gained social and political capital as their children became the earliest black graduates of Harvard College, Radcliffe College, and Wellesley College and their husbands achieved success as professionals and often were among the first black political appointees to respected, influential government posts.[48] Pauline Hopkins never would acquire an impressive academic affiliation or benefit from the powerful institutional imprimatur that accompanied an Ivy League degree. What she did have, however, was a history that marked her as a descendant of black pioneers; her Paul family legacy was the chief cultural and social credential that she could claim. In the years to come, she would use this history deliberately to legitimize her contributions to Boston's black community and to certify her own intellectual and activist potential.

Throughout the 1870s and 1880s, Pauline's connections to the historic black arts tradition of Beacon Hill reaffirmed her identity as a Paul family member and located her squarely within the community's historic and effective black artistic and political traditions. In late August 1884, the Hopkins Colored Troubadours shared the stage with members of the Lew family, descendants of one of the earliest black families in Massachusetts. As a Paul family descendant, Pauline shared an impressive Masonic history and Boston political tradition with this family. The Reverend Thomas Paul, her great-granduncle, had been a founding Prince Hall Mason member and served as the first chaplain of the organization. The Lews, whose family lived alongside the Pauls, also proudly shared that institutional heritage. From 1811 through 1816, Peter Lew, a Belknap Street neighbor of the Pauls, served as fourth grand master of that pioneering organization.[49]

In addition to the stately ancestral patriarchal history that Pauline shared with the Lews, she also could take great pride in the two families' shared history of leadership in African American arts. The Pauls and the Lews organized some of the earliest New England black musical performances, events that laid the foundation for the late nineteenth-century showmanship of their family descendants. Late in the summer of 1884, Pauline and other members of the Hopkins family and members of the Lew family were scheduled to perform in the "Best Concert of the Season" at Oakland Garden.[50] The Hopkinses appeared with four accomplished members of the Lew family, three of whom were brothers: forty-year-old bass James Adrastus; thirty-five-year-old tenor John Henry; thirty-year-old tenor and cornet soloist William Augustus; and nineteen-year-old pianist and accompanist William Edward, James's son.[51] Newspaper notes about the late August 1884 collaboration between these performing families reveal that William Hopkins functioned as the director of the Hopkins Colored Troubadours and that Pauline Hopkins, the "Soprano Soloist," and Sarah Hopkins, who sang contralto, were the only two women involved in the ten-person group.[52]

Like the Hyers Sisters, Pauline Hopkins and William Edward Lew shared the distinction of having family troupes established to showcase and advance their impressive individual talents. Pauline, who had been performing with her immediate family since 1880, was the more experienced former child performer of the two. In 1884, William and his family had just formed a male quartet, the Lew Ensemble, and affiliated themselves with the Sam Lucas Concert Company and also with the Redpath Lyceum Bureau, the organization that had worked closely with Lucas and the Hyers Sisters during the 1879 tour of *Peculiar Sam; or, The Underground Railroad*.[53] The Hopkinses' collaboration with the Lews translated into considerable social capital within Boston's African American community. This musical partnership reinforced the cultural leadership of the Hopkins family and its work as an effective proponent of racial uplift.

A continued association with Sam Lucas, who benefited from Pauline Hopkins's contributions to his career in the late 1870s, also continued to bear fruit for the Hopkins family. In 1883, Lucas invited Pauline to join him for an elaborate show in August at the Park Square Pavilion in Providence, Rhode Island, where she and the Hopkins Colored Troubadours had performed before enthusiastic audiences just two months earlier. Identified in the publicity materials as "Lena Hopkins," she appeared with Sam Lucas, "His Entire Company of Jubilee Singers," Walker's Quintet, and Carrie Alden, the pianist for the Hopkins Colored Troubadours and her duet partner.[54] The Hopkins family and Lucas seemed to enjoy a friendly professional rivalry, one that intensified when William, Sarah, and Pauline began marketing themselves as authentic race singers. Lucas, who had moved with ease from his minstrelsy career to leading roles in various slavery panoramas designed by Charles Hicks, was the chief proponent of "Grand" sacred concerts. These events, which he too may have developed as a counterpoint to the reenactments, became the primary vehicle through which Northern blacks profited, especially during the busy summer and early fall seasons. William Hopkins, recognizing the financial and cultural benefits of these concerts, worked tirelessly to capitalize on the public interest. In the summer of 1884, he preempted Lucas by securing a booking at Oakland Garden for the Hopkins Colored Troubadours at a "Mammoth Jubilee Festival." Accompanied by "10 Solo Artists [and] 20 Camp Meeting Shouters," Pauline, William, and Sarah Hopkins now were engaged in a new but still familiar enterprise to perform authentic black ritual and cultural practices. One week later, Oakland Garden opened its doors to Lucas for a "Mammoth Sacred Concert" with "his Jubilee Serenaders."[55] Although it was now under new management, Oakland Garden still invested in shows that featured black subjects in the most grandiose and exaggerated cultural contexts that it could muster.

The move into the entertainment world had significant implications for the class mobility of Pauline Hopkins, her potential for civic leadership in late nineteenth-century Boston, and her family's claims on middle-class respectability. As she and her parents became part of the African American entertainment circuit, they negotiated the demands of the racially proscribed entertainment world. They benefited from the expertise that William had acquired during his bachelor days in Boston and in performances in some of the city's earliest drama groups; and they also gained considerable insights through their collaborations with Elijah Smith Jr. Pauline's movement between amateur community ventures and public commercial events easily could have derailed her development as a public historian. She, however, had been groomed to capitalize on the political potential of the arts and to discern the ways in which African American performance could facilitate racial uplift and provide accessible critiques and interventions.

In 1880s Boston, Pauline Hopkins had to deal with a complicated cultural and racial legacy of womanhood in America. In her own family, the careers of foremothers like Susan Paul and more recent family relatives like Anna Pauline Pindell, the accomplished concert singer known as the Black Nightingale, revealed the complex intra- and interracial tensions associated with black womanhood as a performed and public identity. Hopkins's own evolution in the public sphere became increasingly bifurcated. As the complicated circumstances surrounding the 1875 *Pauline; or, The Belle of Saratoga* production and the 1880 *Slaves' Escape* shows in Boston suggest, Hopkins's theatrical ventures both reinforced and challenged middle- and upper-class codes of gentility. In the face of public trends that would compromise her vision, she produced scripts with high social relevance, dramas in which she articulated issues, controversies, and solutions relevant to her New England community and to her race. Her desire to become a playwright and to do so in public forums was fueled and legitimized by the phenomenal successes that American and European women performers had achieved by the 1880s. She could look to the careers and influence of popular actresses such as Charlotte Cushman and idealized white European singers like Jenny Lind and Adelina Patti, all of whom shaped nineteenth-century cultural expectations of female desirability, respectability, and virtue. Unfortunately, the cultural and professional status accorded to white women was not necessarily extended to female performers of color. Hopkins was not daunted by this exclusion, though, and as the rich history of her public performance life reveals, she focused her energies on crafting and protecting her work and identity as a gifted writer and honorable public historian.

Pauline Hopkins benefited from her wholly supportive family ties throughout her professional life. The creativity, innovation, and boldness of her immediate and extended families nurtured her as she began her performance career, provided her with invaluable marketable resources such as the Hopkins Colored Troubadours, and helped to secure creative opportunities that honored her cherished ancestry and personal goals. When she moved beyond the community forum in which she had first appeared, in 1875—the Progressive Musical Union—Hopkins stepped onto an increasingly volatile secular stage, a space controlled more often than not by white theater owners and influenced by the appetites of predominantly white audiences and profit margins rather than by motivations of racial uplift. She developed nuanced and overt performance strategies and learned how best to defend her own artistic visions, and these talents served her well as she cultivated herself as an outspoken novelist and journalist in the late 1890s and early 1900s. The power of Hopkins's theatrical innovation lies in its deft challenges of American racial stereotypes, its reappropriations of black agency, and its redirections of the white public gaze away from ahistorical social fantasies and toward sobering political realities of the day. The public intellectual who recognized the flaws of accommodationism, proclaimed the evils of lynching, and allied herself with the most fervent race men of her day in the early 1900s did not just suddenly appear on the twentieth-century American literary landscape. The performance history of Pauline Hopkins demonstrates decisively that *Contending Forces* and the work she began when she was forty years old grew out of the revisionist histories of American slavery and society that she began writing some two decades before when she was barely twenty-one years of age.

7

Literary Advocacy

Women's Work, Race Activism, and Lynching

They say the woman's era dawns at last,
When now this century draws its end,
Old notions of man's lordship, fading fast
Make way for women's aid to help to mend
Affairs that sorely need her presence bright.

ALICE MILLER
"To the Woman's Era Club,"
1895

We cannot cease from agitation while our wrongs
are the sport of those who know how to silence our
every complaint and plea for justice.

PAULINE HOPKINS
1905

 The vocal and politically astute black Boston community in which Pauline Hopkins came of age had long regarded the arts as a vital resource for community rejuvenation, education, and mobilization. Since the late 1700s when African Americans first began to constitute a community in New England, they had promoted gentility, honored cultural traditions, and celebrated artistic achievements often overlooked by the dominant culture. Hopkins's rich cultural education began in her early adolescent years, and it enabled her, during her fifteen-year performance career, to make substantive links between her creative work and local and national politics and race matters. Her ancestral history and contemporary experiences in and beyond the cohesive black Beacon Hill community prepared her to view racial oppression in the context of a larger and empowering narrative of black resistance. Indeed, she clearly regarded herself as encouraged, if not expected by her family and community, to regard her public life as an extension of an organized racial uplift campaign and as part of the historic Paul family tradition of fostering political awareness, race pride, and collective resistance within black Boston.

In the years following her collaborations with Sam Lucas and the Hyers Sisters and her affirming, well-received tours with the Hopkins Colored Troubadours, Pauline Hopkins continued to think seriously about whether she could pursue further a life in theater. The commissioned works she had produced for Lucas and the Hyers Sisters and her contributions to her family troupe had been well received and had provided good supplementary income for her family. Yet her mentors in the world of professional theater, like Fred Williams of the Boston Museum, counseled her against pursuing a life in the entertainment business. Williams, the respected and longtime manager of the Boston Museum on Tremont Street, had on at least one occasion "examined her writing," and Hopkins later credited him for the advice that ultimately led her to "direc[t] her attention finally to fiction in story form."[1] She gained much pleasure from the immediacy of the genre and clearly relished the process by which her prose metamorphosed into stimulating visual performances. She also savored the tangible connections to audiences, and she delighted in the generous community reactions to her work.

As she turned toward fiction, Pauline Hopkins seemed determined not to surrender her early literary passion for drama and to blend theatrical elements into her narrative work. Her acts of storytelling began as and long remained highly interactive enterprises. As a self-described "writer of fiction," she committed herself to producing politically and socially relevant critiques. Her stories addressed "the wrongs of her race" and were "so handled as to enlist the sympathy of all classes of citizens, in this way reaching those who never read history or biography."[2] Her prose narratives, like her plays, would present absorbing astute historical narratives of African American social and political emancipation in an unstable, unpredictable postslavery world.

As a fledgling novelist, Pauline Hopkins first turned her attention to American slavery and contemporary racial violence. Throughout the 1890s, Hopkins saw sharply contrasting realities for African Americans. She had firsthand experience of an evolving, confident African American political resistance movement in the North but witnessed only from afar the increasingly volatile and predatory racial conflicts in the South. Hopkins and fellow Bostonians routinely received shocking reports in the daily city papers about gruesome racial horrors of Southern mob rule and lynchings and widespread, almost routine instances of African American disenfranchisement, intimidation, and oppression. Hopkins was convinced that by exploring the social hysteria, political machinations, and racial prejudice at the heart of these two subjects, she could best analyze and assess her increasingly modern and violent postbellum world. She decided to use slavery—a system of global capitalistic enterprise that sanctioned ruthless dehumanization and relied on cultural disorientation—to explain the increasingly volatile racial upheaval and tension of the 1890s. Now in her thirties, this unmarried aspiring writer who lived at home in Cambridge with her parents, was increasingly convinced that America was still haunted, if not obsessed, by the politics and social agendas that produced and protected slavery, segregation, and lynch mobs. The first novel that Hopkins began to write was *Hagar's Daughter*, a work set primarily in Washington, D.C., and its environs. She returned to the themes that she had explored in *Slaves' Escape* one decade earlier and demonstrated how race and slavery were an inextricable part of all American family histories. In March 1891, Hopkins registered a copyright for the work, even though she only had three chapters completed.

March 1891 was also the month in which W. E. B. Du Bois, who had just earned a master's degree from Harvard College and was a member of the Wendell Phillips Club, one of the city's elite African American men's organizations, addressed Boston's Colored National League. The League was an outspoken political organization formed to protest the weakening of African American civil and political rights. Du Bois's provocative address, published in an early March 1891 issue of the *Boston Courant*, the social and political paper of which Josephine St. Pierre Ruffin was editor, was reprinted in full, taking up eighteen pages. Du Bois argued the connection between literacy and social reform, advocated an intensification of black cultural activities, and "foretold the inevitable decline of a race that lived an unexamined life."[3] While Du Bois's analysis was regarded by many as illuminating, Pauline Hopkins had already anticipated the links that Du Bois made between African American agency and literary production in spring 1891.

The calls for black literature coincided with Hopkins's response to financial pressures and her decision to step away from a full-fledged writing life. Hopkins was feeling that she was "obliged . . . to cease her literary labors for a time and try for something that would immediately help her financially."[4] She acquired clerical training and obtained full-time work as a stenographer in Massachusetts state government offices and the civil service during the early 1890s. In 1892, Hopkins joined the staff of two "well-known, wealthy, and influential Republicans": Alpheus Sanford and Henry Parkman, uncle of Massachusetts state representative and civil rights attorney William Homans Jr., whose legal advocacy and activism in the 1970s contributed to the state's high court decision in 1984 to abolish the death penalty.[5] That Hopkins secured a civil service position was significant, given the long-standing discrimination that kept the numbers of African Americans in government to a minimum. Even as Hopkins pursued full-time administrative and civil service work, though, she maintained a high public profile in African American political circles and affiliated with key community and race organizations. These memberships and her key contributions to them would enable her, when she next was able, to respond fully to the earnest calls for evocative historical black literature.

The first political event that prompted her to offer her literary talents to the struggle for African American rights occurred in Boston on Memorial Day, 30 May 1892, when the Robert A. Bell Post 134, an African American Grand Army of the Republic (GAR) chapter, hosted her as its guest of honor at its post–Memorial Day parade services.[6] Pauline's stepfather, William, was a member and future commander of the Robert A. Bell Post 134, and his fellow members included the beloved and courageous Bostonian and Masonic leader Lewis Hayden, survivors of the acclaimed Massachusetts Fifty-fourth Regiment, members of the all-black Fifty-fifth Regiment, and soldiers from the Massachusetts Fifth Cavalry.[7] Pauline delivered her speech after the veterans' parade and later, accompanied by the Women's Relief Corp Post 67 of which she was a member, decorated the graves of fallen soldiers on Rainsford Island, one of several islands in Boston Harbor.

In 1892, African American Memorial Day exercises, especially those in Boston, were linked to a growing unrest in the African American community. Lynchings and murderous attacks on African Americans, which had been rising steadily in the last two decades of the nineteenth century, peaked in 1892 at an all-time high of 226. The racially motivated aggression continued so relentlessly throughout the nation that it was rightly regarded as an epidemic of violence.[8] The physical threats of lynching were intensified by the psychological and intellectual violence that accompanied segregation and racial bias. These legitimized antisocial practices encouraged and indulged reprehensible behavior even as they mobilized a new postbellum and interracial abolitionist movement. Activists of the late nineteenth and early twentieth centuries confronted the evils and threats of rampant violence and the "primordial racism" that fueled mob violence.[9] Boston was home to one of the most visible contingents of race activists, and it was here that people of color rallied with their white supporters to protest institutional racism, to strategize about how best to counter mob violence and Southern lawlessness, and to engage in ingenious acts of civil disobedience.

Fueled by African American patriotism, chapters like the Robert A. Bell Post 134 used Memorial Day events to protest Southern lynching and to prepare a collective black urban response to Southern mob violence. Hopkins delivered her Memorial Day address at the Charles Street African Methodist Episcopal (AME) Church, a downtown Boston sanctuary with which she was allied through the 1890s and 1900s. The church was linked to major and relatively recent African American political initiatives; in 1889, Josephine St. Pierre Ruffin and colleagues had founded the National Association of Colored Women there, and in the 1890s, the Colored National League used the church as one of its primary meeting sites. When she spoke at the Charles Street AME Church, Hopkins became part of a celebrated roster of speakers who had held forth there, including the eminent Barbados-born lawyer, Reconstruction-era politician, and historian D. Augustus Straker, whose memorable 1885 lecture at the church was sponsored by the William Lloyd Garrison Society and presided over by the influential Boston lawyer George Ruffin.[10] Hopkins championed the African American patriots who, since the late 1700s, had fought and died for the freedom of a country that still denied them equality and civil liberties. Her address, characterized as "a great success," served as a powerful precursor to a major Colored National League meeting that garnered significant press attention.[11] Shortly after Hopkins spoke that day, Colored National League officers took the stage and convened one of the two protest meetings that merited coverage in the Boston Globe. June 1892 articles about the gatherings at the Charles Street AME Church and the Ebenezer Baptist Church began with terse headline captions: "Colored Men Gather. They Resent the Wrongs in the Southern States. Two Big Meetings Held in Boston, with Prominent Speakers. Outrages Denounced and Peaceful Methods Urged in Resolutions."[12] According to the article, Boston African Americans were part of a national protest. "All over this country yesterday," wrote the unidentified reporter, "colored men and women assembled to implore divine aid against the continued outrages on the colored people of the South, hoping through this agency that the sentiment of the American people would be aroused to a point where it will be demanded that the colored people will be given their just right, which the Constitution of the United States guarantees them."[13] The Memorial Day services of 1892 in the Ebenezer Baptist Church and Charles Street AME Church, two of the city's leading black churches, produced declarations of righteous indignation and resolutions that would be sent on to Congress. The Colored National League, led by Edwin Garrison Walker, decided to enact a day of fasting and prayer before "appeal[ing] to their white brethren all over the land to put an end to the cruel hanging and other tortures inflicted upon the colored race in the South." The meeting closed after the assembly adopted "[r]esolutions praying Congress to pass some law that would guarantee protection to all American citizens."[14] The passionate declarations would fall on deaf ears in Washington, D.C., as President Harrison and his successor Grover Cleveland refused to condemn lynching or the continued economic and political abuses of African Americans in the South.

By 1895, the year in which African American women converged on Boston in July for the First Congress of Colored Women of the United States, Hopkins had moved on from her staff position with Alpheus Sanford and Henry Parkman, passed the civil service exam, and become a stenographer in the census division of the Massachusetts Bureau of Statistics of Labor, a pioneering government agency, then headed by Horace Wadlin.[15] Her employment there indicates that Hopkins performed extremely well on the civil service exam and that she had good political connections with her previous employers, since such positions often required endorsement by prominent politicians such as Sanford and Parkman.[16] Since its establishment in 1869, when it became the first such office to be established in the United States, the Bureau had been charged by the state legislature to "collect, assort, systematize and present in annual reports to the legislature, statistical details relating to all departments of labor in the Commonwealth, especially in its relations to the commercial, industrial, social, educational and sanitary condition of the laboring classes, and to the permanent prosperity of the productive industry of the Commonwealth."[17] Hopkins became part of an organization that Carroll Davidson Wright, its second and most celebrated chief, described as an "office [that] makes its initial work that of pure fact" and whose "works must be classed among educational efforts, and by *judicious investigations* and the *fearless publication* of the *results* thereof, it may and should enable the people to more clearly and more fully comprehend many of the problems which now vex them."[18] At the Bureau, Hopkins was a member of the large clerical staff in this division and worked for four years in the branch of this office as it processed the data gathered from Decennial Census returns for 1895 that would determine state legislative representation and provide details about state populations, economic stability, domestic arrangements, social service needs, and education. Hopkins was contributing to the massive editing and tabulation efforts required to publish the information that the more than 1,000 enumerators, field agents, and inspectors began gathering in April 1895.[19]

The employment that Hopkins had during her decadelong hiatus from public creative writing would provide a solid foundation for the literary race work that she would resume in the late 1890s. Hopkins's work for white Republicans not only provided her with the opportunities to see firsthand the workings of state government, but it also gave her political credibility within the city's vibrant black political milieu. Even though she was a stenographer, she was part of the political system and could use her affiliations with Sanford and Parkman, and later her employment with the Bureau of Statistics for Labor, as additional political credentials, ones that would strengthen her own role in the Republican majority that reigned at this point in Boston's West End. Indeed, Pauline became an active member of the city's African American political community during a "period of political supremacy," one that constituted a formidable Republican majority for twenty years, lasting from the 1870s to the 1890s, before redistricting diminished its power.[20] During this period, the African American constituency regularly elected members of its own Republican community to the city council and to the state legislature.[21]

Throughout and following her time of civil service employment, Hopkins was extremely active in the Colored National League and its affiliated circles. She also enjoyed rich kinship ties in this vibrant political culture, since members of her extended family, like John M. Burrell, a Boston attorney who married into Elijah Smith Jr.'s family, thus becoming Hopkins's cousin by marriage, also were intimately involved in race politics and city organizations. The Colored National League, one of the city's most active civil rights organizations, was established in 1876 in response to the lack of enforcement of the Fourteenth and Fifteenth Amendments to the Constitution. As the last of what were considered to be the Reconstruction Amendments, these acts guaranteed citizenship to all who were born in the United States and the right of citizens to vote, respectively.[22] The membership of the Colored National League was drawn from across black social lines, and it enjoyed strong community support. The city's African American churches, especially the Charles Street AME Church, located downtown on Charles and Mt. Vernon Streets, regularly opened their sanctuaries to meetings. The Colored National League diligently marked the anniversaries that had particular importance to people of color and coordinated bold protests of the events and policies that oppressed them. Elijah Smith Jr., Pauline's cousin and early arts mentor, had close ties to the group, and it was he who regularly provided the celebratory odes and poetical tributes that the League used on formal occasions. These included meetings in which members and their supporters celebrated the ratification of the Thirteenth, Fourteenth, and Fifteenth Amendments and marked the birth or passing of leading antislavery heroes like William Lloyd Garrison and Wendell Phillips.

During the era of Reconstruction, the Colored National League was Boston's most daring, outspoken, and unapologetic African American political collective. It predated other African American organizations such as the Afro-American League and the National Afro-American Council founded in 1890 by T. Thomas Fortune and the National Association for the Advancement of Colored People (NAACP), founded in 1909. The Colored National League was an imposing example of black political institutions, as well as an extension of the collective political imperative that black Bostonians had nurtured in their New England community since the early 1800s. It achieved national prominence and provided a forum for well-known black activists like Ida B. Wells-Barnett, the intrepid antilynching activist and journalist, and Edwin Garrison Walker, the only surviving son of the Boston abolitionist David Walker, who addressed its membership on various occasions. This group, which existed for nearly twenty-five years before it disbanded in 1900, had an undeniable influence on Pauline Hopkins's political and literary sensibilities.

The organization's membership roll was a register of Boston's African American political, intellectual, and social elite. In addition to Walker, the all-male leadership of the Colored National League included William Dupree, a Union army veteran and GAR leader and Hopkins's future colleague and president of the *Colored American Magazine*'s board of directors. Dupree, the superintendent of the second largest postal station in Boston, had come of age during the antebellum era and performed courageously as a member of the Fifty-fifth Massachusetts Regiment, the second African American Civil War regiment organized in the state.[23] William Monroe Trotter, a relative of Dupree, was also an emerging political force associated with the group and a dynamic Harvard magna cum laude graduate. He outcourted fellow Harvard student W. E. B. Du Bois and won the heart of Geraldine Pindell, a descendant of the family that fought Boston school segregation and into which Annie Pauline Allen, one of Pauline Hopkins's aunts, married. Shortly after graduating, Trotter began to develop his own distinctive brand of lively, effective, and frequently controversial methods of political protest in local African American political circles. Throughout the 1880s and 1890s, Walker, Dupree, and Trotter collaborated with other highly respected African American civic leaders and accomplished professionals in post-Reconstruction America. All of them eagerly positioned themselves at the forefront of Boston's campaign for black civil rights. They recognized their historic responsibility to continue documenting the plight of Southern blacks and committed themselves to doing so in the most enterprising, effective manner possible.

The air of middle- and upper-class gentility that these local African American leaders achieved did not diminish their capacity for strident protest. Like Pauline Hopkins, Edward Garrison Walker used his rich and incontrovertible legacy of Boston black activism to fuel his postbellum work for black civil rights. His father, David Walker, whose sudden death was rumored to be the work of ruthless proslavery advocates intent on silencing him, was the author of the incendiary 1829 "Walker's Appeal." Edward Walker, whose middle name of Garrison reflected the great respect that his parents had for the *Liberator* editor, inherited his father's courage and unwavering belief that African Americans had the power to emancipate themselves and the right to self-determination. Walker served as president of the Colored Citizens Club, a forerunner of the Colored National League, and he used his status as Boston's "favorite colored attorney"[24] to draw public attention to the Colored National League and its commitment to obtaining the civil rights of African Americans.

The consistently male leadership of the Colored National League leadership kept up metaphorical and increasingly literal calls to arms. Such mandates, although powerful and widely supported, made it a challenge for the League's female members to make full contributions to the League mission. Women members of the League included unmarried working women like Hopkins, genteel but enterprising women such as Lizzie Dupree, wife of Colonel William Dupree, the future editor of *Colored American Magazine* and Colored National League member, and Geraldine Pindell Trotter, devoted wife and professional partner of William Monroe Trotter, *Guardian* editor and vociferous opponent of Booker T. Washington. The separate spheres of this era in some ways were reminiscent of the male-dominated abolitionist forums of the 1830s and 1840s. Ardent abolitionists like Susan Paul, Hopkins's literary and ancestral foremother, and Lydia Maria Child, Paul's contemporary and Boston Female Anti-Slavery Society colleague, were vital to the activist mission, but because of their sex and prevailing cultural codes of the day, they occupied the periphery of predominantly male associations such as the New England Anti-Slavery Society. Female political auxiliaries like the Boston Female Anti-Slavery Society or the postbellum Women's Relief Corp with which Hopkins was affiliated granted women some political autonomy and public visibility. However, these women's groups also symbolized the degree to which women's public behavior continued to be mediated and constrained by social expectations of women's gentility and piety and sanctioned expressions of militaristic masculine prerogatives and rhetoric.

Hopkins also had to negotiate the particular status politics within the women's uplift and social circles. Her status as a single woman was one factor. Many of the leaders, Mary Church Terrell, Josephine St. Pierre Ruffin, and Margaret Murray Washington, were wives or widows of men whose professions and accomplishments helped to secure class privileges and higher social status for their families. In the 1890s, Hopkins was a woman in her thirties with no current marriage prospects. But she did not see herself as a spinster. In 1906, several years later, her explanation about property-related matters and the navy pension of her stepfather, William, culminated in her admission that she had included her mother's name on the mortgage papers for their Cambridge home "in case I contracted a marriage at any time."[25] That she was a property owner signaled that Hopkins was a resourceful woman with strong roots in her New England community, an individual for whom the cause of racial uplift would be an extension of the ethos that informed her own primary family relationships and that had shaped her own impressive New England genealogy.

On the eve of the twentieth century, Hopkins was nearing a personal and professional crossroads. The increasingly deliberate African American feminist advance on the public sphere would now inform her consideration of how best to sustain a purposeful, engaged life on the public stage. Her return to the public stage coincided with an increasingly visible presence of Boston's African American women's clubs and national women's philanthropic organizations in the 1890s. This was prompted by several factors. One related to the desire on the part of African American women to assert their influence as accomplished, visionary feminists. Another grew out of their collective rejection of racial slander. One of the most dramatic and far-reaching examples of this occurred in 1895, when Ruffin and others promptly sprang into action after they received word of a scandalous letter that impugned the honor of African American women. Its author, James W. Jacks, was a Southern newspaper editor and president of the Missouri Press Association. Jacks sent his controversial missive to Florence Balgarnie, a British antilynching activist, in order to smear the reputation and thwart the efforts of Ida B. Wells-Barnett. In the June 1895 issue of *The Woman's Era*, Ruffin purposefully addressed the matter. In a column entitled "A Charge to Be Refuted," she noted that "the letter of Mr. Jacks to Miss Balgarnie is a denouncement of the morality of colored women of America . . . and also a criticism of the peculiar ideas of virtue and morality held by everybody but the people of the south and west." Jacks, she declared, was part of a "host of traducers who are so free in bringing the charge of immorality upon all colored women." After acknowledging Balgarnie's "expression of sympathy and indignation," Ruffin explained that "[a]s the charges in this letter are so sweeping and so base, we [the editors] have decided not to act hastily upon it, but to be very careful in our method of bringing it to the public." "Our line of action has already begun," she assured her readers, noting that "the letter will be printed and forwarded to leading men and women and heads of educational institutions, particular[ly] in the south, people of reputation and standing, whose words carry weight; and in the next issue it is hoped to print the charge, with these signed replies." The "matter is a solemn one," she declared, "and one upon which we shall call all our women all over the country to act."[26] Victoria Earle Matthews, editor of the column that dealt with women's clubs in New York state, agreed whole-heartedly and used her July 1895 report in *The Woman's Era* to articulate her outrage against Jacks and her support for Ruffin's emerging plans. Matthews regarded Jacks's "attack on womankind" as "so noisome and foul." She also maintained vigorously that the letter was more of a reflection on Jacks than it was on women of color. "No man capable of reverencing his mother, or protecting the unsullied fame of any woman would have written or forwarded such a communication to any woman," she asserted. Matthews also noted that Jacks was to be castigated for sending the note to Balgarnie, "one whose life work entitles her to the respect of the least of progressive and wholesome minds, regardless of sex, wherever principle and unselfish efforts to uplift struggling humanity exists."[27] In addition, she suggested that the letter was "merciless in marking to the world the standard of man that the Missouri State Press Club has seen fit to elect as its presiding officer." "He has not only slan-dered the women of negro extraction," Matthews insisted, "but the mothers of American morality and virtue."

Ruffin, Matthews, and others regarded the Jacks letter as an opportunity for unprecedented collective action by African American women. Ruffin urged her readers to consider "if it be not time for us to stand before the world and declare ourselves and our principles."[28] Matthews outlined the practical realities and important opportunities afforded by the outrageous Jacks letter. She suggested first that "it is not to be expected that any good effect can be made by our utterances on the class that the defamer represents." She then was swift to insist that "courageous women should speak through *The Woman's Era* that the world may feel the power of the chaste mentality of the true negro woman."[29] Florence Balgarnie, writing later that summer from London to Florida Ruffin Ridley, co-editor with her mother, Josephine Ruffin, of the *Woman's Era*, requested that Ridley "convey my expressions of sympathy to your friends" at the upcoming convention. "[M]ake it quite clear to them," she requested, "that in sending you the letter I was convinced of its utter and dastardly falsehood from the first. You have a hard fight before you in America, but never fear, right must triumph, and with God on your side you are in a majority."[30]

The Boston clubs, with Ruffin at the helm, made plans to convene an unprecedented gathering of black women in Boston. It was an opportunity, as Matthews saw it, for the "brightest of our women" to "come together" and would "afford an opportunity not only of educating public opinion as to our status as women, but will be a test of the broadmindedness and zeal in the matter of mutual advancement existing between the women of the races."[31] These events prompted participants and observers alike to recall that in Boston the history of black women's activism dated back to the early 1800s. At the forefront of that inspiring history were Hopkins's maternal ancestors like Susan Paul and pioneering social activists like Maria Stewart and Nancy Prince. Black educational and social advancement in the city provided new opportunities for black women's outreach and mobilization. New England women of color had a reputation of organizing impressive forums and ambitious networks. When Hopkins began work in the Parkman and Sanford offices in 1895, she did so as the women of color in her community marshaled forces to defend the honor of African American women all over the nation.

For four days, from 29 July through 1 August 1895, African American women converged on Boston for the First National Conference of the Colored Women of America.[32] They responded to the generous and urgent call that Josephine St. Pierre Ruffin, president of Boston's leading women's club, issued on behalf of her group: "We, the women of the Woman's Era Club of Boston[,] send forth a call to our sisters all over the country, members of all clubs, societies, associations, or circles,"[33] and to "all colored women of America, members of any society or not."[34] The convention was held at Boston's Berkeley Hall and, in its extra day of sessions, at the Charles Street AME Church, the site that the Colored National League used frequently for its antilynching rallies. Harriet Smith, Hopkins's cousin and a daughter of Elijah Smith Jr. and his wife, Eliza Riley Smith, was elected to serve as one of the two Secretaries of Convention.[35]

Led by Josephine St. Pierre Ruffin, black women rallied to protest the ongoing defamation of the character of African American women. Delegates from some fifty-three clubs and nine states participated in the historic meeting. The days were filled with devotional exercises, formal remarks, songs, numerous debates, calls for resolutions, and formation of committees. One of the first orders of business was to address the Jacks letter, and the group did so in private. According to the minutes that Harriet Smith and her cosecretary L. C. Carter produced, shortly after 10 AM on Tuesday, 30 July, the first full day of the convention, "[t]he Convention went into secret session and discussed Jack[s]'s letter." Following a series of resolutions and "discussions by all the women," the group agreed on "a set of resolutions by Mrs. Mathews

Josephine St. Pierre Ruffin, an influential Bostonian, editor
of the *Woman's Era*, and women's club colleague of Hopkins.
*Courtesy of Manuscripts, Archives and Rare Books Division,
Schomburg Center for Research in Black Culture, The New York
Public Library, Astor, Lenox and Tilden Foundations.*

which were adopted by the Convention." Finally, the group agreed to produce
"[l]eaflets on Jack[s]'s letter to be sent to England."[36]

The *Boston Herald*, one of the three city papers that provided detailed coverage of the gathering, offered frank praise of the historic proceedings. On 30 July, the *Herald* devoted a full column to the events. The reporter, who began the article with the somber headline "Colored Women in Council," seemed barely able to contain his admiration or surprise. "The convention was planned and arranged for in six weeks," he noted, "and the result shows that these colored women are of the stamp that know how to pack a valise and read a paper."[37] The capable women described in the article "represent[ed] the brains of the colored nation." These "lawyers, physicians, poetesses, authors, journalists, editors of magazines, publishers, and many women notable as society leaders among the colored people of the country" had achieved impressive professional and social status.[38] Their accomplishments "argue[d] much for the brains of the women," and thus Boston was "honored in having held within its limits the first convention of colored women of America. To say the intellectual centre of the country, the 'Hub' of the universe, the birthplace of freedom, is honored with such a gathering as that which filled Berkeley Hall yesterday is saying a good deal, but such it is," mused the *Herald* reporter.[39]

Pauline Hopkins and fellow members of the newly established Boston New Era Club were the official hostesses of the monumental gathering. It was highly fortuitous for Hopkins to have the world of African American women literally on her doorstep. In the midst of heated debates about lynching, she could immerse herself fully and participate in debates that highlighted social behaviors that produced mob violence. What was especially noteworthy about these circumstances in the summer of 1895, however, was the company in which Pauline Hopkins was discussing lynching, developing domestic strategies for the nation and the home, honing racial rhetoric, and strategizing about how best to groom African American women to enact visible social reforms. The list of speakers scheduled to address the 1895 conference read like a political and uplift who's who of the day. It included Anna Julia Cooper, stately intellectual and author of the incisive 1892 volume *A Voice from the South*; Victoria Earle Matthews, the inspiring writer and enterprising social welfare reform activist; Mary Church Terrell, educator and first president of the future National Association of Colored Women; Professor and Mrs. Booker T. Washington, the increasingly powerful couple at the helm of Tuskegee Institute; Ida B. Wells-Barnett, tireless antilynching and suffrage crusader; William Lloyd Garrison, son of the fearless abolitionist and *Liberator* editor William Lloyd Garrison Sr.; the Reverend Alexander Crummell, the emigrationist; T. Thomas Fortune, regarded as "the most prominent colored journalist in the country" and one of Booker T. Washington's key allies; and Anna Sprague, daughter of Frederick Douglass, the august abolitionist orator who had passed away just five months earlier.[40]

The founding of the National Association of Colored Women in 1896 afforded women like Pauline Hopkins and her local club leader, Josephine St. Pierre Ruffin, a respectable platform from which to enact meaningful social reform for black women and for the race in general. Women in the movement focused on improving African American homes and schools by raising women's awareness about domestic and family matters. Hopkins, the turn-of-the-century clubwoman, had thrived when she was in the public eye during her stage career in the 1870s and 1880s. However, her family history and arts activism could have meant that she would chafe against the conventions of upper-class black gentility and resist messages that true black womanhood was best defined within the home and not in the public arena of black political agitation.

Racial uplift, as Pauline Hopkins understood it, was an inherently public and political undertaking that carried no guarantee of positive public reception or of intraracial support. She certainly would have been aware of Boston's response to Maria Stewart, who in the 1830s became the first woman to speak publicly before an audience of men and women. Stewart, who had married in the African Baptist Church at the time that Hopkins's great-granduncle Thomas Paul presided there as minister, also was an influential model for Susan Paul, the young teacher to whom she essentially passed her mantle when, weary of the mixed responses to her forthright critiques of African American men, home life, and intellectual priorities, she decided to relocate to New York City. Hopkins also could look to the more recent career of Ida B. Wells-Barnett, whose husband had strong ties to the Colored National League. Wells-Barnett's unflappable and tireless campaign for social justice, coupled with her professional development as a journalist and sociologist, provided Hopkins with models of how best to bring a black feminist agenda to bear on thorny social and political issues. In addition, Hopkins could learn much from Frances Harper, the antislavery lecturer who authored the 1892 novel, *Iola Leroy; or, The Shadows Uplifted*. Harper's text, which during Hopkins's lifetime reigned as the best-known novel published by an African American woman, was impressive as literature, advanced African American literary and historical imperatives, and furthered black political agendas of the day. Throughout the 1890s, Hopkins found herself in the middle of a Northern maelstrom, one in which her postbellum community was mobilizing with impressive vigor. The nature of Boston's antilynching campaign and increasingly militant blueprints for resistance recalled the upheaval of the 1830s that her own Paul family ancestors had witnessed firsthand and survived. During those years, Bostonians, including Hopkins's own distant cousin Susan Paul, found themselves fending off the "mob of Boston gentlemen" that metamorphosed into a New England lynch mob desperate for a victim and willing to murder William Lloyd Garrison for advocating African American rights and immediate abolition.

Yet it appears to have been Victoria Earle Matthews who made the deepest impression on Pauline Hopkins at this historic convention. Matthews's compelling message, delivered in a major speech at the 1895 Boston women's convention, provided Hopkins with an invaluable femino-centric blueprint for the writing she increasingly felt called to do. In addition, Matthews's professional trajectory modeled for Hopkins, who was only two years older than Matthews, the next career path that she herself might take. Certainly Hopkins must have been well aware of Matthews, the Georgia-born woman and long-time New York City resident hailed as "the most popular woman journalist among her peers," before she appeared in Berkeley Hall.[41] By the time that she arrived in Boston for the 1895 conference, Matthews, who would found the White Rose mission for African American women, had established herself as a well-known journalist whose articles had appeared in African American– and white-owned newspapers such as the *New York Times*, the *Brooklyn Eagle*, the *Washington Bee*, the *Richmond Planet*, and the *Cleveland Gazette*.

At eight o'clock on Tuesday evening, 30 July 1895, Victoria Earle Matthews took her place at the podium in Berkeley Hall and delivered "a stunning address."[42] Entitled "The Value of Race Literature," the lecture essentially outlined the primary tenets that Pauline Hopkins quickly adopted once she began her professional writing career. First, Matthews defined the nature and objectives of race literature, the genre that she deemed essential to African American literary and social formation. As a "general collection of what has been written by the men and women of [the] Race: History, Biographies, Scientific Treatises, Sermons, Addresses, Novels, Poems, Books of Travel, miscellaneous essays, and the contributions to magazines and newspapers," race literature encompassed all genres and validated all writerly efforts by African Americans.[43] Matthews hastened to articulate the inextricable link between racial oppression and what she deemed an expansive, multifaceted emancipatory canon. According to Matthews, "oppressive legislation, aided by grossly inhuman customs, successfully retarded all general efforts toward improvement, [and] the race suffered physically and mentally under a great wrong, the prejudice of color." In the face of unabating social hostilities, Matthews deemed race literature "a necessity," as a body of work required "to dissipate the odium conjured up by the term 'colored.'"[44] Who better to generate this illuminating canon, asked Matthews, than women: "Woman's part in race literature as in race building is the most important part. When living up to her highest development, woman has done much to make lasting history by her stimulating influence, and there can be no greater responsibility than that."[45]

Pauline Hopkins, a single woman without children, could not claim the ennobling sociopolitical capital that empowered black mothers and celebrated race-conscious wives in the intensely matri-focal arena of the African American club movement. On this night of summer rain showers, however, she could embrace another crucial women's role that Matthews espoused. According to Matthews, the works that Hopkins, the articulate and accomplished arts activist, aspired to produce were "essential for the expression of the inner lives of a suppressed people, just as English or French literature deals with the customs and life of these nations," and were destined to "occupy a prominent place, not only in race, but in universal literature."[46] Four years later, Hopkins's 1899 preface to *Contending Forces* would echo Matthews's 1895 sentiments and acknowledge directly the essence of Matthews's charge. Hopkins's illuminating authorial statement in the novel begins with the following announcement: "In giving this little romance expression, I am not actuated by a desire for notoriety or for profit, but to do all that I can in an humble way to raise the stigma of degradation from my race."[47] Hopkins used the very first lines of her first published book to "dissipate" what Matthews lamented as "the odium conjured up by the term 'colored,'" a word she thought was "not originally perhaps designed to humiliate, but [was] unfortunately still used to express not only an inferior order, but to accentuate and call unfavorable attention to the most ineradicable difference between the race[s]."[48]

Victoria Earle Matthews's persuasive 1895 rhetoric reemerges even more deliberately in subsequent portions of Hopkins's preface. Hopkins wrote, "Fiction is of great value to any people as a preserve of manners and customs—religious, political and social. It is a record of growth and development from generation to generation. *No one will do this for us; we must ourselves develop the men and women who will faithfully portray the inmost thoughts and feelings of the Negro with all the fire and romance which lie dormant in our history*, and, as yet, unrecognized by writers of the Anglo-Saxon race."[49] Matthews's comment about the "inner lives of a suppressed people" reappears in Hopkins's reference to "the inmost thoughts and feelings of the Negro." These frequently quoted lines from *Contending Forces* were penned by Pauline Hopkins at a time when she was part of a self-appointed and highly orchestrated chorus of African American women who were determined to upbuild the race.

Pauline Hopkins left the Massachusetts Bureau of Statistics in 1899. She took a brave step when she left her stable civil service job and began what she imagined would be an autonomous and rewarding professional life as a writer. Hopkins was privileged to be able to make this move. Although a "damn'd mob" of well-published and popular "scribbling women" exasperated Nathaniel Hawthorne in the mid-nineteenth century, the notion of a professional black woman writer, one able to support herself by her craft, was still in its infancy in the 1890s. At this time, African American writers in general, and black women writers in particular, were only beginning to write themselves into the American literary canon. Like most white women authors, women writers of color juggled domestic and work responsibilities and negotiated significant cultural constraints while they wrote.

When Pauline Hopkins dedicated herself to the profession of authorship, she became part of a mighty and empowered tide of black women writer activists and evangelists. She joined the ranks—disparate but functional and ambitious, nonetheless—of women like Amelia E. Johnson, Emma Dunham Kelley-Hawkins, Frances Harper, and Alice Dunbar-Nelson. She was part of an impassioned cohort of literary activists, women who blended social and racial uplift missions into their writing and used the pen to highlight injustices, catalyze reform movements, and educate their readers about African American history, culture, and politics.[50] Hopkins's turn to authorship coincided with her heightened public and political activity. She maintained a high profile in the Women's Relief Corp, the female auxiliary of the GAR veterans' organization, and participated regularly in events organized by African American veterans. She was also committed to club work and was kept busy with responsibilities relating to her membership in the Women's Auxiliary of the Boston Young Men's Congregational Club and in the Woman's Era Club, one of the nation's most influential African American women's clubs.

Although the number of published postbellum African American novels by women was small, Hopkins did have inspiring examples of accomplished writers to consider. Black women writers published short fiction, essays, and poetry regularly in nineteenth-century religious and secular magazines and in newspapers. In addition, the intensity of those women who published— like Frances Harper and Victoria Earle Matthews—more than compensated for their small number. In Boston, Hopkins was part of an emergent New England black literary culture, one that would soon provide literary salons, social forums, and publications in which writers could cultivate their talents and earn their livelihood. In the years preceding the establishment of societies such as the Boston Literary and Historical Association, though, writers like Hopkins gained access to the best and most accomplished figures of their time through the multifaceted political organizations organized around racial uplift, African American suffrage, and antilynching campaigns. Given this intensely politicized backdrop, it is not surprising that Hopkins began to create historical fiction pertinent to the day, narratives that augmented the energetic outreach campaigns to raise African American awareness and political activity, especially in New England.

In 1899, Boston's African American community and its white supporters, in the city and beyond, mobilized in increasingly public venues, to protest lynching, racial intolerance, and African American disenfranchisement. Booker T. Washington's 1895 Atlanta Exposition address ignited sharp and lasting debate within Boston's African American community. In early January 1899, some Colored National League members condemned the Tuskegee president for having "'sold out' his fellow blacks to their oppressors for his own aggrandizement."[51] Washington, who made regular stops in Boston to rally support for his policies, appeared at the Old South Church days later. He "defended himself against [these] charges" and characterized his accommodationist platform as a "policy of patience instead of retaliation."[52] Four months later, in April 1899, the League convened to mark the forty-eighth anniversary of Bostonian Charles Sumner's election to the Senate, and its members were increasingly vocal in their condemnations of President McKinley and Booker T. Washington. On Sunday, 24 April, a large group of "colored citizens" convened in the Massachusetts Club Room at Young's Hotel, the place where the recently deceased Elijah Smith Jr. had presided for years as chief steward in the main dining room. There the group—which included I. D. Barnett, William Monroe Trotter, John J. Smith, Emery T. Morris, future *Colored American Magazine* associate, and John M. Burrell, Pauline's cousin by marriage and her future attorney—"hissed" when the president's name was mentioned. Washington, the man knighted by the white political establishment as the representative of African America, was "sharply criticized." Clement G. Morgan, a close friend of W. E. B. Du Bois and founding member of the Niagara Movement, the predecessor of the NAACP, "invok[ed] the spirit of Sumner." Morgan declared forcefully that "rights had never been won by compromise." Butler R. Wilson, the presiding officer, concurred. "We seek to obtain rights," he noted, "not to surrender them."

The comments of William Lewis, the featured speaker that evening of 24 April, alluded to the growing intellectual divide in black America. His Northern audience included an impressive number of college-educated professionals, many of whom were descended from free families of color or from families that were at least two generations removed from slavery. Lewis argued that white acceptance of Washington's policies indicated the threat that such ideas posed to African Americans: "The gospel of industrial education has been declared to be the negro's only salvation," he noted. "If it is meant by this that through some mysterious process a trade will give to the negro all his rights as a man and citizen, it is a sufficient refutation of the theory to say that the South would not stand for it a single moment." By the meeting's end, the few attempts by members like Edward H. Clement to defend Washington were completely eclipsed when "two black war veterans" called for "violent resistance and retaliation for lynchings." The outraged call to arms by these besieged American patriots constituted "the climax of the evening," according to Boston newspaper reporters who were in attendance.[53]

As news of Southern lynchings dominated the Boston press and black conversation, the increasingly militant Colored National League became the forum in which Bostonians gathered to protest, more than to mourn. Pauline Hopkins witnessed the unabashed defiance of men who were ready to wage another civil war to defend the persecuted members of their race. On 25 April, the day after news that Lige Strickland, a Georgia minister, had been taken from his "little cabin and left his wife and five children to wait and weep over the fate they knew was in store" for him, Black Bostonians responded to the Strickland murder with intense frustration and a murderous rage.[54] "Recent Georgia Outrages—Colored Men of Boston Talk of the Events Just Past—Capt. Williams Says Every Negro Should Be Armed, and after a Lynching the First White Found Should Be Killed," declared the *Boston Herald* caption for the article that documented the League's response. Civil War veterans Captain Williams and Lieutenant Jackson declared that "every Negro should carry a Winchester, and wherever a negro was killed, their brethren should go out on the highways and the byways, and the first white man they saw should be shot down." Their comments were met with "uproarious applause" and prompted Clement G. Morgan to "ris[e] in his seat" and announce, "That's my sentiments, and I wish they could be telegraphed to President McKinley."[55] The shift away from vocal indictments of white Southern mob violence toward African American Northern armed resistance was facilitated by the fact that the nation's segregated troops were embroiled in military conflicts in Cuba and the Philippines. "My country, my country!" exclaimed William H. Lewis, in a comment reprinted in the *Boston Herald* coverage. "[W]hat a spectacle is America exhibiting to the world today! Columbia stands offering liberty to the Cubans with one hand, ramming liberty down the throats of the Filipinos with the other, and with both feet firmly planted on the neck of the negro."[56]

Patience continued to wear thin in many corners of Boston. On 20 May 1899, three of Hopkins's Boston colleagues organized and hosted an extremely well-attended meeting before "an audience of earnest Boston women" in the city's Chickering Hall "to protest against lynchings in the south."[57] Two of the primary organizers of the event were Mrs. Butler Wilson and Mrs. Florida Ruffin Ridley. Ridley brought considerable connections to the event. In addition to her own accomplishments as coeditor of the *Woman's Era*, the nationally distributed newspaper of the women's club movement, she was the daughter of Josephine St. Pierre Ruffin, the president of the Woman's Era Club. Florida was empowered by her stately ancestral history and the accomplishments of her parents. Her father, George L. Ruffin, a former member of Elijah Smith's Progressive Musical Union singing group, was the first African American graduate of Harvard Law School and became the first black municipal judge in the United States. His wife, Josephine, worked in the same uplift circles as Pauline Hopkins, but Hopkins's unflattering portrait of Ruffin as the scheming club leader named Mrs. Willis in *Contending Forces* indicates that the two women were not close. Despite the tension between them, though, it is highly likely that the topic and feminist agenda of the meeting compelled Hopkins to attend.

Also collaborating with Butler and Ridley was Maria Louise Baldwin, the impressive academician who, with help from her African American community in Cambridge, had overcome the prejudice that denied her a teaching job in the city schools. In 1887, her record of excellence led to her appointment as principal of the interracial Agassiz Grammar School in Cambridge.[58] Prominent white women of the day were also invited to participate. Ednah Dow Cheney, the Beacon Hill reformer, women's activist, and cofounder of the New England Woman's Club and the New England Hospital for Women, and Julia Ward Howe, the renowned woman suffrage activist and author of "The Battle Hymn of the Republic," both delivered major speeches.[59] The *Boston Globe* alerted its readers to the event, proclaiming in its dramatic set of titles prefacing the account of the meeting that "Reformers and Colored Women" convened to protest lynching, that they "Demand that Accused Negroes Get Their Constitutional Rights," and that two of the speakers not only criticized President William McKinley but also made "Some Remarkable Allegations."[60]

The multiracial women's meeting at Chickering Hall drew a "representative" audience that "beside a number of prominent reformers . . . contained a good percentage of women of colored blood."[61] The speakers provided statistical figures, stirring critiques of recent debates, and contemplative laments about the state of civic disorder that made such an event necessary. Mrs. Butler Wilson spoke first and delivered a "polished address" that set the tone for the afternoon's proceedings. In addition to providing "figures as to the industrial importance of the negro race," she also insisted that American domestic practice exposed the flaws and hypocrisy of American foreign policy. "The speaker referred to the United States driving the Spanish out of Cuba and the Philippines in the name of humanity," declared the reporter, "while in our own country men were being shot down and burned at the stake, while the attention of the congress was not called by the executive to this grave state of internal affairs, and no steps were being made to remedy it."[62]

Ednah Dow Cheney, a veteran reformer who then was in her sixties, made an effort to sustain the momentum generated by Mrs. Wilson's pointed lecture. She wasted no time in indicting the men of her race, noting flatly that "[o]ur greatest men were going to the south and pandering to the people for their votes, or their admiration, or what not, while acts were being committed in the south that seemed more as if taken from the history of some savage tribe than enacted in a civilized country." Convinced that "[t]here was something deeper behind these lynchings than appeared on the surface," Cheney suggested that "it was the spirit growing everywhere in the south to destroy the right of the negro to be considered an American citizen." Her charge to the audience was to "combat this spirit" and to respond when "called on to face, though God forbid it, another baptism of fire and blood." Her longtime friend Julia Ward Howe impressed the assembly. "Though now 80 years old," noted the reporter, "Mrs. Howe read from her manuscript without the aid of glasses and her voice was strong and clear." Howe advocated a deployment of federal troops to "the states where lynchings occur" and, like Mrs. Wilson, offered a searing indictment of McKinley's accommodation of conservative Southern interests. She declared forcefully that "[w]hat the government permits, [the South] does." According to the *Boston Globe* reporter, Howe's lecture signaled that she "deplored the weakness of the government in meeting the issue."[63]

Mrs. Edwin Mead, another one of the white women invited to speak, followed Howe. She prefaced her remarks by noting that she was "sorry the meeting should have been left to colored women to call," a comment that could have been interpreted as a thoughtless dismissal of African American women's political leadership and initiative. Mead used her time at the podium to urge white women to mobilize and white Southern women to grapple with the stark, often ignored, realities of rape affecting African American women. She reportedly declared that "[i]t would be well for them to remember in approaching the question of the negro that it was their own fathers who were responsible for the mulattoes." Mead also challenged the male journalists present to "see that a line was put in the headlines of their reports of the meeting, bringing out the allegation that only one-fifth of the crimes, of which negroes lynched were accused, were crimes against women." She then "referred in scathing terms to the president" about the Atlanta Exposition "badge incident" and declared forcefully that "[w]hat we need in the south . . . is justice. Crime never was lessened in history by brutality."[64]

The Chickering Hall meeting illuminated the power and agendas that were an integral part of Boston's multiracial women's circles and the larger African American community. Although local women's club leader and newspaper editor Josephine St. Pierre Ruffin was well known for advancing a platform of refined domesticity, moral rehabilitation, and impressive maternal zeal, she also encouraged her sisters to speak out against the "unjust and unholy charges" made by those who accommodated and endorsed lynching. In 1895, at the First National Conference of Colored Women, held in Boston at Berkeley Hall, Ruffin presided over a gathering of women "assembled . . . in the interest of the race and in the cause of oppressed womanhood."[65] Lynching was at the heart of the meeting, but the women rallied around the violent predation on African American men and also on the "lying charge of rape." Their timing was impeccable.

Just three days after the Chickering Hall meeting, the city witnessed a highly controversial event when the Congregational Club hosted former Georgia governor William J. Northen (1835–1913) and AME bishop Benjamin W. Arnett as keynote speakers invited to address the topic of African Americans and the South. When he appeared in Boston in 1899, Northen, a former teacher, farmer, and Confederate Army veteran, had finished two terms as governor and begun a successful campaign to increase investment opportunities in the state.[66] Bishop Benjamin Arnett Jr., a Pennsylvania native, accomplished teacher, and minister, had, by 1899, also made significant forays into American political life. The first African American foreman of an interracial Ohio jury and the first African American to represent a predominantly white district, Arnett was elected to the Ohio House of Representatives in 1886. During his term, he continued his vigorous work to repeal the state's discriminatory and alienating Black Laws. In 1887, legislation that became known as the Arnett bill, because of his lobbying, was passed. It overturned earlier laws that maintained segregated education in Ohio.[67]

Northen and Arnett were slated to present remarks at the Congregational Club's annual "May Festival and Ladies' Night." Organized in 1869 and the oldest Congregational Club in existence in the United States, the group hoped to "encourage among the members of the Congregational Churches and Societies a more friendly and intimate acquaintance, to secure concert of action, and to promote the general interests of Congregationalism."[68] In Boston, the annual ladies' night events evolved into stylish evenings with elegant formal programs that included social hours, devotional services, sophisticated suppers, and music provided by local choral and music groups such as a quartet from the Harvard Congregational Church in Brookline, the Schubert Club, or the Germania Orchestra. The lectures following these social club events would be open to club members, invited guests, and individuals who purchased tickets to hear the speeches. The topics chosen for the annual ladies' night events followed the serious themes that the men's group maintained throughout the year. Discussions ranged from church-related discussions on "Church Going" and the "Right Way to Keep the Sabbath" to contemporary political subjects such as "Present Aspects of Prison Reform." On 22 May 1899, the featured subject was "The Present Situation of Colored People in the South." The *Boston Herald* reported that some "1,000 interested people" assembled in Tremont Temple to listen to the discussion. The *Boston Globe* made even higher estimates and reported that some "1,500 members and friends" had gathered for the "most unusual debate, or discussion."[69] The impressive attendance signals that a great number of Bostonians, and likely many from the African American community in and beyond Beacon Hill, were part of the audience.

The evening discussion featured two views on the proposed question. Northen, charged with presenting "The White Man's View," was given the opportunity to speak first. Arnett's presentation, "The Black Man's View," would follow. In his introduction of the two men, Congregational Club host Rev. Dr. Plumb referred enthusiastically to Northen as "a friend of the colored man, the president of the southern Baptist union and an administrator of the Slater fund for negro education with Booker T. Washington." Plumb also embellished his opening remarks by sharing a telegram sent by "several representative women" of Georgia that underscored "the importance of education to both races" and declared that "the women of Georgia stand ready to aid in organizing and carrying out all practicable educational measures."[70] Though the telegram's language suggested a broad women's coalition, the senders in fact were conservative white women whose husbands were at the forefront of campaigns to enforce white supremacy and to honor the Confederacy.[71]

Northen quickly made it clear that interracial cooperation and any "educational" imperatives for the majority of white southerners were explicitly racialized and designed to maintain white supremacy and ensure African American dependency. He soon brought out myths about African American rapists and white victims, which the Boston women at the interracial Chickering Hall meeting had protested vigorously just three days before. His melodramatic and charged remarks depended on a divisive gendered perspective, and he suggested that the topic of the antilynching platform, rather than a brutal act, was in fact inhumane: "Is there no tender word for the defenseless women of the south who carry with them a living shame in a living death, in a life all too long for its miseries if it lasts but for a day?" In the course of what became a two-hour address, Northen insisted that he was giving an even-handed analysis of the race question. He introduced himself as "the friend of the Negro in my state" and assured his audience that African Americans in Georgia considered him "one of their strongest defenders." "I am not here to defame them," he declared in his first moments at the podium. "God forbid. I am here to speak of their worth, when they deserve it, and to condemn them when their wickedness deserves it."[72] It quickly became clear that "The White Man's View," as Northen was to deliver it, involved his perspectives on Negro lawlessness, white victimization, the complicity of the North in the slave trade, and the impossibility of achieving interracial harmony in the South.

Northen took great pains to illuminate the supposed realities that prevented racial equality. "All history shows," he suggested, "that two races approaching in any degree equality in numbers cannot live together, unless intermarriage takes place or the one is dependent and in some sense subject to the other." This assertion led to his pronouncement that "[m]iscegenation by law will never take place in the south. That may be accepted as an established fact," he intoned, "and settled beyond question. Intermarriage at the south need not be argued for a moment. Unless the south breaks the record of all history, there is only one alternative left, and that is that the negro must be dependent, in a measure at least, upon the white man, as he cannot hope to dominate him."[73] Northen's recommendation exceeded even the terms of accommodationism that Booker T. Washington had articulated at the 1895 Cotton States Exposition in Atlanta. His social solution was shaped, it appeared, by the corruption of race relations that had occurred during Reconstruction. Whites had enjoyed "strong attachments" in the antebellum years with African Americans, but those connections had come undone when people of color aligned "with the carpet-baggers and scalawags, who flocked to the south." "[L]ike vultures over a dying carcass, they ate carrion together, as in all the shame of union leagues and midnight political marauding, they planned for the negroes' antagonism toward the white people that has proved the bane of the negro and the white man at the south. The breach was widened," he suggested, "by the presence of the military all over the south, not only encouraging the schemes of division and domination concocted in the union leagues, but offering support and defence by such arms as might be needed."[74] Northen's revisionary interpretations of Reconstruction and his suggestion that interracial disharmony was the direct result of post–Civil War Northern political aggression supported his persistent effort to claim for the white South an apology and a recognized status as long-suffering and historically misrepresented.

Northen's earnest representations of the wronged white South intensified in his commentary on lynching and mob violence. He included explicit references to brutal attacks by whites upon African Americans that appeared in the Northern press, but he did so in order to revive a transregional commitment to white solidarity. "The policy of the press at the north," he mused, "in condemning simply the lynchings, while they maintain an ominous and painful silence about the crimes that provoke them[,] is incendiary in the extreme." Having alluded to racial violence in the North and Midwest, Northen once again insisted that since no part of the country was blameless, it was appropriate that criticism of the South and documentary journalism be replaced with humanist advocacy instead. "The policy [of reporting on white Southern aggression] is unfair," he announced, "as between lynchings in the north and lynchings at the south, making always fish of one and fowl of the other. Let us be fair," he advised, "and we will sooner be brethren." Northen concluded his heartfelt appeal for Southern autonomy and what he regarded as a long-overdue brand of white accommodationism by reiterating that the representation and mischaracterization of the white South was "a great problem." "[W]e must place our trust in God and do our best," he declared, and as he finally relinquished the podium, the assembled guests in Tremont Temple responded with applause.

Pauline Hopkins and the African American community were outraged by the ex-governor's brazen disregard for African American rights and his willful manipulation of history. However, they also were extremely attentive to the deliberate and problematic seduction of Boston whites, signaled by the enthusiastic and antidemocratic motion that one man made when it was clear that Northen had exceeded his allotted time. "I move that the gentleman be permitted to deliver the whole of his address if it takes all night," motioned an unidentified man just moments after a tap from the Reverend Plumb on Northen's shoulder left the governor "a little confused" and prompted him to admit that "he would like to read the whole of his address if he had the time."[75] The Reverend Plumb failed to assert his authority as moderator; hearing the applause that followed the suggestion from the floor, he hastened to pronounce, without any reported overture to the Reverend Arnett, "It seems to be the sentiment of the audience. And I am agreeable." As a result, Northen was given the opportunity to represent the white man's view of life in the South for some two hours. The enthusiastic response to Northen reconfirmed for Hopkins and individuals in the political circles in which she moved the racial undercurrent in Boston. It was easy for them to believe that Northen's suggestions and their open acceptance would be reinforced by the anti–African American tendencies that undergirded federal legislation and continued to shape national policies on segregation, disenfranchisement, and oppression.

The Congregational Club event failed to deliver a balanced discussion of African American life in the South. When the Reverend Arnett finally gained the podium, he had little time left to him. The *Boston Herald*'s coverage, five modest paragraphs, some of which were made up of only one full sentence, signaled the clear disadvantage to which the evening's organizers ultimately put Arnett. His "hearty welcome" aside, "the hour was late when he began to speak of the black man's view and he abandoned his prepared address."[76] The *Herald* coverage reinforced the brevity that was imposed upon Arnett. The report, which included lengthy quotes from Northen, now offered only general paraphrases that underscored the general diluting of the bishop's perspective. "He made pleasant allusions to Boston," the reporter noted, "and to the debt of his race to the Congregational body. Then he reminded his audience that, while there is one negro brute whose crime has been so thrillingly told, there are millions who are not brutes; many are true Christian men striving to elevate their race."[77]

The *Boston Globe* noted matter-of-factly, "Bishop Arnett did not have more than 20 minutes in which to reply, with the result that he could give scarcely any of the address which he had prepared."[78] Despite the unfairness, the occasion was billed as unprecedented. "It is doubtful," stated a *Globe* reporter confidently, "if such a scene was ever witnessed before on any platform in this country."[79] The *Globe* coverage was more complete than that which appeared in the *Herald*—it included the full text of the remarks of both men. After opening with a salutation to his "Fellow-Citizens and Fellow-Christians," Arnett attempted to refocus the audience's attention on the facts and fictions to which their very surroundings in Boston testified. "I took a walk around your city today," he told the crowd. "I saw Benjamin Franklin out here—he had his hat off and I felt like taking mine off. I looked at Josiah Quincy. He had his hat off, too, but he didn't look at me—his eyes were looking heavenward (laughter)." He then bid his listeners to follow him to one of the city's recently installed historic landmarks, the St. Gauden's memorial to the Massachusetts Fifty-fourth Regiment and to Robert Gould Shaw, their white commander, located directly across from the golden-domed State House and not far from Joy Street, which had its African American historic sites, the African Baptist Church and the Abiel Smith School. "I went up on the common and I stood in front of your capitol and there I saw a sight which filled my heart with joy—I saw Col. Shaw riding down Beacon with his colored soldiers."[80] Arnett's first comments about Franklin and Quincy may have elicited laughter and disarmed the audience, but his remarks about Shaw and the "colored soldiers" represented the first calculated salvo in his response to Northen. Northen, a Confederate veteran, would not have missed Arnett's successful and deliberate rhetorical move. Indeed, Arnett essentially resurrected the Massachusetts Fifty-fourth and celebrated its procession down Beacon Street in the presence of a white Confederate veteran.

Arnett reorganized his address dramatically in order to make use of the precious little time allotted him "to show" his Congregational audience, "if I can[,] that you have not spent your money nor have you labored in vain in the interest of the negro."[81] He did not shy away from the emotional appeals that Northen made as he referenced the much-touted plight of Mrs. Cranford, the white woman who was widowed and allegedly survived a rape by Samuel Wilkes, a man also known as Sam Hose. Wilkes killed Alfred Cranford, his gun-toting employer and Mrs. Cranford's husband, as they were having a dispute. The argument was prompted by Wilkes's request for wages due him so that he, as the primary supporter of his family, could return home to tend to his ailing widowed mother. The completely premeditated and gruesome lynching of Wilkes, which W. E. B. Du Bois characterized as "a crucifixion," showed how deeply the majority of white Southerners claimed vigilantism as a right.[82] The *Atlanta Constitution*, the paper edited by Henry Woodfin Grady, husband of one of Northen's telegram-writing lady supporters, widely advertised the upcoming event that culminated in a public, legally sanctioned vigilante murder on 23 April 1899 in Newman, Georgia, before 2,000 people, in which Hose suffered brutal torture, ruthless mutilation, awful dismemberment, and burning. Mrs. Cranford later admitted that she had lied and that Hose's insistent claim of innocence had been true.

Benjamin Arnett stood before the Congregational Club in Boston less than one month after the Hose lynching and made an expedient and perhaps problematic choice, given Northen's attack on African American violence and unruly behavior. He chose not to take on the argument about Hose and the monstrous extralegal actions sanctioned by then-governor Candler. It appears that at the time of his Congregational Club engagement, Arnett did not have the facts about the lynching victim that Ida B. Wells-Barnett would later publish in *Lynch Law in Georgia* and that described Samuel Wilkes's close ties to his family and reputation as a steady worker. In the absence of such helpful and humanizing details, Arnett declared to his Tremont Temple audience, "I know there are bad negroes, just as there are bad whites, but where there is one Sam Hose there are 7,750,000 that are not of the Sam Hose type." He continued, answering additional charges that Northen had made: "When I read of that crime I felt sorry, my cheeks blushed. I felt sad over the occurrence. But what could we do?" Arnett might have stopped there and successfully have met Northen's request for more sensitive responses to the victims. However, he continued, and as he did, he sacrificed Sam Hose once again to the twisted logic that explains why no antilynching law has ever been passed in the United States. "The class of negroes to which Sam Hose belonged," Arnett stated, "are not the class who are brought under the influence of the teachers of our race; they belong to the class that visit saloons."[83]

As he hastened to share his message, Arnett considered how people of African descent never had acquired equal opportunity. "You put a white apron on yourself and wait on table," was the line he shared as he retold a story about interactions between the founding fathers and a hopeful would-be citizen of color who found no place set for him at the nation's table. "[W]e've been waiting on table ever since," Arnett declared, a comment that should not have been taken as humorous but did nonetheless draw laughter from the audience, despite its sobering truth. Before closing, Arnett cited "statistics of the religious and educational work which was being carried on in the interest of the negro race and the good which was resulting from the same." "It is the silent forces that do the work in this world," he concluded, "not the brass bands." He assured the assembled guests that he and the African American clergy were "preach[ing] against crime . . . all the time. We keep the fires of religion and patriotism burning so that peace between man and man will come into the world." He then shook hands and "had a few friendly words" with Northen, who "invited the colored clergyman to call on him when he came to Atlanta."[84]

Within months of this troubling occasion, it became clear that Pauline Hopkins and the larger circle of African American professionals, activists, and scholars in which she moved were not satisfied with simply stoking the "fires of religion and patriotism" that Arnett mentioned. Nor were they at all content to accommodate the insidious rhetoric of white rights that Northen espoused in the Congregational Club forum. They regarded these local events in the context of national passivity and were determined to mobilize further their supporters and demand that accountability become a federal priority. Already committed to using fiction to articulate the historical legacies and contemporary desires of her race, Hopkins saw a precious opportunity both to serve and to lead her race. A regionalist novel and New England tale would enable her to target her own immediate audience, to capitalize on community familiarity with explosive issues, and to satisfy the increasingly desperate desire to see political resolution and successful popular resistance to white violence and legislative complacency in the face of Southern racism. Hopkins set aside *Hagar's Daughter* and began drafting a new historical novel, one intimately connected to her own apocalyptic time and place. The fruit of these bold literary and political labors, which also became the first twentieth-century novel by an African American woman, was *Contending Forces, A Romance Illustrative of Negro Life North and South.*

8

For Humanity

The Public Work of *Contending Forces*

"Woman's influence on social progress"—
who in Christendom doubts or questions it? One may as
well be called on to prove that the sun is the source of light
and heat and energy to this many-sided little world.
ANNA JULIA COOPER
*Womanhood: A Vital Element in the Regeneration
and Progress of a Race*,
1886

The club woman's task [is] to little by little
turn the desire of the world from things of the
flesh to things of the spirit.
PAULINE HOPKINS
Contending Forces,
1900

Copyrighted on Friday, 25 August 1899, and published just over one year later in October 1900, *Contending Forces* was a direct outgrowth of Hopkins's exposure to the Colored National League debates in Boston about African American civil rights and her participation in local antilynching campaigns. She set her sights on becoming a true public historian and with *Contending Forces* began a lifelong professional tribute to local New England history. The novel was the cornerstone of her literary career, and she promoted it as a testament to brave Bostonians who protested the explicit harm of racial violence and the insidious dangers of accommodationism and to those who endeavored to uplift the race in the wake of a failed Reconstruction. Hopkins also deployed the novel as a vehicle through which she could demonstrate the potential of African American political feminism and evaluate the regional constraints on programs of racial uplift. In this rich, au-

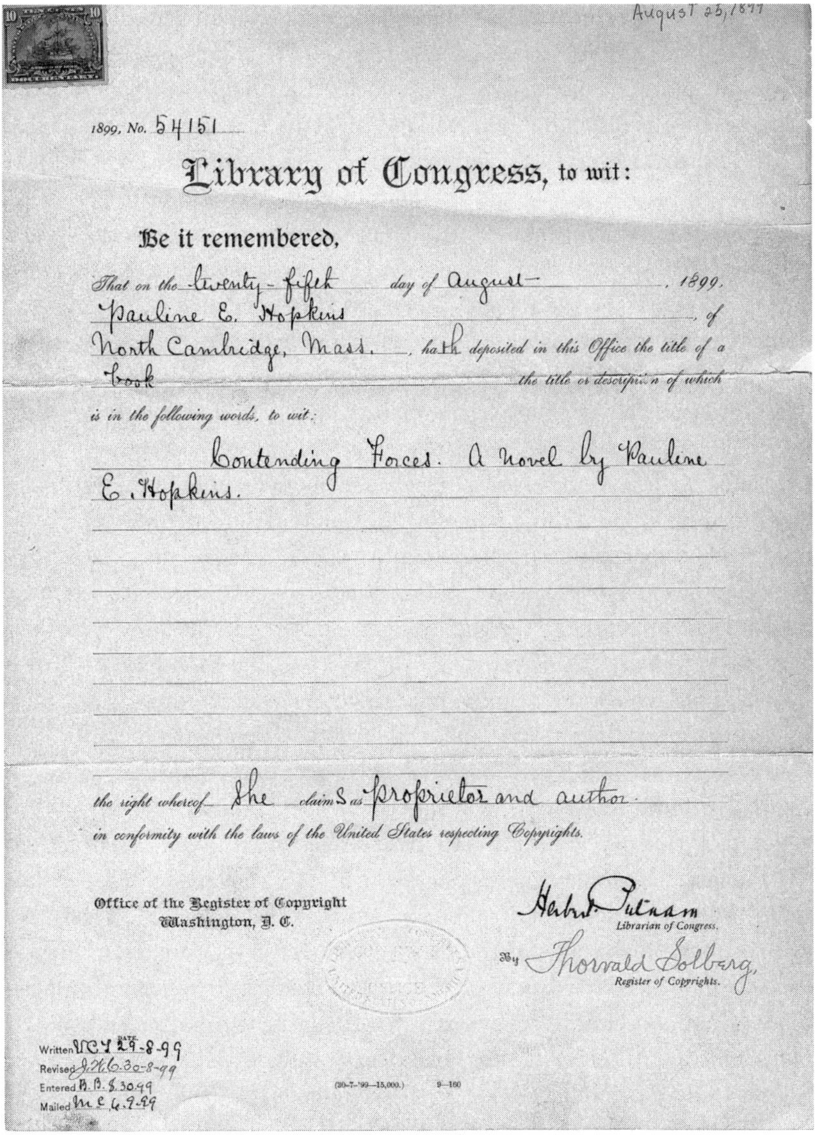

August 25, 1899

1899, No. 54151

Library of Congress, to wit:

Be it remembered,

That on the _twenty-fifth_ day of _August_, 1899,
Pauline E. Hopkins, of
North Cambridge, Mass., hath deposited in this Office the title of a
book the title or description of which
is in the following words, to wit:

Contending Forces. A novel by Pauline E. Hopkins.

the right whereof _She_ claim_s_ as _proprietor_ and _author_,
in conformity with the laws of the United States respecting Copyrights.

Office of the Register of Copyright
Washington, D. C.

Herbert Putnam
Librarian of Congress.

By _Thorvald Solberg_,
Register of Copyrights.

Written _UC 4 24-8-99_
Revised _9.26.30-8-99_
Entered _A.B. $.30.99_
Mailed _M.C. 6.9.99_

(30–7–99—15,000.)   9–100

Approved copyright application for _Contending Forces_, completed in Hopkins's own hand and filed in August 1899 with the Office of the Register of Copyright. _Courtesy of Fisk University, Franklin Library Special Collections._

thentic narrative, Hopkins also redefined the work of uplift and examined the mythologies about the destitute who were in need of that moral, educational, economic, and spiritual help. She created a searing exposé of class tensions within the women's club movement and offered a new model of uplift that merged aristocratic privilege with an unswerving commitment to Christian charity. Her sobering explication of uplift focused on two powerful women's organizations and their markedly different responses to an orphaned young woman whose sexual trauma has made her destitute and transient. Hopkins's efforts illuminate the mythologies, limits, and potential of African American uplift philosophy and suggest ultimately that at least two of the contending forces in the novel are historic feminist organizations, entities that employ different tactics for effecting true social change, self-advancement, and the development of a true black womanhood.

Contending Forces portrayed ruthless antebellum realities in the American South and juxtaposed those scenes against more optimistic, but still politically charged spheres of the postbellum North. The story begins in the British West Indies, moves to the slaveholding South, resumes in abolitionist New England, and finally concludes with two black migrations to New Orleans and London, respectively. *Contending Forces* begins as the Montforts, a British slave-owning family in Bermuda, relocate to antebellum North Carolina in an effort to avoid the financial upheaval brought on by Britain's abolition of slavery in its colonies. The Montforts—Charles, Grace, and their two sons, Charles Jr. and Jesse—arrive in New Bern, North Carolina, a coastal town in which mob rule maintains racial hierarchies and the proslavery sensibilities of its inhabitants. Immediately upon the family's arrival, residents speculate about Grace Montfort's heritage and suggest that her creamy skin and dark features might make her a mixed-race woman. When the Montforts' plan to emancipate their slaves becomes known, the family, already ostracized because of rumors about Grace's mixed-race origins, is targeted to be killed. A gruesome attack on the Montfort plantation results in the death of the elder Charles. Grace commits suicide after she endures a bloody whipping and faces the threat of rape by her attackers. The children, orphaned and traumatized, are remanded into slavery and become the property of Anson Pollock, the man who masterminded the attack on the Montfort estate. Jesse Montfort, enslaved by his parents' murderer and abandoned when a British family friend rescues his brother, eventually finds the opportunity to free himself from slavery. Jesse makes his way to New England and lives in Boston until he learns that his former master is on his trail. Aided by Boston's Underground Railroad network, he is safely transported to Exeter, New Hampshire, and the home of Joseph Whitfield, the local Underground Railroad agent. Almost

For Humanity

a decade later, Jesse marries Elizabeth, one of Joseph Whitfield's daughters, and the couple lives happily together and produces a large family.

The postbellum portion of *Contending Forces* begins in the lively late-nineteenth-century Boston household of the Smith family. The widowed Ma Smith, a daughter of Jesse and Elizabeth Montfort, whose surname reveals connections to the family of Elijah Smith Jr., runs a boardinghouse in an area of the historically black Beacon Hill community known as the West End. She enjoys close relationships with Will and Dora, her two grown children, both of whom live with her. Sappho Clark, a mysterious boarder, takes up residence in their home, and in between her sessions of stenographic work, she builds a close friendship with Dora and becomes the object of Will's romantic dreams. The Smith children and their new friend, all only two generations removed from slavery, become increasingly committed to two major debates in their community. They participate in forums modeled on the Colored National League meetings that Hopkins and her family attended. In these well-attended public gatherings, the Smiths and Sappho Clark debate the necessary roles, social value, and intellectual potential of African American women. They also witness the righteous indignation of Boston's African American community as it mounts an aggressive antilynching campaign.

In the novel's final chapters, the besieged heroine Sappho Clark is forced to leave Boston when an unsavory suitor of Dora threatens her with sexual blackmail. Clark rescues the infant son she has lodged with a relative and flees to New Orleans, the city in which she was raised and brutalized. Rescued by the sisters of the Holy Family, a historic order of African American nuns, Sappho finally begins to recover her social and emotional composure. Will Smith, devastated at losing his sweetheart, travels to Europe and then returns to the United States. His visit to New Orleans to visit his newly married sister results in an unexpected reunion with Sappho. The couple and Sappho's child, Alphonse, then depart for England where, like many nineteenth-century abolitionists and New Englanders of color, they look forward to a more peaceful life, free of racial violence.

Completed in 1899, just three years after the founding of the National Association of Colored Women (NACW), *Contending Forces* also was a club book, and as such offers a rare literary treatment of that world. That an active club woman and officer of the New Era Club, one of the leading groups in the burgeoning national movement, published it in Boston, a city synonymous with club leadership, work, and culture, only underscored the work's social and political authenticity. During November and December of 1899,

Hopkins gave at least two readings from the manuscript, one to the Woman's Era Club of Boston and the second to the members and supporters of the Colored National League. On 15 November, when she appeared before her own Woman's Era Club, her presentation "met with instant success."[1] On the evening of 5 December 1899, she gave a reading of chapters from the as-yet-unpublished *Contending Forces* to the members and supporters of the Colored National League. Addie Hamilton Jewell, a member of the audience that night, recalled that Hopkins was introduced by "a lady who told us that the Book 'Contending Forces' was written in the hope of aiding in putting down lynch law; and that the book would be to the Anti Lynching cause what Harriet Beecher Stowe's 'Uncle Tom's Cabin' had been to the Anti Slavery Cause."[2] These triumphant public readings would prompt the *Colored American Magazine* to proclaim later that Hopkins, who by then would be on staff at the journal, would "be glad to give readings before women's clubs in any section of the country."[3]

Hopkins's club membership and participation in local activities did not, however, prevent her from writing a forceful critique of the movement, of the materialism and the elitism that hobbled its efforts to uplift African American women and families. In these absorbing narratives of turn-of-the-century Boston and club life, Hopkins presents the merits and flaws of uplift ideology and examines the mythologies about the destitute people in need of the moral, educational, economic, and spiritual help that club women purported to offer. Hopkins's novel is a startling critique of turn-of-the-century club life and an unsettling exposé of the class politics, elitism, and caste tensions that permeated club circles. Hopkins was determined to illuminate but not dwell solely on these tensions, and she endeavored to offer a new model of uplift that merged aristocratic privilege with unswerving Christian charity.

In the explication of uplift in this work of historical fiction, Hopkins focuses on two decidedly different women's organizations: a traditional Northern secular women's club and an African American women's religious order in the South, the Sisters of the Holy Family of New Orleans, Louisiana. The women's club is—upon close observation—a thinly disguised depiction of Boston's New Era Club. Its leader, Mrs. Willis, is a troubling caricature of Hopkins's own enigmatic chairwoman, Josephine St. Pierre Ruffin. One of the most clear indications that Hopkins was critiquing Ruffin lies in her repeated use of the word "bright" in her descriptions of Mrs. Willis, whom she characterizes as the "bright widow of a bright Negro politician." The adjective "bright" would have been a clear sign to many of Hopkins's contemporaries, who knew that Judge George Ruffin had died as a result of Bright's Disease, an ailment of the kidneys.[4]

Hopkins does not indulge in artifice or caricature in her representations of the Southern convent. She presents an accurate history of the order and depiction of convent life—the sisters' religious services, public work, and philanthropy. The novel reports that "[t]he convent of the Holy Family was founded in 1842 by three good women, in the very heart of the stronghold of slavery, and under the most depressing influences."[5] The order's first mother superior was a young quadroon woman named Henriette Delille; her two other founding sisters were Juliette Gaudin and Josephine Charles, a mixed-race woman and Delille's girlhood friend. According to order historian Sister Audrey Marie Detiege, Henriette's "elders had all the cultural molds ready to train and educate this little quadroon belle in the traditions of her class and for the same destiny of her female ancestors—to be a mistress of some aristocratic member of the white gentry."[6] By age eleven, however, Henriette was preoccupied with another "dimension of love—celibacy."[7] By the time she was sixteen, Henriette was advocating a moral revolution that had enormous ramifications for herself, her family, and Southern culture. She "announced that the lifestyle of the quadroon was sinful and displeasing to God, because God had ordained that men and women should be united properly in the sacrament of matrimony! With Henriette leading and two cousins about her age following . . . the younger generation in the family completely broke with the customs of the class."[8]

In 1842, Delille and a small number of faithful friends became the new religious community, Sisters of the Holy Family.[9] It was apparently a "sight to see"—Delille, her girlhood friend Josephine Charles, and other young women "going along the muddy streets wearing shoes 'like boots' given to them by friends with dresses that had been darned and patched until they looked like 'Joseph's coat.'"[10] Unfazed by the elements and their lack of material comforts, the young nuns sought out the less fortunate and needy in the antebellum city known as the "slave mart of the country."[11] They did not have to go far from their convent walls: the "city square where the convent was located on Bayou Road had many people living in the vicinity characterized in a local newspaper as 'the lewd, the slewed, and the abandoned.'"[12] The sisters' supervising priest had hoped that the sisters would be a contemplative or cloistered order, but they were very much nuns of the world.[13] Their formal ministry began with the care of elderly ladies, and the sisters absorbed the costs of their upkeep. From the beginning, the Sisters of the Holy Family were devoted to caring for women and girls of color. Their commitment was certainly part of the New Orleans Catholic tradition that goes back to the colony's founding.[14] The Sisters of the Holy Family established numerous agencies to contend with social and moral decay as well as family upheaval. They founded schools, asylums for orphans of color, and homes for the sick and elderly. At the Asylum of the Children of the Holy Family, the poor were "given a rudimentary education in a free school, orphans were sheltered, and the slaves [were] taught religion."[15] The nuns also provided comprehensive training in the domestic arts, including sewing, housekeeping, and laundry. In 1860, enough funds were obtained to build an annex to their hospice; in 1876, they assumed the operation of the Louisiana Asylum for Girls, an institution that was primarily the home of orphans "left in need after epidemics and other circumstances."[16] In 1893 the sisters opened their first orphanage for boys.[17] The order continues to thrive to this day.

Hopkins was the first novelist to treat the Sisters of the Holy Family as a group of pioneering women doing the work of uplift. Apart from her contemporary, Alice Dunbar-Nelson, few of Hopkins's peers incorporated Catholicism, much less African American nuns, into their stories. The majority of post-Reconstruction African American women writers who wrote didactic Christian fiction—Amelia Johnson, Katherine Tillman, and Emma Dunham Kelley-Hawkins, to name a few—developed decidedly Protestant characters as exemplary spiritual models and agents of moral reform. In making the Sisters of the Holy Family the visionary feminists and long-standing proponents of moral and social reform in a novel about uplift, Hopkins rejected the traditional Protestant plot so popular in turn-of-the-century African American writing. She portrayed a new moral high ground based on a now little-known nineteenth-century African American female enterprise.

Hopkins's unprecedented perspective on the Sisters of the Holy Family suggests that feminist Catholic ideology, not Protestant-minded reform, ultimately resolves the principal sexual crisis in Contending Forces. Indeed, the novel is a chronicle of late nineteenth-century Afro-feminist uplift in which Hopkins crafts a reoriented and enabling, rather than disabling, platform that grapples with rape, illegitimacy, and the debilitating social stigma frequently assigned to both. Hopkins creates in the novel three distinct social spaces in which uplift philosophy is imagined, rejected, and finally successfully applied. As she documents one woman's movement through each of these supposedly feminist spheres, Hopkins deftly links class privilege to a traumatic legacy of slavery and racially motivated sexual violence against women of color in America. In so doing, she offers examples of two startlingly different applications of wealth and privilege and challenged her own women's club organization to answer a higher calling—one rooted in Christian virtues and female sensibility.

Contending Forces begins in 1896 Boston, the year in which Hopkins became a homeowner for the first time and with her parents moved to Cam-

bridge. 1896 had great historical relevance for the women's club movement—
it was the year in which African American club women, led by members of
the intellectual and social elite, including Anna Julia Cooper, Mary Church
Terrell, and Josephine St. Pierre Ruffin, founded the NACW. The novel's critique of club politics is dispensed as the plight and history of Sappho Clark
are revealed. Yet Sappho is not just a young mixed-race Southern woman with
a shocking past. She has recently moved back and forth between secular and
religious African American communities as she grapples with her debilitating sexual history. Sappho's shame and frequent migrations are the result of
her multiple social identities: she is an orphan, an adult survivor of rape and
incest, and a single mother to an illegitimate child, a cherubic, blond, blue-
eyed boy named Alphonse, whose name, because it is the same as Hopkins's
maternal uncle, raises additional questions about the Allen family.[18] Sappho
survives abduction, rape, and abandonment in a brothel, before she is rescued
from the lynch mob that her abusive uncle leads in a fiery, murderous attack
on her family. Devastated by the traumatic events, she is nursed back to health
by the African American Sisters of the Holy Family. Upon her recovery, she
changes her name from Mabelle, which in French means "my beautiful one,"
to Sappho, a name evocative of women's community and alternative sexualities. She then begins a series of journeys that will lead her to Boston and,
ultimately, back to New Orleans.

Hopkins's representations of female community, intimacy, and friendship
are borne out by religious and secular scenes. The most graphic illustration
of these social bonds emerges in the tragic tale of Grace Montfort, the novel's
first matriarch, and her maid and confidante, Lucy. The female friendship that
defines the postbellum age, however, is that which develops between Dora
Smith and Sappho Clark. The two first cement their friendship in private, in
a series of conversations that establish Dora's competence as an urban mentor and guide through Northern culture. The young women's relationship
develops in an intensely domesticated and symbolically female arena, the formerly utilitarian room that Sappho quickly transforms into a suitable sphere
for female interaction.

Shortly after renting a room to Sappho, Dora Smith describes her new
tenant as a woman with "the sweetest and saddest face" she has ever seen.
Having met Sappho, Dora now believes that the colloquial expression about
"the woman with a story written on her face" is not simply a "fairytale"
after all.[19] The connection that Dora immediately makes between Sappho and
"a story" invites explorations of women's destitution and African American
female social intervention. The figure and history of Sappho Clark produce
tensions in the world of uplift philosophy, and Hopkins uses the disruptions

to explicate African American uplift ideology and discourse. Over the course of the novel, there are three occasions when Sappho tries to tell, reinterpret, or master her shameful childhood story. All three conversations occur with other African American women: her young landlady and newfound friend Dora Smith, the authoritative and bourgeois feminist Mrs. Willis, and the mother superior of the New Orleans Sisters of the Holy Family Convent, respectively. It is worth noting that the most secular, nonreligious, and decidedly Afro-feminist encounter is framed—or, to be more emphatic, contained—by two scenes marked for their religious imagery, use of traditional religious rhetoric, and espousal of an intense humanistic Christian ethos.

Apparently the first tenant in the Smith boardinghouse to make an "attempt at decoration,"[20] Sappho transforms her plain rented room into a haven of niceties. The "iron bedstead and the washing utensils" are "completely hidden by drapery curtains of dark-blue denim, beautifully embroidered in white floss," and Sappho has used fabric strategically in other parts of the room. She has "thrown" material "over the small table between the windows," and "plain white muslin draperies hid the unsightly but serviceable yellow shades at the windows . . . and a couch had been improvised from two packing-cases and a spring, covered with denim and piled high with cushions."[21]

The room's utilitarian objects—the iron bedstead, washing utensils, and "unsightly but serviceable yellow shades"—have been "completely hidden." Now, "beautifully embroidered" draperies have been "thrown over" various objects so as to make a "very inviting interior."[22] Sappho's exhaustive efforts—all symbolic of her efforts to hide her past—are immediately productive. Dora, Sappho's only female peer in the novel, is "struck at the alteration in [the room's] appearance" and feels instinctively closer to the new boarder, who, in response to her landlady's compliments, "came and stood beside her"; "the two girls smiled at each other in a glow of mutual interest, and became fast friends at once."[23] Sappho's transformation of the rental room enables her to host intimate teas and at least one daylong sojourn with Dora. This "home-making" and housework is the earliest confirmation of Sappho's domestic strengths. Sappho has suitably redesigned her room for discussions about women's worth, marriage, and motherhood. In staging conversations between Dora and Sappho about these very subjects and making them talks that are so clearly versions of the "grown up gatherings" that occur later in the novel, Hopkins indicates the young women's potential for feminist interaction and uplift activities.

In the first of Dora and Sappho's private conversations, Dora introduces the moral and spiritual ethic that cements their friendship and to which Hopkins will ultimately return. Despite their close ages, Dora is cast in the role of mentor and moral guide. By the end of their encounter, Sappho also confers upon her young friend the role of club woman, like the many African American club women of that time who dedicated themselves "'not for race work alone' but for work along the lines that make for women's progress."[24] The scene, which serves as a counterpoint to the more formal women's interactions that follow, provides an important model of idealized uplift ideology.

As Dora takes stock of the improvements Sappho has made to the room, she notices an open Bible with its "illuminated text for the day" clearly visible. "Then she saw an ivory crucifix suspended at the left side of the desk, and stop[ped] in some confusion."[25] In response to Dora's "confusion," Sappho "dropped the dress she was mending and for a moment her eyes took on the far-away look of one in deep thought." When she speaks, she acknowledges Dora's questioning gaze and unspoken questions: "Finally she said, 'I saw you glance at the crucifix. I am not a Catholic, but I have received many benefits and kindnesses at their hands. . . . I am afraid I am not a Christian, as we of our race understand the expression; but I try to do the best I can.'"[26] Dora's "soft" reply takes the form of a gentrified call and response. She takes up Sappho's last words and, although borrowing from the 1863 poem "I Still Live," by Boston spiritualist Lizzie Doten, transforms Sappho's earnest admission into a seeming quote from exhortative evangelical scripture: "And he who does the best he can / Need never fear the church's ban / Nor hell's damnation."[27] Heartened by Dora's assurances, Sappho thanks her for not believing "a woman should be condemned to eternal banishment for the sake of one misstep."[28] Looking at Dora with "two wet eyes," she calls her a "dear little preacher" and "gently" asserts that "if our race ever amounts to anything in this world, it will be because women as you are raised up to save us."[29]

This passage is remarkable because it foregrounds a redemptive feminist uplift philosophy that is explicitly concerned with forgiveness, charity, and salvation while it accepts the host of unknown "circumstances attending" the "fallen sister."[30] The women's language evokes a Miltonic fallen state as it introduces the sexual nature of the fall: references to exile or "the church's ban" and the "eternal banishment" of which Sappho speaks are reminiscent of the "[p]erpetual banishment" of Adam and Eve as described in *Paradise Lost*, a seminal text that Hopkins invoked in her works.[31] Unlike Eve, however, Sappho is a lonely sinner, a sister who is fallen and unmarried. Dora's accommodating and Christ-centered credo is explicitly concerned with forgiveness, charity, and salvation. What remains symbolically covered in this refurbished room are the alarming circumstances that produce a "fallen sister."[32] The informal, private uplift principles that Dora articulates redirect her priorities and appetites; she does not seek to know the details that prompt

Sappho's dramatic statements, nor does she require them in order to offer advice or involve her new friend in the work of uplift. As a result, Sappho never confides in Dora. Like Sappho the interior decorator, who conceals unseemly objects, Dora believes in a type of charitable, ennobling concealment. She emphatically declares that her understanding of the Christian mission requires her to "*cover* [her] friend's faults with the mantle of charity and keep her in the path of virtue."[33] The exchange between Sappho and Dora firmly establishes the Smith home as a site of revisionary social theology—an important feature of the ethos of the sentimental novel about women's power in the domestic sphere. Despite its "updated" and, one might argue, compromised domestic sanctity as a boardinghouse that is open to the public, the Smith house emerges as a reliable and functional site in which women can cultivate each other's moral convictions and address each other's social queries and distress.

On the literal "path of virtue" that the young women follow shortly thereafter, Dora makes practical applications of her Protestant faith and confirms what she believes to be her racial responsibilities. Dora "pilot[s]" Sappho through Boston's African American neighborhoods, initiates her into the world of urban volunteer service, and enables her friend to become "well acquainted with ancient landmarks of peculiar interest to the colored people." The two young women "visited the home for aged women on M— Street, and read and sang to the occupants. They visited St. Monica's Hospital, and carried clothes, flowers, and a little money saved from the cost of contemplated Easter finery. They scattered brightness along with charitable acts wherever a case of want was brought to their attention."[34] Hopkins's Boston readers would have recognized these two institutions and the philanthropic circuit that the two young women establish for themselves. St. Monica's was a Catholic institution affiliated with the Sisters of St. Margaret and one of the few local organizations to admit African Americans. Many of Boston's private charitable organizations and orphanages limited severely their outreach to African Americans. Indeed, historians have suggested that when African Americans in early twentieth-century Boston "f[ell] into the hands of public and private charity" they did so only to a "small and declining extent" and often only after they had exhausted all other possible resources.[35] St. Monica's was one of the few exceptions in a city in which African Americans often were denied access. By 1910, for example, one-fourth of the city's orphanages barred African American children, and the others, if they admitted any, did so in extremely limited ways.

The invocation of St. Monica's enabled Hopkins to blend into her local color narrative a vital but often overlooked element of the city's history and also functioned as a call to her contemporary readers to volunteer. St. Monica's represented the practical, rather than rhetorical, aspects of racial uplift and true black womanhood. The women's home was founded in large part by Reverend Leonard Grimes, the pastor who had presided over the marriage of Hopkins's mother to William Hopkins. Father Grimes, as he was known to many during his tenure at the Twelfth Street Baptist Church, a haven for many self-emancipated former slaves, collaborated on the project with Rebecca Parker, a wealthy white Beacon Hill resident. St. Monica's was a valued haven for the elderly and was, by 1863, located in the heart of Boston's African American Beacon Hill community. The "M— Street" location to which Hopkins refers was a reference to the home's location at 27 Myrtle Street, just a few doors away from where the Ruffins, the characters who inspired Hopkins's creation of Mrs. Willis, lived for many years, at 11 Myrtle Street.[36]

Hopkins's references to the important local resource of St. Monica's resurrected the spirited abolitionist world in which her Paul, Smith, Allen, and Northup family ancestors had worked to secure civil rights and offered vital support to William Lloyd Garrison and organizations such as the New England Anti-Slavery Society. When the home moved from its Beacon Hill site in the early 1900s, it relocated to the former Garrison homestead at 125 Highland Street in Roxbury. At "the last home of the great anti-slavery agitator," the administrators established the "Garrison Ward" in the large formal parlor.[37] In 1905, during the city's Garrison Centennial celebrations, "a goodly number of women and several men" who were able to reach the home, "despite the storm and long, high climb to Rockledge," celebrated the life and legacy of Garrison with the elderly residents.[38] Hopkins's invocation of St. Monica's in the novel also allowed her to pay oblique tribute to her contemporaries, including Geraldine Pindell Trotter, one of the presidents of the St. Monica's Relief Organization and the wife of *Guardian* editor William Monroe Trotter.

Although Sappho's alliance with Dora grants her quick access to and familiarity with the African American community, this friendship is still an amateur, though promising, enterprise. The limits of the young women's bond are confirmed when they move into the more regimented and supervised world of female philanthropy. Sappho's urban migrations no longer involve treks to African American nursing homes and hospitals. Instead, she becomes part of the uplift club maintained by Mrs. Willis with its indoor symposia on subjects such as the role of the Negro woman in contemporary American society. This discernible shift away from public spheres to private domains imposes new behaviors and rigors, involves new modes of discourse about female philanthropy, and offers new rites of initiation and orientation. Exercises and discussions on African American womanhood and the social, racial, and historical obstacles that challenge its existence replace actual charitable acts. As a result of this sociological self-inquiry, discussions of uplift and womanhood inevitably turn to explicit conversations about African American women's sexuality and morality. Hopkins refashions the notion of high moral female domestic discourse, suggesting that the African American Victorian home—in which club meetings occur and over which women preside—is increasingly unable to maintain or sustain itself as a functional female domestic space. Hopkins uses these scenes of formal African American club gatherings in a number of ways: to suggest the tenuous relation between African American domesticity and uplift; to represent the shift from private to public deliberations about African American female morality; and to contemplate the ways in which organized public discourse might actually inhibit not only the cause of uplift but uplifting counsel and feminist-minded guidance.

As a single woman with qualities of good breeding, Sappho becomes a candidate for the regimented feminist and race-conscious programs of Mrs. Willis, the well-known widow of a recently deceased politician. As a widow and as a woman with a strong sense of her responsibilities to the younger generation, Mrs. Willis is reminiscent of the matriarchal figures that prevail in the white sentimental novel paradigm. The profile of Mrs. Willis combines the features of classic matriarchal types found in nineteenth-century works by Harriet Beecher Stowe and Louisa May Alcott with contemporary improvements. Mrs. Willis is, for instance "[k]een in her analysis of human nature" and "contrive[s] to live in quiet elegance."[39] Yet Mrs. Willis's background does not make her similar to the white matriarchal forces in that paradigm. She is presiding over young women who are not her daughters, and lower-class working African American women privately deride her for her "'High Chuch' notions" and criticize her haughty feminist politics. A woman of great appetites—for people, knowledge, and power—Mrs. Willis, like Sappho, is also adept in the art of concealment and decoration. She is "[s]hrewd in business matters. . . . Well-read and thoroughly conversant with all current topics, she impressed one as having been liberally educated and polished by travel, whereas a high school course more than covered all her opportunities."[40]

Mrs. Willis's materialism and hunger for power is in stark contrast to Dora's capacity for spiritual thoughts and tendency toward empathy. Yet Mrs. Willis's personality is rooted in the widow's peculiar social experiences. Upon her husband's death, a penniless Mrs. Willis begins "a weary pilgrimage—a hunt for the means to help her breast the social tide." After "looking carefully about her," she decides that "the best opening . . . was in the work of the 'Woman Question' as embodied in marriage and suffrage."[41] The narrator reports that "in private life she had held forth in the drawing-room of some Back Bay philanthropist who sought to use her talents as an attraction for a worthy charitable object, the discovery of a rare species of versatility in the Negro character being a sure drawing-card."[42] Lest there be any doubt about Mrs. Willis's intent to join the ranks of club women, the narrator offers the following clarification: "The advancement of the colored woman should be the new problem in the woman question that should float her upon its tide into the prosperity she desired. And she succeeded well in her plans: conceived in selfishness, they yet bore glorious fruit in the formation of clubs of colored women banded together for charity, for study, for every reason under God's glorious heavens that can better the condition of mankind."[43] Club work, Hopkins suggests, has been subjected to social ambitions, but she credits Mrs. Willis with the formation of clubs and their subsequent success. Surprisingly, Hopkins's narrator does not bemoan the compromised nature of what should be and is often construed as an organization founded on selflessness and charity. Instead, her narrator seems to have no stake in the club image whatsoever and is able to report, "It was amusing to watch the way [Mrs. Willis] governed societies and held her position."[44] It is not amusing, however, once Mrs. Willis begins interacting with Sappho Clark, a woman for whom social capital is neither a helpful balm nor a resource.

Contending Forces includes only one formal club meeting scene, but it is bold for its unwavering exposé of intraracial and class tensions. Immediately following a reference to Mrs. Willis's ability to "h[old] her own by sheer force of will-power and indomitable pluck," the narrative turns to the first and only Boston club meeting that Sappho attends.[45] Given the lengthy recital of Mrs. Willis's social aspirations, the meeting's focus on "[t]he place which the virtuous woman occupies in upbuilding the race" and the use of the word "upbuilding" suggests here a barely submerged social subtext that threatens to become the new narrow definition of uplift and self-improvement. The word certainly bears a close resemblance to the word "uplift"; Hopkins's revision here, however, suggests an explicit structural project, one in which African American progress and recovery are represented in visible—that is, material—signs. Hopkins also used this occasion in the narrative to address issues about which she would be even more explicit three years later, writing under the pseudonym of J. Shirley Shadrach for the *Colored American Magazine*. Hopkins applied the term "upbuilding" in her forceful February 1903 essay, "The Growth of the Social Evil among All Classes and Races in America," urging readers to "resolve to do what we can the coming year for the substantial up-building of the race while time remains." She then went on at length to decry crime in major American cities, the "haunt of the strange woman," and the "infamy, degradation, and death" that the vices of prostitution, gambling, and theft "inflict" upon the race. In response to contemporary observations about African American criminality, Hopkins lamented immediately the impact of such claims on the "females of our race," individuals like Sappho and the nameless others for whom the club movement offered welcome community protection, and noted forcefully that women of color "suffer from the most malicious slander," a "tyranny of prejudice," and "the power of bad counsel coming from those virtually above us."[46]

Hopkins takes great pains to represent Mrs. Willis as a club woman rather than as a progressive mother. There are, for instance, no scenes of intimacy or strategizing between Mrs. Willis and her daughter. Instead, she is committed to formal gatherings and instruction of other young African American women. This "bright" widow is enjoying a productive postmarriage life and taking great pride in her leadership role in the community, a role she protects by having occasional fits fueled by her intense bourgeois pride and prejudices. The female organization headed by Mrs. Willis prides itself on order and controlled uniformity. This is plainly evident in the prompt beginnings and endings of meetings, the fact that "events of interest to the Negro race which had transpired during the week throughout the country" are "tabulated upon a blackboard," and that these future practitioners of uplift take their club "refreshments in squads of five."[47] Hopkins quickly confirms that Sappho's transient life, assumed identities, and "unacknowledged" illegitimate child are subjects altogether different from the proposed scope of these weekly exercises.

To her credit, Mrs. Willis does not impose her class-conscious motives on the young women who have gathered in the Smiths' home for an afternoon sewing circle in preparation for an upcoming church fair. However, she perhaps cannot help but cast the subject of virtue in economic terms, telling her audience that she is "particularly anxious" that they think about the relationship between virtue and the African American woman because "of its intrinsic value to all of us as race women."[48] With the exception of one spirited contribution by a local schoolteacher named Anna Stevens, Sappho, Dora, and Mrs. Willis essentially carry the conversation that ensues.

Sappho, who has been "very silent during the bustle attending the opening of the meeting," responds to Mrs. Willis's opening remarks by asking for clarification about the seeming presumption that "the Negro woman in her native state is truly a virtuous woman."[49] Mrs. Willis interprets "native state" to mean African origin and says, "Travelers tell us that the native African woman is impregnable in her virtue."[50] Her answer is rather simplistic given the myriad problematic and racially intolerant nineteenth-century anthropological reports about the supposed lack, not abundance, of chastity and sexual interest in African women. When pressed by Dora, the unflappable widow claims virtue as a racial characteristic: "Let us thank God," she says, "that it *is* an essential attribute peculiar to us—a racial characteristic that is slumbering but not lost." Hardly reassured by this, Sappho asks Mrs. Willis whether "Negro women will be held responsible for all the lack of virtue that is being laid to their charge today? . . . [D]o you think that God will hold us responsible for the *illegitimacy* with which our race has been obliged as it were, to flood the world?"[51] Sappho continues, asking whether a "friend" was wrong not to confess her shameful, that is, sexual, story to her future husband. According to Sappho, her friend "married a man who would have despised her had he known her story." Mrs. Willis declares "dryly" that she is "a practical woman of the world . . . of the opinion that most men are like the lower animals in many things—they don't always know what is for their best good. If the husband had been left to himself, he probably would not have married the one woman in the world best fitted to be his wife." Says the widow emphatically, "I think in her case [your friend] did her duty [in not telling her story]."[52]

Sappho's questions about the Negro woman reveal her effort to set the social and sexual experiences of women of color in historical perspective. Her first question about the virtue of the "Negro woman in her native state" elicits an emphatic response from Mrs. Willis. When Sappho presses on to ask how American slavery and Louisiana-style concubinage affect African American female virtue, Mrs. Willis shares her conclusions without hesitation: "I believe that we shall not be held responsible for wrongs which we have *unconsciously* committed, or which we have committed under *compulsion*," she insists. Anxious to stress the difference between acts committed when there is free will and those performed in the context of subjugation, Mrs. Willis concludes that "[w]e are virtuous or non-virtuous only when we have a *choice* under temptation. . . . The sin and its punishment lies with the person consciously false to his *knowledge* of right. . . . From this we deduce the truism that 'the civility of no race is perfect whilst another race is degraded.'"[53] One of the most remarkable elements of this exchange is the decidedly religious—and Catholic—logic that Mrs. Willis uses to deal with a history of amoral co-optation of African American women. Her belief statement about women's virginity, chastity, and virtue is identical to foundational tenets in the Catholic faith. The deliberately crafted theses about virginity developed by early church fathers St. Augustine, St. Bonaventure, and St. Thomas Aquinas are now a critical part of the foundation for Catholic moral theology. The way in which Mrs. Willis qualifies the contexts and conditions that allow for the preservation, loss, or reclamation of virtue clearly echoes the Catholic idea that virginity is a multifaceted state of being, one that exists in the flesh, spirit, and flesh and spirit.[54] According to Catholic doctrine, "the accidental and involuntary loss of physical integrity (e.g., by accident, surgical operation, *rape*) leaves virginity, which is most essential in the will, intact."[55] Mrs. Willis takes great pains not to connect her ideas to this clearly Catholic position. However, her emphases on female choice and will, the connections between volition and violence, and the effect of domination would have prompted young Sappho Clark, a girl educated by Catholic sisters and schooled in Catholic principles and catechism, to recall Catholic ideology as an original source, however unconscious, of Mrs. Willis's sentiments.

As the club meeting continues, the Catholic connection subsides and is increasingly replaced by Mrs. Willis's personal ideology. Yet, just before the sewing circle meeting disbands, the Catholic subtext resurfaces and Sappho again attempts to secure peace of mind using club rhetoric. She and Mrs. Willis draw near to each other in a move that recalls Sappho's step toward Dora that marked the beginning of their "fast friendship." The interaction between the club woman and Sappho, however, is much more maternal. Their conversation, suggestive of the ritual of confession, once again revives the specter of Catholicism. After calling Sappho a "[d]ear child," Mrs. Willis notes that Sappho seems to be "'troubled; what is it? if I can comfort or strengthen, it is all I ask.' She pressed the girl's hand in hers and drew her into a secluded corner."[56] The exchanges that follow confirm that Mrs. Willis is indeed quite willful and that she is not at all spiritually inclined. She thinks nothing of encouraging young women to manipulate and suppress the truth about themselves, their pasts, and their pain. According to this club leader, motherhood is the vocation to be pursued and protected at all costs. The African American woman's next responsibility is to "refute the charges brought against us as to our moral irresponsibility, and the low moral standard maintained by us in comparison with other races."[57] Mrs. Willis downplays the importance of self-revelation, particularly if it jeopardizes a woman's marriageability and subsequent social influence. She values creative redefinition rather than honest self-presentation, silence rather than confession. Mrs. Willis's practicality would prevent Sappho from using her own story, as the eloquent, formerly enslaved and sexually oppressed writer Harriet Jacobs did, to protest racially motivated sexual violence and trauma. The uplift that Mrs. Willis promotes is a sham.

Sappho clearly desires the chance to confess her sins, and, by regarding Mrs. Willis as a potential confessor, she not only relocates Catholic ritual from the church to the catholic, or universal, home, but she also replaces the traditional confessor. The priest and confessor whom Catholics address as "Father" now has become a female figure who has motherly features. Sappho's desire to confess rather than converse testifies to her Catholic upbringing and embrace of confession as a historically powerful "ritual of discourse."[58] Foucauldian meditations on sexuality, transgression, and recovery are especially useful to consider here since they suggest that confession is the "general standard governing the production of the true discourse on sex" and that it has immediate personal and cultural effects.[59] Confession, according to Foucault, "produces intrinsic modifications in the person who articulates it" and also "exonerates, redeems and purifies . . . unburdens him of his wrongs, liberates him and promises him salvation."[60] Hopkins privileges the enduring value and centrality of Western culture, a move not only achieved when she names her heroine Sappho, after the Greek poet and "tenth muse." Hopkins uses naming and an evident investment in confessional discourse to call her readers' attention to the enduring issues of silence and articulation, exile and inclusion, which so often are at the heart of women's experiences.[61]

The limits of female solidarity and feminist social discourse in the secular world, however, are quickly exposed. Sappho is startled by Mrs. Willis's "effusiveness, so forced and insincere"—qualities that emerge as the club woman attempts to assure Sappho of her empathy and willingness to help.[62] The result is intensified concealment rather than long-overdue revelation: "Just as the barriers of Sappho's reserve seemed about to be swept away, there followed, almost instantly, a wave of repulsion toward this woman. . . . Sappho was very impressionable, and yielded readily to the influence which fell like a cold shadow between them. She drew back as from an abyss suddenly beheld stretching before her."[63] Realizing that she has to tell Mrs. Willis something, Sappho lapses into a familiar narrative strategy and transforms her first-person testimony into a third-person narrative. By offering Mrs. Willis a tale about "a woman who had sinned,"[64] Sappho is able to withstand her proximity to the club woman, gain useful feminist perspectives on a supposedly generic situation, and then apply the lessons to her own situation later.

Hopkins reveals the rhetorical priorities of Afro-feminist secular discourse in her re-creation of the women's club meetings and interactions. Mrs. Willis, the more likely of the two Boston women elders on hand to pontificate on this graphic element of African American women's experience, is clearly an unsuitable confessor. Although an authority figure, she is not an "authority who requires the confession, prescribes and appreciates it," or "intervenes in order to judge, punish, forgive, console and reconcile."[65] As a result, she fails to make a space for critical intercourse about, rather than of, sex and sexual violence. When faced with singular rather than general examples of violation, she misses the opportunity to adequately reconstruct the violent and racially motivated sexual encounters, "the thoughts that recapitulated it, the obsessions that accompanied it, the images, desires, modulations, and quality of pleasure that animated it."[66] Sappho's inability to confess her history and true problems do emphasize "the difficulties of 'breaking silence' about rape even in the comfort of a black domestic setting."[67] Sappho's reticence also emphasizes the need for alternative spheres that can accommodate such matters. The Smiths' home in Boston is only one of many places that Sappho has journeyed to, a telling indication that she has yet to find a place in which she can discuss her rape and survival. Once confession finally occurs for this anguished woman, catharsis and reconciliation can begin. Her chronic migrations will end, and she will be able to enjoy stability in her personal, domestic, and professional lives. The meaningful worlds of motherhood, social activity, and community work that Mrs. Willis considers as pressing responsibilities for young black women are hollow pursuits for women such as Sappho unless cathartic revelation and dispensation occur.

In her scenes with Sappho Clark, Mrs. Willis, the new arbiter of African American female morality, boldly compromises the high moral standards on which uplift is supposedly based. In the "Sewing Circle" chapter, uplift becomes synonymous with more veiling; for an already-disguised figure like Sappho Clark, this additional requirement adds to the problem, it does not reduce it. After talking to Mrs. Willis, Sappho is still preoccupied with her past; Mrs. Willis has not mapped out a strategy for Sappho's reintroduction to American society or its postbellum marriage culture. Mrs. Willis, former wife and current club leader, is unable to actually elicit stories of sexual compromise, much less articulate a process of recovery for victims of racially motivated sexual violence. Sappho draws back with a "wave of repulsion" from the woman who has been credited with installing a "mother's law" in the novel. Willis has been equated with a "black matricentric morality . . . [that] privileges a female centered ethical context, and serves as a broader basis for redefining a virtuous woman other than on the grounds of sexual chastity."[68] Such a theoretical premise seems especially promising and valuable to a woman like Sappho Clark, for whom virtue is a concept complicated by her rape, exposure to sexual immorality, and experience of illegitimacy. Sappho herself seems to sense the emancipatory possibilities of Mrs. Willis's uncompromising feminist politics but, as the scene shows, is ultimately alarmed by the message and the messenger. Yet Sappho's "revulsion" and mortified silence suggest that Mrs. Willis has offered a more narrow, not broader basis "for redefining the virtuous woman." A rereading of this scene explains why

Hopkins abandons the North and its rhetoric of uplift and chooses instead to figuratively begin a process of feminist rehabilitation that is marked by descent and humility. Hopkins's slowly emerging feminist protagonist journeys south from Boston to New Orleans, a city whose antebellum reputation was built on frank discourses about race and sex.

Before Sappho enters the Southern discursive space of New Orleans, however, she has to confront her own sexual self—as mother. This is prompted by the unexpected public disclosure of her story at a public meeting in Boston convened to protest Southern lynchings. Luke Sawyer, a former family friend and Sappho's rescuer, reveals Sappho's tale at the mass meeting convened by the Colored American League. Immediately she is subjected to sexual blackmail by the villainous character John Langley. Rather than submit to Langley or allow him to disclose her true identity to her fiancé, Will Smith, Sappho flees the Smith household and the city. She plans to return to the South, but before she does, she faces the now-exposed truths of her situation. This results in a critical act of recovery, an act of confrontation rather than concealment that culminates in Sappho's reclamation of her son, Alphonse. This courageous act of self-assertion is, to a degree, ironic, since it indicates Sappho's veneration of motherhood, a core ideal of uplift, but can occur only after she flees Mrs. Willis and the world of club life.

Upon departing the Smiths' home, Sappho goes directly to her aunt's home, where she has boarded her child. She tells her aunt that she intends to "never part with him again on earth,"[69] a phrase that confirms her increasing readiness to use religious imagery, rhetoric, and practice as she redefines her maternal responsibilities. The scene in which she actually reclaims Alphonse is highly suggestive of the moments following a woman's labor. In this symbolic reappropriation of her traumatic delivery, Sappho replaces the physical pain of labor and the trauma of her adolescent experience with adult joy and an all-encompassing, transcendent pleasure. The pronounced emphasis on the visual in the scene underscores Hopkins's efforts to secure this long-overdue and seemingly impossible moment. Now, Sappho "gazed on the innocent face," and there is a "new light in her eyes as she gazed on the sleeping child," and she "gazed with new-found ecstasy at the rosy face, the dimpled limbs, and thought that he was hers."[70]

In addition to restaging Sappho's labor, Hopkins also uses this pivotal scene to simulate Sappho's symbolic and spiritual rebirth. These episodes, rather than the scene in which Sappho renames herself after her "first" delivery, constitute her truly "heroic self-transformation."[71] When she tells Alphonse that she is his mother, the child "solemnly" replies, "My mamma is gone away to heaven." Sappho responds, "No dear, I am your mamma, come back to keep you with me always."[72] Sappho's explanation, which comes the day after Easter Sunday, cannot be read apart from the Bible's New Testament story of the resurrection. Like Jesus, Sappho rises from the dead and triumphs over the forces of evil. It is a comparison that Hopkins confirms in the narrative: "[T]he risen Christ was a reality," intones the narrator, "and his triumph over sin and death was to [Sappho's] bruised spirit a promise and a blessing."[73] The maternal bond she now intends to honor becomes a sanctified state, reinforced when "something holy passed from the sweet contact of the soft warm body into the cold chilliness of her broken heart."[74] The new romance here is between mother and child, not adult sweethearts, and Sappho experiences love—mother love—for the first time.

Sappho's new confidence in herself as a mother does not send her back to the Smiths and the club world of Mrs. Willis. Instead, she boards a train for New Orleans, where she plans to "lose" her newfound maternal self, "get work," and become yet another one of the city's many mixed-race single mothers. Her intentions contradict some scholarly assertions that Sappho's acceptance of Alphonse and reconciliation with motherhood contribute to the "restoration of Sappho's sense of community."[75] If anything, Hopkins's portrait of Sappho's reunion with Alphonse initially suggests that the young woman is now at peace about living with herself. Yet, given Hopkins's significant efforts to recuperate Sappho as mother and Christian, Sappho's intentions as she journeys south are alarming. Is there to be no benefit gained from the besieged heroine's new appreciation of motherhood? Is this to be a strictly private metamorphosis that secures her no honorable place in the public sphere or the African American community?

As the Southern scenes begin, Sappho is ensconced in a new and monitored women's sphere: the convent buildings of the Sisters of the Holy Family. As she alights from the train in New Orleans, Sappho literally falls into the arms of a nun. Stationed there to solicit donations as well as to "look out for friendless or unfortunate colored women," the nun "put out her arms just in time to receive Sappho's form as she was sinking insensible upon the platform, her strength at last succumbing to the terrible strain upon mind and body."[76] The sisters admit Sappho to the convent hospital and Alphonse to the orphanage. Alphonse's placement there is a shocking nullification of his mother's recent resurrection. Sappho is dead again. Here in Louisiana, however, she has one more opportunity to resurrect herself as mother and rape survivor.

Sappho's return to the nuns' holiness, chastity, and institutionalized purity seems to be the only effective antidote to the postslavery desecration of women of color. Some fifty years earlier, a young woman named Henriette Delille believed that a nun's holiness, chastity, and institutionalized purity

Sisters of the Holy Family, the pioneering African American order founded in New Orleans by Henriette Delille in the early 1840s. The sisters are pictured here around 1899, the year in which Hopkins copyrighted *Contending Forces*, the novel that featured the sisters and their work of racial uplift for women and children.
Courtesy of Library of Congress.

were among the few effective antidotes to the desecration of women of color during slavery. It is within the house of this "early feminist, educator . . . social worker"[77] that Pauline Hopkins lodges her besieged heroine. The documented pre-convent life of Henriette Delille and her first Holy Family sisters illustrates the enormous sexual and moral pressures to which young women of color were exposed in the nineteenth century. When placed alongside the story of Sappho Clark, the history of Henriette Delille and the founding of the Holy Family order suggests that this female community is not only capable, but most perfectly fitted to perform the work that secular uplift "inaugurates" more than sixty years later.

Hopkins places Sappho squarely during the time when the Holy Family nuns were establishing a system of beneficent institutions. As a young Louisiana native, Sappho attends their school; as a rape victim and mother-to-be, she is housed in the convent's Asylum for Girls and her child is delivered in the convent's hospital. As an adult, she is in need of some of these same services—upon her return, she is admitted to the hospital suffering from a nervous breakdown, and her son is enrolled in the sisters' Asylum and Orphanage for Boys during her recovery. Hopkins's readers, particularly those in New Orleans and elsewhere in the South, would have recognized the tribute to these dedicated caretakers and spiritual women.

In 1850, eight years after the founding of the Sisters of the Holy Family, the nuns established the School for the Children of the Holy Family, a school for "free colored girls from families of means" on Bayou Road, New Orleans. According to Holy Family historian, Sister Detiege, after the Civil War "a number of young ladies who had attended this school became outstanding members of the [order]."[78] Closed in 1887 because of the need for substantial repairs, the building was sold in 1890. The Colored Sisters' School to which Luke Sawyer refers as he chronicles Sappho's abduction and sexual assault during the American Colored League meeting in chapter 14 is most likely St. Mary's Academy, the "first Catholic institution for colored girls in New Orleans,"[79] located on Orleans Street. As a student during the 1880s and early 1890s, Hopkins's heroine would have been part of a diverse student body and exposed to an impressive curriculum: "Boarders were attracted to this school from nearly all the southern states, from Central American and the West Indies, as the records show," and as "the only Catholic institution for girls of the race who desired more than a Grammar Grade education, it drew its day-pupils from all parts of the city, with the result that the enrollment exceeded the two hundred mark."[80] The school's prospectus reveals that the "cultural training of the pupils" was emphasized. In addition to all the usual secondary school subjects, "[c]omplete courses were offered in music, instrumental and vocal; painting and artistic needle-work. But it was Christian doctrine that occupied first place, and for which students were awarded prizes for excellence at the annual closing exercises."[81] The sisters' goal was to encourage "the perfect development of religious inheritance of the child," since they hoped "then, as they do now, to give to society through their educational activities, young men and women that would be capable of making perfect adjustments when they will have begun their march with the rank and file of the human race."[82]

Unfortunately for the young girl Mabelle Beaubean, the process of "making perfect adjustments" was difficult to do, in part because she could not fall in step and march with the rank and file of whom Sister Mary Catherine writes.

What we do see in *Contending Forces*, however, is Mabelle Beaubean's/Sappho Clark's repeated attempts to do so. Upon recovering from her ordeal, she embarks upon a new life that barely resembles the old. As an industrious stenographer, she does not reveal the extensive training in gentility and handiwork that she received in New Orleans. Her exposure to various cultures, her privileged background, and her lengthy exposure to Catholic women and religious practice are, for the most part, obscured by the violence she has survived. As Hopkins shows, the links between the Bostonian Sappho Clark and the Louisiana native Mabelle Beaubean have frayed considerably.

The sequences of events related to Sappho's second convent stay and even the implications of her symbolic death there—signaled by the abandonment of her identity as Mabelle Beaubean—need to be more thoroughly assessed than they have been to date. Hopkins uses this stay to produce a series of provocative rejoinders to Northern uplift and ideology. She locates the liberating and empowering African American maternal ethos that Sappho needs within a Southern community of celibate, childless women. The mother superior in the novel is here and her identity is confirmed by both her title and her actions. When Sappho enters the convent grounds for the third time, Sappho is not on the brink of performing an autonomous "heroic self-transformation" but one that depends entirely on others. Sappho absorbs the transformative gaze of the intrigued nuns who attend her and is transformed in that way. The nuns promptly decide that "[s]he is like the angels in the picture of the Crucifixion, so sweet and sad."[83] The spiritually informed gaze of her caring "sisters" displaces and invalidates the lascivious gaze of men, like Sappho's Southern white half-uncle and the Northern mulatto villain who threatened her with sexual blackmail.

Sappho makes her first and only full confession about her past to the mother superior of the Holy Family. The scene is in stark contrast to the tense, unredeeming exchange she has had with Mrs. Willis. Additionally, the interaction between Sappho and the mother superior counters the enduring American stereotype of convents as "prisons of confiding girls."[84] Sappho's confession occurs in the convent hospital, a sanctified place designated for physical recovery that also accommodates spiritual and emotional recovery as well. The entire moment in the convent hospital, the physical and oral response of both women and the mother superior's assessment of Sappho's predicament, establishes a substantial binary opposition between the secular and spiritual worlds. The terms of engagement between Sappho and the mother superior, as well as the nun's assessment of Sappho's predicament, establish two things: the existence of and difference between uplift ideology and practice in the secular and religious spheres. The hospital is a "quiet haven of rest" that "the turmoil and bustle of life did not reach."[85] Here, miles away from the world of Northern uplift and the "hurrying march of humanity," Sappho feels it her "duty" to "make a confidante of the Mother Superior."[86] That Sappho "sent for" the nun indicates her confidence in the quality of the exchange. First, "the Mother" appears, "glid[ing] in, with her noiseless step and gentle, assuring manner." Having established herself in this nonthreatening way, the mother superior invites Sappho's testimony: "The holy woman sat there a long time in silence after listening to Sappho's story. Such confidences were not new to her. At length she placed a toil-worn brown hand upon the girl's head with a murmured "Benedicte."[87] After baring her soul, Sappho kisses the nun's "gentle" and "toil-worn hand" with reverence, is told that they must both "think and pray" about a solution to the problem, and tells the Reverend Mother that she does not wish to become a nun. Sappho admits that she wants to "accept the desire of God in the child . . . take a mother's place and do [her] duty."[88] That both the nun's manner and hands are described as "gentle" assures Hopkins's readers that the woman is predisposed to generating a response to Sappho that is humane, analytical, and practical; the phrase "toil-worn" does not simply speak to the mother superior's years of labor. It also speaks to the years of labors the sisters and their mothers superior have spent combating social ills of this kind. These are hands, perhaps, capable of "upbuilding" as well as "uplifting" the young women who come into their care.

The anticipation surrounding Sappho's confession is gently disappointed when Hopkins fails to provide an explicit account of the conversation between the two women. In fact, Hopkins completely elides it. She presents the moments just before and immediately following Sappho's disclosure: "[P]resently the Mother glided in, with her noiseless step and gentle, assuring manner. The holy woman sat there a long time in silence after listening to Sappho's story."[89] Sappho's words evaporate—they exist in an unwritable space. Sappho's confession forces a narrative caesura—a break in the middle of what could finally have been a catechetical exchange between penitent and confessor. Hopkins honors the Catholic seal of confession that regards all revelations by a penitent as private and confidential.

Hopkins's account of Sappho's interaction with the only woman she calls "mother" reveals a series of shifts between institutional practice and domestic ideology and between religious and secular postures. The physical affection between the two, which includes a kiss and gentle touch to the head, is immediately followed by suggestions about spiritual intimacy obtained through acts of individual prayer and meditation:

"What shall I do, Mother?" asked the girl, as she reverently kissed the gentle hand.

"Ah, we must think and pray. You do not wish to become a Sister?"

"No; I must accept the desire of God in the child. I will take a mother's place and do my duty."

"It is hard for one so young and beautiful to resist the world and its temptation," replied the Mother regretfully; "but we will help you, and the convent will be a home for you always."

Sappho thanked her tearfully.

"My child, I will think over all you have said; I will pray to be shown what it is best to do. Now go to sleep; rest, and pray to the Holy Mother of Sorrow, and Christ will comfort you."[90]

The difficulties of making rape part of the public uplift discourse still persist even as Hopkins shifts from the secular to the religious sphere. However, the convent scene turns the reader and the culture's attention away from the act of rape and toward the issues of recovery.

When Sappho feels it her duty to tell her story by way of honoring a maternal relationship, Hopkins revives for the first, and perhaps only, time in the novel one of the primary conventional and powerful impulses of the sentimental novel form. This is a crucial moment for theorists of the African American sentimental tradition because it symbolizes the alternative racialized maternal ethic at work. This is the third scene in which Hopkins stages Sappho's interaction with another woman around the subject of rape and recovery. Since the opening scene with Dora Smith, the settings have become increasingly spartan: from a decorated rented room, to the Smiths' modest public parlor, and now to a barely furnished hospital room. The mother superior comes to Sappho's "small, bare room," a place lit by "rays from a lamp outside the room [that] came faintly in, dispelling the semi-darkness" and "light from the soft Southern moon" that "gleamed faintly through the windows, making the room like the cloisters of heavenly mansions."[91] The ethereal, holy nature of this place can contain the gruesome details of Sappho's trauma. The power of religious environs and icons, hinted at in Sappho's boardinghouse room by the Protestant pamphlet and ivory crucifix but completely suppressed in the agnostic parlor scene, is finally and fully embodied. Now Sappho's confession becomes a redemptive discourse rather than politic evasion. The mother's law that has been most often located in secular women either hostile to or unaware of Sappho's confession now appears to be capitalistic, opportunistic, and unfeeling. The mother's law that emerges from the meditative, Christian exchange between the mother superior and Sappho now looms as superior indeed—one informed by Christian faith and grounded in personal duty to God and one's offspring. Is it any surprise then, that the novel can, within the next and final two chapters, report that Sappho is finally reunited with her Boston sweetheart with whom she enjoys "happy love—a love sanctified and purified by suffering"?[92]

Hopkins clarifies the novel's enduring leitmotif of resurrection in the final chapter. She uses the Christian celebration of Easter to emphatically secure Sappho's access to true womanhood, a reconstituted nuclear family, and a public career of community outreach. Hopkins can barely contain her enthusiasm for the service conducted by the Sisters of the Holy Family. Indeed, their real customs dovetail with her historic fiction of Southern experiences. The sisters' Easter service is "famous throughout the South," "something to dream of" that "defies description."[93] The rituals of the Easter service allow Hopkins one final meditation on the family—one marked by illegitimacy, a strained engagement, and experience of ostracism, self-sacrifice, and final glory. This final and holy event brings the narrative of disclosure and revelation full circle. It too includes acts of concealment and revelation that signal progress: "Until Easter morning the pictures of Christ, Mary and Joseph were veiled, but now the statues had emerged from their concealment in indication of the spiritual change in us which was wrought by the coming forth of Christ from the tomb."[94] Hopkins seizes upon these details in order to legitimize finally and emphatically the "romance of Negro life," to which the subtitle of *Contending Forces* refers.

Following Sappho's immersion in the convent world, Hopkins turns to Will Smith and prepares him to recognize the solutions that the Afro-Catholic, rather than Afro-Protestant, world will offer him, his compromised sweetheart, and her innocent child. Shortly after Sappho's departure from Boston, Will also leaves, but for Europe, where he pursues his studies. A thoughtful young man whose "imposing, well-developed intellectuality . . . marked him as a thinker and an originator,"[95] Smith "espouses progressive doctrine, promotes and embodies self-development, and represents his race within various circles of the dominant white culture."[96] Yet, for all his studious rationality, Will Smith is a man susceptible to remarkable visions. In the novel, he has two reveries. The first is of Sappho's brutal rape; the second is of her glorious recovery. Smith dreams about Sappho's recovery on the first night of his voyage back to the United States and to Louisiana, where he plans to visit his newlywed sister, Dora. Smith's imaginings occur during a journey that revises the traditional Middle Passage and that modernizes the Montforts' voyage from Bermuda to North Carolina. "He dreamed that he stood in a grand cathedral, and listened to strains of delicious melody chanted by an invisible choir. *Christe eleison, Kyrie eleison*, floated to his ears, and the glad strains of the *Gloria*. Presently upon the altar before him appeared a vision of the Virgin and Child, but the face of the mother was Sappho's, the child by her side was the little Alphonse. He tried to reach her in vain. She smiled and beckoned him on as she receded at his approach; then he awoke. His dream haunted him."[97] This substitution is remarkable for its symbolic license and promise. What Will Smith sees is a Sapphic Madonna—a woman attended only by her child, not by a male consort.

The transformation of Sappho into a Madonna and Alphonse into the Christ Child has important ramifications for critical discussions of literary representations of African American female sexuality, identity, and subjectivity. Will Smith's vision of Sappho Clark as the Virgin Mary represents the most extreme female glorification possible. If the Madonna "connotes a world beyond the confines of . . . Protestant reason and logic,"[98] then this image represents the death of secular feminism articulated by Mrs. Willis and representatives of traditional uplift ideology. *Contending Forces* has been described as the "crisis of a refined, single woman who becomes 'tainted' by sexual scandal and thus 'read' by others as a prostitute."[99] However, the emphatic invocation of the Sapphic Madonna and Holy Family challenge that interpretation. Thus the story of *Contending Forces* can be described as the transformation of a woman traumatized by sexual scandal into one imagined as a holy mother and blessed virgin. This transformative feminist aesthetic relies not on concealment, as illustrated so often earlier on in the novel, but on revelation, the communicating of divine rather than secular truths.

Smith's vision of the Sapphic Madonna and Child removes the volatile issues of African American female virtue, motherhood, and illegitimacy from the secular into the religious sphere. This male character's contribution to Hopkins's uplift relocation project is essential given Smith's interest in ultimately becoming "the father to the youth of his race."[100] Catholic icons signal his inclusion and his place beside Sappho in this redemptive discourse. Newly established as a representative of treasured womanhood, Sappho seems to have reached a position that transcends even the most holy version of Anglo-American true womanhood. Yet Hopkins reassures her readers that Sappho has not become inaccessible—according to the narrator, Sappho has been "fit[ted] . . . perfectly for the place she was to occupy in carrying comfort and hope to the women of her race."[101] United in marriage, she and Will Smith intend to "work together to bring joy to hearts crushed by despair."[102]

Contending Forces suggests that African American progress and uplift often can be enacted only at the cost of certain personal repression. Hopkins uses the figure of Sappho to illustrate that one's sexualized racial identity is not always compatible with the visions and programs of either the oppressed or the dominant group. She uses Henriette Delille and her convent to illustrate that the North does not always offer freedom to the fugitives who run there. As a result, it is in a women's community, rather than in a women's meeting, that Sappho Clark, the unwed teenage mother, is counseled and able to regain her self-esteem and virtue. In the convent of the Sisters of the Holy Family, single women of color, led by mothers superior, dedicate their lives to the spiritual uplift and moral and intellectual education of African American women and girls. As Pauline Hopkins revealed first to her turn-of-the-century readers, nuns, not mothers, have been preparing young women of color for their roles in the secular world long before the formation of the secular NACW organization. It is in this established Holy Family that Sappho is finally able to negotiate the trauma of her adolescence and the artifice of her adulthood. It is a "mother superior," not a superior widow, who correctly prepares Sappho for secular New Orleans and America.

In her first novel, Pauline Hopkins, club woman and member of the Boston New Era Club, makes an unprecedented and potentially impolitic move when she introduces a Southern women's community, and a celibate Catholic one at that, as a viable alternative to Northern uplift organizations. The community, which Hopkins ultimately endorses, overcomes what could well be regarded as its religious handicaps: celibacy, adherence to Catholic dogma, and religious priorities. The Southern black women's community that Hopkins chooses came into being precisely because it celebrated the African American family. At the turn into the twentieth century, this modernized order embodies virtuous black womanhood. The feminist principles at the core of the community's philosophy successfully counter the lingering, unwieldy effects of American slavery.

In her 1901 annual report to the NACW Executive Board, NACW founder and former first president Mary Church Terrell frankly addressed the tension between the organization's ethos and the disposition of its bourgeois elite. A member of the Memphis black elite, Terrell recommended that there was no better way to live up to the organization's credo of "lifting as we climb" than "by coming into closer touch with the masses of our women. . . . Even though we wish to shun them and hold ourselves entirely aloof from them," she confessed, "we cannot escape the consequences of their acts. So, that, if the call of duty were disregarded altogether, policy and self preservation would demand that we do go down among the lowly, the illiterate, and even the vicious to whom we are bound by the ties of race and sex, and put forth every possible effort to uplift and claim them."[103] The ethos of uplift that Terrell advocated recognized the reservations and distaste that contributed to racial hierarchies and class divisions. When she delivered this speech, Terrell not only was a long-standing member of the Memphis and American black elite but also a current member of the Tuskegee Women's Club. Her social and professional commitments illuminated what, in the age of the talented tenth—the group described by Du Bois as the intellectual and professional elite—was becoming a necessary alliance between privilege and the practical.

It is possible to regard Pauline Hopkins as a woman in a vexing public situation. She had no social pedigree to match that of the Ruffins and the Terrells who presided in the uplift circles of which she was a part. Yet Hopkins, nonetheless, was a woman whose political pedigree and genealogy legitimized her increasingly important role as social commentator, activist, and public historian. In *Contending Forces*, Hopkins anticipated Terrell's 1901 injunction to club women. Indeed, the novel may have inspired Terrell to make her forthright comments. Like the NACW chair, Hopkins discerned the ways in which unyielding social hierarchies and their attendant rigid protocols threatened the mission of racial uplift and were essentially incompatible with the more explicit goal of racial "upbuilding." Hopkins deployed a realistic feminist ethos in *Contending Forces* and supplied it with graphic regionalism and persuasive social critique. In the same ways that Sappho Clark's redemption was realized in spite of perennial itinerancy, Hopkins transformed discourses about slavery, concubinage, lynching, and mob violence into itinerant, unstable subjects in need of rhetorical discipline and reinterpretation. Ultimately, the convent[ional] wisdom of *Contending Forces* reveals that racial uplift and emerging contemporary Afro-feminism are understood best when examined in the context of unruly subject matters.

9

Contending Forces
as Ancestral Narrative

O Freedom! . . .
thine enemy never sleeps,
And thou must watch and combat till the day
Of the new earth and heaven.
WILLIAM CULLEN BRYANT
"The Antiquity of Freedom,"
1842

No man, unless he puts on the mask of fiction,
can show his real face or the will behind it.
WILLIAM DEAN HOWELLS
Years of My Youth,
1916

Contending Forces was shaped indelibly by the nadir, a period when America was fraught with contentious politics of division, disenfranchisement, and racial violence. Such tumultuous times influenced Pauline Hopkins's conception of what she might achieve as she published the first significant novel by an African American woman writer since the 1892 publication of Frances Harper's *Iola Leroy.* Her completion of *Contending Forces* in 1899 coincided with what she referred to in the novel's preface as a "crisis in the history of the Negro in the United States." Federal policy, regional divisions, local custom, and even scholarship and social theory that reinforced flawed notions of racial supremacy and myths about the beneficence of American slavery all combined to erode the civil rights, economic advancement, and domestic stability of African Americans. Justifications of racial oppression and notions of the "white man's burden," as articulated first in 1899 by Rudyard Kipling, benefited from majority white political rule. They also were reinforced by politics of racial and social accommodationism advanced by public figures like Booker T. Washington, the influential former slave and founder of Tuskegee Institute, and entrenched by landmark legal rulings such as the May 1896 U.S. Supreme Court decision, *Plessy v. Ferguson*, which upheld racial segregation.

Contending Forces was an eloquent indictment of racial violence and a studied critique of divisive social stratification and the implications of sanctioned economic injustice. Yet the novel also functioned for Hopkins as a vehicle through which to grapple with her family's own experiences of violence, trauma, and loss. Interwoven with the novel's discernible political content is an astonishing set of personal, private, and local facts, details that appear to dictate the terms on which Hopkins considered potent national issues of lynching, women's roles, and activism. The detectable urgency and intense articulations of racial responsibility that pervade the novel are fueled by an accumulated Hopkins family history, one that spans three generations of her maternal family and invokes histories of empire, colonialism, and slavery. Masked, but not completely obscured, is the story of Pauline Hopkins's maternal grandfather and his family, a history embedded in the tale of the novel's founding family, the Montforts. The tragic fate of this family at the hands of slaveholders and their proslavery minions constitutes the opening story of *Contending Forces* and was modeled on the identity and experiences of Pauline Hopkins's maternal grandfather, a man named Jesse Allen.

The fictionalized biography in *Contending Forces* of Jesse Allen is a wrenching narrative of displacement and diaspora, victimization and self-preservation. In the novel, Hopkins recast her maternal grandfather as Jesse Montfort, a man who survives the murder of his father, Charles, the suicide of his violated mother, Grace, the loss of his brother, Charles Jr., and the tyranny of Anson Pollock, his parents' oppressor and the man who enslaves him following their deaths. The fictional Jesse, who as a child was "the young darling of his mother's heart," never is able to avenge the awful wrongs visited upon his family.[1] His sole chance at a peace of sorts once he alights on American soil, according to the watchful narrator, arises when he marries in the North. When he weds, Montfort is "absorbed into that unfortunate race, of whom it is said that a man had better be born dead than to come into the world as part and parcel of it."[2] This usually festive occasion marks the penultimate step in a gruesome immigrant narrative, one in which none of the traditional and uplifting hallmarks of transition, acculturation, and advancement apply.

In *Contending Forces*, the character Jesse Allen is one of three children born to Charles Montfort and his wife. In "A Retrospect of the Past," the novel's opening chapter, Hopkins introduces the Montforts, a slave-owning family of four who in the "winter of 1790" are residing in Bermuda, an island nation regarded at one time as the "Gibraltar of the Atlantic" and that "[o]nce . . . was second only to Virginia in its importance as a British colony."[3] Members of the planter class, the Montforts are among those affected by the British Parliament's passage of the gradual emancipation act. Montfort, who has profited handsomely as an "exporter of tobacco, sugar, coffee, onions and other products so easily grown in the salubrious climate," has approximately 700 slaves. The novel describes Charles Montfort as being born in Bermuda, as were his two sons and the daughter who died in childhood. Charles and Grace wed in the island's Church of England and saw their children baptized in that faith also. The origins of Grace Montfort, a woman who is "a dream of beauty even among beautiful women," are not as precise. A reference to her education in England suggests that she may have been born to British parents outside the United Kingdom and been sent back for schooling, or that, like her husband Charles, she also may have been born in Bermuda. The detailed physical description of Grace Montfort calls attention to her "complexion . . . creamy in its whiteness, of the tint of the camellia," hair of "rich golden brown," "brown eyes, large and soft as those seen in the fawn," and "heavy black eyebrows marking a high white forehead, and features as clearly cut as a cameo."[4] The richness of Grace Montfort's appearance ultimately jeopardizes the sanctuary that white identity often provides in the antebellum American South. The suffering of Jesse, her youngest son, will be complicated in part because he so closely resembles his mother.

The Montforts leave Bermuda for North Carolina sometime between 1790 and 1807, the year in which England abolished slavery in its colonies. They and their significant number of slaves relocate to the coastal North Carolina city of New Bern, but, within a few years, when rumors surface that Montfort might be planning to emancipate his slaves, a slave trader named Anson Pollock mobilizes a violent white proslavery mob to attack the family. Charles Sr. is shot and killed. Grace is brutally whipped and shortly thereafter kills herself by drowning herself in Pamlico Sound. Charles Jr. is saved from further violence and the horrors of slavery by an honorable British mineralogist who is able to purchase one of the boys from Anson Pollock. The family friend, who intends to, but does not, return with funds enough to purchase Jesse, also plans to sue for the children's freedom and obtain restitution for their pain and suffering. When he is sixteen years old, Jesse Montfort, who has been serving Anson Pollock as a valet and has been groomed to act as a purchaser on his behalf, takes advantage of his arrival in New York where he is to conduct business for Pollock. His white skin prompts a group of men to address him as a free man, an empowered but agitated fugitive. He makes his way north to Boston, and there, "beside the stone wall that enclosed the historic Boston Common and as he watched the cows chewing their peaceful cuds," he vows "to die rather than return to Anson Pollock." In Boston, he "cast[s] his lot with the colored people of the community" and earns his livelihood doing "menial work."[5] He is forced to abandon the city when he learns that Pollock, whose actions are sanctioned fully by the Fugitive Slave Law of 1793, is heading north to reclaim him. The vigilant members of the Underground Railroad network in Boston direct Montfort to Exeter, New Hampshire, where he is instructed to seek aid from Mr. Whitfield, "a negro in Exeter, who could and would help the fugitive."[6] It is a fortuitous meeting. While waiting for Whitfield, Jesse Montfort sits in the kitchen, where Whitfield's wife, a "comely black woman," is preparing the evening meal. He offers to comfort the "fretful" baby named Elizabeth in the "little red cradle which stood in the center of the floor." Some fifteen years later, he marries the child whom he "rocked to sleep the first night of his arrival in Exeter," and "by her he had a large family."[7]

Jesse Montfort regains his social composure in New Hampshire, so much so that the narrator reports that he "prospered"; however, an unfortunate business investment in "an evil hour" undoes his economic stability. An employer, "failing to meet his liabilities, involved Montfort in his ruin," and Jesse Montfort is "[u]nmanned by recurring misfortunes" from that time forward. He relocates to Boston with his wife and their twelve children and suffers emotional paralysis. "Born in an evil hour, under an unlucky planet," intones the narrator, "this man's life was but a path of sorrow to the grave, which he welcomed as a refuge from all vicissitudes."[8] Hopkins concludes the substantial Montfort story in Exeter, New Hampshire, returning to it briefly at the novel's close when a descendant of the long-lost son Charles reacquaints himself with his brother Jesse's daughter, Ma Smith, and his grandchildren, William and Dora. Charles Montfort marries the daughter of his rescuer and, in an attempt to preserve his family name hyphenates it with that of his wife. His namesake Charles, a successful and well-traveled businessman who has served in the British Parliament, seeks out the family of Will Smith, whom he had met in Boston a year earlier. In a moving scene of stirring revelations, Ma Smith shares her Montfort history with Montfort-Withington, the "tall elegant white man of distinguished address" who has "been reared in the luxury of ample wealth" and reveals himself as their cousin.[9] The British visitor provides some additional details about the efforts that his grandfather Charles Jr. made to find his younger brother Jesse Montfort and also shares information about a successful lawsuit that Charles Jr. has filed against the United States for recompense in the loss of his parents' lives and their estate.

Tragic romance in *Contending Forces* is embodied first by the Montfort brothers, whose family and childhood are torn asunder in the antebellum South. Charles and Jesse never are reunited, and Jesse suffers this wrenching injury and additional losses of property and morale before his death. Ma Smith muses that her grandfather died of "a broken heart," one undone by childhood trauma and an irrevocable loss of family and identity. "God did not intend that his wrongs be righted," she concludes tearfully, as she narrates the family history, "like one who describes a vision passing before her eyes," and provides the first full "recital" of her family history in this novel.[10] The Montfort story frames the novel's interior narratives of loss, upheaval, domestic practice, and racial violence. However, when she revives this ancestral tale with the coincidental meeting between the Montfort descendants, Hopkins places long-overdue closure on the story that has haunted the Southern and Northern lives of so many characters in this novel.

Pauline Hopkins introduces herself, in the preface and opening chapters of *Contending Forces*, as a scribe of the past, witness to the present, and mollified historian. Yet she is alternately most emphatic and most oblique about the history and details that shape the fictionalized Montfort story, the most keenly autobiographical and explosive interpolated history in this and all of her subsequent writings. She notes that "[a]mple proof . . . may be found in the archives of the courthouse at Newberne, N.C., and at the national seat of government, Washington, D.C.," but provides no specifics to enable a thorough retelling of her riveting family history.[11] The sparse historicity of the ancestral narrative in *Contending Forces* requires a painstaking reconstruction of multiple truths, details that Hopkins regards as illustrative of the irrepressible pains and legacies of bondage. Hopkins exercised creative license as she made her way through a tragic private and public story, but the blending of facts and fictions is symptomatic of an unruly past as well as of an unsatisfied desire for justice long denied. She modified names to protect violated innocents such as Jesse Allen, but readers must still contend with embellished aspects of the family's past that obfuscate, rather than clarify, key elements of the true stories.

Jesse Allen, an enigmatic figure, an elusive patriarch, and the maternal grandfather of Pauline Hopkins, emerges in the historical record as a mulatto who claimed both Bermuda and the city of New Bern, North Carolina, as his birthplace, and as a man born to parents whose forenames are identical to those of the Montfort couple who suffer so dramatically when they relocate to the antebellum South. He also quietly emerges as one who married into the family of an Exeter, New Hampshire, Underground Railroad conductor and who became the father of ten children. These facts mostly correspond to the "fictional" biographical profile of Jesse Montfort, the youngest protagonist in *Contending Forces*. Despite its resurrection by his granddaughter Pauline, Jesse Allen's life story contains some still-unconfirmed episodes or incidents that rely more on circumstantial evidence than on documented facts. What does emerge more fully from the archival records, however, is his life in New England. Jesse Allen's years in the North begin as early as 1813 and span a period of fifty-five years. This period reveals a host of tantalizing clues about his links to Bermuda, his experiences of slavery in North Carolina, and the heartrending family history that Hopkins immortalized in her first and most influential novel.

The key to unlocking the primary family histories of *Contending Forces* lies in the facts of Jesse Allen's parentage. Although there are only tantalizing bits of information in the historical record to tell his story, these are arresting and suggest a thoroughly dramatic history. Jesse Allen's father was a man named Nelson Allen, who, to date, appears only to have been identified secondhand in two U.S. census reports and referenced briefly in his son's death certificate. Nelson Allen, whose birth and death dates, parentage, and racial identity remain unconfirmed, was born in Bermuda. His still elusive history makes it difficult to confirm how closely his life corresponds to that of the entrepreneurial Charles Montfort, the character whose life apparently is modeled on his. This mystery, however, is eclipsed in its potential horror and its value by the even more provocative fact that Jesse Allen's mother was a woman named Grace. Given the awful nature of Grace Montfort's experiences, it seems difficult to believe that Hopkins would have invoked her great-grandmother's name lightly. Do the life and death experiences of Grace Allen and Grace Montfort truly mirror each other? If so, then Pauline Hopkins is but two generations removed from a woman driven to suicide by shame and madness induced by excessive physical, emotional, and psychological violence. The prospect of such a legacy only intensifies Hopkins's declarative rationale about her novel: "In giving this little romance expression in print, I am not actuated by a desire for notoriety or for profit," she notes in the opening lines of the preface to *Contending Forces*, stating that she writes in order "to do all that I can in an humble way to raise the stigma of degradation from my race." The novel is an act of literary catharsis and is essential to a larger campaign for justice.

Unlike the perpetual half-truths that surround Grace and Nelson Allen, it is possible to locate their son Jesse, with certainty, in nineteenth-century America. One of the earliest confirmations of Jesse Allen's existence comes as a result of his inclusion in the "Africans" section of the 1813 Boston city directory. His listed address on Chambers Street confirms that he is the man who gives his occupation as "sugar refiner" in the 1810 Boston directory, in which Boston residents are not segregated by race. Jesse Allen reappears in the 1816 city directory, listed as living on Spring Street. He next is identified in the 1821 roll of taxpayers in Boston, a source that reveals that he is still living on Spring Street in the city's sixth ward, that he has real estate valued at $200 but no identified personal estate, and that the amount of tax owed that year is $3.18. There is some ambiguity surrounding the timeline of Jesse Allen's arrival in Boston, complicated in part by earlier city directory entries for a man of the same name but whose entries would make him significantly older than the man who married Elizabeth Whitfield in the 1820s. The provocative clues raise questions about whether or not Allen was an independent businessman in Boston before he moved to New Hampshire, married, and began a family. They also hint at a trade that may have been derived from direct experience in the sugar business, which depended on the labor of enslaved people in the West Indies, but which also became a key trade for island nations such as Bermuda.

Jesse Allen seems to disappear from Boston city records after 1821, and he surfaces next in the 1830 New Hampshire census entries for Exeter, in Rockingham County.[12] His life there became intertwined with the Whitfields and the Pauls. The Underground Railroad conductor identified only as Mr. Whitfield in *Contending Forces* and the man with whom Jesse Montfort seeks refuge did exist. He was a longtime resident of Exeter, the town to which the orphaned fictional Jesse Montfort fled when he received news of his former master's search for him.

Joseph Whitfield, like members of the Hopkins and Waugh families, was born into slavery in Virginia in 1762. By 1797, he had escaped his bondage and was living in Newburyport, Massachusetts. On 12 December 1797, he married Nancy Paul, daughter of French and Indian War veteran Caesar Paul and Lovey Rollins Paul, and a sister of the Baptist ministers Thomas and Nathaniel.[13] Two years later, the Whitfields were living in the vicinity of Exeter, New Hampshire, but had not yet secured for themselves a stable home. Despite the Paul family's longtime links to Exeter, Nancy's husband, Joseph, was subjected to an increasingly popular town law known as "warning out." This local legislation, which did not always require that individuals leave a town, was a means by which town officials prevented needy individuals ranging from people of color to widows with children from claiming benefits or relief, as it was known, from the town to which they had come. "Warning out" was a defensive social mechanism, one implemented by the appointed town overseers who were responsible for minimizing unwanted and illegal claims on a town's welfare funds and charitable organizations.[14] Joseph

Whitfield weathered the "warning out," established himself and his family in the community which his wife Nancy regarded as home, and quickly demonstrated that he was anything but a needy unemployed itinerant. Locals came to know him as a "famous gardener and hunter" who was "very clever, good natured, [and] enjoyed telling of his hunting escapades with [his] dog Skip."[15] He lived with his wife and family in a simple one-story house on a road that later was known as Court Street. The couple had three children: Elizabeth, who would become Jesse Allen's wife; James Monroe, who would become a respected poet and Masonic leader; and Joseph Jr., who collaborated with Mark De Mortie to support the Massachusetts Fifty-fourth Regiment and later died after being accidentally shot by a man identified in Exeter historical records as Proctor.[16]

Jesse Allen married Elizabeth Whitfield of Exeter sometime around 1825. There is scant information about her, which makes the details in *Contending Forces* about the fugitive Jesse Montfort rocking his future wife, then a young child, to sleep, one of the most tender scenes of the novel. One of the details known about her, however, sheds additional light on her family life in Exeter and on the timeline of Jesse Allen's journeys north and his sojourns in Massachusetts and New Hampshire. On 18 September 1825, Elizabeth became a member of the Baptist Church in Exeter. The church record, which lists her as "Elizabeth Whitfield (Allen)," suggests that she did so either on the eve of or soon after her marriage to Jesse.[17] The couple lived in New Hampshire for almost a decade, and they had the benefit of supportive extended family networks as they began their own family. The first of their ten children was born in 1827, and the family grew quickly over the course of the next seven years. Elizabeth bore some of their ten children in Exeter, New Hampshire, between 1827 and 1834: Frances E., in 1827; Mary E., in 1832; Anne Pauline, in 1834; and Sarah A., the mother of Pauline Elizabeth Hopkins, in 1834. Jesse, Elizabeth, and their four young girls all were in Exeter when Joseph Whitfield died in November 1832, the victim of an apparent stroke. The attack felled the "hunter and skilled . . . marksman," and he was discovered lying dead in the lane leading to his house.[18] The *Exeter News-Letter* paid tribute to him, noting that he had "borne through life the character of a worthy and industrious man" and one who "perhaps more richly deserves to have a paragraph penned in his praise, than many whose riches have entitled them to a column of eulogy."[19]

Jesse Allen's claim on domestic stability may have been shaken again when he lost his affable, protective, and politically astute father-in-law. That event may have contributed to his decision to leave New Hampshire for Massachusetts, and at some point in the next two years, the Allen family relocated to

Boston, where their child, Caroline A., was born in 1836. Two years later, in 1838, their daughter Angelina Grimké Allen was born. In Boston, the Allens situated themselves in the African American community on Beacon Hill. They lived in Boston's sixth ward, the area of the city flanked by Beacon Street and the Boston Common to the south, and Cambridge Street and the West Boston bridge across the Charles River to the north. There they were in close proximity to the historic African Baptist Church and the Abiel Smith School, and their neighbors included mighty men and women like Lewis Hayden, Benjamin Roberts, John Rock, Susan Paul, and Elijah Smith, whose public and political work shaped the local and national abolitionist and equal rights movements.

The family suffered the loss of at least one child once they moved to Boston. In March 1839, *The Liberator* announced the sad news that Angelina, born in May 1838 and the "daughter of Jesse and Elizabeth Allen, aged 8 months," had died on 14 March 1839.[20] The baby's name was chosen as a tribute to the white abolitionist and future Boston resident Angelina Grimké, who had appeared in the historic African Baptist Church, or Belknap Street Church, as it then was known, almost one year earlier. The Allens' decision to name their daughter after the activist was most likely the result of their meeting Grimké, whose public antislavery career had begun by then and had resulted in her frequent speaking engagements before sympathetic audiences in Boston. Indeed, when Elizabeth Allen was pregnant with her seventh child, the family had had the opportunity to hear Grimké speak in the African Baptist Church, the sanctuary through which they shared a close family and political connection to the Pauls. In March 1838, *The Liberator* had reminded its readers that Grimké was booked to "lecture before the colored people on Tuesday evening next at the Belknap-street Church" on the topic, "The universal dissemination of knowledge among all classes of society the only safeguard against oppression."[21] The Allens' choice of name for their daughter, who was born four months after that lecture, signaled their support of the burgeoning feminist antislavery presence in New England and their own proud hopes for their newborn child. Indeed, the circumstances that prompted the Allens to make such a deliberate statement about their own politics are borne out further by Jesse Allen's additional commitments to the antislavery cause and his support of and subscriptions to antislavery newspapers such as *Frederick Douglass' Paper*.[22]

Shortly after Angelina Allen's death in the spring of 1839, Elizabeth once again began to bear children in rapid succession. Daughter Harriet H. was born in 1840, and the family's first sons arrived soon thereafter.[23] George J. M. B. was born in 1842, and Charles H. was born in 1844. The youngest and last Allen child, Alphonse, was born in 1848 when Elizabeth was forty years of age. The information about Alphonse notes that he was born in a home on Belmont Street and that his father's occupation was that of laborer. The latter corresponds to the stated occupation of stevedore listed for Jesse Allen only two years later. However, there is a mystery about Alphonse's birth. In *Contending Forces*, the illegitimate son of the abused Sappho Clark is named Alphonse, and the use of his name in this tragic context hardly suggests an uncomplicated tribute by Hopkins to her maternal uncle.

Despite the trauma that may have affected Jesse Allen's early life, he and his family steadily became an integral part of the middle-class world in Boston and the neighboring city of Charlestown. They inculcated strong abolitionist principles in their children, values that were enriched by the inspiring Paul family history and accomplishments in the ministry, in education, and in the abolitionist sphere. One of the most encouraging signs of the Allens' success-ful assimilation in Boston was their proud participation in the ongoing anti-slavery struggle. In addition to Jesse Allen's donations to the New England Anti-Slavery Society, the Allens were able to stake out a more visible place for themselves in the rich Beacon Hill world before Jesse left the city for New Hampshire. By 1844, Frances Allen, the family's oldest child, was upholding the family abolitionist arts tradition inaugurated by Susan Paul, her mother's first cousin. While still in her late teens, Frances assumed the position of di-rector of one of the city's children's choirs, and did so barely three years after the untimely death of Susan Paul. Her vocation and this leadership position suggest that Frances may have followed the professional examples of her Aunt Susan, Uncle Thomas, and others in the Paul family, and become a school-teacher.

In this all-too-familiar tragic way, though, Frances Allen's professional teaching, musical interests, and racial uplift work were cut short when she died in 1859 at age thirty-two. She had married Robert H. Johnson, of Ithaca, New York, in 1857, and she seemed to be on the verge of a happy life when she left Massachusetts with her husband, "resided for one year in central Illinois, spent [the summer of 1858] at Niagara Falls, and returned to their pleasant and beautiful residence in Ithaca."[24] Tragedy struck shortly after the couple, who were expecting their first child, returned to Ithaca. Just twenty days after she gave birth to a daughter, Elizabeth M. F. A. Johnson, Frances died "after a short illness, of typhoid fever and pleurisy."[25] As the obituary in the 17 December issue of the New York City *Anglo-African* lamented, the "endeared husband," who now was responsible for their child, had "lost an affectionate and intelligent wife, the babe a kind mother, and her death will be regretted by a large circle of relatives and friends."[26] The Allens stepped in quickly to help their bereaved son-in-law, and by the time that the 1860 census was taken, seven-month-old Elizabeth Johnson, the Allens' second grandchild born in 1859, was part of their Charlestown household. She remained there with them through the end of the Civil War. By 1870, she had rejoined her Methodist minister father and Elizabeth, his second wife, in Ithaca. Also in the Ithaca home to which she returned were her blind paternal uncle William and her aunt Mary Augusta.[27]

The tragedy that struck the Allens in 1859 when they lost Frances transformed that year and the ones that followed into bittersweet times. They may have been able to assuage their grief by caring for Frances's daughter, but that may have deepened the keen sense of loss. The Allens may have been distracted by and gained some solace from the successes of their daughter Anne Pauline, known affectionately as Annie, whose singing career was bringing her international acclaim. Annie Pauline Pindell's penchant for composing enabled her to accomplish another family first when the enduring and influential Boston-based music publisher Oliver Ditson and Company published several of her own songs.[28] Of the several works by Pindell that the company distributed, "Seek the Lodge Where the Red Men Dwell" was, according to Pauline Hopkins, "the most widely known" and became "a popular 'hit' of the day."[29]

By 1863, however, the Allens, who had moved to Charlestown in 1850 and were living in a three-family home at 64 School Street, once again were experiencing loss and emotional upheaval. Two of their daughters were in the throes of divorce proceedings. In Boston, Sarah Allen Northup was filing papers to leave her erstwhile husband, Benjamin. On the West Coast, Annie Pauline also was suffering the loss of her marriage, and soon after its formal dissolution, as publicized in the San Francisco–based *Pacific Appeal*, she had to deal with her former husband's speedy return to the altar.[30] Jesse Allen and his family weathered the domestic tribulations as the onset of the Civil War loomed large. While they appear to have been spared the pride but also the agony of seeing sons enlist, they did have the chance to behold the historic assembly of the first African American regiments raised in the North. They also would have been on hand in Boston to salute the companies of the Massachusetts Fifty-fourth Regiment as they paraded proudly through the city streets en route to the ships that would take them into the Southern war zone.

Jesse Allen died in 1868, three years after the Civil War came to a close when Generals Ulysses S. Grant and Robert E. Lee signed the documents of surrender at the Appomattox Court House in Virginia. The family interred him at the Garden Cemetery in Chelsea, the town to which Elizabeth moved shortly after her husband's death. She sold the family home at 64 School Street in Charlestown and began to make a new home in the popular nineteenth-century summer resort town also known as Winnisimet, which was growing steadily as a result of the steam ferries that connected it to Boston, one mile away by boat, and manufacturing.[31] In 1870, Elizabeth Allen was living there with Harriet, her twenty-four-year-old daughter, who worked as a dress-maker, and James Scotron, a thirty-one-year-old hairdresser who boarded with them. In Chelsea, the Allens also were closer to the Garden Cemetery where Jesse had been buried and the site where additional Allen family mem-bers, as well as Pauline and her parents, Sarah and William, eventually would be laid to rest.

The story of Jesse Allen gradually becomes less about him and more about the life of his large family—the accomplishments of his daughters and their professional successes, international travel, and contributions to an estab-lished Paul family tradition of civic and political work. Questions still remain, however, about his origins and the family history that may have dogged him as he survived the era of bond slavery, the kidnappings in the North and in Boston of self-emancipated and free people of color, and the Civil War. The narrative of freedom and acculturation that Allen's granddaughter Pauline relays in *Contending Forces* never can overshadow the untamed and unruly history of Allen family origins that are rooted in the soil of empire and colony, of Britain and Bermuda. To link Jesse Allen to Bermuda makes real the dread-ful story of the Montforts and infuses the biography of Pauline Hopkins with grim echoes of predation and grief. At present, there are few documents that establish the Allen connection to the former British West Indian colony, but the ones that do, despite their limited information, reveal the potential source of Pauline Hopkins's literary and political zeal. To date, the only known legal documents that establish the Allen family's link to Bermuda are census returns that Jesse Allen filed while living in Massachusetts in 1850, 1855, and 1860. These hint at still elusive Bermuda documents that would provide invaluable confirmation of the Allen family history and bear witness to the foundational narrative on which Pauline Hopkins depends so fully in *Contending Forces*.

Jesse Allen's age as given at the time of his death suggests that he was born in the year 1800. If the Allens were in Bermuda in the years prior to and just after Jesse's birth, then they would have been candidates for inclusion in the extensive list of the island's inhabitants that was compiled between 1789 and 1808. The roster was designed "to make a[n] estimate of the real estate of the inhabitants of these Islands distinguishing the parishes and the freeholders in each parish with the names of the several owners or possessors—the quan-tity of acres and value of timber, houses or other improvements to be made to the best of their ability on principles of equity and justice."[32] However, no one by the name of Nelson Allen appears in any of the nine parish surveys of that document. That the Allen family is not included raises both practical and dramatic possibilities about their identity and their link to the island. In the first instance, the document, which was generated over several years, may have been completed before Nelson Allen and his wife, Grace, arrived on the island. The more dramatic possibility is that they were in fact in residence on the island but not as freeholders or "owners or possessors" of real estate. Were the Allens not included in the supposedly exhaustive census because they were part of the community of color that included servants, slaves, and indentured people? Did their son Jesse later identify as a mulatto because of his parents' identity or as a result of generalizations often imposed on individuals in interracial marriages? Such a possibility certainly would fuel the romance of the "story of Negro life" that Hopkins aspires to tell to her twentieth-century readers. The details about the Montforts' involvement in the Anglican Church however, undermine that potentially explosive possibility. The Montforts full participation in the church certainly does not follow the characteristic disregard for religion that historian W. Winterbotham noted in his 1795 study, *America*. According to Winterbotham, Bermudians "seldom go to church, except to attend a funeral or get their children baptized, or hear a stranger."[33] Although the Montforts, according to Hopkins, enjoyed the privileges of marriage, baptism, and access to weekly services, the churches on the island were strictly segregated. Members of the island's enslaved population were prohibited from having church weddings and although "generally allowed to bury their dead in existing churchyards," for example, they were relegated to "burial plots [that] were distinctly separate from the rest of the churchyard." In some cases, as one descendant of Bermudian slaves noted, burials were "[s]o far . . . to the westward, it was not expected the dead would ever see the dawn of Resurrection Day."[34]

Records of the Allens' arrival in North Carolina are as elusive as the Bermuda documents. Hopkins, in *Contending Forces*, suggests that the fictional Charles Montfort sailed several times between Bermuda and North Carolina. That possible activity of Nelson Allen is of little use, however, since it was not until January 1820 that the U.S. government began to require that passenger lists be compiled for all ships entering American ports.[35] The family's arrival in New Bern, though, is consistent with the city's prominence in trade during the late eighteenth and early nineteenth centuries. Between 1785 and 1788, as one of the state's five ports, New Bern contributed to the impressive exports to other colonial ports and to the West Indies, which included some "20 millions of shingles, 2 millions of staves and heading, 5 millions feet of boards and scantling, 100,000 barrels of tar, pitch, and turpentine."[36] As historian Delbert Gilpatrick points out, New Bern's role, along with Edenton on Albemarle Sound and Wilmington on the Cape Fear River, as one of the three most popular trading centers in the eastern part of North Carolina, was financed in large part by the enslaved populations who lived with their planter-owners in towns not far from these frequently plied rivers. The area was home to mighty plantations that depended on the agricultural labor and expertise of enslaved people for their harvests of grains, tobacco, and indigo. In addition, slave labor was essential to the systematic logging that produced the wood products needed for the timber, shipbuilding, and naval markets.[37]

The 1865 Massachusetts State Census, the last census for which Jesse Allen was alive, is the only known extant document that places him in North Carolina and more specifically in the town of New Bern.[38] Searches of local newspapers, wills, probate records, and court documents for both the state and the U.S. Supreme Court provide no conclusive proof that the Allen family was lynched or that Jesse was remanded into slavery. Yet here, as in other parts of the Jesse Allen story, the circumstantial evidence suggests that there may in fact be truth to the story that Hopkins claims to be verifiable even as she shrouds key details relating to the victims and their attackers. For example, an intriguing set of late eighteenth-century documents that revolve around transfers of slaves and of land link the Pollocks to a family named Montfort. In Edenton District, between 1774 and 1787, there were several interactions between "Cullen Pollok" and Joseph Montfort, a resident of Halifax County for whom several transactions were made before and after his death. On 4 July 1774, Joseph Montfort appeared before two witnesses, "Cullen Pollok" and "Michl Payne," as he prepared to "giv[e] his bond to Dr. Robert Lenox of Bertie Co."[39] By 1784, Henry Montfort, the executor of Joseph's will, was "to answer" in the District Court of Edenton to Robert Lenox for debts. The case was resolved, it appears, by two rulings in 1785 and 1787 that gave over to Robert Lenox the Montfort estate of "31 negroes, 900 acres, etc."[40]

Extensive searches of pertinent historical documents have not revealed a man named Anson Pollock. The word "Anson" does, however, have historic relevance and a long-established link to North Carolina. Anson County, located in the southern part of North Carolina and near the South Carolina border, is a substantial distance away from New Bern. The census of 1790 reveals that the county's population included 2,047 white men and women over the age of sixteen and 828 slaves. Anson County's enslaved population was exceeded by several other counties, among them Bertie County, home to Cullen Pollock, where the 5,141 slaves well exceeded the free white population of 3,514.[41] By 1850, Anson County's population of nearly 13,500 was almost evenly divided between free and enslaved people. The hilly landscape also was one of the most fertile in the state; in 1850, Anson County produced 10,864 bales of cotton, the second-largest amount of cotton produced by any North Carolina county that year. Hopkins's use of the word "Anson" may have been tinged with irony or been a more deliberate place and a telling pun. Her effort to reveal the chief aggressor against the Montforts, if not by name then by insinuation, suggests emphatically that he was "a son" or a descendant of the Pollock family.

The narrative that links Jesse Allen to New Bern, North Carolina, is extremely tantalizing and as elusive as his family's connection to Bermuda. Both the historical record and the novel that incorporates it call attention to the Pollocks, a historic and well-documented ruling family of the state. In New Bern, the colonial capital, the Pollocks had far-reaching influence, a longstanding participation in the slave trade, and a dependence upon the labor of enslaved people. Hopkins, in her regionalist re-creation of antebellum North Carolina, intensifies the Pollock family's participation in slavery. This aspect of their history is borne out by their staggering holdings of slaves and also by their uncanny links to other historic and nefarious characters such as James Norcom, the scheming Edenton, North Carolina, owner of Harriet Jacobs, author of the controversial 1861 narrative, *Incidents in the Life of a Slave Girl, Written by Herself*. The Pollocks also had potentially strategic ties by marriage to Boston, the city to which Jesse Allen and his fictional alter ego Jesse Montfort fled.

The Pollock family history reinforces Hopkins's exploration of the legacies of slavery. Her decision to maintain rather than to shroud the identity of the Pollocks can be read as a move to satisfy her own hunger for justice and long-denied financial and psychological restitution. She does appear to make one key fictional overlay, however, in the figure of Anson Pollock, the man who sanctions the brutal attack upon the Montforts before seizing Lucy, the handmaid of Grace, as his concubine, and enslaving the freeborn Montfort children Charles and Jesse. Years later, Pollock's descendant, John Langley Pollock, repeats the sins of his ancestor as he attempts to orchestrate the concubinage of Sappho Clark, a resilient but deeply traumatized woman who already has survived rape and has weathered the birth of a son born as a result of that attack. Hopkins's prefatory remarks about historical authenticity suggest that her invocations of the Pollocks are deliberate. Jesse Allen and the Pollocks shared a link to New Bern, North Carolina.

The history of the Pollock family in New Bern, North Carolina, dates back to the city's founding in 1723 during the colonial period, some thirteen years after its establishment by a group of explorers led by the Swiss baron from

Berne, Christopher de Graffenried, and that included John Lawson, a British explorer, who in 1708 became the colony's surveyor general.[42] Located at the junction of the Trent and Neuse Rivers, New Bern was the second town established in North Carolina and served for a time as the colonial capital.[43] Thomas Pollock (1654–1722), born in Glasgow, Scotland, on 6 May 1654 at the Pollock estate of Bal Gra, traveled to New Bern from Scotland in 1683 "as a deputy for Lord Carteret[,] one of the Lord Proprietors," gentlemen rewarded by King Charles II as overseers of the newly established Carolina colony. It was in New Bern that Thomas Pollock, one of many Scottish men who "regarded themselves as gentlemen" and for whom "[p]ublic office was a legitimate object of ambition," was able to join the ranks of successful Scottish men abroad.[44] He became proprietary governor of North Carolina, holding the post twice, from 1712 through 1714 and again in 1722. He married Martha Cullen West (died 1766) in Chowan, North Carolina, settled in Bertie County, and built a plantation that he named Bal Gra, in honor of his Scottish ancestral home. He also built other plantations, and his holdings transformed him into one of North Carolina's "lords of princely domains." He owned some 22,000 acres and had 10 plantations that thoroughly depended on enslaved labor.[45]

Governor Pollock's wife, Martha Cullen West, also had links to the British Isles. The daughter of Thomas Cullen, of Dover, England, Martha wed Pollock following the death of her first husband, Major Robert West, and with her second husband she had three sons: George and twin boys named Cullen and Thomas. Cullen Pollock and his wife, Anne Boothe Pollock, although childless, became one of North Carolina's wealthiest planter families. Cullen had the greatest number of slaves in all of the state, and his holdings were significantly increased by the substantial bequest that his mother made to him and to his brother Thomas. He and his brother were among the planter elite who owned over 10,000 acres. In 1753, Thomas Pollock of Chowan County dispensed with "40,000 acres and 16 other plantations" in his will.[46] In 1787, Cullen and Anne Pollock bought a house in Edenton, North Carolina, that came to be known as the Pollock House. Built in 1765, the structure was located on West Eden Street. They owned it until 1824. Its next owner was James Norcom, a physician and slave owner whose tactics of intimidation and predation are well documented in *Incidents in the Life of a Slave Girl, Written by Herself* (1861), the landmark account of female bondage by Harriet Jacobs, the enslaved woman who secreted herself in an attic for seven years in order to escape with her children from Norcom and from slavery.[47] Cullen Pollock died in 1795 in Baltimore, Maryland.[48]

The nuanced histories that connect Jesse Allen to North Carolina and to

New England persist also in the histories of the Pollock families that might have had ties to the Allen family's demise. Thomas Pollock, the twin of Cullen and brother of George and one of the great-grandsons of "Colonel Pollock to whom De Graffenried mortgaged his claims" on New Bern, forged an impressive alliance with the Northern intellectual elite when he married in the late 1760s.[49] His bride was Eunice Edwards, "the seventh daughter and eighth child of that great divine, Jonathan Edwards, D.D., president of Princeton College."[50] The couple, who wed sometime around 1767, had four children: George, Thomas, Elizabeth, and Frances. Three of the children remained childless, including George, "one of the wealthiest men in North Carolina, owning many plantations, and some 1,500 slaves." George Pollock owned several expansive plantation properties. These included Ashland Plantation, an 1,100-acre estate named in the 1830s in honor of Ashland, the Kentucky hometown of Henry Clay. Pollock sold the plantation in 1832 to a white slave owner named Thomas Holley, whose slaves completed major renovations and additions to the original structure.[51] George Pollock also owned Willow Branch, a sprawling plantation whose property lines were framed by willow trees, and another property that Pollock sold in 1811 to Thomas Holley.[52] Daughter Frances, who married New Bern resident and Irishman John Devereaux in 1793, was the only Edwards-Pollock sibling to bear children.[53] She also outlived her brothers and, as a result, inherited the plantation home known as Runiroi, as well as significant other plantation acreage.[54] Following the death of her husband, Thomas Pollock, his widow, Eunice Edwards Pollock, married Samuel Scollay, who at the time was a resident of Bertie County. It was through Scollay, a Boston native and a member of the family after whom Scollay Square in Boston was named, that the Pollock family connection to Boston was made.[55]

Charles Montfort chooses to forgo his life in a "land of love and beauty" and to relocate to the "comparative barrenness" of North Carolina. The region functions essentially for the Montforts as a political sanctuary, one in which they can avoid British mandates and thus function above the law. Yet, symbolically, the region was a charged liminal space, one that existed between the state's history as the second-oldest British colony and its more contemporary identity as the twelfth of the thirteen American states to join the Union in the aftermath of the War of Independence. In neither one of its incarnations does North Carolina exist as a suitable site for legal machinations that accommodate individual applications of the American slave code or British emancipation policies. In fact, the "new spot" to which Jesse Allen and the fictional Montforts were linked could not have been more unsuitable to what amounted to an essentially privatized slavery venture. In the early 1800s, North Carolina was "a conservative rural society dominated by a powerful unenlightened elite who detested change and mindlessly ignored the social cost of poverty, economic stagnation, and unresponsive government."[56] It also was a region in which "most of the wealth . . . was in land and slaves," and, as such, a region that would not easily accommodate any gradual or immediate emancipation of slaves.[57]

In New Bern, residents were vigilant about potential uprisings among the people of color. In the summer of 1792, white New Bern residents were "alarmed" by rumors of a potential slave revolt. "The negroes in this town and neighborhood," wrote one resident, "have stirred a rumour of their having in contemplation to rise against their masters and to procure themselves their liberty; the inhabitants have been alarmed and keep a strict watch to prevent their procuring arms; should it become serious, which I don't think, the worst that could befal [sic] us, would be their setting the town on fire. It is very absurd of the blacks," concluded the optimistic writer as he revealed his patronizing views of the people of color in his midst, "to suppose they could accomplish their views, and from the precautions that are taken to guard against a surprise, little danger is to be apprehended."[58]

Statewide antipathy in North Carolina toward change had complex implications for the institution of slavery and for people of African descent. This was due in part to the fact that in the years since the American Revolution, and between 1790 and 1815, in particular, North Carolina was regarded as the "Rip Van Winkle State—a pastoral, lethargic entity within a buoyant, restless new nation."[59] Yet, although this period of post–Revolutionary War lethargy was pronounced enough to generate the state's unflattering moniker, it did not eradicate entirely the turn toward increasing stratification and unforgiving power relations. In fact, "this fluid milieu" encouraged the creation of "fierce loyalties" that shaped the state's "order and predictability." In addition to strengthening ties to "family, church, and local communities," it also fostered a vague but purposeful hostility to change. As a result, native white North Carolinians tended to regard "local social rivals, outsiders, racial subordinates, and powerful institutions generally as 'the enemy.'"[60] The pervasiveness of such perspectives is realized quickly in the tragic tale that thoroughly infuses *Contending Forces*.

While *Contending Forces* may have been in part a cathartic autobiographical exercise for Hopkins, it is clear that as author and as descendant she continued to grapple with the far-reaching implications of decisions that quite literally enslaved her ancestors. Chapter 2, entitled "The Days 'before the War,'" provides the first glimpse of the North Carolina world into which the Montforts have journeyed. The chapter begins with lines from "The Antiquity of Freedom" (1842) by William Cullen Bryant (1794–1878). Hopkins's placement of the epigraph is in and of itself an illuminating confirmation of her own intellectual and political turmoil as she attempted to meld the moving personal history and impersonal political initiatives of family ancestors.

Hopkins exercised considerable restraint in her portrait of Charles Montfort, the man purportedly modeled on her own maternal great-grandfather. She laments his decisions, but she chooses not to condemn him outright. Instead, she chronicles his demise and allows the awful disintegration of his family to rouse the indignation of her readers. However, she does not eliminate all critique of the plan that can be regarded as wholly selfish and self-indulgent. Hopkins's invocation of William Cullen Bryant, a figure with whom her educated readers would have been wholly familiar, introduces the outrage that she herself does not permit herself to utter.

The epigraph from "The Antiquity of Freedom," which Hopkins uses in the novel's second chapter but does not attribute to Bryant, reads

> O Freedom! thou art not as poets dream,
> A fair girl with light and delicate limbs,
>
> . . . .
>
> Thy birthright was not given by human hands:
> Thou wert twinborn with man.[61]

It is first through the words of Bryant, a Mayflower descendant and the Massachusetts-born editor of the *New York Post*, that Hopkins contemplates the quietly unrelenting imposition of tragic reality that invalidates romantic illusions of equality, justice, and innocence. Indeed, Bryant's poem is an eerie overlay on the phantasmagoric scene in *Contending Forces* that unfolds as the Montforts's ship nears the New Bern harbor and enters into the unruly antebellum, pro-slavery space of Southern culture.

"The Antiquity of Freedom," itself a meditation on the natural world and the perversions of the unnatural forces cultivated by humankind, chronicles the first major transition that occurs in the novel: the willful and irreversible move from paradise to hell. Bryant's narrator is one who "linger[s]" in "peaceful shades— / Peaceful, unpruned, immeasureably old" and is able to conjure up "the earliest days of liberty" during this moment of respite as he rests near "old trees, tall oaks, and gnarled pines" where "the ground / Was never trenched by spade, and flowers spring up / Unsown, and die ungathered." He declares:

> It is sweet
> To linger here, among the flitting birds
> And leaping squirrels, wandering brooks, and winds
> That shake the leaves, and scatter, as they pass,
> A fragrance from the cedars, thickly set
> With pale-blue berries.[62]

Unlike the Montforts, Bryant's narrator quickly realizes the unrelenting attacks that Freedom will bear in the real world: "Power at thee has launched / his bolts, and with his lightning smitten thee." "Tyranny himself" also is "Thy enemy," admits the narrator.[63] In a recasting of the prelapsarian days of humankind, Bryant imagines Freedom as "twin-born with man." In a highly evocative scene that suggests Freedom as the first consort of man, Bryant also depicts freedom as an intensely protective ally in a world in which innocence is already threatened. Freedom instructs man how best to "teach the reed to utter simple airs," even as it steps into the "tangled wood" to "war upon the panther and the wolf."[64] Yet, if Freedom emerges as a personification of Montfort the slaveholder and gradual emancipator, it is encouraged to heed life-preserving threats that the Bermuda native fails to appreciate. The narrator declares:

> Oh! not yet
> Mayst thou unbrace thy corset, nor lay by
> Thy sword nor yet, O Freedom! close thy lids
> In slumber; for thine enemy never sleeps,
> And thou must watch and combat till the day
> Of the new earth and heaven.[65]

The vigilance that Bryant advocates is never realized in the early chapters of *Contending Forces*.

Hopkins's invocation of Bryant is not limited to the four-line epigraph that adds considerable nuance to chapter 2. Indeed, her literary overture to Bryant also admits one of the most memorable antebellum indictments of slavery and Bryant's unapologetic excoriation of gradual emancipation and its advocates. In response to the 1863 passage of the Emancipation Proclamation, which did not abolish slavery outright but instead emancipated all those enslaved in Southern territories controlled by Confederate forces, Bryant, according to his biographer, John Bigelow, "portrayed the follies of gradual emancipation in terms as nearly approaching to genuine eloquence, probably, as he ever reached."[66] His strident characterization of slavery and the motives that justify gradual emancipation are riveting. When overlaid on *Contending Forces*, Bryant's powerful rhetoric intensifies the tragic romance out of which the Hopkins family history was born. The fateful decision of Charles Montfort to leave Bermuda for North Carolina is spurred by his desire to enact gradual emancipation on his own terms. He is determined to sustain no financial losses as a result of emancipation and determines that his most reliable route to autonomous capitalism lies in relocation to the former colonies. His decision, though deliberately made, is flawed, however, since gradual emancipation was a more feasible, albeit convoluted, enterprise in the Northern colonies than it was in the Southern colonies that ultimately united as the Confederate States of America.

Gradual emancipation was a policy not limited to British colonies in the West Indies. Indeed, throughout the late eighteenth and early nineteenth centuries, states in the North implemented various timetables for the abolition of slavery. Historians agree that the policy benefited slave owners rather than those enslaved. Statutes such as those enacted in Connecticut, Massachusetts, and Rhode Island, for example, significantly reduced the numbers of slaves. Unfortunately, they often doubly penalized individuals born into slavery—either by eliminating the opportunity to become free if born before the passage of the law or by postponing freedom until an individual had labored for twenty-one or even twenty-five years. Gradual emancipation then, was a staggered and oppressive system. It essentially taxed the enslaved populations so that they not only bought their freedom through years of additional service but also bore the burden of compensating owners who wanted to recoup and to maximize their own investments in the slave trade. Perhaps the clause that most often sparked outrage in critics was the subtle but undeniable resistance to freedom in legislation that was designed to ease the suffering of innocents. Gradual emancipation acts often included elaborate schedules of release and frequently failed to dispense freedom in a humane or timely manner to those who were enslaved. In Connecticut, individuals still were being held in bondage as late as 1848. In this year, six people were freed by an "immediate and comprehensive" emancipation law, passed some fifty-six years after the ratification of the state's 1784 Gradual Emancipation Act. These individuals lived the majority of their lives as slaves in a supposedly "free" Northern state.[67] Such manipulations of the law, which produced numerous cases of lifelong servitude and gross impositions on individuals of color that essentially invalidated the notion of the North as the righteous province of freedom, fueled the protests of writers such as Bryant.

Bryant's tirade against gradual emancipation is bolstered most significantly by his gripping Miltonic portrayal of slavery. He declares with apocalyptic fury and without hesitation that slavery is

> a foul and monstrous idol, a Juggernaut under which thousands are crushed to death; it is a Moloch for whom the children of the land pass through fire. . . . [L]et us hurl the grim image from its pedestal. Down with it to the ground. Dash it to fragments; trample it in the dust. Grind it to powder as the prophets of old commanded that the graven images of the Hebrew idolaters should be ground, and in that state scatter it to the four winds and strew it upon the waters, that no human hand shall ever again gather up the accursed atoms and mould them into an image to be worshiped again with human sacrifice.[68]

He then goes on to insist that gradual emancipation is a wholly political and amoral act, one that depends on the unnatural suppression of human responses to suffering.

Like William Lloyd Garrison, Frederick Douglass, and Sojourner Truth, Bryant invokes domestic and familial imagery in order to further his campaign of moral suasion. He declared:

> My friends, if a child of yours were to fall into the fire, would you pull him out gradually? If he were to swallow a dose of laudanum sufficient to cause speedy death, and a stomach pump was at hand, would you draw the poison out by degrees? If your house were on fire, would you put it out piecemeal? And yet there are men who talk of gradual emancipation by force of ancient habit, and there are men in the Slave States who makes [sic] of slavery a sort of idol which they are unwilling to part with; which, if it must be removed, they would prefer to see removed after a lapse of time and tender leave-takings.[69]

Hopkins's astute readers might well have heard the fiery rhetoric of Bostonian William Lloyd Garrison in Bryant's argument. Indeed, Bryant not only invoked the fiery oratory with which William Lloyd Garrison introduced himself and *The Liberator* to antebellum readers, but also unapologetically appropriated it. Bryant's references to endangered children and houses echo lines that Garrison himself penned some thirty-four years earlier.

The urgency that marked Garrison's abolitionist career continued to inspire his descendants and those of the men and women who worked tirelessly with him in the multifaceted fight against injustice. Hopkins, who took pride in her knowledge of Boston abolitionist politics, was well versed in the *Liberator*'s history and familiar with the eloquent challenges that its editor routinely handed down. In turning to Bryant rather than Garrison, though, Hopkins enveloped her novel in a discourse of genteel literary politics and did not link it explicitly, or predictably, to a history of volatile, uncompromising political critique. Her choice, however, did not undercut the intense pride that Hopkins took in her documented links to Garrison and his era. These ties, which persisted through her own interactions with Garrison family members and the descendants of Boston's African American abolitionists, emboldened her. Her modern-day Garrisonian principles were evident in the forthright and daring manner in which she wrote. The unapologetic documentary style of her works was one of the clearest indications of her commitment to fulfilling an awesome political legacy, and it was one of the most important justifications for the claim she made to take her place on the public political stage of the twentieth century.

One of the lingering tensions that emerges in Hopkins's career is her embrace and romanticizing of the British empire and, by extension, life in its second-oldest colony. In *Contending Forces*, Hopkins's historical indulgence manifests itself first through her narrow view of colonial slavery in Bermuda. Although she strategically invokes Bryant's words and their high moralistic fury in the novel, she also maintains an air of political innocence that can result in restrained and even bucolic characterizations of slavery. In *Contending Forces*, for example, Hopkins assures her readers that, in Bermuda, "slavery never reached its lowest depths."[70] This is the same island, however, on which Mary Prince, the self-emancipated West Indian woman and author of the first published slave narrative by a British woman of African descent, suffered brutal treatment while in bondage and saw firsthand the murderous rage that owners directed toward those that they enslaved. Prince's traumatic experiences in Bermuda, where she was born into a large enslaved family, coincided with the era in which the Montforts of *Contending Forces* were presiding over a contented slave population.

Prince offers one of the most illuminating reports about white involvement in Bermuda slavery in her account of how she and her sisters were sold following the death of their white mistress. "My heart throbbed with grief and terror so violently," she recalled, "that I pressed my hands quite tightly across my breast, but I could not keep it still, and it continued to leap as though it would burst out of my body. But who cared for that? Did one of the many bystanders, who were looking at us so carelessly, think of the pain that wrung the hearts of the negro woman and her young ones? No, no!" She goes on to make the generous qualification that "not all" of the onlookers were "bad," but she does conclude that "slavery hardens white people's hearts towards the blacks; and many of them were not slow to make their remarks upon us aloud, without regard to our grief—though their light words fell like cayenne on the fresh wounds of our hearts. Oh those white people have small hearts who can only feel for themselves."[71] Prince's insightful exposé of daily life in Bermuda provides sobering counterimages and introduces a set of historical contending forces relating to the myths and realities of slavery.

Despite the still-unresolved confirmation of the Allen family's whereabouts in the late 1700s, that the Montforts, that is, the fictionalized Allen family, are deliberately positioned as slaveholders is key to the foundational story that Pauline Hopkins develops first in *Contending Forces*. Although she sidesteps the graphic slavery realities that Mary Prince documented so forcefully, Hopkins does produce a concise and nuanced narrative of Bermuda's response to the slavery question. She also establishes the first of two key invocations of British law that frame the novel. In this instance, she uses the antislavery desires articulated by the empire and the laws that this collective desire eventually produces to effectively discipline and govern unruly colonists. In Hopkins's view of global antislavery history, it is the amorality and willful self-indulgence of this latter constituency that pose real and symbolic threats to the honor of the motherland.

Hopkins invokes the allegory of family in her depictions of Bermuda and of slavery there, and these hint at an environment infused with loving interdependent relationships, maternal indulgence, and paternal beneficence. Such gestures allow her to accommodate, rather than critique outright, the lifestyle and proslavery philosophies attributed to real families such as those that owned Mary Prince and others, or to fictional characters such as the Montforts. Hopkins invests in the notion of the beneficent empire and unabashedly declares that "England's honor and greatness had become a passion with the inhabitants, and restrained the planters from committing the ferocious acts of brutality so commonly practiced by the Spaniards."[72] This is a sweeping redemptive gesture, one that appears at first glance to minimize the inherent horrors of slavery and its manifestations in Bermuda by applying a comparative analysis of degrees. It also runs counter to what Prince, author of the first published slave narrative in England by a woman of African descent, attributed to British colonials. During her time in England, Prince admitted to readers that she was "often much vexed, and I feel great sorrow when I hear that people in this country say that the slaves do not need better usage, and do not want to be free. They believe the foreign people, who deceive them, and say slaves are happy. I say, Not so. How can slaves be happy when they have the halter round their neck and the whip upon their back? and are disgraced and thought no more of than beasts?—and are separated from their mothers, and husbands, and children, and sisters, just as cattle are sold and separated."[73] Prince ultimately confesses that she has "often wondered how English people can go out into the West Indies and act in such a beastly manner. But when they go to the West Indies, she concludes, "they forget God and all feeling of shame, I think, since they see and do such things. . . . [T]hey put a cloak around the truth . . . All slaves want to be free—to be free is very sweet."[74]

Hopkins's perspective here on movements toward emancipation in fact is in keeping with other historical perspectives on the island. Henry Hamilton, a Scotsman, a descendant of Mary Queen of Scots, the island's governor from 1788 to 1794, and the man after whom the island's capital is named, "held an optimistic view about the Bermudian slaves." Hamilton found them in no way "tainted by the turbulent example of slaves in other colonies of which they cannot well be ignorant, so lenient, in general has been the treatment of them."[75] By 1800, however, the island's white authorities were imposing draconian measures to curb established patterns of slave autonomy. The "reactionary legislation" was designed "to stop all retailing of goods by slaves, all butchering, all wandering at night, and every variety of lottery, raffling, dice, and cards."[76]

Although Henry Hamilton believed that slaves "can be trusted under arms" and was a man who "could not regard slavery as an imminent danger or an outstanding problem,"[77] other white Bermudians openly advocated the suppression of the enslaved population. President Henry Tucker, in response to the House of Parliament's move to outlaw the slave trade and anticipating the call to abolish slavery altogether, suggested that white Bermudians apply "some legal restraint" in order to "arrest that progressive influence which [the slaves] are acquiring."[78] Tucker, who was alarmed by the fact that some of the island's "colored people 'are enterprising, sensible, and aspiring in the world,'" also was a chief proponent of antiemancipation practices that included mandates to slave owners that they "not liberate a slave of less than forty-one years of age except to leave the island."[79]

In *Contending Forces*, Charles Montfort's strategic but fatal resistance to British parliamentary efforts to abolish the slave trade is the result of his focus on the economics, rather than the moral question, of slavery. Indeed, as news of the Whig campaigns led by Lord Grenville, Charles Fox, and William Wilberforce reached Bermuda in 1806, many whites responded keenly. The *Bermuda Gazette* was inundated with letters in which citizens welcomed the

Contending Forces *as Ancestral Narrative*

prospect of abolition. One outspoken resident declared that slavery "has long palsied the arm of Bermudian industry, corrupted the morals of our youth, covered our island with poverty and wretchedness." Others insisted that slavery was an "insatiable vulture which preys incessantly on the vitals of her unhappy country" and that it was "the irreconcilable enemy of all improvement, the source of evils, moral and physical, without number."[80]

Bermuda, as represented in *Contending Forces*, emerges as an apolitical space. This is most noticeable when one compares the novel's stirring partisan representations of the proslavery South and the domestic politics and machinations in the post-Reconstruction north. This may signal a troubling ambivalence on Hopkins's part, but the one-sided view of early colonial Bermuda also is produced in part by Hopkins's focus on the heroic English campaign to abolish the trade and slavery. *Contending Forces* opens with an enthusiastic tribute to the British men who worked tirelessly to achieve an end to Britain's slave trade and to abolition in the British colonies. Although she focuses only on the white Britons associated with the campaign, Hopkins easily could have expanded her acknowledgment to include Nathaniel Paul, her great-granduncle, who in 1832 began travels throughout England and Scotland, ostensibly to raise awareness about initiatives such as the Wilberforce Settlement and to lecture widely on the history of slavery and American abolition. During his two years abroad as an agent for Wilberforce, Nathaniel Paul, whom Hopkins profiled as her great-grandfather in her 1901 *Colored American Magazine* biographical profile, spoke with and testified before members of Parliament. In the summer of 1833, he traveled to Ipswich with William Lloyd Garrison, who had arrived in England to raise funds for the American abolitionist cause, and enjoyed a four-hour interview with the renowned Thomas Clarkson (1760–1846). During that memorable exchange with the then "aged and sightless" Clarkson, Paul "described the attitude of Negroes to the American Colonization Society," and his words, according to Garrison, "seemed powerfully to agonize the mind of the venerable man."[81] The Paul family connection to the British Isles and to the ongoing debates there about abolition significantly enriched Pauline Hopkins's appreciation of the historic evolution of antislavery campaigns in and beyond the United States. The legendary family history and the marital history of the Reverend Nathaniel Paul, her maternal ancestor and perhaps the family's most enterprising antislavery activist, also demonstrated for her the inextricable connection between romance and politics.

Hopkins's great-granduncle Nathaniel was a committed abolitionist, a "highly respectable and pious man of color" and a man "distinguished for his intelligence and private virtues."[82] Like his brother Thomas and in-law relation Jesse Allen, Nathaniel lived in Boston and relocated as a result of family upheaval and professional opportunities. When he married Elizabeth (Eliza) Lamson of Hollis, New Hampshire, in 1814, the couple relocated to Boston. There, like Jesse Allen and his wife Elizabeth, the Pauls suffered the devastating loss of a child. Boston city records reveal that a four-year-old son named Nathaniel died of influenza in 1819. The couple left the city for Albany, New York, and it was here in 1828, that Eliza Lamson Paul died. Death prompted Nathaniel Paul to relocate again, and in the wake of his wife's passing, he left their Albany home for the Wilberforce community in Ontario, Canada, where he joined his brother Benjamin in maintenance and improvement of the Negro settlement there. He later returned to Albany and established himself as an earnest advocate for equal civil and education rights and immediate abolition.

In addition to representing African American interests abroad, Paul worked diligently to achieve the spiritual, social, and professional uplift of his parishioners. He lived for a number of years in Albany where he was pastor at the Hamilton Street Baptist Church, an African American congregation, in the city. Paul was recognized for being "of great utility in improving the morals and conduct of that class of the community, which has been but too long neglected. To prepare men for the rational enjoyment of liberty," reflected the editors of *Freedom's Journal* in one of their earliest issues, "their minds must be enlightened to a just sense of their own rights and the duties which they owe to the community. This has been the great object of the pastor of the African church, and we congratulate him on the success which has attended his endeavours."[83] His career there cemented his reputation as "an estimable and eloquent divine and pastor of the Hamilton Street Baptist Church in Albany."[84]

Nathaniel Paul's marital history also echoes in the repeated suggestions that his great-grandniece Pauline makes that Britain, rather than America, was a land in which people of color could truly realize and preserve their romantic passions. Nathaniel Paul's second marriage drew considerable public attention, and it highlighted the social tensions and hypocrisies of American social life. In 1833, during his productive but eventually controversial fund-raising tour of the United Kingdom on behalf of the Wilberforce settlement, Paul married Anne Adey (ca. 1791–?), a white British woman. Known among her friends as an "accomplished, intelligent, amiable and pious woman," she was the daughter of John and Sarah Stanley Adey of Gloucester. There is little documentation of the courtship between Paul and Adey, but it is possible that he was introduced to her through his own contacts with the British abolitionist Edward Adey, an active participant in English antislavery circles.[85] The

Paul-Adey marriage may have been inspired by romance but it was couched in a highly political context. This interracial marriage, imbued with genuine devotion and touted in the abolitionist press of the day, also was strengthened by the couple's political convictions. The Paul-Adey marriage echoes powerfully in the fictional alliances that Hopkins creates in *Contending Forces* and in other works such as *Winona*, where marital bliss and political resolutions posit the value of interracial harmony and suggest that such promise only can be realized if the idealistic though weary protagonists depart immediately for England, the bastion of progressive prohumanity sentiment.[86]

The experiences in the United States of Ann Adey Paul, a stalwart abolitionist wife, contrast sharply with those of the fictional Grace Montfort, a woman whose apolitical identity and residence in the American South intensifies her victimization by racist predators. Unlike Grace Montfort, whose racial identity is conjectured and imposed, the cultural and political significance of her interracial marriage was not lost on Ann Adey Paul. In England, the couple was feted and was "most cordially received by the most respectable and worthy members of society"; her British compatriots regarded the marriage "in a very favorable manner," and it did not "excit[e] surprise or opposition."[87] She was prepared to accompany her husband to the United States, even though supporters like William Lloyd Garrison "frankly told [her] what she would, in all probability, be called to endure, on coming to this country." Yet, as Garrison recalled publicly in a substantial October 1841 *Liberator* update about Mrs. Paul, "she calmly made up her mind to receive, in the spirit of her Saviour, whatever of reproach or obloquy might be cast upon her."[88] Following the relatively sudden decline and death of her husband, Ann Paul became an abolitionist migrant and a recipient of the attentions of the nation's most outspoken abolitionist, William Lloyd Garrison. Garrison regarded Ann Paul as one whose life "strongly appeals to us as the friends of humanity, and especially as abolitionists." "She is indeed a stranger in a strange land," he wrote Benson, "without friends or relatives, without any certain abiding place, and without knowing where to direct her footsteps; and all this, solely because, being destitute of the vulgar prejudice against a colored complexion, she married in England the Rev. Nathaniel Paul, a man of fine personal appearance and talents, but one of those who are regarded by the pseudo democrats and christians of this country as belonging to an inferior race."[89] The itinerancy of her life, brought on by her distance from home and political choice to wed a man of color, transformed her into a beneficiary of temporary kindnesses by leading abolitionist couples in and beyond Boston.[90]

The kind of racialized domestic upheaval that so marked the American life of Ann Adey Paul is a model of the kind of Anglo-American romance that

Pauline Hopkins attempted to rectify in her writings. It is no surprise that England, the land in which Hopkins's great-granduncle Nathaniel received so warm a political and social welcome, continued to exist for her as the sphere in which it was possible to achieve racial equality and to experience meaningful life events such as marriage. The destruction of domestic bliss, so pointedly illustrated in the life of Ann Adey Paul, occurs when one leaves the decorous world of the empire and journeys to America. In America in general, and in the ostensibly free North in particular, Ann Adey Paul experienced "that scorn and neglect which are meted out to all who dare in their practice, to assert, that God has made of one blood all nations of men, and is no re-specter of persons."[91] Certainly Pauline Hopkins's appreciation of the empire, its accommodation of romance, and its leadership in the global turn toward abolition of the slave trade and of slavery was informed by her knowledge of Nathaniel Paul's experiences. It also was shaped indelibly by the clarion calls for self-determination and strategic nationalism articulated by James Monroe Whitfield, the Exeter, New Hampshire, native to whom Jesse Allen became a brother-in-law.

James Monroe Whitfield not only inherited his father's well-known high moral worth and capacity for hard work but also was a gifted poet and writer, an emigrationist, and a beloved leader in the California Masonic movement. Like so many people of color, Whitfield pursued a livelihood that did not rep-resent the full extent of his interests. He used his earnings to finance his ex-tensive travel to political meetings and to support his passionate and engaged commitment to African American civil and political rights. By age sixteen, he was delivering impassioned political speeches such as the one he gave at a Cleveland race convention in which he argued for new Negro settlements on the California border. His barbershop, like those of his contemporaries in cities such as Boston and Providence, may have been an essential forum for the free exchange of ideas, but Whitfield's ambitions went further. He lived a life of the mind, and even as he worked as a barber in upstate New York and on the West Coast for much of his life, he cultivated his skills as a poet, orator, and activist. Bostonian William Cooper Nell hailed Whitfield as a man whose "genius" was "native and uncultivated" but whose works had "much of the finish of experienced authorship."[92] He was one of the most eloquent of race men, his political perspectives enriched by his creative gifts that earned him accolades in the Northern and Western press. Jesse Allen's brother-in-law was a firebrand, a man for whom race was not a tragedy but instead represented a series of opportunities yet to be realized.

The lives of James Monroe Whitfield and Jesse Allen crossed only briefly. Whitfield, who was born in 1822, was a young child when his sister Elizabeth married the Bermuda fugitive Jesse and began her family in the late 1820s. By 1839, when the Allens were living in Boston, James had established himself in Buffalo, New York, and was maintaining his own barbershop near Lake Erie. In Buffalo, which was one of the principal border cities in the Underground Railroad network, Whitfield became an increasingly eloquent advocate of black nationalism, and he began to explore the merits of emigration. Whitfield's creative genius was nurtured in Frederick Douglass's *North Star*, the newspaper that the formerly enslaved antislavery activist and orator had established in Rochester. Whitfield used the paper not only to publish his works but also to carry on a lively dialogue with Douglass and other emerging forces in the African American political network. In addition to being a regular subscriber to the paper, he submitted forthright commentaries on local plans to mobilize people of color and evaluated national platforms advanced in the convention movement of the 1840s and 1850s. In September 1849, he responded, for example, to Douglass's call to establish a National League. "The necessity of such an organization to draw out and embody the moral and intellectual power of the colored people of this country," Whitfield proclaimed, "is too obvious to need argument."[93] Whitfield's keen assessments of African American political issues eventually prompted Douglass to learn more about the New Hampshire native. His impression of the young man was so great that he was moved to comment on the "malignant arrangements of society" that relegated Whitfield to a barbershop rather than having a position of greater public influence. "That talents so commanding, gifts so rare, poetic powers so distinguished, should be tied to the handle of a razor and buried in the precincts of a barber's shop . . . is painfully disheartening," lamented Douglass.[94] By 1853, Douglass had reason to be encouraged by Whitfield's promising career as a poet. The publication of *America and Other Poems*, his first volume of poetry, prompted a reviewer for *Frederick Douglass' Paper*, to which Whitfield's sister, Elizabeth, and her husband, Jesse Allen, subscribed, to herald Whitfield as "a genius, and a genuine lover of the muses." The reviewer speculated aloud that social constraints and the "force of circumstances" that severely limited his professional options in America may have prompted Whitfield to become "somewhat of a misanthropist." The reviewer nonetheless concluded that the volume was magnificent and evocative of the best of European writers. Poems in the volume such as "Yes! Strike That Sounding String" "forcibly remind us of BYRON" confessed the writer, who then closed with a spirited exhortation: "Friends of Freedom!" he wrote, "buy it."[95]

Whitfield, spurred on by the powerful endorsement of his talents and creative abilities, immersed himself in organized politics. He became increasingly visible in the growing Northern campaigns to engineer African American uplift, an agenda reinforced by his work during the July 1853 Colored National Convention in Rochester, New York. Elected to the Committee of Sentiments with Douglass and George B. Vashon, who would marry Whitfield's second cousin Susan Paul Smith, Whitfield heartily seconded the proclamation that insisted that "all the truths in the whole universe of God, are allied to our cause."[96] In the wake of this successful publication, the first monograph published by a New Hampshire native and one of the earliest collected volumes of poetry by an African American, Whitfield became known as "the literary protagonist of emigration and Negro nationalism." On the eve of the Civil War, Whitfield was in Central America, surveying lands that might be ideal for African American relocation. His reconnaissance, sponsored in part by the plan advanced by Representative Frank Blair Jr. of Missouri, complemented the more well-known efforts of Martin Delany, who just the year before had been exploring the Niger Valley in Africa in order to find and then negotiate passage to lands that would support African American emigration.

It is ironic that Jesse Allen, a man who may have lived his American life as a traumatized fugitive orphan, was linked by marriage to the nation's leading emigrationist poet, a man who was convinced that a stable life within American borders was neither desirable nor possible. Such contrasts could reify Allen's perpetual homelessness, but others functioned as potent antidotes to the specter of violence and uncertainty. Hopkins imposes a set of restorative domestic possibilities when she weds Jesse Allen's history to that of the Smiths, the family that included her cousin Elijah W. Smith, her influential mentor and the beloved poet laureate of their African American Boston community. She honors Smith, who passed away before the novel's publication, by naming her protagonist after him and developing for the character Will Smith the formal credentials and honors that Elijah, her mentor, was unable to pursue because of the constraints and prejudices of the time in which he lived. Elijah Smith, the devoted family man and talented artist, had an education that included years at the city's Abiel Smith School, the first public institution in the country built specifically to educate African American children. He lived a rich intellectual life despite his limited formal advanced education, and, as a writer, he demonstrated his literary genius and capacity for creating insightful political art. Will Smith, the protagonist of *Contending Forces*, whose name and close family relationship invokes the figure of Elijah W. Smith, increasingly becomes a Du Boisean figure, one whose intellectual sophistication and European studies contribute to his racial capital when he returns to his Boston family. The life of Elijah Smith most deliberately informs Will Smith's development at a key juncture, however, when the fictional character becomes increasingly aware that his prized education can be of most use to him in post–Civil War America if he becomes a student of the grueling and intense race conflicts that threaten African American families and endanger the nation's cherished democratic ideals. Will Smith evolves as a vitally necessary heroic figure because his intellectualization of lynching, when combined with the emotional testimony, establishes the contours of the new American social education, a public curriculum that can contribute much to racial progress and that also requires activists able to deliver meaningful contextualization and keen analysis.

The horrifying details of the Montfort family's fate expose the insistent documentary impulse of the novel. Yet readers cannot easily avoid Hopkins's insistence that the book is a romance. As the early chapters make clear, the genre of "romantic literature" literally cannot contain either the history of Jesse Allen or the story of Jesse Montfort. Hopkins, in her preface, first characterizes the novel as a "simple, homely tale," which, if "unassumingly told," is capable of "cement[ing] the bond of brotherhood among all classes and all complexions."[97] Even this simple tale is one that is rife with complexities. It is, according to Hopkins, an account of the "inmost thoughts and feelings of the Negro" and the "fire and romance which lie dormant in our history," which remains, "as yet, unrecognized by writers of the Anglo-Saxon race." In this novel, access to that dormant store of "fire and romance" is routed through an explosive tragedy, one that transforms Hopkins, the writer of literary romance, into a documentary revisionary historian. The narrative palimpsest that incorporates facts and fictions, romance and tragedy, testifies to the lasting effects of the inherited family trauma and to the persistence of what stands as "secondary memory." Yet the novel's historical import is made possible by Hopkins's investment in primary memory, the visceral and quite literally unspeakable histories of individuals like Jesse Allen and Jesse Montfort, men who have survived, but been irreparably damaged by, antebellum violence and the sociopolitical realities that sanction such acts.[98]

In *Contending Forces*, Hopkins wields her pen as a historian and uses it to craft a work of testimony. The blend of the two is powerful; indeed the personal here intensifies the overall political agenda and illuminates the primary interdependence between testimony and history. In the novel, Hopkins herself becomes an actor, one who functions as historian and as a "secondary witness," an individual who "undergoes a transferential relation, and must work out an acceptable subject-position with respect to the witness and his or her testimony."[99] As Hopkins performs this complex analytical and historical work, she provides a gripping and invaluable blueprint of her maturation as a political thinker. In the novel's preface, she makes the following plain admission: "I feel my own deficiencies too strongly to attempt original composition" on certain historical topics "at this crisis in the history of the Negro in the United States."[100] It is telling, though, when Hopkins admits that she has made a "somewhat abrupt and daring venture within the wide field of romantic literature."[101] While she confesses an almost reckless application of romance, Hopkins refrains from an unabashed admission about the family narrative that shapes the novel. Still, it becomes clear that Hopkins uses the past, and specifically her own known past, to groom herself as a public thinker and to facilitate the novel's secondary focus on contemporary race relations in post-Reconstruction America.

The accumulated successes of Jesse Allen's children stand in sharp contrast to the interrupted life and traumatic displacements that he allegedly survived during his childhood and young adulthood. The intimacy and interdependence that emerged because of the Allen children's close proximity to their parents may have been a healing balm for Jesse, a man who may have been violently deprived of his own immediate family. Jesse Allen, once absorbed into the race, did become a quiet advocate of major social change. He was well aware of the abolitionist agenda, and he offered financial support to the pioneering organizations and enterprises dedicated to ending slavery. His contributions, coupled with the efforts and successes of his children, created a powerful emancipatory postbellum corrective to the barbarity and vulnerability that *Contending Forces* links to the ante- and postbellum Southern milieu.

Political and historical facts invigorate *Contending Forces* and transform this first published novel of the twentieth century by an African American woman into a potent manifesto for social justice, recompense, and human kindness. It persists as a novel that chronicles gross violations of human spirit and families, yet the reconstructed Allen-Hopkins family history now provides a lens through which to reread this compelling account of Southern pride, Northern industry, and American resilience. This enigmatic narrative succeeds not just because it stands as a work of sobering documentary non-fiction. It also succeeds because Hopkins invokes literary romance to intensify and finance her mission to use the written word as enduring and evocative testimony for individuals denied their opportunity to speak truth to power.

10

Cooperative Enterprises

[W]e believe that a paper devoted to the dissemination
of useful knowledge among our brethren, and to their moral
and religious improvement, must meet with the cordial
approbation of every friend to humanity.

Editorial, *Freedom's Journal*,
16 March 1827

The management respectfully requests that every man
and woman who desires that the present perils, and wrongs
endured by our race, should be averted and dispelled, will
not only aid this work by a . . . personal subscription,
but will so far as is possible contribute thereto.
"Editorial and Publishers' Announcements,"
Colored American Magazine,
May 1900

Pauline Hopkins left the historically black neighborhoods of Beacon Hill and the West End as the twentieth century began and as Boston became home to a thriving multiethnic industrialized metropolis of over two and a half million people. The systematic migration of the city's African American residents to communities such as Roxbury and Cambridge reflected the pace and nature of the social and civic transformations under way. There were definite signs of change that signaled both welcome historic evolutions of the black community and the upward mobility of some of its members, as well as of others in the city, which confirmed what would become an irreversible dispersal of the small but long-standing and cohesive community on Beacon Hill. One of the most noticeable signs of the change on Beacon Hill could be found in the transformation of the African Baptist Church, known to many as the African Meeting House. This symbol of

Hopkins's inspiring maternal heritage and the embodiment of black Boston history was no longer an African American church. Sold in 1898 to a Jewish congregation, the historic church had become, by 1904, a synagogue for the Anshi Lubavitch congregation and would remain so until 1972.[1] The temple came to be surrounded by neighborhoods increasingly crowded with new European immigrants. Many African Americans of the West End migrated to Roxbury, a former Irish enclave.

The Hopkins family was not part of the substantial African American migration to Roxbury. William, Sarah, and Pauline headed instead for the relatively middle-class neighborhoods of Cambridge, where they bought and settled into a modest residence in North Cambridge. Pauline purchased the home at 53 Clifton Street, a street whose houses were built on lands that in 1875 had been a racecourse for horses, for $1,350 and moved in with her invalid mother, Sarah, and her stepfather, William, who was ailing from rheumatism and injuries suffered during his Civil War–era military service.[2] Hopkins listed her mother on the mortgage as co-owner, but, as she later explained, apparently did so in order to protect the property in case "of marriage being made by her in the future."[3] Once in Cambridge, the Hopkins family no longer was close to the white-collar businesses or to the bustling trade districts in downtown Boston. Yet, as new residents of the area known now as the Central Square region of Cambridge, they were a part of the fast-growing urban Boston that saw over one million people living within a ten-mile radius of Boston Common by 1900. At this time, Boston was a city in which just over 30 percent of registered voters were foreign-born, and approximately half of that number were Irish. Boston's Irish American inhabitants shaped the city emphatically, and its African American population was increasingly overshadowed by the influx of European immigrants.

She may have been geographically removed from her ancestral African American community, but Hopkins soon found herself immersed in the newly emerging communities of color that signaled the looming Great Migration, the exodus that would begin in 1910, in which between 300,000 and one million African Americans from the South would relocate to Northern states and to the American West. In the decade preceding the Great Migration, Southern people of color relocated steadily to Boston, and their presence infused new life into the American histories about which Pauline Hopkins had written and performed. Inspired anew to document the increasingly rich history of her race, she welcomed the opportunity to partner with a group of young men whose life stories and accomplishments could stand as idealized examples of the Great Migration. In 1900, four ambitious Virginians in their twenties, Walter Wallace, Harper Fortune, Walter Johnson, and Jesse W. Watkins, were poised to make history for themselves and the race by establishing the nation's first African American literary magazine.

The founders of the *Colored American Magazine* left their Virginia homes, as so many would do during the Great Migration, in pursuit of steady employment in busy urban centers and relief from the oppressive segregation and racial intimidation that permeated daily life. They left a rigidly and brutally maintained segregated South that consistently thwarted and limited the economic, educational, social, and political rights and aspirations of its African American citizens.[4] The four *Colored American Magazine* founders and their immediate families all shared unrelenting and resourceful pursuits of education, and their modest access to the professions provided them with some measure of economic security. Still, the unpredictable nature of Southern life continued to jeopardize, and sometimes even invalidate, such accomplishments and ambitions. In Boston, Walter Wallace would see his "dream and ambition" come to fruition in the *Colored American Magazine*, an elegant, substantive, and absorbing monthly magazine that featured works by leading women and men of the race and that created unprecedented public and national connections between diverse African American communities.[5]

Wallace, Fortune, Johnson, and Watkins left Virginia at a time when the states were encroaching ever more deliberately on the civil rights of their African American residents. By the spring of 1900, when they launched the magazine, they and others in their newly adopted African American community were confronting what Howard University dean Kelly Miller just months later in October 1900 would decry as "a revival of racial arrogance" that was financed by aggressive responses "to the feebler races" as part of a "whole trend of imperial aggression."[6] The country was rocked by race riots in urban centers such as New York City and cities such as Akron, Ohio. It was plagued by lynchings, not limited to the South. Vicious acts of public race violence were reported in Colorado, Indiana, Kansas, and Nebraska, and these events shook communities of color to the core.[7] The African American press, which provided steady documentation of the widespread racial tumult, proposed that this upheaval was like the mayhem that had plagued antebellum America. Leading men of the race published letters in race papers such as the *Cleveland Gazette* and the Washington, D.C., *Colored American* in which they called for a "new allotment of Joshua E. Giddings, Lovejoys and Charles Sumners . . . to [take up] the cause of the down-trodden Afro-American in his humiliated condition."[8] African Americans, bombarded by relentless attacks—rhetorical and physical, social and cultural—began the twentieth century under the pall of "crude rhetoric of negrophobes, the enactment of discriminatory legislation, and the eruption of diverse forms of racial violence."[9] License for these behaviors was rooted in segregationist legislation and the public dissemination of racist diatribes, illustrated well by the careers of figures like Ben Tillman, who crisscrossed the nation giving spirited and very well-received antiblack lectures to huge audiences.

In Boston, the *Colored American Magazine* founders were quickly absorbed into an ambitious African American community that engaged ardently with each other, elected officials, and the nation as a whole about civil rights, racial violence, and the flawed democracy that was America. Ensconced in a Northern environment that sought to combat the racial hostilities by forming effective community organizations, Wallace, Fortune, Johnson, and Watkins soon were challenging the racial myths about African American literacy, ambition, and humanity that were at the heart of Southern campaigns to disenfranchise communities of color. By spring 1900, all four of the *Colored American Magazine* founders were living in Boston, and together they started the magazine, without fanfare, while boarding and living in West End homes that they shared with working-class couples and other young men. They were optimists who would insist that contemporary social and political events compelled them to create the magazine. They drafted a compelling prospectus, and the lengthy and energetic statement was republished frequently in the early issues of the *Colored American Magazine*. The document revealed the men's political awareness and their commitment to black solidarity, civic education, and cultural awareness. "Recognizing an immediate need of a Race Journal, otherwise than our current local periodicals," wrote Wallace, Fortune, Watkins, and Johnson, "we have organized a Company, to be known as the Colored Co-operative Publishing Company." The men were determined that the *Colored American Magazine* would become part of "every Negro family" and emerge as a "magazine of merit" and a "credit to the present and future generations."[10]

Walter Wallace and Harper Fortune lived together at 232 West Canton Street, in the home of William Haygood and his wife, a Kentucky-born couple who rented rooms to five lodgers, all of whom had Southern parents and all but one of whom had been born in the South.[11] Wallace, the chief executive officer for the *Colored American Magazine* and the Colored Co-operative Publishing Company that produced the periodical, was born in June 1874 in Boydton, Virginia, a small town in Mecklenburg County, which lay some ninety-five miles northeast of Richmond and eighty miles north of Raleigh, North Carolina. The area was known as excellent horse breeding country. He grew up in close proximity to Randolph-Macon College, the first Methodist college in the United States to receive a charter, which was built on former racetrack land in Boydton.[12] His mother was Nannie J. Ellerson Wallace.

His father, Merritt R. Wallace, was one of nine children born into a farming family in Powhatan Township, Virginia, identified as mulattos in the 1870 Virginia census.[13] In 1880, two-year-old Walter was living in "close proximity to nature," with a large extended family of five aunts and uncles and two young cousins on the farm of his paternal grandparents, Robert and Elizabeth Wallace. His parents had made arrangements for him to live here while they pursued their educations.

Both of Walter Wallace's parents attended Hampton Normal Agricultural Institute, one of the first African American colleges in the United States. Founded in 1868 by Samuel Armstrong, a former Union army general who had commanded African American troops during the Civil War, it was the institution at which an impoverished young man named Booker T. Washington began his studies in 1872, two years after the institution received its charter, and where he quickly became the founder's most "prized pupil."[14] Walter Wallace's mother, Nannie, "had the distinction" of being one of the school's first graduates, and his father moved on from Hampton to become a teacher in the Mecklenburg County school system.[15] The Wallaces were at Hampton when it admitted its first Native American students, a group of some thirty former prisoners of war recently released from Fort Marion in St. Augustine, Florida, and where in the late 1880s, the family of Geronimo would be held.[16] Although they sought to advance themselves through education, the Wallaces and fellow students like Washington, who served as a housefather to the Native American students, who were segregated from Hampton's African American students, attended a school whose "pedagogy and ideology [were] designed to avoid . . . confrontations [with the planter regime] and to maintain within the South a social consensus that did not challenge traditional inequalities of wealth and power."[17] Many students of color succeeded at Hampton and learned much, even though there were troubling stereotypical perspectives on African American education and autonomy lurking beneath Armstrong's tested and seemingly sincere motives. In 1874, for example, just one year before Booker T. Washington graduated from the school, Armstrong announced to his former Williams College classmates that at Hampton he had developed "a remarkable machine for the elevation of our colored brethren. . . . Put in a raw plantation darkey and he comes out a gentleman of the nineteenth century."[18]

Despite the school's implicit and explicit provincialism and accommodationist leanings, though, Nannie Ellerson Wallace took advantage of Armstrong's "insistence on the education of women."[19] She was part of the small but cohesive group of female students that Armstrong sought to enlist in the battle to maintain a civil society, because he believed strongly that "there is no civilization without educated women."[20] Nannie Ellerson and her female peers were part of a deliberate campaign to advance the power of domesticity. Armstrong was insistent about the crucial contributions that women should make to secure a stable nation, and his slogans about women's roles were an integral part of his recruitment campaigns: "The condition of women is the test of progress. The family is the unit of Christian civilization. Girls make mothers. Mothers make the home." And women like Nannie Ellerson Wallace were essential to his effort to intensify American domesticity.

At Hampton, Wallace's parents worked toward careers as teachers, a profession toward which the entire curriculum was weighted heavily. Indeed, during the admission process, applicants were asked if they planned to "remain through the whole course and become a teacher," and approximately 600 of the schools' first 723 graduates became teachers.[21] The curriculum was made up of "a surprisingly well-rounded program including language, ranging from sentence making through analysis, rhetoric, elocution, and debating; mathematics through algebra; history, American through universal; science through physiology and botany; miscellaneous courses, including Bible study, moral philosophy, music, and bookkeeping; agriculture, from the study of soil to crop rotation and meteorology; commerce, to include accounting, commercial law, and business contracts, with all students required to keep their personal accounts balanced; and mechanics, including printing and industrial, household, and agricultural machines."[22] Wallace's father became "one of the most prominent and energetic citizens of his community," and before he relocated to New Jersey in the early 1900s, he served as "deputy treasurer and commissioner of the county of Mecklenburg."[23] "[B]esides being a prominent Mason," M. R. Wallace also achieved important supervisory positions as a federal employee at the Railway Post Office, where he at one point was in charge of four clerks. He supported wholeheartedly his son's ambitious race venture, and in May 1901, Wallace, who by this time was working "with the Pullman Car Co., in an easy capacity, having been injured in a wreck which disabled him for three years," was featured prominently as the "agent of our Magazine in Jersey City" and identified as "the father of our editor" in R. S. Elliott's historiographic profile of the magazine and its key associates.[24]

Walter Wallace emulated the example of his parents and focused intently on securing as steady an education as was possible. At nine years of age, he was enrolled at the grammar school in Richmond. He completed a two-year preliminary course at a high school in the city and then began a two year college course at the state college in Petersburg, known also as Virginia Normal and Collegiate Institution, where he "was prominent in athletics and a member of the institute band."[25] He began medical studies at Leonard Medical College at Shaw University in Raleigh, North Carolina, the nation's most successful African American medical school.[26] Wallace did not graduate from Leonard, which graduated some 448 physicians and 126 pharmacists during its thirty-six years of operation, but he learned enough to "secur[e] a position as a prescription clerk in a prominent drug store" when he settled in Boston in 1896.[27] In the years preceding his collaboration with the other cofounders of the magazine, Wallace also pursued his gifts as a composer, producing "several creditable pieces of music" and publishing "Alpha Waltzes," which were published in 1896, the same year that he arrived in Boston.

In June 1900, Fortune listed his employment as "teacher of music" when giving his personal information for the 1900 Massachusetts census.[28] The first treasurer of the Colored Co-operative Publishing Company, he was an accomplished pianist who, at least through 1910, earned his living primarily by giving lessons. Fortune's facility with finances began during his youth. In his childhood home of Richmond, Virginia, his first job was in a business owned by Charles P. Stokes, where he learned the broom manufacturing trade, "soon earned a place as trusted employee," and "was given the collecting to attend to, where the handling of a considerable amount of cash was required."[29] Once he arrived in Boston, Fortune began working with attorney John M. Burrell, a fellow resident of Richmond, Virginia. Burrell had close family ties to Pauline Hopkins. In April 1898, he married her cousin Harriet, one of the two daughters of Eliza and Elijah W. Smith, the gifted poet and devoted mentor to Pauline at the time she began her performance career in the mid-1870s.[30] The ties between Burrell and Hopkins lasted just over three decades, and it was he who attended to her final affairs and the probate of her estate when she died in 1930. In Boston, Fortune once again proved himself a steady and invaluable worker; his 1901 *Colored American Magazine* biography noted that he had been "a trusted employee of lawyer Jno. M. Burrell, who in turn, has been of much assistance to him in the accomplishing of his musical studies."[31] It might have been the mutual connection with Burrell and their shared love of the arts and music that enabled Fortune and Hopkins to meet.

Fortune, a man of "quiet and unassuming manner" who was "decidedly plain and frank with all acquaintances and friends," was a dedicated musician who specialized in the violin and music composition but also was able to "handl[e] several instruments with ease and great proficiency."[32] In Boston, he became "a recognized leader" of the Artist, Guitar and Mandolin Club. While in Richmond, he had served "for more than four years [as] President and clarinetist of the First Battalion Band" of that city.[33] He pursued formal music training in Boston. By May 1901, he had completed one-half of "a professional course in music" and had been "three years under competent masters of Boston, Mass." Fortune's organized approach to music translated into quiet competence for the *Colored American Magazine*, and he enabled the *Colored American Magazine* founders to sustain their commitment to the arts and the cultivation of African American artistic talent. The first issue of the magazine included a special note to aspiring musicians. "Young composers" were advised that they "would do well to send in their manuscript to our musical editor, Mr. H. S. Fortune, care of the Colored American Magazine, and we shall publish from time to time, a limited number of the best."[34] In the months preceding its debut and just following its debut, Fortune spent six months as the "active traveling representative" and "met with marked success."[35] The serious way in which he tended to his growth as a professional musician while contributing earnestly to the collective publishing enterprise with his three friends was a sure example of his primary ethos. "Mr. Fortune believes in the steady advance of the race," assured his colleague R. S. Elliott, "and in the establishing of enterprises where the colored man maybe employed by his own people."[36]

Walter Johnson was one of nine boarders living at 9 Trunwell Place, the home of William and Gabrielle Budd, when the *Colored American Magazine* debuted in 1900.[37] The magazine may have made him more of an eligible bachelor, for by 1901, he had left the Trunwells, was married, and was the self-described "proud possessor of one child, Walter Alexander." The enthusiastic Johnson, proud of the *Colored American Magazine* and its historic significance and clearly delighted to have a son and namesake, purchased stock in the company on behalf of Walter Alexander Jr., who then became "the youngest stockholder in the Colored Co-operative Publishing Company."[38]

Johnson's modern-day migration took him from his childhood home in Deep Creek, Virginia, a small town near Norfolk and located on Deep Creek and the Dismal Swamp Canal. Johnson, who was born on 10 July 1876, grew up in an intensely segregated Southern environment marked by its Civil War histories and civil rights struggles. Norfolk was the city in which the *Merrimac* was rebuilt as an ironclad ship and renamed the *Virginia* following its destruction in a shipyard fire in 1861. It also was the place in which Margaret Douglass, a South Carolina native, was imprisoned in 1852 for teaching free African American children in her home. Tensions over equal education rights persisted in and beyond Deep Creek during the Civil War era. In 1863, Union troops insisted that African American children in Norfolk be granted access to the schools formerly attended by white students and promptly banned the white children from the properties. In the backlash that followed the end of the Civil War, however, the schools were returned in 1865 to white students, and the African American children were expelled. No provisions were made for children of color until 1867, when the American Missionary Association established several schools for African Americans.

Johnson, like Walter Wallace, attended a historic African American institution, when he began studies at Norfolk Mission College, a school for African Americans established in 1883 by the General Assembly of the Presbyterian Church, whose 300-plus student body was eager to pursue an education at the first school in the state to offer free high school–level classes.[39] When Johnson left the college prematurely in 1886, it was because he wanted to meet an important family responsibility to "assist his widowed mother in maintaining a home."[40] In Massachusetts, Johnson promptly sought to resume his education in order "[t]o make up as far as possible for the time lost in obtaining an early education [and] being compelled to start work so young." In the evenings, following his days at work as an "elevator-man in one of the large buildings of Boston," Johnson began attending evening schools in the city. It was through his day job, however, that he made professional connections that would enable him to contribute significantly to the *Colored American Magazine* venture. In the course of his interactions with businessmen while working as an elevator attendant, Johnson came to know "the president of a large publishing house, who gave him a responsible position with his company." His fortuitous connection is reminiscent of Paul Laurence Dunbar's strategic use of his position as an elevator attendant during the early 1890s to promote the sales of *Oak and Ivy*, his first book of poems. Johnson's enterprising spirit and confidence made him the likely man to head the advertising department of the *Colored American Magazine*, and, by 1901, his colleagues were pleased at the ways in which he, with a "good corps of agents," was "successfully building up" the department.[41]

Jesse Watkins, the fourth member of the team of *Colored American Magazine* founders, was by far the most economically stable and domestically settled of the group. The only married man of the set when the magazine made its debut, he too was in a boardinghouse, but he presided over it as landlord. Born in 1872, he hailed from Chesterfield County, Virginia, located about twelve miles from Richmond, situated between the James and Appomattox Rivers, and known for its good deposits of coal. The county, in the early 1700s, had been home to one of President Thomas Jefferson's earliest known ancestors and figured in the Civil War strategizing of Ulysses S. Grant as he endeavored to take Richmond despite the defensive troop deployments in the area by Generals Robert E. Lee and P. G. T. Beauregard.[42]

Watkins experienced considerable loss and domestic upheaval during his childhood. When he was one-year-old, his father passed away, and his widowed mother was left to care for three young children. She made a great effort to pursue educational opportunities for her son, despite the family hardships. His *Colored American Magazine* biography gave ample credit to her labors, noting that "[t]hrough his mother's efforts he was enabled to get through the country schools." As a young man, Watkins "left home for the North and worked at various places at quarrying and on the farm." At the time that he arrived in Boston in 1893, he had spent time most recently working at a mine, where he was "looked up to on account of his integrity" and designated the "banker of his companions, as he was the only one among them who had the knack of saving money."[43] His financial savvy failed to protect him in Boston, where, shortly after he arrived, he was targeted by a "smooth-tongued sharper" and found himself bereft of $50 of $75 that he had saved. Undeterred, however, he set to work, "gradually added to his small bank account," and promptly sought to "invest in some real estate."[44] By the time that he was twenty-eight, Watkins was an established head of household that included him, his twenty-three-year-old wife, Cora, and six lodgers.[45] Watkins earned the unstinting praise of R. S. Elliott, his colleague at the *Colored American Magazine* and the person charged with composing the lengthy biographical profiles of the founders, their early contributors, and key supporters throughout the nation. "One who is born 'with a silver spoon in his mouth' is considered lucky," mused Elliott, before suggesting that "he who, with grit, determination and perseverance, pulls up from the slough of poverty and its attendant adversities to a higher level of usefulness, is by far a more fortunate man."[46] Elliott proposed enthusiastically that "[t]he career of our Secretary and Assistant Treasurer, Jesse W. Watkins, Young Colored American may find a record for emulation."[47] Within seven years of his arrival in the North, he had developed a most "keen business foresight" and had become a prosperous landowner whose initial investments had "increased in value forefold [*sic*]," including acquisitions of "two farms in Virginia, one of which contains twenty acres."[48]

Watkins's story of personal uplift and advancement is impressive; he was perspicacious in his endeavors and pursued with vigor the opportunities that would enable him to advance himself. In addition to recognizing the importance of land and property ownership, he also set about advancing his education. Within two years of arriving in Boston, he had graduated from the grammar department of the Boston public night schools, and by 1899, he had successfully undertaken "a complete business course" at the Boston evening high school, while also "studying practical electricity," a trade for which he became "well qualified."[49] Yet Watkins did not rely solely on his own independent ventures or ambitions. Like his colleague Harper Fortune, he too aspired to see the "steady advance of the race" that manifested itself in African American–owned businesses, which could employ and support members of the race. To that end, Watkins invested his time and hopes in successful fraternal organizations whose members shared an intense entrepreneurial appetite and were committed to building a strong set of nationally available resources for their members. As a member and future Noble Father in the Grand United Order of Odd Fellows, he was part of one of the largest African American fraternal organizations in the United States.[50] The organization, which by the late 1880s had nearly 53,000 members in some 1,000 lodges in America and abroad, "provided social insurance benefits; built social-welfare institutions as well as halls that served as meeting places for many black groups; engaged in impressive parades and ritual displays; and attracted the leading men as well as more humble members in countless African American communities."[51] In Boston, Watkins's Odd Fellows membership facilitated his assimilation into the African American community. Members of Pauline Hopkins's maternal family were members of pioneering fraternal organizations like the Prince Hall Masonic Order, which, since the late eighteenth century, had "stressed black heritage and the assertion of civic leadership."[52]

Watkins also was a member and officer in the Grand United Order of True Reformers, based in Richmond, Virginia, an "insurance-oriented fraternal group open to both men and women." The organization had been established in 1881 by the Reverend William Washington Browne, a versatile man, who believed that the "secret society is the colored man's most effective mode of organization" and, who, after surviving enslavement in the South, became a Civil War soldier, educator, temperance worker, and African Methodist Episcopal minister.[53] Watkins belonged to one of the Order of True Reformers fountains, as they were called, and prided himself on his membership in one of the nation's impressive "self-selecting brotherhoods and sisterhoods that provide[d] mutual aid to members, enact[ed] group rituals, and engage[d] in community service."[54] Watkins's membership in this, and in the "many other organizations" of which he was a part, helped him and the *Colored American Magazine* to maintain vital connections to the South and to hundreds of potential subscribers.[55]

In May 1900, Pauline Hopkins allied herself with Wallace, Fortune, Johnson, and Watkins in the venture that would earn them a place in American publishing history. She was a pioneer from the very first moments of her affiliation with the monthly periodical that has been hailed as the first, most substantial, and influential African American periodical of the twentieth century.[56] The only woman to be published in the inaugural issue of the nation's first African American literary magazine and the only one ever to serve as its editor, Hopkins fully endorsed the magazine's noble goals to "offer the colored people of the United States" a journal that was a "medium through which [they] can demonstrate their ability and tastes, in fiction, poetry, and art, as well as in the arena of historical, social, and economical literature."[57] The venture took hold rapidly, and the founders relished the prospects before them. Barely one month after the first issue appeared, Walter Wallace could take great pride in being able to have his profession documented for the 1900 federal census simply and elegantly as "Publisher, Magazine."[58]

The early role that Hopkins played was linked most directly to the founders' plan to use the *Colored American Magazine* to cultivate a high cultural aesthetic. It was in this context that Hopkins first made her contributions and also established the terms on which she would enjoy the most intense professional relationship of her life up to that time. The launch of the magazine was doubly rewarding for her since the debut issue of the magazine included her first published creative work, "The Mystery Within Us," an intriguing short story about mesmerism, the value of life, and the vital connections between the living and the dead. The *Colored American Magazine* embodied the ambitious goals that Hopkins, now a forty-year-old former actress and singer, playwright, civil servant, and novelist had set for herself. This journal, a cooperative venture started by four young men of color, was to become the new stage upon which Pauline Hopkins would intensify her public outreach to African Americans and instigate new campaigns for black social, political, and intellectual advancement.

Hopkins was appointed a member of the editorial staff and charged with important responsibilities before the second issue appeared in June 1900. She responded purposefully and vigorously to the day-to-day demands associated with the production of the magazine. Her administrative and editorial work had a positive effect on her creative genius as well. She began to write furiously and, without much ado, provided appealing and intriguing creative work for readers under her own name and that of Sarah A. Allen, her mother's maiden name. Hopkins soon became an essential presence at the journal, and her political acuity and intellectual strengths quickly influenced the magazine's focus, outreach, and readership. Like Jessie Fauset, characterized so memorably by her colleagues and scholars as the midwife of the Harlem Renaissance, Hopkins dedicated herself to supporting the dream of her Virginia colleagues, encouraging the latent talent of the many who began to submit work for consideration, and championing the purposeful women and men whose activism, civic engagement, and scholarship were advancing the race.

By 1903, she had become "the real work-horse of the magazine."[59] Although the phrase suggests drudgery, it is clear that for Hopkins such labor did not deplete her stores of creative genius or administrative focus.

The *Colored American Magazine* was a wholly cooperative venture from its inception. The Colored Co-operative Publishing Company, which produced the monthly journal, first was based at the West Canton Street home in Boston's South End where Walter Wallace and Harper Fortune were boarders. This arrangement, no doubt made necessary because of the financial pressures associated with starting a magazine, was a familiar tactic used by enterprising writers who had limited funds for the aspects of their publishing ventures. Some three decades later, for instance, Wallace Thurman, Zora Neale Hurston, and their fellow cofounders of the Harlem Renaissance–era publication *Fire!!* created the bold but short-lived literary publication in the Dark Tower, the well-known Harlem apartment building in which they and some of the other cofounders lived.

Within a few months, Wallace and his colleagues were able to secure a prime downtown location for the *Colored American Magazine* offices. The small staff, including Hopkins, moved to 5 Park Square, a location not far from the Boston Common, which was "most central to the regular business heart of the city, and at the same time . . . convenient to the newer business and publishing centre, in the vicinity of Copley square and Columbus avenue." The location also accommodated the magazine's increasing need for more rooms, a pressing reality for its founders, who were striving to "keep pace with the ever increasing demands of the publishing business."[60] Wallace, delighted with the "finely apportioned offices [and] surroundings," hoped that the premises prompted the public to imagine that the *Colored American Magazine* "appears as a Gibraltar of strength."[61] The January–February 1902 issue of the magazine included "a glimpse of our Home," as the editors described it, and there were photographs of the building as well as some of the office spaces and mailrooms that enabled its founders to insist that "[a]t the present time, the Colored American Magazine occupies the most elaborate and best equipped rooms and offices of any race publication, and [with] the complete press-room and bindery that it is proposed to establish in the near future, the Company will possess an equipment that will easily place it at the head of all Negro Publishing Enterprises."[62] Despite the bustle associated with the production, the editors also thought about how best to cultivate relationships with their audiences and to provide valuable space in which community members could nurture their own intellectual and literary interests. In keeping with the ethos that the magazine was devoted to advancing, the editors insisted earnestly that "[i]t affords us much pleasure at any and

THE HOME OF THE COLORED AMERICAN MAGAZINE,
5 PARK SQUARE, BOSTON, MASS.

The second home of the *Colored American Magazine* at 5 Park Square in Boston. This downtown location was the most prominent of the magazine's three Boston offices. *From* Colored American Magazine, *1902.*

all times to welcome any member or friend of the race, and they will find our 'latch string' always out. Our reception room . . . is ever at the disposal of any one who desires to spend a quiet hour in reading or study, or to meet friends by appointment. All our subscribers and readers from all sections, are especially urged to make our building their headquarters when in Boston, where every courtesy possible will be extended."[63] The magazine was housed at Park Square until March 1904 when, during Hopkins's tenure as editor, the offices moved to 82 West Concord Street. This was its last Boston address before the magazine was appropriated by allies of Booker T. Washington and relocated to New York City.

The first formal editorial statement in the magazine revealed the solidarity that the founders felt with Boston's outspoken activists, like those who were members of the Colored National League. "[T]he South is determined to smile upon the servile, fawning, cowardly and sicko fantine negro and to frown upon the brave, manly, and aggressive negro," wrote the editors, and is "bent upon a policy of extermination or subjugation; they will either exterminate the negro or subjugate him." The editors continued boldly, indicting the silence of the "northern pulpits" and the "strange apathy and indifference at the attempt of the South to crush the manhood and self-respect out of the negro."[64] The *Colored American Magazine* was positioned as a stalwart race journal that would not shy away from addressing political and civil rights concerns, even as it was a vehicle of artistic and literary refinement. "What we desire, what we require, what we demand to aid in the onward march of progress and advancement is justice; merely this and nothing more," the editors insisted in May 1900. They wanted "[n]ot a justice tempered with policy, or trammeled with prejudice, neither a justice semi-hoodwinked, that discriminates invidiously or with unequal balances constantly throwing the weight in one direction, but justice, simple, pure, unbiased, unabridged, unadulterated, and undefiled."[65] Editorial statements such as these established the monthly journal as a resource for the increasingly mobilized African American organizations that were rallying to end lynching and institutionalized racism and inequality.

The early editorial statements in the *Colored American Magazine* demonstrated a powerful intertwining of racial activism, high cultural aesthetics, and intellectual endeavor. Such deftly intertwined priorities continued to anticipate theories of race and public culture advanced by individuals like W. E. B. Du Bois, who, by 1905, was articulating publicly his own assertions of how best to use journalism to combat social and racial upheaval and to empower vulnerable and outraged communities of color. When Du Bois endeavored to acquire funding for a race journal, the rationale he sketched out for Jacob Schiff, a successful German Jewish banker, philanthropist, and donor to Tuskegee Institute, already had been embodied by the *Colored American Magazine* founders. Du Bois imagined "a literary digest of fact and opinion concerning the Negro in particular and all darker races," a "compendium of the News among these people gathered by staff correspondents in the larger cities and centers of the U.S. and in the West Indies, West and South Africa, etc.," regular "interpretation of the current news of the larger world from the point of view of the welfare of the Negro," "short, pertinent, and interesting articles," and "illustrations attempting to portray Negro life on its beautiful and interesting side." "Above all," he concluded, "the Journal should be cast on broad intelligent lines, interpreting a new race consciousness to the modern world and revealing the inner meaning of the modern world to the emerging races. It should rise above narrow interests, personal likes or dislikes and seek about all practical united effort toward ideal ends."[66] In 1900, Wallace and his three associates apparently realized a long-cherished dream of Du Bois, though the formidable academic likely would have disagreed on that point, since, in 1905, in one of his few references to the magazine, he acknowledged it as one of two African American monthly magazines in existence at the time but criticized it and the *Voice of the Negro* as lacking editorial professionalism and reliable sources. "They are fairly good periodicals of the ordinary sort," he admitted, but he believed they failed to provide "(a) careful editing on broad lines, (b) timely, readable articles, (c) an efficient news service, (d) good illustrations, (e) modern aggressive business management."[67] Du Bois's criticisms however, could not invalidate the enterprise of the *Colored American Magazine* founders, nor their strategic enlistment of their Northern community and the Southern networks in heroic efforts to finance and distribute the magazine.

During the Boston tenure, *Colored American Magazine* readers and supporters consistently were encouraged to enhance the quality and broaden scope of the magazine. The editors made earnest solicitations for materials, urging many readers who never before had published to try their hand at writing, to share their perspectives on current events, and to become self-appointed cultural delegates for the race. The calls to the masses complemented the editors' growing relationships with more accomplished professional writers such as Hopkins, Braithwaite, and Cyrus Field Adams. Their outreach challenged Du Bois's 1905 musings about a "proper Journal," for which "Negro writers and artists could be encouraged to write of themselves and depict the things nearest to them and thus to speak more naturally and effectively than they usually do."[68] Indeed, the call for submissions never wavered. In 1902, issues included calls for "short articles or stories from any section of the world, that show the real progress that the race is making." "What we especially desire," wrote the editors, "are articles illustrated by photographs of the homes owned by the race, together with the business enterprises conducted by or for our people." Aspiring composers were encouraged to share their work, while amateur and professional photographers were invited to "'snap' everything which comes your way" and submit works to a magazine competition that would allow the *Colored American Magazine* to "show to all the world that we as a people are not only rising with great rapidity in the business world, but that we are determined soon to claim our share in the higher walks of life."[69]

The *Colored American Magazine* also provided welcome coverage of African American military men and used its profiles of courageous African American veterans to reinforce its claims for true American democracy and social justice. Subscribers could purchase photographs of the veterans, such as the "large and handsome mounted photograph of Company 'L'" that was previewed "under the frontispiece" of the first issue. Offered as incentives to readers, such items could "be had at fifty cents each at the office of the magazine."[70] In addition to articles written by soldiers in the field, there were regimental histories and copies of personal letters and travelogues like the one that "Captain W. H. Jackson, U.S.A. now at Manila" wrote to his mother after his "long, long sail over the blue Pacific."[71] Readers often had direct access to soldiers participating in American domestic and international campaigns, and the magazine also catered to those who might prefer to moon over images of debonair black regiments standing at attention in full dress uniform. The articles and images constituted strong affirmations of the platforms being advanced by veterans groups and those affiliated with organizations such as the Colored National League, groups determined to protest the hypocrisy of weakened black citizenship and civil rights in the United States.

The *Colored American Magazine* board members were keenly aware of the need for an assertive black history, a revisionary record of African American contributions, frustrations, and triumphs. In their first "Editorial and Pubisher's [*sic*] Announcement," in which the misspelled word suggested the haste and newness of their venture, they acknowledged that although African Americans were "liberally and kindly treated" in numerous white publications, "the Anglo-Saxon race, fails to sufficiently recognize our efforts, hopes and aspirations."[72] Expressed in phrases that would be repeated in Hopkins's prefatory remarks in *Contending Forces*, the editors' mission was clear. They wanted to address a pressing cultural and racial hunger for representation: "The *Colored American Magazine* proposes to meet this want, and to offer the colored people of the United States, a medium through which they can demonstrate their ability and tastes, in fiction, poetry, and art, as well as in the arena of historical, social, and economical literature. Above all it aspires to develop and intensify the bonds of that racial brotherhood, which alone can enable a people, to assert their racial rights as men, and demand their privileges as citizens."[73] The request for patronage was thus presented as an opportunity for African Americans to demonstrate their political commitment and to reinforce their commitment to collective racial advancement. Subscriptions were touted as investments in race history. The editors declared, "We therefore appeal to you separately and collectively to lend your assistance toward the perpetuation of a history of the negro race."[74] The crisis, as they saw it, lay in the ever-present threat of black invisibility, the suppression of African American history, and the concomitant and demoralizing effects of such erasure.

The *Colored American Magazine* founders approached the monumental task of building a publishing house and producing a successful monthly publication with lofty goals and an acute sense of urgency. Undaunted by the high illiteracy rates among African Americans nationwide, which in 1900 were at 45 percent, the editors pressed ahead in the spirit of their antebellum journalistic forefathers, refusing to believe in a diminished power of the black periodical press and using their energies to create reading communities in which the magazine's contents were dispersed broadly and generously in ways that promoted new literacies.[75] That noble strategy was good, but J. Max Barber, the dashing *Voice of the Negro* editor who would hire Hopkins to write for his magazine in 1905, articulated the insistent and unmistakable social triumphs of which the *Colored American Magazine* editors were well aware. "To the casual observer," Barber noted in 1904, "there is nothing interesting in the launching of a Negro magazine; but to the careful observer, to the philosopher of history, to him who is a reader of the signs of the times it means much. It means that culture is taking a deep hold upon our people. It is an indication that our people are becoming an educated, a reading people, and this is a thing of which to be proud."[76]

The antebellum African American press, by nature and through circumstance, was an enterprise that both encouraged and required collective reader response. When the *Colored American Magazine* was started in Boston, it tapped into a resourceful, receptive network, one that could date its support of the African American publishing tradition back to its very beginnings and to Hopkins's own ancestors—like Thomas Paul, who had been one of the first

Cooperative Enterprises

subscription agents for *Freedom's Journal*, the nation's first African American newspaper. By May 1901, when the magazine marked its first anniversary, it could claim "one hundred thousand readers at the present time."[77] That number represented an impressive 35 percent of the nation's literate African American readers; indeed, the reference to readers rather than to subscribers reconfirms that circulation figures not only included individual subscriptions but also accounted for the collective reading supported by women's clubs, church organizations, and reading clubs, such as the Putnam, Connecticut, group founded by a Miss Josephine Hall, named after the magazine, and dedicated to providing for the "literary and social advancement of its members."[78] The Putnam-based Colored American Magazine Club embraced the *Colored American Magazine*'s ambitious goal of achieving racial uplift and contributed by "read[ing] the articles, and hav[ing] general discussions," efforts that, they concluded proudly, ensured that "not only the members but the families which they represent are benefited."[79] Collaborative reading practices such as these, and the magazine documented a substantial number of them, enabled the cultivation of a broad spectrum of readers across class, faiths, and region. While the board authorized numerous sales and distribution agents who lived in urban areas, it was by no means limited to a middle-class reading audience in that milieu.

The editors of the *Colored American Magazine*, men familiar with the power of collective racial uplift efforts through their own Southern and fraternal organization experiences, also sought to formalize the work of the steadily growing number of literary agents. The founders were astute and recognized that they could thrive if their readers, especially African American readers, regarded the magazine and the Colored Co-operative Publishing Company as a mutual race enterprise, one with direct beneficial implications for their public, professional, workaday lives and their private, social, and spiritual experiences. To reach this goal of collective race investment, the founders, in what was becoming a trademark gesture for them, immediately encouraged their potential collaborators. Wallace, Fortune, Johnson, and Watkins insisted that all people were capable of contributing to their platform of race advancement, and created organizations that facilitated the outreach that was essential to both their political and financial viability. The Literary Agents' Business Club, for example, "organized for the purpose of canvassing the literature of the Colored Co-operative Publishing Company of Boston," was represented by the motto "Let All Be Combined" and an emblem of an open book emblazoned with an acronym of the motto, the initials "L.A.B.C." Members would be deployed into communities where they might use the company's publications to "create among our people a taste for good reading matter suitable for the Home, that shall give inspiration and encouragement to our boys and girls to aspire to high ideals and high aims in life."[80] As an affiliate of the Boston company, the club also positioned itself as key support for "ambitious young men and women seeking positions of trust and responsibility in other lines of work, for the advancement of the race," and offered to provide vital references to potential employers.

The *Colored American Magazine* staff recognized the political alliances that would give their publication cachet and enhance its national profile. In addition to allocating pages to partners in uplift such as the National Association of Women's Clubs, Wallace and his fellow editors built formal relationships with groups dedicated to the eradication of segregation, racial disenfranchisement, and social inequality. Their overtures bore immediate fruit; within six months of its founding, for example, the *Colored American Magazine* declared that it would "hereafter be the official organ" of the Constitutional Rights Association of the United States. The announcement, detailed over three pages that included the constitution and bylaws of the association, gave no indication that the magazine had been co-opted. In fact, the statement had precisely the opposite effect. The magazine had a new subscriber pool. Association members were instructed to become "regular subscriber[s]" of the magazine, since that was where information about the organization's "latest efforts for the betterment of the race" would be published. The group, based in Richmond, Virginia, the city to which Wallace and Fortune had close ties, formed to prove the unconstitutionality of Jim Crow segregation laws. Founded "for the purpose of defending and contending for our every right, guaranteed to us by the Constitution of the United States," the association was determined to "invoke the aid of the proper courts . . . and have these unholy, degrading and discriminating laws reviewed by the highest court of the land." The association chose the *Colored American Magazine* as the vehicle through which its "colored brethren in the North and West [might] help . . . in [the] struggle for right and justice."[81]

In providing forums for organizations such as the Constitutional Rights Association, the *Colored American Magazine* contributed to the growing polarization between African American camps that endorsed and those that opposed accommodationist politics. In the wake of Booker T. Washington's 1895 speech at the Cotton States and International Exposition in Atlanta, the fervent rhetoric in articles published in the *Colored American Magazine* by black nationalists and race men who were members of the Constitutional Rights Association was deliberate and pointed. Their condemnation of the South's mob rule flew in the face of Washington's proposed model of tolerance that depended on the notion that "in all things that are purely social we can be as separate as the fingers, yet one as the hand in all things essential to mutual progress."[82] However, in its early years, the magazine refrained from staking out an explicit political position that could jeopardize its efforts to establish a broad national readership. The editors recognized the diversity of opinion about accommodationism and industrial education, to name but two of the primary issues associated with Washington's work, and they published articles that bolstered readers for whom industrial education provided a long-awaited means of rising above the poverty engineered by antebellum enslavement and postbellum disenfranchisement. Their shared Southern backgrounds contributed to their distaste for alienating former colleagues and community partners who, through diligence and force of will, were organizing mutual aid societies throughout the South, establishing and defending African American schools, and developing successful businesses. The editors catered to their progressive Northern readers, members of the intellectual and social elite, and the large numbers of Southern migrants who, like them, had come to the North in order to improve their opportunities. Such generosity and marketing explained, for example, the promotion of the Negro Business League that Washington founded in Boston in 1900 and of the increasingly outspoken anti-Washington organizations such as the Boston-based Colored American League. Eventually, though, the combination of continued race violence, federal disregard, and increasingly insistent African American community mobilization prompted the editors to favor and feature even more fully the organizations that regarded Washington's philosophies as liabilities that the race could not afford.

Four years later, when the magazine was struggling to defend itself against a politically motivated takeover financed by Washington, it accepted financial and political support from the Colored American League. The League, which included a number of *Colored American Magazine* staffers and board of directors members, chose the phrase "For Humanity" as its motto. This was the very phrase that Hopkins had immortalized in 1900 in her *Contending Forces* dedication. The *Colored American Magazine* was to be not only the official publication of the League but the embodiment of the organization. The League believed that it was vital that its "white brothers and sisters realize the work we are doing, and that, in a single generation after the abolition of slavery, we have produced not only farmers and mechanics, but singers, artists, writers, poets, lawyers, doctors, successful business men, and even some statesmen." Hopkins, now installed as editor, declared that the magazine would "be the means by which we shall make known not only our aspirations but our accomplishments, as well as the efforts we are ourselves making to uplift our race."[83] Evidence of the formal affiliations with groups such as the

Constitutional Rights Association and the Colored American League provide enlightening details about how the magazine marketed and sustained itself. Its unprecedented and multifaceted agenda was sustained by the flexibility of its editors and their unwavering desire to create an unassailable record of racial enterprise.

Pauline Hopkins joined the staff of a magazine run by men who were literally half her age and who, like their predecessors in the field, "were a relatively idealistic, optimistic group who, despite a myriad of problems and frustrations, continued to be unified in their newspaper columns on messages aimed at the vindication, uplift, and acceptance of blacks into mainstream America."[84] The first roles that the all-male board devised for Pauline Hopkins, their first female staff member, were rather matronly and maternal. Hopkins's responsibilities, in spite of their direct correlation to regional black politics, reinforced traditional gender roles. The May 1900 edition announced that Hopkins's first official assignment was to "begin a department devoted exclusively to the interest of women and the home." Wallace and his board believed that Hopkins was "well fitted for this work among the women of her race," in large part because of her "heartfelt desire to aid in every way possible in uplifting the colored people of America, and through them, the world."[85] Hopkins set the same tone in the June edition. In her "Editor's Note," she appropriated the language of the collective enterprise and made a confident overture to her readers. "We bring to this column an enthusiastic desire to do good and pleasing work for our lady patrons," she declared, "and to that end would be pleased to receive suggestions from all our friends." Recognizing the potential value that her column of "articles . . . of special and practical value to all women" could have to the club movement, Hopkins made a deliberate overture to club leaders and members. Hopkins offered to use the column to advertise upcoming events and announced her plan to institute a "Club Record," a regular list "in descending order, of national, regional, and local women's club organizations and their officers."

Hopkins quickly developed an alternate method for engaging club women, and the "Women's Department" evolved into a collaborative club enterprise featuring columns and articles authored by club leaders. This new format resurrected the highly successful format of *The Woman's Era*, founded in 1890 by Josephine St. Pierre Ruffin and her daughter Florida Ruffin Ridley, the first newspaper edited, published, and created for and by African American women. Hopkins's reorganization of the "Women's Department" in the *Colored American Magazine* may have flattered Ruffin, then the reigning leader of Boston's active club network. Hopkins's actions also may have revived a local rivalry between the two women, a tension already documented in her aggressive and unflatteringly frank caricature of Mrs. Ruffin in *Contending Forces*. Whatever the social costs, though, the new format strengthened the *Colored American Magazine*, and Hopkins was able to position herself both to serve the extensive women's club network and to shape the discourse about women's work, service, and leadership. She developed productive work relationships with prominent club women such as Mrs. Albreta Moore Smith, an "energetic and businesslike" woman, who was "the embodiment of many other thrifty qualities so characteristic of true Westerners."[86] Smith, president of the Colored Women's Business Club of Chicago, and the first elected vice president of the Negro Business League, which had close ties to Booker T. Washington, became a frequent contributor to the *Colored American Magazine*.[87] Hopkins also enjoyed professional collaborations with talented Boston writers, chief among them Olivia Ward Bush, an active member of the Women's Era Club, published poet, and one of the first women that Hopkins enlisted as a contributor.[88]

Lauded by her editors as "one of our foremost contributors," Pauline Hopkins became indispensable to the *Colored American Magazine* and critical to the ambitious marketing plans and the plans for growth. She did not balk at the myriad requests for her expertise but rose to the challenge with a sense of purposeful determination. The arrangement was mutually beneficial to both parties. The *Colored American Magazine* founders had a local author who was willing and thoroughly able to produce a range of work that would help them to realize their dream of a periodical that was "rich in social, literary and business details concerning Afro-Americans in every section of the country, who have and are vindicating the just claims and worthy aspirations of the race."[89] The cooperative relationship between the founding editors and Hopkins was enhanced greatly when their cooperative publishing house published *Contending Forces*, a work that they embraced wholeheartedly and to which they committed vital resources and much publicity.

It was within the pages of the *Colored American Magazine* that *Contending Forces* was celebrated most enthusiastically. In issue after issue, Pauline Hopkins was hailed for creating a work that intensified race pride and encouraged racial advancement. On the one hand, the magazine was committed to implementing a strategic publicity campaign. The editors, who seemed genuinely taken by the historicity and relevance of Hopkins's novel, believed that it would increase sales of the *Colored American Magazine* and that it would support their efforts to build a national reputation for the monthly journal. The editors invested themselves wholeheartedly in the advance publicity campaign for *Contending Forces*. It was one of four books and the only novel that the company endeavored to publish during its first year of existence. The others included *The Story of the American Negro*, a book by Chaplain Steward that the press envisioned as a "valuable addition to Negro literature."[90] Also produced by the press was *In Free America*, a volume by Ellen Wetherell, which the magazine marketed as "the most powerful book on the wrongs and injustices heaped upon our race in the South as well as in the North."[91] Wetherell was the daughter of a man who "for many years helped in conducting an 'underground railroad,' back before the war" and the publishers insisted that she, as his daughter "has inherited a spirit of equality that makes her one of the most steadfast friends of the Negro race."[92] In December 1901, the magazine recommended to readers Wetherell's *In Free America* and Hopkins's *Contending Forces* as "most acceptable Holiday Gifts."[93]

Of the first four books published by the Colored Co-operative Publishing Company and advertised regularly in the *Colored American Magazine*, *Contending Forces* was the only text accorded full-page advertisements in the opening pages of the magazine. In September 1900, the notice of the novel was a full-page advertisement that appeared opposite the table of contents. Entitled "Prospectus . . . of the New Romance of Colored Life," the advertisement delivered to its readers a stately message fashioned after a formal calling card. "We beg to announce to the friends of Miss Hopkins of Cambridge, and the public," read the piece, "a romance written by Miss Hopkins, entitled 'Contending Forces.' This is pre-eminently a race-work dedicated to the best interests of the Negro everywhere." In addition to believing that the work would "certainly create a sensation among a certain class of 'whites' at the South," the promoters believed that the novel also would "awaken a general interest among our race, not only in this country, but throughout the world."[94] The tantalizing suggestions about the work resulted in "enormous" advance sales. Editor Wallace insisted that the press "want[ed] an active agent in every town and city to represent us" and to coordinate sales of the book, which had eight original illustrations, was priced at one dollar and fifty cents, and was forthcoming in October. He also solicited agents who would market the book, and to "persons who desire to become agents for it," Wallace requested only fifty cents for an "Agents' Outfit" that would include a copy of the novel.

This coordinated and enthusiastic publicity for *Contending Forces* revived the public persona that Hopkins had had during her performance years of the 1870s and 1880s. In the fall of 1900, she seized the opportunity to reclaim the political autonomy that she had been unable to enjoy fully as a playwright in the commercial theater circles. She capitalized on the exuberance and optimism of her younger colleagues and began to cultivate a writerly identity for herself, one inspired by her increasingly celebrated capacity to generate affirmative African American historical perspectives. The *Colored American Magazine* board knew that in Hopkins they had an established link to the uncompromising black Republican intellectual and social elite of Boston. Through her, they had direct connections to the city's substantial history of black activism, enterprise, and civic leadership.

Hopkins's affiliation with the Colored Co-operative Publishing Company and the *Colored American Magazine* reflected extremely well on the magazine and its founders' dedication to African American equality and advancement. Within months of offering her services as a *Colored American Magazine* staffer to African American women, Pauline Hopkins emerged as "one of the leading writers of the race" and as an uncompromising, fair-minded arbiter of the "wrongs and injustices perpetrated on the race." It was *Contending Forces* that prompted her sudden elevation. A woman knighted as a race writer quickly replaced the woman who had only recently been the magazine's scribe of women's club activity. Hopkins was celebrated as a "woman of great versatility, deep thought and wide scope of observation."[95] The magazine proudly acknowledged its associate as a conscientious and articulate author upon whom African American readers could depend for enlightening works that were "startling in the array of facts shown and logical in the arguments . . . present[ed]."[96] The magazine editors touted Hopkins's first novel as tangible proof of what the race could and should produce in order to reinforce its collective pride and progress.

It remains difficult to determine how many copies of *Contending Forces* were published. In 1905, Hopkins provided the only information about the publishing run in a letter written after her ouster from the magazine. In her gripping correspondence with J. Max Barber, she described the hostile take-over of the magazine staged by men loyal to and funded by Booker T. Washington. Hopkins noted that, in the process, the new owners also acquired 500 copies of her novel and all of its printing plates.[97] The Colored Co-operative Publishing Company appears to have published a substantial number of copies in 1900. In November of that year, the editors made a special point of discussing publicly the status of Hopkins's work. "The advance sales of Miss Pauline E. Hopkins's 'Contending Forces' have been enormous," they exclaimed, "considering this to be her first work published in book form." After praising her as "a woman of great versatility, deep thought, and wide scope of observation," the editors confidently stated, "We predict for her book (now in publication) the success it merits."[98] Such positive news has long added to the puzzle of why Hopkins's work seemed to fade into obscurity.

The details about the loss of the plates—or as she regarded it, their theft by her professional adversaries—does explain in large part why no additional editions were ever printed. However, the relative obscurity of the novel and the lack of formal responses or casual acknowledgments by her contemporaries encourages additional speculation about the distribution of the novel and the avenues that were open to review her work. As enthusiastic as the *Colored American Magazine* editors were about *Contending Forces*, they were concerned primarily with the success of their publication. They did not dedicate their resources to advancing Hopkins's career separate and apart from their own collective venture. As a result, information about the book may have actually been mostly confined to *Colored American Magazine* circles, attentive and national though they might have been.

To date, there are only a handful of published responses to the novel. There is no evidence that Hopkins's novel drew attention from white newspapers such as the *Boston Globe* or from white Northern literary journals. This may have been a mixed blessing. Writers like Paul Laurence Dunbar and Charles Chesnutt benefited immensely from their publication in the white press and the support they received from the white literary establishment. Yet, as William Stanley Braithwaite, Bostonian and poet whose works appeared regularly in the *Colored American Magazine*, noted, such prominence came at a high price and by no means indicated a full or honorable welcome. Braithwaite recalled his shock and disappointment upon learning from a colleague that "it was common in literary and publishing circles, to refer to that superb and tragic artist, Charles Waddell Chesnutt, as 'Page's darky!' because Walter Hines Page, as editor of the *Atlantic Monthly*, had discovered and printed Chesnutt's earlier stories in the magazine, and persuaded Houghton Mifflin to publish his books."[99] With the exception of the lengthy review that Bostonian Addie Jewell wrote in the form of a private letter and in which she evaluated Hopkins's reading before the Colored National League of Boston, all of the reader responses to *Contending Forces* appear to have been published in the pages of the *Colored American Magazine*. As a rule, these reviews were not formal critical responses to Hopkins's work but rather comments included in letters to Hopkins and to her colleagues at the *Colored American Magazine*.

The most autonomous and formal comment on Hopkins and *Contending Forces* was published in February 1901. In his article entitled "The Opening Century," Robert W. Carter provided readers with a grand assessment of the African American literary tradition and hailed the new era in which they were now. "We were unknown as authors of books, and had not then a Paul Laurence Dunbar to make a favorable impression in the literary world," he wrote. "We could not then as now gaze with pride and pleasure upon a Pauline Hopkins, from whose vivid pen came forth 'Contending Forces.' Nay, we could not then look back upon the eighteenth as we can now upon the nineteenth century and point to a cluster of bright stars in the constellation of human thought who in their days of nature and activity bravely pleaded the cause of human liberty, and now leave to us monuments of fame—men such as Dr. J. C. Price, Douglass, Bruce, and Langston."[100] The only woman writer that Carter mentions, Hopkins becomes part of a cultural, political, and literary pantheon. Nonetheless, she is part of a segregated literary marketplace, one that clearly had yet to contend with the revisionary racial histories that were Hopkins's specialty.

By May 1901, seven months after the publication of *Contending Forces*, the magazine prepared to disseminate the novel across the country. The editors were "prepared to offer a limited number of copies of this powerful story FREE." Walter Wallace used his "Editorial and Publisher's Announcements" column to explain the motivation. "[W]e feel sure that a few copies in each town will immediately sell a still larger number," he stated. It is likely that Hopkins was able to bring attention to her novels as late as 1905 when she was delivering lectures throughout the Northeast, but there is documented evidence that reveals how the book was received shortly after its publication. *Contending Forces* was read, for instance, in Chicago club circles, and it prompted one of the city's urban and club leaders to register publicly her deep satisfaction with the book. In October 1901, Wallace was delighted to reference a letter received from Mrs. Albreta Moore Smith, president of the Colored Women's Business Club of Chicago. Smith, who had by this time become a contributor to the *Colored American Magazine*, may have been solicited to write the highly complimentary review. Regardless of the circumstances, though, her thoughtful assessment of the work stands as one of the few direct reviews of the work. "It is undoubtedly the book of the century. Ethiopia is stretching forth her arms in all branches of learning," announced Smith. "The only disappointment to me was to read 'Finis,'" and "[i]n point of composition, plot and style of writing, it cannot be excelled." Smith closed with the following heartfelt benediction: "May God encourage and inspire Pauline Hopkins to give to the reading world more gems of thought from her storehouse of knowledge."[101] Hopkins's role as a public historian was certainly legitimized by such impassioned responses. While it was unfortunate that such widespread black enthusiasm for her work did not translate into even more notice by the press, the silence from white literary quarters only intensifies the unmistakable call that was emanating from the national black community. This was the constituency of readers and fellow social activists that gave Hopkins its imprimatur and that eagerly awaited her next productions.

Behind the scenes at the company, however, the decision to produce books now was emerging as a weighty and perhaps overwhelming responsibility. In May 1901, Wallace approved of the details pertaining to the magazine's finances and structure in R. S. Elliott's informative profile of the magazine. In that article, Elliott had declared to readers that "[t]here has been no attempt to seek the aid of philanthropists" and emphasized that "every cent of surplus, after the payment of publishing bills, office expenses, etc., has been devoted to spreading the influence of our publication and increasing the circulation."[102] On 6 August 1901, however, Walter Wallace could bear the financial pressure no longer. As the person with primary responsibility for the magazine, he endeavored to solicit patronage that would help him avert the "shoals ahead."[103]

The person to whom Wallace wrote in August 1901 was Booker T. Washington, the longtime Tuskegee University president and, like Wallace's parents, a former Hampton Institute student. Wallace, since the outset of the magazine, had encouraged his readers to be generous in their assessments of Washington, noting in the first issue that "[m]uch has been said about Mr. Washington's plans or methods in conducting his school. His plans may not be yours, but . . . if they reach the many poor boys and girls in many different sections of the South, you nor I should take exception to them. . . . Surely, whatever else he deserves," suggested the editors, "he does not deserve censure, criticism, and calumny. Sad would it be, indeed, if it were said of him, as it was said of another of earth's great benefactors 'He came unto his own and his own received him not.'" Such endorsements of Washington, in the wake of strident calls for racial preservation in an era of predatory mob rule, revealed that the *Colored American Magazine* editors were not making explicit links between white Southern intimidation and African American accommodationism.[104]

Wallace was circumspect as he made his overture to Washington. "My dear Sir," Wallace wrote, "I am about to make a disclosure to you which is strictly confidential, asking your indulgence of a careful perusal and advice." He then spoke plainly: "The future affairs of the Colored American Magazine are in a critical condition." Its plight and current debt of $1,000, he explained, was brought on in part by flawed financial counsel and the "ill advice of a party who has had fifteen years experience in the publishing business," who recommended that the company "dabbl[e] in the publishing of books." This was, admitted Wallace, "an expensive luxury" and one that drained the "surplus proceeds of the magazine to such an extent that we find the summer dullness upon us with no sinking fund to meet increased expense."[105] The outstanding debt could be met easily if the company's agents, some of whom likely were members of the touted Literary Agents' Business Club, "were prompt with their remittances."[106] He also recognized that slow stock sales could be explained in part by the conservatism of potential investors, who "are waiting to see the business built up before taking the Stock, not realizing that we need the money now when the concern is in its infancy."[107] Wallace sought from Washington an immediate loan of $500 to help him meet the expenses due by mid-August. He and his colleagues, it appeared, had agreed that "[r]ather than consider the complete failure [of the magazine] after reaching this advanced stage," they would "consider allowing affairs to run to the limit and rescue the magazine from the debris (at an expense of $1000) with a change of affairs and to move on from where it left off."[108]

When Wallace wrote to Washington, the magazine enjoyed an impressive monthly circulation that Wallace estimated as being between 15,000 and 16,000 readers. Such numbers represented part of the "gigantic stand" that the magazine had taken, an accomplishment that exceeded Wallace's confessed "sanguine expectation." In the first year, the magazine had become "an indisputed [sic] success," Wallace claimed, as he called Washington's attention to the "accomplishment of $15,000 worth of business from its inception in May 1900 to May 1901." In his earnest summation, Wallace declared emphatically that "[a]ll communications [are] strictly confidential and I give you my word as a man, I believe on oath that every cent received or expended by the Company has been used for (what the Directors thought was) the good of the Company." He also offered complete transparency and noted he would be "willing to open our books to any Attorney you may name for your benefit." "May you see fit to aid us," he urged Washington, before closing with the assertion, "Ever yours for the Race through the magazine."[109]

Despite the sincerity and shared Southern history that infused Wallace's letter, Washington offered a decidedly qualified response. He purchased fifty dollars of stock, an action that, as he explained later to Francis Jackson Garrison, was done "simply for the purpose of helping the magazine out when it was in Boston."[110]

Hopkins refused to be daunted by the financial concerns and was determined not only to maintain her impressive literary output but to think creatively about how she might tailor it so that it contributed to the stability of the magazine. Her decision to use the serialized novel form was no accident. She was well aware of the literary precedents and financial successes enjoyed by British and American writers such as Charles Dickens and Harriet Beecher

Stowe. This style of episodic and intensely commercialized writing may have deprived her of the professional satisfaction of creating monographs, but it enabled her to pursue her craft and to sidestep any protests from her colleagues that their organization no longer could afford to "dabble," as Wallace described it, in book publishing. Wallace and his three colleagues may not have been as fully aware as Hopkins, an individual with a keen literary eye, that the early twentieth-century American literary marketplace was one still shaped by patterns of the mid-Victorian period. During that era, in which the serialized form enjoyed its highest level of popularity, popular authors regularly contracted with magazines, owned increasingly by book publishers, to provide material.[111] Publishers, striving to avoid a paper tax, had implemented the serial form in England in the late 1600s, but readers continued to delight in the format long after it made financial sense to use it. In America, influential magazines such as *Godey's Ladies Book* and publications such as the prestigious *Atlantic Monthly* invested to great profit in the serial format. When the *Colored American Magazine* shifted away from the publication of monographs and toward novels that were serialized in its issues, it made a strategic financial move. Certainly, serialized materials whet the appetites of readers and created a keen desire for the next issues. In so doing, the serialized novels of Hopkins and the few other authors whose work was presented in this form during the magazine's Boston years also helped to inculcate a capitalist ethos in the magazine's readership. In *Hagar's Daughter*, *Winona*, and *Of One Blood*, Hopkins provided material that functioned as an "exemplary tool of capitalist production," precisely because it depended on intriguing replication, continuity, and repetition.[112]

Hopkins's response to financial stresses corresponded directly to the ethos of industry and entrepreneurship that the *Colored American Magazine* founders encouraged in others. Hopkins saw an opportunity to transform the company's financial necessity into a literary benefit for herself. In her quest to become a professional writer, she transformed herself into a "hired pen,"[113] a writer whose weekly salary of seven dollars was only a little more than double the three-dollar wage for the office typist, whose responsibilities included handling the office correspondence.[114] Hopkins's modest income from the *Colored American Magazine*, which would have amounted to less than $400 per year, may not have been enough to stave off financial concerns that she as the sole provider for her family may have had. She secured additional professional security by working her way into a formal position as literary editor of the magazine. Although that promotion enabled her to make more deliberate decisions about the magazine's content, it did not bring a substantial increase in pay. As Hopkins noted in a lengthy letter that she penned to

William Monroe Trotter, her political ally and the editor of *The Guardian*, her promotion to literary editor raised her pay to eight dollars, but financial pressures prompted the dismissal of the secretary so that Hopkins found herself now "doing her work of correspondence and my own editorial work," as the magazine "jogged along" until its next financial turning point.[115]

The profession of authorship, as Pauline Hopkins experienced it, was rigorous and empowering; the daily production work, clerical responsibilities, and pressures resulting from being the lone woman in an editorial office could have taxed her creative genius. Hopkins did not sacrifice her own editorial agendas and writing even as the founders' dependence on her increased steadily and as the magazine worked its way toward first anniversaries and other milestones. As a result, the work that she produced and the writings of others that she invited, shaped, and edited made manifest the political ideals and racial perspectives that the visionary Southern editors first imagined. Hopkins discerned the power and promise at hand, and she invested herself fully in the *Colored American Magazine* to realize her modern-day goal of becoming a public historian whose career was built on writerly innovation, community empowerment, and emancipatory political ideologies.

11

(Wo)Manly Testimony

The *Colored American Magazine* and Public History

You must cease to dwell upon your wrongs in the past,
however bitter, however cruel. . . . Your duty is to forget the
past, at least, to put it behind you and to advance bravely,
with your faces to the dawn and the light.

JOHN CHRISTIAN FREUND

January 1904

The American Negro must remake his past
in order to make his future. . . . History must
restore what slavery took away, for it is the social
damage of slavery that the present generations must
repair and offset. . . . There is the definite desire and
determination to have a history, well documented,
widely known at least within race circles, and
administered as a stimulating and inspiring
tradition for the coming generations.

ARTHUR A. SCHOMBURG

"The Negro Digs Up His Past,"

1925

Pauline Hopkins responded purposefully to the urgent call from the *Colored American Magazine* editors for work that would "perpetuat[e] a history of the negro race."[1] In November 1900, just seven months after the magazine's debut, she inaugurated an impressive series of historical biographies that demonstrated the inclusive and ambitious pan-Africanist perspective of the magazine and became the first African American woman to publish a serialized historical biography series. Her work constituted a significant model for public history narratives and inspired contemporaries, most notably W. E. B. Du Bois, editor of the *Crisis* magazine, who would imitate her to great benefit.[2] The extensive narrative nonfiction pieces that Hopkins produced just months after joining the *Colored American Magazine* exuded what bibliophile Arthur Alphonso Schomburg revered as "a true historical sense" and was a substantial component of her effort to maintain the work of historical recuperation and cultural reinterpretation that she began so powerfully in *Contending Forces*.[3]

From November 1900 through October 1902, Hopkins produced a total of twenty-three richly textured and absorbing articles in two biography series for African American men and women. The first series, simply and assertively entitled "Famous Men of the Negro Race," began with a stirring profile of Toussaint L'Ouverture that included an image of the Haitian leader taken from an oil painting that Hopkins's stepfather William owned. Subsequent articles included profiles of abolitionist, orator, and statesman Frederick Douglass, industrial education proponent Booker T. Washington, politician John Mercer Langston, and pioneering lawyer, statesman, ancestor of the Harlem Renaissance, and poet Langston Hughes. Hopkins engineered a smooth transition in November 1901 from profiles of famous men to famous women of the race, focusing on women who had distinguished themselves in the arts, club movement, and racial activism and uplift movements of the antebellum and postbellum eras. The series on women featured pieces that were more dense and collective in nature than those in the "Famous Men" series. Hopkins honored the achievements of intrepid activists such as Sojourner Truth and Harriet Tubman. She also focused on the ways in which women as educators, club women, writers, and performers represented powerful racial ideals and how they, through generous outreach, had an impact on the public sphere. Several additional biographies profiled prominent New England writers such as Lydia Maria Child; John Greenleaf Whittier; Elijah W. Smith, her mentor, cousin, and Boston's African American poet laureate; and the South African journalist A. Kirkland Soga, with whom she worked closely on pan-African unity projects. She also endeavored to launch a third biographical series, entitled "Heroes and Heroines in Black," highlighting the achievements of contemporary African Americans such as David Wilder, the first man of color to graduate from the Springfield, Massachusetts, YMCA Training School.

Hopkins crafted evocative and stirring biographies that endowed the *Colored American Magazine* with an impressive scholarly legitimacy, a feat that was ironic, given her lack of formal advanced academic credentials. Yet she was more than qualified, as educator Charles Chesnutt insisted in 1899, when, in reference to his biography of Frederick Douglass, he announced that he could "claim no special qualification for this task, unless perhaps it be a profound and in some degree a personal sympathy with every step of Douglass's upward career."[4] The rich prose and impressive intertextuality of Hopkins's writing authorized her to be a steward of the African American historical and cultural record. Indeed, in the years just prior to Hopkins's affiliation with the *Colored American Magazine*, there was a genuine flowering in the publication of African American history and an opportunity for Hopkins to study a compelling body of general African American historical works and biographies. Compiled by ministers, lawyers, abolitionists, and educators, these works were part of a growing effort to strengthen collective African American identity, assess the prevailing white canon, and reconstruct a more true and inclusive record of American history and society.[5] Hopkins was motivated by what scholar V. P. Franklin has described as "an overarching commitment to 'race vindication,'" a determination on the part of African American intellectuals engaged in a wide-ranging set of professions and scholarly fields to "put their intellect and training in service to 'the race' to deconstruct the discursive structures erected in science, medicine, the law, and historical discourse to uphold the mental and cultural inferiority of African peoples."[6] Thus, Hopkins became a public defender in the most stirring of contexts. She represented individuals silenced by circumstance, environment, and force and testified on behalf of those whose lives provided powerful evidence of the race's noble endurance and invigorating resilience.

As she began to write historical documentary narratives, Hopkins was increasingly convinced that the realities of the antebellum and postbellum ages legitimized her writerly projects. "[T]he same reasons exist at present, and quite as potent," she asserted in 1902, "for the preservation of all records pertaining to persons or events connected with our remarkable history, as existed before emancipation."[7] She welcomed the chance to be a part of the historical continuum that positioned her as an extension of the professional work that individuals like William Still had achieved. Indeed, she rallied the race to sustain the collective race pride and study of African American history that antebellum African Americans had begun. She cited Still's belief, articulated first in his stirring preface to his 1872 *The Underground Railroad*, that African American history "must never be lost sight of."[8] Still, having completed what Hopkins and many others regarded as a "remarkable work," essentially bequeathed his place to the next generation. Hopkins took seriously his urging to her generation the mandate to maintain a high and revitalizing sense of African origins and American history. "The race must not forget the rock from which they were hewn," he insisted, "nor the pit from whence they were digged. Like other races, this newly emancipated people will need all the knowledge of their past condition which they can get."[9] She now aspired to honor the liberation historiography work of early African American historians who had dedicated themselves to assembling and reconstructing the African American past, even as they contended with widespread disbelief about African American achievement and divisive racial slander aimed at preserving the myths of innate black inferiority.[10] The intrinsic value of the *Colored American Magazine* was linked to Hopkins's unswerving devotion to retelling the African American story; she was motivated by what Arthur Schomburg later would describe as the race's "definite desire and determination to have a history, well documented, widely known at least within race circles, and administered as a stimulating and inspiring tradition for the coming generations."[11]

The historical materials in the *Colored American Magazine* represented a new dimension of African American scholarship and biographical writing. Publishers like Boston's Small, Maynard, and Company were aware of the significant responsibilities of "the average busy man and woman" and marketed their books accordingly. In an effort to make intellectual growth possible and complementary to everyday activities, this Beacon Street press developed a biography series that would "furnish brief, readable, and authentic accounts of the lives of those Americans whose personalities have impressed themselves most deeply on the character and history of their country."[12] To meet that goal, the press recruited "writers of special competence . . . who possess in full measure the best contemporary point of view" to generate volumes that would contain "everything that such a reader would ordinarily care to know," "equipped with a frontispiece portrait, a calendar of important dates, and a brief bibliography for further reading . . . [and] printed in a form convenient for reading and for carrying handily in the pocket."[13]

Hopkins and her contemporaries at the *Colored American Magazine* also had a keen sense of their reading public. As a result, Hopkins too was departing from some of the traditional aspects associated with the form. She was developing works that were markedly different in scope and overall presentation from the larger African American biographical tradition established through a host of nineteenth-century monographs, many of which were published in both the North and the South in the 1890s. Her narratives were enriched by her alternately gentle and demanding interrogative narrative voice. The pieces featured conventional life stories that evolved into patriotic discourse and provided glimpses of the meaningful private emotional bonds experienced by the men and women revered publicly for their ambition, fortitude, and vision. Hopkins's serialized biographies differed significantly in format and distribution from the monographs published by her male peers. Like them, her works were commissioned by a publishing house. However, the similarity was in some ways technical, since the national reputation of the Colored Cooperative Publishing Company had yet to be established and, at the time, could not rival the distribution and marketing of presses such as Funk and Wagnalls. Second, her biographies truly aspired to be public history. Incorporated into an appealing periodical, they were designed to be completely accessible to "the average busy man and woman" targeted by the Beacon Biographies editors, but also to those without access to what they perceived to be scholarly tomes.

In the decade before Hopkins became one of the few published nonacademic women historians, African American writers began to produce broad and comprehensive historical overviews. These important efforts included Edward A. Johnson's *A School History of the Negro Race in America, from 1619 to 1890, with a Short Introduction as to the Origin of the Race; Also a Short Sketch of Liberia* (1890); and P. Thomas Stanford's *The Tragedy of the Negro in America: A Condensed History of the Enslavement, Sufferings, Emancipation, Present Condition and Progress of the Negro Race in the United States of America* (1897). In addition, Hopkins lived in close proximity to prolific Boston historians such as Archibald Grimké, the nephew of white South Carolinian abolitionists Angelina and Sarah Grimké and Harvard Law School graduate, who was active in the Colored National League and local African American civil rights organizations. Grimké, one of the first American scholars to publish on the giants of the antebellum age, produced biographies of William Lloyd Garrison and Charles Sumner in 1891 and 1892, respectively.[14] In 1899, the Beacon Biographies of Eminent Americans series, edited by M. A. De Wolfe Howe and produced by Small, Maynard, and Company, featured Charles Chesnutt's study of Frederick Douglass, the first volume on an African American ever included in the series, which at the time featured works on John Brown, Aaron Burr, Thomas Paine, and Daniel Webster.[15] The impetus for historical writing continued to be the acquisition of social order and African American freedom. In his dedication, Stanford suggested that his "short story of Negro life in the United States" represented his "hope of helping create a strong, healthy public opinion that will make it impossible for outrages and lynchings to be much longer continued."[16] Chesnutt, in his preface to the Douglass biography, was quite forthcoming about the emotional appeal of the historical matter. "The more the writer has studied the records of Douglass's life, the more it has appealed to his imagination and his heart," he confessed.[17] Chesnutt's goal was to "revive among the readers of another generation a tithe of the interest that Douglass created for himself when he led the forlorn

(Wo)Manly Testimony

hope of his race for freedom and opportunity." If he achieved this, he wrote, he would regard "his labor . . . amply repaid."[18]

Hopkins heeded the exhortations for intellectual rigor that shaped the work of leading male authors of the day and endeavored to broaden the nature of female-authored pieces on religious matters and domesticity. She managed this academic triumph despite her subtle social marginalization in Boston, a city with a growing, self-conscious, and self-selecting African American elite who prided themselves on their Wellesley College and Harvard College degrees. She was a pioneering lay historian, one of the many who began to emerge in the 1890s. All shared a lack of formal training or institutional affiliation—fewer than ten women earned doctorates in history before 1950.[19] Twenty-five years before the Oberlin-trained feminist educator Anna Julia Cooper earned her Ph.D. from the Sorbonne, in 1925, and became the first African American woman to earn a doctorate degree in history, Hopkins was only a high school graduate with professional training and experience in stenography and related clerical work. She was motivated by an ancestral rather than academic mandate to document race history and, through her work, to enlist new soldiers in the battle to secure equal rights and sustain the race by correcting the historical record. History, for Hopkins, was a significant cultural and political tool. She had no advanced academic degrees of her own. It was also extremely important to Hopkins that she was heir to a powerful ancestral record of public writing through maternal second cousin Susan Paul, granduncle James Monroe Whitfield, and cousin Elijah Smith. All three of Hopkins's writerly kinfolk defended the honor and integrity of the race with passion, translated their fervent political convictions into stirring public actions, and created lyrical pieces that enabled their readers and audiences to behold the often unspeakable realities and frequently obscured truths of African American life, culture, and history.

The growing canon was marked by its intertextuality and innovative hybridities. Hopkins harnessed the power of the interdisciplinary text and blurred the precise boundaries between fact and fiction in her evocative profiles. Her works thus were in keeping with the "grander nineteenth-century tradition" of socially conscious interdisciplinary writing.[20] The tenor and breadth of Hopkins's biographies also allowed them to function as a "vehicle for all sorts of ideas about the purpose and destiny of human life in general."[21] Hopkins's capacity to create absorbing narratives with richly detailed settings and engaging characters made her an invaluable asset to the magazine's editors. Her contributions compensated in some ways for the more traditional narrative nonfiction articles penned by writers who offered more staid and matter-of-fact reports on African American military endeavors, pan-African conferences, and the like. In time, her prodigious literary production and demonstrated versatility as a writer would justify her promotion to editor. During the magazine's tenure in Boston, Hopkins was the only editor to publish articles other than editorial reports, many of which were issued under the title of "Here and There."

Hopkins could easily have written compelling articles based on the lives of her distinguished male ancestors, such as the minister brothers Thomas and Nathaniel Paul or the poet activist and barber James Monroe Whitfield. Yet she refrained from doing so. It was a choice that may have been influenced by her desire to achieve total objectivity and to avoid charges of partiality. Hopkins did make references to family members, and these comments enriched the material at hand. She referred to the connections that her family had to William Wells Brown and John Mercer Langston, for instance. In one intriguing comment, she writes of the adventures that occurred when her stepfather, William Hopkins, was a traveling companion to William Wells Brown, the future Chelsea, Massachusetts, resident and the man who would bestow upon her the ten-dollar gold prize for her high school essay, "The Evils of Intemperance." Hopkins and Brown were together during an abolitionist lecture tour in the early 1840s featuring the celebrated author of *Clotel*, which included a memorable and potentially violent stop in western New York state.[22] Brown, who "always told [of the incident] with great pride," managed to outsmart the "howling set of men and boys, waiting to give me a warm reception."[23] In 1902, she included a short but glowing portrait of Annie Pauline Pindell, her maternal aunt, in her profile of accomplished female concert singers. Hopkins exercised considerable restraint, however, and never revealed her close family link to Pindell, a talented diva known as the "Black Nightingale," whose voice "embrace[d] twenty-seven notes, from G in bass clef to E in treble clef."[24] Hopkins's reticence may have been generated by a lingering grief; Pindell had passed away only five months earlier, in May 1901. On at least one occasion, Hopkins used resources from her own immediate family to augment her work. In her article on L'Ouverture, for instance, the rare oil painting of the Haitian leader, which her stepfather owned, was the source of the evocative image that accompanied the article.[25]

The decision of the *Colored American Magazine* editors to launch twelve biographical articles testified to their confidence that their new magazine would succeed. References to the upcoming series began appearing in August 1900 in the "Editor's and Publisher's Announcements" column. It was

(Wo)Manly Testimony

presented as a vital offering, one that would enable the magazine "not only to give [their] patrons a periodical that will entertain, but instruct as well."[26] Hopkins, who had now assumed the weighty responsibility of creating the magazine's first yearlong series of articles, did much more than this, however. She used the "Famous Men of the Negro Race" series as a vehicle through which to advance her own interpretations of black history, using the articles to reconstruct black history, cultivate civic awareness, and provide corrective and unmediated evaluations of the past.

The first series was a successful addition to the monthly issues. Once it concluded, Hopkins immediately began publishing a second series, "Famous Women of the Negro Race." She was clearly committed to generating an inclusive black historiography. Hopkins used both series, but especially the first, to develop an ennobling and romanticized black history. She posed affecting rhetorical questions to her readers, and these queries, often delivered in sequence, made up interludes of call and response between the writer and her audience. She employed this narrative engagement most memorably in her tribute to pioneering lawyer Robert Morris, who, in the early years of his career, represented six-year-old Sarah Roberts in her 1849 Boston public school integration suit. "Shall we not prize these great men of ours, and crown them?" she asked. "Do they not reflect upon us as the radiant light of nobility? Are they not centers about which we may rally, these standard-bearers, in our hard struggle against the adverse winds and tides of life?"[27]

Hopkins's indulgent prose, palpable race pride, and unself-conscious displays of sentimental fervor provided her readers with a richly textured escape from the rigors of daily life. Many of the pieces were absorbing because Hopkins recreated the nurturing aspects of antebellum black life. Like Susan Paul did in her account of how she taught lessons about slavery in her antebellum Northern classroom, Hopkins softened the gory details of racial oppression and violence. She conveyed the horror, but did so by setting it in sharp contrast to the essential and universally cherished aspects of kinship ties, home, and family life. As a result, Hopkins's historical writings clarified the ways in which she defined romance. For her, romance was a state of existence that persisted in the face of oppression. It offered unwavering protection to certain persons, and it prevented moral, physical, and emotional damage in the face of social and political evil. Indeed, such protections fueled her inclination to find the messianic dimensions of the men that she chose to profile.

Hopkins created biographies of famous Negro men that were shaped by her intensely feminized historiographic vision. That perspective was shaped by Hopkins's enduring conviction, expressed especially well in her "Famous Men" tribute to John Mercer Langston, that "[t]he true romance of American life and customs [was] to be found in the history of the Negro."[28] As a whole, the series anticipated the call from white literary circles for writers to "re-wed literature with journalism" and prompted Julian Hawthorne, the only son of the renowned New England author Nathaniel Hawthorne, to worry that the "fundamentally 'material'" elements of journalism threatened the "spiritual" qualities of literature.[29] Hopkins's insistent effort to link romance and history represented a "higher journalism," a professional pursuit that was being hotly debated in elite white Northern literary circles at the time. Contributors to the *Atlantic Monthly*, the Boston-based journal associated most often with its longtime editor William Dean Howells, were among the most earnest discussants. In 1899, for instance, Gerald Stanley Lee declared that American journalism was about to make an epic shift. He predicted that the "next great writer who shall succeed in making headway in the public mind" would be the one who was a "transfigured journalist," a reporter who is "more of an artist than the artist, an artist who is more of a journalist than the journalists."[30] When one considers Lee's prophecy in the context of the African American audience to whom Pauline Hopkins was introduced in the spring of 1900, it is impossible to locate Hopkins anywhere else but within the evolution of the dominant, that is, white, American periodical press. The editors of the *Colored American Magazine* did not obsess about whether or not their publication could or should be measured against its white contemporaries, but it is clear that its writers were cognizant that reportage was itself an enterprise in flux.

The twelve biographies in the "Famous Men of the Negro Race" series were absorbing social histories in which Hopkins frequently underscored the global, rather than local or narrowly defined African American, potential of each man. Hopkins clearly reveled in the opportunity to provide her readers with long-obscured and rarely published facts about the heroes of the race. The series quickly and emphatically proved her editors' assertions in the first issue that "[a] vast and almost unexplored treasury of biography, history, adventure, tradition, folk lore poetry and song, the accumulations of centuries of such experiences as have never befallen any other people lies open to us and to you."[31] Hopkins often was moved to make fervent declarations about the power of history and the privileges it could accord a people. "We delight to honor the great men of our race," she explained, for example, in her tribute to attorney Robert Morris, "because the lives of these noble Negroes are tongues of living flame speaking in the powerful silence of example, and sent to baptize the race with heaven's holy fire into the noble heritage of perfected manhood."[32]

Hopkins certainly invoked the past to great effect in the series, yet she also offered the pieces as meditations on the present that could contextualize and contain the turbulent events of the day. "Circumstances are arising every hour in these momentous times, when the Negro is making wonderful and lasting history through the medium of the very oppression placed upon him, designed to force him into unredeemable inefficiency," she declared in February 1901.[33] Such circumstances may have prompted her to focus on men of New England, a move that would bolster regional readers in particular as they continued to confront on a daily basis the ways in which "Negro ambition, enterprise and culture" were difficult for "fellow-citizens of Caucasian descent to consider."[34]

Hopkins's mission at the *Colored American Magazine* was to provide "encouragement of those who faint, or would slavishly bend under the weight of a mistaken popular prejudice," and "inspiration and aid of all . . . noble men and women, who [were] fearlessly and successfully vindicating themselves and [their] people."[35] In October 1900, this campaign began in earnest when the *Colored American Magazine* debuted the "Famous Men of the Negro Race" series. The first subject was Toussaint L'Ouverture, a "Negro of unmixed blood,"[36] whom African American activists like James T. Holly lauded for his instigation of "the grandest political event of this or any other age," which "[i]n weighty causes and wondrous and momentous features . . . surpasse[d] the American Revolution, in an incomparable degree."[37] Hopkins's first biographical essay was a studied exercise in contained and tentative political assessment, signaled by the deferential parenthetical remark in tiny print just below the author credit: "The extraordinary fortunes of Toussaint L'Ouverture bespeak for him more than the passing interest of a dry biography," she contemplated in hushed tones, before giving in to a rapturous consideration of her responsibilities as biographer. "[Y]et how few the words, how stifled must be the feelings of the heart when we endeavor to cramp the passionate flow of holy emotion aroused by a studious contemplation of the character of our hero, within the narrow limits of a magazine article."[38] Black history had, it seemed, exceeded the form that Hopkins was supposedly primed to create for it. In addition, she hinted here at the greater scope of writing and book-length projects that she might be willing to take on at some point. Hopkins's sentiments did reflect the way in which L'Ouverture had fared in nineteenth-century literary works.

Hopkins lamented that L'Ouverture, or "[t]his Negro," as she referred to him, had "left hardly a line for history to feed upon," but she could compensate for that lack by consulting a substantial range of biographies, novels, poems, and pamphlets published in Dutch, English, French, and German that memorialized, mythologized, and critiqued the formidable political and military leader who had achieved Haitian independence.[39] Hopkins's rich political education would have ensured her familiarity with leading African American writings on the island, chief among them the 1841 *A Lecture on the Haytien Revolutions; With a Sketch of the Character of Toussaint L'Ouverture*, by New Yorker James McCune Smith, the first African American physician, and the 1857 *Vindication of the Capacity of the Negro Race for Self-Government and Civilized Progress*, by Episcopal minister James Theodore Holley, a staunch proponent of colonization, who advocated repatriation not to Africa but to Haiti. There also were several sources produced by leading Bostonians, including her great-granduncle Thomas Paul, who had served in Haiti as a missionary in the early 1800s. Prince Saunders, a teacher at the African Baptist School and the "most persistent advocate of Haitian emigrationism," emigrated to the island in 1807, became the nation's attorney general and architect of its criminal code, and hoped that both his 1816 *Documents Relative to the Kingdom of Hayti, with a Preface* and his 1818 *Haytian Papers* would "excite a more lively concern for the promotion of the best interests, the improvement, the definite independence, and happiness of the Haytian people."[40] Hopkins also likely turned to the substantial writings of the prolific and accomplished writer and editor Lydia Maria Child, who considered L'Ouverture in both her pioneering 1833 *An Appeal in Favor of That Class of Americans Called Africans* and her 1865 volume *The Freedmen's Book*. In the final published piece, however, Hopkins reprinted in its entirety William Wordsworth's 1803 sonnet on the Haitian hero, using the poem to underscore her continuing argument about L'Ouverture's status as a "hero [who] had the pity and sympathy of all generous spirits of the time" during the time of his imprisonment and mysterious death.[41] She relied most heavily on the 1841 novel *The Hour and the Man: A Historical Romance*, by Harriet Martineau, a contemporary of William Lloyd Garrison and member of the Paul family, and included two lengthy excerpts from one of the best-known writings on L'Ouverture that demonstrated L'Ouverture's capacity for deep emotional solidarity and bravery. Both Hopkins and Martineau reveled in the chance to claim L'Ouverture, the man whose history, according to Martineau, "admits of romance . . . furnishes me with story . . . [and] will do a world of good to the slave question."[42]

The Hour and the Man, one of the best-known writings on L'Ouverture, stirred Martineau's contemporaries to high compliments. William Ellery Channing told Martineau that "he knew no grander conception of heroic character." The diarist Crabb Robinson regarded it as "her masterpiece, despite its faults." Florence Nightingale hailed it as "the finest historical romance in any language."[43] Thomas Carlyle, in a fashion symptomatic of the time, waxed poetic and lapsed into racial stereotyping, as he reminded Mrs. Ralph Waldo Emerson of Martineau's achievement. "You saw her *Toussaint L'Ouverture*," he reminded her emphatically in a February 1841 letter, "how she has made such a beautiful 'Black Washington,' or 'Washington-Christ-Macready,' as I have heard some call it, of a rough-handed, hard-headed, semi-articulate gabbling Negro. . . . It is very beautiful. Beautiful as a child's heart,—and in so shrewd a head as that!"[44] The power of Martineau's writing, completed while living as a semi-invalid in a house near the River Tyne, lay in her re-ordering of autonomy and obedience that, according to her biographer, succeeding in introducing new "moral considerations" into public discourse on race matters. "Toussaint not only frees the Negroes of Haiti from French rule, not only works in obedience to the voice of God within him," observed her biographer, "but presides over a quite automatic reform of the island in which morals become pure, labour is honoured, inventions are made by ingenious labourers able to work for themselves, and every cottage has two rooms!"[45] Pauline Hopkins was quite taken with Martineau's acts of literary and historical reclamation, and, as her biographical writings quickly revealed, seemed especially intrigued by the compelling "moral considerations" of Martineau's historical fiction.

The "Famous Men of the Negro Race" series was the platform on which Hopkins sought to assert the high morality, ethics, and bravery of men of African descent. In documenting first the life of L'Ouverture, she honored him in matters both domestic and national, using the realm of the intimate to show his manliness and godliness. Martineau's novel facilitated Hopkins's agenda, and the *Colored American Magazine* writer eagerly invoked *The Hour and the Man* to underscore her point about L'Ouverture's "great moral heroism," his purity of heart, and the sanctity of his familial relations. Martineau's novel included riveting scenes in which justice trumped romance, a theme that Hopkins would use in her first serialized novel, *Hagar's Daughter*, to great effect. Hopkins told her *Colored American Magazine* readers of the circumstances leading to the death of General Moyse, L'Ouverture's nephew and the fiancé of his daughter Genefrede. Hopkins reported that Moyse was "sacrificed . . . for disregard of orders for the protection of the Colonists" and used Martineau's work to illuminate the point that "for the sake of what he called justice," L'Ouverture was compelled "to destroy his nephew—the betrothed of his daughter—the only child of a wifeless brother." Martineau's tautly rendered scenes of the overwrought Genefrede learning the fate of her beloved infused the *Colored American Magazine* biography with great drama. On the verge of contemplating suicide in a "deep and brimming reservoir," Martineau's tragic heroine stood with "her hands . . . clasped above her head for the plunge when a strong hand seized her arm and drew her irresistibly back. In ungovernable rage she turned and saw her father."[46] Hopkins, caught up in a breathless literary solidarity with Martineau, transitioned seamlessly from the quoted material into her own critique of the scene, and the distinction between historical fictions and facts blurred altogether as Hopkins marvels at the might of a man whose "moral heroism" enabled him to accomplish, according to Hopkins, "such a course" that "would have been beyond us of the present day and generation."[47]

Hopkins's turn to Haiti, which accommodated her immersion in a deeply evocative romance, also was informed by her documented ancestral links to the island. In the spring of 1823, less than two months after Thomas Paul buried his father, Caesar, at the Copp's Hill cemetery in Boston, he petitioned the Massachusetts Baptist Organization for permission to become a missionary to Haiti. His letter of request to the trustees was "expressive of the deep interest which for a long time he had felt, in relation to the moral and religious condition of the Haytians," and his desire to "mak[e] known to the inhabitants, 'the unsearchable riches of Christ.'"[48] Paul was granted a six-month commission and, on 31 May 1823, boarded a schooner, the *Alert*, for a twenty-two-day voyage to the island.[49] Paul traveled to Haiti at a time when the island nation figured prominently in the imagination of free and enslaved peoples of African descent in America. Just five years earlier, in 1818, the African American crew of the *Holkar*, an American ship, mutinied while sailing off the coast of Curaçao and immediately set a course for Haiti.[50] In 1823, he was sailing for the island just one year after Denmark Vesey, who had cultivated ties to Haiti's postcolonial rulers, had instigated a slave revolt in Charleston, South Carolina, that clearly was inspired by the Haitian independence movement.

Paul took with him "letters of introduction to the most distinguished persons in Hayti," provided by "several respectable merchants" in Boston and from the American Bible Society, some "100 Bibles, and 100 Testaments, in the French and Spanish languages—committed to [his] care . . . for sale, or gratuitous distribution among the inhabitants of the island, and also an elegant Bible, which is to be presented to the President."[51] The letter that he received from Daniel Sharp, the organization's secretary, shared the board's hopes for Paul's visit. "Your object in visiting Hayti, is purely religious," he reminded him. "We wish you to make known to such of the inhabitants as are disposed to hear you, the way of salvation by Jesus Christ. Our prayers will be answered and our most enlarged desires realized, if you should be instrumental in teaching men to deny themselves of all ungodliness and worldly lusts, and to live soberly, righteously, and godly, in this present evil world."[52] The

Massachusetts Baptist Organization urged Paul, in his audiences with Haitian president Jean-Pierre Boyer, to "take this opportunity of assuring him of the deep interest which the Board feel in the moral and religious welfare of his fellow-citizens, and of the joy with which we behold the republic of Hayti so rapidly rising to take her place among the freest and most enlightened nations of the earth."[53]

Pauline Hopkins inherited the deep spiritual and political convictions that prompted the Reverend Paul's evangelical mission to the island. Hopkins admitted unself-consciously that she simply was unable to suppress the provocatively imagined "stifled" feelings and the "cramped . . . passionate flow of holy emotion." Such transcendence prompted her to make grand narrative gestures aimed at transfixing her readers. "Races are tested by their courage, by the justice which underlies their purposes, by their power and endurance—the determination to die for the right, if need be," she declared, before going on to apply the lessons of the Haitian past to the African American future. "If the Negro race were judged by the achievements and courage in war of this one man, by his purity of purpose and justice in times of peace, we should be entitled to as high a place in the world's relation of facts respecting races, as any other blood in the annals of history."[54] Her arresting rhetorical flourishes, delivered in hypnotic rhythmic cadence, became sermons on racial salvation able to convince all who heard them of their earthly worth and potential.

The "Famous Men of the Negro Race" series gained momentum through the autumn of 1900, and Hopkins grew increasingly confident of her ability to appropriate and to racialize the genre. She was positively gleeful as she imposed a lively interdisciplinarity on the form, superimposed the intellectual and emotional needs of her audience upon the canonical and white-authored history, and furthered the pan-Africanist agenda that the *Colored American Magazine* espoused. Such deft reworkings of the form enabled Hopkins to "translat[e] the familiar lives" of men like Toussaint L'Ouverture, Frederick Douglass, and Booker T. Washington into "participatory exemplary texts" that "relaxed into the conventions of essential biography, wherein the life described becomes an extended allegory."[55] In addition, Hopkins's writings defied the linearity and racial exclusivity of Western history by conjuring up a black meta-historical chronology. Her aggressively corrective discourse, though, like the white-authored history against which she was writing, also depended on deliberate elisions and strategic suppression of facts.

As Pauline Hopkins devised it, the "Famous Men of the Negro Race" series constituted a systematic reconstruction of African American manhood. Hopkins wrote that conventional American biography was tailored to maintain an exclusive white American history and to perpetuate mythologies of white superiority. In her profile of Charles Lenox Remond, the Salem-born man who was the first African American abolitionist lecturer, she stated her case for distinctive and revisionary black biography quite directly. "Ordinarily a biography is expected to begin with some genealogical narrative intended to show that the person presented to the reader was descended from ancestors of renown," she noted, before making observations about specific cultural practices and cherished national genealogies. "They boast in England of a descent from William the Conqueror. In our own country, New Englanders date from the landing of the Pilgrim Fathers, while the boast of the South is from the colonization in the time of Queen Bess," she concluded.[56] Hopkins's references to Northern and Southern traditions, however, were neither applicable to nor available to African Americans. Hopkins recognized that the enslavement of Africans and their transport to the New World was a violent act of displacement, and she insisted that bondage constituted a savage de-historicization and lasting alienation from the supposedly all-encompassing national genealogy.

Hopkins offered a definitive intervention in order to counter the erasure of black history from the founding narratives of England, New England, and the South. Since this erasure is inextricably bound up with slavery, Hopkins's three geographical references are momentarily re-presented as key vectors of the triangular slave trade.[57] Hopkins then deprives these literal and politically symbolic sites of their traditional power over black people, and by extension, over their history. "[T]hese men of the Negro race whom we delight to honor," she exclaims, "had no ancestors. 'Self-made,' they traced their lineage from the common ancestor, Adam. Their patent of nobility is found in the sacrifices that they made to lift the yoke of human bondage from their over-burdened, down-trodden race; their crown of glory was the victory that crowned their efforts."[58] Hopkins performs a striking erasure of her own, one that successfully links black people to a prelapsarian moment and the first human father, an ancestor far greater than English kings or queens.

Hopkins's explanatory remarks about mythic black origins may have been successful as defensive cultural maneuvers enacted in the face of an exclusionary national historical discourse. Over time, it appeared that she had even transcended that long-deployed white practice. She generated an alternative thesis of origins that claimed for her male subjects an impressive and deliberate black autonomy. Midway through the series, Hopkins wrote about John Mercer Langston, former slave, American statesman, and ancestor of Harlem Renaissance poet Langston Hughes. She began the Langston profile with a substantial quote about paternity, agency, and vocation. Citing a "great English writer," she wrote, "Unquestionably, the greatest thing that can be said of a man is, that he had no father; that he sprang from nothing, and made himself; that he was born mud and died marble: but the next best thing is, that having something he made it more; being given the fulcrum, he invented his machines, and wrought his engines, till he made conquests that gave lustre to his name."[59] In closing, Hopkins notes that "Mr. Langston accomplished his own success in life. His determination was supreme. His motto, 'Self Reliance, The Secret of Success.'"[60] The rhetoric of collectivity had no place in Hopkins's empowering hagiographic tributes.

It is possible to read Hopkins's depiction of the self-made black man as a strategic intervention against the decimated and abusive genealogies of slavery. In some ways, this aspect of the biographies situated them squarely within the long-standing tradition of what Arthur Schomburg would refer to in 1925 as the "[v]indicating evidences of individual achievement [that] have as a matter of fact been gathered and treasured for over a century."[61] However, Hopkins's work succeeded where many early efforts at African American historiography had failed. Schomburg does not reference Hopkins, or, for that matter, any other women lay historians, in the article that he prepared for the historic 1925 African American issue of *Survey Graphic* that Alain Locke edited and later transformed into the *New Negro* collection, the touchstone anthology of the Harlem Renaissance. Yet had the visionary bibliophile, whose collections formed the impressive foundation for the Schomburg Library Collection, considered Hopkins's work, he would have been much encouraged. Her narratives defied the pattern that he suggested was a dominant characteristic of early considerations of African American achievement. He referred to books written on the "less-known and often less discriminating compendiums of exceptional men and women of African stock," and he lamented such works: "[T]his sort of thing was on the whole pathetically overcorrective, ridiculously over-laudatory." "[I]t was," he declared, "apologetics turned into biography."[62]

The intervening that Hopkins accomplished in the biography series also included the relegation to the margins of interracial origins and the explosive subject of sexual concubinage of enslaved black women. By doing so, she reclaimed long-contested psychical territory for descendants of enslaved Africans in America. She refers by name to the white slave owners who fathered famous black men like John Mercer Langston, but the terse statements about other mixed race men suggest the narrator's barely contained rage. Of William Wells Brown, noteworthy abolitionist and her Boston mentor, she allocates just three curt sentences to the circumstances of his birth: "William Wells

Brown was born in Lexington, Ky., in the year 1816. His mother was a slave, his father a slaveholder. The child was taken to Missouri in his infancy, and his boyhood was passed in St. Louis."[63] There is a dramatic shift in tone between the first and third sentences, the lines that literally contain Brown's vexed genealogy. The initial and intense subjectivity, achieved by her use of all three of Brown's names, contrasts with the alienating reference to "the child." Hopkins's hyper-repressive prose here suggests that even broaching the circumstances of such a birth can induce a paralyzing and sympathetic trauma. When appropriate, Hopkins invokes the "stock" from which men like Edwin Garrison Walker, only surviving son of David Walker, the author of the incendiary 1827 "Walker's Appeal," have come. It is clear, though, that Hopkins came to realize how necessary it was for black biography to contend with and even circumvent this historic abuse. The foundation of Hopkins's *Colored American Magazine* reputation had been established with *Contending Forces*, in which she staged an unprecedented post-Reconstruction interrogation of black women's sexual objectification and the sociopolitical implications attached to their reproductivity.

Hopkins invokes the rhetoric of self-determination most deliberately in the profiles of mixed-race men. One-third of the men featured in the series were the sons of their white slave masters: William Wells Brown, Frederick Douglass, John Mercer Langston, and Booker T. Washington. Of the other eight men, Robert Browne Elliott is described as a "Negro of unmixed blood,"[64] and only Toussaint L'Ouverture and Robert Morris are described as descendants of African men. In the case of Morris, Hopkins endows his biography with dignity, even as she makes reference to his grandfather's corrupted childhood and experience of the horrific middle passage: "Cummono Morris was the first member of the Morris family in America. He was a native African, and was carried to Ipswich, Mass., when very young."[65] Here, Hopkins's first statement confers an unmediated and dehistoricized American domesticity upon the African man. Only after imposing this sociocultural caesura does she refer to his dehumanizing and emasculating American bondage. In doing so, she applies the word "carried," a popular euphemism like the word "brought" that writers as ancient as Phillis Wheatley used when referring to their abduction from their African homelands. Hopkins, determined to maintain the dignity of her subjects, uses phrases that give the real history but do not resurrect the trauma associated with bondage or overshadow the individual's New World accomplishments.

Hopkins's efforts to contain and then create an empowering revisionary story of American enslavement for African American readers was even more pronounced in the "Famous Women of the Negro Race" series that she began

(Wo)Manly Testimony

in November 1901. Overall, the articles were much more contemporary in subject matter and the individuals mentioned represented a much wider geographical range than that found in the "Famous Men" series. Hopkins focused on the present-day accomplishments of black women and addressed directly the ongoing debate about how the public work of women affected contemporary notions of African American womanhood. With this series, she continued the tradition of women's public writing to which Gertrude Mossell and Anna Julia Cooper had contributed so importantly in the 1890s. Hopkins would have been encouraged by Mossell's assessments of the professional opportunities that awaited American women, and which also were of particular value to African Americans. Noting the cultural transformation that now provided opportunities beyond the "dressmaker's arc" or the work of "teacher," Mossell celebrated the fact that the profession of author and the advance of African American women in the field of journalism and public writing was proceeding apace. "The success of this line of effort is assured and we hail it with joy," she declared. She was quick to insist, though, on the civic responsibilities that attended such professional ventures. "Our women have a great work to do in this generation," she intoned before discussing the powerful intermediary place that women on the verge of the twentieth century now held: "[T]he ones who walked before us could not do it, they had no education. The ones who come after us will expect to walk in pleasant paths of our marking out. Journalism offers many inducements. It gives to a great extent work at home; sex and race are no bar, often they need not be known; literary work never employs all one's time, for we cannot write as we would wash dishes. Again, our quickness of perception, tact, intuition, help to guide us to the popular taste."[66]

The articles in the "Famous Women" series were infused with practicality and industry, but that did not diminish the rhetoric of high romance that so deeply permeated the series on men of the race. Nonetheless, Hopkins's unmistakable emphasis on domesticity was key to her assertion that the daily life of all women merited documentation and that their experiences in the domestic realm—broadly or narrowly defined—were an essential part of African American history. The "Famous Women" series celebrated a number of living subjects, and that contemporaneity created a vital cultural immediacy, one that created role models with whom most of the Colored American Magazine's African American women readers could identify easily and could immediately begin to emulate.

Hopkins's overarching purpose in the "Famous Women" series was to acknowledge the public value of women's work, activism, and artistic talents. Hopkins devised a new presentation for the series, which brought a new and distinctive character to "Famous Women" and allowed Hopkins to cover more individuals over the course of the year. Hopkins made only two exceptions to the grouped format of the "Famous Women" series. She wrote separate profiles for Harriet Tubman, the fearless fugitive slave, intrepid Underground Railroad leader, and resourceful Union spy, and Sojourner Truth, the formerly enslaved, self-confident evangelical itinerant. The series, which began with a rousing article entitled "Phenomenal Vocalists," subsequently included articles, a number of them offered in two- and three-part installments, on "Literary Workers," "Educators," "Artists," "Club Life among Colored Women," and the "Higher Education of Colored Women in White Schools and Colleges." The patriarchal discourse of exceptionalism that emerged in the "Famous Men" series here was replaced by a matriarchal rhetoric that was rooted in a celebratory black female gentility and enterprising domesticity.

The revisionary history agendas that shaped so much of Hopkins's work emerged also in the "Famous Women" articles in which she countered popular misconceptions of slavery as a Southern phenomenon. Her essays on Harriet Tubman and Sojourner Truth, for example, featured vigorous treatments of Northern complicity and moral corruption during the antebellum era. After musing that "[a]ll our ideas of slavery are connected with the South," Hopkins stated frankly that "[v]ery few people of this generation realize that slavery actually existed in all its horrors, within the very cities where, perhaps, we enjoy the fullest liberty today; but so it was."[67] Then, with barely repressed disdain and righteous indignation, she provided a systematic and bulleted history of slavery and the trafficking of Africans in New England and the North. She recalled that in late eighteenth-century New York, "[t]he legislature of the state . . . declared . . . that 'all encouragement should be given to the directed importation of slaves; that all *smuggling* of slaves should be condemned as *an eminent discouragement to the fair trader*." In wry tones, she remarked that "[i]t is also interesting to note that in 1807, no less than fifty-nine of the vessels engaged in that trade were sent out from the State of Rhode Island, which then could boast of but 70,000 inhabitants." Of Massachusetts, she declared that "[t]he history of slavery and slave trading in Massachusetts is one of the most surprising volumes ever issued by the American press." She concluded with damaging comments about two more Northern states. "New Hampshire, too, held slaves," she insisted, before noting that "General Washington himself, while President of the United States, hunted a slave woman and her child all the way into that State."

Hopkins spent little time invoking the antislavery past of New England. The only example that she did give referred to an 1808 fugitive slave case that was argued in Vermont before a judge named Harrington. She may have turned to the well-known *Colored Patriots of the American Revolution*, by Bostonian William Cooper Nell, for details about the case involving a New York slave owner who tried to reclaim a formerly enslaved man, now living as "a person of color in Middlebury" but whom the court rebuffed when it noted that although there was "evidence of title that was good . . . the chain had some of its links broken."[68] Hopkins celebrated the boldness of that moment, and by amplifying the reports that Nell provided, she assured readers that "the brave Judge Harrington stunned the remorseless claimant with his decision that 'nothing less than a bill of sale from the Almighty could establish ownership' of his victim." Having given her New England readers a dizzying and unsettling tour of their own region, Hopkins dared her audience to come to any conclusion other than the one she offered. "Thus we see that slavery was a sin and crime of both North and South," she declared confidently. "It was sustained by the government, it was sanctioned by almost the whole religious world of the United States, and this crime of slavery became the 'sum of all villainies.'"[69] The formidable moral rectitude expressed here not only reinforced Hopkins's role as a lay historian but also suggested the valuable objectivity that she brought to divisive, and often alienating, subjects.

Early on in the "Famous Women" series, Hopkins provides a forceful chronicle of slavery and riveting "details" about the bondage of women like Sojourner Truth, "who experienced all the horrors of Northern servitude."[70] Like Harriet Wilson, a member of the Beacon Hill community in the 1850s and the first African American woman to publish a novel, Hopkins knew full well that "slavery's shadows [fell] even there," in and beyond the New England city that was home to Faneuil Hall, the celebrated "cradle of liberty." Yet she refused to allow the awful dehumanizing aspects of enslavement to define those who were enmeshed in it. This was especially clear in her tributes to two of the race's most beloved foremothers, Truth, who passed away in 1883, and Tubman, who was living in the Auburn, New York, home that she had built for indigent and elderly people. Hopkins related the evolution of her own regard for Tubman, the intrepid self-emancipated woman whose career included work as a Union army spy and nurse, as well as a suffragette and legendary Underground Railroad conductor. "In giving a sketch of the life of Harriet Tubman we find that this woman, though one of earth's lowliest ones[,] has shown an amount of heroism in her character rarely possessed by those of any station of life," Hopkins wrote forcefully. "Her name deserves to be handed down to posterity side by side with those of Grace Darling, Joan of Arc, and Florence Nightingale," she insisted, "for none one [*sic*] of them has shown more courage and power of endurance in facing danger and death to relieve human suffering than has this woman in her heroic and successful endeavors to reach and save all whom she might of her oppressed and suffering race, and pilot them from the land of bondage to the promised land of Liberty."[71] Hopkins's fervent tribute to Tubman even offered readers glimpses of Tubman's potential experience of the afterlife that would bring long-overdue elevation to the woman, naming her Moses because of "her being the leader of her people in their exodus from the land of bondage" and "Moll Pitcher' for the energy and daring by which she delivered fugitive slaves from the South."[72]

Hopkins's early treatment of slavery in the "Famous Women" series and her writings on New England's history of enslavement enabled her to repoliticize the social activism of Northern women. She now was able to characterize the activities of African American women of the North as a type of modern antislavery work. This bold, and even controversial, redefinition challenged black middle-class complacency, and it reminded women within and outside of the club movement of the need to remain vigilant about their still-fragile freedoms. Hopkins also offered a striking corollary between slavery in the Americas and the intellectual advancement of individuals of African descent. She did not simply suggest that some rare individuals such as Phillis Wheatley, Benjamin Banneker, or Jupiter Hammon had managed to cultivate and to demonstrate their creative genius during the colonial and antebellum eras. Instead, she wrote, even more forcefully, that "[f]rom the time that the first importation of Africans began to add comfort and wealth to the existence of the New World community, the Negro woman has been constantly proving the intellectual character of her race in unexpected directions; indeed," she concluded, "her success has been significant."[73] She did not focus on the oppression of slavery but rather on the positive contributions that Africans made to New World culture. She asserted the inherent capacity for upbuilding that was possible because of, and even dependent upon, African contributions. Having done that, she then imagined the early and "unexpected directions" of early creative genius by Africans in America. The political narrative that she crafted here challenged racial stereotypes and cultural mythologies that were used to justify the mistreatment and dehumanization of African Americans. It insisted instead that slavery had failed to corrupt the inherent, unshakable intellectual core of the race; she would return with vigor to this concept in her serialized novel *Of One Blood*, the narrative nonfiction work that she published in the *Voice of the Negro*, and ultimately in the *New Era Magazine*, her short-lived but ambitious periodical.

Hopkins also used the "Famous Women" series to provide explicit political commentary and pointed assessments of current-day problems. In "Literary Workers," she stated pointedly, "We know that it is not 'popular' for a woman to speak or write in plain terms against political brutalities, that a woman should confine her effort to woman's work in the home and church," but such restrictions were impossible to honor since, as she asserted, "[t]he colored woman holds a unique position in the economy of the world's advancement in 1902."[74] Hopkins reassured herself and her readers about the rightness of this venture and the high responsibilities of such work, declaring fervently that "the colored woman must have intimate knowledge of every question that agitates the councils of the world; she must understand the solution of problems that involve the alteration of the boundaries of countries, and which make and unmake governments."[75] These were modern-day tenets for the acquisition of true black womanhood. The cult of true womanhood, fashioned as a template for nineteenth-century white women, already had been refashioned to honor the realities of African American women's experience. Its original tenets of piety, purity, submissiveness, and domesticity here were revised so that cultural submissiveness was replaced with political assertion, and domesticity was expanded to ensure that women, according to Hopkins, could "continue to help raise the race by every means in their power, and at the same time raise our common country from the mire of barbarism."[76]

The "Famous Women" series demonstrated Hopkins's belief in the fragility of freedom and the value of women's work in a volatile postslavery America. As she evaluated the importance of black women writers, for instance, she first defined them as "Literary Workers" and then considered the political implications of their vocation and the oppressive social circumstances in which they wrote. The life of Frances Harper spoke directly to such objectives, and Hopkins profiled at length the author of *Iola Leroy; or, The Shadows Uplifted* (1892). Hopkins also used the Harper essay to contextualize the unpredictability of life in relation to the steadying assurance provided by a devout Christian life. Hopkins indicated here her growing interest in a faith-based approach to early twentieth-century life as she began her tribute to the woman who "is lovingly spoken of and known to her friends and acquaintances as 'Mother Harper'": "[W]e feel more than glad of an opportunity to add our mead of praise to the just encomiums of many other writers for the noble deeds of an eminent Christian woman," she wrote in the last installment of the "Literary Workers" article.[77] The essay provided an especially engaging overview of Harper's life and the dreadful events that propelled her to become an ardent abolitionist. Hopkins enriched the profile by citing an array of primary sources, ranging from Harper's own letters to newspaper reports that confirmed Harper's gifts for persuasive political outreach. Hopkins continued her focus on the enduring legacy of antislavery work and the lessons that modern American women could learn from the women who, like Harper, began to "use time, talent and energy in the cause of freedom."[78] She described Harper as one who, though "freeborn . . . yet partook of the cup of woe under the oppressive influence which was the heritage of bond and free alike under slave laws."[79] In her assessment of Harper, Hopkins underscored the fictional nature of freedom. She suggested that, given the African American past and the present-day challenges to the race, no woman of color could consider herself immune from racism or social upheaval.

Throughout the "Famous Women" series, Hopkins invoked moving abolitionist speeches and referred to antislavery events in which many New England men and women had participated. She made repeated references to figures such as William Lloyd Garrison, Wendell Phillips, Lydia Maria Child, and Frederick Douglass and the vital interactions between these influential individuals and the subjects about whom she was writing. She was unwavering in her conviction that antislavery activism was an illuminating and viable model for early twentieth-century race activism. As she established herself as the primary historian for the *Colored American Magazine*, Pauline Hopkins became increasingly dedicated to the concept that African American history was an antislavery, and therefore an emancipatory, discourse. As a result, activists, writers, and lecturers such as Mary Ann Shadd Cary, the pioneering journalist and "brave-hearted, daring [woman] of the race who stood shoulder to shoulder with the men in the times, not so long ago, that tried men's souls,"[80] Frances Harper, abolitionist lecturer, poet, and novelist, and Maria Baldwin, the accomplished principal of the Agassiz School in Cambridge, were engaged in restorative social work. Their efforts were what would preserve and protect Hopkins's postslavery readers, a constituency that, Hopkins noted more than once, was less than forty years "removed . . . from the maelstrom of slavery."[81]

Hopkins celebrated the mythic dimensions of her subjects in "Famous Men" and did not dwell on mundane or practical issues pertaining to the livelihoods or domestic needs of her male subjects. In the "Famous Women" series, however, as she herself grappled with the sizeable work expectations at the *Colored American Magazine*, low pay, and growing family responsibilities, she was much more forthright about the material and financial needs of even the most venerated women that she discussed. Where she minimized the hardships that men like Douglass and Washington faced as slaves, Hopkins used the "Famous Women" series to advocate philanthropic responsibility in her readers. On behalf of Harriet Tubman, the elderly slave who nursed the ravaged survivors of Massachusetts's own all-black Fifty-fourth Regiment, for instance, Hopkins asked for "all the financial aid that a generous public can bestow."[82] Such unabashed advocacy on behalf of Tubman was part of

Hopkins's desire to see African Americans providing tangible evidence of their racial responsibility.

The "Famous Women of the Negro Race" essays are significant for their dissemination of a doctrine of high black female morality and divinely ordained political intervention. Throughout, Hopkins uses vivid evangelical prose to underscore the tenets of an emergent early twentieth-century Afro-feminist nationalism and advances her belief that "the colored woman holds a unique position in the economy of the world's advancement in 1902" and beyond. Hopkins also describes a visionary domesticity and model of spiritually informed civic activity and conceptualizes women's work as "sacred" work. She speaks repeatedly of God's "commands" to black women and of how self-advancement is a sanctified means of improving the race. The religiosity of the "Famous Women" articles depends on an inverted gender hierarchy, one that charges women with the task of creating and protecting the manhood of their race. In the first installment of the series, Hopkins, certainly influenced by her own experiences on the stage, argued that arts performances were an inherently political act of uplift. Even the manner in which these vocalists presented themselves fueled Hopkins's argument of the link between black womanhood, divine plans, and American social evolution. Elizabeth Taylor Greenfield, a singer born into slavery in Mississippi, separated from her parents, and educated by her wealthy white Quaker mistress, was a case in point. Hopkins concluded that "[God] sent an angel's voice to dwell within a casket ebony-bound, with the particularly carved features of racial development indelibly stamped upon it, to confound the skepticism of those who doubted His handiwork."[83] Hopkins's description of Greenfield's black body as a "casket ebony-bound," which reveals an uncharacteristic weariness on her part, succeeds precisely because such images enable reclamation of that female body—vulnerable during and after slavery—as a tool for the enlightenment of all those who encountered Greenfield.

Hopkins found a unique way to discuss female reproduction and labor—in work and in childbirth—and devised striking metaphors for the current rebirth of the race. She revisited the argument that Anna Julia Cooper had made in her 1892 *Voice from the South*, about the links between enlightened and politically astute American womanhood and the domestic life of the nation. Like Cooper, Hopkins reassures her readers that "[e]ducation has not cause[d] . . . women to shirk the cares and responsibilities of private life," invokes the voice of a unified collective "that feels the blessing which her example must be to the entire race," and endorses the intellectual advancement of women. "Education, with us," she insists, "does not encourage celibacy but is developing pleasant homes and beautiful families."[84] Hopkins also hints at a mobilized maternal ethos like that which enabled Mary Ann Shadd Cary to "rais[e] recruits in the West" in response to the federal decision to "put colored men in the field to aid in suppressing the Rebellion." Cary, according to Hopkins, "brought [the men] to Boston with as much skill and order as any recruiting officer under the government. Her men were considered the best lot brought to headquarters."[85] Cary and Tubman, both of whom Hopkins features in the "Famous Women" series, had lives that challenged conservative notions of African American womanhood. Yet, even as Hopkins asserts the essential link between their gender and their achievement, she incorporates a subtle feminine rhetoric. Keen to showcase the intrepid modern woman of color and to assert that the postbellum age required such individuals, Hopkins assured her readers that "[n]o record of the *fruitful* work of colored women would be complete without the name of Mary Shadd Carey [*sic*]." By characterizing Cary's work as "fruitful," Hopkins accomplished much. She invoked a distinctively Christian and womanly aura, but also strategically complimented Cary's "strong determined will" and the fact that Cary "could not be checked in doing what she conceived to be her duty."[86]

The "sacred" nature of women's work infused the profiles of Elizabeth Greenfield and Annie Pauline Pindell, and Hopkins couched their life stories in holy tones and imagery. "[F]or to them it was given to help create a manhood for their despised race," she declared forcefully.[87] Hopkins insistently proposes here and throughout the series that African American women from all walks of life were not only required, but, by virtue of their gender, were fully equipped to "teach the embryo man the duties of good citizenship."[88] Even as she proposed such ennobling ideas, though, Hopkins was fully aware of the conservatism and traditional ideas that some of her readers had about what constituted appropriate female behavior. Without hesitating, she addresses those in her audience who regarded it as "not popular" for a woman such as herself "to speak or write in plain terms against political brutalities" and who believed that "a woman should confine her efforts to woman's work in the home and church."[89] Hopkins and other women writers carefully crafted their proposals in order to minimize potentially devastating male resistance.[90] Hopkins spoke to these potential skeptics as one who had her own doubts about the political dimensions of a women's public life. As recently as 1900, she had revealed the limitations of her feminist ideology when, in a "Women's Department" column, she referenced female suffrage and declared, "We believe it to be a good thing if limited in some degree." At that time, Hopkins's reservations were rooted in her fear that "the politician's life" would bring about a dreadful change in women. "[W]e should deplore seeing woman fall from her honorable position as wife and mother to that of the common

(Wo)Manly Testimony

ward heeler hustling for the crumbs meted out to the 'faithful' of any party in the way of appointments to office," she confessed. Nearly two years later, however, Hopkins was much more specific about women's political activity and the forums, such as those provided through the women's club movement, in which they could sustain themselves as watchful and effective citizens.

Throughout the "Famous Women" series, Hopkins demonstrated her solidarity with prevailing women's club ideology. She also used the persistent controversy relating to integration of the national federation of clubs to underscore the continuing need for collective action and confident assertion of race identity and history. In "Club Life among Colored Women," the ninth essay in the "Famous Women" series, Hopkins provided readers with a thrilling account of the behind-the-scenes networking and conspiracies designed to thwart the advancement of African American women's clubs. She relayed "exciting news" gleaned from reports that Josephine St. Pierre Ruffin, head of the Woman's Era Club of Boston of which Hopkins was a member, delivered, in which she described travels to national club meetings that had enabled her to collect "interesting relics" that she meant to transform into objects that would "form the basis of a law suit against the General Federation of Women's Clubs."[91] Such tensions made Hopkins's initial efforts in the "Women's Department" column and the decision to feature more prominent and regular contributions from African American club women in the magazine seem all the more vital. Hopkins and the *Colored American Magazine* club correspondents reaffirmed African American women's efforts to maintain a functional femininity, one that would accommodate their purposeful work to achieve racial uplift, to debunk stereotype, and to confront the persistent evils of racism that dogged their campaigns to advance in social and professional arenas. As Josephine Turpin Washington, a mathematics instructor at Tuskegee Institute and wife of the school's physician, stated in her preface to the 1893 volume *Women of Distinction*, by Lewis Scruggs, "Whether in the home as wife and mother, or struggling in the ranks of business or professional life, [the true woman] retains her womanly dignity and sweetness, which is at once her strength and her shield."[92] Hopkins endeavored to address the domestic issues that pertained to the home and also the larger domestic issues involving regional and national conflicts. Her assessment of the ongoing resistance to the membership and full participation of African American women's clubs, especially the resistance of Southern white women to such integration, prompted Hopkins to imagine the issue as events that simply were "renewing the old conflict" between the states. "Thrice before in the history of our country," she reflected, "the 'spaniel' North has grovelled before the South, but, thank God, the time came when the old New England spirit of Puritanism arose and shook its mane and flung off the shackles of conservatism. So it will be this time," she predicted.[93] Hopkins's effort to cast the postbellum age as one that required activism and race work akin to that practiced during antebellum days was justified by the shenanigans engineered by members of the national club movement. Hopkins did not hesitate to cast aspersions on white Southern women, individuals whom she believed had "given us a terrible blow and in a vital part" by their outspoken resistance to African American women. "Club life has but rendered her disposition more intolerable toward the victims of her husband's and son's evil passions," Hopkins declared, her remarks revealing the disgust and frustration that she felt on behalf of her disenfranchised sisters.[94] However disappointing were the conflicts within the national club movement, they did serve to reinforce Hopkins's points about the need for women of color to be politically savvy and ruthless in their determination to expose the failings of society and the potential of the oppressed.

The "Famous Women" series concluded with "Higher Education of Colored Women in White Schools and Colleges," and Hopkins used this moment to pose a set of probing queries of her readers. "Can the Negro woman learn anything? Is she capable of the highest mental culture?" Noting that these "questions . . . have been conclusively answered in the series of articles closing with this number," Hopkins rallied against the Southern racism and sexism that she held responsible for current threats to national order and to African American domesticity.[95] The article title suggested that Hopkins meant to document the educational experiences of African American women, but it quickly became clear that in doing so she was going to blast the South. "We have seen that every slave State had laws against the education of the Blacks," she wrote emphatically, "and that the present régime of State government in the South land is in opposition to the highest educational development for the race." Yet Hopkins lambasted white Southern women in a moment that recalled the outrage caused some years earlier when the Tremont Temple address of former Georgia governor J. W. Northen at the Congregational Society gala had been prefaced by the reading of a seemingly innocuous telegram from white Southern women who essentially sanctioned the aggression advanced by their white supremacist advocate husbands. Hopkins took aim at the explicit obstructionist work of white Southern women and characterized their actions as antithetical to the godliness that they invoked on a regular basis. After charging that "we have seen, too, that the Anglo-Saxon woman, in convention assembled, has sought to place the indelible stamp of hopeless intellectual inferiority upon the Negro race in spite of voluminous testimony to the contrary," Hopkins then quite pointedly asked, "Is the course adopted toward the unfortunate Negroes of this country according to the teaching

and spirit of the Gospel which is so proudly and austerely heralded to hea-
then nations at an annual cost of millions?"[96] Her indictment here recalls
the rhetoric of those committed to the nineteenth-century anticolonizationist
platform. Her castigation of the flawed Christian oppressors spiraled into an
impassioned critique of the "condition of woman in Palestine and the European states" and the era of Queen Victoria.[97] Ultimately, she used this global
overview to justify her unrelenting call for equal rights for women of color.

Hopkins's tirade against the evils of sectionalist thinking and segregation
gave way to a set of five delightful profiles of young women who had succeeded in predominantly white schools and colleges. They were part of the
cohort whom Hopkins imagined as "a new race of colored women" whose
presence and ambition signaled a "new tide set in, new forces called into play,
a new era in the world's history and through all this the moral and social
regeneration of a race." She also was pleased to report that members of this
sanctified group had "entered the sacred precincts of celebrated institutions
of letters, and successfully combatting great obstacles have demonstrated
to the world their peculiar fitness for service in the sacred inner courts of
intellectual preeminence, regardless of race."[98] Hopkins turned first to the
achievements of Harriet H. Allen, a young woman from Charlestown, Massachusetts. In what now functioned as characteristic journalistic reserve, she
neglected to mention that Harriet Allen was her aunt, the younger sister of
her mother, Sarah, and the daughter of her grandfather Jesse who, with his
family, had been living in Charlestown, Massachusetts, since 1850. In this
veiled family biography, Hopkins established yet another facet of the social
emancipation that sorely was needed in New England and throughout the
United States. Hattie Allen's educational bildungsroman began on the eve of
the Civil War when the "bright, intelligent girl" who was "well known and
liked by the white citizens" finished grammar school classes and then "because
of her Negro blood was denied admission to the high school." Thanks to a
multiracial local effort, Allen was admitted to the local seminary, where she
gradually joined the curricular mainstream, having been "received at first as
a special pupil." Three years later, she graduated, and, "as a special mark of
favor," noted Hopkins, "the colored girl was the valedictorian of her class."[99]
Allen eventually accepted an offer to join the faculty of a private academy in
Canada. She emigrated to the country "where her color was no bar" and in
which her maternal granduncles Nathaniel and Benjamin Paul had lived and
worked in the Negro settlements.[100] Hattie's experiences on the one hand
justified Hopkins's question about "the right of the woman of color to live
in the world on the same terms as a white woman does—to work as she
does, to be paid as she is, to elevate herself, intellectually and socially as she

does—to make use, in short, of all that is elevating in life." Her achievements also furnished the second major issue that Hopkins sought to address in the final essay of the "Famous Women" series: "the question as to the colored woman's competency" to live on the same terms as those that applied to white women.[101]

The additional profiles that Hopkins included reinforced her argument about the necessary and honorable marriage of African American gentility and intellectual ability. Where Harriet Allen enjoyed a local success at the Charlestown Seminary, the next set of women profiled embodied an indisputable high culture aesthetic. Through their own college work at selective universities and prestigious Seven Sister schools and their marriages to Ivy League graduates, they became part of the upwardly mobile and highly educated African American elite. Hopkins offered an intimate glimpse into the life of Marie Elizabeth Hartley. Known to many as Mrs. George W. Forbes, Hartley had graduated from Kingston Academy in New York and had married an Amherst College graduate and Colored National League member, who was the only "colored man in Massachusetts . . . selected for library work by the city government" and one who, "from the fearless position he has assumed in race matters . . . is being felt in all race questions."[102] Hopkins might have been especially inclined to honor Marie Forbes since her husband George was the cofounder, with William Monroe Trotter, of the recently established *Guardian*. Hopkins's admiration of Trotter, at this moment, was in its early stages, but *The Guardian*, since its first issues in December 1901, had been outspoken in its criticism of accommodationism and Booker T. Washington's political agendas. Hopkins also celebrated the achievements of Elizabeth Baker, the Wellesley College–educated wife of William H. Lewis, a Harvard College alumnus and member of the Massachusetts Legislature, who had been elected from Cambridge "solely by white voters."[103] Following the highly romanticized accounts of educational and social success, Hopkins underscored for her readers the beneficial aspects of women's intellectual advancement. "[W]e must not fail to note one important fact," she told her audience; "three of [these young women] have become the wives of progressive college men. Education has not caused these women to shirk the cares and responsibilities of private life; rather, we believe, each feels the blessing which her example must be to the entire race."[104] Clearly Hopkins hoped to stave off a domestic crisis, one that some constituencies imagined would be the inevitable product of women's increasing access to education and the workplace, and to public life in general. Yet the end of the article also suggested that, despite her eloquent and affirmative commentary on the meaningful advances for African Americans, she also was haunted by the prospect of how such ambitions might lead to another race war, one instigated in modern times by women of the unruly South. The telling clues to Hopkins's uneasiness were not signaled by the article's rather splendid and rousing narrative conclusion but by the poetical postscript that she appended to it. She used seven lines of an unidentified poem that began,

> The firmament breaks up. In black eclipse
> Light after light goes out. One evil star
> Luridly glaring through the smoke of war,
> As in the dream of the apocalypse,
> Drags others down. Let us not weakly weep
> Nor rashly threaten. Give us grave [*sic*] to keep
> Our faith and patience.[105]

The word "grave," a misspelling of the word "grace," may have been an unwitting printer's error, but it was quietly appropriate to the melancholy and trepidation that exuded from this last article. Once again, Hopkins may have counted on the collective Northern familiarity with the lines of John Greenleaf Whittier, author of "A Word for the Hour," the poem from which Hopkins drew her conclusion to the "Famous Women" series. The poem, which Whittier penned in January 1861 soon after the first four Southern states had seceded from the Union, resurrected for Hopkins's twentieth-century readers a sobering set of antebellum tensions and resolutions. Whittier proposed in the poem that those states that would rather "break the lines of Union" be allowed so to do. "Draw we not even now a freer breath," he asked,

> As from our shoulders falls a load of death . . .
> Why take we up the accursed thing again? Pity, forgive,
>   but urge them back no more
> Who drunk with passion, flaunt disunion's rag
> With its vile reptile blazon.[106]

The lines that Hopkins included in the *Colored American Magazine* illuminated the degree to which she was concerned about a destabilizing social and racial rift. They also hinted quite effectively at the unstated possibility that the white South could be disenfranchised itself, before African Americans and their Northern supporters "weld anew the chain / On that red anvil where each blow is pain."[107]

Hopkins completed "Famous Women of the Negro Race," a provocative and extended meditation on the politics of black womanhood and African American feminist ideology, late in the fall of 1902, the same year in which Susie King Taylor, the intrepid nurse and educator, published what today still stands as the only known Civil War account by an African American woman. Hopkins's second published biography series was a multifaceted consideration in which she strategized for and with her readers about how best to facilitate the political education of women, to achieve the spiritual enlightenment of the race, and to direct the progress of a multicultural nation. The masterful historical enterprise that she had sustained for two years concluded as African American women continued to mobilize as political writers, literary activists, and social reformers. Hopkins herself was part of that dynamic enterprise. Her nonfiction works, including installments of these biography series that appeared alongside serialized chapters of *Hagar's Daughter*, her gripping Southern melodrama, provided evidence of her formidable scope as a writer and her tireless commitment to articulating the political desires of her people.

As she became an accomplished race historian, Hopkins also demonstrated her capacity for broad analyses of American history. Just before the "Famous Women of the Negro Race" series began, she published the first of a small set of profiles on leading white New England abolitionists. "Whittier, Friend of the Negro" appeared in September 1901, and in spring 1903, she published two articles on Lydia Maria Child. The Whittier article in no way competed with the rhetoric or narrative politics of the "Famous Men" series and was more in the vein of conversational journalism than documentary writing. Hopkins was prompted to write on Whittier because of activities in which she participated with fellow members of the "now famous Woman's Era Club, Boston." Her club "had contemplated making a pilgrimage to Amesbury, Mass., the home of the late John G. Whittier, 'High Priest of the Anti-Slavery Party,' and the Walter Scott of this legendary section of New England, for some time," and they did so on Independence Day, 1901.[108] Hopkins, Ruffin, and other members enjoyed a splendid tour of the home and gardens. "Nothing would delight us more," Hopkins assured her audience, "than to be able to take our readers into the spacious, rambling old house so quaint and comfortable, filled with reminiscences of a good, great man."[109] She emphasized the sanctity of this New England home and was unself-conscious as she admitted that "[t]he spirit of the poet was upon us from the moment we entered the 'garden room' at once sitting room and study, looking upon the garden . . . where he wrote many anti-slavery poems." In her closing paragraphs, she returned again to the holiness of the place, admitting that "[w]e left the homestead reluctantly. We had come in close communion with the spirit of one of our great American heroes, who have filled the pages of history with their renown, and all demonstration was hushed into silent reverence."[110] The New Era club members were accorded a great honor, it seems, but they also appear to have been quite determined to maintain a regimen that is highly reminiscent of the club meeting scenes depicted in *Contending Forces*. Unfazed by their new location, they proceeded with established rituals. "As is customary," reported Hopkins, "the Woman's Era Club held exercises in the garden." The proceedings included remarks by Josephine St. Pierre Ruffin, a historical sketch of Whittier by Hopkins, a reading of Whittier's eulogy by Agnes Adams, and closing remarks by Hopkins's cousin, Hannah Smith.[111]

Hopkins revived the fervent encomium that pervaded the "Famous Men" series as she concluded her article on Whittier. She was convinced that "[w]e, of this generation, cannot realize the difficulty and dangers encountered by the men identified with the anti-slavery struggle." After offering a dramatic word about their sacrifices and physical deprivations, she returned to contemplate the power of the written word. "But, withal their treatises on slavery, written often by the feeble light of a tallow candle," she mused, "were masterpieces of literature, for the Abolitionists embraced the flower of American intellectuality."[112] Once again she invoked the power of political thought and reiterated the idea that political activism was not simply about protest and obstruction but was rather a nuanced, sophisticated combination of efforts designed to achieve liberation and widespread social progress.

In November 1902, she appropriated the biography form even more deliberately for the cause of social justice. The essay entitled "Munroe Rogers" was a calculated effort to rouse readers to protest the de facto legal oppression of African American men. "It has been truly said that there is nothing new under the sun," began the seemingly demoralized narrator. Hopkins then proceeded to consider the huge chasm between the promise of Emancipation and the bloody realities of the postbellum age. "Who among the rejoicing millions could have been persuaded that in less than forty years from the day they celebrated—Emancipation day—this American people would have turned their backs upon the lessons of humanity learned in the hard school of sanguinary war, and repeated in their entirety the terrible acts exemplified by the surrender of Sims and Burns by a conservative North at the brutal demand of a domineering South!"[113] Hopkins tells the story of Munroe Rogers, a man who, after repeated incidents of unfairly docked wages, maligned character, and ultimately a physical encounter with a foreman at his North Carolina factory job, left for the North. Just before leaving, his act of turning off a spigot under the house where his sweetheart worked as a domestic led to the accusation by the foreman that he was trying to set fire to a white man's home. The threat of lynching prompted him to leave quickly and he made his way north to Brockton, Massachusetts. Shortly after he arrived, however, he was arrested, and law enforcement from North Carolina began to seek his extradition back to the state. Hopkins received her details, and perhaps even the prompting to write the piece, from Clement Morgan, a local attorney and one who "was in the forefront of the legal battle" to protect Munroe Rogers and to prevent a modern-day reenactment of the Fugitive Slave Act of 1850.

The article about Munroe Rogers represented Hopkins's most explicit attempt to use the *Colored American Magazine* as a platform from which to rally the public to immediate and urgent protest. She proved herself to be a vital ally of the men of the Colored National League, among them William Monroe Trotter and Archibald Grimké, both of whom attended and spoke "at some length" at the State House hearings on the Rogers case. Hopkins characterized the proceedings as ones "destined to be memorable in the history of extradition cases in Massachusetts and in the annals of Negro history in the North."[114] Unfortunately, the case was a grim reminder of the perilous situations that threatened the daily lives, free speech, and general domestic arrangements of African Americans in the South. Governor Winthrop Murray Crane, whom Hopkins later revealed as a candidate for the Republican National Committee chairmanship and thus a man willing to compromise himself in order to secure the post, sided with the North Carolina parties and signed the extradition papers. Hopkins did not even try to suppress her disgust. "What is the chief end of man?" she asked plainly. "The answer used to be, 'To glorify God and enjoy him forever,'" she stated. "But today times have changed and we have a new catechism.—What is the chief end of man? To put dollars in the hands of our political bosses."[115]

The "Famous Women of the Negro Race" series, well under way when the case of Munroe Rogers began to develop in the Massachusetts courts, cast a new light on Hopkins's efforts to create a record of stalwart African American leadership and perseverance. The grim modern-day realism that the Rogers case illuminated tinged her invocations of the mythic greatness of men such as L'Ouverture and Douglass. Hopkins's authorship of the two biography series and articles such as that on Rogers confirmed that the *Colored American Magazine*, for all of its innovative recruitment of amateur photographers and aspiring writers, was not sacrificing its commentary on the persistent targeting of African Americans and their continued subjection to unpredictable and politically sanctioned forces. Hopkins was so bold as to suggest that they were living in the age of a revived Fugitive Slave Act and that such pernicious legalized harassment haunted their every move. At this moment, she took up the mantle of the abolitionists, a mantle that she previously had deemed too weighty for a modern woman such as herself to carry. As the past hurtled into the present, however, she became increasingly convinced of the vicious cycle of oppression and of the damnably porous nature of the Mason-Dixon Line that required ordinary people to take extraordinary measures to preserve their families and freedom.

Hopkins's evolution as a public intellectual and lay historian strengthened her political commitments to racial advancement and effective agitation through enlightenment and collective resistance. She did not have to utter blatant and controversial rejections of accommodationism, the platform associated with Booker T. Washington that he advanced with much success. Nonetheless, her historical writings broke out of the narrow script of African American resistance that often failed to acknowledge the sophistication and wide platforms that Americans of color had claimed in their pursuit of the nation's cherished democratic ideals.[116] Hopkins was poised to build significantly on the successful series and political advocacy that she had initiated through the monthly profiles. But that opportunity was not one she would obtain easily. Eventually, Washington would set his sights on Boston, the city in which the African American press, of which *The Guardian* newspaper and the *Colored American Magazine* were a chief part, represented the greatest threat to his political influence and stature. When Hopkins finally assumed the editorship of the *Colored American Magazine*, she would find herself and the journal to which she had devoted herself directly in the line of Washington's deadly political fire.

12

Love, Loss, and the
Reconstitution of Paradise

Hagar's Daughter and the
Work of Mystery

I hate the dreadful hollow behind the little wood;
Its lips in the field above are dabbled with blood-red heath.
The red-ribb'd ledges drip with a silent horror of blood,
And Echo there, whatever is ask'd her, answers Death.

ALFRED, LORD TENNYSON
Maud; A Monodrama, 1855

The great political problem which is required to
be solved, is the recovery of the free negroes from their
false position in this slave-holding community.

CALYX
"Two Great Evils of Virginia,"
1880

1901 began with a literary and historical flourish for Pauline Hopkins. Heralded in the *Colored American Magazine*'s first issue of the year as "The Popular Colored Writer," she was feted in the pages of the magazine that confidently proclaimed itself to be "the only high-class illustrated monthly devoted exclusively to the interests of the negro race."[1] It was in this deliberate and self-conscious context of race work that the magazine prepared its new and established readers for Hopkins's next writings. The magazine praised her creative abilities and substantial literary output but emphasized most her gift for shrewd political critique. "Yours for humanity," the eloquent pledge that she coined and used beneath portraits and in written works such as *Contending Forces,* underscored the wholehearted and selfless commitment that she brought to her professional work and community activism. The *Colored American Magazine* valued Hopkins because as a race woman and a race writer her politics and craft were inextricably and obviously intertwined. As her powerful antilynching and racial uplift novel, *Contending Forces*, and journal writings circulated in the American literary marketplace, Hopkins was consistently celebrated by her peers and admirers as a staunch supporter of equality and African American civil rights who was willing to tackle such knotty questions as "shall the race have a fair chance?"[2]

To answer the question about viable opportunities for African American stability and advancement, Hopkins invoked American race and labor histories and examined, without artifice, the romantic rhetoric explicit in founding notions of an American nation indivisible and blessed by God. Hopkins and others had long experienced the United States as a nation riven by uneasiness about race, caste, and class and the ways in which these central social entities defined American society. In March 1901, Hopkins launched *Hagar's Daughter: A Story of Southern Caste Prejudice*, her first serialized novel and a work that confronted some of the most troubling race matters in American history. The novel, like *Contending Forces*, was steeped in American history and focused deliberately on the lingering manifestations of slavery—haunting histories of loss, deprivation, greed, and lust—that challenged notions of a reunited nation in which justice and democracy prevailed. Advertised as a "powerful narrative" of "love and intrigue," it was notable for its competing plots and subtexts in which ruthless ambition, social climbing, and personal angst threaten domestic stability, innocence, and romance and invalidate sacred hallmarks of society such as marriage vows and family bonds. *Hagar's Daughter* moves back and forth between the antebellum and post-Reconstruction periods, between countryside estates and city mansions, and between the bustling American Midwest of the self-made man and the political minefields of the Southeast, specifically Washington, D.C., and the nearby environs of Baltimore, Maryland. The novel's slate of diverse characters represents the full spectrum of American society: the white Southern elite and the Northern aristocrats, restored gentry, enslaved families of the South, and Northern communities of free people of color. However, it is a group of itinerant and alienated characters whose personal dilemmas fuel the novel's most deadly plots.

The novel revolves around the Ensons, a Southern aristocratic family represented by two brothers with starkly contrasting natures and aspirations. Ellis, the steady firstborn son, lives abstemiously at Enson Hall, the ancestral estate that is located just beyond the city of Baltimore, Maryland. A seemingly confirmed bachelor, this forty-year-old man lives quietly in the elegantly appointed Maryland estate that encompasses gardens, conservatories, and plantation lands, which support a variety of crops, as well as farm animals and dairy and poultry manufacturing. Ellis unexpectedly falls in love with Hagar Sargeant, the gentle and sophisticated daughter of the neighboring estate, but, in an austere moment of foreshadowing, the death of Hagar's mother on the eve of the wedding casts a dark shadow over the celebration. Because of the tragedy, the couple hosts severely modified nuptials. The two settle into an otherwise blissful domestic arrangement, and when they are blessed with a daughter, it seems as though this branch of the Ellis family is poised to enjoy uncomplicated and satisfying lives. St. Clair Enson is the complete opposite of the responsible Ellis, who is fifteen years St. Clair's senior. A young man whose birth came late in his parent's marriage and that tragically cost his mother her life, St. Clair Enson seems never to have recovered from the anguished circumstances of his birth or from the maternal void in his formative years. Unlike his laconic namesake from Harriet Beecher Stowe's 1852 antislavery novel *Uncle Tom's Cabin*, St. Clair Enson is a devilish rapscallion whose exploits are legendary and lamented widely in the community and in the several schools that he attends. His wild behavior in college eventually culminates in a deadly duel, and the awful incident results first in his expulsion from college, banishment from the family home by his father, and then severely limited access to the family money. Persona non grata for five years, until his father's death, St. Clair develops desperate financial problems and becomes widely known as a reckless gambler.

Both Ellis and St. Clair Enson reinvent themselves dramatically over the course of the novel. As a result of St. Clair's acts of violent treachery, Ellis survives a physical attack and involuntary enlistment in the Confederate Army. After a corrective three-year stint in the Union army that is of his own arrangement, he metamorphoses into Chief J. Henson, a legendary detective and chief of the Secret Service Division, who solves high profile federal cases that earn him the deep respect of many in the capital. When Henson is drawn into a tangled case that involves murder, blackmail, and kidnapping, he finally is reunited with his family. His daughter, known throughout the novel as Jewel, who believes herself the biological daughter of Senator Zenas Bowen, approaches him first to work on the case. Jewel's servant, Venus Johnson, collaborates with Ellis to solve the case, once it escalates and leads to the abduction of Jewel and Aunt Henny Sargeant, Venus's grandmother. In a riveting courtroom scene, the reserved detective breaks down and reveals his true identity, and his admission allows the newly widowed Estelle Bowen to declare that she is Hagar, his long-lost wife. The couple is reunited after years of tortured separation, years in which each had believed the other dead and their only child lost to them forever.

Zenas Bowen is one of the most mysterious figures in the novel, a man whose presence is both vital and least influential, a man of high station with great political power, who falls in love with a working woman, adopts a foundling, makes a fortune, and then comes to the capital to represent the interests of "the people." The kindly patriarch lives with his second wife, Estelle, and his daughter Jewel in a mansion located on Sixteenth Street, N.W., that is "in close proximity to the homes of many politicians who have made the city of Washington famous at home and abroad."[3] The descriptions of Bowen hint at a racial background that would best be applied to the other characters, but he is, at best, black by association as the husband of Hagar, the tragic mulatto and the adoptive father of Jewel, her quadroon daughter. Once Zenas Bowen succumbs to an untimely and much-lamented death, his bereaved wife and daughter are ultimately reinstated as the long-separated kin of Ellis Enson.

St. Clair Enson also works for the Treasury Department, but, unlike his Secret Service brother, he does not have the government's best interests at heart. On one occasion, he even admits complicity in the plot to assassinate President Lincoln. As General Benson, St. Clair uses his position to engineer unsavory deals and swindles that could provide him and his cronies with substantial profits. He becomes the father of a child born out of wedlock, murders the unfortunate mother, Elise Bradford, who loves him, and frames his secretary, Cuthbert Sumner, for the murder. He then forges ahead with his plan to claim the heart and fortune of Jewel Bowen, the daughter of Senator Zenas Bowen and the stepdaughter of his wife, Estelle, one of Washington's most powerful and socially elite couples. St. Clair ultimately is revealed as the criminal, unmasked as the ne'er-do-well Enson son, and consigned to prison, where he dies in a botched escape attempt. Both Enson men are slave owners, but their places in the worlds of slavery vary dramatically. Ellis depends on slave labor to support the agricultural business of Enson Hall. However, his experience of it is minimized: he appears to have no dealings with the men and women who tend the estate's crops, is not featured in any conversations with overseers, drivers, or patrollers, and does not have any substantial encounters within or beyond his home with enslaved people. Despite the seemingly separate spheres here, though, Ellis, and eventually his small family, benefit most directly within the Enson home from the domestic labor of an industrious slave family. The family matriarch is a middle-aged woman named Henny Johnson, whose daughter, Marthy, is a maid to Hagar Sargeant and whose granddaughter, Venus, works for Jewel.

Three generations of women in Aunt Henny's family provide manual labor and emotional affirmation that compensates for unpredictable white patriarchal support and that also is used to ensure the intellectual and professional advancement of the young men in the family. Despite these taxing demands and potentially demoralizing family responsibilities, Aunt Henny and her female kin move with much confidence and easy self-assertion in and beyond their prescribed white domestic spheres. Henny's job as a maid in the capital, and in the offices of the Treasury Department in particular, both empowers her and endangers her. As a result of her sturdy work ethic, she is on site when a crime is committed, and she becomes a key witness against General Benson in the murder of Elise Bradford. Aunt Henny also is transformed into a damsel in distress, a role usually reserved for delicate white heroines, as a result of her presence in the general's offices on that fateful night. Her granddaughter, Venus, becomes an intrepid detective, the earliest known example of an African American female sleuth, and it is her resourcefulness and intuition that solve multiple mysteries, including the murder of Elise Bradford, the kidnapping of Jewel Bowen and of Aunt Henny, the framing of Cuthbert Sumner, and the blackmail of Estelle Bowen. It is sobering, though, to see that no matter their perspicacity, the rewards and advances for African American women always are linked to labor. Hopkins underscores this most emphatically when Aunt Henny helps to solve a celebrated federal case while dusting in the Treasury Department, as she prevents villains from seizing a sizeable amount of money that she discovers out of place. The government rewards her with a lifetime domestic appointment as a housekeeper.

The Johnson family, which has ties to both the Enson and the Sargeant families and estates through slavery, plays a central role in the convoluted serialized plot of kidnappings, blackmail, and treachery. Ultimately, it is this family of formerly enslaved people that stands the best chance of reclaiming upstanding postbellum domesticity and family morals. Unfortunately, Isaac Johnson, who clings like a shadow to his nefarious owner, St. Clair Enson, is not part of this promising reconstruction of the American family. He dies in prison in a daring but unsuccessful escape attempt aimed at securing St. Clair's freedom. The Johnson women—Henny, her daughter Marthy, and her granddaughter Venus—represent the domestic, social, and professional complexities of the African American past, present, and future. Venus, the novel's most appealing character, chafes at the gender constraints that prevent her steady, professional evolution. Her resourcefulness defies the stereotypes of domestic servants, and by novel's end, her marriageability and prospects for upward mobility and high respectability allow her to transcend very deliberately the stereotypical contexts associated with her classical mythological name of Venus, an identity that reflected the cruelly ironic naming practices of American slave owners.

The first white heroic figure that Pauline Hopkins creates is Cuthbert

Sumner, a handsome New Englander and the novel's promising suitor. His surname evokes the Massachusetts senator Charles Sumner who fraternized with African Americans in Boston and was a legendary advocate for the race. In *Hagar's Daughter*, this historic example never takes hold. Hopkins uses this opportunity instead to contemplate thwarted white power, and the character Sumner never realizes his heroic potential. Sumner works in Washington, D.C., as private secretary to St. Clair Enson, known as General Benson, a high-ranking officer at the Department of the Treasury. The plot intensifies when Sumner's former fiancée, Aurelia Madison, arrives in the capital as he prepares to wed Jewel Bowen. Sumner becomes the unwitting victim of an ambitious plot that the spurned Aurelia hatches with her father and his employer, the wily General Benson. The three villains conspire to end the Sumner-Bowen engagement, provide an opportunity for General Benson to wed Jewel Bowen himself, gain access to her substantial inheritance, resulting in the Madisons getting one million dollars for their efforts to make the plan succeed. Benson and the Madisons systematically undo Sumner, so much so that he ends up on trial for the murder of Elise Bradford, his coworker and Benson's tragic paramour. Cleared by the resourceful detective work of Venus Johnson and Chief Henson, he is able to pursue once again his plans to marry Jewel. Unfortunately, despite his tried-and-tested love for her, he hesitates to claim her when he learns that she is of mixed race, the quadroon daughter of Ellis and Hagar Enson. When he comes to his senses and rushes to the Baltimore Enson estate to declare himself, he finds that he is too late. His beloved has been struck down by Roman fever, and his prospects for true happiness have evaporated. The novel closes with an image of Cuthbert Sumner, a man denied matrimonial happiness and emancipation from his unnecessary but deadly racism, surveying the grounds of the Enson estate. There, playing on the lawn is the unclaimed child of St. Clair Enson and Elise Bradford. Sumner watches the boy and is overcome by the child's innocence, a state that counteracts the treachery and stigma of the union that produced him. The novel closes as Sumner contemplates the definition of true national progress and concludes that if the child of a villainous racial hypocrite and a victimized single mother can succeed, then America truly will be a nation in which the pursuits of freedom and liberty ultimately may be possible.

The prepublicity for *Hagar's Daughter* began two months before publication of the first installment, the novel's first three chapters. The enthusiastic prose of the advertisements that dotted the pages of the January and February 1901 issues of the *Colored American Magazine* whetted the appetites of subscribers and potential new readers. Notices about *Hagar's Daughter* boldly claimed that it would be "one of the chief attractions of the year," not only because Hopkins was the author but also because its chapters would be "beautifully illustrated" by Alexander Skeete, the "regular staff artist" of the *Colored American Magazine*. Although the magazine's editors hoped that this "powerful narrative of love and intrigue" would appeal to its female readership, publicity materials quickly linked these elements to an even larger national romance. Advertisements noted, for instance, that the novel's "love and intrigue" was "founded on events which happened in the exciting times immediately following the assassination of President Lincoln." Such details capitalized on the high interest in Lincoln, fueled at this very moment by works such as Ida Tarbell's 1900 *Life of Abraham Lincoln*, which included a great number of previously unpublished letters and telegrams and a never-before-published image of Lincoln that the president's son, Robert Lincoln, had bestowed upon the enterprising investigative journalist. Ultimately, *Hagar's Daughter* was billed as a "story of the Republic in the power of Southern caste prejudice toward the Negro."[4] That defining characterization reasserted the political nature of the work and dismantled any reader notions that the work simply was an entertaining love story set in the waning years of the Civil War. When *Colored American Magazine* advertisements emphasized the novel's focus on Southern racial intolerance and its author's belief that the nation itself was "in the power" of that prejudice, Hopkins could be charged with making monumental and potentially offensive claims. Yet it was precisely these kinds of assertions that raised Hopkins's political profile. *Hagar's Daughter* was marketed as a work that examined whether or not the South had a stranglehold on American democracy and if pervasive racial intolerance, rooted in Southern culture and politics, rendered the nation essentially powerless.

Many white Americans sidestepped the evidence that Southern interests governed the nation. History confirms that regular newspaper reports of and protests against lynchings and white mob violence, the evidence of widespread black poverty, and the public manifestations of disempowering segregation were not enough to compel federal legislation or national outrage. The characterizations of a hobbled nation that appeared in the days leading up to the publication of *Hagar's Daughter* were capable then of widening the already-enormous gap between Hopkins and the white American and New England literati. She was writing at a time when influential editors and writers such as William Dean Howells and publishers like Walter Hines Page had confirmed their interest in African American writing and were exploring the potential and marketability of such literature. A favorable alliance with individuals such as Howells, Page, or others could provide a talented and prolific writer like Hopkins with useful editorial support, career-changing endorsements, and the wide dissemination of her work and place her alongside writers like Paul Laurence Dunbar and Charles Chesnutt, who represented the small but influential emerging African American literary establishment.

The project of race writing, demonstrated in the careers of Charles Chesnutt and Paul Laurence Dunbar in particular, was in a decidedly promising but fragile position when the twentieth century began. As Hopkins moved on from *Contending Forces* and turned toward serialized fiction projects such as *Hagar's Daughter*, Chesnutt was enmeshed in trying negotiations with the dominant white literary publishing world in which he had achieved ground-breaking success. By 1901, Chesnutt, who had published the first works of African American literature in the prestigious *Atlantic Monthly* and had been mentored by William Dean Howells, was suffering through fraught dealings with the man known to many in his circle as "the Dean." The uneasiness between the two men had everything to do with the politics of race writing and the romance of American realism, the literary movement with which Howells was synonymous. Despite her distance from the inner circles of the African American literary brotherhood to which Chesnutt, Dunbar, Douglass, Du Bois, and others belonged, such issues had direct implications for Hopkins. She, after all, was part of a politicized African American literary phalanx that included Chesnutt, Ida B. Wells-Barnett, Victoria Earle Matthews, and Mary Church Terrell, and whose collective abilities to improve the lives of African Americans depended heavily on bold and unflinching writings.

Hopkins was crafting a writing career for herself in the early 1900s that depended in large part on subjects that tapped into the literary appetites that her fellow Bostonian William Dean Howells was interested in fulfilling and, as it turned out, also trying to suppress. The degree to which Howells and, by extension, the larger world of white publishers were willing to support African American writers depended on the accounts of blackness and American history being palatable. Certainly, some overtures were made, and professional goodwill and the commitment of white publishers and patrons did transform some poets such as Paul Laurence Dunbar into nationally celebrated figures. Yet there were defined boundaries as to what would pass muster as race literature, subject to white literary approval. In correspondence with Chesnutt in the fall of 1900, for example, Howells asserted that he desired "something about the color-line, and of as actual and immediate interest as possible—that is of American life in the present rather [than] the past, even the recent past."[5] Such preferences as these would seem to have eliminated Hopkins from consideration. She was inclined to create narratives that functioned as political and sociocultural excavations. Her narrative incursions into the past were not fueled solely by her love for bygone eras but rather by her unwavering belief that such cultural study was vital to American social redemption and true national emancipation.

The opening scenes of *Hagar's Daughter* are astounding for their vivid resurrection of the days just preceding the onset of the Civil War. Certainly, Hopkins's re-creation of the Confederate Congress in Charleston, South Carolina, would have been enough to disqualify her promptly in the eyes of Howells, who was leery of material that veered toward "clichés of racial melodrama or sentimental evocations of antebellum southern life."[6] Yet there were other exquisite details in the novel that might have prompted Howells, a figure so emblematic of high literary culture, to think twice about turning away from Hopkins. Her confident appropriations of canonical British literature complicated essentialist evaluations of her as a "race writer," and she challenged readers on both sides of the color line to broaden their expectations of the subject matter to which writers of color might gravitate and also of the literary tools that they might employ as they created race literature.

Hagar's Daughter is a highly textured literary palimpsest, an ambitious work whose primary layers depend on the Old Testament, British epic poetry and romantic tragedy, and African American memoir and fiction. The novel metamorphoses from a twentieth-century story of the American South into a timeless American allegory of *Paradise Lost*. Hopkins's wholehearted investment in Milton's epic poem, part of an established cultural and literary trend, enabled her to illuminate the mythic alienation between South and North and suggests that at its core, the alienation between the states is a story of damnation and unattainable redemption. The novel begins with colorful re-creations of rowdy Southern debate and proceeds in its first chapter to document the intensification of Southern nationalist fervor and the inevitable resulting disintegration of the Union. The opening chapters of *Hagar's Daughter* offer a microcosm of a Miltonic Hell and chronicle the feverish turn away from union with the divine and toward bold, unapologetic secession. Chapters 4 through 6 explore a Southern paradise that is akin to Eden. These chapters also document the incursions into this earthly heaven by devilish forces, show the fall from innocence, and replicate the Miltonic account of a marriage undone. The narrative handiwork in the early sections of *Hagar's Daughter*, though, lies in Hopkins's deft recasting of the War between the States as a holy war that could best be understood through the lens of *Paradise Lost*, the majestic seventeenth-century epic poem that the blind and ailing Milton narrated aloud to daughters who transcribed their father's words. In addition, Hopkins liberally invokes works by William Wells Brown, one of her local inspirations and mentors. Finally, Hopkins turns to Tennyson, as she over-lays the story of sectional pride with a mantle of tragic love, treachery, and overwhelming disappointments. Like Chesnutt, Hopkins drew on pained and delicate romantic lyrics from Tennyson to convey the pathos of tortured love affairs and the undying faithfulness of sweethearts. Chesnutt's "The Wife of His Youth," the tale of a devoted wife's unrelenting search for a lost hus-band—in which the author made highly evocative references to Arthurian legend and Tennyson's writings about Lancelot, Queen Guinevere, and the Lady of Shalott—may have been an especially useful model for Hopkins. She broadened that Tennysonian gaze in *Hagar's Daughter* and invoked the tragic melancholy of *Maud; A Monody*, the poem that Tennyson completed in 1855 and then published ten years later in England in its polished form just as the American Civil War ended.

Hagar's Daughter is striking for the early and emphatic intertextuality that intensified readers' engagement with the *Colored American Magazine*, as a whole, and with Pauline Hopkins, its chief writer, in particular. Readers of all races could cultivate and take pleasure in a rich narrative literacy of transhis-torical and transnational dimensions. Works such as *Hagar's Daughter* com-plemented the classical knowledge that well-read and educated subscribers brought to bear on their consumption of the magazine and provided elegant introductions and the prospect of new literacies for those less tutored.

Hopkins essentially sidelined vexing questions about white reader re-sponses to African American writing and African American political critique when she used a foundational white canonical text like *Paradise Lost* as the lens through which to regard the American South.[7] The first set of villains was modeled on the promising but corrupted figure of Lucifer and his henchmen, and her besieged heroic characters evoked aspects of Adam and Eve both before and after the seduction and fall. Her masterful use of *Paradise Lost* demonstrated her literary versatility at a time when African American writers were negotiating calls for stereotypical race plots, ones that the majority of white readers preferred and were not prone to challenge. Hopkins's applica-tions of the epic poem enabled her to explore the complexity of seduction, or the loss of favor and innocence, but also to deflect the uncomplicated bi-nary oppositions that all too often pitted the North against the South, blacks against whites, and men against women.

Initially, *Hagar's Daughter* reflects Hopkins's strong desire to engage with *Democracy in America*, the influential 1835 treatise by the French legal scholar Alexis de Tocqueville, which discusses but never fully indicts or sanctions American slavery and its vast attendant economies and heinous practices. *Hagar's Daughter* opens in the autumn of 1860, a moment of deep national chaos and strife, and as its first scenes unfold, Hopkins enlists a Tocquevillean observer, who notes that "a stranger visiting the United States would have thought that nothing short of a miracle could preserve the union of the states so proudly proclaimed by the signers of the Declaration of Independence, and so gloriously maintained by the gallant Washington."[8] Hopkins's ingenious invocation of Tocqueville, which inserts her work of historical fiction into canonical discourse, may have been inspired by her close study of William Wells Brown, the writer whose work shaped indelibly the form and early focus of *Hagar's Daughter*. Like a number of prominent African Americans, Brown traveled throughout Europe as part of a successful abolitionist campaign, and while in France for the September 1849 Second General Peace Congress, he met Tocqueville at the reception that the French foreign minister and his wife hosted for congress attendees.[9]

In antebellum Maryland, one of the primary sites that Hopkins features in *Hagar's Daughter*, Tocqueville learned firsthand from a lawyer there that "the incoming Legislature may pass unjust and oppressive laws against the blacks. People want to make it intolerable for them to remain in Maryland. One must not hide it from oneself; the white population and the black population are in a state of war. They will never mix. One of the two must give way to the other."[10] Such direct and alarming sentiments were at the heart of what Tocqueville characterized as an "all-pervading disquietude" in antebellum America.[11] In *Democracy in America*, Tocqueville writes that the "danger of a conflict between the white and the black inhabitants of the Southern States of the Union—a danger which, however remote it may be, is inevitable— perpetually haunts the imaginations of Americans."[12] He continues, noting, however, that in the South such tension is suppressed and that "the subject is not discussed: the planter does not allude to the future in conversing with strangers; the citizen does not communicate his apprehensions to his friends; he seeks to conceal them from himself; but there is something more alarming in the tacit forebodings of the South, than in the clamorous fears of the Northern States."[13] Hopkins speedily explodes the sense of nagging unease to which Tocqueville refers. However, rather than offer a simplistic race war, of enslaved Africans rising up against white planter society, she homes in on another aspect of the haunting domestic crisis. *Hagar's Daughter* depicts white Americans under siege, and it is this condition that realizes Tocqueville's prophecy.

Hopkins also creates an alternative battle, one in which the race conflict that Tocqueville imagined implodes behind white battle lines. Whiteness is undermined by blackness, and Hopkins applies yet one more striking aspect of Tocqueville's musings about that looming struggle. In 1835, just four years after the bloody struggle that began with Nat Turner's revolt in Southampton, Virginia, Tocqueville speculated on the aftermath of a battle waged between whites who possessed "an immense superiority of knowledge and of the means of warfare" and the "blacks [who] will have numerical strength and the energy of despair upon their side." Tocqueville suggested that the white Southerners might not fare well and that their "fate . . . will, perhaps, be similar to that of the Moors in Spain. After having occupied the land for centuries," he wrote, "it will be perhaps forced to retire to the country whence its ancestors came, and to abandon to the negroes the possession of a territory, which Providence seems to have more peculiarly destined for them, since they can subsist and labor in it more easily than the whites."[14] These references to the most foundational of American documents and to the first president cast a patriotic shadow over a set of states that, as the novel begins, are experiencing fractious discontent and demanding sovereignty, even as they suppress the rights of significant numbers of their inhabitants. Of course, here, the carefully articulated "undertell" challenges the existence of this seemingly uncomplicated colonial paradise to which Hopkins refers in the opening lines of the novel.[15]

Hagar's Daughter essentially is a narrative account of a monumental battle to preserve and reinstitute bondage and chattel slavery, as well as of calculated and political efforts to taint and invalidate personal freedoms. Hopkins invokes George Washington but does so in the context of slavery rather than in the grand fight for freedom to which he so often is linked. The Washington that Hopkins refers to here was a slaveholder who regarded himself as empowered by the Fugitive Slave Act of 1793. Some of her contemporary readers might have been familiar with the reports of the particularly aggressive way in which Washington, with the direct assistance of his nephew Burwell Bassett and some amenable proslavery contacts in New Hampshire, pursued a female fugitive who had relocated to Portsmouth, New Hampshire, after she emancipated herself from slavery at Mount Vernon.[16] Indeed, certain descriptions of the wooded Enson estate and the Washington, D.C., residence of the Bowen family ensconced within clusters of trees and located at the end of a long winding wooded drive also bring aspects of Mount Vernon to mind. Hopkins insistently repositions the first president of the United States in an era of unruly American politics that is directly related to enslavement. By so doing, Hopkins reconnects Washington to the fractious secession of states, all former colonies that he helped to unite, and thus undermines thoroughly the union for which Washington fought. In citing Washington and, by extension, the

Declaration of Independence and other key aspects of the nation's founding history, Hopkins effectively debunks the mythologies of self-determination and equality cultivated so earnestly during the formative years of American democracy.

Rather than remain in the realm of political innuendo, though, Hopkins begins her first serialized novel with a deliberate Miltonic recasting of key moments in Southern secession history and American antebellum politics. Hopkins models much of *Hagar's Daughter* on the narrative structure of *Paradise Lost*, a strategy that intensifies the overarching biblical connections and that infuses the work with an undeniable and haunting symbolism. The epic poem, which opens in the gripping moments after Lucifer's fall into Hell, is made up of twelve books prefaced by informative overviews entitled "Arguments" and focuses on two falls from grace. The first is that of Lucifer, the archangel; the second is that of humankind, represented by Adam, Eve, and their sons, Cain and Abel. The poem portrays the prelapsarian delights of the lovers Eve and Adam, before chronicling their loss of innocence and subsequent exile from Paradise. Both *Paradise Lost* and *Hagar's Daughter* invert time and reject linear progression; events are reported in media res; and in Hopkins's novel, scenes move swiftly into and out of the antebellum past and present. Such narrative chaos challenges readers who hold simplistic "cause and effect" ideas about the Civil War and suggests to them that there was an inevitability, an inborn political predetermination that America from its inception would be a paradise in name only, a land destined to suffer a brutal fall that would include secession, civil war, and an uneasy, flawed reunion.

It is the specter of slavery in the Southern public sphere that cements for Hopkins the parallels between that region and Milton's Hell. The brevity of her novel's first chapter hardly hides the chaos and upheaval that will lead to the sectional outrage and divisiveness that precedes the Civil War. Although noticeably devoid of dialogue or characters, the opening chapter provides an illuminating historical overview that revolves around antebellum responses to the Republican nomination of Abraham Lincoln for president. According to the sober narrator, the very nomination of Lincoln outraged his enemies. They were "drunk with rage at the prospect of losing control of the situation," intones the narrator, who then notes that the populace was outraged especially because "up to that time, [Democratic Party members] had needed scarcely an effort to bind in riveted chains impenetrable alike to the power of man or the frowns of the Godhead; they had inaugurated a system of mob-law and terrorism against all sympathizers with the despised party."[17] The chapter ends with the terse and dreadful apocalyptic announcement that Lincoln's election was "the signal for secession, and the South let loose the dogs of war."[18] Hopkins's spirited introduction reinforces what historians of the South have identified as a key moment in antebellum politics, one in which many, including planter politicians, regarded secession as a long-anticipated response to the election of a president "committed to the nonextension and eventual demise of slavery."[19]

Hopkins refers baldly to the deep resentment and excessive free will that fueled the rebellious Southerners intent on secession, or on self-exile from the Union. These temperaments to which Hopkins refers echo the subjects documented in the early chapters of *Paradise Lost*. Milton's first books focus on the excessive pride of self that leads to the irreversible schism that occurs in Heaven and to the exile of Lucifer, a cherished angel, from that blessed place, and other sons of Light. Hopkins's characterization of Lincoln's Southern foes as a "proslavery Democracy," if one sets aside the real political affiliation here, is a raging oxymoron, since a proslavery stance is inherently undemocratic. As the chapter unfolds, Hopkins slips into tangled prose that recalls the august lyrics of epic poetry. Her bulky description of the erosion of the white Southern proslavery culture suggests that white Southerners are enraged not because slavery is under attack but because work is now required to maintain it. She calls attention to malevolent malaise and to its invulnerability, since neither "the power of man or the frowns of the Godhead" are able to challenge it.[20] By invoking *Paradise Lost*, Hopkins foreshadows the downfall of the aggressive proslavery democracy, even as she uses references to Hell and to the fall of Satan to segue into the introductions of the novel's primary villains.

Hopkins uses Satan's war on Heaven as an allegory through which to reexamine the Civil War as the South's war on the North. However, she avoids simplistic characterizations of the North as the good, holy, and godly North. The implicit comparisons emerge for readers nonetheless, though, as she focuses intently on the Southern milieu and the resemblance between its military response and the unholy war on Heaven. Hopkins's suggestion that there are genuine parallels between the American Civil War and Satan's attack resound with symbolism for her postbellum readers. *Hagar's Daughter* begins with Hopkins's straightforward assertion that the Civil War was a direct result of Southern secessionist outrage and proslavery practice. Embedded here also are Hopkins's evaluation of post–Civil War America. Milton scholars have noted that *Paradise Lost*'s "war in heaven seems more than a simple finished event" and that it was "ambitious, impious, proud, vain, and resulting in ruin."[21] Such analyses dovetail with interpretations of *Hagar's Daughter* and the ways in which the novel hints that Reconstruction, the equivalent of the aftermath of the Miltonic war between the holy and unholy states, is a period not of reconciliation but rather of continued unrest and striving.

One of the clearest applications of *Paradise Lost* in the serialized chapters of *Hagar's Daughter* successfully casts the proslavery characters of the novel in roles similar to those of Satan and his chief associates. As a result, Hopkins transforms the proslavery South in general and the novel's chief scoundrels in particular into epic villains who are destined to face severe punishment and awful exile. The doomed men of Hopkins's include the characters of the legendary and heartless slave trader Walker, the dissolute slave owner and treacherous brother St. Clair Enson, and the wily enslaved man Isaac Johnson, who has served St. Clair Enson since their childhoods. These are nefarious characters, and their collective laissez faire, proslavery passion, sectional pride, dishonesty, and love of money are substantial. All of these unsavory qualities enrich Hopkins's highly detailed and persuasive creation of southern Pandemonium, a sphere modeled on the palace of Satan that Milton imagined, and using the term he coined in *Paradise Lost* from the Greek words "pan" (all) and "demonia" (demons).

Walker, Enson, and Johnson, the first set of villains in *Hagar's Daughter*, traffic in human flesh, gamble, and drink. These men, along with the five named influential politicians whom Hopkins imagines at the scene of the December 1860 Confederate secessionist convention, constitute a group of eight who mirror the group of eight principal vanquished archangels featured in Book I of *Paradise Lost*, as well as the angels' predilections and the evils that they elicit in others. Milton's cabal includes Satan, his primary henchman, and six other principals, and it is this group that is most prominent in the first Hell convention that is depicted so richly in Book I. There are legions of other unsavory archangels, of course, including Belial, whose unfortunate honor it is that there is no "Spirit more lewd" or "more gross to love / Vice for itself" than he.[22] In Hopkins's novel, too, there are numbers of other participants, some named briefly and others who form the thundering mass that supports secession from the Union. By identifying Walker, Enson, Johnson, and the legendary Confederates whom she willfully positions on scene in Charleston at the secession convention, Hopkins effectively proposes that they are of the same mold as the overly confident angels, whose brash pride, willfulness, defiance, self-confidence, and jealousy enabled Satan's war on Heaven.

Hopkins first locates the devilish men of *Hagar's Daughter* and their hell in Charleston, South Carolina, a city that was "the center of the lower South and the stamping ground of intransigent opinions."[23] Her use of the site is delib-

The Reconstitution of Paradise

erate and for her readers would have had significant slavery, antislavery, and Civil War resonances. It was the birthplace of the pioneering white Grimké sisters, whose abolitionist work led to their disinheritance and their embrace of their mixed-race nephews, Archibald Grimké and his brother Francis, both of whom became influential public figures and accomplished American statesmen. Charleston also was the site of the legendary 1739 Stono Rebellion and of the foiled insurrection that Denmark Vesey conceived in 1822. Many of Hopkins's readers also would have been quick to associate the city with the first shots of the Civil War in April 1861. Fort Sumter, located in the city's harbor, was a Union garrison that initially refused to surrender to Confederate forces and, as a result, came under direct fire from Brigadier General P. G. T. Beauregard and his troops. Hopkins easily could have focused on these more-well-known aspects of South Carolina history, but she chose instead to mine the symbolic and political ramifications of another notable Charleston event. In December 1860, one of the nation's most historic secessionist conventions occurred in Charleston, at which "the best men the State possessed" passed by a unanimous vote of 169 to 0 an Ordinance of Secession that allowed South Carolina to become the first American state to withdraw from the Union.

Hopkins was well aware that Charleston's "secessionist" history began much earlier than the white abolitionist careers of the Grimkés or the shots fired at Fort Sumter, and that the nature of its rejection of national policy was rooted within its community of color. Almost four decades earlier, in 1822, Denmark Vesey undertook "a most remarkable experiment" and endeavored to eradicate slavery by marshaling an estimated 9,000 coconspirators to emancipate all slaves and overthrow all owners.[24] Vesey was a formerly enslaved African who gained his freedom, won a $1,500 lottery, and invested the money in a carpentry shop, where he could practice his acclaimed artisan skills. The plot was foiled, though, and Vesey and some thirty-four others were hanged. The aftermath of Vesey's plot and the trials against him and the individuals charged with conspiracy elicited much impassioned discussion by whites about the state of relations between the races. A South Carolina writer named E. C. Holland declared on behalf of fellow whites in *A Refutation of the Calumnies Circulated against the Southern and Western States Respecting the Institution and Existence of Slavery among Them* that "[w]e regard our negroes as the '*Jacobins*' of the country, against whom we should always be on our guard, and who, although we fear no permanent effects from any insurrectionary movements on their part, should be watched with an eye of steady and unremitting observation."[25] Such sentiments only deepened as other key events such as the confrontation at Harper's Ferry and secession approached.

In the wake of John Brown's failed raid on Harper's Ferry in 1859 and on the threshold of South Carolina's secession from the Union in 1860, Charleston's free people of color began to experience violent attacks on their homes and status. Until this increasingly explosive moment, the free people and elite of color had enjoyed a community life that was "calm, even nonchalant," and which had featured "routines of work and family life," as well as "revivals and May festivals[,] . . . lavish weddings and receptions," and freedom of movement.[26] In August of 1860, however, "Charleston authorities began to go door to door through the free colored community demanding unassailable proof of free status and proceeding to enslave those without it." In the course of these raids, white authorities remanded into slavery "not only slaves who had enjoyed de facto freedom but also individuals who had lived all their lives as free people, some of them free for two generations."[27] James Marsh Johnson, author of one of the rare extant notes by a free Charlestonian person of color, summed up the situation in the newly seceded state. Writing from Charleston on 23 December 1860 to his brother-in-law Henry Ellison, just three days after the secessionist convention, Johnson described the "situation" of his community as "not only unfortunate but deplorable." He offered the shrewd recommendation that "it is better to make a sacrifice now than wait to be sacrificed *our selves*."[28]

Charleston early on became a city crucial to the maintenance and spread of Southern chattel slavery. The primary economic markets of this city that "had achieved fame and notoriety as a bustling port and lively center of antebellum culture" were linked to the production of indigo, cotton, and rice.[29] In this "commercial capital of the South," though, the "enormous profits" came not from the iron foundries, brickyards, mills, or places where grist or lumber were processed but rather from "the trade in black flesh."[30] In 1860, South Carolina had a slave population of 402,406, which constituted 57 percent of the total population; the free population of color numbered 9,914.[31] Among Charleston's population of 40,522, whites numbered some 57.7 percent, and people of African descent numbered 42.3 percent.[32] Of the 17,146 blacks in the city, just over 81 percent, or approximately 13,909, were enslaved. Some 3,237 people of color, or 18.8 percent, were free.[33] There were daily auctions of men and women of African descent, and the popular and heart-wrenching sales often were held in the Old Exchange Building on Broad Street, a site also known then as the Customhouse, built in 1767 and still standing today. A selective history is noted on the historic bronze plaque that the Sons of the Revolution of South Carolina placed on the building in 1899. The plaque, created as part of the festivities marking the centennial anniversary of George

Washington's death and characterized in the "Notes and News" section of *American Historical Review* as "one of the most interesting" commemoration activities, calls attention to several key dates and events in the building's history.[34] These include the fact that the building was the first site of America's first independent government, that it served as a prison that held Revolutionary soldiers, and that it was where President Washington was "entertained by his grateful countrymen." References to the building's centrality in Charleston's slavery landscape are nonexistent, and Bancroft asserts quite rightly that "[w]ith no less historical importance," the Sons of the Revolution might easily have added the following testimony to the building's most lasting and influential function: "From colonial days until after the middle of the nineteenth century . . . several hundred to many thousand slaves were annually sold to the highest bidders, in front or just north of this building."[35]

Once the Civil War ended and Reconstruction began, the free people of color in early Reconstruction-era Charleston were visibly perspicacious and many were actively involved in local politics. In the early postbellum years, some 234 men of color were active in political circles, including 39 of whom were affiliated with the proslavery Democratic party.[36] Among the prominent residents were men whose ancestries reflected the multiracial and interracial genealogies of the South and testified to the restrictive intraracial codes that made it difficult for formerly enslaved men to advance in political circles.[37] The well-known political endeavors of individuals like Martin Delany, whose successful studies at Harvard Medical School in the early 1850s ended abruptly due to racist administrative policies, also informed Hopkins's narratives about the South and its ever-evolving political culture. Delany, the author of *Blake*, campaigned in South Carolina in 1874 for the post of lieutenant governor as part of a reform party ticket, and many of Hopkins's readers would have recalled his name as they immersed themselves in the serialized novel whose opening scenes were set in a major city of the Confederacy.[38]

Some historians have referred to Charleston as a "backwater," but others have identified it as a critical Civil War site, a place that was "essential to the morale and economic strength of the Confederacy."[39] Antebellum Charleston had an "ancient, quaint, and foreign appearance" that elicited frequent comparisons with European cities such as Venice.[40] That the city's oldest white family was descended from the royal Venetian Priuli family only encouraged comparisons that Charleston was "like Venice in its heyday." It was "a city-state ruled by an intelligent and cultivated oligarchy of great families who managed to monopolize control, generation after generation."[41] Despite such grand comparisons, though, the city's "narrow streets were much more numerous than the broad, and often lined with rude, ill-shapen, neglected structures, showing that comfortable living, neatness and thrift were virtues not generally practised by a large portion of the white inhabitants and were unknown to the colored."[42] Despite such unsightly scenes, though, almost one-fifth of the state's wealthiest planters had homes in the city.[43]

When Hopkins focused on South Carolina's secession, she tapped into a volatile era of American history, one that provoked intensely aggressive and illuminating assertions of national discord and alienation and that exposed the breadth and depth of white male power. In *Hagar's Daughter*, such sentiments and evidence highlighted the ways in which Southern white manhood had suffered, which in turn made the novel all the more evocative. The move toward secession by Southern whites was one that South Carolinians had attempted unsuccessfully several times before they succeeded in late 1860. Scholars have asserted that South Carolina believed the best way to "make the move" that would compel the South to secede was "for her to lead off with an irrevocable act with or against which every other State would be obliged to act."[44] The successful move toward secession tapped into what convention attendee Dr. James H. Carlisle characterized as "wild passions of that mad hour."[45] It also justified the long-held beliefs of former South Carolina governor and United States senator James H. Hammond, who announced during the 1858 session of Congress that "cotton is king." April 1860 found Hammond, who resigned his seat in the Senate in protest against Lincoln's election as president, proclaiming the inviolable power of the proslavery South even more vociferously. "I firmly believe," wrote the long-standing secessionist, that "the slaveholding South is now the controlling *power* of the world. . . . The North, without us, would be a motherless calf, bleating about, and die[ing] of mange and starvation."[46] The South Carolina secessionists and the men whom scholars have referred to as "Charleston fire-eaters" also attached aggressive extrasecessionist items to the Ordinance.[47] These sobering amendments were the grounds on which individuals would be punished for treason against the state and the declaration that all people of African descent were denied citizenship.[48] The document was signed in "a stately two-hour ceremony" in Institute Hall, where some 2,000 members of the public witnessed "the 170 delegates affixed their names to the document" that ended "the Union between the State of South Carolina and other States United with her under the Compact Entitled '*The Constitution of the United States of America.*'"[49]

Hopkins reconstructed the defining pre–Civil War moment in 1860 Charleston that the *Carolina Spartan* referred to as "the glorious act of secession, which is to make the Southern States the greatest people under the sun, and South Carolina the greatest State of them all."[50] In the spring of 1860, for example, when Jefferson Davis and other Democrats convened in Charleston to engineer the removal of Stephen Douglas as the party's presidential nominee, they did so in "the most picturesque of American cities, the last general muster of the old Democratic party." At the time, Charleston was "second to no city in the country in culture and charm" because "[i]n luxury and enjoyment of life it was quite unique in America. Here the planter aristocracy, in complete control, extended a gracious hospitality to the delegates from the whole country . . . and Northerners and Westerners fell under the spell of the quaint old town dressed in all the flowery beauty of the Southern spring."[51]

Hopkins located the primary scene of Democratic mayhem in the fictional St. Charles Hotel, a palatial structure in the historic city that was a popular destination for Democratic party political gatherings. She creates in the hotel a "magnificent hall" that, while "always used for dancing," on this occasion, is "filled with tables which spread their snow-white wings to receive the glittering mass of glass, plate, and flowers." The physical scene seems antithetical to any hell or even routine mayhem. In fact, it seems more reminiscent of a pastoral or interior Edenic scene. The room is filled to bursting with "[p]alms and fragrant shrubs" that are "everywhere," and "garlands of flowers decorated the walls and fell, mingled with the new flag—the stars and bars—gracefully."[52] The fleet of "Negro servants in liveries of white linen" moves "noiselessly to and fro."[53] Once the white Southern hordes of convention delegates and their wives appear, however, the peace is replaced by an increasingly frenzied scene. This striking change is one of several important allusions to the foundational scenes that feature Satan and the fallen angels in the opening books of *Paradise Lost*.

This meeting of staunch proslavery Southerners is modeled on the gathering in *Paradise Lost* where Satan convenes his fallen angels, not on the burning lake of fire where the former archangel first awakens, but in an ornate golden hall that rises out of Hell. At the helm of this construction project is Mammon, "the least erected Spirit that fell / From Heav'n," and whose

> looks and thoughts
> Were always downward bent, admiring more
> The riches of Heav'n's pavement, trodden gold,
> Than aught divine or holy else enjoyed
> In vision beatific.[54]

Mammon directs his "crew" to a hill "whose grisly top / Belched fire and rolling smoke," and under his supervision they there "Opened into the hill a spacious wound and Digged out ribs of gold."[55] The gathering place is "built like a temple, where pilasters round / Were set." It has "Doric pillars overlaid /

With golden architrave," and there is no lack of "Cornice or frieze with bossy sculptures grav'n." The "roof was fretted gold." The structure is an "ascending pile," and when its doors open, their "brazen folds," all behold

> from the archéd roof
> Pendent by subtle magic many a row
> Of starry lamps and blazing cressets fed
> With naptha and asphaltus yield light
> As from a sky.[56]

Its appearance, overseen by the fallen angel named Mulciber, a formerly acclaimed celestial architect, who was well known in Heaven for creating "many a towered structure high, / Where sceptred angels held their residence, / And sat as princes."[57] The appearance of the hall is not heralded by a hellish cacophony or discordant choir but rather by the angelic noises of "dulcet symphonies and voices sweet."[58] The parallels between the summit sites in Paradise Lost and those in *Hagar's Daughter* also are strengthened by the seemingly magical ways in which the halls are transformed into celebratory venues. The implicit discordance between the venue's appearance and the agenda that calls for such unruly political behavior as secession helps to strengthen the links between the two works. It emphatically sets the stage for the next phase of Hopkins's Miltonic allegorization of Southern rebellion and her attention to the calls for secession.

Having emphasized the domestic order achieved in the St. Charles Hotel by the hall's design, its ornamental elements, and the polished service of the liveried staff, Hopkins seeks out the origins of another kind of domestic disorder. She suggests quite practically that it is the marriage of sectional politics and individual expression that produces the mayhem that ensues in the St. Charles Hotel. In *Paradise Lost*, the assembly of fallen angels that Milton's narrator refers to as a "hasty multitude" makes its way into the hall "Admiring." In *Hagar's Daughter*, a similar procession occurs as the "delegates filed in to their places at table." In both works there is musical fanfare: Milton imagines "wingéd heralds," who "with awful ceremony / And trumpets' sound throughout the host proclaim / A solemn council forthwith to be held." In *Hagar's Daughter*, the secessionists file in to the St. Charles hotel ballroom "to the crashing strains of 'Dixie.' Within moments, someone raised the new flag aloft and waved it furiously; the whole assembly rose *en masse* and cheered vociferously, and the ladies waved their handkerchiefs."[59]

Hopkins uses the convention moment to re-create an antebellum version of the awakening in Hell that finds Satan coming to consciousness, finding himself and his angels strewn across the burning lake, and then marshaling his legions and rallying them to the next phase of their work against Heaven. This awakening, which is a central aspect of Book I in *Paradise Lost*, is the first description of Satan's primary allies. The scene on the burning lake where the fallen angels are "o'erwhelmed / With floods and whirlwinds of tempestuous fire"[60] reveals the prostrate form of Satan as well as that of his chief coconspirators. First among these is the angel Beëlzebub, the "bold compeer" of Satan and one whom Satan himself describes as "One next himself in power, and next in crime, / Long after known in Palestine."[61] The other primary angels who emerge alongside Satan and Beëlzebub include the "horrid king besmeared with blood" named Moloch, the chameleonic Chemos who "enticed Israel . . . To do him wanton rites," Astoreth, "to whose bright image nightly by the moon / Sidonian virgins paid their vows and songs," Thammuz, "whose annual wound in Lebanon allured / The Syrian damsels to lament his fate," Dagon, a "sea monster, upward man / And downward fish," and Rimmon, the angel who "also against the house of God was bold."[62] This assembly of fallen angels is notable for its powers of seduction and love of gold.

Hopkins departs from the historical record of the secessionist convention and replaces its leading participants with five men whose political power, strategic allegiances, and proslavery positions reinforce the connections between this convention and Milton's account of the angelic assault and resulting exile from Heaven. She places in Charleston five leading antebellum Southern politicians who were not present at the historic meeting. In *Hagar's Daughter*, when the convention's "business of the day began in earnest," the following men are listed as being present: "There was the chairman, Hon. Robert Toombs of Georgia; there was John C. Breckenridge of Kentucky, Stephen A. Douglas, Alexander H. Stevens, and Jefferson Davis."[63] According to the historical record of the convention, not one of these was present. Her deliberate rewriting of history here allows her to constitute an antebellum version of the archangels who align themselves with Satan's unsuccessful celestial battle. She underscores Southern solidarity by including well-known figures who were both controversial and celebrated for their connection to secession, the creation of the Confederacy, and endorsements of slavery. The first evidence of Hopkins's bold retelling of the 1860 South Carolina secession scene involves a dramatic substitution. She replaces David Flavel Jamison, the actual chair of the convention, with Robert Toombs, an "irrepressible charmer,"[64] highly effective lawyer, wealthy planter whose estates relied on the work of 300 to 400 enslaved people, and Democrat who served as a U.S. representative from Georgia from 1846 through 1852 and in the U.S. Senate from 1853 to 1861. Jefferson Davis appointed Toombs to the cabinet position of secretary of state in his newly formed Confederate government.

Toombs and his family were well acquainted with the Davises, and Varina Davis remembered Toombs as a "university man" with a "lordly air," "long, glossy black hair," "hands . . . beautiful as a woman's," and "eyes . . . magnificent, dark and flashing" that "had a certain lawless way of ranging about that was indicative of his character."[65] Toombs worked in Washington, D.C., alongside Davis, the future president of the Confederacy, when the two men served in the U.S. Senate, but there was no love lost between them. Decorum kept matters civil, even though Toombs regarded Davis as "not only incompetent but a scoundrel."[66] Davis regarded Toombs as "a whole-souled man," precisely because he was able to act honorably despite their differences. In 1860, Toombs and Davis were members of the Committee of Thirteen, a Senate group formed to create a political compromise that would preserve the Union.[67]

Toombs, whose "knowledge of finance" made him especially valuable to Davis as he began to build his Confederate administration, complemented Hopkins's strategy for re-creating Miltonic pandemonium. Toombs was well known for his "mercurial temperament and drinking problems,"[68] and he apparently possessed a "wild streak" that "would have made the quiet Davis nervous."[69] Yet, even more significantly, Toombs led Georgia's secession from the Union, a political act that could be recontextualized in relation to Satan's own war against Heaven.[70] In his opening speech in *Hagar's Daughter*, Toombs delivers melodramatic confessions about his grief in the face of disturbing political events and defines the secessionist meeting not as one bent on rebellion but rather as a meeting "assembled to discuss the rights of humanity and Christian progress."[71] He urges the "most loyal, high-spirited and patriotic body of men and their guests and friends," to defend themselves and their interests most vigorously. "[L]isten to no vain babbling," he urges, "to no treacherous jargon about overt acts," and "[d]efend yourselves; the enemy is at the door; wait not to meet him at the hearthstone,—meet him at the door-sill, and rive him from the temple of liberty, or pull down its pillars and involve him in a common ruin." The great danger that could result from ineffective resistance, cautions Toombs, is a sickening transaction: the passing of the federal government "into the traitorous hands of the black Republican party."[72]

Hopkins deftly replicates the tenor of Toombs's secessionist fervor, and the address that she attributes to him recalls quite effectively the speech that Toombs delivered on 13 November 1760 to the Georgia legislature. On that occasion, he also began with a self-indulgent lament. "I can bring you no good tidings," he declared, before going on to announce that the "stern, steady march of events has brought us in conflict with our non-slaveholding confed-

The Reconstitution of Paradise

erates upon the fundamental principles of our compact of the Union."[73] In a speech that historians have declared devoid of "invincible logic or stunning abstraction" and replete with "the emotional fury of the secessionist," Toombs assured his audience of its victimization and thus rightful indignation. "We have not sought this conflict," he intoned, "we have sought too long to avoid it; our forbearance has been construed into weakness, our magnanimity into fear, until the vindication of our manhood, as well as the defence of our rights, is required at our hands."[74] Such incendiary oration strengthens Hopkins's suggestion that Toombs is reprising the role of Beëlzebub, the attentive second to Satan and the chief ally, who helps to preside at the first Hell convention. Having accomplished this first Miltonic recasting, Hopkins then continues to fill the dais on which Toombs stands and works her way toward the unveiling of the Satan of the South. She places a number of prominent Southerners next to Toombs, who, although not present at the actual convention, had Confederate sensibilities and careers that contribute to her efforts at creative historical reconstruction. These Southern politicians and Confederate generals become vital in her persuasive fictional recasting of the convention as the first gathering in Hell.

Hopkins places Alexander H. Stephens, the slight and physically misshapen Whig politician and vice president of the Confederacy, at the side of Toombs. Stephens, whom some colleagues came to regard in the postbellum age as one of the South's "*representative* men of the true conservatism," succeeded despite his unfortunate physical image and pathetic personal history.[75] Born into poverty, he had been orphaned at a young age and became a "lonely abstracted warrior" whose "hairless face" and "higher-pitched tones of a woman" rendered him a clear opposite to enormous, portly, masculine men like Toombs.[76] Here, in the opening scenes of *Hagar's Daughter*, the appearance of Stephens, whom Hopkins refers as "Stevens," underscores the unpredictability of this volatile political moment, and Hopkins deliberately uses Stephens as a symbolically intermediary figure. On the eve of the Civil War, Stephens was a highly visible Confederate Party member who actually was skeptical about secession, had "rumored reconstructionist leanings," and believed that as vice president in Jefferson Davis's newly established secessionist government he could better "promote 'harmony' among the people and . . . prevent 'strife, factions, and civil discord.'"[77] In his 14 November 1860 speech before the Georgia legislature, which came one day after that of his longtime colleague Toombs, Stephens scored a "stunning oratorical triumph."[78] He acknowledged that "[n]ever, since I entered upon the public stage, has the country been so environed with difficulties and dangers that threatened the public peace and the very existence of society as now."[79] Yet, despite these unprecedented threats, Stephens lobbied for reason and moderation. "Though new storms now howl around us, and the tempest beats heavily against us," he told the assembly that was reeling from the election of Abraham Lincoln, "I say to you, Don't give up the ship,—don't abandon her yet. Let us not, on account of disappointment and chagrin at the reverse of an election, give up all as lost; but let us see what can be done to prevent a wreck." When a member of the audience shouted out that "the ship has holes in her," Stephens maintained his composure: "And there may be leaks in her," he concurred, "but let us stop them if we can; many a stout old ship has been saved with richest cargo after many leaks; and it may be so now."[80]

Hopkins also transports Stephen A. Douglas and John Breckenridge of Kentucky into the Charleston gathering. Frederick Douglass regarded the Vermont-born Douglas as "the standard-bearer of what may be called the western faction of the old divided Democratic party" and noted that "[t]he name of Douglas stood for territorial sovereignty, or, in other words, for the right of the people of a territory to admit or exclude, to establish or abolish, slavery, as to them might seem best."[81] Known as the "little Giant," Douglas was "quick-witted, energetic, and resourceful" and "a tireless stump campaigner who instinctively knew how to build rapport with an audience, had a winning manner and an instinct for leadership."[82] The Illinois Democrat had sparred with Abraham Lincoln in the legendary debates during their congressional campaigns of the 1850s and had become a staunch advocate of what became known as "popular sovereignty," a position that held that local, rather than federal, law would govern the peculiar institution.[83] When the move toward secession intensified after the 1860 elections, Douglas collaborated unsuccessfully with other politicians, especially Kentucky senator John J. Crittenden, to create a compromise that would preserve the Union.

John C. Breckenridge was a wealthy landowner, former attorney general and U.S. senator for the state of Kentucky, and Confederate Army major general, and he eventually served under Jefferson Davis as secretary of war. Frederick Douglass characterized Breckenridge as "the standard-bearer of the southern or slaveholding faction of that party" who rallied his political comrades to "erec[t] the flinty walls of the Constitution and the Supreme Court for the protection of slavery at the outset."[84] It is to this man that Hopkins in *Hagar's Daughter* gives the honor of toasting Jefferson Davis following the Confederate president's rousing speech to the conventioneers. According to Douglass, who offered succinct characterizations of Breckenridge and Douglas in his 1892 memoir, *Life and Times of Frederick Douglass: His Early Life as a Slave, His Escape from Bondage, and His Complete History*, the "doctrine of Breckenridge was that slaveholders were entitled to carry their

The Reconstitution of Paradise

slaves into any territory of the United States and to hold them there, with or without the consent of the people of the territory—that the Constitution of its own force carried slavery into any territory open for settlement in the United States, and protected it there."[85] Hopkins's invocations of such influential national antebellum politicians and their agendas put a chilling political layer over the emerging *Hagar's Daughter* plots, which feature individuals wrested from freedom and pitched into slave markets—from states of privileged whiteness into milieus of uncertain, destabilizing blackness.

The last Confederate whom Hopkins places at the 1860 South Carolina secessionist convention is Jefferson Davis, the slave owner who often referred to those he held in bondage as "our people." He receives a rousing hero's welcome as Toombs introduces him to the convention and knights him as "the guardian and savior of the South."[86] As he rises from his seat, the band strikes up "See the Conquering Hero Comes" and "a lady in the gallery back of him skilfully dropped a crown of laurel upon his head."[87] During his years on the American public stage, Davis combated antislavery ideologues with the assertion that "[c]hattel slavery never existed in this country." He insisted that the words "chattel slavery" constituted a phrase used only "to excite prejudice" and to distract from the fact that one could only buy "a lifelong right to service and labor." Slave owners, he argued, were not in fact purchasing rights to the bodies or to the souls of human beings.[88] Hopkins's readers, especially those who were familiar with the key battles and cities at the heart of the Civil War, would have been struck by her decision to link Davis to Charleston. One of Davis's most important military decisions occurred when he assigned the defense of Charleston to the legendary general P. G. T. Beauregard, a "flamboyant, much adored" Southern hero. Beauregard, in his relations with Davis, shared an experience similar to that of Robert Toombs. The general had a lifelong loathing for Davis, but he did not allow those feelings to compromise their collaborative work on behalf of the Confederacy.[89]

Davis's efforts to establish Southern order on the eve of the Civil War are contrasted in *Hagar's Daughter* with the complete mayhem that ensues as he takes his place to advocate for secession. He suggests that the fight to preserve the Southern economy, culture, and identity will be swift and victorious. "Yes, friends," he assures the convention attendees, "all is ready; every preparation is made for a brief and successful fight for that supremacy in the government of this nation which is our birthright."[90] He castigates the North, insists that it is "but a conglomeration of greasy mechanics, filthy operatives, small-fisted farmers, and moonstruck Abolitionists." Hopkins presents Davis as a man able to excite a crowd into a frenzy by imagining Southern domination of the United States and couching that aggressive program of political domination in a seductive rhetoric of democratic fairness and gentility. "I believe that when our principles shall have been triumphantly established over the entire country—North, South, West—a long age of peace and prosperity will ensue." The narrator states matter-of-factly that the secessionist convention crowd "went mad" and describes their destruction of the ballroom that was so carefully prepared for their gathering. "They tore the decorations from the walls and pelted their laurel-crowned hero until he would gladly have had them cease," reports the narrator, before suggesting that "such is fame."[91] He concludes that true madness prevails. The meeting "passed the bounds of all calmness," "intemperate sentiments were voiced by the zealots in the great cause," the "vast crowd went wild with enthusiasm," at least one attendee "swept the dishes aside, and was standing upon the table, demanding clamourously to be heard," and there is a ceaseless amount of "cheering and waving of handkerchiefs."[92] "Pandemonium reigned," asserts the narrator, and the brevity of this evaluation highlights the excessive expressions of solidarity reigning at the convention.

It is in the context of this political rally that Hopkins situates the two primary villains of *Hagar's Daughter*. Present as the St. Charles Hotel ballroom becomes a veritable frenzy are Walker, a "vile dealer in human flesh," and St. Clair Enson, who is in Charleston on political business as "one of the most trusted delegates."[93] Hopkins's focus on Walker, which precedes the Confederate secession scenes, highlights the absolute complicity between proslavery advocates and the Confederacy. Indeed, Hopkins's first invocation of lines from *Paradise Lost* appear as she notes that slave traders "paused in their hurried journey" to sell their "gangs of slaves chained together like helpless animals destined for the slaughter-house" in order to "participate in the festivities which ushered in the birth of the glorious Confederate States of America."[94] Chief among these is a nefarious Missourian named Walker. Walker, a "repulsive looking person, tall, lean and lank, with high cheek bones and face pitted with the small-pox, gray eyes, with red eyebrows and sandy whiskers," reigns indisputably as "the terror of the whole Southwest among the Negro population, bond and free."[95] He arrives in Charleston with a "gang of human cattle," establishes them and himself in a building that functions essentially as a prison and that is replete with the awful trappings of slavery: "iron collars, hobbles, handcuffs, thumbscrews, cowhides, chains, gags and yokes."[96] This listing of horrible tools serves to completely destroy the fictions of Southern antebellum slavery society.

Hopkins commits a strategic historical intervention when in *Hagar's Daughter* she privileges the historical perspective of a Southern man of color rather than that of the self-proclaimed white Southern patriots who supported the secession movement that she documents. She uses both the actual life and the fictional writings of William Wells Brown, a native of Kentucky whose mother was enslaved and whose father was the relative of the man to whom his mother was in bondage. Brown in his later years lived in close proximity to Hopkins's maternal grandparents and was a generous mentor for Hopkins. His pioneering 1858 play *The Escape; or, A Leap for Freedom* had greatly influenced her popular and long-running 1870s play *Peculiar Sam*. In the early chapters of *Hagar's Daughter*, Hopkins showed that nearly twenty years after Brown's death, in 1884, he continued to be an influential role model for her, an American patriot whose stories she still regarded as richly intriguing and extremely marketable. *Hagar's Daughter* was a tribute to the much-beloved abolitionist, who, in 1900, had just been hailed by his biographer Alonzo Moore as an orator and writer whose works "exhibit depth of thought, flights of eloquence, and a conception of statesmanship calculated to throw the haughty master of such a man far in the background."[97]

The powerful antislavery message and sentimental pathos that Hopkins creates in *Hagar's Daughter* are indebted to three works by and about William Wells Brown. Brown was the author of two of these works: the 1847 autobiography *Narrative of William W. Brown, an American Slave, Written by Himself*, which Brown published in London, and the controversial 1853 novel, *Clotel; or, The President's Daughter: A Narrative of Slave Life in the United States*, also published in London.[98] The third is *Biography of an American Bondman*, the memoir that Brown's daughter Josephine published in 1856 with the Boston-based printer R. F. Wallcut, whose business was on the historic Cornhill Street, near the longtime offices of *The Liberator*. A close reading of *Hagar's Daughter* reveals that Hopkins did more than just imitate the plot of *Clotel*. In fact, she transported Brown's text and two of his characters into her work, using his language verbatim to expose the harsh economics of slavery. She also borrowed freely from Brown's own life experiences during his indenture to a St. Louis slave trader.

The most unmistakable link between *Hagar's Daughter* and Brown's writings comes in Hopkins's first introduction to the slave trader and villain Walker. Her use of Walker allows her to pay tribute to Brown and to benefit from his literary renderings of the slave trade. She describes Walker as a "most conspicuous" trader, "a noted man from St. Louis, by the name of Walker," who "started in St. Louis as a dray driver, and now found himself a rich man."[99] Over the course of chapter 1, Hopkins outlines the deceptive marketing practices that Walker uses to maximize his profits during the slave auctions. She also reveals the heartlessness that enables him to separate families and drive women deprived of their children to suicide. The slave trader of whom Hopkins writes orchestrates the first attack on the Southern paradise that is the Ellis Enson estate. The Walker of *Hagar's Daughter* is taken directly from the life and writings of William Wells Brown, who was apprenticed to Walker.

Hopkins taps into the 1856 biography by Josephine Brown as she creates the first details about the unsavory Walker. In chapter 1, Brown refers to Walker as "a noted trader," and in chapter 6, Brown offers the following description of her father's employer: "Walker was an uncouth, ill-bred man, with little or no education. Before embarking as a negro-driver, he had been a dray-driver in St. Louis, and had earned, by his own hard labor, the capital with which he commenced in trade. Money was the only God he worshipped, and he knelt at no altar but that erected at the expense of suffering humanity. William shuddered at the idea of having such a man for a master, but there was no alternative."[100] Hopkins condenses these lines dramatically but uses Brown's first two pointed critiques of Walker. Hopkins, as mentioned earlier, refers to the trader as "a noted man from St. Louis" and as an *"uncouth, ill-bred*, hard-hearted, [and] illiterate" person. She borrows liberally again when she notes that her villain has come up in the world since his early days as a dray driver.[101] Josephine Brown, writing about Walker's efforts to transport and sell human beings, refers to the unfortunates in his clutches as "human cattle," and Hopkins uses this term also, referring to Walker's "gang of human cattle" as she prepares to detail the horrors of their pending sales and separations.[102]

The most significant borrowing that Hopkins undertakes brings William Wells Brown's own writings into clear view for her twentieth-century readers. In appropriating Brown and his writings, she follows the admonition of Alonzo D. Moore, the Buffalo native and Brown biographer, who had witnessed the pioneering abolitionist writer dodge rabid antiabolitionist crowds in Buffalo. Moore, whose work Hopkins cites and uses to conclude her 1901 *Colored American Magazine* profile of Brown, insists that "[i]t is well for us to ponder the history of these self-made men of our race, and mark the progress they made with nothing but the husks of living to stimulate the soul thirsting for the springs of knowledge."[103] Hopkins takes these words to heart and brings Brown's writings to bear on her novel. She uses similar scenes of inspections of the enslaved individuals before the auctions, includes a slave trader named Walker and his enslaved assistant named Pompey, and incorporates comments of the deep hypocrisy that allows ministers to condone the slave trade and also to participate in it. These borrowings raise the issue of plagiarism in *Hagar's Daughter*, even as they confirm the deep respect that Hopkins had for Brown's work.

In the early chapters of his 1847 memoir, *Narrative of William W. Brown, An American Slave*, Brown recounts the stressful year that he spent working for Walker, a slave trader in St. Louis. Brown later would enjoy an apprenticeship with the abolitionist printer and eventually martyred abolitionist Elijah P. Lovejoy. He was thoroughly devastated by the awful aspects of his job with Walker, the man whom he regarded as a "soul driver" and whom his daughter described as a "monster in human shape."[104] William Wells Brown was powerless to aid the suffering men, women, and children whom the trader collected for sale, separated from each other, priced matter-of-factly, and terrorized with his absolute power over their immediate destinies. He became "heart-sick at seeing my fellow-creatures bought and sold."[105] Brown was in this situation because Dr. Young, his master and "near relative," had arranged a yearlong loan of Brown to Walker. Brown sought out Young and asked him to cancel the yearlong contract, but his request was denied. In the course of that terrible year, Brown witnessed unforgettable and traumatic events. He recorded many of the haunting scenes of desperation, brutality, loss, and death in his 1847 memoir. He returned to these scenes again some six years later and deployed them to fuel outrage and raise the awareness of all who read *Clotel; or, The President's Daughter*, his bold 1853 work of historical fiction.

Brown did not create an alter ego when he invented, in *Clotel*, the character of Pompey. There were substantial differences between him and the enslaved man, who "was of low stature, round face, and, like most of his race, had a set of teeth, which for whiteness and beauty could not be surpassed; his eyes large, lips thick, and hair short and woolly." Unlike Brown, Pompey had no visible qualms about his work and worked diligently to meet the expectations of his owner and of the marketplace. Another key distinction between Brown and Pompey lay in their genealogies. Brown was a mulatto whose mother was subjected to the sexual advances of her owner's relative. Pompey, according to the observant narrator, was "of real Negro blood, and would often say, when alluding to himself, 'Dis nigger is no counterfeit; he is de genewine artekil.'"[106] In *Clotel*, Pompey prepares enslaved people for display and purchase; he instructs them on the answers that they must give about their ages and grooms them strategically so that they appear to be ten years younger than they actually are. These were the same tasks that Brown performed. His daughter Josephine recalled this phase of her father's early life. Josephine Brown's recounting though, is noticeable for the deliberate narrative distance that it installs between Brown as the subject of the biography and as a powerless enslaved subject. "Soon after leaving St. Louis," writes Brown's daughter, "William had to commence preparing the slaves for the market." Josephine Brown then provides additional specifics: "The old men's gray hairs were plucked from their heads, and their whiskers shaved off clean; and where the white hairs were too numerous, hair dye was used to bring about the desired color. These old men and women were also told how old they were to be, when undergoing an examination by those who might wish to purchase."[107] Brown clearly distances her father from these deceptive practices and intimate physical activities. Her use of a passive construction to report the work hints at the depth of distress that Brown felt during these sessions.

William Wells Brown asserts in *Clotel* that time takes a dreadful toll on those who are forced to deal with the slave trade. He states that assisting Walker has taken a dreadful toll on Pompey and diminished severely the man's capacity for sympathy or for protest. Brown writes that Pompey "had long been with the trader, and knew his business; and if he did not take delight in discharging his duty, he did it with a degree of alacrity, so that he might receive the approbation of his master." A few lines later, he repeats the impact that Pompey's indenture has had on his conscience and on his heart: "Pompey had been with Walker so long, and had seen so much of the buying and selling of slaves, that he appeared perfectly indifferent to the heartrending scenes which daily occurred in his presence."[108] Brown's passages about Pompey and his activities are central to Hopkins's writing of the Southern scene in *Hagar's Daughter*. Hopkins borrows most heavily from Brown here, and in her references to Pompey in chapter 1, she changes only the last four words of Brown's account. The biography that she provides for Pompey reads as follows: "Pompey had been so long under the instructions of the heartless speculator, that he appeared perfectly indifferent to the heart-rending scenes which daily confronted him."[109]

Hopkins also borrows heavily from *Clotel* as she describes the men and women who make up Walker's most recent lot. The group includes two women who clearly are suffering in the wake of separations from husbands and family, an older man known as Uncle Jeems, and Tobias, a polished "gentleman's body servant educated at Paris, in medicine, along with his old master."[110] Both Jeems and Tobias appear in *Clotel*. Pompey had an energetic interaction with "a man who, from appearance, was not less than forty" and who, when asked his age, declared, "If I live to see next corn-planting time I will either be forty-five or fifty-five, I don't know which."[111] Pompey quickly intervenes. First he renames the man, who says his name is "Geemes," and calls him "Uncle Jim." He says that Jim will be punished if he declares himself older than thirty and insists to Jim that he "must have off dem dare whiskers of yours, an when you get to Orleans you must grease dat face an make it look shiney." According to the narrator, "This was all said by Pompey in a manner which clearly showed that he knew what he was about."[112] In *Hagar's*

Daughter, Hopkins veers away from *Clotel* after borrowing the slave identities when she creates dialogues between Walker's slaves in which they bemoan their situations and in their interactions with potential white buyers.

The next significant act of borrowing of Hopkins echoes the critique of the clergy that Brown incorporates into *Clotel*. A "tall, thin-faced man, dressed in black, with a white neckcloth, which immediately proclaimed him to be a clergyman," separates Althesa and Currer, the mother-daughter pair who are the novel's chief protagonists. Even as Althesa "clung to her mother's side," the clergyman focuses instead on the domestic skills that Walker attributes to the mother. He is unmoved by the prospect of separating the two and states matter-of-factly, "I only want one for my own use, and would not need another." Moments later, the trader and minister seal the deal in a saloon, and the unnamed clergyman is in possession of a bill of sale and has "the understanding that the woman should be delivered to him at his house."[113] Such concise and pointed anecdotes pepper the Brown narrative, biography, and novel and transform the texts into virtual encyclopedias of the slave trade. Like Brown, Hopkins focuses on the desires of the clergy and other individuals, who otherwise have reputations for godliness, honesty, and kindness. She creates a hypocritical minister who fails to honor his vocation and prefers instead to market his own wares just as the slave trader does his. The Reverend Pinchen tours the Charleston slave pen where Walker has installed himself. There he announces that "a man in your business of buying and selling slaves needs religion more than anybody else." With this we might agree, but what is shocking comes next. Mr. Pinchen proposes that religion will not convict the trader and lead him to cease his predation on God's creatures but will "mak[e] you treat your people well."[114] Despite the fact that *Clotel* and *Hagar's Daughter* were ante- and postbellum works, both Brown and Hopkins were witness to ongoing cultural and religious accommodation. Brown experienced it in the context of enslavement, while Hopkins saw it made manifest in continued white acceptance of race violence and entrenched segregation.

Brown did enrich *Clotel* by drawing from his own experiences and the observations he made during his travels with Walker through some of the South's most notorious slave markets. He created in Pompey, though, not a variation of himself but rather an extension of Walker. Brown's tactic here suggested an awful interracial complicity and the intraracial treachery that enabled slave traders like Walker to profit so significantly from his evil work. Hopkins grasped Brown's suggestions about complicity and embellished them in her creation of Isaac, the attentive and ingenious enslaved man whose name suggests his favored status in the eyes of St. Clair Enson, his erstwhile and long-time owner. The early scenes with Isaac and Enson also are indebted heavily to *Clotel*. In that novel, Brown calls attention to the range of markets that exist within slave culture. Aboard the *Patriot*, the steamer ship on which his enslaved heroines are being transported, are high-stakes games that without warning become slave markets and auctions of enslaved men and women held as collateral or offered as winnings. Such scenarios, writes Brown, reveal the "uncertainty of a slave's position. He goes to bed at night the property of the man with whom he has lived for years, and gets up in the morning the slave of some one whom he has never seen before!"[115] In chapter 2, "Going to the South," Brown describes the prevalence of gambling on the ships that plied the Mississippi River between slave markets. "Thousands of dollars change hands during a passage from Louisville or St. Louis to New Orleans on a Mississippi steamer," the narrator tells his readers, "and many men, and even ladies, are completely ruined."[116] He directs his readers' attention to a scheming character named "Mr. Smith," who owns "a fine looking, bright-eyed mulatto boy, apparently about fifteen years of age."[117] Faced with a losing hand, Smith bets on "the whole of the boy" and sees him become the chattel of his opponent. The winner, Mr. Johnson, instructs Jerry to "not forget that you belong to me" and bids him to "be up in time to-morrow morning to brush my clothes and clean my boots." Jerry, apparently saddened by the quick exchange, "wiped the tears from his eyes" just moments before his former master, Mr. Smith, hands over the bill of sale that gives Johnson legal right to the young boy. In that moment, Smith declares, "I claim the right of redeeming that boy, Mr. Johnson. My father gave him to me when I came of age, and I promised not to part with him."[118] This scene drew Hopkins's interest and prompted her to make liberal and creative use of the passage. Brown's quiet indictment of gambling and the far-reaching nature of the slave trade becomes key for Hopkins as she begins to spin the web of subterfuge that makes *Hagar's Daughter* the complicated mystery and detective novel that it is.

Hopkins's final appropriation of Brown's work appears in scenes that follow the raucous secession convention in Charleston and as Enson and his slave, Isaac, journey north to Maryland aboard the legendary steamer the *Planter*. Her narrator emphasizes the political significance that envelops this scene and notes that this is the steamer's "last trip up Chesapeake Bay" before it becomes part of the Confederate fleet. Not one to miss an opportunity for literary or political foreshadowing, Hopkins launches into a concise recollection of the abduction of the *Planter* that a man named Robert Smalls orchestrated with breathtaking precision. Smalls, a native of Beaufort, South Carolina, was born into slavery and went on to become a five-term congressman from South Carolina. He worked aboard the *Planter* before the historic moment in May 1862 that Hopkins proudly characterizes as "[o]ne of the most daring and heroic adventures of the Civil War."[119] Before daylight on 13 May, he boarded the ship with his wife and children and a twelve-man crew. He successfully absconded with the boat, piloted it through Charleston Harbor, and then turned it over to Union forces.[120] When Hopkins introduces this history into her account of Enson's passage home to Maryland, she effectively rends the veil of fiction. This incursion on the fictional tale not only reminds her readers that she is creating a "story" but it constitutes a double set of postbellum disciplinary acts imposed upon the rebellious antebellum South. Hopkins is able to disprove in both the fictional realm and the historical sphere that the antebellum conviction that "a few short months would make [Southerners] masters of the entire country" was, even then, already a fiction.[121]

The role of Satan, the rebellious archangel, challenger of God, and interloper, metamorphoses in *Hagar's Daughter* as Hopkins assigns various aspects of the fallen angel's identity and endeavors to characters with different levels of investment in Southern autonomy and white power. Once Hopkins shifts the novel away from South Carolina, St. Clair Enson clearly becomes the antebellum devil. St. Clair is a marked man, one whom the authoritative Aunt Henny regards as not just born under the sign of the devil but fathered by him. "Ef de debbil ain't de daddy" of St. Clair, she announces with vigor, "den dat ol' rapscalion neber had a borned servant in dis sinful wurl."[122] Aunt Henny's proclamations are rooted in events that transpired on the Enson family estate. St. Clair apparently was born just moments after the "debbil just showed he face" and "grinned" at his mother. According to Aunt Henny, the awful apparition occurred on a night when a "turrible thunder storm came up" and "tored up eberythin." That chaos occurred when Uncle Ned, an enslaved man on the Enson estate, pledged his lifelong faithfulness to Satan if the fallen angel would "stan by" him "in dis [his] trial hour" and prevent an impending whipping.[123] Ned's appeal for lifelong immunity from whippings was granted, but his outreach gave Satan free access to the estate. On the same night that St. Clair was born, the overseer reportedly saw "hell wid all its torments an' de debbil dar, too, wid his clove foot, an' a struttin' 'bout like he know'd he was boss." The specter was so terrifying that the overseer, who was scheduled to whip Ned the next morning, left the estate abruptly. Aunt Henny, the plantation historian, takes distinct pleasure in telling her daughter Marthy that after beholding that amazing scene, the overseer "run, an he run, an' he run an' he never stop runnin' tell he git plum inter Baltymo'."[124]

St. Clair becomes synonymous with references to the devil, and it is Aunt

Henny, a redemptive force of Negro darkness, who successfully maintains the links between the white Enson and the wickedness of Hell. She does so in the privacy of her perch in Ellis Enson's home and in full view of the American public when she testifies in the murder trial of Cuthbert Sumner. Henny not only refers emphatically to St. Clair as "dat lim' o' Satan" and as "dat imp ob de debbil" but also insists with utter conviction that "ef eber der was a born lim'o' de debbil it's dat same St. Clair Enson."[125] Like Milton, who moves his protagonist between the two magisterial but sharply contrasting spheres of Hell and Eden, Hopkins transports St. Clair Enson from Hell to Paradise. In the Paradise that is the Enson estate, St. Clair the unclaimed prodigal son allows his evil and devoted allies to wreak havoc and oversees himself the disruption of domestic bliss.

Like the "delicious paradise" that is Eden, the Enson estate is a romantically wooded place, a "sylvan scene," to which Milton's images of "a rural mound" and "steep wilderness" with "thicket overgrown, grotesque and wild," would apply.[126] Just as Milton's Book IV features the first glimpses of Eden, set within a "woody theatre / Of stateliest view" and behind a "verdurous wall of Paradise," so too does chapter 4 of *Hagar's Daughter*.[127] Enson Hall is set amid "deep, mysterious woods where the trees waved their beckoning arms in every soft breeze that came to revel in their foliage." The built structures, which include the brick home and nearby offices and outbuildings, are "reached through a long dim stretch of . . . woods, locusts and beeches—from ten to twelve acres in extent," and the "mellow, red-brick walls [of the manor house are] framed by a background of beechtrees."[128] The preponderance of woods evokes an air of both privacy and mourning. Hopkins repeatedly makes mention of the beeches in her accounts of the novel's two primary residences, the Enson estate outside Baltimore and the Bowen home in Washington, D.C. Greek mythology suggests that the beech, symbolic of oracle and divination, is dedicated to Zeus and Jupiter. Its leaves also figured in mythology. Apollo, the sun god born to Jupiter and Latona and creator of the Pythian Games, decreed that winners at the Games be crowned with wreaths of beech leaves.[129] The beech also is suggestive of "prosperity and pleasant memory."[130] It is telling, though, that Hopkins frequently places locust trees alongside these clusters of beeches. The locust tree, symbolic of "affection from beyond the grave," gives voice to the dead—those killed, presumed dead, or silenced—in the novel.[131]

Enson Hall intrigues Hagar Sargeant, the young woman who becomes the wife of Ellis and the mother of the child eventually known as Jewel Bowen. In her youth, Hagar is drawn to the Enson grounds, and it is this angelic figure, rather than a demonic one, who is cited first as the one who makes incursions there. "Sometimes Hagar would trespass," the narrator tells us, and "would cross the parklike stretch of pasture, bordered by the woodland through which it ran, and sit on the edge of the remnant of a wharf, by which ran a small, rapid river, an arm of Chesapeake Bay, chafing among wet stones, and leaping gaily over rocky barriers."[132] Hopkins's descriptions of Eden echo the impressions that Tennyson registered in his 1863 tribute to Milton, in which he mused about the "brooks of Eden mazily murmuring / And bloom profuse and cedar arches / Charm."[133] In this Southern Eden, Hagar also appropriates the position usually ascribed to Satan once he has taken the form of the serpent. Just moments before she makes her first fall, quite literally, into the arms of Ellis Enson and accepts his proposal of marriage, Hagar creates a hammock beneath the "strong, straight branches of a beech" and, crawling "cautiously into her nest . . . let down the long braids of her hair, and . . . lolled back in her retreat." She lies there, "with nothing in sight but the leafy branches of the trees high above her head, through which gleams of the deep blue sky came softly," and she feels "as if she had left the world, and was floating, Ariel-like, in midair."[134] That feeling is replaced moments later by the first of many descents that Hagar experiences. In her effort to extricate herself from the hammock when Ellis Enson discovers her, Hagar rolls out of the "turned up" hammock, and he turns "just in time to receive her in his arms as she fell."[135] His confessions of love, her awakening to him, and their mutual decision to wed lead to Hagar's installation in Enson Hall. There she becomes a mother and, according to Hopkins's admiring narrator, "Eve's perfect daughter."[136] Such details would seem to sidestep, if not altogether to reverse, the usual Edenic plot found in the Bible and in *Paradise Lost*. However, Hopkins is only intensifying the imminent and multifaceted fall and exile from Paradise that Hagar will endure.

Most of the key battles for money, love, and power in *Hagar's Daughter* are staged in gardens, sites that are natural and contrived, external and internal, wild and cultivated. Noble and nefarious characters alike rely on these flowery, tamed, and untamed spaces and in them allow themselves to be compromised, advance their own unsavory agendas, declare and lose love, and stage seductions and abductions. The garden at Enson Hall includes "huge conservatories" that are "gay with shrubs and flowers."[137] In Washington, D.C., the conservatories in the Bowen home are central to Aurelia Madison's efforts to win back her former love, Cuthbert Sumner, and to General Benson's tactical maneuvers to seduce Jewel Bowen. The natural gardens accommodate acts of love only in the first chapters of the novel when Ellis Enson and Hagar Sargeant enjoy a prelapsarian romance that culminates in the birth of their only child. Once the relationship of Ellis and Hagar is destroyed, natural gardens never again function as paradise; they are perverted for other uses and become treacherous spheres that must be overcome, reclaimed, and conquered. In the wake of the Ellis Enson family tragedy at the hands of St. Clair Enson and his associates, manmade gardens become the primary sites of action. It is in these ornate spaces, which symbolize wealth and mastery over nature, that trickery and false seductions flourish. Jewel Bowen, kidnapped by her dastardly uncle St. Clair and his trusted sidekick Isaac Johnson, is unaware that she has been imprisoned at her ancestral home. When she finally gains access to a window, she surveys "extensive gardens filled with ruins of what must once have been buildings and offices of a large plantation." She sees "once well-kept walks" that now are "overgrown with weeds, and a heavy growth of trees obstruct[s] the view in all directions."[138] Even when the Enson estate falls into ruin, the decay only highlights the tendency of the natural landscape to return.

Hopkins's reliance in *Hagar's Daughter* on gardens as realms that facilitate critical actions and reactions may be read as more than just religious symbolism and as part of a larger trend in post-Darwinian fiction. In the years following the publication of *Origin of the Species*, which appeared in the year that Hopkins was born, writers had to contend with new interpretations of foundational Western myths. Writers grappled with the impact of Darwin's scholarship and the evolutionary theory that implied a new myth of the past, one originating not from a garden paradise but rather from "the sea and the swamp. Instead of man, emptiness."[139] A canonical work like Milton's *Paradise Lost*, with its lush and attentive accounts of creation, apparently "gave Darwin profound pleasure" and confirmed "how much could *survive*, how much could be held in common and in continuity from the past." Yet the scientist apparently "was to rejoice in the overturning of the anthropocentric view of the universe which Milton emphasises." As a post-Darwinian writer, Hopkins's return to the garden followed the new evolutionary theory and her focus on the "emptiness" made her portraits of antebellum and postbellum America that much more powerful.

The publication of *Hagar's Daughter* coincided with the turn away from American literary realism toward literary naturalism, an era dominated by the gritty visions of writers Frank Norris, Stephen Crane, and Theodore Dreiser and in which the realists came to the sobering conclusion that "there was no American Eden and no American Adam."[140] The belief in an American Eden, formulated most spectacularly when James Madison assumed the presidency in 1828, was gradually undone. Darwinian scholarship had an impact on American literature directly, as it privileged European discourse on nature rather than the lofty humanism that emanated from all cherished national documents and appeared so frequently in white canonical American literature of the antebellum period.

As the twentieth century began and the age of naturalism ensued, Hopkins wasted no time in lamenting the death of an American innocence that was intertwined to racially exclusive notions of human destiny and blessed potential. Her riveting portraits of American landscapes under siege signaled her already advanced treatment of American vulnerability and fallibility. She clearly was crafting a cultural narrative that stood in sharp contrast to *Contending Forces*. *Hagar's Daughter* was altogether different from her debut novel, a work whose subtitle proclaimed its investment in romance and whose modern-day protagonists at the novel's end quite literally sailed off toward the motherland of Britain and into and toward a postcolonial sunset.

The first emotional, racial, and economic conflicts in *Hagar's Daughter* occur on the grounds of Enson Hall, a place that has both a wilderness and lush conservatories. St. Clair Enson, accompanied by the slave trader Walker, wrest the Edenic place from the grasp of its patriarch, Ellis, and his bride. They accomplish this at Enson Hall with brash pronouncements and acts of physical intimidation. Not only do they invalidate the legal and social rights to residence of Hagar, the woman identified as "Eve's natural daughter," but they also uproot its rightful patriarch and owner. The two stage the murder of Ellis Enson, and, in an effort to make it look authentic, they leave a dead body at the edge of the property where the "remains of the old wharf enter the stream."[141] The body that many believe to be that of Ellis Enson suggests a violent end. A doctor called to the estate reports the grisly find to St. Clair Enson, and Enson reveals his despicable nature and even his guilt as he continues to eat hotcakes as he receives the news. According to the physician, the corpse has "been there two or three days," and it has "an ugly wound in the head that completely disfigures the face, and an empty pistol by the side of the body [that] tells its own pitiful tale."[142] The theme of fratricide in this tale about a Southern Eden undone also reveals another set of strong literary allusions that enrich Hopkins's tale. The 1855 poem, *Maud: A Monody*, by Tennyson, haunts the key underlying plot of *Hagar's Daughter* and infuses the work in subtle ways.

Maud, which Tennyson began to write as early as 1836 and completed in 1855, is a poem that chronicles the violence that plagues a family. In the work that Tennyson himself described as "a little *Hamlet*," a young man loses his grip on reality in the wake of his father's suicide.[143] In the course of his delusions, he accidentally kills the brother of Maud, the woman whom he loves and to whom he refers as "my jewel."[144] He imposes an exile upon himself and leaves for France. Eventually, he learns that Maud has died. That news prompts him to commit himself to fighting in the Crimean War. In this work that "lurches from death to death," Tennyson "announces the death of an *ancien regime* of privilege and injustice, to be purged in the great common bloodletting of war."[145] The work, which appeared in England just six years before the American Civil War began, is a sobering and relevant text to consider in relation to *Hagar's Daughter*. Like Hopkins, Tennyson had the specter of war on the horizon when he published *Maud and Other Poems*, which critics tended to disregard but readers loved so much that Tennyson was able to reap financial rewards, enabling him to purchase Farringford, his Isle of Wight estate, and then see the production of some twenty editions between 1855 and 1884.[146] Tennyson invokes the Crimean War, which England joined in the spring of 1854 and in which it suffered early and devastating losses, such as in the ill-fated Charge of the Light Brigade at Balaklava. The Crimean War functioned for Tennyson as the source of "extra literary parentage" for his poem *Maud*, and it provides an instructive way to regard the reality of the Civil War, which informed *Hagar's Daughter*.[147]

Hopkins uses *Maud* in the same bold way that she does the other major works that she uses as models for her works. She borrows key elements from the poems and appears to have been most struck by the opening images of the poem, the gripping and bloody images of the landscape that haunt Tennyson's protagonist. "I hate the dreadful hollow behind the little wood," declares the unnamed narrator as the poem begins. "Its lips in the field above are dabbled with blood-red heath, / The red-ribb'd ledges drip with a silent horror of blood, / And Echo there, whatever is ask'd her, answers 'Death.'"[148] These lines are ones that Hagar Enson, the bereaved wife and traumatized woman, easily could utter. The use of land transformed into a bloody scene and the perpetual and unrelenting echo of "Death" are realized in the chaotic chapters that see Ellis Enson allegedly murdered in the lower field of his estate and his disoriented wife attempting to comprehend her transformation from a cherished white woman to a commodified, objectified woman of color. There is speculation about the manner in which the patriarch in *Maud* dies, and the poet's account of the worry and wonder also enrich the reading of *Hagar's Daughter* and the demise of Ellis Enson. In *Maud*, the body that is retrieved lay in a "ghastly pit," and, like the unidentifiable body believed to be Enson's, this one is "[m]angled, and flatten'd, and crush'd, and dinted into the ground."[149] The distraught narrator, coming to terms with the idea that suicide was the cause of death, can only wonder, "Did he fling himself down? who knows? for a vast speculation had fail'd, / And ever he mutter'd and madden'd, and ever wann'd with despair / And out he walk'd when the wind like a broken world-

The Reconstitution of Paradise

ing wail'd."[150] *Maud* is riveting for its opening portrait of overwhelming loss, both emotional and financial. Hopkins underscores these same subjects in the opening chapters of *Hagar's Daughter* as the slave trader Walker schemes and as the disinherited St. Clair Enson gambles wildly and fails to win.

Hopkins's investment in the symbolism of the garden is buttressed by *Maud*, a work whose numerous references to flowers and landscapes resound in *Hagar's Daughter*, as it too employs natural spheres, gardens, and flowers in its tangled plots of deception and thwarted love. In *Maud*, the young man courts the eponymous heroine and often meets her in the woods. The courtship between Ellis Enson and Hagar Sargeant, who early in their romance enjoy "walks and drives and accidental meetings in the woods" that contribute to the feeling that the "sun was brighter and the songs of the birds sweeter that summer than ever before," is almost stereotypical.[151] This pastoral splendor in the woods gives way in *Hagar's Daughter* to less delightful experiences for the Ensons' daughter, Jewel. After a session with Mr. Henson, the famed Secret Service detective, who is, unbeknownst to both of them, her father, Jewel accepts his escort home. However, Henson, who had enjoyed the woods when he was courting Jewel's mother, fails to walk his daughter and client directly to the front door of her elegant Washington, D.C., home. Her "rapid gait" notwithstanding, Jewel quickly becomes unsure of the landscape that lies between the gates and her home: "Along the edges of the drive the underwood was so thick, and the foliage of the trees arching overhead so full and dense that towards the centre of the drive it was in semi-twilight, and thick shades of darkness enveloped all things."[152] This realm of untrimmed woody excess that lies in close proximity to a scrupulously maintained conservatory inside the house accommodates treachery and jeopardizes innocents. Jewel is abducted just steps from her home and is transported to an even wilder and more unnatural sphere, the long-abandoned Baltimore Enson estate.

Hopkins makes her first and only direct citation of Tennyson's work in the "The Ball," the novel's fifteenth chapter and the site of key introductions. The chapter opens with a scene that recalls the preparations for the secession convention mentioned in chapter 2. Here in the Washington, D.C., home of the Bowens, "Flowers wreathed the gallery, the national colors hung in the angles, [and] banks of roses were everywhere." In the moment before Hopkins attempts to introduce Jewel, she invokes Tennyson: "Inglass of satin, / And shimmer of pearls," she writes. Those lines, which she does not attribute to Tennyson, are almost verbatim from one of the most passionate sections of the otherwise somber *Maud*. In the poem, these lines are prefaced by a lyrical injunction to Maud from her unsuccessful suitor. "Come into the garden, Maud," he declares and repeats emphatically. "Come into the garden," he implores, and then relates the revealing dialogue that he has had with the flora and fauna in the woods where he would meet her. The section metamorphoses into a meditation on the ways in which the suitor enlists nature in his cause and how the flowers and trees, gloriously personified, share the hopes of the suitor. The lines that Hopkins uses occur in stanza 9 of this section:

> Queen rose of the rosebud garden of girls,
> Come hither, the dances are done,
> In gloss of satin and glimmer of pearls,
> Queen lily and rose in one;
> Shine out, little head, sunning over with curls,
> To the flowers, and be their sun.[153]

The ill-fated suitor in *Maud* seeks an audience with a woman who has mastery over the natural elements. Maud's movements in the natural sphere demonstrate her power to create desire. The suitor declares to her,

> From the meadow your walks have left so sweet
> That whenever a March-wind sighs
> He sets the *jewel*-print of your feet
> In violets blue as your eyes,
> To the woody hollows in which we meet
> And the valleys of Paradise.[154]

Hopkins is inspired by Tennyson's visions in *Maud* of a responsive, emotive landscape and of a young woman who ultimately succumbs to the unnatural forces of human actions. In the context of *Maud*, which her novel confirms that she read, some of her creative choices thus become especially telling. For instance, the specter of *Maud* looms large in *Hagar's Daughter* when Hopkins names the beautiful but tragic heroine Jewel, creates nicknames for her that are based on flowers, places her often in close proximity to the woods or in rooms decorated with lush floral arrangements, and, in the course of the novel, allows Jewel's suitor, Cuthbert Sumner, to meditate in moments that are both loving and desperate on the variety of flowers that she embodies. Like Tennyson, Hopkins uses the Victorian language of flowers to intensify the symbolism associated with her tragic heroine. In chapter 13, for example, the narrator offers the following pronouncement: "Aurelia was a gorgeous tropical flower; Jewel, a fair fragrant lily," and then declares that "even though a lily lies above their hearts," men demonstrate time and again their "unfortunate weakness for tropical blooms."[155] The very first time that Aurelia Madison, Jewel's chief rival, beholds her, she too imagines her in this context. The presence of the celebrated Polish actress Madame Helena Mojedska acting in

The Reconstitution of Paradise

the title role of "Camille" on a Washington, D.C., stage cannot hold Aurelia Madison's attention; she becomes enraptured by the sight of Jewel Bowen and ultimately compares the young woman to a "strain of lilies."[156] The lily, "since time immemorial," has been regarded as "the sacred flower of motherhood." In Greek mythology, it is symbolic of Hera, the "goddess of the moon, earth, air, woman's life, marriage and childbirth; and in ancient Rome it was the emblem of Juno, the goddess of light, sky, marriage and motherhood." Used to represent virtue and chastity, the flower also symbolizes the resurrection of Jesus Christ during the Easter season. However, as folklore scholars indicate, the lily in ancient Semitic legends is linked directly to Eve: "[T]he lily sprang from the tears of Eve when expelled from the Garden of Eden, she found she was approaching motherhood."[157] Jewel Bowen is the embodiment of the delight and pains of marriage, the joys and heartaches associated with motherhood. As one who is regarded by others as a lily, she confirms the true experiences of Hagar Enson, that is, Estelle Benson, her mother. Yet for all the attendant symbolisms of the word "lily," Jewel Benson is denied full and unmediated access to marriage and to motherhood. Hopkins uses this unrealized symbolic potential to advance her characteristic investment in contrasts; the experiences and unattainable symbolic power of Jewel Benson highlights for readers the outrageous crime committed against the young woman and those who treasure her.

Ultimately, *Hagar's Daughter* diverges significantly from the plot of Tennyson's poem. This Hopkins novel presents a multitude of characters with collective tragedies who experience plights and passions that are comparable to those delineated in Tennyson's poem. Hopkins appears to have been influenced by Tennyson's efforts to "concentrat[e] on the mind of the grieving survivor rather than on the dead friend."[158] She rehearsed the poet's "favorite themes," which focused on "morbid withdrawal from the world and the necessity for political commitment on the part of the artist."[159]

Hopkins, like many in her African American community in and beyond Boston, believed that the tumult of post–Civil War America made it neither politically feasible nor socially useful to withdraw, as Tennyson imagined it in *Maud*, from the world. In *Hagar's Daughter*, Hopkins meditates thoroughly on the cooptation of the natural world, whether it be through the interiorization of the natural as seen in the construction of elaborate conservatories or through potentially lucrative industries such as mining. She combines both of these examples when she arrives at the Washington, D.C., mansion of Zenas Bowen, a capitalist whose successful mining ventures finance the political bid that brings him to Washington as a U.S. senator. Bowen's story is the often-savored embodiment of the American dream, and Hopkins's narrator concurs, characterizing Bowen's life story as "an example of the possibilities of individual expansion under the rule of popular government."[160] Bowen likely saw the same chaotic scenes of which William Wells Brown wrote; he worked aboard a Mississippi steamboat as a young boy, eventually joined the Union forces, mustered out with the rank of major, and became a millionaire after he "invested his small savings in mining property in the Black Hills." The Bowen estate hosts a party that rivals the South Carolina secessionist convention.

The most strategic space in the Bowen home is its conservatory, a lush and expansive site that gives way to numerous greenhouses and "many arbors and grottoes."[161] Amid greenhouses that are "softly lighted" by "silvery lamps" are intimate spaces, "transformed for the time being by draperies of asparagus vines and roses into a charming solitude for two."[162] Hopkins employs the pastoral bower here, but her postbellum tale quickly becomes one of betrayal rather than sanctified love. It is here, for example, that General Benson sits with Jewel Bowen and waits for the performance that his accomplice Aurelia Madison has promised to stage. Aurelia and Cuthbert Sumner make their walk into the conservatory "where all was coolness and shadow" and, in a moment that recalls vividly the alluring woods of Tennyson's *Maud*, the two find "one of the grottoes, where from between the folds of the rose-curtain drapery a rustic seat held its inviting arms toward them."[163] The artfully constructed Eden in the Bowen mansion quickly becomes the province of Lilith rather than of Eve. Aurelia refuses to let Cuthbert deny her; she throws herself into his arms with great drama, and her weeping prompts Jewel to seek out the source of the woman clearly in the throes of "desperation and the abandonment of grief" and "sobbing hysterically, with low, quivering moans."[164] Cuthbert is discovered; Jewel, "pallid as a ghost" and "with frightened, woeful eyes and despair in every feature," beholds her fiancé standing in the "garden" with another woman, one who is "faltering and shivering, and clinging to him," and whose "lovely wet face was pressed close against his cheek."[165] The scene, memorable for the palpable heartache that Hopkins conveys, successfully identifies this postbellum American Eden as a compromised space.

In literature and in certain religious traditions, the loss of Eden is attributed to, or suggested as depending upon, the treachery of a woman. Although the figure of Eve figures most prominently in these accounts, Hopkins once again veers away from the traditional interpretative expectations and offers new readings of widely accepted stories. Certainly the biblical woman at the forefront of the novel is Hagar, the Egyptian handmaid whose child Ishmael was the firstborn son of Abraham. The biblical tale of Hagar is relevant to a consideration of the loss of Eden, since after Eve, it is Hagar who suffers one of the notable and early exiles reported in the Old Testament. The

The Reconstitution of Paradise

metaphorical loss of Eden to which Hopkins refers in her use of the name Hagar enriches the larger meditation on the compromised American South, a sphere corrupted by sin and penalized for a war that can be interpreted as a war on goodness and order. Yet, in the novel's references to gardens and the unruly behaviors that occur there, Hopkins also turns her readers' attention to a more aggressive biblical woman, one whose life is extratextual in many traditions but powerful nonetheless for the specter of sexual predation, aggressiveness, and disdain for domesticity that she represents. Hopkins uses the figure of Aurelia Madison as the foil for Eve's daughter, or Hagar, and in Aurelia re-creates the persona of Lilith. In Jewish cosmology, Lilith exists as a demonic figure, a "queen of evil" created alongside Adam, one "whose lust was awakened by Eve's sin in the Garden of Eden and who was out to avenge herself on Eve and all Eve's female descendants."[166]

Aurelia Madison, who also is known fleetingly as Amelia, mirrors the invasive behaviors, seductive behavior, and conniving that St. Clair Enson first imposes on his family and the novel's chief victims. After *Contending Forces*, a work in which Hopkins worked diligently to restore and to defend African American female virtue, the novelist now stepped away from conventional notions of African American gentility. Aurelia is a study in emotional excess and full disclosure of her desire. She is prone to "breathless misery," can harbor "rage and hatred in her heart," and the "precarious life" that she has lived prompts her to regard "[h]onesty . . . as a luxury for the wealthy to enjoy."[167] Aurelia is the female manifestation of the devil, a figure that is the "antithesis of female virtue," the "paradigm for the rebellious woman," and the "antiheroine" whose power "is a measure of the unease engendered by the strictness of the female role deemed proper by the rabbinic authorities themselves, a tradition to which Lilith serves as a potent countercurrent."[168] In *Hagar's Daughter*, she not only becomes essential to the scheme that seeks to defraud the Bowens of their money but also suffers a devastating fall that mirrors the ultimate exile imposed upon Satan when he is hurled into the fiery lake created especially for him and his traitorous legions.

The two-pronged narratives of deceit in *Hagar's Daughter* feature St. Clair Enson and Aurelia Madison as twin forces of wicked subterfuge. They depend on the contrived natural spaces and the untended wilderness; their ultimate undoing, however, is staged in a most sterile environment, one completely devoid of natural adornment or signs of life. Their denouement, presented during the murder trial of Cuthbert Sumner, consigns her to a hell that racial intolerance and stereotypes maintain. As soon as the woman who once stirred the heart and blood of Cuthbert Sumner is revealed to be the daughter of a white man and an enslaved woman, she becomes unlovable and physically repulsive. "I think that the knowledge of her origin would kill all desire in me," intones the just-exonerated Cuthbert Sumner in an uncanny conversation with the man who will be revealed as his father-in-law. "The mere thought of the grinning, toothless black hag that was her foreparent would forever rise between us," he concludes brutally. Sumner's words themselves become the most repulsive elements of this scene; his all-too-quick racial nightmare recalls the slow descent that befalls Rena Walden in Charles Chesnutt's *House behind the Cedars*, the notable American novel published in 1900 with which Hopkins was certainly familiar. The tragic heroine, Rena Walden, who possesses a "sweet smile . . . soft touch [and] . . . gentle voice," is rejected by George Tryon, her white lover, when he learns of her racial background. Tryon, the earnest but challenged suitor, then has dreams in which Rena, "by some hellish magic was slowly transformed into a hideous black hag," and he, "[w]ith agonized eyes . . . watched her beautiful tresses become mere wisps of coarse wool, wrapped round with dingy cotton strings; he saw her clear eyes grow bloodshot, her ivory teeth turn to unwholesome fangs."[169] The transformation that is imposed upon Aurelia Madison constitutes a recognizable echo of the gruesome blackening that Chesnutt devised in his novel. Hopkins goes even further though, rendering Aurelia, the mulatto, an irredeemable figure, one whose wanton sexuality and dreadful romantic history trumps her mixed racial background. Unlike Chesnutt, who preserves the innocence and conscience of his tragic mulatto, Hopkins proposes that race is not the determining factor in matters of physical and emotional rejection; it is rather the amoral, wanton use of one's body and the capacity to pursue in rapacious fashion the bodies of others. Hopkins thus reasserts the central characteristics of Lilith, and the legends, such as the ninth-century North African account that tells of Lilith's creation from slime rather than from dust of the earth, note her sexual insubordination and her own departure "out of the Garden of Eden" to a cave by the shore of the Red Sea, where she "took for lovers all the demons who lived there, while Adam, left alone, complained to God that his woman had left him."[170] Yet, in *Hagar's Daughter*, even as Aurelia is despised for being the "incarnation of lust," she succeeds in exposing the inherent desire that all men possess, even the now high-minded, racist Cuthbert Sumner, who played out his role as Adam when he embraced the weeping Aurelia in the conservatory grotto created in the Bowen mansion.

The publication of *Hagar's Daughter* made Pauline Hopkins the first, known African American woman to publish a work of detective fiction and the earliest creator of the first, known African American female detective.

The popular serialized novel also brought honor to the *Colored American Magazine*, which, with its publication of the work, became the first African American periodical to feature a detective novel by a writer of color. Hopkins's second novel, which appeared some thirty-five years after Metta Fuller Victor's *The Dead Letter*, the first American detective story and the first published by an American woman, also placed her squarely within the relatively recent American feminist literary tradition of domestic detective fiction. *Hagar's Daughter* extended the work of Louisa May Alcott, Victor, and highly successful writers like E. D. E. N. Southworth. These women writers accomplished ingenious applications and interweaving of literary models such as the gothic form and sentimental fiction that transformed the domestic sphere into an unpredictable and volatile forum, one that required women's deft manipulation of themselves and their environments in order to counter villainy, theft, and seduction.[171] Even in *Contending Forces*, which she copyrighted in the same year that the abolitionist and best-selling author Southworth passed away, Hopkins was employing key aspects of detective fiction—multiple identities, blackmail, and murder. By 1902, however, she was situating herself even more deliberately within the genre by creating a detective, a principal figure whose powers of deduction, capacity for stealth, and passion for justice would result in triumph over seemingly insurmountable odds and supposedly unsolvable mysteries.

The significant counterplots in *Hagar's Daughter* have prompted some critics to suggest that the novel is "ultimately only partly a detective story" that uses "detective motifs." Such assertions threaten Hopkins's place in the overwhelmingly white canon of women's domestic detective fiction and the incursions that Hopkins made into the field. It is Hopkins's investment in the genre and her enterprising creation of the first genuine African American female detective, however, that warrant serious consideration of the novel as domestic detective fiction. *Hagar's Daughter* succeeds as the first African American detective novel not only because it uses detective tropes but also because it reconfigures the classical detective tradition and experiments with elements that emerge later in "hardboiled detective fiction."[172] Indeed, the substantial subplots and intricate character development also can be read as evidence of the literary sophistication that Hopkins brings to the detective genre.

Hopkins used the detective genre to support her efforts to challenge racial hypocrisy and to promote civil political discourse about race matters. Her ambitious effort of detective fiction also met the demand for serialized fiction and allowed her to alleviate, to some degree, the pressing financial needs of the *Colored American Magazine*. Indeed, *Hagar's Daughter*, in particular, reveals an even more expansive Gilded Age moment of high literary creation, especially since its landmark creation of a female detective of color occurred in the shadow of work by Anna Katherine Green, the writer who in 1897 was hailed as the creator of the first female detective in American fiction and whose mysteries inspired Agatha Christie to create the intrepid Miss Marple. As an avid reader and astute observer of American literary culture, Hopkins was likely aware of Green's quick-fire trilogy that featured Amelia Butterworth, the detective who emerged first in *That Affair Next Door* (1897), published by the New York–based G. P. Putnam's Sons, and then reappeared in rapid succession in *Lost Man's Lane* (1898) and *The Circular Study* (1900), which were published by Putnam's and by McClure's, respectively.[173]

Although the literary imagination and creations of Edgar Allan Poe influenced the contingent of emerging women detective writers, Hopkins, in characteristic enterprising style, proposed that a white male detective like Poe's Dauphin, no matter how cultured and capable, was not powerful, malleable, or mobile enough to restore the peace in a world where racial tension, disenfranchisement, and social disgrace loomed large. In response to the nagging social anxieties and racial hysteria on which she focused in *Hagar's Daughter*, Hopkins created a more effective detective agent, an African American female detective who had both the ability and the willingness to subvert racial stereotypes and to cross gender lines. These attributes made Hopkins's innovative and unprecedented American detective essential to the restoration of postslavery social law and domestic order.

It is extremely fitting that Hopkins hid the identity of the author of *Hagar's Daughter*. She published the work under the name of Sarah A. Allen, a coy but simultaneously transparent pseudonym. Anyone who knew Hopkins well would have known immediately that Sarah Allen was her mother, well before the *Colored American Magazine* editors revealed that truth in the pages of the journal. Astute *Colored American Magazine* readers who had developed a fondness for Hopkins's writings and been attentive readers of her biographical profiles also might have recalled the name of her mother mentioned there. Scholars have speculated that Hopkins employed the pseudonym of Sarah Allen to deflect attention from the fact that, for all intents and purposes, she was the chief contributor to the *Colored American Magazine*. Yet by using the familial and maternal name, Hopkins also hinted at her own perspectives on truth and fiction. This pen name suggested that she saw truth and fiction as inextricably intertwined and detectable entities. Readers of the *Colored American Magazine*'s first serialized novel would have been well advised to ask, What is the fiction and what are the facts folded into the novel *Hagar's Daughter*? It was the first lengthy fictional project that Hopkins published after *Contending Forces*, the novel with which she made her authorial debut and an especially bold story in which she declared the authenticity of key scenes and also infused the narrative with her own gripping maternal family history. The autobiographical links in *Hagar's Daughter* are at first glance circumstantial. The novel opens in Charleston, South Carolina, on the eve of the American Civil War. However, it quickly moves to Washington, D.C., the ancestral home of William Hopkins, the writer's stepfather, one of its key primary settings. When *Hagar's Daughter* was published in 1901, Hopkins still had ties to the capital city. Anna Warrick Jarvis, her stepfather's first cousin, was a longtime resident of Washington and had worked as a teacher at the 16 and L Street School for many years.

Modern literary criticism of *Hagar's Daughter* has tended to focus on the race politics of the novel, the ways in which Hopkins implemented racial critique, and the social realities and political mayhem resulting from deliberate and unconscious race mixing. These have also concentrated on reading *Hagar's Daughter* as a tool with which Hopkins worked to dismantle racial hypocrisy.[174] Such primary issues do connect the novel to prevailing debates about African American rights, social mobility and its connections to racial passing, and the evolving cultural responses to multiracial identity politics. They also establish an effective political trajectory between *Contending Forces* and *Hagar's Daughter*. Like the reconstructive work of *Contending Forces*, *Hagar's Daughter* employs strategic intertextualities that Hopkins uses to reclaim and to recontextualize the American Civil War. As the Victorian age ended and the modern era began, Hopkins redirected readers into the nineteenth century and reintroduced them to the chaos of a civil war that was unparalleled in American history, a heart-wrenching, fratricidal, and deadly enterprise that she recast as an insidious race war of epic and unholy proportions.

13

"Boyish Hopes" and
the Politics of Brotherhood

Winona: A Tale of Negro Life in
the South and Southwest

The plain truth is, our relations with the red and
black members of the human family have been one almost
unvaried history of violence and fraud.

LYDIA MARIA CHILD

An Appeal for the Indians,

1868

American social development has been continually
beginning over again on the frontier. This perennial rebirth,
this fluidity of American life, this expansion westward with
its new opportunities, its continuous touch with the simplicity
of primitive society, furnish the forces dominating American
character. The true point of view in the history of this nation
is not the Atlantic coast, it is the Great West. Even the slavery
struggle . . . occupies its important place in American history
because of its relation to westward expansion.

FREDERICK JACKSON TURNER

*The Annual Report of the American
Historical Association,* 1893

Just two months after she concluded *Hagar's Daughter*, Hopkins
launched the first installment of *Winona: A Tale of Negro Life in the
South and Southwest*. The novel appeared in six installments from
May through October 1902 and continued Hopkins's considerations of
kinship ties, privilege, masculinity, and heroism that she had developed to
great effect in *Contending Forces* and in her other *Colored American Magazine*

writings. This new novel featured a winsome quadroon named Winona, her half-brother, Judah, a cast of abolitionist fighters led by John Brown, and the allure of a substantial and long-unclaimed British inheritance. *Winona* explored antebellum constructions of race, the notion of justifiable violence, and the ways in which slavery inhibited African American heroic potential, romance, and desirability. The enthusiastic reception and marketing success of Hopkins's first serialized *Colored American Magazine* novel had shown her how important it could be for the magazine to launch another absorbing serialized novel. Hopkins set about the task promptly, inspired by the sketches of a promising but unpublished story that she had penned more than twenty years earlier.

In the 1880s, as she savored the successes of *The Slaves' Escape; or, The Underground Railroad*, which had included celebrated performers headlining its cast and its tours of major American cities, Hopkins began to draft a second play about slavery and kinship. Its protagonist is Zach, an earnest enslaved seventeen-year-old boy who communicates directly with the spirit world and a dead man known as the colonel. The directives that the colonel gives Zach prompt the young man to take personal responsibility for his sister, Winnie. The two consider themselves kin, but Winnie is the only biological descendant of the dead Colonel Carlingford and the sole heir to the significant family fortune. Despite his challenging circumstances, which include living in a community of enslaved people, Zach is an idealist, and his "spirit . . . pants to break all bonds; to do such deeds of glory, as shall convince the world, that all men were created free and equal, and that the whitest soul may be found beneath the blackest skin."[1] When he discovers that his sister has been denied her rightful inheritance, Zach strives to unveil the treachery. He does so without any agenda and seems to be motivated primarily by his desire to do good. His final lines, uttered as the play comes to a close, are to the colonel. "I have tried to act," he says, "as I thought you would have had me; and in this moment I realize all my boyish hopes."[2] Hopkins abandoned the sketch for some twenty-two years until she transformed it in 1902 into *Winona: A Tale of Negro Life in the South and Southwest*, a richly historical serialized novel published in the *Colored American Magazine*.

The real tale of "Negro Life in the South and Southwest," to which the subtitle of *Winona* refers, is represented most starkly through Judah, the son of an enslaved woman who dies while trying to emancipate herself and her infant child. After being rescued by a "handsome well-educated mulattress who had escaped from slavery via the underground railroad," whom White Eagle takes as his wife, Judah becomes the only son and first child of Captain Henry Carlingford, the future father of Winona. Carlingford, who is living as a man named White Eagle, is a British man who fled the country to dodge false murder charges and execution. As White Eagle, he enjoys an American life that is best characterized by its frenetic and unruly domesticity. Following the death of White Eagle's mixed race wife, Winona's mother, the Native American housekeeper Nokomis becomes the primary maternal figure in the island home and forges close ties with the motherless girl. Nokomis introduces Winona to Native lore, and her tender storytelling recalls her literary namesake, the comely and victimized character Nokomis in Henry Wadsworth Longfellow's 1855 best-selling epic poem *The Song of Hiawatha*.[3]

White Eagle and his family, despite their residence on an island in the middle of Lake Erie, are inundated by outside forces of good and evil. Warren Maxwell, an envoy of the British government, seeks them out as part of his mission to locate the lost Carlingford heir. Colonel Titus and his sidekick Bill Thompson invade the island, kill White Eagle, and remand Judah and Winona into slavery in Missouri. Ebenezer Maybee, the crusty old proprietor of the Grand Island Hotel, who does "not hesitate to use methods of the Underground Railroad when he deemed it necessary," spearheads the efforts to rescue the children from slavery. He enlists Maxwell, his newest hotel guest, in the effort. Once freed, the children, Maxwell, and Maybee seek sanctuary in a Kansas camp with the legendary abolitionist John Brown, who, in the years leading up to his bold interracial attack on Harper's Ferry, is waging war against slavery and its defenders in the Midwest. Both of White Eagle's children become intimately linked to John Brown. Winona is embraced by the uncompromising abolitionist and welcomed into the bosom of the camp. Judah joins Brown's fighting force and has the opportunity to wage war against slavery and its proponents. Judah develops romantic feelings for Winona, but it is Maxwell who wins her hand. After much mayhem, violence, and conflict between pro- and antislavery forces, the novel closes as Winona marries Maxwell and is ensconced in the British aristocratic circles of her father, while Judah, unable to exist apart from her, pursues honor in the court of Queen Victoria and marries into high British society.

The double bildungsroman structure of *Winona* is muddied by issues of American slavery and Native American removal and westward expansion. Hopkins does not delve as deeply as she might into issues of Native American genocide, treaty conflicts, or wars. The narrative, with its embedded critique of acculturation and forced relocations, does touch on ongoing political maneuvering, such as the 1887 Dawes Act—federal legislation that was initiated by Massachusetts senator Henry Dawes and designed to eliminate reservations and reassign Native Americans to individual agricultural plots and homesteads that would facilitate their acculturation and assimilation into white society. Hopkins seems to acknowledge these contemporary histories of white incursion and Native suffering, but she treats slavery most fully and explicitly. She also focuses on its maintenance and growth, as well as its dependence on government mandates empowered by legislation like the 1850 Fugitive Slave Act, which essentially invalidated freedom for all people of color in America by authorizing the recapture of self-emancipated people. Hopkins uses *Winona* to stage an implicit and spirited rebuttal of the 1854 Kansas-Nebraska Act, legislation that undid elements of the Missouri Compromise and reauthorized the expansion of slavery in the territories. It is in this explosive historical milieu that Hopkins deploys John Brown, the Connecticut-born antislavery fighter, who in the mid-1850s fought mightily and amid great controversy in Kansas. Hopkins had long held Brown in high regard. In November 1900, she lauded him in one of her first *Colored American Magazine* articles as a man whose "spirit . . . marched on and on until it swept this country like an avalanche, and freed six millions from oppression."[4] *Winona* also honors the eloquent musings about the man by Henry David Thoreau, whose encounter with Brown during one of the abolitionist's visits to Massachusetts prompted him later to declare, "Of all the men who were said to be my contemporaries, it seems to me that John Brown is the only one who has not died. I meet him at every turn. He is more alive than ever he was."[5] The May 1854 massacre of five men at Pottawatomie Creek, which Brown's sons, under his direction, committed, is a centerpiece in the novel *Winona*, and Hopkins uses this controversial event to deliver her most vigorous endorsement of justifiable violence. Her unapologetic tribute to Brown, which suggests her complete investment in his politics, is reminiscent of the perspectives advanced by Franklin Sanborn, one of Brown's key supporters and the Concord educator with whom Hopkins shared the Faneuil Hall stage in 1905 at the Garrison Centennial event. Sanborn, who published one of the most thorough accounts of Brown, noted matter-of-factly that Brown's "theory required fighting in Kansas," since, in his mind, "it was the only sure way to keep that region free from the curse of slavery. [Brown's] mission . . . was to levy war on it, and for that to raise and equip a company of a hundred well armed men who should resist aggression in Kansas, or occasionally carry the war into Missouri."[6] The most explicitly violent of all Hopkins's works, *Winona* follows Brown's trail into and out of Kansas, portraying bloody skirmishes and massacres in which his men and her fictional characters are pitted against proslavery forces. It is in these highly tense and graphic scenes that Hopkins demonstrates most emphatically the corrupting and corrosive nature of slavery.[7]

Slavery, with its willfully applied reclassifications of those who can exist as free or unfree, undergirds the convoluted plots and dramas in *Winona*, which showcase race and identity as volatile categories, ones that can subject bodies of color to perpetual indeterminacy and disorienting states of limbo. Hopkins sets the novel's narratives of racial and social mayhem against established African American histories, a maneuver that highlights the extreme chaos of the antebellum world of *Winona* and pays tribute to American Northern antislavery communities that shaped her own conceptions of race, power, and privilege. The novel's first setting is on an island that "[lies] close in the shadow of Grand Island," a historic Lake Erie community that still exists today and is close to the shores of Buffalo, New York. Hopkins reminded her readers that it was "an antislavery stronghold, — the last most convenient station of the underground railroad," and she used the city as the stabilizing backdrop for the increasingly vulnerable island that is home to the widowed White Eagle and his family.[8] Her familiarity with Buffalo was linked to her family history, since it was here that her maternal granduncle, James Monroe Whitfield, established himself as a gifted poet, abolitionist, and leader in the emigrationist movement. The grandson of French and Indian War veteran Caesar Nero Paul and his wife Lovey, Whitfield lived in Buffalo for two decades after he left the Exeter, New Hampshire, home of his parents, Joseph and Nancy Paul Whitfield. He worked as a barber, and his places of business frequently were listed as "on the lake" or in busy central locations such as the Buffalo Hotel.[9] Hopkins's choice of setting also allowed her to conjure up the power of Frederick Douglass, editor of the Rochester-based *North Star*, who, in 1850, sought out Whitfield, the young man who subscribed to his newspaper and published stirring and sophisticated poems in its pages.

Hopkins explores the vulnerability of all American antebellum locations, and it is no surprise, then, that the island on which White Eagle lives is subject to deadly invasion by slave catchers. Despite Buffalo's ardent and watchful abolitionist community, the city and its environs were frequently assailed by proslavery forces determined to impede Underground Railroad travel to Canada, which lay just across the lake, or to reclaim self-emancipated people who were newly settled in the city. The fragility of this fictionalized island place in *Winona* is heightened by both its proximity to and distance from Buffalo and the city's history of antislavery resistance. Hopkins further justifies the susceptibility of White Eagle's island by linking it to Grand Island, a place that historically has been subject to settlement and expulsion and has been at the heart of debates about property and rightful ownership. The eight-mile-long, 17,381-acre place that Seneca Indians in the mid-1600s referred to as Ga-we-not, "great island," was used primarily as hunting grounds because of the substantial seasonal flocks of game birds, ducks, and geese and the teeming schools of fish like black bass, yellow pike, and sturgeon that inhabited its waters.[10] Claimed as part of the British Empire after the French and Indian War, Grand Island was once again American territory by the second decade of the 1800s, and it became home to "hardy individuals" who constructed log cabins, cleared the land, and started making barrels from the white oak trees growing there. The burgeoning barrel market seems to have irked citizens of Buffalo, and after intense legal and vigilante protests, Martin Van Buren, then the attorney general of New York, helped to pass a state law that authorized the region's sheriff to "see that the settlers were removed." Grand Island families were confronted by the sheriff and his posse of twenty-four militia men, subjected to readings of the legislative act, and directed to gather their belongings, leave their houses, and resettle either in Canada or on the American mainland. Then, the homes were burned to the ground.[11] Grand Island's history of destruction eventually gave way to eras of reconstruction, such as that which occurred in the mid-1820s when Major Mordecai Manuel Noah purchased 2,500 acres and made plans to establish a thriving "colony for the Jews of the world" in a city that he wanted to name Ararat.[12] These regional histories of land transfer and abolition, essential to the overall story of *Winona*, however, give way to another pressing chapter in American history, that of Native American possession, dispossession, and imposed exile.

The novel opens with bucolic views of Lake Erie in the 1850s, and the narrator happily surveys the shoreline and beaches where "Indian squaws sat in the sun with their gaudy blankets wrapped about them in spite of the heat, watching the steamers upon the lakes, the constant traffic of the canal boats, their beaded wares spread temptingly upon the firm white sand to catch the fancy of the free-handed sailor or visitor."[13] The picturesque qualities of this scene, intertwined with evidence of the seductive ethnic marketplace, are undermined subtly by the quiet discomfort of the "Indian squaws," women who use blankets despite the hot weather and who, by doing so, hint at efforts to secure their Native identities and protect their bodies from unwelcome scrutiny and gestures by "free-handed" individuals. The seemingly idealized ethnic images do not hide the history of displacement that by the 1850s was playing out in wars and forced Native American migrations across the West, the South, and the Great Plains. Hopkins does not refer directly to the key events—the 1830 Indian Removal Act, the 1834 creation of the U.S. Department of Indian Affairs, or the early 1850s federal acquisition of some 175 million acres of Indian territory. Nor does Hopkins allude to conflicts such as the 1832 Black Hawk War, the 1855 Yakima War, or the Third Seminole Uprising that ended in 1858 after three years of violence. Instead, she hints at an uneasy but seemingly sedate coexistence between Native Americans and

American society, one that recalls Lydia Maria Child's nineteenth-century proposals from her activist writings on Native rights.

Hopkins uses the gaze of the silent Native to focus first on the characters, who continually are rendered "other" to themselves and to the communities to which they are remanded or in which they are hidden. Having surveyed the colorful scene of Native women plying their wares on the shores of Lake Erie, the narrator then directs readers to an image beyond the shore where "on the bosom of Lake Erie floated a canoe." The boat's occupants include a "lad who handled the paddle so skilfully [that he] might have been mistaken for an Indian at first glance" and a girl wearing a "dress of gaily embroidered dark blue broadcloth" who "leaned idly over the side trailing a slim brown hand through the blue water."[14] These children, Judah and Winona, are alternately clothed, unclothed, and reclothed in ways that draw attention to their Native genealogies, their African heritage, and their proximity to Anglo-European history.

Ethnic and racial veils persist in *Winona* and take a number of forms, including adopted names and ethnic costumes. White Eagle bears the most noticeable and persistent of ethnic masks. Despite the emphatically delivered early accounts of his life and immersion in Native American culture, his European ancestry and powerful legacies are not confirmed until the novel's end. The scheming villains of the novel, the slave catchers Captain Thomson and Captain Titus, also use veiling to advance their nefarious schemes. When they first appear on the Lake Erie Island, they give no signs of their native Southern identities but are seen first as "white men in hunter's dress."[15] The acts of self-transformation that obscure regional origins or gender often are prompted by desire, some romantic in nature and others thoroughly capitalistic. The novel's most ambitious transformation occurs when Winona transforms herself into a male nurse, but it becomes a short-lived exercise in cross-dressing and gender reorientation when her overwhelming female desires prompt her to reveal her true self to Maxwell, her sick and imprisoned love interest.

Over the course of the novel, Hopkins ponders identity and the ways in which one's state of being is stymied or nurtured by environments, events, and politics. She seems persuaded, by the time she is publishing *Winona*, that one's identity is thoroughly informed by cultural environment.[16] Hopkins repeatedly invites readers to examine their notions of "the natural" as it applies to the world, status, gender, and race. To enhance this exercise, Hopkins repeatedly presents characters who are consistently misread and whose silence, or inability to define for themselves what is "natural" or "unnatural" about their existence and situations, renders them tragically complicit in the upheavals that follow. A character's survival or demise depends much more heavily on

The Politics of Brotherhood

the acts of misinterpretation that others commit. The patriarch White Eagle, for example, quickly becomes a mythic and strangely powerless figure in the novel. He never speaks, his biographies are narrated and misstated by others, he is murdered by persons who remain unknown for many years, and his children are snatched from their island home by slave catchers. White Eagle's use of the ethnic veil is linked to his close ties with the Native Americans to whom he attaches himself and to whom he provides helpful medical intervention. His name is almost exactly opposite of that of Black Hawk, a historic Native American leader. The Sauk chief and narrator of his 1833 memoir, *Life of Ma-Ka-Tai-Me-She-KiaKiak, or Black Hawk* gained national prominence in the antebellum era because of his determination to reassert the ownership rights of his people. His resistance led to an awful massacre of the tribe, his imprisonment, and his objectification by Andrew Jackson, who insisted that the imprisoned chief be transported from his prison cell and exhibited and displayed in American cities before his eventual release.[17] Even White Eagle's European whiteness raises questions about the identity politics that Hopkins is dealing with in her serialized American romance.

In *Winona*, Hopkins once again drapes historical facts over intriguing fictional stories in order to intensify her critiques of race, origin, and privilege. There are substantial differences between the unfinished 1880s sketch and *Winona*, the serialized novel, but in both, Hopkins invests heavily in the surname of Carlingford. In the 1880s, she may well have become familiar with the name Carlingford because of the prominence of Chichester Parkinson-Fortescue, the Irish politician, statesman, and member of Prime Minister William Gladstone's cabinet, who was elevated in 1874 to the peerage and acquired the title Baron Carlingford.[18] Born in 1823, the Oxford-educated Parkinson-Fortescue became the chief secretary for Ireland and in the 1880s the Lord Privy Seal. Parkinson-Fortescue's political career was memorable for its successes and his resistance, which included his withdrawal of support for the British home rule cause and Britain's Irish policy. The Baron enjoyed a lively marriage to Lady Frances Waldegrave, an influential social leader, but the couple had no children. Upon Carlingford's death in 1898, having no heirs, his title died with him. The biographical resonances in this late nineteenth-century story might have intrigued Hopkins; indeed her use of the name hints again at the impressive political awareness that she cultivated throughout her career and at the potentially useful global histories that she often applied to her American narratives.

It is more likely, though, that Hopkins's choices in *Winona* were shaped by her own extensive reading of British literature and that her serialized novel was influenced heavily by the writings of Margaret Oliphant, the popular and resourceful nineteenth-century Scottish novelist who died in 1897, just five years before the revised *Winona* appeared in the *Colored American Magazine*. In the early 1860s, Oliphant began publishing *Chronicles of Carlingford*, a multipart series of "gently realistic comedies of manners about a mythical English town which she called Carlingford."[19] The connection between Oliphant's *Chronicles of Carlingford* and other writings and Pauline Hopkins's *Winona* go beyond the fact that both works were popular serials that used sensationalism to great effect. Both revolve around tangled plots of thwarted inheritance, unexpected bequests, and family reunion; both have similarly named characters; and both feature women who preside grandly over their respective domains. On one occasion, Oliphant, referring to a character named Lucilla, states that she exists as the "queen of Carlingford." This is a role that Hopkins also attributes to the child Winona, who is "queen of the little island" in Lake Erie and whose "faithful subjects were her father, Judah, and old Nokomis."[20]

Hopkins may have been inspired to create her untitled 1880s play and the 1902 serialized *Winona* after reading "The Executor," an early installment of Oliphant's *Chronicles*, which first appeared in the May 1861 issue of *Blackwood's Edinburgh Magazine*. If one imagines an American reader taking up the story, the first lines immediately take on additional and explosive meaning. "'The woman was certainly mad,' said John Brown," the attorney who finds himself "holding up to the light that extraordinary scrap of paper, which had fallen . . . like a thunderbolt" upon the group dressed in mourning clothes and assembled in a "parlour of very grim and homely aspect, furnished with dark mahogany and black haircloth."[21] An American reader like Hopkins immediately would have thought of the insurrectionist John Brown, the leader of the raid on Harper's Ferry who figures prominently in the 1902 *Winona*. In "The Executor," the town of Carlingford and the Christians, the dispossessed family, grapple with the news that the deceased Mrs. Thomson was the richest woman in the town's history and also a mother. Despite the fact that she had been a resident in the town for more than thirty years and had "settled down in Carlingford—with no child, nor appearance of ever having had one—an old witch with three cats, and a heart like the nether millstone," in death she insisted that her maternal history be privileged and honored. The community is stunned because Mrs. Thomson's will leaves "all the property of which Mrs. Thomson of Grove Street died possessed, to John Brown, attorney in Carlingford, in trust for Phoebe Thomson, the only child of the testatrix, who had not seen or heard of her for thirty years." The deceased also provided for the fact that her long-lost daughter might never be found: "[I]n case of all lawful means to find the said Phoebe Thomson proving unsuccessful," read the will, "at the end of three years the property was bequeathed to John Brown, his heirs and administrators, absolutely and in full possession."[22] Intriguing details such as these transform ordinary tales about community life and women's experiences into extraordinary chronicles of great dimension.

Winona extends the considerations of racial, social, and economic bequests that emerged so fully in *Contending Forces* and in *Hagar's Daughter*. Hopkins turns toward the sensational elements surrounding the location and reinstallation of legitimate heirs and away from a rehabilitation of Zack, the idealistic but multiply constrained male in the 1880s drama. *Winona* becomes a treatment of feminine rehabilitation instead, and this is confirmed in part by the fact that the Sioux name of "Winona" not only means "giving" but "first-born girl-child."[23] In *Winona*, Hopkins subjects families to increasingly drastic schisms, ones prompted by their different eligibilities as heirs to material fortunes and also in terms of their social and emotional dispossessions. Judah, the young man who is saddled with appellations such as "the Negro," has his individuality shrouded, and he has to withstand repeated and inappropriate generalizations of his background and ancestry. Judah struggles mightily against marginalization throughout the novel, despite his unmistakable and powerful physicality and increasingly racialized blackness.[24] The character of Judah enables *Winona* to offer the "Tale of Negro Life in the South and Southwest," to which the novel's subtitle refers. Given the name that she confers upon the young man who figures prominently in her Americanized bildungsroman, it would seem that she was creating a narrative built on justice and unbridled power. Her use of the name Judah rather than that of Zack confers upon him apocalyptic might. Both Zachariah and Judah have biblical connections, but Hopkins tapped into much more heroic potential by using the name Judah. The name Zachariah linked her original protagonist to the unfortunate Old Testament history of the son of Jeroboam, who assumed the throne after his father's death but enjoyed only a short reign of six months. An ungodly man, Zachariah "did that which was evil in the sight of Yahweh," and his reign ended when Shallum, a son of Jabesh, "smote him before the people and slew him, and reigned in his stead."[25] Zachariah is an unfortunate ruler in the kingdom of Judah, which included in its substantial geography lands to the south of Palestine and the city of Jerusalem. The Biblical genealogy of Judah is much more promising. The name, known in Hebrew as "yehudhah," which means "praised," identifies him as the fourth son born to Jacob and Leah, the sister of Rachel and the wife whom Jacob was tricked into marrying. Judah, who became the leader of one of the twelve tribes of Israel, was the intercessor who saved their father's favorite son, Joseph, from death and who persuaded his brothers to sell Joseph into slavery rather than kill him. Finally, the Book of Revelation refers to Jesus Christ as the Lion of Judah, a reference that envelops in rich redemptive possibility the past and present of Hopkins's aspiring protagonist. Despite the explicit power that is evoked by the biblical name and meanings of Judah, in Hopkins's *Winona* Judah cannot evade his progressive descent into an unforgiving and hierarchical raced culture. Judah is exiled from Native American circles, subjugated in antebellum Southern plantation culture, relegated to the margins of white antislavery resistance, and then absorbed by the most powerful circles of whiteness when he "entered the service of the Queen" of England. Between these transatlantic poles, however, Judah bears the burden of racial stereotype, a responsibility that has been imagined as a direct result of Hopkins's attempt to use sentimental romance to advance her campaign for racial justice.[26] Barely five months later, though, perhaps because of her deliberate contemplations in *Winona* of race and romance, Hopkins, writing on race and marriage under the pseudonym J. Shirley Shadrach, would conclude in the *Colored American Magazine* that "[w]e have no desire to eulogize the Negro in treating this subject" and declare that "[t]he purpose of every race lover should be to familiarize the public mind with the fact that the Negro is a *human being*, amenable to every law, human and divine, that can affect any other race upon the footstool."[27]

Hopkins assumes the role of cultural facilitator by steadily distancing Judah and Winona from the ethnic and racial communities that render them alien to the whites and Europeans who gaze upon them. The methods by which Hopkins engineers the reorientations are quite dramatic, especially for Judah. He, of all the characters, is the least subject to veiling. When the novel opens, despite the fact that he stands practically naked and is not swathed in any protective mantles or disguised by regional costumes, he is mistakenly identified as an Indian. From this point on, Judah is clothed, but not well, by the narrative veils that others place upon him. His enduring island contact, the crusty Mr. Maybee, demonstrates the manhandling of biography that occurs throughout the novel. As a violent storm rages, the children arrive at Maybee's house, a place where he boards "Western or furrin" people. The children earnestly solicit help from Maybee, who functions as a "sort of justice of the peace and town constable," but he resists their initial pleas to return with them and tend to their wounded father. As he explains his hesitation to Maxwell, Maybee gives the Englishman a coarse and emphatic biography of Judah and Winona. He is prompted to give the information only after he brands the children with a racial epithet that elicits an exclamation from Maxwell. To explain himself, Maybee, whose name conveniently suggests the indeterminacy that he exudes, despite his proclamations that he delivers "a fac'," declares the following. He identifies Judah as "a fugitive slave picked up by White Eagle in some of his tramps and adopted." He then explains that Winona is "a quadroon. Her mother, the chief's wife, was a fugitive too, whom he befriended and then married out of pity."[28] Maybee's story deprives White Eagle and his family of the truth of the significant emotional effort, physical determination, and legal protection that shaped their evolution as a family. The real story, delivered by the narrator, positions White Eagle not as the itinerant savior to whom Maybee refers but rather as a passive recipient who makes a place for survivors of "the hard struggle to reach the land of Freedom."[29] White Eagle is the champion of domesticity; he builds a "four-room cottage," and it is to this that he one day brings "a handsome well-educated mulattress." Judah is no unattached waif but rather a "mite of humanity" who benefits from the generosity, care, and protection of his future adoptive mother, an persistently unnamed fugitive who is determined to save him when his mother succumbs to the rigors of escape.

Hopkins contemplates in *Winona* the vulnerability of male authorship and male subjectivity, provocative issues that she addressed in *Contending Forces* and *Hagar's Daughter*, and to which she would return again in her last serialized novel, *Of One Blood*. She departs from the traditional representations of objectified female subjects, women rendered voiceless by their powerlessness within and beyond the domestic sphere. Instead, Hopkins focuses on unreadable bodies and rewritable histories, and the ways in which these unreliable, perpetually shifting entities complicate claims on justice—social and political. Judah's inaccessible and malleable histories subject him to faulty objectification, and, like White Eagle, he has no recourse available. In fact, he himself participates in and enables these constant revisions, some of which only serve to alienate him further from the patriarchal environments in which he could claim membership. In one especially significant moment, he refers to White Eagle, the man whose death he plans to avenge, as his "master." His use of that term contributes to Judah's systematic exile from the comforts of home and the delights of family romance. Judah's exile reaches its zenith when he and Winona become part of the camps that the abolitionist John Brown has established on the banks of the Pottawatomie. Their experiences in the camp are starkly different. Winona quickly forms deep, restorative emotional bonds. She is "quartered at the Brown domicile" and in a short time "became Captain Brown's special care[,] and the rugged Puritan unbent to spoil and pet the 'pretty squaw,' as he delighted to call her."[30] In the Brown camp, Winona experiences once again the romantic dimensions of Native American life. That context also prompts her to give in to the natural world that was so much a part of her life on the Lake Erie island. In the middle of Kansas, Winona is drawn to the woods that border the Brown camp; the forest "calmed her," and its "grays and greens and interlacing density of stems, and . . . whisper of a secret that has lasted from the foundation of the world, replac[es] her fever with the calmness of hope." In this natural world just beyond the militaristic Brown encampment, Winona also surrenders to the "impulse of the wild things among whom she had lived." This "impulse," emphatically reports the narrator, "drove her to a hole in under the bluff" and to a "tunnel which led into a cavern." Buried under the woods, Winona "made herself a divan of dried moss," and it is in this subterranean bower that she often "flung herself down at full length to think."[31]

Judah also participates in acts of burial and submersion; only it is his thoughts rather than his body that he strives to hide as he contemplates his romantic prospects with Winona. Judah also inhabits the woods in ways that evoke his early life with Native Americans. Captain Brown soon realizes Judah's "capabilities," and the fugitive is "appointed special aid and scout to the camp." "Nothing could have suited him better," the narrator assures readers, before reporting that "[a]ll day [Judah] scoured the woods, following the trail of parties of desperadoes or bringing in the fruits of the line or rifle to supply the needs in fish or meat."[32] Judah lives beyond the white community of abolitionists, and it is from that unencumbered space that he enjoys his first substantial upward trajectory: "[S]oon his name was heralded with that of Brown as a brave and fearless man bold to recklessness." Judah's mythic self finally takes on positive qualities. Yet the "recklessness" that causes this redemption confirms that in antebellum America his black body still remains in jeopardy. Judah eventually finds safety and the prospect of a full life. The unveiling of Winona's true ancestry and her inheritance finance Judah's migration from the American South and Southwest to England. Enveloped in monarchical power, Judah is gentrified dramatically. The extent to which his physicality and outlooks change is considerable, even if evidence of this is consigned to a few brief lines at the novel's end. The "untamable torrid ferocity of his tribe" that is "not pleasing to see" when it emerges in Bloody Kansas is transformed in England into "daring bravery and matchless courage."[33] The domesticated Lion of Judah "had honors and wealth heaped upon him," and after acquiring these material advantages, he "finally married into one of the best families of the realm."[34] Judah's trajectory is a sure sign that Hopkins has departed from the racial script that she deployed in *Contending Forces*. This insistently blackened character—who is colored in terms of race and moodiness—is never inclined to "draw on the romantic machinery of the feudal South" that Hopkins and her peers, Frank Webb and Paul Laurence Dunbar, all portray. Judah also does not commit himself to "a search for a place to be somebody," nor does Hopkins's tamed protagonist "come to grips with the myth of [his] Afro-American past."[35]

Despite the racial objectification that contributes to Judah's eventual rejection of the United States, African Americanist critics do propose that Judah occupies an enabling place in the novel. The novel has been read as a "triangular love story" in which "honorable love . . . has two faces: the white Warren Maxwell from England and the black Judah who has grown up with Winona."[36] Such a hopeful assessment notwithstanding, though, there is no place for Judah's "honorable love" to flourish. Winona can refuse him on both social and racial grounds. Their familial intimacy as children of White Eagle casts the shadow of incest, despite their dissimilar origins, upon any love relationship. In addition, her incremental and welcome approach toward whiteness installs a significant racial divide between them. Warren Maxwell, the well-meaning English lawyer, usurps Judah's place as a suitor, and Judah understands this in distinctly racial terms. After engineering Winona's successful escape from slavery, Judah realizes that his goal "to work for her and a home in Canada" is "shattered," and he is despondent. The narrator observes that Judah "saw that the girl would not be satisfied with his humble love." Judah, however, is even more direct about the juxtaposition of class privilege, of which he has little, and whiteness, of which he has no certifiable amount. "'So it is,' he told himself bitterly. 'The white man has the advantage in all things. Is it worth while struggling against such forces?'"[37] Maxwell's whiteness, ancestry, and professional credentials enable him to enjoy an easy usurpation of an untutored man of African descent. Over the course of the novel, Maxwell's privileges also provide him with buffers that ease his romantic hesitations and soldierly nervousness and his extralegal persecutions.

Hopkins's privileging of legitimacy and reconstruction of authentic families highlights the persistent illegitimacy, as it were, of African American protest. Yet it is Judah, the motherless and essentially fatherless man with negligible sibling ties and a desire for an increasingly unattainable lover, who possesses the most reliable of family histories. This is no simple suggestion on Hopkins's part that the black folk memory trumps the white aristocratic mind. Judah is hardly a representative of the folk; he hovers in between racial myth and apocalyptic traditions. However, in a novel that is motivated by the desire of white empire and in which black desire repeatedly is tempered, one cannot ignore the fact that Judah possesses and maintains an unshakable grip on his past. The scene that confirms the differences between racial and ethnic memory occurs in the novel's penultimate chapter. Having forced his evil tormentor, Bill Thomson, to choose between a suicidal leap or a point-blank shot, Judah stands "like a statue" atop the cliff above the Pottawatomie River. The sudden physical paralysis unleashes a torrent of mental recall: "He was back in the past. His thoughts ran backwards in an unbroken train until the scene before him changed to the island and the day when the careless happiness of his free youth was broken by the advent of the strangers, Colonel Titus and Bill Thomson. Then had followed the murder of White Eagle." Judah's actions, though, prove quickly to be only vaguely emancipatory because he has in fact threatened the transatlantic investigation that brought Warren Maxwell to the United States in the first place. As if aware of this, Judah's rare moment of self-absorption gives way to wrenching turmoil. It is "[a]s through a mist, queries and propositions and possibilities took shape, there on the cliffside, that had never before presented themselves to him. As he stood in the blazing sunlight, his brain throbbed intolerably and every pulsation was a shooting pain." Judah is tormented by self-defeating and seemingly unanswerable questions. "Why had he been so dull of comprehension?" he wonders beratingly, before considering, "What if a thought just born in his mind should prove to be true. O, to be free once more!"[38] The onset of physical pain as his "brain throbbed intolerably" signals Judah's return to blackness, the state that makes him so valuable to the insurrectionary forces of John Brown and so unsuitable to Winona, his "sister." Judah's actions are softened, and in some ways undone, by Winona, Maxwell, and the assembly of John Brown's men who transport the badly wounded Thomson from the riverbed to his deathbed in the Brown camp. There, before an audience that includes "Judah's dark, handsome face and stalwart form . . . in the background," Thomson provides the sought-after and long-buried Carlingford family history. A folk representative of white Anglo-European aristocracy, a former valet, finally provides the novel's most valuable narrative. This memoir, with its great financial and social implications, enables Winona to transcend the deprivations of American life, to elude the shadow of melancholic and racial blackness cast by her half-brother, and to realize true romance as a member of the British elite.

Against a backdrop of righteous antislavery warfare and bold assertions of white masculinity, *Winona* explores the ways in which the racialized heroic potential for men of color is undermined by imposed racialization of their bodies, motives, and actions. At key moments, black subjects like Judah become objects of the white gaze. This interaction is not reciprocal, and the analysis of the African American actor's performance has significant implications for his potential for assimilation into white American society and his ability to claim a stable and functional African American domesticity. This specular crisis is illustrated most keenly in chapter 15 in the scenes depicting Judah confronting Bill Thomson, his former slave owner and the accomplice in the murder of White Eagle, his adoptive father. Hopkins, clearly inspired by Frederick Douglass's 1852 novella *The Heroic Slave*, delivers a cautious narration of the moment in which Judah enacts justice for himself and his family. Just "a moment" has passed since Judah's foe chose to leap into the Pottawatomie River, and he is in a reverie, standing as a statue while his mind leaps to and fro, recalling the past and grappling with his future prospects now that he has committed this deed. As Judah articulates inwardly a longing to be "free once more," there is behind him "a rustle of leaves, and out from the shadow of the trees filed a number of anti-slavery men headed by Captain Brown and Parson Steward."[39] It is John Brown who, on behalf of the group, declares, "Well, Judah . . . we've been watching your little drama. You promised to kill him and you've done it." Brown's description of Judah's death-struggle as "your little drama" may be interpreted as a patronizing assessment of the heroics from which Judah has emerged unscathed. Brown's words, if read with late nineteenth-century definitions of the word "drama" in mind, are less dismissive. Hopkins may indeed have meant to invoke the word here to call attention to the long-standing, long-suffering reality bound up with Judah's aggressive victory. She well may have intended that readers understand the word "drama" as a reference to "a series of actions or course of events having a unity like that of a drama, and leading to a final catastrophe or consummation."[40] Judah's response accommodates both the prevailing contemporary definition of the word and the performativity that it implies. He does not simply respond to Brown, he "returned" in response, suggesting that he offers Brown a response that constitutes an act of reportage "in answer to . . . some official demand for information."[41] Judah effects a skillful rhetorical maneuver, one that demotes Brown momentarily and transforms him from "Captain" to one of the "Boys." He also takes on the role of performer and suggests that they formalize their casual but explicit behavior as audience. "'Boys,' returned Judah, 'and all of you, I leave it to you,'" he says boldly, "'if I'm not right in ridding the world of such a beast as Thomson.'" Judah places the burden of evaluation upon the band of fighting men who refrained from aiding him as he fought Thomson, and he elicits a decidedly positive assessment: "The men set up a cheer that echoes and re-echoed among the hills." Their exuberance even reaches the women of the camp inside the cave where they have sought protection during the most recent melee, and, without being privy to the cause of the cheer, the women "heard [the noise] with joyful hearts."[42] The affirmation is unanimous and Judah is able to exit yet another public stage that had left him vulnerable to censure and misreading by whites.

Winona opens in 1850, a period in which Native Americans were embroiled in major negotiations and transfers of land, increasingly oppressive treaties, and violent conflicts. This is a historical moment barely removed from the Mexican War, in which a majority of tribes in the Southwest became subject to U.S. policy when the war ended in 1848. Many tribes, such as those in the Southern plains, were also dealing with cholera and other life-threatening diseases. Hopkins does not address directly this Native upheaval and chooses instead to contrast Native experiences with the more static institution of slavery. Even though Hopkins has ample opportunity and cause to incorporate contemporary and historic dimensions of Native American history and experience, she repeatedly resists direct advocacy. The novel's central characters live in close relation to Native American culture even as they live beyond its reach. They are within sight of the Native women who sell their wares on the banks of Lake Erie. Yet in this moment they are not subject to Native culture and are free to form their own interpretation of the culture and to challenge it, as Judah does when he dismisses the folk teachings of Nokomis that Winona cherishes. Hopkins also could have highlighted the Native American background of John Brown, who at the age of five moved with his family to Ohio, a region that Brown's biographer James Redpath described in his 1860 tribute to the abolitionist as a "wilderness filled with wild beasts, & Indians."[43] Hopkins's treatment of the campaigns of John Brown and his band of resisters fits with her closing commentary on the national sickness, one that like the cholera and influenza epidemics of the late antebellum period eradicated hundreds of thousands of people in America. In *Winona*, Hopkins suggests that slavery is a most deadly national sickness, a debilitating malady that threatens the American "constitution"—the legal document as well as the national psyche and collective health.

Racial transformations in *Winona* represent the novel's dramatic exodus or reversal of the Middle Passage. The young girl whose "slim brown hand" slips through the waters of Lake Erie becomes a "noble woman" whom "all" in England "worshipped [as] the last beautiful representative of an ancient family."[44] Judah becomes a knight and devotes himself to the missions and mandates of Queen Victoria. These departures do not quite constitute an abdication of a culture because neither Judah nor Winona claim a righteous and empowering place in African American, Native, or white American communities. Hopkins does try to compensate for the absence of nonwhite leadership that persists in *Winona*. In the final pages, she explores the untapped political power of blackness and also exposes its oppressive subjectivity in antebellum America. The final passages in *Winona* focus on Aunt Vinnie, a minor character who now becomes an authoritative African American cultural critic and race historian. As she attempts to deliver the coup de grâce to slavery and race prejudice, Hopkins depends once again and most dramatically on William Wells Brown, her New England mentor and literary role model.

To achieve a resounding political critique of race matters, Hopkins resurrects the indomitable matriarch, who emerged to great effect in *Hagar's Daughter* in the character of Aunt Henny. In *Winona*, Aunt Vinnie provides a counterbalance to the escapist and romantic narrative of Winona's good luck; she tells the "groups of curious neighbors, white and black," that the girl has "strange fortunes."[45] Aunt Vinnie astutely realizes that her newfound value as a storyteller and historian can be turned to more explicit political agendas. As a result, she merges the tale of Winona with a colorful political commentary and set of prophecies. "She invariably ended the tale [of Winona] with a short sermon on the fate of her race," remarks the narrator. It is this "short sermon" that Hopkins takes almost verbatim from *My Southern Home; or, The South and Its People*, the volume that William Wells Brown had published in Boston in 1880, just four years before his death. Hopkins adapts key portions of Brown's documentary history of his wide-ranging and formative experiences in the South, especially the segments where he focuses on 1 January 1863, a historic moment of national transformation and military assertion. Brown recalls for readers his time in South Carolina, on a night when "rain descended in torrents from the black and overhanging clouds and the thunder, accompanied with vivid flashes of lightning, resounded fearfully as [he] entered a negro cabin."[46] In characteristic and absorbing narrative style, Brown re-creates the moment of anticipation preceding the enactment of the Emancipation Proclamation that is read by a "Yankee soldier, in the Union blue," with help from a "stout negro boy" who "held a torch which lighted up the Cabin." Midnight arrives and the assembled group "threw themselves upon their knees" and began to give thanks. The heavens seemed to respond, and "a sharp flash of lightening was followed by a clap of thunder, such as is only heard in the tropics," Brown reports. He then notes that the group follows Uncle Ben, a "white-haired man," who leads them "in prayer, and such a prayer as but few outside this injured race could have given." Immediately following the prayer, Uncle Ben begins to sing, and it is from these lyrics about aid from on high and angels coming down to earth that Hopkins chooses the last lines of *Winona*.

Hopkins inverts Brown's account of this historic moment, which he recalls with stirring detail. She uses first the set of exchanges between the South Carolinians whom Brown profiles. These include references to three sets of signs that are offered up as corroborations of Aunt Vinnie's assertion that "we's boun' to be free."[47] In *Winona*, the three reporters include an "elderly white woman" who "drew a long breath, and declared that she had been lifted out of her bed three times the previous night"; "a colored brother" who muses about "[d]e mule [that] kicked me three times dis mornin'" and who "never did dat afore in his life"; and 'Tavius, the trusty man who works for Mr. Maybee, and who reports with great conviction that "[a] rabbit run across my path twice comin' through de graveyard las' Sunday."[48] These three colorful and earnest testimonies are taken directly from Brown's memoir. He recalls how "[a]ll sorts of stories were soon introduced to prove that angelic visits were common" and that there were signs that "[d]e angels of de Lord is wid us still," even as the shackles of slavery begin to fall. Brown includes five testimonies, and Hopkins uses three of them. Her reference to the "elderly woman" is a verbatim reproduction from Brown's chapter, the mule-kicking episode is altered only slightly in the very last phrase, and the report about the rabbit is attributed to a man rather than to Uncle Ben's wife. Hopkins practices editorial restraint as she concludes *Winona* and incorporates the Negro spiritual that Uncle Ben performs during the thanksgiving ceremony. Hopkins focuses on the middle portion of a song that is filled with invocation and requests for "breth-er-en" to "send dem angels down" because "my way's cloudy"; "[t]here's fire in de east an' fire in de west" and "fire among de Methodist."[49] Hopkins skips these references and homes in on the prospect of bedevilment of the fallen archangel himself. *Winona* closes as Aunt Vinnie "retired to the kitchen" and sang clearly enough that "her voice came back to [the curious neighbors] in song":

> Ole Satan's mad, an' I'm glad,
> Send de angels down.
> He missed the soul he thought he had,
> O, send dem angels down.
> Dis is de year of Jubilee,
> Send dem angels down.
> De Lord has come to set us free,
> O, send dem angels down.[50]

Hopkins quotes these lines directly from Brown's text, and, unlike the incorporated narrative sections, she sets them off with quotation marks. This is the extent of her signal that the lines themselves are borrowed; like other quotes from poems of Longfellow and from William Shakespeare's *Merchant of Venice* and *The Tragedy of Richard III* that appear in *Winona*, Hopkins does not attribute the lines of the folk song to Brown's text. These literary borrowings, which give the novel substantive literary and historic overtones, recall the creative license that Hopkins accorded herself in *Hagar's Daughter* to great effect. In that work, she also relied on Brown, lifting whole passages from his autobiography and memoir to enrich her reconstruction of the gory and fractious antebellum Southern world. A final assessment of *Winona* should not minimize the complex literary politics and the inspired acts of borrowing that Hopkins performs. However, these assessments should not overshadow the final image of nonnegotiable blackness that concludes the novel.

The issue of racial authority, which remains unresolved through most of *Winona*, finally is addressed when Hopkins steps away from the high drama of politicized warfare and turns instead to the trusted, intimate wisdom of the folk. It is through Aunt Vinnie that Hopkins ultimately achieves the racial authority that she could not realize in Judah, the most manly and capable of original characters that she ever would create. *Winona* begins in a state of racial indeterminacy and familial mayhem; it ends with a return to authentic domesticity, the realm of the African American female provider. It hardly seems coincidental that the name "Vinnie" appears to be derived from Venton, the surname of the white Englishwoman who evokes passion in both of the Carlingford brothers and ultimately seals their awful fate. Both women are central to the plot but once again are constrained severely in their ability to impose narrative control on the his-stories that abound. Miss Venton never materializes in the novel; Aunt Vinnie perennially haunts its margins. Yet, in this tautly structured novel about perpetual recuperation, honorable restorations, and the power of ancestry, Hopkins lodges most power in the folk historian. By so doing, she can insist on the value of the black word in a white world and claim that black historians are well suited to the task of assessing national, public, and private unions.

14

The Souls and Spirits
of Black Folk

Pan-Africanism and Racial Recovery in
Of One Blood and Other Writings

In any case, the modern world must needs remember
that in this age, when the ends of the world are being
brought so near together, the millions of black men in Africa,
America, and the Islands of the Sea, not to speak of the
brown and yellow myriads elsewhere, are bound to have
great influence upon the world in the future, by reason
of sheer numbers and physical contact.
W. E. B. DU BOIS
"To the Nations of the World,"
1900

The regeneration of Africa is upon us,
but blood and tears flow in its train.
PAULINE HOPKINS
"The Dark Races of the Twentieth Century,"
June 1905

Questions about legitimacy, authority, and the power of blackness intrigued and haunted Pauline Hopkins throughout her career as a professional writer and public intellectual. These unruly topics, like relentless articulations of the unconscious, emerged in some of her most popular works. Hopkins grappled in her popular fiction and compelling narrative nonfiction with the complete upheaval wrought by illegitimacy, usurped political power, and underestimated blackness, and contemplated the potential of ennobling ancestry, restorative justice, and cherished race history. She mined the evocative metaphor of darkness, using it both to discuss villainous deeds by dastardly characters and to urge the recollection in fictional and non-fictional contexts of African pasts and ancestors. Hopkins endeavored also to alleviate the darkness, or obscurity of information about Africa, and to illuminate the political, social, intellectual, and material riches of the continent. Such gestures responded directly to those who lamented perpetually inaccessible African histories. As Hopkins's fellow Girls High School alumna Jane Davis Sharp, a teacher and educator who emigrated to Monrovia, Liberia, in the early 1880s, noted, such revelations could be utterly transformative. "I never knew what pride of descent was . . . until I went to Africa," Sharp confessed to Hopkins, before announcing that her African experiences only deepened her belief that "one unfortunate phase of this question of the races is the fact that we do no [*sic*] know enough about our ancestors."[1] Such observations motivated Hopkins to use her role as a public writer and race historian to contribute to a vital African re-education endeavor.

Hopkins began to turn her attention more fully to political and writerly reclamations of Africa by 1902. Her primary contribution to the growing pan-Africanist movement was her solicitation of potential *Colored American Magazine* articles from Africans active in the international conference movements and African expatriate press. Yet, unsurprisingly, Hopkins saw her own major contribution as historical fiction of a mythic and empowered Africa. *Of One Blood*, the third and last of Hopkins's serialized *Colored American Magazine* novels, defied the prevailing literary movement of naturalism and gave readers a blend of fantasy, romance, and local color that included a fantastic view of Africa, acts of mesmerism, and hauntings in the shadow of Harvard College. The novel, which began its yearlong serialization in November 1902 just one month after the death of celebrated naturalist writer Frank Norris, chronicled the change of a melancholy light-skinned man able to pass for white into an optimistic and empowered African demi-god. This elaborate Africanized bildungsroman also advanced Hopkins's belief that women—their history and contemporary lives and work—were central to both African history and to the growing twentieth-century pan-Africanist efforts. *Of One Blood* was most explicit in its celebration of Meroe, a site that Hopkins would extol in 1905 as "the queen city of Ethiopia," the "seat of all ancient greatness," and the "centre of trade between the north and south, east and west," and into which "poured all the caravans of Africa laden with frankincense and gold and fine fabrics."[2] Hopkins crafted a tantalizing vision of a prodigal Ethiopia recovered from "her arrogance and her stiff-necked idolatry," a nation returning to a state of favor with its hands stretched out in earnest supplication to God.

The distinctive core of Hopkins's pan-Africanist fictional enterprise, however, was its juxtaposition of African matriarchal power against African

American female subjugation. *Of One Blood*, like several of Hopkins's earlier works, confronted the devastation that the "peculiar institution" of American slavery brought upon women, girls, and families. Hopkins's incorporation of African and, in particular, Ethiopian and Meroitic histories made possible assertions about nations in which "[q]ueens frequently reigned . . . and royal women were treated with greater respect in the united kingdom than in any other ancient monarchy." She relished the opportunity to enact a corrective and more expansive African history in which there were "celebrated Ethiopian queens," such as those Ethiopian women who, upon their ascension to the throne, became known as Candace and the queen of Sheba, known in Arabic traditions as Bilqis and with whom King Solomon is believed to have inaugurated a monarchical line that included King Menelik.[3] When Hopkins delved into this regal African matriarchal history, her critiques of American antebellum assaults on African American women's virtue, their illegitimized progeny, and suppressed power became all the more melodramatic and the sense of loss and violation that much more graphic and mournful.

Hopkins systematically positioned *Of One Blood* as a reliable fictional interpretation of historical materials on Africa, and more specifically on the Cush kingdom and on Meroe, the ancient capital city. Hers was a bold act of reconstruction, given the historical dearth of original materials on the kingdom about which so little evidence and scholarship existed. The kingdom of Meroe, which spanned some one thousand years, has a history that is regarded by archaeologists and historians as one vital to the history of humankind, and its ruins are believed by many to be "among the great monuments of the ancient world."[4] *Of One Blood* would have recalled for some of Hopkins's readers the earlier nineteenth-century forays into the region. These journeys included "a thin stream of travelers including F. Calliaud, Linan de Belfonds, G. A. Hoskinds, and above all, the great German Egyptologist Karl Richard Lepsius." Unlike the damaging visits of the Italian Joseph Ferlini in 1834, which were "little more than a treasure hunting expedition and resulted in serious damage to the site including the destruction of several pyramids," many early explorers and scholars were more restrained when they "visited Meroe," and they produced "descriptions and drawings of what they saw that remain of fundamental importance both as a record of the condition of the ruins of the major centers of Meroitic civilization at the time of their discovery, and sometimes as the sole surviving evidence of monuments now destroyed."[5]

Hopkins's studies of African history and Meroe enriched *Of One Blood*, and the work in turn may have contributed to the flurry of interest in the ancient city. *Of One Blood* anticipated intriguing published accounts of archaeological explorations of Meroe, such as those that documented the efforts of Sir John Garstang, who from 1910 through 1914 conducted extensive excavations of the city. Garstang's findings confirmed that Meroitic peoples were skilled in ironworking and that their advances in this area enabled them to influence weapon design and tool creations throughout Africa. The scholarship of A. H. Arkell, author of *A History of the Sudan to 1821*, also contained impressive theories about this flourishing city, which was located 120 miles north of where the Blue and White Nile Rivers converge, situated "roughly six hundred miles south of the first cataract of the Nile at Aswan," and "well known in the first millennium B.C.E. and the early first millennium C.E. as an important center of civilization."[6] Hopkins found the elusive romantic history of Meroe appealing, an enterprising and resilient kingdom that had been invoked in foundational Greek histories, cited in Egyptian hieroglyphs, and referenced in Hebrew genealogies of Moses. Indeed, she invested substantially in an African paradise, one that had come to the attention of Western geographers only 130 years prior, following its rediscovery in 1772 by James Bruce.[7] *Of One Blood* gave a powerful and defining role to Meroe, a kingdom not only relegated to the margins of historical scholarship but a civilization that also had a "geographical position on the extreme southern periphery of the ancient civilized world" and whose "separat[ion] from Egypt by the harsh and forbidding terrain of lower Nubia, ensured that the history of contact between it and its northern neighbor would be episodic in character."[8]

The speed with which *Of One Blood* appeared in the *Colored American Magazine*, despite Hopkins's prodigious production of other writings and intensified editorial responsibilities, underscores the deep enthusiasm with which she tackled this multifaceted African and pan-African diasporic subject. She had much to gain for her fictional enterprise from the historical record. Spotty as the published scholarship was, it was rich when she delved into robust African American treatments of the continent, including works by William Wells Brown, George Washington Williams, Martin Delany, and Rufus Perry. *Of One Blood* also gained historical authenticity from its proximity to other key documentary works by Hopkins that preceded or appeared alongside the eleven installments of the novel. The novel began immediately after Hopkins concluded, in October 1902, her pioneering series, "Famous Women of the Negro Race." In that series and the preceding one on illustrious men of the race, Hopkins sharpened her skills as a historian before she began *Of One Blood*. Hopkins thus emerged not only as the author of the brilliant serialized *Of One Blood* but also as a member of the respected set of women historians and educators, which included women like Gertrude Mossell. *Of One Blood* rightly was celebrated by the *Colored American Magazine* as the most recent work of one of the nation's first African American women historians, a writer instrumental to the effort to create a published record of African and African American achievements.

Of One Blood opens in Hopkins's own Cambridge, Massachusetts, but eventually transports readers to Virginia estates, busy British port cities, and mysterious African deserts and elusive buried cities. The protagonist, Reuel Briggs, is a moody medical student who, despite his tendency toward suicidal thoughts, becomes best known among his colleagues for restoring life and reanimating lifeless bodies of patients that his fellow doctors have given up for dead. Reuel, whose name is derived from the Hebrew and means "friend of God," exists as a man with no discernible ties to heaven or to earth. He lives in a sparse apartment located in a "third-rate lodging House near Harvard Square."[9] His room is marked for its "bareness and desolateness," has no carpet, is heated only by a "cylinder stove," and has "ugly white-washed wall[s]." Despite this overwhelming interior melancholy, his quarters manage to "serv[e] both for living and sleeping."[10] Reuel's closest friend at the medical school is a good-looking, wealthy Virginian named Aubrey Livingston who lends Briggs money that enables him to continue his studies. Livingston is the closest friend that Briggs has, but the friendship between the two men highlights Briggs's perpetual powerlessness and indebtedness.

Briggs and Livingston share complicated links to the mysterious Dianthe Lusk, a character provocatively named after the wife of abolitionist John Brown, and to bubbly Molly Vance, sister of a Harvard student who knows Briggs and Livingston, and it is this foursome that fuels the romance, intrigue, and tragedies of the novel. Molly and Aubrey become engaged, but an awful turn of events leads to Molly's death by drowning in the Charles River when her traitorous fiancé refuses to save her and instead rescues Dianthe Lusk. Dianthe Lusk comes into the novel in a series of events that pique the interest of the sober Briggs and his lustful associate, Livingston. Lusk appears first to Reuel as a disembodied and breathy vision and then is seen mounting the stage at the historic Boston Tremont Temple to sing with the touring Fisk Jubilee Singers. On Halloween night, she appears again as Briggs approaches a reportedly haunted house. When she lapses into unconsciousness and is hospitalized, Briggs rescues her from a state of suspended animation and endeavors to ease her recovery from amnesia. Thanks to his urging, she becomes "Felice," a woman with no sense of her past or her African background. The dizzying transformations continue, as Dianthe/Felice is courted by, married to, and then speedily left by Briggs, saved and then "murdered" by Livingston

The Souls and Spirits of Black Folk

so that he can steal her from Briggs, and then resurrected as Livingston's wife. Ultimately, Dianthe is transformed into the long lost daughter of the kingdom of Meroe, but she never fully experiences the privileges and protections due her as a royal princess. Instead, she becomes a tragic heroine, one who allows herself to die by her own forced hand because she cannot imagine herself recovering from her inadvertent acts of bigamy, incest, and attempted murder.

The African narrative in *Of One Blood* begins as a result of Briggs's honorable, if desperate, effort to provide for Dianthe/Felice by embarking on an African exploration. Unfortunately, his journey, which begins just hours after he marries Dianthe, has been orchestrated by Livingston so that he can have access to the vulnerable Dianthe. The African expedition transports Briggs to what he discovers to be his ancestral African home. The kingdom of Meroe, a thriving community that has been waiting for the long-prophesied return of their monarch, hails him as their king. Reuel becomes King Ergamenes, but only after dodging life-threatening encounters with leopards and the clumsy efforts of an undercover contract killer named Jim, who also happens to be a former valet of Briggs's nemesis Aubrey Livingston. Having received news, albeit false information, about the death of his new bride, Dianthe, the newly crowned Briggs pledges to marry a bronze Venus named Queen Candace and to immediately "inaugurate a dynasty of kings."[11] When Reuel's stately mentor Ai provides him with a glimpse into his former American life, the new African king discovers that his wife Dianthe not only is alive but that his former friend Livingston has claimed her for himself.

Hopkins's portrait of Africa also is informed by her naming of Livingston, the villain who ultimately is revealed to be a mixed-race man and not a white Southerner. Hopkins's choice of surname here emphatically recalls Africa and the illustrious Scottish explorer David Livingstone, who achieved what the London *Times* hailed as "one of the greatest geographical explorations of the age."[12] The historical Livingstone was determined to find the source of the Nile, and Hopkins's readers likely would have remembered him in the context of his well-documented 1870 encounter with the intrepid *New York Herald* reporter David Stanley, who, when he encountered the explorer in Tanzania, is said to have uttered the memorable phrase, "Dr. Livingstone, I presume." The University of Glasgow memorialized Livingstone as "a man whose name would be remembered as long as the great lake and the noble rivers he discovered, . . . and who had, perhaps, made the most important advance ever yet made towards the civilisation and the Christianisation of Africa."[13] Hopkins enacts a dramatic inversion of nineteenth-century history, white agency, and African exploration when the fictional Aubrey Livingston commits crimes that compel Africa to seek him out. Livingston is punished for his murderous treachery against Briggs, the newly recovered monarch of Meroe, and for his incestuous relationship and violent manipulation of Dianthe, a woman revealed to be his sister.

Hopkins locates American slavery at the periphery of the central melodramatic plots of *Of One Blood*. The two women who represent that "peculiar institution" and have survived the worst of chattel slavery, however, are the individuals who facilitate the recovery of long-buried Southern histories and reify the connection between Africa and its far-flung descendants. Stalwart Aunt Hannah, the Briggs family historian, outlives the men who have sexually subjugated her and the next two generations of women in her family. Hannah's status as a formerly enslaved woman never diminishes her hold on the glorious African past to which she is linked by a lotus-shaped birthmark on her chest. Hannah's daughter Mira is a more nebulous character, one prone to ghostly appearances and unexpected appearances on the Virginia estate where she once lived. Mira, whose name in Spanish is translated as a command to see or to behold, is a long-suffering woman who has survived the incestuous encounters with a slave master that produced Reuel, Dianthe, and Aubrey. Although a decidedly restless figure, Mira refuses to relinquish her claim on the children from whom she was ruthlessly separated. Her transient state underscores her traumatic exodus from reality, but she endeavors nonetheless to overcome her own pain, and she exhorts Reuel at key moments and comforts her increasingly besieged daughter Dianthe. The life stories of Hannah and Mira are presented as historical ephemera, but their histories haunt the dominant narrative. It is through the unspeakable and invisible stories of these women that Hopkins reenacts antebellum concubinage, child rape, domestic oppression, and savagery. The unflinching narrative gaze and majestic power of this vindicatory narrative recall insistently the testimonies that Hopkins embedded in *Contending Forces* and that made that early novel such a commanding historical and revelatory documentary narrative.

Although *Of One Blood* privileges the masculine and replaces a matriarchal monarchy with a conventional patriarchal structure, Hopkins also wanted to produce a womanist narrative that would assert the enduring power of Africa's women and their inherent value as social historians and moral arbiters. Her besieged tragic heroine, Dianthe Lusk, and the perpetually traumatized Mira were not candidates whom Hopkins could appropriate for this political statement, though. As she grappled with their subjugation in the New World, Hopkins began to invest more deliberately in their recuperation. The Meroitic homeland—symbolic of so many others damaged irrevocably by the Middle Passage and New World bondage—for both women became a restorative cultural balm. Contending with heroines bound by physical scars that seemed to prevent them from transcendent reverse diasporic migrations, Hopkins endeavored to bring Africa to them. Dianthe Lusk never sees the African kingdom to which she belonged, but Hopkins brings it to bear on this character's American life. In this moment of reconnection, Hopkins's tragic heroine achieves a powerful disembodiment, one that allows her to escape the sexualization and trauma that as the child of women enslaved in America she inherits and experiences. Hopkins, whose first published *Colored American Magazine* story, "The Mystery Within Us," confirmed her interest in mesmerism, spiritualist performances, and mysticism, applied elements of these controversial nineteenth-century fields wholeheartedly as she completed *Of One Blood*, a story in which moral triumphs were few and trauma rampant.

Hopkins's appreciation of spiritualism and mesmerism and their powers was linked to the extensive literature and conversations—many of them in New England intellectual circles—about the forms. Her familiarity with the works of Harriet Martineau may have extended to her knowledge of mesmerism as the cure of Martineau's much-discussed dramatic recovery from illnesses that she long imagined as potentially fatal. Hopkins's incorporation of New England spiritualists like Lizzie Doten into her fiction also provides invaluable hints about the public demonstrations that piqued her interest. Unlike Nathaniel Hawthorne, who regarded mesmerism and spiritualism as representative of either "the birth of a new science, or the revival of an old humbug," Hopkins embraced the opportunity to consider the explosive connections between these states and women's abuse and the traumas resulting from acts of sexual aggression.[14] Contemporary late nineteenth- and early twentieth-century conversations in and beyond the academy to which Hopkins had access considered primarily the symptoms, plight, and histories. Recent considerations of *Of One Blood* note Hopkins's invocations of philosopher William James, Harvard professor of philosophy and psychology and author of *The Principles of Psychology* (1890), and her allusions to works of leading practitioners and theorists such as Sigmund Freud and Alfred Binet. Undeterred by her lack of academic credentials, Hopkins makes emphatic use of the prevailing psychoanalytic thought on hysteria, in particular, and considers it in the context of American antebellum realities of sanctioned racially aggressive abuse, sexual predation, and rape of enslaved and free girls and women of African descent. Hopkins's forceful critiques of hysteria and melancholia, which transpire in emphatically historicized milieus, constitute "act[s] of critical memory that both refram[e] the notion of melancholia and resituat[e] the possibilities for African American community."[15] Hopkins's insistent construction of historical frameworks within which she would conduct analyses of melancholia, mesmerism, reanimation, and unresolved trauma underscored her bold engagement with definitive contemporary scholarship. Her efforts to illuminate the deracialized nature of the prevailing discourse also constituted an unprecedented early call to leading figures in the field for more inclusive and rigorous academic and professional analyses and diagnoses.[16] Hopkins's vigorous applications of realism over manifestations of hysteria spoke directly to what William James, a scholar essential to Hopkins's construction of *Of One Blood*, imagined might be the "positive, practical fertility" of current psychoanalysis and its possible application to the relief of human misery."[17]

Even as *Of One Blood* opens and quickly begins to dispel myths about the gendered nature of melancholia and hysteria, Hopkins quickly performs new, although now characteristic, acts of textual veiling. The first hints of overwhelming despair emerge in the shadow of the nation's oldest and most respected institution of higher learning, as one of its medical students, Reuel Briggs, "a close student of what might be termed 'absurdities' of supernatural phenomena or *mysticism*," contemplates the pointlessness of his existence. In his boardinghouse room that is symbolic of the pervasive seamlessness between living and dying—the latter represented here as sleeping—Reuel finds himself harangued by the "tormenting persistency" of "voices and hands . . . beckoning him all day to cut the Gordian knot and solve the riddle of whence and wither for all time." Briggs's current dismay about his "place in the world" and the "eternal movement of all things onward" occurs as he attempts to study, but the natural world enhances his downward spiral and also curtails his contemplation of a major new work that is "eagerly sought by students of mysticism" and one that "deal[s] with the great field of new discoveries in psychology."[18] Although Hopkins suggests that the popular work, entitled *The Unclassified Residuum*, is that of Alfred Binet, the portions quoted in the novel are excerpted from William James's March 1890 *Scribner's Magazine* review, entitled "The Hidden Self," in which he ruminated about the "unconscious mental life" and the scholarship about it.[19] Although Briggs's depression renders him thoroughly lethargic in the face of such work, it is clear that the novel's author is enthusiastic about the "rich reward" to which William James alluded as he encouraged those who might follow a "path of study" inspired by the probing work of French philosophers like Pierre Janet. The novel, whose subtitle honors and directly invokes James's *Scribner's* ruminations, is a sustained and comprehensive consideration of a plagued "double consciousness." Yet, while informed by Du Boisean notions of racial perspectives and contested African genealogies, *Of One Blood* also aspires to solve the mystery emerging from what James hailed as the "ascertain[ment] that the secondary self, or selves, coexist with the primary one, the trance-personalities with the normal one, during the waking state." In 1890, James mulled over the possible outcomes from such new discoveries, suggesting that "just what these secondary selves may be and what are their remoter relations and conditions of existence, are questions to which the answer is anything but clear."[20] These musings resound in *Of One Blood*, a novel defined by the quest to encounter and quiet the damaged secondary self, one troubled by an unspeakable past and vital to a livable present.

Dianthe Lusk and Reuel Briggs, the characters in *Of One Blood* whose shared genealogy ordains decidedly different fates, are the first to animate the mystical scenes in *Of One Blood*. The first scenes feature Reuel, alone in his room near the Harvard University campus, while a storm rages beyond his windows. He sits "with his back half-turned to catch the grateful warmth" from his cylinder stove, while he stares "out into the dim twilight across the square and into the broad paths of the campus, watching the skeleton arms of giant trees tossing in the wind, and the dancing snow-flakes that fluttered to earth in their fairy gowns to be quickly transformed into running streams that fairly overflowed the gutters."[21] The fate of the snowflakes foreshadows the downward spiral that Dianthe soon will endure, from the exotic Fisk Jubilee Troubadours singer to a woman imprisoned in a doubly incestuous relationship. There is no hint of this sexual scandal now, however, and in its absence, the protagonist Reuel Briggs "fell into a dreamy state as he gazed, for which he could not account."[22] Reuel's passivity and lack of agency here create a rare opportunity for one of Hopkins's female characters to prevail. A "passing shadow" appears before Reuel; he attempts to move, but is "power-less."[23] The vision that appears before him has all the markers of whiteness, but, as Hopkins reveals discreetly and in short order, the voluptuous woman that piques Reuel's interest is in fact an embodiment of American blackness. Hopkins grants Reuel a powerful moment of agency in this scene that other-wise overpowers him. It is he who inaugurates the transition into a full visceral and corporeal experience. He sends a "penetrating gaze into the night," and, as he does, "gradually the darkness and storm faded into tints of cream and rose and soft moist lips. Silhouetted against the background of lowering sky and waving branches, he saw distinctly outlined a fair face framed in golden hair, with soft brown eyes, deep and earnest—terribly earnest they seemed just then—rose-tinged baby lips, and an expression of wistful entreaty. O how real, how very real did the passing shadow appear to the gazer!"[24] This highly romantic moment of encounter exudes a lush but unattainable sexu-ality. When Reuel regains his senses, he does so "like a man awakening from a heavy sleep"; he finds himself "alone in the room; all was silence and dark-ness." The female form that he has just beheld, tantalizing even though he saw only her face and had no opportunity to survey her figure, is one that he defines easily and quickly as "the lovely vision of Venus."[25] His characterization is rooted in classical Greek mythology and conjures up traditional European images of a white-skinned beauty. However, at this moment, Hopkins inserts an innovative corrective history, one that veers toward and away from the corrupted Africanized nineteenth-century history of Venus, the story of the South African woman named Saartjie Baartman, who became Sarah Bartman, the Venus Hottentot.

The nineteenth-century history of Sarah Bartman overlays an unequivocal blackness on the evasive, shifting race story that Hopkins dispenses in *Of One Blood*. Bartman was a nineteenth-century legend in her own right, an African who suffered one of the greatest public objectifications when the French scientist Georges Cuvier claimed her smallpox-ridden corpse and subjected it to explicit anatomical investigation.[26] Cuvier transported Bartman's body to the Jardin du Roi and there began "his groundbreaking anatomical study," which he intended would allow him to "decipher her body, to undress the body" through acts of "dissection," since that was, in the nineteenth century, the only procedure through which "the hidden secrets of the body are fully revealed to the medical gaze."[27] After completing his findings, Cuvier was proud to be able to conclude his study of Bartman with the assertion that he "had the honor of presenting the genital organs of this woman to the Académie, prepared in a manner so as not to leave any doubt about the nature" of her sexual organs. Cuvier's research on the body of Sarah Bartman enabled him to become "the first [naturalist] to dissect a black female cadaver of Bartmann's stature and to solve definitely" one aspect of the enduring questions about African female genitalia.[28]

Reuel Briggs in no way approaches the body of Dianthe Lusk as Georges Cuvier sought out the body of Sarah Bartman. However, the encounters that Hopkins stages between Briggs and Lusk do call to mind that awful history of encounter, hyper-sexualization, racial objectification, and punishing isolation. Hopkins creates moments that can be read as correctives of the Bartman tragedy; her scientist reanimates, rather than feasts upon, the bodies of women who have succumbed to disease and abuse. Dianthe's life also stands as an emphatic reversal and purification of the itinerant life to which Bartman was yoked. On the verge of her own death, Dianthe, for example, recalls her persistent itinerancy. As "memories crowded around her, wreathing themselves in shapes which floated mistily through her brain," the beleaguered woman recalls "humble school days at Fisk" and the moments when "her little heart leap[t] at the well-won prize" and she enjoyed "merry play with her joyous mates." She also remembers her wholly satisfying years as a performer that began with the "first triumphant throb when wondering critics praised the melting voice, and world-admiring crowds applauded" and led to "glorious days of travel in Rome and Florence," and "classic scenes of study; intimate companionship with Beethoven, Mozart, and Hayden [*sic*]."[29] Despite Dianthe's ability to recall these portions of her past in such empowering detail and the fact that performance—experienced as her animation of her own self—figures so heavily in these memories, Dianthe ultimately shares a fall into despair, and her self-conscious melancholy once again evokes the history of Bartman. Hopkins laments Dianthe's "fall into unscrupulous hands, and the ruin that had come upon her innocent head," and her observations conjure up aspects of the imposed losses and increasing vulnerabilities that Sarah Bartman also endured.[30] Unfortunately, none of the greatness in Meroe is capable of interrupting the savage sexualization of Dianthe Lusk. The symbolic and historical might of the continent cannot undo her lustful appropriation by an obsessed "brother," nor does it prevent Dianthe's own turn toward self-destruction. Despite these failed, and even unattempted, acts of reclamation, though, Hopkins refuses to allow her tragic heroine to die alone and grants Dianthe access to an African-centered moral authority. The figure of Aunt Hannah, whose bearing and interventions are reminiscent of the mother superior who is essential to the recuperation of Sappho Clark in *Contending Forces*, overlays Dianthe's disgrace and corruption with a purifying maternal love and matri-centric African history.

Hopkins uses *Of One Blood* to explore the deeply contrasting American and African cultural responses to women. The powerful and redemptive actions that Hannah takes lead to her eventual installation as a grand matriarch in Meroe. In the former colonial world of Virginia, though, she can only exist on the margins of civilization, and does so as a hoodoo woman. The true emancipator of *Of One Blood* lives in the woods, and it is in this "natural" realm that her granddaughter Dianthe finally meets her and receives the liberating but damning information about her past. This marginalized matriarch has survived repeated violations, but Hopkins insists that Hannah is a resilient New World link to the old African world embodied by the golden city of Meroe and the hundreds of protected, sanctified virgins who live there. Hopkins's first attempt at description is conservative. She notes that Hannah is "very aged, but still erect and noble in form," and is a woman whose "patched figure was neat to scrupulousness" and whose "eye [was] still keen and searching."[31] Hopkins augments her portrait of Hannah with images borrowed from "The Black Princess (A True Fable of My Old Kentucky Nurse)," by the Kentucky-born poet Sarah Morgan Bryan Piatt, whose work Hopkins had also incorporated into *Contending Forces*.[32] Hopkins uses practically all of the first two stanzas of Piatt's poem to achieve her transformation of Hannah into a figure capable of being romanticized.[33]

The encounters between Dianthe and Aunt Hannah provide closure for three generations of African-descended women: Hannah, her daughter Mira, and her granddaughter Dianthe. Hopkins performs both a textual and a historical reclamation of Dianthe, the woman who believes herself to be an irredeemable pariah. She accomplishes this restoration in a passage that recalls the heart-wrenching deathbed scene that her ancestor Susan Paul recorded in her pioneering 1835 memoir of James Jackson, a gifted freeborn child of color. Scholars of the nineteenth century agree that the moment of dying often afforded individuals an unprecedented access to power. It also was a moment of high performance, often overflowing with spirit-filled exclamations, visions of angelic figures, and irresistible entreaties from heaven to leave the earth behind. Hopkins squarely places Dianthe within this triumphant and sanctified moment of death. As Dianthe continues to suffer from the poison she has ingested, her grandmother Hannah and a devoted maid attend to her. The three women eventually hear an all-encompassing sound that is "[c]lear as the vesper bell" and that gives way to "strains of delicious music, rising and falling in alternate cadence of strong martial measure."[34] In sharp contrast to the localized and private deathbed scenes that dotted antebellum literature, though, Dianthe's death becomes an entirely public and almost apocalyptic moment of transition. "Glorious echoes" first become audible to the women in the sickroom and then become "music as of a might host" that local villagers cannot ignore: "Louder it grew, first in low and wailing notes, then swelling, pealing through arch and corridor in mighty diapason, until the very notes of different instruments rang out as from a vast orchestra. There was the thunder of the organ, the wild harp's peal, the aeolian's sigh, the trumpet's peal, and the mournful horn . . . ever and anon the muffled drum with awful beat precise, the rolling kettle and the crashing cymbals, kept time to sounds like the tramping of a vast but viewless army." The scene intensifies as the sounds signal the steady approach of an unrelenting invisible legion: "Nearer they came. The dull, deep beat of falling feet—in the hall—up the stairs. Louder it came and louder. Louder and yet more loud the music swelled to thunder! The unseen mass must have been the disembodied souls of every age since Time began, so vast the rush and strong the footfalls. And then the chant of thousands of voices swelling in rich, majestic choral tones joined in the thundering crash. It was the welcome of ancient Ethiopia to her dying daughter of the royal line."[35]

The kingdom of Meroe initiates Dianthe's final reanimation, and it is an undeniable restoration that defies the Southern hell in which she has been trapped. She leaps, "[u]pspringing from her couch, as through the air the mighty hallelujah sounded," and she makes "frantic gestures" and has "wild distended eyes" as she "cried": "I see them now! the glorious band! Welcome, great masters of the first world's birth! All hail, my royal ancestors—Candace, Semiramis, Dido, Solomon, David and the great kings of early days and the great masters of the world of song!" In a slightly surprising invocation of the European masters Beethoven and Mozart, Dianthe then asks the African "Divine ones" if they have "come to take me home?" She hopes that it is so, and beseeches them, "O, let me be thy child in paradise!"[36] The novel does not deny Dianthe one last moment of adult romantic desire, even as she requests that she be installed as a "child in paradise." Reuel finally arrives, and when he crosses the threshold of Dianthe's room, she utters "one wild scream of joy," and races into his arms. Hopkins is ever vigilant, even as she crafts this intensely moving and melodramatic scene. She returns to the moment of female mastery of which Dianthe was a part in the novel's opening chapters, and, once again, it is Dianthe who controls the nature of the specular realm. It is with "fond wild tenderness" that she "gazed upon [Reuel], gazed in his anxious eyes until her own looked in his very soul, and stamped there all the story of her guilt and remorse." Once she accomplishes this most primal imprinting, Dianthe finally acquiesces to death and "laid her weary head upon his shoulder and silently as the night passed through the portals of the land of souls."[37] The mighty feminized narrative of *Of One Blood* ends here. In this richly textured final scene, Hopkins allows Africa to reclaim its daughters, and she privileges the female gaze. Hopkins also allows silence to become a realm of peace, one that generously accommodates long-anticipated reunions with the African motherland.

Of One Blood—the first installments were published late in 1902 and appeared just months before *Souls of Black Folk* by W. E. B. Du Bois emerged in 1903—offered full-bodied interpretations of the term "double-consciousness," in which Du Bois also invested heavily. Hopkins's perspectives on African identity, pan-African politics, and African American consciousness, which may well have been informed by Du Bois's newly accessible meditations, had been shaped by vigorous transatlantic debate and intellectual exchanges. Chief among these was the impressive emerging institutionalization of pan-Africanist thought and activism, represented keenly in the organization and proceedings of two historic meetings, the 1893 Chicago Congress on Africa and the 1900 Pan-African Conference in London. These two conventions brought together luminaries of African descent and notable

American and European whites and recalled for some the stirring antislavery meetings in America and England that had invigorated the political cause at hand, reaffirmed the veteran heads of the struggle, and knighted new leaders. The Chicago meeting truly articulated the principles of pan-Africanism and preceded the 1900 moment that Du Bois proposed as the first formal deployment of the term. It was a gathering that the *Chicago Advance* celebrated as "unquestionably one of the most notable convocations of recent years in any country." "We have had pan-Presbyterian, pan-Methodist, pan-Anglican, pan-missionary and pan-Congregational councils," noted the article, but "none signified more than this pan-African conference."[38] Attendees at the weeklong meeting included important African American scholars and accomplished religious leaders such as Alexander Crummell and the Reverend Henry Mc-Neal Turner, as well as well-known race men such as Booker T. Washington. Also participating were African statesmen, such as Edward Wilmot Blyden, the Liberian minister, *Lagos Weekly Record* reporter, *Sierra Leone News* editor, and self-taught and "able and versatile linguist, classicist, theologian, historian, and sociologist" who served as the Liberian ambassador to Britain and France.[39] Both of these meetings sparked and complemented additional African-oriented initiatives. These included, for example, the organization by Gammon Theological Seminary of an African Congress meeting in Atlanta, Georgia, in December 1895, and, under the guiding hand of Trinidadian lawyer Henry Sylvester Williams, the formation of the African Association in England in 1897.[40] The meetings were directly indebted and linked to the flurry of published scholarship on Africa.

Hopkins was familiar with the participants who attended the 1893 and 1900 conferences. Her affiliations with Boston's race groups, such as the Colored National League, facilitated her access to some participants, and her close attention to the domestic and international news events of her day, which refined the political literacies that she brought to the *Colored American Magazine*, ensured her awareness of others. The papers given at the 1893 Chicago meeting, which the African American press commented on widely, included provocatively titled pieces such as "What Do American Negroes Owe to Their Kin beyond the Sea" and other presentations such as "The African in America" and "Liberia as a Factor in the Progress of the Negro Race."[41] The 1900 London meeting, held over a three-day period in late July, brought together thirty-seven delegates from organizations such as the Afro–West Indian Literary Society of Edinburgh, as well as high-ranking African religious leaders such as Bishop Colenso of South Africa, successful African and Afro-European professionals such as the lawyers A. Ribero of the Gold Coast, F. R. S. Johnson, the former Liberian attorney-general, and R. Akinwande Savage, a Nigerian physician from Lagos. The American delegation included two visionary women, Anna Julia Cooper and Anna H. Jones, and the enterprising W. E. B. Du Bois.[42] The London attendees enthusiastically endorsed the conference's eloquently articulated objectives. The larger mission of the meeting was touted as an effort to "bring into closer touch with each other the peoples of African descent throughout the world; second[,] to inaugurate plans to bring about a more friendly relation between the Caucasian and African races; third, to start a movement looking forward to the securing to all African races living in civilized countries their full rights and to promote their business interests."[43] During his three days at Westminster Town Hall, Du Bois served as chair of the conference committee that created the compelling document entitled "To the Nations of the World." It was an appeal that featured for the first time his assertion that "the problem of the twentieth century is the problem of the colour line."[44]

The 1893 Chicago Congress and its most substantial counterpart, the 1900 London conference, were events notable for their predominantly male participants and attendees. However, women like Hopkins and Gertrude E. H. Bustill Mossell ensured that women not only were a part of the formal collective efforts but evaluated them and provided alternative interpretations of the prospects of African vitalization and success. Unlike the Harvard men, W. E. B. Du Bois and William Monroe Trotter, the distinguished Anna Julia Cooper, or other enterprising peers like John E. Bruce, Hopkins was not an active participant in the thriving pan-Africanist conference culture of the early twentieth century. Despite her lack of documented formal participation, though, Hopkins was committed to helping her like-minded peers achieve the goals established by the organizers of the first and historic 1900 conference. The primary goals of those participating in meetings such as the 1900 gathering were fourfold: "[T]to campaign for effective legislation to secure civil and political rights for Africans throughout the world; to encourage educational, industrial and commercial enterprise among peoples of African descent; to produce information and statistics about peoples of Africa and African descent; and to raise funds."[45] In her editorial role at the *Colored American Magazine*, and also later when she contributed to *Voice of the Negro* and became editor of the *New Era Magazine*, Hopkins contributed significantly to these articulated objectives. Her outreach to Africans, such as Plenyono Gbe Wolo, Kwegyir Aggrey, S. F. C. C. Hamedoe, and others, strengthened the intellectual and political clout of the *Colored American Magazine* and later the *New Era Magazine*. Hopkins solicited works that would enable both of these New England journals to offer informative profiles of contemporary and historic African events, politics, and protest. She eagerly took on the role of cultural facilitator and endeavored to provide a rich and intriguing array of materials that could generate more sales of the magazines.

Hopkins became increasingly convinced of the political and cultural potential of literature about Africa, materials that she imagined could help to sustain international attention to the ongoing atrocities throughout the continent by colonial forces. As a woman self-taught in some key anthropological and historical subjects, Hopkins also aspired to provide creative works that were enriched by her own readings of African American canonical studies of Africa and contemporary accounts of explorations, culture, and social Darwinism. *Of One Blood* was produced in the shadow of, if not borne of, the powerful pan-Africanist ideology that was articulated in the 1890s and opening years of the 1900s. Hopkins, the writer and passionate scholar, turned to the rich canon of African American writings about Africa as she developed the perspectives that would shape her creative writing. Her immersion in this field of historical, anthropological, and race literature certainly was shaped by the male-dominated political discussions that occurred in and beyond the Chicago and London conferences. Also shaping her understanding of the stakes and issues were feminist evaluations of African and African-American "literary ventures." One of the most notable of these feminist texts was *The Work of Afro-American Women*, the sophisticated volume that Mossell published first in 1894, a work that began with a deliberate and stately preface, to which the author appended "A List of Afro-American Publications." The unadorned bibliography included references to over seventy works by authors such as Phillis Wheatley, James Monroe Whitfield, William Wells Brown, Josiah Henson, I. Garland Penn, Ida B. Wells, Daniel Payne, and Frances Harper. The list was an essential guide for anyone striving to gain familiarity with the central African American texts, and Mossell invited all who perused it to inform her of "the names of omitted volumes" so that she could incorporate them "in a possible future edition."[46] Mossell provided for Hopkins an invaluable model of scholarship and strategic historical assessment, and Hopkins enthusiastically applied it in her writings on Africa. Mossell's bibliographies include works that likely informed *Of One Blood* and that certainly figured prominently in Hopkins's subsequent Africa writings, including her 1904 *Voice of the Negro* ethnological writings and her 1905 *Primer of Facts Pertaining to the Early Greatness of the African Race*. The most foundational texts for Hopkins, and ones that she privileged in her writings, included Martin Delany's 1879 *Origin of Races*, also known by its full title, *Principia of Ethnology: The Origin of Races and Color*; William Wells Brown's *The Rising Son; or, The Antecedents and Advancement of the Colored Race*; Rufus Perry's *The Cushite; or, The*

Descendants of Ham; and George Washington Williams's 1880s *History of the Negro Race in America.*

Hopkins's 1905 political manifesto, *A Primer of Facts Pertaining to the Early Greatness of the African Race and the Possibility of Restoration by Its Descendants — with Epilogue Compiled and Arranged from the Works of the Best Known Ethnologists and Historians,* illuminates the ways in which Hopkins was conceptualizing the African landscape and history so essential to the race triumphs and social critiques in her serialized novel. The *Primer of Facts* revisits the history and Africanist agendas of *Of One Blood* and allows a more full articulation of the serialized novel that, interestingly enough, Hopkins did not cite in the list of her works on the primer's cover.[47] Readers of the *Primer of Facts* are assured, however, that each of the pamphlet's seven chapters and the lengthy epilogue have been "Compiled and Arranged from the Works of the Best Known Ethnologists and Historians by Pauline E. Hopkins."[48] The pamphlet embarks on an intensive educational intervention by employing catechismal questions throughout. Readers are alternately grilled and enlightened about the creation of humankind, early governments, the origins of the races, biblical prophecy, African political and religious history, and literary references to Ethiopia. The sequence of chapters, offered practically, are titled "Original Man," "Division of Mankind into Races," "The Brotherhood of Man or the Origin of Color," "Early Civilization of the Africans," "Progress in Religion and Government," "Progress in Science, Art, and Literature," and "Restoration."

Launched by the newly established Cambridge publishing house of P. E. Hopkins, the *Primer of Facts* was imagined as the first in a series entitled "Black Classics." The pamphlet was an ambitious compendium of historical facts, political critique, biblical exegesis, and racial exhortation. Hopkins addressed both "facts" and "theory" embedded in biological and social constructions of race and global histories of power and dominion. Her opening analyses advanced traditional readings of Old Testament scriptures and highlighted Hopkins's investment in the New Testament declaration that God "hath made of one blood all nations of men for to dwell on all the face of the earth."[49] As she reviewed a substantial body of literature, scholarship, and myths, Hopkins consistently equipped her readers to study the material themselves. Focused and pithy questions formatted in block capital letters spanned the entire primer, and each could engage and inform both culturally and biblically illiterate readers and sophisticated learned individuals. Questions included "What was the Original Man?" "How many sons had Cush?" "What other cause is sometimes given by writers for the color of the African and his descendants?" and "What may be said of the Ethiopians in literature?" Hopkins confidently used a range of sources that demonstrated her broad reading as well as her capacity for synthesis, analysis, and critique. Hopkins rehearsed familiar biblical discourses of racial origins in the first four chapters, moving on from declarations that "[u]ntil the entry of Noah's family into the ark, all people were of the one race and complexion" in the opening statements of chapter 1 to detailed delineations of the sons of Ham and their governance of lands in "the land of Midian" and within "the Nilotic borders of Egypt in toward the interior of darkest Africa, and known as Ethiopia."[50]

The *Primer of Facts* gradually gained in political intensity and barely suppressed outrage at perspectives that obstructed the greatness of Africa and undermined and discounted the potential of its far-flung descendants. Hopkins's authoritative voice dominated fully by the final chapter and epilogue, and she shifted noticeably from historical critiques to engagement with materials that exemplified the problematic dimensions of both liberal and conservative white analyses of race relations. Having moved from discussions of classic texts by Heliodorus and Diodorus that buttressed her claims of what John Cullen Gruesser so eloquently describes as a "usable African past," Hopkins used a list of "phenomenally intellectual" men and women "produced in Africa and America" to transition her critique from ancient histories to current assessments of American race realities and interactions.[51] She focused on science, art, and literature and also included lists of Revolutionary War patriots by name and Civil War patriots, including nine well-known and tested African American regiments. The Africanist honor roll included native Africans and American-born individuals, as well as those born into bondage, those who achieved freedom, and those who were born free. The forty-two named individuals were not new to those familiar with Hopkins's writings; indeed, she had profiled many of them in her *Colored American Magazine* articles or solicited their work or works about them for the periodical. Hopkins did make special mention of those with native or unmixed African origins, such as the Reverend Tiyo Soga, father of her fellow *Colored American Magazine* contributor A. Kirkland Soga, whom she designated as "Native Kaffir"; and the Reverend Mojolo Agbebi, a "Learned Divine, Orator, Missionary," who was the founding pastor of the first independent church in Lagos, Nigeria. She also advanced the African lineages of Henry Highland Garnet, whose father was a Mandingo prince and whom she claimed as a man of "Pure African descent," and the West Indian–born Dr. Edward Wilmot Blyden, whom she categorized as "Native West African."[52] Citations of these accomplished heads of state, learned philosophers and educators, gifted artists, and ambitious scientists might almost have rendered unnecessary Hopkins's question about the possible fulfillment of biblical prophecies about Ethiopia's reemergence. Yet she forged ahead, citing "the many significant happenings of the past few years," calling for "Africans in America" to "help forward the time of restoration," and to do so not through emigration, necessarily, but by "becoming thoroughly familiar with the meagre details of Ethiopian history, by fostering race pride and an international friendship with the Blacks of Africa" and through "[f]riendly intercourse and mutual aid and comfort."[53]

Hopkins ultimately wields the *Primer of Facts* as a political tool, and its epilogue changes dramatically in tone and focus. She addresses problematic extensions of Washingtonian-like accommodationism, such as that espoused just three years earlier by the Reverend Charles H. Parkhurst, a Presbyterian minister and Framingham, Massachusetts, native, who in 1892 blasted corruption, licentiousness, and vice.[54] Hopkins took direct aim at Parkhurst's suggestion that the acquisition of African American rights would be possible if "the Negro talks [less] about civic rights under the constitution, particularly the right of suffrage," and at his patronizing account of interracial efforts, writing that "[t]he Northern and Southern friends of the Negro are now counselling him to keep quiet upon the whole suffrage matter, to keep out of politics, not to talk about the constitution, not to insist upon his rights, but to attend industriously to the work of getting himself well read—which he is not now—for what God and the country and the future have in store for him."[55] She barely restrains her outrage, though, when she considers the "work of Southern whites against the Negro." Rather than critique leading white citizens and prominent elected officials, though, Hopkins lambastes Jeannette Robinson Murphy, a Southern white woman whose works on African music, African American spirituals, and race relations had appeared in *Century Magazine* and *Appleton's Popular Science Monthly*, as well as in the 1904 monograph, *Southern Thoughts for Northern Thinkers [and] African Music in America*. Hopkins devoted considerable space to Murphy and incorporated lengthy quotes that illuminated what she regarded as narrow-minded, ill-informed, and decidedly divisive perspectives on race, culture, and history. Empowered by the formidable African history laid out in the early chapters of the *Primer of Facts* and bolstered further by the indisputable lists of Negro success, Hopkins took direct aim at Murphy's simplistic references to history and her shallow comments on the realities of African American advancement, noting, for example, that Murphy believed that "[i]nstead of the South wasting any more of its hard-earned money upon the impossible higher education of the Negroes, let us give them as a whole domestic training and sound Bible teaching," and then "expend all our surplus money and energy in colonizing the race somewhere as Abraham Lincoln suggested." Murphy proposed that one "temporary" site might be New England, "since the historic underground railroad has already given the Negro a taste for travel," and that that relocation might provide "the race" with "a chance to show if it is really capable of self-government and higher culture."[56] Hopkins's response to such "desire and commands" of "enemies" like Murphy was to rally the race to claim the ballot: "We cannot cease from agitation while our wrongs are the sport of those who know how to silence our every complaint and plea for justice. NEVER SURRENDER THE BALLOT."[57]

The professional challenges that Hopkins weathered in the months leading up to the publication of the *Primer of Facts* certainly intensified her outrage in the face of accommodated or, as she identified it in the *Primer of Facts*, socially sponsored racism that was preventing full and frank discussions of the "burning question" of race and the "iron heel of oppression." Hopkins made it plain, both as a novelist and as a pamphleteer, that "abject submission" to political and racial intimidation was not acceptable. She commandeered the written word, as *Of One Blood* and *Primer of Facts* confirmed so decisively. In her own works and in the activism and writings of others whom she cultivated as colleagues, Pauline Hopkins proved that activism, assertive citizenship, and rigorous re-education constituted a potent triple threat to white supremacy and privilege.

15

Witness to the Truth

The Public and Private Demise of the
Colored American Magazine

The people must know before they can act,
and there is no educator to compare with the press.

IDA B. WELLS
The Free Speech,
21 May 1892

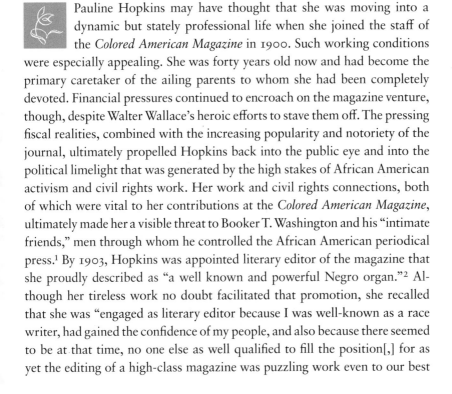

Pauline Hopkins may have thought that she was moving into a dynamic but stately professional life when she joined the staff of the *Colored American Magazine* in 1900. Such working conditions were especially appealing. She was forty years old now and had become the primary caretaker of the ailing parents to whom she had been completely devoted. Financial pressures continued to encroach on the magazine venture, though, despite Walter Wallace's heroic efforts to stave them off. The pressing fiscal realities, combined with the increasing popularity and notoriety of the journal, ultimately propelled Hopkins back into the public eye and into the political limelight that was generated by the high stakes of African American activism and civil rights work. Her work and civil rights connections, both of which were vital to her contributions at the *Colored American Magazine,* ultimately made her a visible threat to Booker T. Washington and his "intimate friends," men through whom he controlled the African American periodical press.[1] By 1903, Hopkins was appointed literary editor of the magazine that she proudly described as "a well known and powerful Negro organ."[2] Although her tireless work no doubt facilitated that promotion, she recalled that she was "engaged as literary editor because I was well-known as a race writer, had gained the confidence of my people, and also because there seemed to be at that time, no one else as well qualified to fill the position[,] for as yet the editing of a high-class magazine was puzzling work even to our best scholars."[3] Her "unique position" as an African American "woman editor" had prompted some of her supporters to be "chivalrous in their desires to help" her sustain, if not improve, the magazine's circulation and prominence. The *Colored American Magazine* staff was adamant that its race politics would not be sacrificed in order to achieve some semblance of fiscal stability. That stance, which Hopkins shared, would make her especially vulnerable in the increasingly volatile and male-dominated intraracial war that pitted spirited antiaccommodationists, many of whom were based in Boston, against the allies of Booker T. Washington, the Wizard of Tuskegee.

The public race work that Hopkins performed in the early 1900s and that raised her profile as a formidable public intellectual and activist, occurred in and beyond the *Colored American Magazine*. Just as she was formally recognized as literary editor, she began to move in Boston's most distinguished and powerful political circles. In the spring of 1903, the Boston Literary and Historical Association, one of the city's recently established and most progressive new societies, invited Hopkins to lecture before its distinguished audiences. The invitation was significant, especially because many association members belonged to Boston's most radical political sectors. Eloquent, cultivated, and credentialed members, such as William Monroe Trotter, Archibald Grimké, George Washington Forbes, Clement Morgan, and Butler Wilson, shaped New England's African American early twentieth-century political agenda. Modern-day Garrisonians, these individuals were determined to achieve immediate emancipation for all those who were denied their freedoms—economic, educational, political, and social. Hopkins welcomed the prospect of participating in the spirited association gatherings and of reinforcing her reputation as a spirited and capable race woman.

The Boston Literary and Historical Association, established in 1901, was a product of the city's African American intellectual and professional elite. Its founders, William Monroe Trotter and Archibald Grimké, were two dashing and highly educated men who were well known within and beyond Boston. Trotter, an 1895 graduate of Harvard University and the nation's first African American Phi Beta Kappa, was editor of *The Guardian* and a man establishing himself as the "most relentless Boston critic" of Booker T. Washington.[4] Grimké, the first president of the association, was an attorney, nephew of white South Carolina abolitionists Angelina and Sarah Grimké, and the father of future poet, playwright, and teacher Angelina Weld Grimké. According to Trotter, the association was established in order to "improve and quicken the intellectual life of the Colored people of Boston and to have a body to represent their best interests."[5] It actively promoted the values of higher education and sought to admit members who were actively committed to racial advancement and uplift. Association by-laws confirm the intellectual urgency that motivated founders and members, and one of the most eloquent declarations reads that the association's "special purpose is to arouse men and women to the grave danger of mental starvation as a result of their absorption in the strife of commercialism so characteristic of the age." Founders also recognized the importance of asserting and claiming the past, which would enhance their claims on the present day. To support their campaigns for civil rights and civic equality, they stipulated that another "special purpose" of the organization was to "collect and preserve hitherto ungarnered data of historical value to so-called colored Americans."[6] The association's dual mission and its full acceptance of women as members, officers, and speakers made it a logical partner with Hopkins and her *Colored American Magazine* colleagues.[7]

The association did have concerns about Booker T. Washington's prominent industrial education model and the social and racial stratifications on which his systems depended and were authorized.[8] Certainly, these issues explain in part why association forums demonstrated and focused on intellectual advancement, high culture, and the diversity of African American political opinion. However, the impressive range of lectures delivered by accomplished academics and professionals also grew out of a substantial antebellum Boston tradition of spirited intellectual debate and cultural performance. During the mid-1800s, William Cooper Nell and others established organizations such as the Adelphic Literary Union and the Afric-American Female Intelligence Society to encourage literary pursuits, academic development, and professional interests in the African American community. The Boston Literary and Historical Association successfully modernized the intellectual consortiums that Boston's antebellum community of color had used to honor, celebrate, and enrich its members. Its impressive roster of speakers between 1901 and 1905 included community leaders, clubwomen, scholars in the humanities and social sciences, ministers, and judges. Association audiences gathered to hear from the gifted mathematician Kelly Miller of Howard University, the Reverend Francis J. Grimké, Judge Robert H. Terrell, Charles Chesnutt, Albert Bushnell Hart—a white Harvard University historian and the former academic adviser to W. E. B. Du Bois, ministers from Congregational and AME Zion churches in Salem and Cambridge, respectively, and Du Bois himself, who returned again to the warm welcome that he had come to expect from Bostonians.[9]

The spring 1903 association calendar that featured Hopkins was begun just two months earlier by W. E. B. Du Bois, then an Atlanta University professor of economics and history, who was on the threshold of seeing his influential *Souls of Black Folk* appear later that spring. He was enjoying a growing reputation as a "distinguished Negro thinker."[10] The lecture he delivered as the association's first spring 1903 event, entitled "Outlook for the Darker Races," gave Bostonians a tantalizing glimpse of the elegant analyses that shaped *Souls of Black Folks*, a work that would appear six weeks after Hopkins appeared before association audiences. Du Bois, reiterating his incisive statements about the politics of the color line, exhorted his audience to "do away with the Color line, to strive to the end that the dominant whites may be willing to give the dark skinned individual the place in social, civil, religious, and in political life that his individual merits entitle him to without regard to the condition of his race or class."[11] Hopkins, who was most likely part of the large contingent of Bostonians who flocked to hear him speak, may well have felt once again an intellectual kinship with Du Bois. The sentiments that he espoused about the importance of equal opportunity echoed the last and most emphatic points that she herself had articulated in the 1902 close to her series, "Famous Women of the Negro Race."

One of the "prominent intellectuals" who appeared before the association and the "city's black elite," Hopkins participated on Monday, 9 March 1903, in the season's only symposium.[12] Her fellow panelists, Agnes Adams, Olivia Ward Bush, and Addie H. Jewell, were well-known Bostonians and active club women who were highly familiar with Hopkins and the *Colored American Magazine*. Jewell, a future association vice president, had penned a detailed review of Hopkins's reading of *Contending Forces* chapters, and Hopkins had recruited Adams and Bush to publish in early issues of the *Colored American Magazine*. Hopkins's participation in the symposium represents one of the first known moments when she was formally invited to participate in the upper echelons of African American society. Despite her impressive genealogy and the central role that her New England ancestors had played as abolitionists, educators, and activists on the international stage, she had remained on the margins of Boston's professional and social elite.

Hopkins's prominent contributions to the Boston Literary and Historical Association programming helped to consolidate her place in New England's anti-Washington circles. There were some bold suggestions from some quarters that the association in fact was "intended by its founders to be a direct attack on the leadership and racial politics of Booker T. Washington and his by-then considerable 'Tuskegee Machine.'"[13] It may have had such priorities, but the association consistently offered succinct assessments of its goals, and the programs distributed at events noted simply that the society's "purpose, briefly stated[,] is 'to promote the intellectual life of the community.'"[14] The roster of speakers did not all share antipathy for Booker T. Washington. Professor Albert Hart made several overtures to Washington in the late

1890s, tried earnestly to forge a connection between his former dissertation advisee, Du Bois, and Washington, and even facilitated the Tuskegee leader's early interactions with future president Woodrow Wilson.[15] Francis Grimké, another association speaker, was an enthusiastic supporter of Washington during and after Reconstruction. However, by the early 1900s, Washington's muted response to widespread African American disenfranchisement prompted Grimké to join the national conversations, including those held as part of the National Negro Conference of 1900 that led to the formation of the NAACP in 1909. Grimké's past, which included his history as a formerly enslaved man and former valet to a Confederate officer, as well as his undergraduate triumphs at Lincoln University, and professional success as the longtime pastor of Fifteenth Street Presbyterian Church of Washington, D.C., also confirmed that the association was not promulgating escapist and unrealistic ideas about African American history and the future development of the race. Grimké's gripping and well-known past was yet another way in which the reality of enslavement and the legacy of abolitionist activism continued to educate the postbellum African American communities and to shape the politically informed intellectual work of activist communities such as those established in Boston. Grimké's storied life and purposeful turn toward progressive race politics also highlighted the allure of advancement that Washington, who enrolled his daughter at Wellesley College rather than at Tuskegee Institute, also appreciated. Judge Robert Terrell, husband of the influential Mary Church of Memphis, was one of the Tuskegee president's "adherents" and "loyal friends." Indeed, Terrell's appointment to the Washington, D.C., bench, where he became the first African American judge in the district's history, was directly due to Washington, whose endorsement and "arrangement" made it possible for the law school graduate and principal of M Street High School to make history.[16]

Pauline Hopkins's lectures before the Boston Literary and Historical Association brought invitations to speak at St. Mark's Musical and Literary Union, the second of Boston's two most prominent turn-of-the-century African American societies. Founded in the spring of 1902, St. Mark's had close ties to the Boston Literary and Historical Association. Its first president was Maude Trotter Steward, wife of Charles Steward, a Boston dentist, and future president of the Boston Literary and Historical Association. She was also the sister of William Monroe Trotter, the association's cofounder and editor of *The Guardian*. Yet St. Mark's Union evolved as a distinctive women's organization, one in which artistic and literary women such as Maude Cuney Hare, an accomplished musician, an educator, and one of the members of the Union's executive committee, created the agenda and calendar of events.

Some may have regarded it as a female auxiliary to the Boston Literary and Historical Association, but it forged its own reputation as an autonomous organization that had "for its object the moral and intellectual improvement of the community."[17] Through its home at St. Mark's Congregational Church, the organization also had ties to the Garrisonian past that continued to influence Hopkins and many other New Englanders. Founded in 1895, it first was known as the William Lloyd Garrison Memorial Church.[18] The Union, which operated from October through May of each year, held its Sunday afternoon meetings in rooms at the church's Tremont Street location in Roxbury. On 27 December 1903, Hopkins was the keynote speaker scheduled to address Union members. It is likely that she continued to receive invitations to speak, but the events surrounding the tumultuous battle for ownership and distribution of the *Colored American Magazine* may have effectively absorbed her completely during that two-year period. It would be 1905, some two years hence and in a most significant city forum, before Pauline Hopkins would appear again as a public speaker.

In late 1903, as she participated in meetings such as those hosted by St. Mark's Musical and Literary Union, Hopkins was working diligently at the *Colored American Magazine* and drafting a provocative call for submissions that would enable the magazine to publish "material from writers of prominence and influence."[19] What she developed in 1903 anticipated what would just over two decades later be one of the most memorable cultural debates that her contemporary, W. E. B. Du Bois, with his trusted editor Jessie Fauset, would stage in the *Crisis*, the journal of the National Association for the Advancement of Colored People. In 1926, Du Bois, who may have recalled Hopkins's idea for the series and her successful solicitation of him for a contribution, collaborated with Fauset and solicited from writers such as Countee Cullen, Sinclair Lewis, H. L. Mencken, and Walter White articles that would be suitable for inclusion in a series, "The Criteria for Negro Art." Du Bois and Fauset were responding to the tendency toward self-indulgent, untamed, representations of African American life that increasingly rankled Du Bois, who prided himself on creating and soliciting works that upheld high cultural depictions and insights about black culture.

Hopkins, perhaps reinvigorated by her proximity to antiaccommodationists at the Boston Literary and Historical Association, focused on the politics of industrial education and its ramifications for African American society and advancement. The limited resources of the *Colored American Magazine* required that she be thoroughly enterprising. Knowing that she had no funds with which to offer payment for articles, she developed "a circular which [she] knew would touch the people in a kindly vein" and solicited essays on "[i]ndustrial education; will it solve the negro problem?" The primarily male public figures that Hopkins contacted included an array of African American, African, and white editors, educators, and writers, such as Booker T. Washington's nephew and the man who would usurp her place as *Colored American Magazine* editor, Roscoe Conkling Bruce, W. E. B. Du Bois, William Lloyd Garrison, Howard University professor Kelly Miller, J. Kirkland Soga, and poet Ella Wheeler Wilcox. The series worked well, both as an intellectual venture and as a financial enterprise. Only Miller charged a fee for his work, and William Dupree, the president of the Colored Co-operative Publishing Company, was "greatly pleased with [her] success."[20]

The growing scrutiny of the political literature published in the *Colored American Magazine* signaled the increasingly explicit link between the magazine's success and its political identity. Dupree, a veteran of the heroic Massachusetts Fifty-fifth Regiment and successful superintendent of Station A., a branch of the U.S. Postal Service, began to take a great interest in preserving the right to free speech for the *Colored American Magazine* writers. He also was committed to creating a visible united political front for the magazine, one that would signal to opposition forces that the magazine had the support of vigilant African Americans for whom the journal was a proud extension of their own activism. From 1901 through 1904, when the magazine was wrested away to New York City and a pro-Washington staff, Hopkins built a strong relationship with Dupree and benefited from his efforts to preserve the literary and editorial integrity of the magazine. Her connection to him also improved her access to William Monroe Trotter. Dupree and William's father, James, were relatives through marriage. Both shared family connections to the Monticello estate of Thomas Jefferson and a Civil War history as officers of the Fifty-fifth Massachusetts Regiment, and both had survived the battle at Honey Hill that in its first thirty minutes claimed the lives of one hundred soldiers in the African American regiment.[21]

Dupree, a Petersburg, Virginia, native, had been president of the Colored Co-operative Publishing Company board since July 1901, a moment when the officers concluded that the "reports of the several departments of the business showed great progress for the first year's work."[22] Hopkins and her colleagues believed earnestly that Dupree held "a position worthy of his history and one which will aid the race materially."[23] In July 1901, the magazine featured a highly complimentary profile of their company president, one likely authored by Hopkins, who at the time was publishing her "Famous Men of the Negro Race" series.[24] The biography portrayed Dupree's patriotism, demonstrated commitment to racial uplift, entrepreneurial strengths, and substantial political prominence in New England and established him as a mighty defender of the Colored Co-operative Publishing Company and the jewel in its crown, the *Colored American Magazine*.[25] Dupree also had considerable influence in white circles, achieved primarily through his work at the U.S. Postal Service, where he rose through the ranks to oversee the city's second-largest postal station and supervise a predominantly white staff of "fourteen clerks and forty-four carriers," who carried out "a business in stamps and other sales of $100,000 and money orders to the amount of $125,000."[26] In addition, he had the immense respect of high-ranking white Massachusetts public officials and was appointed in 1890 by Governor John Q. A. Brackett as chairman of the otherwise all-white group of commissioners charged with disbursing the Firemen's Relief Fund of Massachusetts. His *Colored American Magazine* biographer assured readers that Dupree could have "undoubtedly secured the position" of state auditor—that he had been "mentioned for the office" and would have been appointed "if he had been persistent."[27] At the *Colored American Magazine*, Hopkins and the staff championed Dupree, believing him well equipped to fight for "the maintenance of the rights of all men," the issue that they regarded as the primary "battle-ground of the twentieth-century Negro."[28]

In late 1903, one of Dupree's Postal Service colleagues and "a man of noble character," knowing of his interest in racial matters, called his attention to "a series of articles which had been printed in a New York paper on the condition of the Negroes in the Island of Jamaica, in the British West Indies." The articles, by John Christian Freund, a portly white newspaper editor and music critic of German ancestry, excited Dupree, primarily because "there are some seven hundred thousand colored people and, in all, about fourteen to fifteen thousand whites" living in the island nation. He obtained copies of Freund's work, "read them through," and then "thought it would be a good thing if we could induce Mr. Freund to permit us to republish them in our magazine."[29] Freund was delighted by the prospect and speedily granted the request for republication. His letter to Dupree also contained "a promise of material help to testify to his good will towards our enterprise." As Hopkins confirmed later, Freund "gave us the articles, furnished cuts of a size suitable for our magazine and gave us $15 per month toward defraying the expense of manufacturing same."[30] The correspondence that ensued between Dupree and Freund and with "the editor of our magazine, Miss Hopkins," Dupree recalled, soon led to Freund's statements that "he would be glad to be of service to us and expressed a desire to meet some of the representative colored people of Boston, so we might lay out some comprehensive plan of action."[31]

A festive formal dinner at the renowned Revere House in Boston, hosted by Freund, was arranged to achieve these very goals.

The March 1904 issue of the *Colored American Magazine* featured Pauline Hopkins's thoroughly detailed account of the January gathering at the Revere House. Her thoughts about it evolved substantially; in hindsight, one year after the event, she regarded as the first in a series of cataclysmic events that led to the undoing of the publication to which she and her colleagues had committed their energies so completely. Hopkins's private recollection of the Revere House dinner figures prominently in the single most explosive item of her extant correspondence.[32] Dated 16 April 1905 and addressed to William Monroe Trotter, this letter is the single-most-damning account of how the *Colored American Magazine* was targeted and infiltrated. It provides an unprecedented view of the magazine's office dynamics and of the interchanges that occurred between Hopkins, the editorial staff, and influential members of the board. What emerges is an absorbing account of the intense race politics with which the magazine had to contend and the intellectual attacks that Hopkins did her best to withstand.

The Revere House dinner, reported Hopkins, left the *Colored American Magazine* staff feeling "greatly surprised not to say overwhelmed by the honor thrust upon us."[33] The location of the dinner alone was significant. It was held at one of the city's best hotels, the former mansion of Kirk Boott, the founder of the Massachusetts town of Lowell and the site to which novelist and *Atlantic Monthly* editor William Dean Howells sent Bartley Hubbard and his wife, Marcia, the ill-fated newlywed protagonists of his 1882 novel *A Modern Instance*, when they arrived in Boston shortly after their ceremony.[34] Located in Bowdoin Square, the Revere House had hosted American presidents Millard Fillmore and Ulysses S. Grant, celebrated divas Jenny Lind and Adelina Patti, and the Prince of Wales, the future King Edward VII, when he visited the city in 1860. By the 1890s, it had become a fashionable site for elegant dinners for groups such as the Mermaid Club, a Harvard University drama society.[35] The house also was "celebrated in the annals of the abolition movement." On this occasion, however, the evening in many ways represented for Hopkins and her fellow guests the beginning of a political bondage for the magazine and the irreversible loss of the dream that its four idealistic Virginia founders and their devoted supporters had worked so hard to realize. Pauline Hopkins became the de facto historian of the *Colored American Magazine* and its efforts to survive the "distressing experiences" that threatened the founders' "heroic endeavor to keep the magazine alive."[36] She recounted positively for *Colored American Magazine* subscribers, and later with outrage for William Monroe Trotter, the spirited toasts, thoughtful speeches, and ambitious plans

John C. Freund, editor of the *Musical Times*, whom the
Colored American Magazine staff referred to as "Papa Freund"
when he first became their patron. Freund, who directly
challenged Hopkins's work and activism, initiated the undoing
of the *Colored American Magazine* and its relocation to
New York City. *Courtesy of Library of Congress,
Arnold Genthe Collection.*

discussed that led to a formal place for "Papa Freund," as he came to be called, and the creation of the Colored American League, whose members would "do everything in their power to aid the work [of the magazine] by personal efforts for subscription and business."[37]

The man who introduced himself to the *Colored American Magazine* emphasized his literary upbringing, lengthy career as a music journalist, and capacity for objectivity about American race relations, as a result of his inter-

Witness to the Truth

national experiences and perspectives. Born in 1848 in London to German parents, Freund was the son of J. C. H. Freund, a physician "of great note," and Anna Louise Freund, a writer who published under the pseudonym of Louisa Lewis.[38] His mother's literary connections and his father's prominence often meant that luminaries of the day visited the family home. One of Freund's favorite childhood recollections was of the time when Lajos Kossuth, the Hungarian revolutionary leader, "took him on his knee, and told him of his grief." He also delighted in telling the story of his encounter with Thomas Carlyle, the Scottish writer and mathematician who, "with a rich Scottish burr," responded memorably when Freund "expressed his firm ambition to become a writer." Freund recollected that Carlyle's vigorous response was "What! Ye want to be a writer! Better be a bricklayer, or tinker, a tailor or a candlestick maker. It took me years to write ma' History o' Frederick the Great' an' in those years I nearly starved."[39] Freund studied music at Oxford University before emigrating to the United States in the early 1870s. The *Chicago Daily Tribune* would report in its obituary notice for him that Freund graduated from Oxford, but he in fact attended only for three years and left before obtaining a degree.[40] While there, he edited the literary magazine *Dark Blue* and during his tenure published works by Algernon Charles Swinburne, Dante Gabriel Rossetti, and William Morris.[41] Despite his immersion in aspects of school life, Freund maintained that he endured a difficult childhood and also painful years as a student in the British system. He "felt the prejudice," he recalled, "that existed at that time in England, and particularly in the English schools and universities, against the man with a foreign name, who had anything but orthodox, Protestant-Episcopalian blood in his veins." He came to America, he said, in part because he "had been told there was neither prejudice of caste, nor prejudice of religion, nor prejudice of race, but where a man could make himself what his ability, his industry and his courage entitled him to be."[42] When he discovered the fallacies of that description of the United States, however, he "took an ever increasing interest in the colored race problem, not because . . . I have any particular interest in the colored people of such," he declared, but "because of the principles which had appealed to me, and because I believed that a man should be what he makes himself, whether his face be white or black, his hair straight or kinky, his eyes blue or brown, whether his nose curves one way or the other."[43]

Freund's career as a musical editor began in 1871, when he joined the staff of the *Musical and Dramatic Times*. In the 1890s, he launched a series of music magazine ventures. In 1890, he began publishing the commercial magazine *Music Trades*. In 1898, he established *Musical America*, his most successful venture. The weekly magazine that he began on the eve of the twentieth century exists today as *Musical America International*, a web-based directory of the performing arts.[44] Freund published thirty-six issues of the journal, from October 1898 through June 1899, before halting distribution for six years. In mid-November 1905, having "martialed financial support" for the magazine, he and his colleague Milton Weil began publishing weekly editions once again. The revitalized issues focused entirely on music, and the journal enjoyed consistent publication for nearly twenty-five more years. Three years before his death, in 1924, Freund published the first edition of a comprehensive volume known as the Guide, a directory that was "the forebear of the current International Directory of the performing Arts" and that was "organized by state, listing cities and their local newspapers, managers, hotels, and railroads, as well as music schools and festivals."[45]

Freund came to be known as a biting editor, something that Hopkins and the *Colored American Magazine* staff would experience firsthand. His weekly editorial columns in *Musical America* often were "sharp polemical articles denouncing composers and music critics who disagreed with his viewpoint."[46] He also harbored conservative views about women and the professions and discouraged American women from pursuing their art abroad because they would jeopardize their chances of becoming "the gentle, loving wife of some good American, and the mother of children, and so fulfill woman's noblest destiny."[47] Freund's perspectives on appropriate roles for women surfaced in his interactions with Pauline Hopkins, who, when she met Freund in 1904, was an ambitious unmarried professional woman.[48]

Despite his primary connection to the music world, by 1904 Freund considered himself a veteran of journalism, and the *Colored American Magazine*'s Dupree cemented this notion in his Revere House introductory comments, in which he lauded Freund as one who, since coming to America, had been "continually at work as newspaper editor and writer" and as "the oldest publisher of a musical paper in this country." In addition, Dupree referred to Freund's accomplishments as "a playwright, as a writer on politics and social economics," roles that he used to present himself as an alternately embattled and successful journalist.[49] Freund expanded on Dupree's comments and pontificated at length about the business of journalism and his "long and somewhat arduous newspaper career, with all the ups and downs, failures and successes that come to a man who has struggled for over a third of a century."[50] It well may have been these reports that encouraged the *Colored American Magazine* staff to welcome Freund with "a generous reception" at the Revere House and to grant him full access to the magazine headquarters. He, however, was representing himself in duplicitous ways to Dupree, Hopkins, and those associated with the *Colored American Magazine*.

The grand overture that Freund made in January 1904 to the *Colored American Magazine* staff and board members occurred at a time when he was combating major financial worries. This set of pressures had prompted him to cease publication of *Musical America* for four and a half years, and it would be two more years before he was able to resume publication. Was Freund seeking solidarity with the Boston group in order to secure money for himself? Was his talk of the lofty "principles that must guide us in every effort" merely rhetorical rambling? Did he receive any recompense or helpful indulgence at all from the takeover of the magazine that he in large part initiated? Was his ability to resume work on *Musical America* in some way tied to the end of his role at the *Colored American Magazine*? Despite insisting that he had "not come here to say pleasant things to you," Freund certainly courted intently the ambitious people of color before whom he appeared at the Revere House. He mentioned nothing of his own financial straits or the suspended state of his music magazine. He chose instead to underscore his deep sympathy with the cause of uplift, to suggest his deep admiration for American mothers, and to preach the gospel of divine order that insisted on the potential of all people to "rise above the brute."[51] His approach worked. "So genial, so kind, so disinterested did he appear," Hopkins reflected. "[H]e very soon won our entire confidence. . . . I thought it a case of pure philanthropy, one of those rare cases which are sometimes found among wealthy, generous and eccentric white men."[52] What Hopkins did not know then would come back to haunt her and her colleagues.

Pauline Hopkins and her comrades were completely unaware that Freund had had an altogether dismal and scandalous financial past. In 1880, almost twenty-four years to the day before which they gathered in the Revere House for a sumptuous repast, Freund had been suspected of committing a major swindle against "every prominent house in the piano, organ, and music trade" in New York City and in Boston. It was estimated that he owed or had bilked his clients out of $60,000 to $70,000. His treachery was so extensive and his disappearance in the wake of its discovery so worrying that the *New York Times* was moved to document the details of the case in articles such as the one published in January 1880, entitled "Why Mr. Freund Left the City," and illuminated by the equally intriguing subtitle, "Boston Creditors and Others Anxious to Learn His Whereabouts."[53] According to the report, Freund was a successful businessman and through his popular publication, the *Music Trade Review*, had built an impressive client list of "[p]ianos and organ manufacturers and dealers in music and music instruments" who "patronized the advertising columns of the paper liberally."[54] Unfortunately, Freund's "expenditures . . . soon outgrew his income. He adopted an expensive style of living" and in 1878 "built a splendid residence in Tarrytown. On this house he spent, it is said, nearly $100,000, nearly all of which was raised by mortgages." In addition to creating this luxurious lifestyle for himself as a bachelor, Freund "kept 'open house' for all his friends." Freund also spared no expense in his professional office, where "the fittings" were estimated at $5,000. The *New York Times* reporter remarked dryly, "All these expenditures taxed his resources heavily."[55] The solution that Freund devised, when faced with the considerable debts that he had amassed, showed a clear and premeditated turn toward illegal actions. Nonetheless, Freund's friends, "as well as a majority of his victims," believed that "he did not really mean to cheat anyone out of the money." According to one friend interviewed for the article, "Freund couldn't stand prosperity; that was the only trouble with him."[56]

The unfortunate fiscal mayhem that dogged Freund and his family, even after his death, creates questions about the motives that prompted his involvement with the *Colored American Magazine*. The details of his introduction to the magazine seem to be genuine, but one may begin to doubt Freund's supposed intolerance for prosperity when he turned his attention to the ambitious but beleaguered members of the Colored Co-operative Publishing Company. When he appeared at the Revere House in 1904, nearly two and a half decades had passed since he had become "too deeply involved to extricate himself" from financial mayhem and had "fled" his home and business. Even in 1904, though, financial disarray dogged Freund, and he still was ill equipped to finance even his own musical periodical. Unfortunately, his association with the *Colored American Magazine* and its publishing house would bring financial misery to them as well.

The connection between John Freund and the *Colored American Magazine* introduced for the first time to the magazine the specter of white paternalism and influence. Initially, Freund attempted to minimize the obvious racial dynamics that could emerge in any interaction between himself and the group. However, as Hopkins would note in 1905 with characteristically insightful prose, he "held with each one of us the patriarchal relation of ancient days. He was spoken of by us in our conversations together as 'Papa Freund.'"[57] In Boston, in January 1905, Freund cited his commitment to his new "friends" and insisted at various moments that he had no "particular interest" in African Americans per se but rather in the common universal goals that all humans had for enlightenment and success. Those may have been his words in public, but in private he was making dismissive and disrespectful comments about the enterprising men and women whom he was courting so vigorously. In a note to Stephen Fiske, the sixty-four-year-old writer and journalist who still was well-known for his work as a Civil War correspondent for the *New*

York Tribune, Freund made remarks that may have been meant to illustrate the great accomplishment of the magazine's staff and board but that bordered on racial caricature. "The editress is a colored woman," he remarked blithely, not deigning to provide Hopkins's name. "What do you think of a colored editress, whose salary is eight dollars a week when she gets it—with a bedridden mother to support?"[58] Hopkins may have cringed at the callous representation of herself and characterization of the family whom she worked so hard to provide for and to protect. He continued with his acerbic profile of the Boston organization, referring to the visionary and earnest Jesse Watkins as a "coalblack Negro," before going on to say that Watkins, whom he also did not identify by name, "has put the savings of his life, from day's labor, to help it along, because he thinks it may give people a better idea of his race." Finally, Freund referred to William Dupree, who had the elegant bearing and the disposition of a gentleman, as a "grizzled veteran, who came out of the War an emancipated slave, unable to read or write, but has educated himself until he is the superintendent of the second largest branch of the Boston post office."[59] Such comments were uttered in private correspondence, but Fiske, in his capacity as the long-standing dramatic editor at *Sports of the Times*, made them public as he praised Freund's unceasing generosity toward and his interest in the downtrodden. Fiske's evaluation of Freund's details about the magazine's staff hardly softened the hard blows of prejudice that the Boston group would have felt. "It is a far cry for Mr. Freund of Oxford University and the society of distinguished authors, actors and musicians to the association with Negroes," observed Fiske, who then concluded that such a connection was understandable because Freund "throws his whole heart into every philanthropic mission."[60] Such portraits painted the *Colored American Magazine* as a needy venture and a charity case that could not even begin to approach the lofty intellectual circles in which Freund circulated. In truth, however, the magazine staff and its contributors were honest and ambitious. The tragedy here was that they became entangled in the web spun by an Oxford University dropout whose reputation depended on a magazine that he had used to finance his excessive lifestyle and who lied in claiming that he was a graduate of one of the world's most prestigious institutions.

The injustices that would result from Freund's involvement also caused intraracial mayhem that ultimately linked the *Colored American Magazine* and Booker T. Washington. Freund became the vital conduit through which Booker T. Washington gained inside information about the periodical's financial status and the politics of its writers and staff. As Hopkins noted in her letter to Trotter, Freund "had interviewed our creditors, examined our books, [and] knew our weakest as well as our strongest points."[61] Thanks to Freund's presence in the magazine headquarters, Washington was able to strategize about how best to co-opt the magazine that, if funded fully, was poised to become the nation's most dynamic commentator on the status of African Americans and an influential resource for those striving to protect African American civil rights, social progress, and political advancement.

John Freund harbored decidedly conservative political racial perspectives and endeavored to suppress the progressive civil rights ideology to which the *Colored American Magazine* staff had been committed wholeheartedly from the magazine's inception. Freund began to reveal his stance on these matters at the Revere House dinner, and he used the work of Pauline Hopkins to do so. "I notice, in one of the articles written by your worthy, most talented and self-sacrificing editress, Miss Hopkins, a tendency to refer to her people as a 'proscribed race.' You must cease to speak of yourselves as a proscribed race," he insisted. "You must cease to dwell upon your wrongs in the past, however bitter, however cruel."[62] Such remarks likely caused Hopkins consternation. His interpretation of her use of the phrase "proscribed race" was narrow, and his injunction against thinking about "wrongs in the past" essentially was a draconian call for censure of African American historical perspectives. His sentiments seemed rooted in the political mythologies that prompted him to emigrate to America and hardly seemed appropriate utterances by a man informed about the racial mayhem of the day that manifested itself in acts of lynching, segregation, and economic disenfranchisement throughout the South, for example. Hopkins's writings, in general, and *Contending Forces*, most notably, were vivid interrogative texts, ones that did not dwell in maudlin ways on previous acts of injustice but rather historicized the disregarded lawless acts perpetrated against people of color and created an uplifting record of African American achievement that could not be divorced from the history of racial violence and extensive disenfranchisement. "Your duty is to forget the past, at least, to put it behind you and to advance bravely, with your faces to the dawn and the light," Freund proposed, as he segued boldly into an appropriation of Hopkins's signature phrase. "This is not a fight for the colored people," he declared. "This is a fight 'for humanity.'"[63] As he proposed what amounted to political and historical amnesia, Freund also made dramatic overtures, conjured up images of an unforgettable African American past, and invited his audience to indulge in intense emotional responses as they considered the realities of postbellum life. "I will scarcely even touch upon the distressing situation in which many of your people find themselves in the Southern states to-day," he remarked. "To understand that, a man must have the ability to place himself not only in your position, but in the position of the Southern people who emerged from a terrible war, ruined, and with that legacy which war always leaves and which it will take more than one generation to obliterate."[64] Freund continued, throughout his Revere House address, as coffee and cigars were offered, to oscillate between invocations of an impatient American universalism and a seemingly benign but inherently suspect racial sentimentalism.

As early as January 1904, at the Revere House dinner, Freund had proposed that the *Colored American Magazine* relocate to New York City. James H. Wolff, one of the magazine's staunch allies, reacted strongly to that proposal when Freund introduced it. A Civil War veteran and commander of a local GAR post, Wolff was one of the city's "prominent Negro attorneys." A distinguished man of light complexion with a bushy mustache, he, like fellow Revere House dinner guests Butler R. Wilson, Archibald Grimké, and William H. Lewis, was one of the city's leading race men. Although Hopkins did not allude in her *Colored American Magazine* article to Freund's New York City musings or reference the "opposition" that Wolff mounted in response to Freund's suggestion, she did confide in William Monroe Trotter that Wolff "spoke decidedly against our accepting any overtures leading to a removal to New York before the close of the Presidential campaign, and he concluded by predicting that such a move would involve the loss of the magazine."[65] On this last point, unfortunately, he would prove to be absolutely correct.

The grand Revere House dinner—featuring delectable offerings that amounted to two dollars per plate and presented "in a style worthy of the giver," Mr. Freund—proved to be the first salvo against the *Colored American Magazine*.[66] The formation of the Colored American League, although a worthy endeavor, was not especially shaped by any explicit political agenda such as the antilynching platforms that had mobilized the Colored National League. A full two-page ornamental and photographic layout was included as a supplement to the March 1904 edition of the magazine, and surrounding the handwritten text about the formation of the league were photographs of the Revere House dinner attendees who founded the organization. These cameo images were a stirring snapshot of earnest, respectable Americans. There were images of the *Colored American Magazine* founders, editor Pauline Hopkins, and the men of the Colored Co-operative Publishing Company. In addition, each image, where appropriate, was placed next to an image of the board member's or founder's wife. This presentation defined the magazine as a family enterprise, and it further humanized the investment in the publishing company and the race that these founders and their immediate supporters had made. Included in the gallery was the stately and somewhat formidable Mrs. Nellie B. Mitchell, wife of attorney Charles Mitchell, an older woman pictured with a substantial strand of hair curled deliberately at the center of her forehead. Also included were Mrs. Lizzie Dupree, pictured with a steady gaze, Mrs. Cora B. Watkins, with a ribbon sitting atop her high and full pompadour, and the winsome Mrs. Anna West, with curls splaying around her head and above the high collared dress she wore. The image of a bespectacled, white-haired Mrs. Mary Wolff, wife of attorney and staunch magazine supporter James Wolff, suggested a rather grandmotherly air. The highly romantic image of Mrs. Katherine Brown, wife of Edward Everett Brown, clearly was the most glamorous of the group. Her dress was cut to reveal bare shoulders, accented further by her delicate up-do and half smile. Taken as a whole, the portraits illustrated quite effectively the high domesticity, exquisite femininity, and self-conscious respectability of *Colored American Magazine* readers and of the wives of the founders and board members.

The images of the newly formed League were part of a calculated marketing strategy, one developed in response to Freund's suggestion that the magazine generate attention for the league as it changed the magazine's price and the incentives for subscribers. The twenty-one published images also framed a handwritten signature list that identified each member, as well as a brief description about the league. These two pieces revealed the enduring political consciousness of the members, even though, according to the explanatory note about the organization, "the League . . . has no political purpose to serve." The note continued, informing readers that the organization had taken for its motto the phrase "For Humanity." The primary objective of the Colored American League, explained its members, "is to encourage virtue, industry and patience among the colored people to the end that they may serve as an example to the oppressed, and to those who suffer from prejudice at the hands of their fellow men, from whatever cause, the world over."[67] New supporters of the league would be provided one of the 5,000 badges that the *Colored American Magazine* had designed and ordered. In addition to this red, white, and blue button that had the motto emblazoned upon it, new members also would receive a similarly colored receipt. The organization and the publicity generated to showcase it demonstrated the high respectability of the *Colored American Magazine* staff and the publication's appeal and value to the African American middle and upper classes. Its overtures, though supposedly apolitical, also confirmed their unabating interest in "the oppressed," the very individuals whose lives were affected by the very forces that Freund hoped that the magazine staff would set aside as they "advance[d] bravely, with . . . faces to the dawn and the light."[68]

That John Freund was given complete access to the *Colored American Magazine* operation, from publication issues to financial matters, suggests that the founders and board may have been feeling quite desperate about the state of affairs. But it may not have been as simple as that. Pauline Hopkins and her colleagues were committed to maintaining the magazine. They valued Freund's expertise, and although they were aware that there might be political motives for him, they were not convinced that those would prevent them from producing more issues. Two days after the Revere House dinner, James Dupree approached Hopkins and asked for her impression of the recent proceedings. She told him that she thought "it is a political move" but concluded that "if you can get your money back why, we can say nothing as long as we keep the magazine afloat."[69] Quite soon after the Revere House dinner, Freund "took hold" of the magazine's business. He did so, recalled Hopkins, "ostensibly to correct our errors made in ignorance of the needs of a successful publication." He created additional financial hardship for the magazine even as he assured them that he was helping them. He implemented new prices for the magazines, cutting the cost of individual copies by five cents and reducing yearlong subscriptions by fifty cents. "All this was for the good of the cause," Hopkins thought, "but made a marked shortage in our receipts which he generously made up from his private purse."[70] Given Freund's own financial difficulties at this time, it is curious that he had the resources to provide such financial buffers. His generosity at this juncture raises questions about his symbolic and political investment in the magazine. At the Revere House, he began his speech by insisting that he had "absolutely no interest in the publishing company—hold no stock in it—and, indeed, only recently became aware of the existence of the enterprise through my friend, Mr. Barker of the Post Office, and my subsequent correspondence with Colonel Dupree."[71] Freund would compensate for his initial lack of awareness about the magazine, however, and in a tragically ironic moment, would insist that Pauline Hopkins provide for him an introduction to Booker T. Washington and the world of the Tuskegee Machine.

Shortly after the January dinner at the Revere House, Freund turned his eye to the production of the magazine. He quickly became a tyrannical force, a man who "criticised our work harshly," remembered Hopkins. However, the staff "cared not for that," she said. "[W]e were bent on keeping his friendship and profiting by his experience and ripe judgement."[72] The staff had been "late in the month in getting out" the magazine, and Freund, according to Hopkins, "strove hard to have us out on time."[73] They had been struggling since the beginning of the year, but it was more than editorial difficulties that kept them from meeting deadlines. Hopkins and the publishers noted in their March 1904 announcements that the year had not started smoothly at all. In addition to the "prodigious" work associated with producing "the magazine in its new spring dress," the staff had to deal with "the annoyances to which the inclement New England weather has subjected us. Water-pipes have burst," they wrote, "machines have broken down, snow-storms have made roads impassable, and travelling perilous, but still we have struggled to have the book appear each month, and have not missed an issue."[74]

Freund recognized the key role that Hopkins played on the staff and began to focus intently on her work and influence. Indeed, Freund's sometimes explicit and sometimes subtle overtures provide a troubling mix of intrigue and political subterfuge. His efforts to determine the scope and subject of her writing suggest emphatically that he, a man who had no self-professed interest in the Negro, had a decided interest in the message disseminated to the broad African American readership to which the *Colored American Magazine* dedicated itself. The intensity of Freund's work with and against the *Colored American Magazine* was staggering. In May 1904, just two months after the March issue appeared with its detailed account of the Revere House dinner, Freund would be writing congratulatory notes to Fred Moore, one of Booker T. Washington's devoted allies, in which he praised Moore for acquiring the magazine. Were it not for the scrupulously detailed letter that Hopkins typed painstakingly to her ally William Monroe Trotter, there might be no firsthand confirmation of the professional tyranny that she withstood.

In her 1905 manifesto to Trotter, Pauline Hopkins outlined the ways in which Freund endeavored to distract her from her professional work. In February 1904, he bombarded her with gifts, which included "a bouquet of Russian violets . . . an expensive set of furs, [and] a \$25-check." He also bestowed upon her copies of *Eternalism: A Theory of Infinite Justice* (1902), by philosopher Orlando J. Smith, and *Self-Help: With Illustrations of Character and Content* (1859), by the Scottish writer, outspoken reformer, and inspirational philosopher Samuel Smiles.[75] These were popular works of the day that the New York music editor apparently imagined would resonate with Hopkins's own commitment to uplift. Orlando J. Smith was perhaps best known for his recently published work entitled *A Short View of Great Questions* (1899), a "mysterious, multilayered tract" and "a popular polemic endorsing the theory of reincarnation and metempsychosis (transmigration of souls)."[76] The automotive entrepreneur Henry Ford believed that this document "changed his outlook on life."[77] Smiles's book, *Self-Help*, a Victorian-era best seller that was distributed regularly to British schoolchildren, was filled with inspirational biographical profiles of industrious British workers and tradesmen and became known for its memorable and pithy phrases such as "Heaven helps those who help themselves," the maxim with which Smiles began his lengthy book.[78] Uncomfortable with this generosity, Hopkins admitted that she "seemed to be a favorite with our benefactor" but noted that his "special attentions made my position in the office very uncomfortable." In one of her most frank and personal comments, she confided to Trotter that "[a]s I am not a woman who attracts the attention of the opposite sex in any way, Mr. Freund's philanthropy with regard to myself puzzled me, but knowing that he was aware of my burdens at home, I thought that he was trying to help me in his way." Yet she chided herself for not being more savvy and discerning. "I was so dense," she confessed, "that I did not for a moment suspect that I was being politely bribed to give up my race work and principles and adopt the plans of the South for the domination of the Blacks."[79] Within a very short time, though, Hopkins confirmed the nature of Freund's dastardly agenda. "Little by little he opened his views to me," she recalled, "and I found that he was curtailing my work from the broad field of international union and uplift for the Blacks in all quarters of the globe, to the narrow confines of the question as affecting solely the Afro-American."[80] Hopkins had been instrumental in helping the *Colored American Magazine* to build its connections to pan-Africanist thinkers and activists, such as the South African Allan Kirkland Soga, who used his base in London to disseminate *Izwi Labantu*, the newspaper that he cofounded in 1897 and that was published in Xhosa, Sesotho, and English editions.[81] Soga, whom Hopkins had profiled in the *Colored American Magazine* in 1904 and had recruited as one of the magazine's most influential international contributors, went on to establish a political organization that has been hailed as a forerunner to the powerful African National Congress. Hopkins's overtures to Soga began to bear fruit just as Freund began to protest the pan-African aspects of the magazine.

Hopkins bore the brunt of the increasingly rabid political conservatism that Freund brought to bear on the organization. She was taken aback by his protests of the global awareness and pan-African dimensions of the articles by and about accomplished Africans and relevant political events. Her dismay was transformed into outrage when Freund sought to eliminate all meaningful political matter from the publication. "He told me there must not be a word on lynching, no mention of our wrongs as a race, nothing that would be offensive to the South," she told Trotter. To illustrate her point, she quoted from one of the more confrontational letters that she received from Freund, one in which he laid down the exacting terms on which he would continue to support the magazine and solicit additional funds on its behalf. He wrote, "If you are going to take up the wrongs of your race, then you must depend for support absolutely upon your own race. For the colored man today to attempt to stand up to fight would be like a canary bird to face a bulldog, and an angry one at that. The only line of work must be conciliatory, constructive, and that is where Booker T. Washington is showing himself to be such a giant."[82] The aggressive and patronizing points that Freund made in his letter may have recalled for Hopkins the vexedly ironic words from Smiles's *Self-Help*: "Help from without is often enfeebling in its effects," reflected Smiles, "but help from within invariably invigorates."[83]

The *Colored American Magazine* entered a new phase when it accepted the overtures of John Freund. Within months, the magazine was inundated with complimentary letters of support from prominent individuals, many of whom praised Freund and hinted at their willingness to support the magazine. In March, eighty-two-year-old Isabella Beecher Hooker of Hartford wrote directly to Pauline Hopkins, addressing her as "Dear Friend." The pioneering educator and longtime woman suffrage activist proceeded to share with Hopkins her impressions of the recent issue, to comment on the value of Freund's role, and to offer her assistance in the drive to increase subscriptions. "To begin with the cover is admirable and the contents match the cover," Hooker mused, before declaring that "In Mr. Freund you have discovered a noble champion, a trustworthy leader in the cause of humanity." So struck was Hooker by the Hopkins article on the Revere House dinner that she specifically requested that Hopkins send her Freund's address "that I may thank him for every word of his late utterance at your dinner." Hooker also took time to offer potential marketing arrangements that might benefit the magazine. Though she did not have "a thousand dollars to spare" to support the *Colored American Magazine*, Hooker did think that there were other potentially helpful white Americans. The one individual she mentioned may have struck Hopkins and the magazine staff as an unlikely choice. Hooker suggested that James Vardaman, then-governor of Mississippi and known as the state's "Great White Chief," was a likely candidate to help "get people to read this number of your magazine and subscribe for it." "Somebody ought to get Governor Vardaman to do this," she proposed, "and every decent newspaper in the land ought to lend a hand in its circulation." Hooker envisioned the message of the *Colored American Magazine* as one that would dovetail with Vardaman's white supremacist views, or she imagined that the magazine would have a transformative effect. When Hooker recommended Vardaman to Hopkins, he had just begun to serve his term as the thirty-sixth governor of the state, following a campaign in which he traveled to some Mississippi towns dressed completely in white and on a wagon drawn by snow-white oxen, all of which symbolized his belief in white supremacy.[84] Vardaman was well known for his fierce resistance to racial equality, his belief that the Fourteenth and Fifteenth Amendments should be revoked, and his opinion that public education opportunities for African

Americans should be suspended altogether because people of color were fit only for the lowest echelons of society.[85] Offers for support and attention from the white elite intensified the pressure with which Hopkins already was grappling. Such tantalizing prospects of significant support competed with the race-based support that the staff was genuinely seeking. As the letters from upper-class whites such as Isabella Beecher Hooker and others arrived, Hopkins and her colleagues had to remain focused on their primary message and their shared desire to occupy what Butler Wilson, a leading attorney in the city and one of the Revere House dinner attendees, referred to as "a broader plane—the plane of humanity."[86]

In the days after the January dinner at the Revere House, the staff had accepted "a large number of subscribers" and were so encouraged by the apparent success of the Colored American League that Hopkins could conclude publicly in her March 1904 article on the dinner with Freund that "there is every reason to believe that within a year or more, the League will have tens of thousands of members, who will be working for the noble purpose announced by its founders."[87] The staff knew that they could not depend entirely on even a national network of good-willed subscribers. They still recalled their early struggles with subscription agents whose inability or failure to send in subscription payments had placed the fledgling journal in serious financial jeopardy as early as 1901. Three years later, Hopkins could recall, in a "most eloquent and touching account of the struggles of the magazine," those early times when "there was not a dollar in the treasury, and when the darkness of despair settled upon the little band of men and women who had devoted themselves to the cause."[88] The staff and founders thus were acutely aware of the cultural cachet and the financial capital that were within reach if they were able to sustain the attention of the "very distinguished men and women, both in Boston and New York," who had "become interested in the cause."[89] It was clear, though, that gathering expressions of support from leading white and African American figures was part of a master public relations move that Freund was engineering. The letters published in the spring issues of the magazine certainly sounded a common theme: praise for Freund and good wishes for the magazine that had the good judgment to accept his advice. Writing from the Hotel Carlton in Boston, Mrs. Robert Floyd noted that she had heard of the magazine "[t]hrough our friend Mr. John C. Freund" and that if it was "agreeable" to Hopkins, she "would like to call, with my friend Miss Snelling, and have the pleasure of meeting you personally."[90] Howard H. Smith, of Yonkers, New York, invited Hopkins to correspond with Julian Hawthorne, son of the legendary New England writer Nathaniel Hawthorne, whom he was happy to note "has just confided to me his willingness to do all in his power for your Magazine." Smith's closing note, that Hawthorne "is already acquainted with Mr. Freund," was yet another public and provocative confirmation of Freund's web of connections.

Invocations of an even more foreboding type began to appear in the spring 1904 issues of the magazine. Florida Ruffin Ridley, daughter of national club leader Josephine St. Pierre Ruffin and George Ruffin, the accomplished judge, wrote to William Dupree, praising him for "the general excellent appearance" of the April 1904 issue and "express[ing]" her "humble approval of your series of articles by distinguished men on the Industrial question." Ridley's praise may have been predictable, given that her mother had long worked closely with fellow women's club leader Margaret Murray Washington and that she also vacationed regularly with the Washingtons. In February 1904, just two months before her daughter's letter was published in the magazine, Josephine St. Pierre Ruffin was ensconced in Tuskegee where, as Booker T. Washington would report in a newsy letter to Francis Jackson Garrison, son of *Liberator* editor William Lloyd Garrison, she was "spending the winter with Mrs. Washington and me."[91] It was telling that a number of the published letters were from individuals who were on intimate terms with Washington. The growing number of references to him in the magazine seemed to be summoning up the man, and his shadow began to loom over the *Colored American Magazine* enterprise.

Freund, who rightly considered himself a maverick, insinuated himself into the bosom of the magazine, believed himself capable of invigorating the *Colored American Magazine* enterprise, and successfully persuaded sober women and men that he could do so. Freund emphasized his common bond with the magazine staff and their audiences, insisting that race and racial difference were necessarily outweighed by an egalitarian shared concern for human progress. At strategic moments, however, Freund stressed his identity as a white man. He took great pride in his role as a self-professed expert in journalism who had ties to white philanthropy, a world that had genteel but unbending terms according to which it would provide money to those who were deemed needy. One of the most startling ways in which Freund began to wield the power that the magazine staff and board accorded him was in his strident editorial ultimatums. He began to deliver these immediately after he gained access to Booker T. Washington, an introduction that, in the most frustrating of scenarios, he demanded that the magazine and Pauline Hopkins arrange.

In late March 1904, Hopkins received a telegram from Freund in which he asked her to compose a "letter of introduction" that he could use to gain access to Booker T. Washington. Hopkins may have been aghast because of the politics involved in such a request, which came through clearly in her letter to Trotter where she emphasized, through the use of capital letters, that "I had NO PERSONAL ACQUAINTANCE WITH MR. WASHINGTON." She apparently had to be coaxed and then even directed to do what Freund asked. "Mr. Dupree and the staff requested me to comply strictly with Mr. Freund," she told Trotter, and she composed a letter, which she regrettably did not copy for her own files, "detailing our situation, recounting Mr. Freund's kind acts and craving Mr. Washington's good offices as a race man in our favor."[92] Her letter achieved what Freund hoped it would. On 31 March 1904, Washington and Freund met. Six days later, Freund's editorial directives became sharp and narrow, and he began a savage attack on Hopkins.

The March issue of the *Colored American Magazine* was a hefty issue and one in which the publishers took great pride. It was, they said, "a work of art and eighty pages of choice matter, devoted to the interests of the Afro-American in every quarter of the globe."[93] In a prophetic move, the issue also debuted a new "cover design," one that the staff celebrated as "a miracle of artistic beauty." "The reading of the design is prophetic," stated the announcement, "thorns and thistles for our past mingled with roses which indicate hope for the future."[94] There would be deadly thorns with which to deal. On 6 April 1904, a "firebrand" landed in the *Colored American Magazine* offices. Colonel Dupree received a letter from Freund that Hopkins described as one that "made my position unbearable."[95] It read in part:

> There is, however, one rock right squarely ahead of us. That is the persistence with which matter is put into the magazine, which has no live interest, and furthermore, is likely to alienate the very few friends who might help us. Now, I have spoken on this subject already more than I care to. Either Miss Hopkins will follow our suggestion in this matter and put live matter into the magazine, eliminating anything which may create offense; stop talking about wrongs and a proscribed race, or you must count me out absolutely from this day forth. I will neither personally endorse nor help a business proposition which my common sense tells me is foredoomed to failure. Every person on the subject is with me. IT IS MR. BOOKER WASHINGTON'S IDEA.
>
> If you people, therefore, want to get out a literary magazine, with article[s] on THE FILIPINO, I refuse to work one minute longer with you. That is my ultimatum and I shall say no more on the subject.[96]

Freund's aggression and his patronizing references to the staff succeeded in driving Hopkins out of the office. She was absent "for a number of days" but used the time to confront him in writing. Their correspondence was heated and revelatory. Hopkins "outlin[ed] to him some of the difficulties [she] was encountering not knowing that they were caused by him." Freund turned on the woman whom, just weeks earlier, he had courted with flowers, furs, and books. He told Hopkins "of the unflattering comments made upon [her] work (the work so recently eulogized by himself) by Boston people."[97] Hopkins knew immediately that the criticisms to which Freund referred were from biased sources. As she told Trotter, her "Boston critics were all men working for and under Mr. Washington." These included Charles Alexander, a Tuskegee graduate and Wilberforce University teacher of printing, who, in 1904, was the recently installed editor of the *Boston Colored Citizen*. That weekly newspaper, which individuals like the Reverend Bradley Gilman, a white Unitarian minister in Canton, Massachusetts, and loyal Washington supporter, described as "not as good as the *Guardian*," could be used to obstruct the work of Boston's African American progressives movement.[98] The paper was one of several that Washington was known to have established, and the *Colored American Magazine* staff had always been wary of it and of Peter Smith, one of the first coeditors. According to Hopkins, Smith, an "employee and intimate friend of Mr. B. T. Washington," had asked "us to allow him to remove his plant to our office at 82 West Concord St. as his quarters on Charles St. were too cramped." They rejected Smith in "very few words," fully aware of his affiliation and because they "mistrusted his intentions knowing the man." They were right to do so, especially because Smith soon proved to be a liability, even to his backers. By 1904, he had badgered Washington for numerous loans and payoffs, and he eventually succeeded in getting the Tuskegee office to send him sixty-five dollars each month, even after he was no longer affiliated with the paper.[99] The surreptitious manner in which Washington arranged Alexander's tenure, insisting that there be no invocation of his name in any proceedings, revealed the lengths to which he would go to avoid the appearance of what some might perceive as meddling and others as an extension of his political control.[100]

John Freund's March 1904 histrionics were designed to alter the basic identity of the *Colored American Magazine*. He who had been espousing the value of humanity now claimed that the magazine's "international policy" was entirely problematic, unsuitable for readers, and wholly inappropriate to share with potential "friends" and investors. Indeed, the magazine's growing pan-African dimension and publication of articles on South Africa, the Philippines, Cuba, and Ethiopia, for example, was what made it appealing to its growing readership of color. Hopkins and the staff had succeeded, for example, in providing the *Colored American Magazine* audience with engaging and informative articles about the Caribbean and the contributions of African American soldiers fighting in Cuba and on other fronts in the Spanish American War. Such pieces, including the original set of articles by Freund on Jamaica that prompted the magazine's connection to him, sought to broaden the horizons of readers, as well as to continue the work of historical and ethnographic reclamation for which Hopkins, Trotter, and others had called. Hopkins sought out a number of accomplished African writers and scholars whose writings and activist work she wanted to bring to African Americans and to the larger American public. As Jessie Fauset would do in her role as editorial assistant at the *Crisis*, Hopkins ensured that the work of her protégés was published in the *Colored American Magazine*. She introduced them to American readers, and she provided a dynamic forum in which they could build new ventures to achieve African autonomy. Indeed, the magazine, under Hopkins's supervision, had the potential to create a mobilized and progressive international coalition of people of African descent.

One of the most influential international writers that Hopkins featured in the *Colored American Magazine* was Alan Kirkland Soga, a man who had "grown familiar to the readers of the Colored American Magazine as a writer of able papers on racial matters of South Africa." The son of a prominent African family, he was "closely connected with most of the stirring events of colonial frontier life." Soga's father, the Reverend Tiyo Soga, "was the first ordained native minister to the Kosa Kafirs." He was part of the "last of the old line of retainers who had followed the fortunes of the royal houses faithfully throughout the stirring incidents connected with the white invasion and the inter-tribal wars of the last and preceding century."[101] In 1898, Soga became editor of the newly established East London–based newspaper *Izwi Labantu*, whose editors sought to provide Cape Africans with a publication friendly to the interests of the region's Progressive Party, and began his rise to prominence as one of the most influential political thinkers in the colony.[102] Soga's affiliation with *Izwi Labantu* led to a close working relationship with Walter Rubusana (1858–1936), a British-born man of African descent and Congregational minister who also was a cofounder of the African National Congress, through which Nelson Mandela and others would continue the fight against apartheid in South Africa.[103] In London, Soga immersed himself in ventures that celebrated Queen Victoria and that advanced the progress of native Africans.[104] He also cultivated his interests in American education, kept himself apprised of American race politics, and, after reading *Up from Slavery* "with great pleasure," became a "great admirer" of Booker T. Washington.[105] Hopkins also cultivated a professional relationship with Professor S. F. C. C. Hamedoe, a scholar and writer "well versed in history, a traveler who has visited nearly every corner of the globe," and a "colored linguist who has mastered seven modern languages and thirteen Chinese dialects." His contributions to the *Colored American Magazine* included essays on great men of the West Indies, Pacific Rim, and Africa, such as Cuban general Antonio Maceo, Filipino patriot José Protacio Rizal, and the Ethiopian ruler Menelik. Hopkins appreciated Hamedoe's "gracefulness of . . . diction and the power of his thought on race matters," sentiments that generated even more ire from Freund, who, as part of his campaign to squelch the pan-Africanist tenor of the magazine, railed against Hamedoe's work and its "glittering generalities."[106]

Freund discerned correctly that Hopkins was building a promising global network of scholars, writers, and activists whose campaigns against ongoing colonial oppression in Africa and racial tyranny at home in the United States directly threatened the white status quo and the advocates of accommodationism, who were vital to continued American social and economic hierarchies. Hopkins's connection to Hamedoe, for example, extended beyond their publishing relationship and linked her and the *Colored American Magazine* to simmering Afro-British activists and African reform movements. One of these was the Congo Reform Association that Hamedoe's colleague Edmund Dené Morel, a white French activist who sought to expose colonial fraud and violence in African nations, established in 1904. The organization formed to challenge the corruption imposed on the Congolese people by King Leopold and Belgian forces, and historians have credited it with being the first to expose the "nightmarish visions" of suffering in the Congo and for being "dedicated to inform[ing], shock[ing], and mobiliz[ing] public opinion against the autocratic rule of King Leopold II" and note that it was central to the king's eventual abdication.[107] Freund's war on Hopkins and the politics of the *Colored American Magazine* systematically deprived her and the journal of sustaining global connections such as these and hampered the magazine's growing international presence and contributions.

The editorial commitments that Pauline Hopkins made to scholars like Hamedoe and political journalists such as A. K. Soga were central to the *Colored American Magazine*'s mission to educate African Americans about African conditions and its efforts to promote a collective colored American investment in global uplift. Such agendas aligned Hopkins, whose contributions were made in print and not at international conferences, with W. E. B. Du Bois, whose participation in the Pan-African Conference in London, for example, allowed him to pursue more fully the notion of African uplift and to counter the "aggressive humanitarianism" that emerged from other such gatherings.[108] Although the *Colored American Magazine* was strapped financially, its editorial policy and political outreach succeeded magnificently and could have become the magazine's saving grace. The journal, for example, was positioned to broker productive international connections, had proved itself open to invitations to serve as an American liaison for and official publication of English- and African-based organizations, and was willing to introduce African Americans interested in extending their racial uplift efforts to African communities interested in partnering with them.

The global political potential of the *Colored American Magazine*, made evident in the steady stream of articles about pan-African gatherings abroad, was also confirmed through the passionate editorial commentaries about colonial savagery. In the debut issue, for example, the Editorial and Publishers' Announcements section included a lengthy note about the "existing conflict now in progress in South Africa" and the ways in which divine forces were at work so that "vengeance is being answered now tenfold."[109] The magazine also maintained its steady focus on African history and identity by publishing gripping fiction, most notably Hopkins's serialized novel, *Of One Blood*, which ran from November 1902 through October 1903. The magazine's diverse content, plus the evidence of Hopkins's own successful inroads into international pan-African circles, represented a most substantial aspect of its reputation. Thus it was not surprising that Washington ultimately deployed Freund to eradicate without delay this vital dimension of the magazine.

John Freund's increasingly intense attacks upon Hopkins compromised her working relationships with the founding editors. She found herself unable to negotiate effectively with her colleagues about the importance of the magazine's established attention to international matters. Nor did she have an opportunity to emphasize the potential place that the magazine could take on the pan-African platform. A flurry of financial transactions began, and the formal encroachment by Booker T. Washington began. Hopkins would recall that it was "[a]bout the last of April or the first of May 1904, [that] [n]egotiations were opened with Mr. Dupree by Mr. Fred R. Moore, National Organizer of the Business League, looking to the purchase of the Colored American Magazine. It was planned to remove this plant to New York and have T. Thomas Fortune as the Editor and Pauline E. Hopkins as Associate Editor. It was understood by the force that Mr. Moore represented and covered Mr. B. T. Washington." The arrangements reveal the degree to which the magazine was to become an extension of the Tuskegee Machine. Dupree was entering into talks with Frederick R. Moore, one of Washington's most enterprising and faithful associates. Indeed, Moore was actively consulting with and being monitored by Washington. He received a note from Washington, penned on 18 May, that congratulated him on finalizing the acquisition of the magazine. In addition, Washington urged Moore to proceed with great discretion. "[I]t

Booker T. Washington, ca. 1908, the Tuskegee Institute
president whose interference in the African American press
contributed directly to the downfall of the *Colored American
Magazine* and the encroachment on Hopkins's professional
life as a journalist and prominent race woman.
Courtesy of Library of Congress.

will be best, considering all things, for me not be represented in it as you
suggest," he wrote.[110] Moore responded promptly. On 20 May, he wrote to
his benefactor about the arrangements. "I agree with you as to magazine," he
wrote conspiratorially. "Shant connect you with it in any way—you can rely
on this. I shall work out its policy in my own way with your quiet advice—
shall be glad to receive suggestions from Scott. I find Fortune agrees with
my plans of making it the exponent of the material progress of the race."[111]

Witness to the Truth

Frederick R. Moore, a staunch ally of Booker T. Washington
and president of the Negro Business League. Moore became
the editor of the *Colored American Magazine* when it relocated
to New York City. *Courtesy of Photographs and Prints
Division, Schomburg Center for Research in
Black Culture, The New York Public Library, Astor,
Lenox and Tilden Foundations.*

Moore's potential ally here was T. Thomas Fortune, "the lanky, alcoholic New York newspaperman who had given the teenaged Du Bois his first crack at journalism."[112] Washington relied on both Moore and Fortune in the effort to acquire the magazine but had to facilitate the working relationship between them. On 9 June 1904, for example, Washington endeavored to reassure Fortune that he would help to establish an acceptable role for him at the new magazine. "As soon as I reach New York," Washington wrote, "I think I can help in your coming to an understanding with Mr. Moore regarding your work on the Colored American Magazine as well as other matters."[113]

The National Negro Business League, for which Moore served as general manager, spearheaded the purchase of the *Colored American Magazine* and its transfer to New York City. The League's involvement made plain that the magazine now would be marketed to an African American entrepreneurial and rising middle class constituency that embraced the League's mission. It was a sobering irony that the League, which Booker T. Washington had established in Boston in 1900, financed the buyout of the *Colored American Magazine*. Even more ironic is the fact that W. E. B. Du Bois was the impetus for the League's founding. In 1898, Du Bois presided over the Fourth Atlanta Conference, a gathering whose subject that year was the "Negro in Business," and two years later, in August 1900, three hundred African Americans from thirty-four states convened in Boston for the League's first meeting. Its chapters grew significantly over the next two decades. Washington was elected to the presidency of the organization, and he held that position until his death in 1915.[114] The League's purpose was to promote African American "commercial, agricultural, educational, and industrial advancement" and to "encourage more of our people to go into business."[115] In his speech to the convention, Washington touted the value of future annual meetings that would "bring together annually those of our race who are engaged in various branches of business, from the humblest to the highest, for the purpose of closer personal acquaintance, of receiving encouragement, inspiration and information from each other." He also suggested that the League would be devoted to more than the appreciation of "material possessions." Such objects, he said, "are not, and should not be made, the chief end of life, but should be made as a means of aiding us in securing our rightful place as citizens, and of enlarging our opportunities for securing that education and development which enhance our usefulness and produce that tenderness and goodness of heart which will make us live for the benefit of our fellow-men, and for the promotion of our country's highest welfare."[116] That same rhetoric about the power of the material to support educational enrichment and domestic harmony in 1904 would be overlaid on the *Colored American Magazine*. Yet it would not signal the unification and cooperation to which Washington referred.

The June issue of the *Colored American Magazine* reprinted the notice about the New York City relocation and announced the goals of the new management. "It is our purpose to publish a magazine that shall record the doings of the race along material lines," the statement read, "and to demonstrate to mankind generally that we are worthy to have the door of opportunity kept wide open for us as for other men."[117] Under Moore's watchful eye, the process of justifying racial worth now was the modus operandi, and this represented a huge shift away from the rhetoric of intrinsic worth that the magazine's founders and staff had espoused. Readers now were turned away from a domestic and international program of high moral racial uplift and instead directed toward an insular, self-serving promotion that many of the stalwart early subscribers regarded as an essential tool in the persistent subjugation and the highly selective advancement of African Americans.

Just six months after the January 1904 Revere House dinner, the *Colored American Magazine* announced its formal relocation to New York City, in June 1904. Yet weeks before the confirmation, written by Frederick Randolph Moore, appeared in the "Publisher's Announcements," a set of pro-Washington men based in New York City had been forging ahead with their plans to use the magazine once it was in their hands. These plans, corroborated in correspondence included in the Booker T. Washington papers, show that the *Colored American Magazine* was under siege shortly after Freund gained entry to its inner circle. The tidy statement about the magazine's relocation could not suppress what some might have characterized as the self-satisfied gloating of Fred Moore, its new publisher. The magazine "will hereafter be issued from 181 Pearl Street, New York City, N.Y.," Moore announced, before stating that the "management appreciates the cordial support given it during its stay in Boston, and hopes for a larger measure of support now that it has been located in the great Metropolis."[118] Moore could speak with such grandiose rhetoric because he was an established and tested colleague of Washington and a man who did not hesitate to defend or to advance the interests of his powerful Tuskegee associate. Given the explicit but hidden political agendas surrounding the *Colored American Magazine* takeover, it is highly significant that Moore was selected as publisher of the magazine. His appointment was not based on his expertise in running a periodical but rather on his impressive political connections to powerful federal officials and thus on his political value to Booker T. Washington. Moore had established his own political identity and mobility before he became an instrumental part of the Washington machinery. He, however, would benefit professionally and politically from his relationship with Washington, the power broker who reviewed, endorsed, and nixed all federal appointments of African Americans during the Theodore Roosevelt and William Taft presidential terms. In 1905, Washington recommended Moore for a position as a New York City deputy collector of internal revenue. In 1912, during Taft's presidency, Moore was given the plum assignment of U.S. minister to Liberia.[119] As Moore's 1943 *New York Times* obituary would note, following his education in Washington, D.C., and subsequent work selling newspapers in the capital, the Virginia-born native "served as messenger to five Secretaries of the Treasury during the Grant, Hayes, Arthur, and Cleveland administrations."[120] His post placed him in "close proximity to cabinet members and presidents," a fact demonstrated most clearly in 1881 when he "was with President Garfield when the latter was assassinated."[121] In 1893, following an eighteen-year stint as clerk in the Western National Bank, a position bestowed upon him by Daniel Manning, a former secretary of the treasury, Moore established the Afro-American Investment Building Company in Brooklyn, New York. His turn toward real estate development and African American entrepreneurship caught Washington's interest, and the alliance between the two men began in earnest. It was Washington who, despite his categorical public denials of any involvement in the *Colored American Magazine*, appointed Moore editor of the publication, once the financial takeover was complete. In 1907, Washington repeated that maneuver when he purchased the *New York Age*, granted Moore part ownership, and appointed him editor of the pro-Washington publication, which became one of the best-known African American weekly newspapers of the early twentieth century.

The move of the *Colored American Magazine* to New York City implemented one of Freund's earliest, most enthusiastic, and frequently mentioned suggestions to the Boston founders and their magazine staff. Indeed, Freund could hardly suppress his self-righteous glee about the turn of events. His haste and delight, expressed in a letter to Moore, is but one more piece of evidence that suggests his ultimate, if not initial, collaboration with the pro-Washington set. Freund expressed his satisfaction at the move and generated a set of lofty pronouncements that suggested he considered himself an insightful expert on race matters. "Let me congratulate you that you have secured possession of the Colored American Magazine, and that it will in future be published in New York City, where I believe it will have a better chance of success." He then urged Moore to "not forget that all those who have heretofore been interested in this enterprise have shown great self-denial, a most worthy purpose and a devotion to the *cause* of their race, which have commanded the respect and the admiration of all those who like myself have become acquainted with the facts."[122] Such sentiments might have been genuine, but his use of the phrase "secured possession" raises the possibility of a battle for ownership and the successful suppression of competing forces. The misrepresentation of the proceedings only fueled Hopkins's determination to stay with the magazine as long as possible.

When the *Colored American Magazine* relocated to New York City, Pauline Hopkins went with it. She was the only Boston staff member to do so, and her refusal to relinquish her connection was based on deep moral and professional reasons. Personal financial issues also spurred her to maintain whatever official link she could to the magazine. Her investment in the *Colored American* was substantial. It was her primary source of employment, of course, but it also represented part of her considerable stake in the company and her own profession as an author. The transfer between the company and Moore also included Hopkins's property. As she shared with Trotter, "They held, also, the plates of my book 'Contending Forces' and 500 bound and unbound copies of the same. The book had been sold to the former management on the monthly installment plan, and when the company failed they still owed me $175. So being a creditor and a shareholder and a member of the Board of Directors, I had a deep interest in the business of the corporation."[123] She was determined to hang on, and the only thing that she could imagine that would prevent her from doing "all I could to keep the magazine alive" would be if she was "asked . . . to publicly renounce the rights of my people."[124] As it was, she was able to maintain her position there for less than four months. Despite the fact that "many promises were made" to her, Hopkins discovered that she was "being frozen out for Mr. Roscoe Conklin SIMMONS[,] a nephew of a MRS. B. T. WASHINGTON."[125] The cumulative editorial, managerial, and location changes all favored Booker T. Washington. As Pauline Hopkins surveyed the emerging skyline of New York City in the summer of 1904, she could be certain that she was facing an unrelenting co-optation of the earnest goals that she and four young ambitious Virginians had set out to achieve as the twentieth century began.

16

The *Colored American Magazine* in New York City

[W]hat a magazine should be, is plain enough.
It should be a record of what mankind are doing,
what they are thinking, what they are dreaming, with the
greatest emphasis on what they are doing in their intellectual
strivings, in their industrial efforts, in their commercial
activities, in their religious aspirations, — but always
results as the sequence of efforts.

T. THOMAS FORTUNE
Colored American Magazine,
June 1904

Don't give up, and don't go over to your enemy
any farther than you can help to keep living.

PAULINE HOPKINS
to J. Max Barber,
18 April 1905

Pauline Hopkins left her parents and the familiar environs of New England in the summer of 1904 and journeyed south to New York City, the "great Babylon" about which Lydia Maria Child had mused so eloquently. More than six decades had passed since Child published her observations about the city in which she began a two-year stint as editor of the *National Anti-Slavery Standard*. Still, Hopkins could have echoed Child's own words and matter-of-factly assured her fellow New Englander, "Well, Babylon remains the same as then." In the city, Hopkins was within reach of a "thousand and one mechanical conveniences" and could behold the already legendary skyscrapers, "steel-cage structures" like the Flatiron Building that the writer Henry James described as "extravagant pins in a cushion already overplanted."[1] Broadway dazzled all comers with electric lights that became "multi-coloured bouquets of luminous advertising" and unforgettable shows, including *In Dahomey*, which in 1903 became the first African American musical to open there.[2] Times Square, another new city phenomenon, also was coming into its own just as Hopkins relocated to New York City. The former Long Acre Square area now was becoming home to a "very substantial and handsome building being put up in the metropolis at the corner of Broadway and Forty-second Street" that would house the venerable *New York Times*, and the Strand Theatre, located on Broadway and Forty-seventh Street, seating 3,000 people, also was established there.[3]

Hopkins may have found unexpected similarities to her Boston life in the innovative and spirited world of popular entertainment. She may well have recalled her times at New England summer venues, such as the Oakland Garden, as she encountered all the advertising for the adventures awaiting New Yorkers and visitors to the city. One could go easily, assured the advertisements, from the "wonderland after dark"[4] that was Broadway to the splendid illuminated parks at Coney Island. In the summer of 1904, thirty cents would buy passage aboard the newly renamed "Dreamland," one of four "swift excursion steamers" that offered a quick forty-minute voyage to all who wanted to partake of the excesses of Dreamland at Coney Island. Once there, fun seekers and the curious could linger on boardwalks that could accommodate 60,000 people, visit the "largest ballroom in the world," where 8,000 people could dance simultaneously on a 25,000-square-foot dance floor under 10,000 electric lights, witness the "Fall of Pompeii," replete with "[f]ire, lava, ashes [and] electrical effects," take "[r]apid rides through mystic glades" aboard the "Scenic Railway," or venture into "Midget City," which purported to house "[a]ll the midgets in the world."[5] In the city proper, Hopkins could feast her eyes on the displays at the grand Macy's building on Herald Square and also indulge, free of charge, her passion for history. Public history was an increasingly grand characteristic of New York City, and she would have enjoyed the connections to her New England roots that some art and artists provided. On Fifth Avenue and Fifty-ninth Street, for example, Hopkins would have been able to admire the statue of General William Tecumseh Sherman. Unveiled in May 1903, the work was designed by the sculptor Augustus Saint-Gaudens, the artist who created the still-imposing tribute in Boston to the Massachusetts Fifty-fourth Regiment and its captain, Robert Gould Shaw.

In 1904, though, Hopkins was trying her best to preserve her integrity in the face of professional treachery and financial disaster. Some may have regarded her as only a symbolic escort of the *Colored American Magazine*. As the only Bostonian on the newly organized editorial staff, however, she alone knew the full history of the journal, and it was she who could bear witness to the cherished dream of its founding editors. The city that Lydia Maria Child imagined as a realm of "rapid fluctuation, and never-ceasing change"[6] may have been a perfect foil for Hopkins. In Manhattan and in the *Colored American Magazine* offices on Pearl Street in the Wall Street area, Hopkins began a rapid time of adaptation. She had to establish a new home for herself, negotiate a charged and unpredictable office, and maintain an air of professional composure, even as the antics of Washington's allies like Fred Moore continued.

Although she was in a tenuous professional position, Hopkins was bolstered enormously by a circle of longtime and devoted *Colored American Magazine* agents, who had been steady supporters of the venture since the magazine's inception. These enterprising women and men were teachers, temperance activists, school founders, and devout churchgoers with strong community connections linked to their memberships in the Concord Baptist Church and the Mt. Olivet Baptist Church, two of the city's largest African American churches. Nathaniel Barnett Dodson and his wife, Sarah Elizabeth Goode Dodson, the leaders of the cohesive New York *Colored American Magazine* agents, would have alerted the group and prepared for Hopkins's arrival. The welcome party likely included Annie L. Connelly, Daisy Foarns, Aaron Ferribee, Mrs. Lola Ferebee, Mrs. K. H. Spriggs, Mr. E. N. Brodnax, Mrs. Sadie Price, and Mrs. S. J. Winters, all of whom represented well the *Colored American Magazine*'s readership. Daisy Foarns, a member of Mt. Olivet Baptist Church, was known as a "young woman who is intensely interested in the material advancement of the race."[7] She had a kindred spirit in Mrs. Sadie Price, a fellow Mt. Olivet member and one of the most enterprising representatives of the magazine. Despite having no official status as an agent or detailed instructions about how best to sell it, Price quickly sold the first fifty copies that she received, consulted with Daisy Foarns about the terms on which agents were hired, "took out her commission and came down to [the] office, introduced herself to Mr. Dodson, and reported the money."[8] Equally tenacious was Aaron Ferribee, a native of North Carolina who was "fortunately situated" and whose "education and experience, coupled with his untiring energy," enabled Dodson and the *Colored American Magazine* in its early days to "snatch success from the very jaws of seeming failure."[9] Feribee, who in 1920 was still living in Brooklyn and working as a clerk, was, during the early years of the magazine, a "trusted lieutenant" of Dodson who "proved himself to be a great worker."[10]

The Dodsons were enterprising individuals who cherished their hard-won domestic stability. Nathaniel, a self-professed "lover of good books," had pursued a teaching career in Virginia before migrating to New York in 1887,

Nathaniel Dodson, Brooklyn-based general agent for the
Boston-based *Colored American Magazine* and father of poet
Owen Dodson. Dodson and his wife, Sarah, provided key
support to Hopkins during her brief tenure with the magazine
in New York City. *From* Colored American Magazine, *1902.*

Sarah Dodson, wife of Nathaniel Dodson and a leading
member of the Concord Baptist Church. Dodson maintained
contact with Hopkins once the journalist returned to Boston.
From Colored American Magazine, *1902.*

where he first became employed as an elevator operator at the Pierrepont
Hotel. Three years later, he left to attend Wayland Seminary in Washington,
D.C., but upon his return in 1892, he returned to the Pierrepont, was promoted to the position of second clerk, and in this "position he showed marked
ability."[11] He and Sarah married in Virginia in 1898, and, following the birth
of Lillian, their first child, they returned to New York City and settled in
Brooklyn.[12] By 1901, Sarah, who worked as a laundress and performed substantial community work, was complementing her husband's early efforts to
build what would become a successful and lengthy career in publishing.[13] The
Colored American Magazine praised her generously as "the accomplished wife

of our general agent" and noted that she was "doing good work in behalf of our publication."[14] Her *Colored American Magazine* responsibilities eventually afforded Sarah stability and remuneration enough that she was able to set aside her physically taxing work as a laundress and become a social worker.[15] When the Dodsons met Hopkins in 1904, they had been married for five years and were parents to five-year-old Lillian and to two-year-old Nathaniel. They were some years away from the tragedy that would befall Sarah, who would bear eleven children in a fifteen-year period, including the future poet and dramatist Owen Dodson.[16]

The Dodsons, like the founders of the *Colored American Magazine* and Pauline Hopkins's stepfather, William, were part of the substantial migration that brought thousands of southern-born African Americans to the North. Their hard work and efforts to acquire advanced degrees enabled them to create a respectable middle-class and professional life for themselves and for their growing family. The Dodsons showed great initiative in their promotion and distribution of the magazine and were primarily responsible for the strong subscriber base in the region. The highly complimentary May 1901 *Colored American Magazine* profile of Nathaniel Dodson described him as "one of the most enthusiastic supporters of our magazine" who was "building up the work in Greater New York by leaps and bounds."[17] As early as 1901, Nathaniel had organized "a club among his sub-agents in Greater New York for the purpose of facilitating in every way possible the work of extending the influence of our publications."[18] In addition, he sought to apply the principles of racial uplift to club members, the "ambitious young men and women seeking positions of trust and responsibility in other lines of work, for the advancement of the race."[19] Such dedication prompted him also to make arrangements so that "each district of the city will soon have its special agent to attend to the literary needs of all members of the race."[20]

Hopkins benefited from the fact that the Dodsons were a devoutly religious family and longtime members of the Concord Baptist Church, a vital and powerful community resource for Brooklyn's African American residents. Founded in 1848, the church had grown exponentially during the nineteenth century, and by 1900 its congregation was estimated to be between 10,000 and 15,000, perhaps the largest African American church in the United States.[21] It is highly likely, while in New York City in the summer and early fall of 1904, that Hopkins attended Concord with the Dodsons. Her own strong and impressive Baptist genealogy, coupled with her professional identity and the reasons for her sudden relocation to New York City, all would have resulted in a hearty welcome and sincere encouragement from the Dodsons' church community.

Hopkins may also have developed ties to the Mt. Olivet congregation located in Manhattan, which in 1904 was under the stewardship of the Reverend Matthew William Gilbert. Gilbert, who would in 1910 become president of Selma University, was active in New York's progressive African American political circles. Indeed, at the very time that Hopkins was settling herself in New York City, Gilbert was working actively with fellow ministers to hold a "private conference of Negro citizens of New York, New Jersey, Connecticut and Rhode Island" in the Abyssinian Baptist Church in New York City. According to the circular distributed about the event, the conference was organized so that attendees could "take into consideration how the political power of the Negroes of these States can best be put into operation to break up Southern disfranchisement."[22] Such efforts alarmed members of Washington's widespread network; Charles Anderson dispatched a confidential note to the "dear Doctor" as soon as he found out about the event, characterizing the organizing group of ministers as "hold up men" and asking if he should "better attend this conference and find out their plans." Whether she moved in the Mount Olivet or the Concord Baptist circles, Hopkins was part of a progressive and watchful African American constituency. The Mt. Olivet commitment to uplift and intellectual advancement would last well after the high jinks associated with the *Colored American Magazine*. In 1922, for example, the church was one of the primary sites that helped to host the first spring conference of the Association for the Study of Negro Life and History. That occasion brought Du Bois's Harvard University adviser Albert Bushnell Hart to Brooklyn, and attendees gathered at Mt. Olivet heard his "informing address on 'Involuntary Servitude.'"[23] It is also worth noting that in November 1931 the association held one of its two opening assemblies at Concord Baptist Church.[24] Such activity is yet another indication of the progressive and unwavering commitment to intellectual advancement of the race. Both the members and the activities of the New York City African American community buoyed up Hopkins. Like them, she was doing her part to protest disenfranchisement and Washington's relentless efforts to suppress African American free speech.

During her New York City sojourn, Hopkins would have had the privilege of hearing sermons by the great Reverend William T. Dixon, a theologian who was "[d]ignified in bearing, mild in disposition and a wise counsellor." Dixon's tenure at Concord lasted for fifty years, and in Baptist church history he is regarded as "one of the 'Fathers in Israel.'"[25] Hopkins had a unique connection to Dixon, a son of Virginians who migrated to New York City in 1833. In 1851, Dixon was baptized into the faith in the Abyssinian Baptist Church, the historic congregation that her great-granduncle, the Reverend Thomas

Paul, had shepherded into existence in 1809 and who, for four months, had served as its first pastor.[26] Hopkins also would have benefited from the ways in which Nathaniel Dodson merged his interests in literature and publishing with his activities at Concord Baptist Church. Dodson, who had been the church's Sunday school superintendent since 1892, also was elected to serve as president of the Concord Baptist Literary Circle during the mid-1890s. Once again, he sought to use his position for extensive good. In 1894, his reelection to the presidency was documented in the local papers. The *Brooklyn Daily Standard Union* praised him for his "singleness of purpose and faithfulness to duty" and prophesied that "[i]f his future career is to be judged by his past record, his name will some day be written high on the scroll of fame."[27] The prediction was partly realized, because, unlike the Boston founders of the magazine, Dodson managed to preserve his livelihood in the publishing industry. That was explained in part by his political versatility. He had political sympathies for the positions advanced by W. E. B. Du Bois. He also was an active member of the National Association for the Advancement of Colored People and its Brooklyn branch. Those ties did not prevent Dodson from working as a general agent for the *Voice of the Negro* and as a correspondent for the pro–Booker T. Washington newspaper, the *New York Age*.[28] By 1910, he was working as an editor and in subsequent years would become president of the National Negro Press Association.

The daily trek that Hopkins made to the New York City offices of the *Colored American Magazine* took her into the Wall Street district, not far from Battery Park where the southeasterly stretch of Pearl Street began. The magazine, housed at 181 Pearl Street in what is now known as Lower Manhattan, was located on a street that originally had been part of an East River inlet called Coenties Slip but was renamed Pearl Street "because of the sea shells found there in the days when the East River almost reached this street."[29] Pearl Street in earlier days "commanded a magnificent view of the harbor," and one could see "tallmasted, ocean-going ships resting in the East River docks, where they towered above the ferries and brigs and sturdy Dutch sloops designed for the local river traffic."[30] It was near the Fraunces Tavern, one of the oldest buildings in New York City. In the late eighteenth-century it was run by Samuel Fraunces, a West Indian man of African and French heritage, who, in addition to being an earnest patriot, deft spy against the British, and chief steward of George Washington's Philadelphia mansion, also was "a public benefactor." He "established a course of lectures on natural philosophy, and opened an exhibition of wax figures, seventy in all, for the amusement of New

Yorkers."[31] Hopkins also was traversing a street that had been home to some of the nation's most accomplished literary figures and artists, including John Howard Payne, the theater pioneer and creator in 1823 of the winsome song "Home, Sweet Home," and the writer Herman Melville.

Pearl Street was also a major business area in New York, and its proximity to the harbor drew merchants and encouraged construction of warehouses and shops. It included a substantial section that contained manufacturing concerns, textile merchants, stationers, purveyors of dry goods, and auction rooms where jobbers, also known as wholesalers, bid on an array of imports.[32] In the 1880s, large brick buildings at number 142 housed the C. W. Durant Sugar Refinery, and it was here on Pearl Street where Thomas Edison, funded by the wealthy industrialist J. P. Morgan, established experimental power stations that were an essential part of the move to create electrical power stations to provide light for the city.[33] Edison paid $150,000 for two four-story buildings on a 50-by-100-foot lot located at 255–257 Pearl Street, even though he characterized it as "the worst dilapidated street there was."[34] Despite his complaints, Edison thrived in that location and made great strides with his research and construction efforts.[35] In the early 1900s, Pearl Street was home to a variety of businesses, including saloons like those located at No. 414 and run by a Mrs. Cook, whose estranged husband offered three men a sum of two dollars to "throw vitriol into his wife's face."[36] The area had housed the offices of the 1850s-era weekly *Police Gazette*, "a byword in American pink-page literature," and the *Morning Telegraph*, a "sports, theatrical and turf newspaper" that was "standard equipment in every barber shop" and that had been located at 442 Pearl Street in 1900. In 1904, the Broadway Magazine Company was located at number 497 in the Hallenbeck Building.[37]

Hopkins used her time in the Pearl Street office to gain more information about the machinations that had resulted in the magazine's relocation and that contributed to the mounting intrigue in this annex of Washington's New York City sphere. Hopkins witnessed the ongoing efforts to disguise Washington's involvement with the magazine and parallel efforts to keep the influential African American apprised of all details. She and T. Thomas Fortune developed an intriguing relationship. This bespectacled man with long wavy hair, whom her contemporary Ida B. Wells had described as "more like the dude of the period than the strong, sensible, brainy man I have pictured him," provided Hopkins with titillating facts and confirmations of many of her suspicions.[38] She benefited from Fortune's vacillation between high professional anxiety and giddy confidence in the Washington team. Indeed, the man whom Theodore Roosevelt, during his term as governor of New York, once described as "an able and rather discontented black man," proved to be one of Hopkins's most useful, though unwittingly so, resources in New York City.

Fortune, who was three years Hopkins's senior and a seasoned journalist, was born into slavery in Marianna, Florida, in 1856, the third child and first son of Emanuel and Sarah Jane Fortune. His schooling included his first lessons in a school established by two Union army soldiers, as well as a short stay at Howard University. Fortune's early immersion in journalism sparked a life-long career that afforded him opportunities to work for pioneering Southern papers like the *People's Advocate* and leading Northern dailies such as the *New York Age*. He was an early supporter of African American women's activism and had close ties to Ida B. Wells. As historians have noted, it was Fortune who was the first to find and tell Wells that the Memphis newspaper office of the *Free Speech* had been destroyed by an outraged and bloodthirsty mob. In 1895, Fortune was in Boston for the historic women's meeting that Josephine St. Pierre Ruffin and others convened and was one of the only three men invited to address the gathering. Fortune held forthright women in high regard and freely promoted the activism and efforts of women like Ida B. Wells. He admired Wells especially, because he thought that the antilynching crusader had "plenty of nerve, and is as sharp as a steel trap, and she has no sympathy with humbug."[39] His delight in such purposefulness may have meant that he was drawn to Hopkins as well. Her Boston background, demonstrated journalistic zeal, and dogged determination could have prompted Fortune to engage her in conversation. Her battle against Booker T. Washington also may have prompted him to share his own stories of victimization. Although some historians assert that Fortune was Washington's closest African American political ally in the North, it is clear that Fortune regarded the relationship as extremely costly and problematic. In the summer months of 1904, Hopkins savored all of the details that Fortune shared with her about Washington's campaigns to undermine African American publications that he deemed problematic or combative. It was a difficult time for her, but Hopkins seemed to thrive on the intrigue.

Hopkins spent a great deal of time with Fortune and his wife, Caroline Smiley Fortune. The couple, who would separate just two years later, had survived personal stresses that included the deaths in infancy and early childhood of three of their four children, as well as the turmoil brought on by Fortune's loss of employment at various points following their marriage in 1877. Hopkins elicited a great deal of information from the Fortunes, and in 1905, when she recalled that she "learned much in New York," the majority of that insight was due to her conversations with the Fortunes. The information that she acquired shed light on Fortune's professional slights and financial difficulties. The longtime editor of the *New York Age* had, for instance, seen his newspaper transferred to Jerome Peterson, whom Booker T. Washington then recommended for an ambassadorship to Venezuela. In addition, "from the lips of Mr. and Mrs. Fortune" she had heard "that Mr. Fortune wrote "Up from Slavery" and the famous Atlanta speech "separate as the fingers of the hand," and that Fortune "writes many of Mr. Washington's magazine articles at a great sacrifice to himself, financially as to do this he has had to give up his work on white organs that netted him a good monthly income."[40] Hopkins may have had sympathy for Fortune as she heard his tales about Washington's manipulations, but she resisted any inclination to side with him. Despite his reputation as an outspoken and autonomous journalist, Fortune regularly accommodated the Republican Party platform and enjoyed the benefits of such strategic affiliations. Hopkins never lost sight of the fact that Fortune, despite his woes, was one of what she called "Mr. Washington's active agents and trusted allies," that he attended the "[m]eetings . . . held frequently at the Stevens House, Broadway, New York," and that he was privy to the "[p]lans . . . laid for 'downing' opposing Negroes," as well as the ways in which "wires are pulled for paying political jobs, and 'ward-heeling' schemes are constantly resorted to."[41]

Hopkins, the displaced but resilient journalist, was determined to acquire as much information as she could about the tangled financial arrangements that benefited Washington and the political indebtedness that kept individuals like Fortune and Moore yoked to various pro-Washington enterprises. She shared all evidence with Nathaniel Dodson, who was being pressured by Washington's henchman Fred Moore, urged not only to align himself with the new *Colored American Magazine* but also to take a significant cut in his commissions and to give up his business relationships with other periodicals such as the Atlanta-based *Voice of the Negro*. Hopkins could see that Washington was about to stage an intervention at the *Voice*, one much like that which she and the Boston magazine founders had experienced. According to Hopkins, not only was Dodson "expecting to have a call from Mr. Washington at any time," but also "Mr. Moore has been after Dodson."[42] In a letter dated 22 April 1905, Dodson told J. Max Barber and the publishers of the *Voice of the Negro* just how Washington's representatives had harangued him. Dodson noted that an agent of the New York–based *Colored American Magazine* approached him and "asked me to give him a list of my agents and their addresses and wanted to write them with my authority and send them a few copies of the Colored American to work in each month until they displaced the Voice." Dodson was indignant. "This I refused to do," he told his friends, but then went on to note that he soon heard that the *Colored American*

Magazine was "running behind and that the Wisard [*sic*] of Tuskegee, Ala. had issued orders that the [*Colored American Magazine*] must secure my services at any cost and at once." "Then came the information from one that worked with them," wrote Dodson, that "if I did not come over, they would spend money to put the Voice out of New York City and that I should not represent the Voice here in the National Negro Business League when it meets here, Aug. 15–16, and they would have things out and dried so that if any of the editors came to the meeting, they would be howled out."[43] Once again, Hopkins may have been the individual who provided Dodson with the vital inside information that helped him to sound the alarm and seek out the publishers of the *Voice*, a journal that he thought had "fine courage" and one that "speaks out in open meeting 'Vox Populi.'"[44] Hopkins undoubtedly warned her friend about the mercenary tactics that Washington could employ in order to eliminate any unflattering political critique. As she told her colleague J. Max Barber, "Mr. Washington is so powerful among white men in New York that if he works against Dodson in the firm where he is employed, it will settle it." However, Hopkins was well aware of Dodson's determination to secure his own professional advancement and could see that her friend was willing to negotiate. "Dodson wants to get into the Office of the [New York] AGE to work," she told Barber, "as he feels that it will advance him a step in literary work, and he is willing to meet Moore more than half way."[45] Yet, even as he considered acceptable compromises, Dodson was actively disseminating the work of Barber and other Booker T. Washington rivals in places such as the reading rooms of the Brooklyn Young Men's Christian Association.[46]

The summer of 1904 was full of indignant denials and endless obfuscation about the ownership of the *Colored American Magazine* by the Washington camp. Moore and his allies sought to deflect the rumors that the Tuskegee president had imposed himself on the resourceful and enterprising African American press. Much was at stake, including the notion that Washington enjoyed wide support from African Americans and that his opposition, though unruly and loud, was miniscule and thus irrelevant. Behind the scenes, Washington concentrated his efforts on directing Moore, finessing the working relationship between Moore and Fortune, and otherwise fielding suggestions about how best to use the magazine as effective political capital. "I want to be of whatever service I can," Washington assured Fortune, even as he claimed that he had no financial stake in the periodical. Despite his delicate sidestepping, however, the belief that Washington was the primary financial backer of the takeover continued to spread. It was even suggested that Washington had collaborated with white publishers and that he and the New York City–based house of Doubleday and Page were co-owners of the *Colored American*

Magazine. As Austin Jenkins, the publisher of *Voice of the Negro*, explained to Washington's devoted secretary, Emmett Scott, he had "received *quite definite* information that Doubleday-Page and Professor Booker T. Washington practically own the Colored American."[47] Jenkins had received that revealing information from an unidentified informant, who also insisted that John Freund had provided editorial advice to Fred Moore. The cloak-and-dagger role that Pauline Hopkins began to play while at the magazine in New York makes it thoroughly likely that she was the source of that controversial information.

Washington responded swiftly to all mounting rumors, and he fired back, writing from South Weymouth, Massachusetts, to Doubleday. "It has been stated by a certain publishing firm that you and I own the *Colored American Magazine* now being published in New York. Will you be kind enough to write me a letter on this point that I may show to other persons if necessary. For myself, I do not own a dollar's worth of interest in a single Negro publication in the country. Whether or not you have such interest I do not know."[48] Washington did have connections with the firm and had himself solicited the company to take out advertisements in the magazine.[49] Emmett Scott wrote back to Jenkins and used a range of rhetorical strategies to undo the growing damage to Washington's reputation and that of the magazine. "You are entirely—absolutely—completely off in your statement that you have 'definite information that Dr. Washington has purchased the Colored American Magazine,'" he insisted with great urgency. "Now here is a case where 'definite information' is positive misinformation," he declared, before resurrecting now-familiar denials of Washington's involvement or interest. "He has no interest in any publication of any kind," maintained Scott, "never has had and has no such thing in contemplation, and your definite information has doubtless come from the malicious newspapers which abuse, slander and misrepresent Dr. Washington on every possible occasion. Will you permit me to say that I am greatly surprised that you should have (in forming your opinions) trusted unauthorized and prejudiced sources of information when you could have been advised correctly at the only place to secure the information straight."[50]

Washington was so perturbed by these allegations that he drafted an additional corrective to Jenkins and his publishing partner, Mr. Hertel, one that he hoped would "serve in a small degree to bring them to their senses."[51] His letter to Jenkins sounded the same note as Scott's. "I never give any attention to ordinary street corner gossip," said Washington, despite the fact that his collected correspondence is filled with many missives of precisely that nature. "[I]t seems to me rather extraordinary unless you have definite information upon which to base your assertion. . . . I do know that so far as I am concerned the statement has no basis and is untrue." Despite such thorough and immediate responses, however, Booker T. Washington failed to convince certain members of the watchful African American press of his complete disinterest in the field. The very next month, even the *Dallas Express* was insisting on Washington's intimate connection to the magazine, and Scott once again had to insist that "Dr. Washington has not purchased THE COLORED AMERICAN MAGAZINE."[52]

Washington continued to respond quickly to the increasingly public charges of his interference in the larger African American press. His supporters rallied around the purloined and increasingly beleaguered *Colored American Magazine*. They published enthusiastic and transparent endorsements of the journal, praising it as an independent venture of Moore. The June edition featured a number of congratulatory notes, including an upbeat and complimentary letter from Fortune. "I am very much pleased to learn that you have secured control of the COLORED AMERICAN MAGAZINE which has had such a creditable existence since its first publication in Boston," he wrote, as if he had been completely unaware of the transactions that resulted finally in the acquisition of the magazine. "There is a very large field for a good magazine which shall be a record of the industrial and intellectual activities of the Afro-American people, the Negro at work, if you will." Fortune was confident that "[s]uch a magazine should appeal to thoughtful and industrious Afro-American people of the country as well as to the very considerable number of the general citizenship who are desirous of knowing at first hand what the Afro-American people are thinking and doing."[53]

The magazine made visible the problematic fact that a monumental shift in political perspective had occurred and that Washington was the primary beneficiary. It immediately became the official publication for the National Negro Business League, the group with which Washington was connected, and the first set of issues produced in New York City promoted the benefits of and continuing need for industrial education. The August issue promoted industrial education in two of its seven lead articles, focusing specifically on Washington's Alabama institution in pieces entitled "Little Journey to Tuskegee," by Elburt Hubbard, and "How Electricity Is Taught at Tuskegee," by Charles W. Pierce, and touted the "inestimable value [for] the education and elevation of the Colored Race in America" that Washington was achieving. The ever-vigilant Washington, concerned that the magazine's focus on Tuskegee-related items was a liability, directed the associate editor, his nephew, Roscoe Conkling Simmons, to be careful. "I very much hope that there will be nothing whatever in the June issue of the Colored American Magazine about the school or myself," he wrote pointedly. He continued, admitting plainly that "I think it was little unfortunate that there were two articles from members of the school in the April number and still another in the May number." Washington then gave Simmons explicit instructions about advertisements that he wanted to see pulled and asked Simmons to convey his wishes to Fred Moore. "Explain to him fully that I am doing this purely as a matter of caution," he urged. His next point was illuminating for its unself-conscious sense of entitlement and involvement: "I do not want the public to feel that the Colored American Magazine is our organ. Later on I will put it in again."[54]

Hopkins, assigned editorial work when she joined the New York staff, was part of the all-African American production team of which Fred Moore was so proud. By November 1904, though, she was on the verge of final exile. The announcement of her departure from the magazine hints at a variety of distresses and truths about what it was that dislodged Hopkins from the Pearl Street offices. Fred Moore, in his November 1904 "Publisher's Announce-ments," offered the following statement: "On account of ill-health Miss Pauline Hopkins has found it necessary to sever her relations with this Maga-zine and has returned to her home in Boston. Miss Hopkins was a faithful and conscientious worker, and did much toward the building up of the Magazine. We take this means of expressing our appreciation of her services, and wish for her a speedy return to complete health."[55] Hopkins made no public final statement, nor did she publish a farewell in the Colored American Magazine. The appointment of Roscoe Conkling Simmons, nephew of Washington's third wife, to the post that Hopkins had held confirmed the increasing co-optation of the journal.[56] Simmons's limited creative abilities and passionate commitment to Republican politics also helped to sound the death knell for the Colored American Magazine.[57] Hopkins had provided enticing fiction and ensured that a set of diversified, pertinent, and absorbing articles appeared each month. The loss of her editorial vision and creative contributions was enormous, and in no time the Colored American Magazine became a rather dry compendium of reports about industrial education and Republican politics, a journal whose new editorial staff abandoned the historic African American feminist readership that Hopkins and her women's uplift cohort had culti-vated and educated with delight during the magazine's first three and a half years. Moore also had no appreciation of the powerful race romance that the Colored American Magazine had fostered. No longer were there covers that featured gorgeous children of color holding the American flag, images of debonair African American regiments in uniform, or newsy reports from the front and reflections about international campaigns in the Philippines and Cuba that had made early issues altogether riveting and marketable.

Pauline Hopkins, who never published in the pages of the *Colored American Magazine* after its takeover and relocation to New York City, appears never to have made any explicit public reference to the significant professional and personal losses she endured at the hands of Booker T. Washington. However, in correspondence to important allies like William Monroe Trotter, she lamented loudly that the magazine became a "pitiful rag" and "a shadow of its former self." Despite Freund's policies of "'not a word of complaint,' no 'literary' efforts, 'no talk of wrongs,' or of a 'proscribed race,' no 'glittering generalities,' no 'international aspect' of the Negro question, no talk of 'Filipinos,'" the magazine failed to succeed. "What was the result? A rain of dollars into the treasury?" she asked pointedly in her letter to Trotter, before concluding, "Far from it." She could assert that sales plummeted and that customer interest withered dramatically. "The agents in every city have complained bitterly of the change of policy," she reported to Trotter. "It has hurt their sales; many of them have given the book up." New York City sales dropped precipitously, the typical range of $800 to $1,500 in monthly purchases dropping at least 300 percent to $200.[58] Apparently not many of the huge numbers of National Negro Business League members were flocking to purchase the magazine. Hopkins suggested that the venture would be "out of business were it not for the fact that it is supported from Mr. Washington's private purse." Those who dropped their subscriptions or refused to sell the magazine, she said confidently, turned to another independent journal, the Atlanta-based *Voice of the Negro*, edited by J. Max Barber, a man whose solidarity with Hopkins would prove vital in the days after she was ousted forever from the *Colored American Magazine*.

Hopkins composed a detailed documentary narrative about the demise of the *Colored American Magazine* when she sat down and typed a ten-page single-spaced letter with multiple attachments to William Monroe Trotter. In some respects that correspondence was probably a therapeutic exercise, but the effort to recount the devolution of the business enterprise that was the *Colored American Magazine* also sharpened her perspectives on the treachery and high stakes involved in intraracial race politics. One of the most poignant assessments of the experience was a four-line statement that read: "We needed money. Mr. Freund assumed the character of the disinterested philanthropist with no 'axe to grind.' Dissentions entered into the little business family. The editor and writer was maligned and 'turned down.' The rest was easy."[59] She could sum it up so succinctly, but her use of the third person signaled trauma and conjured up images of the wide chasm that had been established between her and the magazine that had given her the opportunity to shape public opinion and to inspire readers to creative and substantive action. She was left with "a feeling of honest indignation and contempt" for Washington. In the aftermath of the financial debacle, professional mayhem, and intellectual assault, she was deprived of a public platform from which to address her race. Like her ancestor, Susan Paul, who, in the wake of a racial outrage that victimized the children whom she taught, wrote to *The Liberator* editor William Lloyd Garrison, Pauline Hopkins picked up her pen to write to the city's most fiery newspaper editor of her day. In 1904, it was the bold editor of *The Guardian*, William Monroe Trotter, to whom she related her "necessarily personal" chronicle of the *Colored American Magazine* takeover.[60]

Pauline Hopkins did survive the tragedy that saw the *Colored American Magazine* stolen from its founders in Boston and ultimately doomed by the scoundrels who wrested it away. She also outlived the Wizard of Tuskegee. Unfortunately, though, the effect of her trials was significant, and the machinations and professional interruptions deprived Hopkins of substantial advancement as one of the nation's most eloquent and industrious race writers. She never recouped her journalistic momentum or again contributed so fully and publicly to the national collective race enterprise as she had during her early years at the *Colored American Magazine*. Her losses were broad and deep, individual and collective, private and wholly public. The one she could and did hold directly responsible was Washington, a man whom she regarded as a heartless thief who was determined "to defraud a helpless race of an organ of free speech, a band of men of their legal property and a woman of her means of earning a living."[61] It was not right that such predation should go unanswered. In the years that followed, Pauline Hopkins endeavored to restore the battered honor of the African American periodical press and to contribute definitively to the ongoing uplift of the race for which she had such great and high hopes.

17

New Alliances

Pauline Hopkins and the *Voice of the Negro*

America will be the field for the demonstration
of truths not now accepted and the establishment
of a new and higher civilization.
GEORGE L. RUFFIN
1892

This human striving for supremacy is the primary
movement of the age in which we live. The observant eye
can trace the impress of Divinity on sea and shore as He,
in mighty majesty, protects the weak in the great battle
that is now on between the Anglo-Saxon and
the dark-skinned races of the earth.
PAULINE HOPKINS
March 1902

Pauline Hopkins returned to Cambridge in late 1904 from New York with a considerable amount of professional resolve. Her ouster from the magazine that she had shepherded into becoming a substantial race journal made her a veteran and a victim of an unfortunate and vicious intraracial war. She had no patience with martyrdom, though. Her taxing sojourn in New York City only intensified her belief in the political power of the written word. She regarded this next professional transition as one that would accommodate her deep interest in pan-African matters and deepen her belief that African history was a vital step in the advancement of people of African descent in and beyond America. She knew well, too, that an informed Africanist consciousness could expose the petty and pedestrian dimensions of the race politics to which Booker T. Washington was wedded.

The distractions and upheaval of the past year had stifled her creative genius, but she did not surrender to self-indulgent moping or disabling regrets. She had quite impressively preserved her writerly sensibilities even as she waged war with ideologues and slick political operatives in the decidedly subversive galaxies that were part of Booker T. Washington's Northern networks. She possessed amazing fortitude and responded to the intimidating tactics of Fred Moore and others with a gritty determination to undo their enterprise. Hopkins's resilience, which emerged in her spirited correspondence with William Monroe Trotter, shaped her interactions and correspondence with J. Max Barber, the dashing and enterprising twenty-six-year-old editor of the *Voice of the Negro*. Hopkins and Barber had much in common; both were recognized as eloquent race writers, and their talents elicited substantial intraracial professional harassment. Once Washington and his cabal corralled the *Colored American Magazine*, Barber and the Atlanta-based *Voice of the Negro* became Washington's next primary target. Barber's politics of dissent and the lively journal threatened the already fraying hold that the relocated *Colored American Magazine* had on its declining readership.

Jesse Max Barber was a son of the South. His impressive professional trajectory embodied the unrealized and widely suppressed ideals of Reconstruction. He was born in 1878 in Blackstock, South Carolina, where, during the antebellum era, large plantations were populated with sizeable enslaved populations that tended to expansive cotton fields. His parents, Jesse and Susan Barber, were formerly enslaved and "a poor and respectable man and wife."[1] In spite of his material disadvantages, though, Barber prospered. As his biographer, William Pickens, observed wryly, "The lad's parents were poor, which was bad for the parents; and so the lad was self-dependent, which was good for the lad."[2] Barber grew up in Chester County, forty miles north of the South Carolina capital city of Columbia, where Jesse Barber Sr., who was identified as a mulatto in the 1880 South Carolina federal census, worked as a farmer. His mother, Susan, who in 1880 was caring for five children, ranging in age from one year to nine years of age, kept house."[3] Jesse Max, the youngest of five children and the second son, had vigilant and ambitious parents who ensured that he had access to all the educational opportunities available. He began formal schooling at age six and early demonstrated his intellectual prowess. His first teacher, who referred to Barber as "little Jesse," regarded him as an "embryon which needs only time and opportunity to develop into a leader of men." Barber apparently had a "'special tact' in mathematics; he had a disposition to commit and quote 'wise sayings;' was

Jesse Max Barber, the Virginia native who became editor of the
Atlanta-based *Voice of the Negro*. Hopkins published articles
in the *Voice* and offered support to her fellow journalist, who
was also targeted by Booker T. Washington and his supporters.
*Courtesy of Photographs and Prints Division, Schomburg Center
for Research in Black Culture, The New York Public Library,
Astor, Lenox and Tilden Foundations.*

'courteous and gentle,['] and became a member of the Baptist church 'early
in life.'"[4] Barber was the valedictorian at Friendship Institute in Rock Hill
and then, "still achieving, still pursuing," enrolled at Benedict College in the
state capital.

Barber's arrival at Benedict College, which was overseen by the American Baptist Home Mission Society, provided his future colleagues with an
excellent opportunity to debate the merits and mandates of industrial education. An impassioned Pickens declared in his 1906 reflective essay on Barber's

evolution, "Would it not have been better to send this Negro youngster of grit and genius and artistic bent to some trade school? Right here is where the cross-road is. Right here is where two groups of educators are formed. Right here is where the worlds divide."[5] A. C. Osborn, one of the presidents of Benedict College, insisted that the institution was "not a trade or industrial school, in that it does not give the industrial work the foremost place."[6] Barber flourished at Benedict and was able to "foll[ow] his instinct,—his star." He completed his studies there in short order, relocated to Richmond, Virginia, and enrolled at Virginia Union University. His two years there were full and splendid. "He is reported to have taken 'pleasure in going to the bottom of things,'" reported his friend Pickens. One of Barber's professors insisted that "[t]his University will have done the human race noble service when her history shall be complete, if Jesse Max Barber alone shall be her intellectual contribution to the world's thinking."[7] Just as Pauline Hopkins and the *Colored American Magazine* were thinking about the possibility of a solvent publication in 1903, Barber was graduating from Virginia Union and beginning a short-lived career as a "teacher and travelling agent for an Industrial School in Charleston, S.C." However, that venture proved highly unsuitable for "this emulator of master spirits" who was "not destined for narrow confines."[8] Within months of leaving Virginia Union, Barber was "called to the controlling editorship" of the *Voice*, a publication whose founders were determined that it should be "an organ worthy of the race's VOICE in this strenuous and warlike age."[9]

Barber and Pauline Hopkins were kindred spirits, and not only because they shared a passion for journalism and had to withstand the rage of Booker T. Washington. Both were passionate and gifted writers who were determined to provide their readers with articulate evaluations of American politics and culture, analyses of the merits and limits of industrial education, and discussions about the pitfalls of Washington's primary emphasis on insular Southern African American experience. Barber may have been encouraged by Hopkins's gravitas, expressed so deliberately in her 1903 profile of William Pickens, a former "colored orator of Yale" as well as his dear friend and biographer.[10] In the early 1900s, both Barber and Hopkins were refining their perspectives on colonialism, imperialism, and the increased global mobilizations of pan-Africanists.

The *Voice of the Negro* and Barber, its most well-known and ultimately controversial editor, had an alternately ironic and symbolic connection to Booker T. Washington and to the complicated race politics to which Washington so often was tied. The magazine was created and at first financed by the white Naperville, Illinois, publishing firm of J. L. Nichols and Company, the company that produced Washington's *The Story of My Life and Work*. Barber's introduction to the *Voice*, in fact, occurred during his student days at Virginia Union when Austin Jenkins, a vice president of the publishing house, was in Richmond visiting John A. Hopkins, a fellow student of Barber's at the university who also worked as a sales agent for J. L. Nichols and Company. In short order, they began sketching plans for an African American magazine. A few months later, John Hopkins was installed as "head of [the] Negro department" at the publishing house, Barber was appointed magazine editor, and the editor-in-chief of the new magazine was John Wesley Edward Bowen, a university professor and future president of Gammon Theological Seminary in Atlanta. Bowen's status was important here, even though in 1906 during the Atlanta riot it would not protect him; he was targeted by a policeman, who beat him badly with his rifle butt. In 1903 Bowen was especially proud of the new publication venture, and he and John Hopkins appear to have been unaware of the havoc that Washington was wreaking on the most ambitious African American periodicals of the day.

John Hopkins wrote to Washington in 1903, sharing news about the collaborative venture and seeking an endorsement for the magazine. Washington was of two minds about the project. First, he told Hopkins that one of the "prominent wants of the Negro race for a number of years" was for a "first class well edited and well printed magazine."[11] Then, two days later, Washington urged his longtime secretary, Emmett Scott, to make a speedy intervention. "Dear Mr. Scott," he wrote from Tuskegee on 4 November 1903. "A magazine is to be issued in Atlanta called "The Voice of the South," December 1st or January 1st. The thing is under the control of J. L. Nichols & Co., Naperville, Ill. . . . A colored man by the name of Hopkins, whom you will find in the Atlanta office of Nichols & Co., is to be in general control of the magazine, and a young man from Richmond is to edit it. I am very anxious that you have a good confidential talk with Hopkins and be very sure that we get an influence with this magazine that shall keep it working our way or at least not against us. Hopkins seems to be a very sensible fellow, but we want to be sure that he does not get under wrong influences, which is very easy to be done at Atlanta."[12]

Scott had more than a "good confidential talk" with Hopkins. The very first issue of the *Voice of the Negro*, when it appeared in January 1904, included, on page eight, a photograph of Scott alongside one of Hopkins, the business manager. The caption below Scott's portrait identified him as associate editor. Also serving on the board was the Reverend Henry Hugh Proctor, a former Fisk University student who had been in Nashville when W. E. B. Du Bois arrived to begin his schooling there and remembered that "there was something about [Du Bois] no other seemed to possess." He would enjoy a lasting professional relationship with Du Bois.[13] The *Voice of the Negro* gained a powerful ally when Proctor joined the editorial board. By then, the former Fisk student, whose college studies had taken six years to complete because he had had inadequate schooling in his home town of Fayetteville, Tennessee, had graduated from Yale Divinity School and been appointed in 1894 to the prestigious, resourceful, interracial First Congregational Church in Atlanta.[14] In Atlanta, Proctor was fast becoming "one of the African American lights of Congregationalism, a powerful speaker, opinion maker, and staunch Republican with a girth matching that of William Howard Taft, his favorite president."[15] Proctor, who was committed to wholesome values, the elimination of vice, and the enfranchisement of African Americans, brought to the *Voice* an impressive reputation for bold community political work.[16]

The editorial, appropriately titled "First Words," provided a clear and modest overview of the editors' perspectives on the journal and its potential value to African Americans: "The *Voice of the Negro* enters the field of magazine literature modestly but with a high purpose. In these strenuous days of literary and commercial competition, none but the best is able to stand and receive the patronage of the reading public." After eschewing politics and stating dramatically that the magazine was not "a political magazine . . . [or] owned by any party or clique in church or state," the editors proclaimed that the *Voice* would not "become the tomb of dead men's bones, whether these bones are found to be the ancient sermonic literature of the ministry or in the bombastic fire-eating speeches of the disappointed politicians of the day." The editors, who seemed single-minded in purpose, believed themselves poised to "endeavor, with conscience, to prevent the Magazine from degenerating into a medium for the bombastic talker or the fire-eating anarchist, black or white."[17] For all their collective assertions, though, the very first issue of the magazine confirmed the magazine's dueling platforms. First, the incorporation of a sizeable number of materials favorable to Booker T. Washington, including articles written by his supporters, suggested an already-established close tie between the magazine and the Tuskegee Machine. Second, J. Max Barber's editorial debut confirmed that he was ready to become a muckraker, a writer unafraid, as he put it, to oversee "times when literature we publish will rip open the conventional veil of optimism and drag into view conditions that shock."[18] Such pronouncements unnerved Washington and Scott, especially as stinging criticism from Tuskegee made its way to Barber.

Misunderstandings, arguments, and spats between J. Max Barber and Scott and Washington of Tuskegee quickly escalated as Barber attempted to preserve the magazine's autonomy. J. L. Jenkins became embroiled in a testy correspondence with Tuskegee about Washington's rumored ownership of the *Colored American Magazine* and how that made Emmett Scott's editorial role at the *Voice* seem increasingly inappropriate. As Washington's denials of any connections to the magazine arrived at the Atlanta offices of the *Voice*, Barber was becoming extremely frustrated by secondhand criticism of his writing and by Scott's refusal to provide him with access to Republican officials during the 1904 presidential campaign. The "peppery Barber" and the "supercilious Scott" butted heads so vigorously that Scott was driven to resign his position at the magazine, and he had nothing good to say about Barber. Scott complained about Barber's "malevolent spirit . . . his nagging propensities, his studied affectation of superiority; the man's overweening egotism and acceptance of everything as an insult."[19] The board did not so much side with Barber as it did agree with Scott's decision to step away from the board in light of the Tuskegee connection to the *Voice*'s contemporary and rival, the New York–based *Colored American Magazine*. In the autumn of 1904, J. Max Barber, the most forthright ambassador and defender of the *Voice*, was buoyed up, even emboldened, by the collective defense of the magazine and the exodus of Tuskegee from its ranks.

The editors at the *Voice of the Negro* soon realized that they had to marshal their writerly and political sensibilities in order to keep the magazine afloat. Shortly after their last tussles with Washington, sponsors such as the established Afro-American Realty Company, based in New York City and run by Philip A. Payton, withdrew their advertising. Payton acted on specific instructions from Scott, and when Barber challenged him, he suggested that his decision was based on the magazine's lack of support for the National Negro Business League, a stalwart Washington entity. Barber, insistent that "[t]here must be some other reason," told his fair-weather client that the magazine would "wear no man's yoke" and would "remain independent and jealously guard the interests of the Negro race if every advertiser withdraws from our pages."[20] As advertising contracts dissolved, Tuskegee supporters such as Emmett Scott celebrated. "It rather shows them that 'The Wizard' has friends who resent the untoward position of that publication," wrote Scott in a self-congratulatory letter to Washington's personal attorney Wilford Smith.[21] The Wizard, however, was not the only one with friends. As 1904 came to a close, Barber sought out new colleagues like Hopkins, rallied his supporters, and prepared to meet 1905 with editorial vigor.

The November 1904 issue of the *Voice* heralded Pauline Hopkins as a new contributor, less than one month after Fred Moore and his editorial board had ended her career at the *Colored American Magazine*. Hopkins was well aware that the message and politics of the *Voice* constituted a serious challenge to journalists like Moore. Her decision to become a contributor signaled her full endorsement of its pledge to keep its readers "posted on Current History, Educational Improvements, Art, Science, Race Issues, Sociological Movements, and Religion."[22] A full-page advertisement to publicize "Our Christmas Number" delivered the exciting news about Hopkins's impending debut in the December 1904 issue, "the finest and most beautiful number ever got up by the editors."[23] Barber and his associates were determined that the "Christmas number in point of artistic beauty and timeliness of matter will surpass most of the magazine on the market" and promised that it would feature "a new and handsome cover design by one of the leading Negro artists of the land" and that the "entire number [is] . . . profusely illustrated." The enthusiastic advertisement celebrated Pauline Hopkins and three additional authors: Silas Xavier Floyd, a frequent contributor of fiction and poems that elicited the "keenest pleasure" in *Voice* readers, Mary Church Terrell, the accomplished women's club leader who is "always doing something nice" and was about to publish something "new and novel," and Kelly Miller, the gifted Howard University mathematician and "no literary lightweight."[24] Such attention to detail justified the high praise that Barber and the magazine earned from contemporary journalists like L. M. Hershaw, an African American journalist who later collaborated with Du Bois on the publication of the magazine *Horizon*, who declared in a "national news magazine" that "*The Voice of the Negro* [is] one of only two Black magazines of real merit."[25] The enthusiasm in the November issue about Pauline Hopkins, however, revealed real enthusiasm, and it also provided evidence of her national reputation. "Miss Pauline E. Hopkins is a well-known literary star among the Boston magazine writers," the announcement proclaimed, before revealing how the *Voice* succeeded in signing her to publish in its pages. "By any amount of coaxing and begging and paying we have been able to secure her services as one of our regular contributors." Hopkins was to "signalize her appearance" in the magazine with an article about the New York subway system. The November announcement enthusiastically characterized Hopkins as "by far the best staff writer on The Colored American Magazine when it was published in Boston" and insisted that "[s]he has made her mark and is entitled to be considered as one of the best young writers in the race." The fervor with which Hopkins was introduced may have distracted some readers from the references to the *Colored American Magazine* and to its interrupted tenure in Boston. To be sure, though, such references would not have escaped the watchful eyes of Emmett Scott or his vigilant boss, Booker T. Washington. They may have seen to it that Moore stymied her even more, because she told Barber that she also intended to advertise her novel *Contending Forces* in issues of the *Voice of the*

Negro. Ultimately, she would reveal to Barber that "Mr. Moore holds my matter in the shape of 500 copies of my book 'Contending Forces' along with my plates." Moore's vindictive claim on the material meant that Hopkins was denied yet another potential source of income and professional renaissance. As she concluded plainly, "In this way I had nothing to advertise," and she never did promote her work in the pages of the *Voice of the Negro* or in any other publication. Yet, despite these difficulties, the announcement of Hopkins's new contract with the *Voice* did not dodge the facts. Before noting in its final line that Hopkins's "Christmas article will be well illustrated," the announcement offered the tantalizing detail that "Miss Hopkins is no longer connected with The Colored American Magazine."[26]

Hopkins joined the *Voice of the Negro* at a propitious time in its and her own history. Fresh from a round of enterprising and also unsavory African American literary politics, she had the potential to become a good mentor to Barber should he need one. He certainly was the most publicly aggressive editor with whom she had worked to date. In the inaugural issues, for example, Barber underscored for his readers the moral platform and professional intensity that would shape the forthcoming issues. By year's end, Barber was taking an aggressive tack, spurred on more by the Tuskegee machinations that aimed at compromising the financial stability of the *Voice* than by more general injustices. Barber and his colleagues, however, had succeeded against significant odds.[27] Editors celebrated, in January 1905, that the magazine had begun "with no subscribers at all," and they now were required to "print copies for twenty thousand this month." Such "phenomenal growth" was unique, they insisted, and "had not been hitherto recorded in magazine history."[28] From its inception, the *Voice of the Negro* articles that offered "vivid interpretation to the current history of the day" were borrowed and reprinted, often without Barber's permission or even acknowledgment of the *Voice* as the source.[29]

The steady growth in circulation and subscribers, coupled with the *Voice*'s apparent editorial value to peer publications, was key to the *Voice*'s recruitment efforts, too. The impressive subscriber list enabled Barber and the board to make "full arrangements with the leading men and women of our race" and to "produce a better magazine than ever."[30] The tables of contents confirmed these editorial boasts. The prominent members of leading African American organizations and institutions, such as Mary Church Terrell, Josephine Silone Yates, Fannie Barrier Williams, brought the power of the National Association for Colored Women to bear on the magazine. The *Voice* created a special 1904 issue entitled the "Negro Women's Number."[31] The *Voice* successfully demonstrated the breadth and regional power of the African American intellectual elite. It published some of the most brilliant scholars of the time and counted among its contributors individuals who had earned doctorates at Ivy League institutions, had integrated prestigious universities, and had achieved leadership positions in higher education and in law. These intellectual luminaries included Du Bois, the first African American Ph.D. graduate of Harvard, Kelly Miller, the nation's first African American graduate student in mathematics, and Archibald Grimké, the distinguished lawyer who was the second African American graduate of the Harvard Law School.

The *Voice of the Negro* contributors also were the sons and daughters of enslaved, self-emancipated, and free people of color. Some had been born into slavery. Daniel Payne Murray, historian, visionary bibliophile, and a pioneering librarian at the Library of Congress, was a *Voice* contributor who was part of the first generation of freeborn people in their families. The *Voice of the Negro* consistently published some of the nation's most accomplished, intrepid, and creative scholars, professionals, and writers. In so doing, the magazine underscored absolutely the resilience, drive, and abilities of the "proscribed race" of which Hopkins often spoke. The lives and successes of these contributors to the *Voice of the Negro* also offered incontrovertible proof of the substantial dimensions and realities of racial uplift.

Barber employed Hopkins as a contributor to the *Voice of the Negro* in late 1904, just months after he assumed the position of editor. In the aftermath of her exhausting struggle to maintain and then to defend the *Colored American Magazine*, she did not seem to consider for even a moment that she should curtail her actions or lay down her pen. Within one month of the publication of the official *Colored American Magazine* notice that she no longer was part of the staff, Hopkins saw her name appear in print once again. The December 1904 issue of the *Voice* featured her essay "The New York Subway." Her topic, and her turn to a local issue about urban development and expansion, illustrated her highly practical and industrious sensibilities. She clearly had been taking stock of her surroundings in the city, even while she was gleaning information from the beleaguered T. Thomas Fortune, taking dictation from Fred Moore, and otherwise gathering details that corroborated her claims that Washington was the architect of the *Colored American Magazine* takeover.

Hopkins must have been well pleased to see herself featured prominently in the announcements published in the January 1905 issue. The editorial overview of the year and its potential articles included profiles of the most prominent contributors. In addition to Hopkins, who was pictured with hair upswept and in a striped dress with high dark collar, there were formal images of accomplished university professors—including Kelly Miller of Howard, W. S. Scarborough of Wilberforce, C. H. Turner of Clark University, and Du Bois of Atlanta University. Of the thirteen individuals presented, Mary Church Terrell, Fannie Barrier Williams, Nannie Burroughs, and Hopkins were the only women. Of the group, Hopkins had the lengthiest biographical narrative and list of upcoming contributions. Barber negotiated with Hopkins for a set of materials that would appear throughout 1905. "She will open up in February in her first of a series of articles on 'The Dark Races of the Twentieth Century,'" he was able to announce. The series was to "compose a historical regime of the history, habits, customs, and locations of the several dark races now brought prominently before the world as 'perils' to civilization." Barber was confident that such timely and important material would appeal to his readers and would "be well worth a year's subscription to the magazine."[32] Despite Barber's public enthusiasm about the project, Hopkins did have to prod him to commit to the entire series. In April 1905, in response to a note from him, she wrote asking that he "kindly forward me what you can for my work as I need it for immediate use in meeting a bill." She then made a delicate but direct request. "Will you also, let me know if you wish the last number of the series or not so that I may not spend my time in needless labor if it is not wanted," she wrote, before insisting that "[b]y doing this you will greatly oblige me."[33] Barber responded forthwith, and arrangements for the final essay appear to have been finalized promptly. Hopkins published the set of five "Dark Races" articles, plus her debut essay on the New York City subway, over a period of seven months, from December 1904 through July 1905. All of the signed pieces were works of nonfiction. They confirmed Hopkins's versatility and to some degree did suggest that she was appearing in the *Voice of the Negro* as an author who was pursuing different goals than those she sought as the *Colored American Magazine*'s gifted writer of gripping serialized historical fiction and absorbing short stories. The *Voice of the Negro* articles were most closely related to the substantial nonfiction history and biographies in the *Colored American Magazine*. However, now Hopkins developed further her scholarly and political interest in African history and ethnology.

In January 1905, readers familiar with Hopkins's work, or even more generally with the early *Colored American Magazine*, might have been delighted to hear from Barber that "Miss Hopkins will also contribute a few short stories during the year."[34] However, as the year unfolded, there were not any fictional pieces attributed directly to her. It is possible, though, that she did contribute fiction to the *Voice of the Negro* and that she did so by using pseudonyms once again. Since Hopkins did not use previously employed *Colored American Magazine* pseudonyms, such as Sarah A. Allen and J. Shirley Shadrach, it is difficult to confirm the true identity of the serial novelist whose gripping Civil War–era novel debuted in the *Voice* alongside the first article that Hopkins contributed to the magazine. *The Welding of the Link—A Story Dedicated to the Unfinished Work of the Civil War* was the creation of a writer who, according to a disclosure by the *Voice of the Negro*, had chosen the pen name of Gardner Goldsby. In March 1905, Barber promoted the novel as the "leading serial for the year" and noted delightfully that the story was "creating a great deal of interest, especially among the ladies."[35] It was a novel that had all the hallmarks of Hopkins's style and perspectives and that was reminiscent of her mastery of the serialized novel. The story's form and content suggested, much as *Contending Forces* and later works such as *Hagar's Daughter* and *Winona* had done, that "there can never be any permanent and lasting peace between the white North and the white South, if the civil and political rights of the Negro are not guaranteed and maintained by the so-called superior race."[36] In addition to Gardner Goldsby's *Welding of the Link*, the only serialized novel published in the magazine, there were poems by aspiring writers such as Clarence Emery Allen and multiple pieces by Silas Xavier Floyd, an Atlanta University graduate who earned the Doctor of Divinity degree from Morris Brown College in 1902.[37]

Hopkins's first *Voice of the Negro* article was a departure from the conventional women's uplift and biographical profiles that she had published frequently in the *Colored American Magazine*. Characteristically, her account of urban planning triumphs concluded with a reminder about the need for racial justice. The article also had some unexpected debts to her association with John Freund and the period in which the aggressive benefactor of the *Colored American Magazine* was inundating her with gifts. Hopkins opened her article with a stirring tribute to New York City, a place that she referred to as the "living embodiment of true Americanism."[38] She moved on quickly, though, to celebrate the marvelous feats of engineering and the substantial cooperative effort that enabled the completion of the forty-million-dollar subway system. Hopkins invoked the "common saying among men of affairs" that suggested "there is always a way to 'make good' any bright business scheme, on a decently honest basis, in New York." She then shored up her point by incorporating a rather lengthy excerpt from the 1882 *Self-Help*, by Samuel Smiles, one of the books that Freund had bestowed upon her. The section that she chose touted the invaluable work of "[p]atient and persevering laborers in all ranks and conditions of life, cultivators of the soil and employers of the mine, inventors and discoverers, manufacturers, mechanics and artisans, poets, philosophers, [and] politicians." It was this broad spectrum of individuals, she suggested through her citation of Smiles's work, who were part of a multigenerational success that had led to this auspicious day in the history of New York City and of the world.

Hopkins provided colorful and earnest accounts of the subway that suggested her attendance at its opening on 28 October 1904, her participation in the first ride through Manhattan to Harlem, and her firsthand assessments of the beautiful subway stations where "Rockwood pottery, faience, and marble are used in many tints and in countless designs."[39] She provided intriguing details about the infrastructure, innovative engineering, and aesthetics of the system, as well as commentary on the business arrangements that provided a forty-year lease to John B. McDonald, the contractor and chief engineer. "Wonderful, indeed, is the country which produces so magnificent a metropolis," she declared, after offering additional tidbits about the feting of key financiers at the restaurant called Sherry's. Hopkins underscored the transformative effect of such substantial construction and business efforts and celebrated their positive impact on the nation. Yet she could not divorce such progress from the still-troubling political undercurrents that threatened African American progress and stability. "[W]e hope that the warning words of Emerson will forever impress this country and citizens," she wrote, and then cited in full the same lines from the transcendentalist writer Ralph Waldo Emerson that she had incorporated some four years earlier into *Contending Forces* and its chapters on women's club work and racial uplift.

Hopkins thought it entirely appropriate to recall Emerson and his incisive 1 August 1844 address for her 1904 audiences. Sixty years earlier, Emerson had delivered the speech in Concord as part of the celebrations marking the anniversary of British abolition of slavery in the West Indies. Having considered the "formidable task calling for a union of all the arts of modern engineering" that took some "six years to lay out the route and plan the make-up of the great tunnel,"[40] Hopkins felt obligated to caution those who might allow this advance to overshadow the disturbing realities of racial conflict, economic distress, and social violence. During the six-year period in which the subway, its ingenious labyrinth of tunnels, and its gleaming stations were built, some 642 African Americans had been lynched. Such violence, which was linked to social and economic intimidation, as well as political harassment, countered the glossy veneer of success that monumental urban achievements such as the New York subway represented to Americans and to those abroad. Hopkins invoked what Emerson characterized as a "very elevated consideration" and a "doctrine alike of the oldest and of the newest philosophy": "The civility of no race is perfect whilst another race is degraded."[41] Even in a contemplation of modernity and marvelous feats of engineering, Hopkins refused to unyoke American race matters from chronicles of the nation's social and industrial progress.

In 1905, Hopkins resumed her focus on African history and politics. Having set herself the substantial task of consolidating and mining large and nagging ethnological questions about racial origins and global hierarchies, she created for the *Voice* a series entitled "The Dark Races of the Twentieth Century." Five articles of modest length included colorful photographs taken from recently published books, travel postcards that depicted foreign royalty in full regalia, natives in traditional dress, and individuals photographed against the backdrop of villages.[42] Hopkins launched the series in February 1905 with "Oceanica," a piece that focused on the "dark-hued inhabitants" of the Pacific, including Hawaii, Fiji, and the New Hebrides. The March issue featured her article on the islands of Borneo, Java, Sumatra, and the Philippines, and the piece published in June 1905 focused on Africa and included assessments of the Abyssinians, Egyptians, Kaffirs, Hottentots, and the "Negroes of the United States." The final installment, published in July 1905, opened with a discussion of Native Americans in North America and concluded with a piercing analysis of race and culture, the "Negro Problem," and of the "persistent rise of the dark men" that constituted "a source of constant menace" to the Anglo-Saxon population.[43]

The "Dark Races" essays were the primary acknowledged contributions that Pauline Hopkins made to the *Voice of the Negro*. The writing, her confident use of secondary sources, and the contemplative analyses she incorporated into the ethnographic articles strengthened her reputation as a thorough journalist and pan-Africanist race writer. J. Max Barber had considerable confidence in Hopkins, a colleague whom he regarded as part of a vital Afrocentric phalanx whose work enriched the monthly journal. Although openly committed to providing exhaustive critique of American race issues, Barber too was intrigued by African histories and their potential to reshape early-twentieth-century African American political and cultural discourse. Although he did not explore this fully in the pages of the *Voice of the Negro*, in 1904 he published the monograph, *Negro of the Earlier World: An Excursion into Ancient Negro History*, with the African Methodist Episcopal Concern in Philadelphia.[44] His colleague Hopkins followed suit barely one year later. In 1905, she self-published *A Primer of Facts Pertaining to the Early Greatness of the African Race and the Possibility of Restoration by Its Descendants—With Epilogue.*

It is notable that when Hopkins joined the *Voice of the Negro* she did so as a writer who was prepared to tackle key racial, sociological, and political questions, rather than as a writer of fiction. The "Dark Races" series further solidified her rightful admission to African American intellectual circles and highlighted the solidarity with pan-Africanists that she had established during her tenure at the *Colored American Magazine*. It also cemented her extension of the political activism that so defined the Paul, Northup, and Hopkins families in antebellum and early postbellum periods. When they became formal colleagues in the early 1900s, Hopkins and Barber were invested in redirecting attention away from inflammatory and misleading discussions about African American inferiority and toward African superiority and what Barber would describe as "the golden age of Negro power."[45] The elegant Africanist rhetoric of Barber's pamphlet shaped Hopkins's writings on the peoples who constituted the "Dark Races" of her time. Barber may well have shared his work with her, and that welcome collegial exchange may have sparked her own ideas about generating a treatise. The *Voice of the Negro* issues in which Hopkins published reveal that she responded generously to her editor's interest in the African "noble past." Barber believed strongly that it was Africans who "rocked civilization in the cradle," and Hopkins used her writings to reinforce this view for the magazine's steadily growing readership throughout the winter and spring of 1905.[46]

Hopkins endowed the "Dark Races" series with rich literary allusions and scholarly citations that demonstrated her awareness and evaluation of key contemporary and historic anthropological, political, and cultural texts. Once again, Hopkins brought the power of intertextuality to bear on her efforts to use literature to achieve political intervention and to provide her readers with substantial, though concise, access to valuable intellectual debate. The role that Hopkins took for herself in this debut piece and the subsequent installments of the series was that of a cultural and scholarly interlocutor, a role she reprised in her 1905 *Primer*. She posed questions of her readers and of the published scientists, explorers, and military men whose writings and actions had an impact on the historic debate about race and identity. She also positioned herself as a reader sympathetic to all others who might feel oppressed by the sheer volume of sometimes unwarranted mountains of literature produced in response to these questions. "So strong is the question of color that all information possible is sought for in reply, and every theory imaginable is advanced by men who should know better."[47] In the *Voice of the Negro*, Hopkins aspired to become a trusted voice of racial reason and cultural insight.

The voice of Hopkins the novelist shaped the "Dark Races" series that saw the first article begin with a lyrical and persuasive meditation on Shakespeare and his considerations of race and oppression. The first essay focused specifically on Oceania, which Hopkins routinely referred to as "Oceanica," and on "[t]he dark-hued inhabitants of New Guinea, the Bismarck Archipelago, New Hebrides, Solomon Islands, Fiji Islands, Polynesia, Samoa and Hawaii."[48] Although there was an imposing photograph of the Hawaiian monarch King

Kalakaua, almost full-page in length, directly opposite the opening page of the first "Dark Races" article, Hopkins began by citing literary materials produced almost an entire world away from Hawaii. The piece begins with an epigraph from *The Merchant of Venice*, two lines taken from a speech that the Prince of Morocco delivers when he first meets Portia, the young woman who is compelled by the wishes of her dead father to allow suitors an opportunity to win her hand. Hopkins offers the first two lines of the Prince's speech, in which he advises Portia to "[m]islike me not for my complexion[,] / The shadowed livery of the burnished Sun."[49] By quoting, however briefly, the *Merchant of Venice*, Hopkins achieved several key interventions and reorientations. She drew in readers who might have been daunted by the densely subtitled ethnographic essay and captivated those who might have been interested. Once again, the truly literary historian maximized her access to readers and provided them, regardless of their formal education, class status, or professions, with empowering literary and cultural capital.

Hopkins's invocation of Shakespeare, in which she demonstrated her confidence as a reader and revealed her familiarity with high Western literary discourse, also created a valuable moment of extratextual recollection for her readers. Her seemingly straightforward citation had great resonance and would prompt many to recall Ira Aldridge, the impressive nineteenth-century tragedian of color and highly regarded American actor who triumphed in his performances of Shakespearean plays and on stages throughout nineteenth-century Europe.[50] Hopkins uses only the first thirteen words that the white-robed Moroccan prince utters to perform direct and emancipatory cultural and political rereadings of key elements of the white Western world. Hopkins moves quickly in the "Dark Races" series to legitimize herself as a race writer who is immersed in ethnographic, sociological, and biological debate. She first positions herself as a student of influential literary giants, and it is literature, not history or politics, that validates critiques of "color prejudice" and the "science of ethnology." "So important was the quality of color that we find the greatest of all English poets making place for this question in the greatest work of his hands," she insists. She relies not on her own interpretations but on evaluations by acclaimed poets such as William Wordsworth, who had high praise for *Othello*, the play that was one of the "four great tragedies" and which many "assign[ed] the foremost place" in their evaluations of Shakespeare's works. Hopkins transforms Shakespeare into a meaningful muse for her work; her highly politicized ethnographical writing becomes tribute to the playwright who "left, in perhaps his greatest work, a silent protest against the unjustness of man to man."[51] Hopkins's "Dark Races" meditations on race,

New Alliances

origin, and culture make audible the enduring and powerful "silent protest" that influenced some of the greatest works ever published in the West.

Hopkins moves from her meditations on Shakespeare to a substantial invocation of Martin Delany and his ambitious postbellum treatise, *Principia of Ethnology: The Origin of Races and Color.* Delany, with whom James Monroe Whitfield, Hopkins's granduncle, worked closely on African American emigration plans, was a figure with whom Hopkins was well acquainted. Delany had close ties to South Carolina, the state in which Hopkins opened *Hagar's Daughter*, her thrilling serialized novel that was published in the *Colored American Magazine.* One of the most prominent African Americans to emerge in South Carolina Reconstruction-era politics, he also distinguished himself in the antebellum era. He served with distinction in the Civil War, was an editor of the early African American newspaper *Mystery*, and author of *Blake*, the serialized work that also was one of the first published antebellum African American novels. Like Hopkins, Delany also had ties to Cambridge, Massachusetts, but his memories of the city were far from happy. He was an aspiring medical student studying at the Harvard Medical School when he was summarily dismissed. The decision, which coincided with the egregious Compromise of 1850 and the Fugitive Slave Act, was initiated by administrators who chose to yield to race prejudice rather than to defend the rights of Delany and the small group of highly motivated and capable young men of color with whom he had enrolled.[52]

Hopkins relied heavily on Martin Delany's *Principia of Ethnology*, which she refers to by its partial subtitle, "The Origin of Races," as she transitioned in her first "Dark Races" essay from a contextualization of ethnology in terms of the Western literary tradition to an examination of the anthropological dimensions of ethnology. His work, in her eyes, was an "eminent work," and one in which he answered "explicitly and clearly" the most foundational of questions about racial difference: "What causes the color of the dark races of the globe? What is it and of what does it consist?"[53] Hopkins also cited Delany when she sought "the benefit of scientific opinion"; her use of his work corroborated her emphatically religious perspectives and advanced her thesis that "[t]he word of God as given to Paul should settle the question of color origin of the human species beyond a peradventure."[54] Here she referred to the assertion that she embraced wholly in her last serialized *Colored American Magazine* novel, that "God hath made of one blood all the nations of men for to dwell on all the face of the earth." In this essay, Hopkins went further than she had elsewhere when she quoted this utopian vision of the earth. Rather than attempt to redeem Ham, the unfortunate son of Noah from whom all

African peoples were believed to have descended, she focused instead on Japheth, the son "with the least of the same color," identified as the father of Europeans. "[T]he sons of Japheth are a stiff-necked people," she writes, before declaring that they are individuals "prone to improve upon God's work, if possible," and it was they who created the notion of "'perils' yellow and black" and subjected them to being "born alone on an unreasonable insanity on the question of color."[55]

Having delivered biblical injunctions, Hopkins then comments on the geography and landscape that specific peoples inhabited, noted traditional customs, and mentions the impact of European contact with these populations that once existed as "sterling race[s]."[56] She does not develop a raging indictment of colonialism in the "Dark Races" series, nor does she discard her own Western perspectives on practices such as cannibalism that were not part of American and Western culture. She states plainly in her essay, "Oceanica," for example, that "Bismarck Archipelago lies to the east of New Guinea, and belongs to Germany."[57] In her account of the Fiji Islands, she observes that the islanders "have greatly declined in numbers since white men brought them the vices of civilization" and then declared, "They were cannibals and still practice this horror at intervals."[58] Her conservative perspective on European activity throughout the Eastern and African worlds, however, does not eliminate altogether her critique of colonial practice. The "Dark Races" articles were marked for the wry ways in which Hopkins evaluates and even bemoans the unfortunate predatory and invasive incursions of the white West. One of the most memorable examples of this aspect of Hopkins's rhetorical style emerges in her discussion of Borneo. She remarks that "[n]umerous ruins of Hindu temples are scattered over the island," and that such sights "remin[d] one forcibly of the first immigrants to this country. But always predominating, we find the incisive Anglo-Saxon marching along triumphantly toward the sovereignty of the world."[59] By the fourth and fifth essays of the "Dark Races" series, though, Hopkins has rendered the Anglo-Saxon a "persona non grata" throughout the globe. In so doing, she relies on the rhetoric of complicity and sympathy that she develops earlier on in the series, and thus the set of essays concludes on a note of fierce political outrage.

Hopkins also makes strategic use of the rhetoric of complicity. On these occasions, she invokes the collective as she details the economic benefits that African Americans, whom she regards here as Westerners, gained from their far-flung global communities of color. "All of our spices—cinnamon, cloves, nutmegs, and pepper—are raised on these islands," and "[f]rom the Philippines we receive sugar," she states in the opening paragraph of her second essay, a study of the islands that make up the Malay Peninsula: Borneo, Java,

Sumatra, and the Philippines. The last essay, which took the Native American Indian as its subject, also contained gentle chiding. "We are apt to forget in the enjoyment of the luxuries of our food products," observes Hopkins, "that maize or Indian corn which furnishes a large part of the world's food was the gift of the Indian to civilization."[60] These invitations to African Americans to consider themselves as fellow consumers in global economies encourage polarized perspectives. The "we" that Hopkins uses in her overtures to all of her Western readers in her fourth "Dark Races" essay becomes a polarized constituency. The Western collective gives way to a reconstituted pan-African community, and Hopkins, somewhat predictably, implements this major rhetorical and political shift in her essay on Africa.

Hopkins asserts herself with increasing boldness as the "Dark Races" series progresses. She becomes unabashed about enlisting her readers of color in her campaign to reclaim the history of African supremacy. In a rhetorical style that recalls her purposeful outreach to readers in her *Colored American Magazine* fiction and essays, she deployed the empowered voice of the collective as she intensified her exposé of ethnological myths and falsehoods. "When we consider the fact that there are 1,300,000,000 people in the world and that only about 375,000,000 are white (or one-quarter of the globe's population)," she declared in the opening lines of her essay on Africa, "we are not surprised that the dominant race dreads a 'dark peril,' and sees in every movement made by the leading representatives of dark peoples, a menace to his future prosperous existence."[61] Glimmers of Hopkins's outrage emerged throughout the essay and especially in moments when she described the deliberate suppression of potentially emancipatory knowledge. This was particularly clear in her musings about links between African peoples and the Jews. After observing that "[s]o striking is the resemblance between the modern Abyssinian and the Hebrews of old that we are compelled to look upon them as branches of one nation in spite of strong evidence to the contrary. As this theory is forbidden us," she noted impatiently, "how are historians to account for the existence of this almost Israelitish people, and the preservation of a people so nearly approaching to the Hebrew in [sic] inter-tropical Africa?"[62] One of the tactics that Hopkins uses effectively here, and in her general resistance to prevailing anti-African ethnology, is the charge of compromised scholarly endeavor and stifled intellectual inquiry. Those charges ultimately culminate in her thoroughly positive call for more expansive research and contemplation. One of the immediate benefits of such practice, of course, is not just a more dependable body of research but a more globally and racially inclusive discourse.

The power of pan-African identity emerges plainly in Hopkins's fourth essay and is signaled first by the most extensive subtitle in the "Dark Races" series. The populations she attends to in this essay are identified as follows: "Abysinians [*sic*], Egyptians, Nilotic Class, Berbers, Kaffirs, Hottentots, Africans of Northern Tropics (including Negroes of Central, Eastern and Western Africa), Negroes of the United States." The noticeable transition from the exotic dark other to the local dark known confirms how Hopkins's conceptions of race were situational. The "Dark Races" essays also reveal an uneven aspect in Hopkins's thinking on global race matters such as imperialism, which she envisioned both as "benign" and as a "more explicitly identified imperialism with a secular notion of domination."[63] Despite these inconsistencies, the series as a whole did demonstrate the strengths upon which Hopkins called as she donned the role of the impassioned twentieth-century race writer. On the one hand, Hopkins brought an established perspective on race, color, and prejudice to bear on her work. It was squarely faith-based and rooted in the tenets of uplift ideology that championed collective enterprise, professionalism, cultural development, and fully developed pursuits of excellence. When she tackled these questions, she did so authentically, as an individual immersed in the culture of reading. There were significant ways in which others might regard her as far removed from contemporary conversations about pan-Africanism. Unlike Anna Julia Cooper, for example, Hopkins did not attend the 1900 Pan-African Congress in London and so was not privileged to converse directly with influential Africans or to take her place on the public international stage in the ways that Cooper did. Hopkins compensated for this remove, however, and became part of the vigilant home guard, an attentive commentator whose keen historical consciousness was shaped indelibly by the early pan-Africanist work of her maternal forefathers. Hopkins was thoroughly empowered to continue her family's ancestral work of empire rebuilding for the race.

The political critique of the "Dark Races" series begins to gather momentum as Hopkins offers a number of readings, some cursory and others rigorous, of canonical historical texts on Africa and Asia. She also develops counterreadings of the works that historically have shaped the prevailing theses about race and origins. This two-pronged approach begins as early as the second essay and hints at Hopkins's mastery of the existing discourse. She blends her overviews of historical events, such as Magellan's discoveries of the Philippines, with references to more recent anthropological forays, such as the sojourn in those islands of explorer Abraham Hale, which produced "valuable information" for the Anthropological Institute of Great Britain. Her commentary on the Negritos, "descendants of African tribes" that include the Sakai people, could be read, for example, against the newly published *Negritos of Zambales*, a three-part study of the Negritos in Zambales, Benguet, and Paragua that

William Allen Reed published in Manila in 1904. His work, part of a series entitled "Ethnological Survey Publications," was produced under the auspices of the Department of the Interior and was the fruit of field work over a two-month period in May and June of 1903. In his preface to the volume, Reed explained that his access to the Negritos was sketchy, "owing to the fact that most of them would remain only as long as they were fed" and also because he only could spend a "short time at a place." As a result, he conceded that "it is evident that an exhaustive study of the people of any particular locality could not be made." Reed promoted his work, nonetheless, and noted that even in the face of such realities, "the culture plane of the entire area is practically the same, and the facts as here presented should give a good idea of the customs and the general condition of the Negritos of Zambales Province."[64] In some ways, the concise narrative tours and brief introductions to various tribes and peoples that dotted Hopkins's "Dark Races" series suggested a similar kind of constraint as she negotiated her own fast-paced "field work" through the anthropological literature.

During her tenure as a *Voice of the Negro* contributor, Hopkins encouraged her readers to focus on her strengths as an observer and an advocate. She promoted herself not only as a writer offering insightful contextual information about contemporary debates but also as one striving to reiterate with, and on behalf of, her readers the real stakes at issue in ethnological studies of race and culture. She provided tantalizing scholarly morsels, and they could deploy the facts that she offered or explore the sources and writers more fully. Time constraints and editorial pressures about word limits may have prevented Hopkins from offering consistently full biographical information about the scholars that she mentioned, so she crammed strong citations and promising scholarly allusions into the articles. As a result, though, the series featured at times a kind of rhetorical impatience, evident most often in her abbreviated overviews and speedy citations of major scholars and scientists whose research was legendary and whose reputations continued to impact the fields over which they had presided. She offered readers no information about George Louis Leclerc, known as the Comte de Buffon, for example, when she noted the similarity between her theses and his ideas. In the second essay, she expounds earnestly on the idea of "one centre of creation and a triple complexion in the family of Noah." Once she is satisfied that "we can conclude that the Negritos of the Philippines and the other dark races of Australasia are of the family of Ham," she quickly seeks scholarly confirmation. "Buffon supports the theory of three fundamental types of man—white, black, and yellow," she wrote, her phrasing suggesting readers' familiarity with the individual she mentioned. "We believe this theory to be true," she concluded tersely and without noting that Buffon, the eighteenth-century naturalist who "had the status almost of a living classic," was regarded by Thomas Jefferson as the "best informed of any naturalist who has ever written" or that he was the author of a mighty forty-four-volume work entitled *Histoire Naturelle* that was published over the span of fifty-five years, from 1749 through 1804.[65] Hopkins also let pass the opportunity to expound on the distinguished career and scholarly importance of Louis Figuier, the nineteenth-century French scientist. Hopkins may have been one of those individuals to whom the writer John Fiske referred in his 1904 volume *The Unseen World, and Other Essays* "who find pleasure in frequenting bookstores" and there discover "one or more of the profusely illustrated volumes in which M. Louis Figuier has sought to render dry science entertaining to the multitude."[66] Unlike Fiske, however, Hopkins did not regard Figuier's writings as "pretentious books [that] belong to the class of pests and unmitigated nuisances in literature," for which even the "sensational pictures of the 'dragons of the prime that tare each other in their slime'" barely compensated.[67] In her minimalist reference to Figuier, whom she only mentioned by surname and for whom she did not provide the source of the lengthy quote that she incorporated, Hopkins may have imposed another kind of disciplinary citation style. She homed in on Figuier's admission that "[n]ations whom we find at the present day but little advanced in civilization, were once superior to other nations."[68] She may have found other central arguments in Figuier's writings objectionable, but Hopkins applied sources that strengthened her own arguments and that also featured the works of others with whom she desired to make common cause. In this instance, for example, Figuier's comments dovetailed with ideas that journalist John Edward Bruce expressed in the bristling 1883 speech that he gave when Congress nullified the 1875 Civil Rights Act. In Washington, D.C., Bruce, after bemoaning the trials endured by those "whom the finger of God has painted black," insisted that "[t]he white race, whose ancestors belonged to the criminal classes of Europe and wore collars of Iron and Brass around their necks, were not always in the ascendancy, not always. Lord of Creation," Bruce intoned, "they were not always independent."[69]

The "Dark Races" series represented Hopkins's efforts to perform acts of cultural resurrection, racial elevation, and interracial and cross-ethnic equalization. There were two nations in particular that were key to these efforts, as she wrote for the *Voice of the Negro*: Egyptians and Ethiopians. In the wake of *Of One Blood*, the rich historical and mythic fiction about Ethiopia published in the *Colored American Magazine*, Hopkins took advantage of the opportunity to focus also on Egypt and to reclaim this nation for her defiant project of African recuperation. Hopkins was familiar with the holy and hushed invocations of Ethiopia, especially those that lent power to numerous antebellum speeches delivered by her maternal ancestors and in historic Boston sites such as the African Baptist Church on Beacon Hill and the Tremont Temple on Tremont Street. In the early twentieth century, though, Hopkins and others who were striving to establish a corrective racialized ethnology, also focused on Egypt. Its history was central to African American rallying cries for freedom, political equality, and psychological recovery from the devastating cultural realities borne of enslavement, segregation, and racism in America. Hopkins's attention to Egypt also justified again her place in the global conversation about historic African might and the blueprints for a collective pan-African recovery. Her work in the *Voice of the Negro*, combined with her serialized novel and future publications such as the 1905 *Primer of Facts*, kept the arguments of influential pan-Africanists such as James Africanus Beale Horton in view. Writing in 1868, this Sierra Leonean writer of Nigerian descent and longtime British Army officer declared in his well-known work, *West African Countries and Peoples, British and Native*, that Africa was "the nursery of science and literature," that Africans were "a permanent and enduring people," and that people of African descent "must live in the hope, that in process of time, their turn will come, when they will [again] occupy a prominent position in the world's history, and when they will command a voice in the council of nations."[70] In contrast to sentiments such as Horton's, the "Dark Races" series was noticeably forthright and unsentimental. The absence of emotional language in Hopkins's work also reaffirmed her studious effort to participate fully in pan-African discourse and also to cultivate the impression that she could be a promising leader in those same global circles.

The "Dark Races" series ended in June 1905 with "The North American Indian." Despite its announced focus, the article reflected Hopkins's unwavering interest in African subjects and issues. None of the six illustrations included in the article, for example, featured Native American subjects. Pictured instead were prominent men of African descent such as Alexander Dumas Sr. and Alexander Dumas Jr., the African chiefs Bathoeng, leader of the Bangwaketse, and Sebele, leader of the Bakwena. In addition, there was a photograph depicting unidentified Africans, with a caption that read "Group of Natives, Showing the Mode of Wearing Ntama," and a black-and-white graphic that depicted an "Ashante Captain in His War Dress."[71] Hopkins made initial points about Native Americans, though, and, under the watchful gazes of the African chiefs and writers of African descent positioned alongside her paragraphs, she honored the contributions of Native peoples and revisited the politics of assimilation and segregation that had dogged them in America. Here, as in her essay on the Africans, Hopkins endeavored to equalize her historically oppressed subjects. "Whatever value is placed upon them, whatever rank may be assigned them in the scale of human efforts," she wrote, "they were at least his own, and compare favorably with Anglo-Saxon advancement in the scale of progress."[72] Hopkins allocated less than one-half of the essay to Native American subjects, and overall this essay fell short of the others in style and substance. It lacked descriptive accounts of landscapes and references to specific tribes and historical moments of encounter with Europeans, and it was devoid of any scholarly citations like those that she had incorporated into the earlier pieces in the series.

Hopkins tackled the subject of the Native American Indian as one of the dark races with dispatch. It soon became clear that she did so in order to make space for her overview and conclusions, points that she offered "having viewed the origin, customs, and situations of the living dark races, from a scientific view-point, as explicitly as possible in magazine articles."[73] She divided these final thoughts into two categories: conclusions and questions. The queries that she posed, she declared, were the "most serious questions of the hour" and were "the Negro Problem and its fellow—Capital versus Labor." She quickly justified her attention to economics in a series focused on ethnological matters. After asking "How will capital and labor bear upon a question of ethnology?" Hopkins insisted that "sociological conditions have more to do with developing civilizations than racial descent" and that, historically, it was economics that explained the downfall of major empires. "Great estates ruined Greece," she reminded readers, and the "tyranny of concentrated wealth on the one hand, and social, industrial and economic enslavement on the other, caused the ruin of the Roman Empire." Hopkins believed that it was in the context of economics that Africans and their descendants could begin to succeed again. Focusing on labor and capital, she argued ardently, was absolutely necessary and was as much a calculated psychological strategy as it was economic. "Six thousand years of isolation in Africa," she contemplated, "two hundred and fifty years of slavery in America, savagery, barbarism and semi-civilization in other quarters of the globe give us people burdened with helplessness, melancholy and stifled aspiration to whom the 'door of opportunity' is but a fairy tale."[74] African peoples, she suggested, could immunize themselves against such disabling morbidity if they focused instead on the "great labor contest." This was the field of challenge on which they were guaranteed success and could "teach the Anglo-Saxon that 'all men are created equal' and that 'all men' are not *white* men."[75] Hopkins brought the "Dark Races" series to a close with this powerful note. As an African American, descended from enslaved and free women and men, Hopkins recommended a step away from the disempowering elements of the shared African past. The key to a bright future for the dark races was a collective and purposeful effort that quite literally involved working for the future.

Hopkins's "Dark Races" articles signaled the interest of *Voice of the Negro* editors in attending to and monitoring global affairs, but Hopkins became the primary and almost lone commentator on these subjects. Indeed, her 1905 series essentially was the magazine's attention to global matters, and the "Dark Races" articles made up the most sustained focus in the *Voice* on Africa and on international ethnic topics. Other writers, such as J. E. Bruce, whose article "The Song of Solomon" appeared in the June 1905 issue, certainly shored up the call for unapologetic black pride that Hopkins and others were making and also called attention to the scholarly resistance to African origin theories. Yet Bruce's *Voice of the Negro* publications did not offer the depth of scholarship or political commentary that Hopkins used in her writings.

Articles penned by leading Africans in America complemented the pieces that Hopkins published. This group of industrious and enterprising Africans included individuals who agreed with the philosophies and political perspectives of Booker T. Washington. In addition to Hopkins's articles on global history and the evidence of African origins, the *Voice of the Negro* also published articles by native African writers. One of the most notable Africans to write for the *Voice* was James Emman Kwegyri Aggrey, a celebrated Ghanaian whom many regarded as "an internationally known educator, an advocate of racial harmony, a noble Christian gentleman, and one of the beloved sons of Africa."[76] His article "The Dawn of Antioch" appeared in the July 1905 issue, which also included the last installment of Hopkins's "Dark Races" articles, an essay by Du Bois entitled "Serfdom," an article on race prejudice in America by Emma F. G. Merritt, and an article on strategies that Southern women of color might use to ease their acculturation in the North by Frances H. Keller. Aggrey, a member of the Fante tribe, might seem to be a man who would have given Hopkins and her firebrand colleague Barber some pause. By 1915, Aggrey, who developed a close relationship with nationalist writer John E. Bruce, whom he referred to as "Daddie Bruce," would himself be known in patriarchal terms, as the "Father of African Education." At this time, however, he also was becoming known as the "Booker T. Washington of Africa."[77] Aggrey taught for some twenty years at Livingstone College, the institution in Salisbury, North Carolina, that was named in 1882 after David Livingstone, the white explorer of Africa, funded primarily by the AME Zion Church. Licensed as a doctor of osteopathy, Aggrey became an effective elder and minister of two AME Zion Methodist churches in North Carolina. Although his sermons sometimes focused on "strange subjects," his audiences apparently delighted in them and were heard to say, "There's gravy in his sermons; plenty of good strong meat, but gravy to make them savoury."[78]

Hopkins and Aggrey had a shared belief in the power of the periodical press. In 1913, two years before Hopkins launched the *New Era Magazine*, Aggrey was endeavoring most earnestly to become an intern for W. E. B. Du Bois at the offices of the *Crisis*.[79] This did not happen, and it may well have been because Du Bois "castigated the industrial arts focus of both Washington and Aggrey for putting too much stress on teaching blacks manual skills rather than educating them to think." Despite the frequent linking of Aggrey and Washington, the African pioneer, in fact, was "critical of both the 'bread and butter' and the 'knowledge for knowledge's sake' approaches to education," and in the lectures that he delivered throughout the world, he "emphasized that the ultimate aim of education was 'the development of the socially efficient individual.'"[80] In this regard, Aggrey and Hopkins were of like minds, and both writers used the pages of the *Voice of the Negro* to exhort and to educate the races.

The *Voice of the Negro*, a new source of employment and political succor for Hopkins, exposed Booker T. Washington's continued interest in the African American press. Its editor, Barber, abandoned the professional diplomacy that his coeditors espoused and resisted the incursions, dictates, and models of race leadership advanced by the Tuskegee Machine. He quickly came under extensive and daunting siege by Washington, and his victimization, which he fought against quite spiritedly, caught the eye of Pauline Hopkins. She encouraged him and wanted to protect him. "Don't give up," she urged him in an earnest letter penned in April 1905. She promised to "keep [Barber] posted on all that I hear or can learn of" and also pledged to "help you in ways you know not of."[81] Hopkins did not confide in Barber to the same degree that she did in William Monroe Trotter. But her correspondence with the earnest South Carolinian journalist reveals that, as she resettled herself in Boston and attempted to reorient her professional life, she recognized the ways in which her experiences could benefit and protect others. She intended to challenge Booker T. Washington's calculated acts of trespass and his relentless appropriations of the African American press. Hopkins wanted to honor Barber's politics and journalistic integrity, both of which he asserted frequently in the *Voice*, when he insisted, for example, "We wish to have it well understood that the editorial and business management of the *Voice* have consciences and convictions that are not in the market for sale."[82] His editorial policies in the face of increasingly volatile intraracial politics had all the trappings of a true Garrisonian journalistic credo and would have reminded Hopkins of Garrison's legendary declaration in the first issue of *The Liberator*, where he swore to be "as harsh as truth, and uncompromising as justice," insisting, "I am in earnest, I will not equivocate, I will not excuse, I will not retreat a single inch, and I will be heard."[83] Hopkins found Barber's determination familiar, and she responded warmly to his idealism, energy, and ethics. Even in her last days at the *Colored American Magazine* in New York City, she was gathering facts that would help her colleague in arms.

Evidence of Hopkins's steady commitment to J. Max Barber emerges in the informative note that she penned to her colleague in April 1905, just over one week after she compiled her lengthy manifesto to William Monroe Trotter that bulged with attachments and copies of supporting documents. In her letter to Barber, which also included her request for his formal editorial commitment to the last essay of the "Dark Races" series, Hopkins alerted him to impending assaults from Washington and his allies. These attacks, warned Hopkins, were ones that would target specifically Barber and the *Voice of the Negro*. "With regard to the future of the Voice let me say," she wrote, "I believe that the same forces are at work that crushed the C.A.M. [*Colored American Magazine*] into the pitiful rag that it is at present. . . . The taking over of the C.A.M. to New York was a dastardly trick and they are about to play the same tactics on you unless you go under."[84] Hopkins revealed that Fred Moore and Thomas Fortune, Washington's main allies in this planned attack on the *Voice of the Negro*, were motivated by what they regarded as upstart tactics by Barber's publishers. "In some way it was learned that your firm has made advances towards buying the C.A.M. This fact enraged [Moore] and Fortune. Fortune said to me then," recalled Hopkins, "Wait, and you will see us put the Voice out of business; It will take a little time but it will come."[85] Hopkins then revealed to Barber the way in which the *Voice of the Negro* was to be undone. In her overview, she described how Barber's "book" (periodical) was to be sidelined through a combination of strong-arm tactics and editorial savvy. In her passionate letter to Barber, Hopkins revealed the following details:

> Moore's plan is, as far as I could learn, to get back all the old force that he can—writers, agents, etc., get the best matter and infuse new life into the book; then, he will work to drive you out of the field. Some of the Agents are asking Mr. Washington to make the fact known that he is the owner of the magazine and in this way their work will become easier in regaining old subscribers. The League will bar you and your

representatives from the convention and advise the people to buy the other book. . . .

Here is an illustration of the way they are working: Roscoe Simmons has been to the Y.M.C.A. Brooklyn, where your book has been placed in the reading rooms by [Nathaniel] Dodson, and has spoken there two Sundays in succession and has offered a prize of $5 to the men for the one who brings in the greatest number of the new members before their anniversa[r]y in May. Mr. Moore follows him in speaking for the C.A.M. Such tactics will naturally win with the men even before M. Washington addresses them in May.[86]

Hopkins revealed to Barber the seedy politics of the African American press and provided details about the aggressive and systematic bribing of his potential audience. She expected Barber's dismay when confronted with these facts and realized, too, that there were limitations on the ways in which she could help him. In 1905, she was an exiled *Colored American Magazine* writer who also was subject to the blackballing procedures that Washington's cronies used. Even though she insisted to Barber that "[s]o far as advice is concerned" she could not counsel him, Hopkins did offer rousing support and pledged, "I can do what I can to help you to [take] a stick to break your enemy's head." One of the coming opportunities that Barber would have to strike back was in the form of strident criticism of the *Colored American Magazine*. Hopkins assured him, "There will be, in a short time, material for you to make a stinging editorial against the C.A.M without seeming to go out of your way to do it in malice." Hopkins closed by urging Barber to stay in close contact with her. "Let me know how you come on," she encouraged him. "Don't give up." After noting the *Voice*'s recent "write up of Tuskegee" that she hoped was included only "to illustrate your impartiality," she counseled Barber not to "go over to your enemy any farther than you can help to keep living."[87]

As soon as Barber received Hopkins's letter, he attempted to enlist W. E. B. Du Bois, one of his most influential peers and a man whom Washington always kept within his sights. He apparently talked in person with Du Bois immediately, and then, on 27 April 1905, barely days after he received Hopkins's revelatory letter, he wrote to the Atlanta University professor. "My Dear Sir," he began, "I am sending in this letter the information for which you asked when I was at the University last Saturday." The enclosures included correspondence between Barber and the Reverend D. J. Jenkins, clippings from the *Messenger*, the paper that Jenkins edited, and a copy of Hopkins's recent missive. "I am sending you a letter from Miss Pauline Hopkins of Boston," Barber explained. "The letter speaks for itself." Barber also enclosed correspondence from Nathaniel Dodson in his effort to communicate to Du Bois what the future *Crisis* editor and others had realized about Washington's connections to the African American press and been protesting for some time. "It is perfectly evident from these two letters that the Business League machinery is being mustered against The Voice of the Negro," Barber declared. He then urged Du Bois to be politically astute as he responded to the information that the letters revealed. "If you can use these facts in any way to help the cause of decent journalism and fair play, you are perfectly welcome, not only to the facts, but to use my name in sending these letters to the Editor of the Post," offered Barber. He did caution Du Bois to practice some restraint if he chose to contact Oswald Villard, editor of the New York City–based *Evening Post*. "Please ask [the Post editor] not to make the facts public, for the reason that if Mr. Washington finds out that we are aware of his plans, he can easily switch off between now and August and resort to some other plan. We have got to protect ourself in this matter," exclaimed Barber, "and at the same time, catch this man in the very act of using the Business League to do a dirty deed."[88] Du Bois, whose own journalistic ambitions piqued his interest in the fate of the *Voice*, received this news from Barber, and by extension from Hopkins, barely one month after he had been involved in a heated tussle with Villard about the extent of Washington's treachery and subterfuge. Barber was quite familiar with this since the trouble Du Bois had experienced after the Atlanta professor's essay "Debit and Credit: The American Negro in the Year of Grace Nineteen Hundred and Four" had appeared in the January 1905 issue of the *Voice of the Negro*. Du Bois had made his boldest public accusations about Washington's control of the African American press in this article. With facts and suggestions presented in an essay that was "arranged like a balance sheet, in part to satirize the inconsistencies in Washington's philosophy of material accumulation as the basis of racial equality," Du Bois made a series of noteworthy allegations.[89] He suggested that Washington drew money from funds provided by Andrew Carnegie designed to create mayhem in the African American press and that the Wizard of Tuskegee also had offered bribes to members of the press in 1903 totaling some $3,000.[90] Hopkins's letter to Barber, which may be the closest she came to corresponding with Du Bois, did not prompt any significant action by the Atlanta scholar on Barber's behalf. It also does not appear to have prompted Du Bois to acknowledge Hopkins either directly or indirectly. It is unfortunate and telling that Hopkins's overtures to Barber, and, through him, to Du Bois, failed to produce any noticeable resistance to the acts of which Hopkins spoke.

Hopkins's relationship with the *Voice of the Negro* and with J. Max Barber was part of a complex moment of transition in her professional life. In spite of the relatively brief time of Hopkins's connection with the publication, her interactions with Barber and her publication in the magazine underscored the intensity and the extent of the professional battle that she had been waging since Washington had launched his first assaults on the *Colored American Magazine*. The "Dark Races" series and the New York subway article that showcased Hopkins's historical writing enabled her to develop further her position as a cultural critic. Hopkins was willing to go to great lengths to uplift and defend her race, but the enemies she faced were brutal and unrelenting. J. Max Barber eventually became a dentist, a career change prompted by his conclusion that it was the only profession into which Booker T. Washington could not follow him. The professional exile that Barber ultimately experienced was one that Hopkins endeavored to prevent. Despite the ultimate demise of the *Voice of the Negro* and the gradual dissolution of the ties between Hopkins and Barber, she still represented, for him, for Du Bois, and for others familiar with the intense and bitter struggles within the African American periodical press, a sure and even "voice of the negro." Pauline Hopkins emerged from her time with Barber and his ambitious journal as a woman ready to offer steady professional contributions and generous observations, and as one who would not hesitate to summon an unwavering ferocity whenever she joined a fight for African American freedoms.

18

Well Known as a Race Writer

Pauline Hopkins as Public Intellectual

[T]he question of deepest moment in this nation today
is its span of the circle of brotherhood, the moral stature of
its men and its women, the elevation at which it receives
its "vision" into the firmament of eternal truth.

ANNA JULIA COOPER
"The Ethics of the Negro Question,"
1902

1905 was a year that began well for Hopkins. Settled anew in Cambridge, she began preparing articles for the *Voice of the Negro*, and she also rekindled her connections to the circles of Boston's social and intellectual elite. It was a year that held much promise for African American women and that also brought to the city a steady stream of the nation's most influential and successful men and women of color. Charles Chesnutt held forth in May when he came to attend commencement services at Harvard, which also brought Major Charles Douglass, the Civil War veteran and son of the orator and diplomat Frederick Douglass, to Cambridge for the celebrations. The presence of such luminaries, crowed the editor of *Alexander's Magazine*, was "the occasion for many of the brilliant entertainments projected by Bostonians."[1] Memorial Day services in the city were especially memorable, in no small part because ninety-two-year-old Harriet Tubman, the Civil War nurse, spy, and redoubtable Underground Railroad conductor, traveled to Boston from her Auburn, New York, home to honor the sacrifices and courage of African American veterans. A delegation of GAR members, which likely included William A. Hopkins in the Robert Bell group and members of the Shaw Veteran Association and the Peter Salem Garrison, conducted a program at the St. Gaudens memorial on Beacon Hill. That impressive statue of Robert Gould Shaw on horseback followed by men of his heroic regiment could have included Tubman's figure as well. The *Boston Globe* coverage of the Memorial Day event and Tubman's visit reminded readers that it was "Mrs. Tubman, who gave the Colonel his breakfast the morning he was killed and nursed his soldiers."[2] August 1905 saw "[h]undreds of ladies" descend on the city for the ninth annual meeting of the Northeastern Federation of Women's Clubs, including Mrs. Booker T. Washington, who "came from her summer home in South Weymouth to address the convention" and to speak on "the value of mother's meetings, and . . . how the mothers in the neighborhood of Tuskegee are reached and interested in matters of practical value—such as simple dressing, the care of the home and the proper preparation of foods."[3]

Hopkins was a visible contributor to the vibrant events of 1905 that occurred in Boston, and she also participated in well-attended events in New York. Hopkins appeared at three important public events in Boston, which reflected her ongoing diversification as a public intellectual and her investment in racial advocacy. In addition, her close ties to the supportive Brooklyn community with whom she spent time in 1904 helped to finance her writing life. She returned to New York City as a guest of the Dorcas Home Missionary Society to deliver a lecture at the Concord Baptist Church. The event reflected the church's unswerving commitment to racial uplift, intellectual development, and professional support, a position that led in 1922 to its selection as the site of the first spring conference of the Association for the Study of Negro Life and History.[4] In Brooklyn, Hopkins was the celebrated keynote speaker at the evening events that followed a day of lectures, interaction between church women and their invited guests, and afternoon services that began at 3:30 P.M. and included "congregational singing, scripture reading by Miss Christina Goode and prayer by Mrs. N. B. Dodson."[5]

The collegiality and friendship that Hopkins enjoyed with Nathaniel and Sarah Dodson continued to bear fruit even after she returned to Massachusetts. At the Dodsons' church, Hopkins was part of services geared specifically toward African American women that focused on the high moral outreach and activism that they as ardent Christians could and should perform. Once again, Hopkins was part of an impressive slate of speakers; the day's program began with a lecture entitled "Pearl of Great Price," by Ella Alexander Boole, a white temperance reformer who in 1920 would run unsuccessfully for the U.S. Senate and in 1925 would begin an eight-year term as president of the Women's Christian Temperance Union.[6] The evening program began at 7:30 P.M., and Hopkins must have been quite pleased with the enthusiastic reception. "[E]very seat in the auditorium was occupied and chairs were used in the aisles" to seat the individuals who flocked to Concord Baptist for a riveting lecture by one of the nation's most insightful women intellectuals. "Miss Pauline E. Hopkins of Boston, Mass. was the speaker," reported the review of the meeting. "Her subject was 'Women.'" Hopkins "held the interest of her audience for forty-five minutes and closed with an earnest appeal to young women to take a position in the front in the work of temperance, religion, and reform."[7] On that day, Hopkins was able to hold her own as an ardent social activist, one who from her early school days had extolled the virtues of godliness, temperance, and fortitude. Her conversations with Ella Boole and her Dorcas Society hosts tapped into the persuasive call that she made in her prizewinning school essay, "The Evils of Intemperance and Their Remedies." In this eloquent piece, which she signed "Pauline E. Allen," Hopkins admitted unself-consciously in an elegant cursive script that she felt "it to be the task of Hercules, to endeavor to enumerate . . . the sin, and the depths of degredation [sic] to which . . . man has been reduced by the demon of excess; not only in strong drink, but in all the train of evils which it entails."[8] No doubt, by 1905, Hopkins felt more empowered than she had as a teenage writer to recommend bold moral and cultural reform.

During the spring of 1905, Hopkins delivered a series of public lectures in Boston that focused less on temperance and more on the power of feminist thought and effective masculinity. On 5 March, she returned to the Boston Literary and Historical Association venue at the Prince School, located on the corner of Newbury and Exeter Streets in Boston. Her address, entitled "The Crown of Manhood," was part of the spring series, which included Charles Chesnutt, who delivered the lecture "Race Prejudice: Its Causes and Its Cure" when he came to the Society in May.[9] In mid-November, Hopkins lectured before members of the St. Mark Musical and Literary Union for a second time. The opportunity to move once more in the mixed social, professional, and intellectual circles of the Association and the Union reinforced Hopkins's sense of the cultural authority that she could bring to bear on contemporary questions. Though some might regard her as a woman without reliable professional credentials, throughout 1905 she took advantage of her prominent contributions in the African American public sphere and promoted her perspectives, record of achievement, and future goals.

Hopkins had important allies on whom she could depend and with whom she could strategize about regional protests and outreach efforts. William Monroe Trotter, one of the nation's most tireless, ingenious, and outspoken journalists, would prove to be her most trusted adviser and helpful patron. Trotter moved easily between worlds that Hopkins could only glimpse from afar. When the year began and Hopkins was reorienting herself to a new life in Boston, for example, Trotter was organizing strategic sessions with the nation's leading scholars. On 15 January 1905, he convened in his Boston office a group that included W. E. B. Du Bois, Kelly Miller, and Archibald Grimké

William Monroe Trotter, Phi Beta Kappa graduate of Harvard,
editor of *The Guardian*, outspoken race activist, and ally
of Hopkins. *Courtesy of Photographs and Prints Division,
Schomburg Center for Research in Black Culture, The New York
Public Library, Astor, Lenox and Tilden Foundations.*

and set them all the task of "draft[ing] a petition to President Roosevelt asking
the federal government to enforce laws protecting Negro voting and guaran-
teeing equal accommodations in interstate travel."[10] Trotter had audiences
with presidents at the White House, attended international conferences, and
endured stints in jail as a result of his unrepentant civil disobedience, propen-
sity for disturbing the peace, and ingenious political resistance. Trotter carried
proudly the imprimatur of the nation's most elite university. He was a Phi Beta
Kappa graduate of Harvard and one of the school's earliest graduates of African descent. At Harvard, Trotter moved in an interracial circle that included
many friends from his high school alma mater, the Boston Latin School, and
"won a reputation as an aggressive advocate of social equality."[11] Trotter's

Advertisement for *The Guardian*, the paper founded and edited by
William Monroe Trotter that was known for its outspoken criticisms of
accommodationism and Booker T. Washington. This notice appeared
in the short-lived *New Era Magazine*, which Hopkins founded in 1916.
Courtesy of Moorland-Spingarn Research Center, Howard University.

class position and educational privilege gave him a particular immunity; his
brilliance, fortitude, and potential never were in question, even as his opponents ridiculed his critiques of accommodationism or protested his mischievous tactics for creating political disruptions. As an editor whose handling of
the day-to-day operations of his lively newspaper, *The Guardian*, Trotter also
could lay direct claim to the city's substantial journalistic history, especially
that history represented by William Lloyd Garrison's *Liberator*, which was
one of the primary models on which Trotter based the layout, scope, and
editorial components of his own newspaper.

Pauline Hopkins reconnected with her maternal Paul family antebellum
history when she forged her professional friendship and camaraderie with
William Monroe Trotter. They were of a like mind about the damage that
they believed Booker T. Washington was doing to the race. They also were
outraged by the favor bestowed by the white press on Washington and the
ways in which the mainstream media disregarded African American criticism
of the Tuskegee leader and power broker. As she forged new alliances with

members of the antiaccommodationist African American press and drafted ambitious publication plans of her own, Hopkins became part of a dynamic and outspoken group whose members considered themselves the political descendants and heirs of the antislavery cohort that included fearless individuals like William Lloyd Garrison, Thomas Paul, Susan Paul, James Monroe Whitfield, and Frederick Douglass.

The friendship between Hopkins and Trotter deepened considerably in 1905, when she found herself targeted by the networks that Trotter deemed inherently destructive to African American interests. Hopkins was well aware, in the summer of 1905, of Trotter's latest ambitious endeavor: to assemble the leading race men of the day to Niagara Falls, where they would "discuss serious matters like gentlemen" and create a "nonpartisan organization to define objectives and strategies for the race."[12] These meetings, which became known as the Niagara Movement, included attendees such as J. Max Barber and W. E. B. Du Bois. The annual gatherings eventually led to the historic formation in 1909 of the National Association for the Advancement of Colored People. Despite the fact that Hopkins was well qualified to participate in such foundational discourse, as were a significant number of other accomplished American women of color, she would once again remain on the margins. Hopkins's politics identified her as an ally of the Niagara Movement, but the times and circumstances prevented her from realizing fully her own public political potential.

The professional and public high point for Hopkins in 1905 came just a few weeks after she delivered her lecture at the St. Marks Musical and Literary Union meeting. On 10 December, Pauline Hopkins joined other luminaries to mark the centennial of the birth of William Lloyd Garrison, one of Boston's most enterprising and tireless abolitionists. A photograph of a meditative Hopkins adorned the front page of *The Guardian* and appeared above the fold. The paper, which traditionally used multiple columns on all pages, included its report of the event and Hopkins's memorable contributions in the center column of the front page. Hopkins's stately and composed image looked out from beneath the paper's celebratory banner, which proclaimed, "Greater Boston's Two Days' Garrison Centennial an Unprecedented Success."[13] She was part of what Trotter, with great gusto, referred to as a "galaxy of orators," and his spirited report still conjures up the intensity of that historic moment.

There were nationwide celebrations of Garrison's birth in December 1905, but none rivaled the citywide, multivenue, and collective celebration, tribute, and memorial that Bostonians organized. Booker T. Washington, writing from Tuskegee on 11 October 1905 to the editor of the *New York Times*, had urged Americans to ensure that the historic dates "not pass without proper recognition on the part of the white people." He alluded to the "[s]teps . . . being taken by the colored people to have the event celebrated by members of their race throughout the country" but felt compelled, "as a member of the race which [Garrison] most served, [to] urg[e] upon the public the importance of seeing that the celebration of his one hundredth anniversary shall be of such a character as to do credit to our entire country."[14] Some constituencies may have heeded Washington's words, but whether or not their efforts, such as those organized at the People's Institute at Cooper Union in Manhattan, honored the legacy of Garrison was debatable. The *New York Times* coverage of the Garrison Centennial events was sparse and included only two pieces, both of which suggested that Garrison's pioneering commitment to interracial solidarity had not fully permeated twentieth-century New York.[15] Apparently the event, held in a Cooper Union auditorium, though "crowded to the doors," featured not even one "negro man or woman in the big hall."[16]

The Boston effort, with its ambitious scope, interracial collaboration, and African American leadership, easily eclipsed all other national Garrison celebrations. The centennial was a rallying moment that provided some of the nation's most hardworking and visionary citizens with an opportunity to mobilize around a thoroughly edifying history. Trotter was the recognized general of the enthusiastic regiments that devoted hours to committee work, site preparation, hosting, presenting, and programming. Trotter created several committees, and the groups organized reunions for members of the *Colored American Magazine* network, as well as introductions to descendants of the city's stalwart families whose ancestors had been at the forefront of key campaigns, such as those relating to abolition and antislavery resistance, school desegregation, and Civil War recruitment. One of the sure signs that the 1905 event was one that understood the core principles of Garrison's life and his passionate commitment to social justice, equality, and freedom was the designation of the Centennial's primary planning group as the "Citizens Committee." The subcommittees read like a who's who of Boston—and the list reflects the thoroughly heterogeneous mix of social and working classes, young and old, veterans and pacifists, women and men. Ever mindful of the power of the people, Trotter allocated considerable space to full listings of the committee members, and his efforts provide invaluable insights into the community leadership that Pauline Hopkins and close friends of the Hopkins family played in this momentous celebration. Mark De Mortie, the lifelong friend of Pauline's stepfather, William Hopkins, chaired the all-important Committee of Arrangements, and the sizeable group with whom he worked closely included two men who figured prominently in the *Colored American*

Magazine enterprise, William H. Dupree and J. H. Wolff. Also included in the equally mixed group of men and women was Mrs. Virginia Trotter and Mrs. C. G. Morgan, wife of prominent Boston attorney Clement G. Morgan. Pauline Hopkins agreed to serve as chair of the Committee on Printing, and in that capacity she had the critical task of overseeing the production of all event publications. Her committee included fellow Boston writer Olivia Ward Bush, *Colored American Magazine* contributor Dr. Charles G. Steward, and Mrs. W. M. Trotter. Other committees tapped into the considerable artistic strengths of Boston's music and arts constituency. Julius B. Goddard, who worked as a messenger at the Republican state committee headquarters in Boston,[17] as chair of the Committee on Music collaborated with Mrs. Maud Cuney Hare, the gifted pianist, student at Boston's prestigious New England Conservatory, and the future music editor of the *Crisis*,[18] and with George Lewis Ruffin, the former Progressive Musical Union member and barber who eventually became one of the city's leading judges and the Boston Consul for the Dominican Republic.[19]

The Resolutions Committee membership list was one of the most inspiring assemblies involved in the Garrison Centennial. Its members were linked to powerful moments in American publishing history, to far-reaching local advances in education, and to national triumphs for African American women. Chairman T. P. Taylor worked alongside the celebrated poet William Stanley Braithewaite, whose wife, identified as "Mrs. W. S. Braithewaite," was on the Committee on Reception. Also serving on the Resolutions Committee with Braithwaite was Mrs. Addie Jewell, the Bostonian whose forthright evaluation of Hopkins's public reading of *Contending Forces* just before the book's publication is one of the rare firsthand accounts of Hopkins's self-presentation. The committee included Miss Maria L. Baldwin, the beloved and highly respected Cambridge teacher, who, in 1916, would become master, or principal, of the Agassiz School and hold "the most distinguished position achieved by a person of Negro descent in the teaching world of America."[20] Maude Trotter, the activist sister of William Monroe Trotter, also was involved on the Resolutions Committee.[21] Also on the committee were Emery T. Morris, the nephew of pioneering attorney Robert Morris, treasurer of the Colored National League, and the assistant sealer of weights and measures for the city of Boston,[22] and two of Hopkins's cousins, Mrs. Hannah Smith and Miss Hattie Smith.

Alexander's Magazine reported that Hopkins took a "conspicuous part" in the events. At the Monday afternoon event where she was featured most prominently, Hopkins had the opportunity to talk with eighty-six-year-old Julia Ward Howe, author of "Battle Hymn of the Republic," and to mingle with Francis Jackson Garrison, a man whom she would have regarded with additional interest given his publishing connections at Houghton, Mifflin & Company. The celebration overall constituted a most timely moment for Hopkins, one that enabled her to reassert the ancestral links that she had to Boston's unsurpassed history of antebellum activism and interracial leadership. At this moment in her life, recently deprived of the professional platform for which she had sacrificed much on behalf of the race's advancement, Hopkins could revel in the attention to Garrison and its explicit affirmation of her and her family. On Sunday evening, Hopkins and her community heard the Paul family history acknowledged once again for its fearless alliances with Garrison.

Francis Jackson Garrison, son of the *Liberator* editor, delivered a stirring speech at the Joy Street Church, the sanctuary to which Hopkins referred the very next day in the preface to her Faneuil Hall speech. The church, which since 1898 had been serving as a temple for the congregation Anshi Lubavitch, was opened to the Boston public for the Garrison celebrations. Centennial organizers took care to honor the holy practices of the new congregation. "There was some effort necessary at first," Trotter admitted, "to make the men understand that they should keep their heads covered in accord with the custom of the Jews in their synagogues."[23] Eventually, the protocols were established, and the old African Church was "filled to overflowing." This dramatic sight may have softened the mortification that Hopkins felt about the fact that the church of her ancestors had "done more than change its coat—it ha[d] changed religions, too," and her conviction that "[i]f brick and mortar can mourn—even stone possesses life—how many tears that venerable building must have shed over its fall from Christianity."[24] In the place "where many stirring events in those days took place," Bostonians filled the galleries and "people standing reached out in the corridors. In fact as many as it was deemed safe for the building's strength were crowded into it," reported Trotter.[25] Garrison was accorded a place of honor at the front of the sanctuary, and "[s]eated on the small altar platform were Mr. Francis J. Garrison, son of the Abolitionist and head of the great publishing house of Houghton, Mifflin & Company, and Butler R. Wilson, Esq., president of the Boston Literary Association. On the first step, Miss Maude A. Trotter, president of the St. Mark Literary[,] was seated[,] and below and in front of the altar sat Misses Lillian Chapelle and Bessie V. Trotter, secretaries of the St. Mark's and of the Boston Literary[,] respectively[,] and the speakers."[26]

The Guardian delighted in the historic reunion, announcing enthusiastically on the front pages of its Saturday, 16 December 1905, issue not only that the "Son of Garrison Speaks at Smith Court Church" but that "Reminiscences of

Those Who Knew Garrison Delight Audience That Fills the Edifice."[27] In this "sacred spot in the anti-slavery history of Boston," Francis Garrison spoke proudly about his father's visionary zeal and unrelenting social justice work. "I do not recall anything in my father's career that illustrates more strikingly this sure instinct, his indomitable courage, his unwavering confidence in the power of truth over all obstacles, than the stand he took that stormy winter evening in the little schoolroom downstairs."[28] Garrison here was referring to the formation of the New England Anti-Slavery Society in the basement schoolrooms of the African Church, a scene that wide-eyed William Cooper Nell witnessed from the window, even as the snow fell about him. Garrison praised the fidelity and vigilance of men like Hannibal Lewis, Solomon Alexander, Thomas Cole, and Hopkins's relative, John B. Cutler, the nephew of Nathaniel Paul, her great-granduncle and son of Dorothy Paul Cutler and her husband, Tobias Cutler. Francis Jackson Garrison made mention of Cutler and his peers as he held in his hand a "roll of members" of the New England Anti-Slavery Society, which included "the names of many well-known Colored men of that day." Cutler was one of *The Liberator*'s earliest promoters and, from the 1830s, was president of the Massachusetts Union Harmonic Society and another active member of the city's sophisticated African American cultural scene. He used his barbershop on the corner of Poplar and Chamber Streets as a political forum and regularly promoted the paper, also using his shop as a ticket agency for the events that it advertised.

Francis Garrison represented another cherished link to the antebellum past that Hopkins and so many other Bostonians held dear. "I know not how many of them will be recognized by members of this audience," said Garrison, "but some of them were household names in my boyhood, and I know in what warm esteem my father held John T. Hilton, the barber in Howard Street . . . Phillip A. Bell . . . and John E. Scarlett, a chimney sweep, and one of the little band of Colored men who constituted themselves a body guard to my father and sometimes followed him on his dark and lonely midnight walks over the Boston Neck to his Roxbury home."[29] Although he worried that his 1905 audience might be unfamiliar with the antislavery leaders he mentioned, his audience knew them all intimately. Garrison made direct mention of the Paul family, recalling that "finally there was Thomas Paul, the Negro apprentice boy who was the only visible auxiliary of my father when Mayor Otis' police officers entered the attic printing office of the 'Liberator' on a detective hunt to oblige a southern senator."[30]

The Garrison Centennial celebration also provides information about the women's networks of which Hopkins was a part. Information about her personal friendships still remains sketchy, but it is likely that her passion for

Well Known as a Race Writer

literature and the arts eased her into conversations and collaborations with ambitious and talented local women such as Olivia Ward Bush and Nellie Brown Mitchell. Hopkins had been involved with both women in professional and feminist work. Bush, one of Hopkins's National Association of Colored Women colleagues, was part of the historic women's meetings that led to the formation of the national organization. During the festive Garrison celebrations, Bush had the daunting task of overseeing the "several hundred Sunday school children from the various Colored churches in Boston and Cambridge [who] assembled in the corridors of the Public Library" in anticipation of the walk through Copley Square to the Garrison statue.[31] She prevailed so graciously during the Sunday afternoon procession on Commonwealth Avenue that Trotter could assure his readers that the parade "was a most inspiring sight" that demonstrated clearly "the interest and devotion shown [to Garrison] by the school children and by the old men."[32]

The Garrison Centennial celebrations also reaffirmed Hopkins's quiet interest in the elderly women of color in Boston. The Sunday proceedings included a service at 125 Highland Street in Roxbury in the last home in which Garrison had lived while in Massachusetts. In *Contending Forces*, she demonstrated the philanthropic leanings of the characters Sappho Clark and Dora Smith by sending them off to deliver baskets to St. Monica's, a home for the elderly located, at one point in its history, on Myrtle Street on Beacon Hill. They "visited the home for aged women on M— Street, and read and sang to the occupants."[33] Five years after Hopkins incorporated St. Monica's elderly home and hospital into her novel, Bostonians could once again get a glimpse into the vital institution. "Touching Service by Colored Women at Homestead," declared *The Guardian*'s front-page coverage of the Garrison Centennial events. It focused on the events held at Garrison's home and provided respectful information about the aged occupants of St. Monica's Home for Sick Colored Women and Children. The session was the only one of the weekend that was shaped directly and primarily by Boston women. Members of St. Monica's Aid Sewing Circle and of St. Monica's Relief Association, identified as "two organizations of Colored women that give financial aid to this hospital," were on hand in full, as were "a goodly number of women and several men" who, "despite the storm and long, high climb to 'Rockledge,' as Garrison's home was known, "were present to show their devotion."[34] The group included Mrs. William Goodell, Relief Association secretary; John D. Willard, a Garrison family friend and former organist in the church of Theodore Parker; Mrs. George Glover; and Geraldine L. Trotter, the woman whose heart W. E. B. Du Bois had lost to his Harvard colleague William Monroe Trotter. All gathered in the "Garrison Ward," a "large rectangular room, formerly used as the parlor of the homestead," where a number of elderly women now rested in single beds or in rocking chairs. The session at St. Monica's illuminated the care with which William Monroe Trotter, Pauline Hopkins, and so many others in leadership positions on the planning committees honored the life of William Lloyd Garrison and the efforts of the often unsung extraordinary citizens with whom he had worked, strategized, and triumphed. As 1905 drew to a close, Hopkins had succeeded in restoring her public profile and deploying with aplomb her inspiring ancestral legacies.

In the years after Pauline Hopkins's marvelous contributions to the Garrison festivities, she and her mother suffered the loss of William Hopkins. His death occurred in early 1906, the first and only year in which Pauline appeared in the Cambridge city directories with the profession "writer" listed after her name. On 16 February, William Hopkins succumbed to apoplexy and complications from "calcarious blood vessels" that his doctor, George A. Miles of West Somerville, could not overcome.[35] His devoted wife and stepdaughter made arrangements with a local undertaker, Timothy T. A. Danehy of Cambridge. Within days of his passing, William was laid to rest in the Allen family plot in the Garden Cemetery in Chelsea, Massachusetts. In the years after the death of William Hopkins, Pauline appears to have escaped into the working world and to have set aside her writing life while she tended to her mother, Sarah, and provided for them both. The Cambridge directories again confirm Pauline's presence in the city only after her mother passed away in the fall of 1914. Until then, it was entries that read "Hopkins, Sarah A. wid. William, 53 Clifton" that indicated the family's presence and resilience.

The impassioned speech that Pauline delivered at Faneuil Hall in December 1905 prompted William Monroe Trotter to turn to her again six years later, in 1911, when Bostonians marked the centennial anniversary of the birth of Charles Sumner. In January 1911, Hopkins responded once again to William Monroe Trotter, her tireless ally, and accepted his invitation to serve on the Citizens Auxiliary Committee for the Sumner Centennial. She agreed to deliver a speech in honor of Sumner, the lawyer who had argued forcefully with Robert Morris in 1849 for the desegregation of Boston public schools and for providing the children in Beacon Hill's Abiel Smith School and other segregated institutions with all the resources and equal opportunities that were due them. When she joined the Sumner celebrations, Hopkins was sobered by recent family losses, and she also may have been exhausted by the labor that now consumed her days. Trotter reported that "Miss Hopkins spoke briefly"

Well Known as a Race Writer

but noted that the length of her presentation did not diminish her capacity to speak "with much point and ability, upholding and defending the radical liberty spirit of Charles Sumner and decrying compromise." Trotter seemed especially pleased to emphasize that Hopkins "said no one knew the latest potentialities of the Colored Race which might yet punish its oppressors."[36] There was a characteristic vigor in the concise review that Trotter provided of Hopkins's speech at the Sumner celebration. Her words were powerful and demonstrated that the accomplished author had not relinquished her command of race politics. She used lines from Elijah Smith's poem "Our Lost Leader" as the final statement in her speech, another sure sign of her enduring investment in her family's tradition of race leadership. Nor had she stepped away completely from the ongoing national and international efforts for racial justice, political reform, and social stability. Her enduring ties to Trotter kept her abreast of the efforts that sought to deny African Americans a rightful and protected place in American society. In 1911, as he planned the Sumner events, Trotter was collaborating with fellow members of the National Association for the Advancement of Colored People to "defeat a bill in the General Court that would have banned interracial marriage in Massachusetts."[37]

The fall of 1913 brought with it another episode of deep loss for Pauline Hopkins. Sarah died on Wednesday, 24 September, after fighting a painful battle against severe nephritis and arteriosclerosis. Three days later, on Saturday, 27 September, Hopkins laid her mother to rest on the Lilac Way in Chelsea's Garden Cemetery, near her parents, Jesse and Elizabeth Allen, and alongside her husband, William, whom Sarah had loved for decades. In the weeks and months following her mother's death, Hopkins worked to improve her finances. She began to rent rooms in her home, and in so doing, began the transformation from owner to boarder that would not change until her own death in 1930.[38]

Hopkins suffered greatly when, during a period of seven years, she lost her father and mother, who had been her closest friends. She rallied herself, though, taking comfort from the fact that she had been a steadfast daughter and for years had met, honorably and lovingly, the responsibilities that came from caring for elderly parents. Now fifty-six years of age, she had the benefit of considerable work experience and had more than proved herself a powerful standard bearer of the activist past that she had inherited from all three of her parents. This was a moment to be seized, and she wasted no time in preparing to take Boston and the world by storm once again.

19

The *New Era Magazine* and a "Singlewoman of Boston"

Let us make, if we can, the rough places smooth;
let us write naught that need cause a blush to rise to our
cheek even in old age. Let us feel the magnitude of the work,
its vast possibilities for good or ill. Let us strive ever not to be
famous, but to be wisely helpful, leaders and guides for
those who look eagerly for the daily or weekly feast
that we set before them.

MRS. N. F. MOSSELL
"Our Women in Journalism," in
The Work of Afro-American Women,
1894

[F]rom New England we expect an influence will yet go
forth that will at least help win for the Negro in the South
the advantages that are accorded him in the North.

P. THOMAS STANFORD
The Tragedy of the Negro in America,
1897

Booker T. Washington had been dead for sixteen weeks when the long-awaited professional resurrection of Pauline Hopkins occurred. She made her debut in the spring of 1916 as the editor of the *New Era Magazine*, the nation's newest race magazine. The moment was complicated by the triumphs, the possibilities, and the past that came to bear on her literary renaissance. Hopkins had outlived her nemesis, but his passing might have heightened her sense of mortality and the unpredictable turns of life. Now she was fifty-seven years old, the same age that Washington had been when he died in November of 1915, just hours after reaching Tuskegee in a dramatic railroad and overland ambulance journey that brought him from New York City to Chehaw, Alabama, and then to Tuskegee. He was returned to the American South where he was "born . . . lived and labored," and, as he told reporters, where he "expect[ed] to die and be buried."[1] That last journey out of New York could have been read by anti-Bookerites like Hopkins as a final and long-overdue retreat, an epic journey of a powerful man now disabled, unable and at last disinclined to wield the power that silenced many and consigned others to professions not of their first, or even second, choosing. The New Year of 1916 would bring long-deserved possibilities for individuals like Pauline Hopkins, a woman whose sense of mission and calling had survived the professional deprivation that Washington had so effectively sanctioned.

In March 1916, Hopkins proudly introduced the first issue of what promised to be a bold and substantive new periodical. The magazine reflected her deep New England roots, her partnerships within the highly organized African American women's club network, and the pan-Africanist connections that she had first cultivated at the *Colored American Magazine*. The *New Era Magazine* had a distinctive New England flair that seemed to defy the global mayhem and upheaval sparked by the January bombings of Paris by German zeppelins, the withdrawal of Allied Forces from Gallipoli, and Pancho Villa's recent incursions into New Mexico that prompted President Woodrow Wilson's retaliatory dispatch of 12,000 American soldiers into Mexico to apprehend him. The prospectus for the magazine testified to the earnest and sincere hopes of the publishers and their high expectations for the *New Era Magazine*. It was to be "an illustrated and thoroughly up-to-date magazine" and "devoted exclusively to the best interests of the colored race, not alone in this country, but throughout the world." The journal was a purposeful response to the "rapid progress made by the race in this country during the past twenty to twenty-five years," and, as a documentary vehicle, it would "deal fully and frankly with all questions affecting the progress of the race." The magazine pledged to "do its utmost to assist in developing the literature, science, music, art, religion, facts, fiction, and tradition of the race throughout the world."[2]

The *New Era Magazine* is situated rather memorably between three major African American journals that became synonymous with the Harlem Renaissance. The *New Era Magazine* debuted six years after the *Crisis*, the official publication of the National Association for the Advancement of Colored People for which W. E. B. Du Bois was the founding editor. The *New Era Magazine* preceded by nine months the *Messenger*, the socialist periodical developed by A. Philip Randolph and Chandler Owen.[3] It also preceded by six years the journal *Opportunity*, which appeared in 1922, with sociologist Charles S. Johnson as editor. Hopkins's Boston journal, from the outset, seemed determined to sidestep the "graveyard of ambitious and worthy ventures" to which W. E. B. Du Bois had referred in his 1912 *Crisis* retrospective assessment of the *Colored American Magazine* and the *Voice of the Negro*.[4]

The publication of the *New Era Magazine* revived the professional shadow dance in which Pauline Hopkins and W. E. B. Du Bois had been silent partners for years. Though there is not a single known letter between them, no known photograph that confirms their physical proximity to one another, and no extensive commentary about each other in any extant correspondence that either one of them generated with their friends and colleagues, it is clear that Hopkins and Du Bois were well aware of each other. She, like many, knew him best as the luminary intellectual who presided on the national stage and was feted in Boston's African American social and professional circles. He knew of her more distantly, but she must have stood out. She was a professional writer, an outspoken woman whose political victimization and professional trials were brought to his attention. Her work as a journalist and editor with the *Colored American Magazine* anticipated, and even shaped, his conception of the race periodicals that he hoped to produce. Du Bois benefited from Hopkins's early journalistic trials and her innovations in publishing, but he might have thought that to acknowledge Hopkins publicly might diminish his own professional stature and the hard-won reputation that he had scrupulously created and protected.

In 1916, the roles of Hopkins and Du Bois were reversed. The *Crisis* now was the established race journal of the time, and it is apparent that Hopkins and her associates studied it. Just as there were ways in which the features, layout, and editorial presentation of the *Colored American Magazine* influenced the proposals that Du Bois articulated in the early 1900s, the *Crisis* functioned as an important model for the *New Era Magazine*. One of the most discernible ways in which the *New Era Magazine* attempted to situate itself in the periodical marketplace was to revive the important biographical series that Hopkins had shaped. In 1916, however, for those who might have been unfamiliar with the *Colored American Magazine*, the *New Era Magazine* appeared to imitate the *Crisis* and "Men of Mark," its regular, tidy, and illustrated feature that, despite its gender-specific title, included, on occasion, "women of mark" as well. In 1910, that was one of the first elements that Du Bois incorporated into the *Crisis*.

The *New Era Magazine*'s first issue, made up of sixty-one pages and ten crisp black-and-white photographs, focused insistently on America, although its contents revealed an editorial focus on an American landscape that raised the specter of significant turmoil within American borders. Adorning the magazine's cover was an evocative image of a contemplative William Stanley Braithwaite. The Boston poet and editor was presented in profile, his head bowed, his forehead and face illuminated partially by a soft light. The table of contents revealed the strong foundation and body of Hopkins's own work on which she and her small staff were building. Interspersed between short articles on "Musical Appreciation" by Clarence Cameron White, spirited dialect fiction written by Hopkins using the Sarah A. Allen pseudonym, and "Helpful Suggestions for Young Artists" by Meta Vaux Warrick-Fuller were essays on distinctive New England institutions and events. These included the tribute to the Home for Aged Colored Women, the institution for which Hopkins had a tender regard, and articles noting the fiftieth-anniversary celebrations that marked the passage of the Thirteenth Amendment, the statute that abolished American slavery. A promising series, entitled "Men of Vision," dedicated to profiles of accomplished African American men and energetic articles about Wendell Phillips, Abraham Lincoln, and the Home for Aged Colored Women transported readers back into the golden age of abolition, emancipatory Republican legislation, assertive social work, and unapologetic racial uplift. These very themes underscored the new era in which Hopkins now was writing.

It is difficult to separate the professional rebirth of Pauline Hopkins from the death of Washington, and it seems to have had its challenges for her. The magazine's second issue began with a page that preceded, or even usurped, the table of contents. The April issue opened first to a full-page advertisement that included a large formal photograph of the Wizard of Tuskegee at its center. The "Excellent Portrait" of Washington, the "Great Race Leader," was "beautifully executed and mounted with tinted border, size 11 × 14 inches, and suitable for framing."[5] It was "NOT FOR SALE" but would be given free of charge to all those who subscribed to the *New Era Magazine*. Those who knew the unfortunate history of Hopkins's interactions with Washington and his allies might have found this portrait a jarring image to behold. Hopkins might have explained the uncomfortable situation by recalling her own advice to *Voice of the Negro* editor J. Max Barber about not "go[ing] over to your enemy any farther than you can help to keep living."[6] The Washington advertisement exuded an immediate and wry irony. The use of Washington to sustain, rather than to sap, the periodical, may have been a most satisfying revenge for Hopkins, even as the commodification of him revealed the unemotional and practical decision making that Hopkins required of herself.

Hopkins never gave any public indication that she regarded the *New Era Magazine* as a fortuitous second chance or as a precious opportunity to recoup the noble aims and sincere intentions that had undergirded the *Colored American Magazine* in its Boston years. She crafted an impassioned statement of intent, one fueled by a discernible and unwavering commitment to racial uplift. "We are sparing neither time nor money to make this Magazine the most authentic historian of the race's progress," she declared emphatically in the "Editorial and Publisher's Announcements," the most prestigious perch in any publication, which now was hers.[7] It was almost impossible to detect in her editorial comments any scars from the tussle over the intellectual and editorial rights to the *Colored American Magazine*. She was fervent about the collective race venture, and her overtures to readers, couched in easy prose that seemed like an exchange between friends, were infused with optimism. "Put yourself out to make it known to your friends," she encouraged readers, "that they have a race Magazine, which shall be a Magazine from all stand-points and we *must* have their support in building this monument to future generations, and the satisfaction that we have lived in this world not as para-sites, but have helped make the world better and wiser by our lives."[8] The rhe-toric of possession in her words certainly hinted at lessons that Hopkins may have learned during the *Colored American Magazine* years. They also revealed, however, the strategy that Hopkins and the New Era Publishing Company needed to use to sustain their dream of a "large Publishing House for the race, which will issue books, pamphlets, music and art works of our people at a minimum cost, and see that they are distributed where they will do the most good."[9] The power of the people was what Hopkins and the company had to marshal; indeed, their venture epitomized the self-help principles of the age. There was practical labor involved if intellectual capital was to be acquired and deployed. "Are you with us?" Hopkins asked pointedly. "Get busy and place your shoulder to the wheel with us today, not tomorrow, but NOW."[10]

The *New Era Magazine* often has been portrayed in contemporary literary criticism and in African American history as the publishing company that Hopkins founded. She certainly played a key role in the company's major, albeit short-lived, project, but announcements and the *New Era Magazine* prospectus assert that the company was established by four male colleagues of Hopkins. Like her former Colored Co-operative Publishing Company col-leagues, this small band of men also were willing to commit their own funds and to secure backing for the company. The New Era Publishing Company was "formed by a number of successful business and professional men of the race," whose shared concern with "matters of racial interest" fueled their "ultimate aim of establishing in Boston, not alone a strong and helpful maga-zine, but a *Race Publishing House*, that shall stand as a permanent and lasting monument of race progress."[11] The company founders included resourceful

J. H. Blackwell, president of the New Era Publishing Company,
which sponsored Hopkins's *New Era Magazine*. *Courtesy of
Moorland-Spingarn Research Center, Howard University.*

men—like Hopkins's uncle, the Boston African American poet laureate and
longtime Young's Hotel headwaiter Elijah Smith—who worked at demanding, labor-intensive jobs and used their wages to finance their real and otherwise frustrated professional and creative dreams.

The president of the New Era Publishing Company was forty-year-old Virginia native James H. Blackwell. In 1916, Blackwell was living with Mazie,
his twenty-four-year-old Canadian-born wife, and their two daughters, five-
year-old Verna and two-year-old Mazie J.[12] The company's vice president

Emery T. Morris, nephew of famed Boston attorney Robert
Morris and a prominent Bostonian in his own right. In 1916 at
age sixty-five, Emery Morris invested in the *New Era Magazine*
venture spearheaded by Hopkins and became vice president
of the New Era Publishing Company. *Courtesy of Moorland-
Spingarn Research Center, Howard University.*

was Emery T. Morris, at sixty-five the oldest man on the company board. At
the time that he joined the New Era venture, Emery, the nephew of the beloved pioneering attorney Robert Morris, was living in Cambridge with his
wife, Elizabeth, in a multifamily home on Parker Street that they shared with
sixty-five-year-old Ida Chapman and her three adult children. The Morris
home was the only African American residence on the block, which included
white families of Italian, Irish, and British descent who worked as teachers,
chauffeurs, junk dealers, salesmen, electricians, piano tuners, stenographers,

Walter Wallace, cofounder of the *Colored American Magazine* and the Colored Co-operative Publishing Company, which published *Contending Forces*. Wallace also worked closely with Hopkins as managing editor of the *New Era Magazine* and served as secretary of the New Era Publishing Company. *Courtesy of Moorland-Spingarn Research Center, Howard University.*

and servants. In this neighborhood, Morris had the most prestigious of jobs. His longtime city white-collar post of assistant sealer of weights and measures added considerable prestige to the family and also to the New Era Publishing Company enterprise. Walter Wallace, who was affiliated with both the company board as secretary and with its magazine as the managing editor, was trying his luck again in the publishing industry. He now had invaluable experience from the impressive venture that he had pursued in 1900, along

Arthur Dunson, a Bostonian whose father worked in a local
hotel, served as treasurer of the New Era Publishing Company.
He was the youngest member of the company. *Courtesy of
Moorland-Spingarn Research Center, Howard University.*

with good local connections and a sober maturity that enabled him to complement and to lead this collective New Era effort. Arthur Dunson, the treasurer,
was the youngest member of the four-man publishing company board. Born
in Boston in 1896 to Arthur and Severina Dunson, he was the oldest of three
children. He too shared the connection to the service industry and the thriving
public/private subculture of African American activism through his father,
who in 1900 was working as a waiter at an unidentified Boston hotel.

The arrangement between the New Era Publishing Company and the *New
Era Magazine* revealed a gender dynamic similar to the one that had governed
the *Colored American Magazine*. In this instance, though, Hopkins was the

Emery T. Morris-Gordon, an earnest writer, joined
the *New Era Magazine* as its associate editor. *Courtesy of
Moorland-Spingarn Research Center, Howard University.*

editor in chief, a role that she had never formally had during her years at the
Colored American Magazine. She may have chafed at the patriarchal structure
of the company, but, in giving up certain important responsibilities to her colleagues, she freed herself to generate the most ambitious and polished journal
that she could. As once again the creative genius on whose shoulders rested
the mission of visionary men, Hopkins seemed to relish her creative freedom.
She immersed herself fully in the effort to educate a national and international readership, to facilitate stimulating and meaningful debate among the
race's promising new leaders, and to provide meaningful connections between
modern Bostonians and their impressive nineteenth-century New England
history.

In addition to editor Hopkins and managing editor Wallace, the *New Era
Magazine* staff included Gertrude Cromwell and Emery T. Morris-Gordon,

two associate editors who brought fresh perspectives, good resolve, and an appreciation of Hopkins's unwavering resolve. Cromwell and Hopkins both were in their fifties, lived in Cambridge, and had established ties to the local and national women's club movement. When she joined the *New Era Magazine* in 1916, the fifty-four-year-old Cromwell, wife of the Wisconsin-born William L. Cromwell, who had English and American parents, was celebrated as "one of the best known literary and club women of the race in this part of the country."[13] The *New Era Magazine* founders were confident that Cromwell would "keep our readers constantly informed as to the doings among all department of the women's clubs throughout the country."[14] Emery T. Morris-Gordon also was touted as a "well-known contributor to the leading race publications in foreign countries" and promoted as one who would bring to the *New Era Magazine* "a wealth of world-wide information on all matters affecting our interests."[15]

The *New Era Magazine* was marketed deliberately as "An Illustrated Monthly Devoted to the World-Wide Interests of the Colored Race."[16] Hopkins made shrewd publishing arrangements with contributors and contracted with several to provide multiessay series to the magazine. The prospectus promised "A Word from Africa," a "series of articles that will give our readers a few comprehensive happenings in the life and struggle of the natives of Liberia."[17] It also heralded the forthcoming series "Porto Rico and the United States," autobiographical essays by a Puerto Rican native who would focus on "his native country and its relations to America, especially those which concern the economic relations of our race here and there."[18] Hopkins was a discerning editor, and it showed in some of the first decisions that she made about her contributors. The two young Harvard graduates she recruited as writers for the African and Puerto Rican series went on to become internationally recognized representatives of their respective nations and helped to shape the role of the Western world in nations of the Third World.

Plenyono Gbe Wolo, a Liberian student at Harvard and treasurer of the Harvard Cosmopolitan Club, was the author whom Hopkins chose to write the series "A Word from Africa."[19] In 1916, Wolo had been "honored by election" to serve as the treasurer of the Harvard Cosmopolitan Club. As recently as 2000, Wolo, whom the *New Era Magazine* described as "the son of a savage African chieftain of Liberia" and "splendid specimen of the native African," was remembered as one of the "stalwart sons of Liberia."[20]

The author of the Puerto Rican autobiographical essays was Pedro Albizu Campos, a twenty-five-year-old native of the island, who in 1916 was almost ready to graduate from Harvard University, where he was president of the Cosmopolitan Club. Within the next fourteen years, Campos would become "[o]ne of the most controversial figures of the twentieth century," known for "voic[ing] his protests of U.S. imperialism and racism as he rose through the ranks of the Puerto Rican Nationalist Party to become its President in 1930."[21] One year after the *New Era Magazine* published him in the magazine, Campos enlisted to fight in World War I, joined the segregated U.S. Army, and fought with an African American unit.[22] The *New Era Magazine* prospectus that highlighted the pending contributions of Wolo and Campos alongside its mention of articles on prejudice, the African American Masonic tradition, the historically black American colleges and universities, and reviews of the "Business Progress of the Race," suggested that the magazine would be a well-rounded journal. According to the pre-publicity materials created to pique the interest of potential subscribers and advertisers, the monthly magazine would blend works on American culture, history, and literature with international narratives on race, imperialism, and resistance. The first two issues of the *New Era Magazine* did strive to meet these published goals, but it was clear that the magazine was being marketed directly to New Englanders in particular and to Northerners in general.

Although the *New Era Magazine* prospectus announced that the magazine would be available "early in the fall" of 1915, the first issue did not appear until February 1916. There were twelve articles listed in the opening pages, but an additional nine items not itemized in the formal table of contents also filled out the issue. Among the works not listed in the table of contents was "Converting Fanny," a short story that Hopkins published under her time-tested pseudonym of Sarah A. Allen, an article on Puerto Rico by Pedro Campos, and a splendid history of the "Home for Aged Colored Women of Boston" written by Emery T. Morris, the New Era Publishing Company's vice president. The magazine featured three pieces directly related to contemporary artists and artistic technique and two works of fiction. One was *Topsy Templeton*, a serialized novella for which Hopkins took full credit. The other fictional piece was a short story by J. I. Morehead that was highly reminiscent of Hopkins's own story on mesmerism, "The Mystery Within Us," with which she had made her publishing debut in the *Colored American Magazine* in May 1900. In addition to providing Hopkins with a welcome forum in which to write fiction and document American history, the *New Era Magazine* also accommodated Hopkins's passion for African American history and her belief that twentieth-century audiences had much to gain intellectually, socially, and emotionally from the stories of the past. The February 1916 issue included four historical articles, two on prominent white men and two that focused on unsung African Americans of New England. The first of the four historical articles was devoted to Wendell Phillips, the dedicated abolitionist and longtime comrade of William Lloyd Garrison. The article was not attributed to any named author, a fact that suggests that it was the handiwork of Hopkins herself. It concluded with lines from the powerful 1884 "Monody," by New Hampshire writer Thomas Bailey Aldrich. The narrative may have been the result of a savvy marketing strategy. The poem, with its noble eulogy of Phillips, certainly did heighten the appeal of the *New Era Magazine* for white elite Bostonians, who cherished the legacy of Phillips, a Harvard College graduate and the son of Boston's first mayor. Many of the members of the *New Era Magazine*'s targeted audience also cherished Aldrich, the New Hampshire native whom many regarded as the father of the American novel and the man whose *Story of a Bad Boy* inspired Mark Twain's best-selling *Tom Sawyer*. William Stanley Braithwaite hailed Phillips as a "Wondersmith in vocables" in "On the Death of Thomas Bailey Aldrich," his lengthy 1907 tribute, which he composed on the occasion of Aldrich's death and published one year later in his collection, *The House of Falling Leaves, with Other Poems*. Braithwaite's tribute suggests the level of cross-racial familiarity with Aldrich and is a helpful gauge of the potential reception that Hopkins's readers—white and African American New Englanders—brought to their encounter with the *New Era Magazine*.

Hopkins's inclusion of Aldrich also may have been a calculated marketing gamble, one that counted on the lasting appeal emanating from the endearing and tragic love story that featured Aldrich vying for the opportunity to marry the daughter that Wendell and Anne Phillips adopted. The tale would have appealed to her older readers, those with an abiding set of memories about antebellum days coming from the city's dedicated abolitionist circles. The story revolved around an earnest Aldrich who broke his engagement in order to pursue, albeit in a thoroughly melodramatic and ultimately unsuccessful fashion, Phoebe Garnaut Phillips. Garnaut was the child of a woman who nursed Phillips when he was deathly ill. Phillips recovered, but his nurse died and left an orphaned daughter. Phoebe became a beloved member of the Phillips family. Some years later, Aldrich met Phoebe and found her wholly irresistible. His attraction and her appeal was explained in part by some who believed that by coming of age in a staunchly abolitionist milieu, Phoebe's presence had been endowed with "a kind of fire shining through and about her like the lights in a jewel."[23] Phillips resisted Aldrich's request for Phoebe's hand and insisted that they communicate only occasionally by letter over the course of a year. If, at the end of that time, the ardor was still intense, then a courtship might be possible. Unfortunately, although their passion weathered the separation, Phoebe was so ill from the nervous strain brought on by the threats from proslavery mobs against the family that she was unable to accept his attentions and Aldrich was unable to claim her as his wife.[24] This tangled romantic tale was an especially haunting backdrop for the Phillips article, and one that enabled Aldrich's poem, and by extension Hopkins's tribute to Phillips, to resonate profoundly with Bostonians. Aldrich, one of many city residents who was devastated by the news of Phillips's passing, penned the piece in just one night and did so in the hours immediately following Phillips's death.

A rather exultant narrative tribute to Abraham Lincoln immediately followed the Phillips material. The placement hints at Hopkins's efforts to engage white audiences by demonstrating the all-American dimensions of the magazine. Her choice of layout also may have been shaped by her effort to rally African Americans by telling of the influential figures who had become synonymous with African American freedom and the abolition of American slavery. The Lincoln piece provided a rather staccato biography in its subtitle, describing the former president as "Citizen—Patriot—President—Martyr." It was an unself-conscious panegyric from start to finish, one that began with the exclamation, "Lincoln!—Before that name all bow in reverence and awe." He was a man "[c]alled to the highest honor by the rightful suffrage of his fellow-citizens." The unidentified author noted that Lincoln "administered the laws with conscientiousness and impartiality" before being "assassinated by a villainous fanatic."[25] "LINCOLN. There will never be another," declared the writer in closing. The intensity of the piece was offset slightly by "Lincoln's Rules for Living," a set of aphorisms that included broad recommendations such as "[d]o not worry, eat three square meals a day, say your prayers, [and] be courteous to your creditors."[26]

The final two historical pieces in the debut issue of the *New Era Magazine* featured the riveting and previously unpublished stories of two important Bostonians, Mark Réné De Mortie and Eliza Gardiner. Hopkins endeavored to confer upon these two Bostonians a long overdue authority and institutional identity. The biography of De Mortie, the first installment in Hopkins's "Men of Vision" series, demonstrated her goals to publish essays that "will include the lives of those men of the race who have clearly demonstrated by their achievements that they are really 'Men of Vision,' and the entire series will be fully illustrated." To reinforce the heft of the series, Hopkins quoted directly from the Book of Proverbs, reminding readers that "[w]here there is no vision, the people perish."[27]

Hopkins seized the opportunity to honor De Mortie, the stalwart Colored National League member and close family friend with whom she had worked on the 1905 William Lloyd Garrison Centennial celebrations. She drew much of the essay from a profile of De Mortie that had appeared three years earlier in *The African Abroad* by William Ferris. Hopkins also reconnected with the Rhode Island community in which her father Benjamin Northup had come of age. De Mortie had married into one of the best-known and most influential families of color in Providence when he wed Cordelia Downing, a daughter of George T. Downing and his wife. De Mortie shared with his father-in-law a zeal for politics and promptly began to stake his claim in Rhode Island matters. When he and Cordelia relocated to Virginia, De Mortie ran for public office, "was a successful candidate for the Fourth Congressional District, but was deprived of [his] seat by fraud." He then was appointed "deputy collector of internal revenue," and in that capacity, he was able to travel to Chicago for the National Republican Convention in 1880, serving as an alternate delegate. Hopkins characterized her De Mortie biography as "a record of an active life of love for humanity," and she endeavored to provide the longtime family friend with a platform from which to tell his own story. The five-page article included four pages in De Mortie's own words. Hopkins offered a stirring introduction and also a final note about his passing. Hopkins placed De Mortie's autobiographical narrative, which began with thrilling tales of his work with the Underground Railroad, in the larger context of American idealism and patriotism. She performed a bold narrative act of equalizing. She insisted that widely cherished figures such as the Puritans and Christopher Columbus were motivated by the same desire for freedom that compelled African Americans to seek their freedom. "It is an unquestionable fact that the colored men who took the liberty denied them and followed the North Star blindly were of the same class as the hardy Puritans," she intoned, before suggesting that the self-emancipated men and women were individuals "whose dauntless courage should be inspiring to the young people of the present generation."[28] Hopkins also prepared her audience to accept the dreams and visions discussed in De Mortie's autobiography; she proposed that his creativity was of the same ilk as that which fueled the scientific advances of Isaac Newton and "other adventurous visionaries of olden times." It was the "visions of the dreamers," she declared, that were the foundation for the "colossal modern vigor" of the contemporary "materialistic world."[29]

De Mortie was a good storyteller, and his autobiography was one that included long-obscured details about some of the city's legendary people of color. His talents for giving compelling accounts of the past emerged in the testimonial that he contributed to William Hopkins's Civil War pension application. In his autobiographical statement, De Mortie reviewed his marvelous evolution in public and private life, as a citizen and as a patriot. He was an enterprising Underground Railroad conductor, a politician, a community organizer, a shrewd businessman, a labor activist, and an antilynching activist, whose resourcefulness served him and his fellow soldiers of the Massachusetts Fifty-fourth Regiment extremely well when they were denied equal and regular pay during their Civil War service. De Mortie also was a leading African American member of the Know-Nothing Party, who counted among his close colleagues key men in Boston, including the Reverend Leonard Grimes, the pastor who had presided over the 1864 Christmas Day wedding of William Hopkins and Sarah Allen. De Mortie collaborated successfully with Lewis Hayden, the city's most legendary Underground Railroad conductor and antislavery worker, and Benjamin F. Roberts, the father of Sarah, in whose name the city of Boston was sued for maintaining segregated schools. The three men worked with others and "secured the removal of the abbreviation 'Col.,' which was always attached to a colored man's name on the voting lists."[30] During the early postbellum years, De Mortie collaborated again with Lewis Hayden on labor issues and helped to negotiate terms that enabled some "120 ablebodied colored men to fill the places of the strikers" and the freight handlers for the Boston & Albany Railroad Company. He and Hayden "sent notices to all the colored churches asking able-bodied men desiring work to meet us at the rooms of the Union Progressive Association, corner of Cambridge and Chambers Streets."[31] They informed the men about the strike and the request for men that Judge Russell, a representative of the company, had made, and they organized the response.[32]

The tribute to De Mortie that Hopkins published in the *New Era Magazine* is the only detailed extant profile of the Virginia native and "race man of distinct individuality," who was "generously endowed with the humble virtue called mother wit."[33] One of the best examples of that "mother wit" emerges in De Mortie's reminiscences in a story that likely touched many of the *New Era Magazine*'s readers who cherished the history of the Massachusetts Fifty-fourth. This regiment, led by Robert Gould Shaw, was the first African American regiment organized in the North, the group that suffered devastating losses at Fort Wagner, South Carolina. In 1863, Governor John A. Andrew offered to De Mortie the "position of Sutler of the 54th Massachusetts Colored Troops by Governor John A. Andrew." "I accepted," De Mortie recalled proudly, "and was appointed by Col. R. G. Shaw."[34] The position carried with it an enormous financial obligation and "requir[ed] the expenditure of considerable ready money." De Mortie did not have immediate access to large quantities of cash and so sought out a partner who could finance the arrangements and allow him to meet the expectations of his role as provider to the regiments. De Mortie tapped into the Hopkins-Allen-Paul family connections and was directed to make contact with Joseph Paul Whitfield, the son of James Monroe Whitfield and the great-grandson of Caesar

Nero Paul. "I offered an equal partnership to Joseph Paul Whitfield, a New England black man, who had located in Buffalo, New York, and accumulated about sixty thousand dollars in money and real estate." The two men became a force unto themselves when "Mr. Whitfield accepted [De Mortie's] offer and chartered a ship and stocked it with supplies of all kinds and we sailed with the regiment."[35] De Mortie was the unsung voice of reason who counseled the regiments to "stand firm" against the discrimination and encouraged the soldiers to refuse salaries that were considerably less than those they had been promised and those offered to white soldiers. De Mortie was clear about the political dimensions of the pay controversy but equally aware of the intense hardship presented by the regiments' boycott of the lower wages. "I told the men in my regiment not to accept the seven dollar," he recalled, "and I would give them credit to the amount of two dollars per month if they would stand firm for the amount they had enlisted for. They took this advice and after a wait of eighteen months they received their pay at the rate of thirteen dollars per month, the original amount promised them. They owed [me and Whitfield] about $14,000, which they paid like men. The 54th had but three pay days during the war; they were mustered out in 1865."[36]

The first installment of the "Men of Vision" series closed with De Mortie's earnest invocation of the opening lines of "Battle Hymn of the Republic." "Mine eyes have seen the glory of the coming of the Lord," De Mortie assured his audience. "My work is done." Hopkins appended a brief note about the paralysis that De Mortie suffered in his later years and acknowledged his daughter and son-in-law, Irene De Mortie Wheatland and her husband, Dr. Marcus Wheatland, of Newport, Rhode Island, for welcoming Mark De Mortie into their home and caring for him until his death, on 3 September 1914. Hopkins concluded the piece by invoking three moving quotes from poems by William Cullen Bryant and Henry Wadsworth Longfellow. The Longfellow quote, which Hopkins used as her final statement, captured eloquently the life and triumphs of her stepfather's bosom friend, a man who knew "how to read and write, but [was] practically uneducated and penniless, without the application of this or that elaborate law of eugenic or other scientific training warranted to manufacture men" and who "made himself invaluable to his people, and also to the United States Government at a critical period in its history."[37] The lines from "The Ladder of St. Augustine" emphasized the impressive work ethic and unflagging desire to achieve freedom of so many New England women and men of color, individuals whom Hopkins was determined to honor in the pages of the New Era Magazine.

One of Pauline Hopkins's principle contributions to American history and journalism was her attention to the history, accomplishments, and strivings of African American women. New Englanders and Americans owed a considerable debt of gratitude to countless numbers of unsung female heroes, women who, though relegated to the margins of society, left indelible imprints on the politics, literature, and culture of the ante- and postbellum age. When she took the editorial helm of the *New Era Magazine*, Hopkins built on the good feminist and women's history work that she had begun at the turn of the century. Now, though, she invited the elders among the Boston community to tell their own stories. In so doing, Hopkins transformed a traditional oral history phenomenon into a culture of published reminiscences that predated the Works Public Administration interviews of the 1930s and that accorded deep respect to the veterans of antebellum and postbellum wars for freedom and justice.

The first issue of the *New Era Magazine* was enriched by the contribution of Eliza Gardiner, a longtime Bostonian whose experiences and firsthand eyewitness accounts of historic moments allowed her to give voice to a rich collective race history. Gardiner, who brought her audience at the 1905 Garrison Centennial to tears, published her first memoirs in the pages of the *New Era Magazine*. "Many times I have been asked to give some personal reminiscences of the early days of the anti-slavery struggle—my own recollections," she said. On this historic occasion in 1916 and in response to the request that Pauline Hopkins lodged, Gardiner acquiesced. Eliza Gardiner, whose name was spelled as Gardner in the *Guardian* reports of the Garrison Centennial, was one of a "number of capable women whose influence was for race advancement."[38] She was part of an admirable cohort, one that, according to the dynamic Washington, D.C., club woman and educator Leila Amos Pendleton, also included Mark De Mortie's daughter Louise, as well as pioneering journalist Mary Ann Shadd Cary, educator Fannie Jackson Coppin, sculptress Edmonia Lewis, and teacher and writer Charlotte Forten Grimké. The *New Era Magazine* counted itself extremely privileged to have the promise of "Miss Gardiner's recollections."[39] Hopkins valued her because she was "perhaps better fitted than any person" to provide readers with "the real personal touch with those great leaders of fifty years ago, both white and colored, who played such an important part in the Civil War, and the exciting days that preceded that struggle."[40] It was of especial value to Hopkins, given her attention to the rich history of family friends like Mark De Mortie and the Reverend Leonard Grimes, that Eliza Gardiner would offer memoirs that were "in every case personal." As she had with the Harvard students Wolo and Campos, Hopkins contracted with Gardiner for a multipart series, and that agreement enabled her in the magazine's prospectus to declare proudly that the articles would be "fully illustrated by rare prints and photographs" and would "run for several months."[41]

Gardiner, who held audiences captive during her 1905 speech at the unforgettable Boston Garrison Centennial celebrations, was an engaging narrator and a powerful historian. It also was clear that she was a vital resource for Hopkins; early on in her first essay, Gardiner recalled the rising tension between North and South. After noting that Northern abolitionists such as Garrison, Wendell Phillips, and Parker Pillsbury "commenced to thunder in the ears of this guilty nation," she recalled that such effective protest "only made the slave holders more insistent upon their rights to carry their slaves anywhere in the United States." She recalled that "Toombs of Georgia," the man whom Hopkins positioned as chair of the South Carolina secession convention depicted in *Hagar's Daughter*, "impudently asserted his belief that he would yet 'call the roll of his slaves beneath the shadow of Bunker Hill.'" Gardiner was sure to note here, though, that Massachusetts responded without hesitation to the Southerner's taunt: "Massachusetts in reply, said 'the day you bring your slaves upon our soil, that day they are free men.'"[42] The power of the memoir certainly emerged in Gardiner's references to leading women and men of the day. It also was a compelling piece because she provided a rare glimpse of African American childhood. She privileged this perspective and did so to great effect. "When a very little girl not more than eight or nine years of age I learned about the cruelties of slavery," she wrote in the opening lines of her first essay. Not only did she learn "to be in sympathy with those in bondage 'as bound with them,'" but she also "knew at that tender age what bondage meant." She described the home of her parents as one that "often sheltered the oppressed," a demure way of confirming that it was one of Boston's Underground Railroad stops and a vital gathering place for self-emancipated people. In that home, she "sat and listened with a beating heart and heard the refugees tell the story of their cruel bondage." That powerful history, which some might discount as too emotional, complemented the intellectual analyses that Gardiner was privy to as well. "Very early, too," she told her readers, "I knew something of the political history of the country and the relation of the parties to the bondman. I knew the difference between the Whig and Democratic parties, for in those early days we knew no other."[43] The first installment of Gardiner's memoir embodied one of the key hopes of the *New Era Magazine*. It was a publication that was determined to "deal full and frankly with all questions affecting the real progress of the race." One of the most powerful ways in which Hopkins achieved this end was the privileging of testimony. This narrative form accorded its author immediate authority and allowed writers like Eliza Gardiner to reconsider the past in the context of usually marginalized issues such as domestic instability caused by the Fugitive Slave Law, familial anxieties produced by the threat of lynching, and community solidarity created through collective events ranging from classical music performances to civil rights marches on the State House.

The second, and unexpectedly final, issue of the *New Era Magazine* maintained its New England focus even as it intensified its analyses of race prejudice and Southern racial violence. The second issue, which appeared in April 1916, included four substantial historical articles that focused on Crispus Attucks, the great Shakespearean actor Ira Aldridge, the beloved Boston minister Leonard Grimes, and the dramatist John T. Trowbridge. The creative pieces included the second installment of Hopkins's latest serialized novella, *Topsy Templeton*, a dialect anecdote, poems by William Stanley Braithwaite and Ella Wheeler Wilcox, short stories by writers identified by pseudonyms, such as "The Growing Up of Jeanette" by "August Day," and new clippings from newspapers, including the Scottish *Glasgow Rotary Gazette* and the *Boston American*. An article by Plenyono Wolo, "The 'Colored' Peoples and The War," and an article from the *African Times* on the West India Regiments fulfilled the editors' pledge to discuss international events. That spring, though, Hopkins gave considerable attention to a case that was garnering public attention and that highlighted the ongoing challenges that African Americans, and, in particular, the rising generation of African American women, were facing in the still inhospitable public workplace.

The Bosfield case, which centered on a dignified twenty-two-year-old woman named Jane R. Bosfield, clearly touched Hopkins. Bosfield, like Hopkins in her later life and the tragic character Sappho Clark in *Contending Forces*, was a stenographer who had to confront workplace prejudice. A talented young woman from Allston, Massachusetts, she was the daughter of Samuel Bosfield, a man of Bahamian ancestry who had moved from his work as a newspaper editor on the island to Cambridge, Massachusetts, where he gained employment at the Riverside Press. Bosfield had schooling and credentials that hint at what Pauline Hopkins may herself have acquired as she moved from high school, through her years on the stage, to office work. After graduating from city schools, including the Latin School of Cambridge, she "worked at the Riverside Press" and pursued additional studies at the Boston Evening High School. She emerged with training as a bookkeeper, stenographer, and typist.[44] Bosfield sought "employment as a clerk and stenographer at the Medfield State Hospital." Her time there was dreadful; she was forced to work separately from other employees and also to eat her lunch alone and in a room beyond the main cafeteria. She was fired when she protested the segregation and went into the cafeteria to obtain food. The presiding governor at the time, David Walsh, did intercede on Bosfield's behalf in order to get her the job, but the hospital's superintendent discharged her. The Board of Trustees upheld his decision, noting that "the action of Superintendant French in discharging Miss Jane R. Bosfield, the 22-year-old colored girl stenographer, was entirely warranted on the grounds of insubordination and that there was no question of race prejudice whatever."[45]

According to articles reprinted from Boston newspapers and incorporated into the *New Era Magazine*'s coverage of the case, Jane Bosfield "was not the first colored girl turned away" by the Medfield State Hospital superintendent, Dr. French. In addition, there was evidence that in his requisition orders for administrative support, he made, on at least two occasions, specific requests for white applicants. Bosfield's case was sustained by the determination that she and her family brought to her case. It also was greatly supported by the "determined effort of the colored citizens of Massachusetts," as noted in one article that appeared in the *Boston Traveler*. There was an institutional counter-response to Bosfield's plight that came "through the National Equal Rights League," an organization determined "to eliminate the denial of civil service and segregation for color in the civil service and the state institutions." The League, noted the *Traveler* reporter, "decided to fight this alleged color discrimination to the last degree."[46]

Hopkins included this riveting profile of the Bosfield case in the section entitled "Around the World of Color," and in so doing attempted to rally the public to Jane Bosfield and her cause. She made plain her thoughts on the matter, offering additional commentary on the situation in a piece entitled "The Question of Segregation." Hopkins explained the Bosfield case in a most memorable manner, suggesting that it was "a startling example of how subtly the devil works in human affairs." She used this occasion to give voice to her own professional frustrations, doing so with considerable restraint but noticeable fury. "Who would believe that such abuses could exist in Massachusetts! But there were rumors along this line way back in President McKinley's time," she noted. The subsequent recurring use of the collective "we" hinted at the personal relevance that this case had for the editor. What followed in the short commentary was a startling set of admissions and observations: "We have been sitting on this lid for a number of years. We ourselves have waded through the bitter waters of prejudice in silence and in tears. We know of cases where girls have accepted traveling expenses and a week's wages in lieu of the position which was rightfully theirs rather than cause trouble," she wrote. "And so we have compromised and compromised until we are sick at heart."[47]

In many ways, the *New Era Magazine* was shaped by a recurring call for advocacy, manifested in articles that documented vital interventions on behalf of hunted enslaved peoples and life-sustaining support for brave and patriotic men like those in the Massachusetts Fifty-fourth Regiment, who sacrificed much in order to acquire pay equity. Hopkins certainly was the chief architect of the group of articles that together provided a substantial contemporary and watchful gaze on the African American past and on what the title of one aptly named submission termed as the "Relation of the Black American to Twentieth Century Civilization." Hopkins carried this theme of creative advocacy over into the primary work of fiction that she envisioned as her first signed piece to appear in the *New Era Magazine*.

Topsy Templeton was a story "of a modern Topsy," declared the preview announcement of Hopkins's pending work of fiction. Just as the editors of the *Colored American Magazine* saw the great appeal and high sales that good fiction could provide, so too did Hopkins and her new associates at the *New Era Magazine*. The story of Topsy was to "be one of the early attractions" of the magazine and was scheduled, like the other nonfictional series, to "run through several issues."[48] Hopkins focused on the plight of orphans, revisited the sentimental dramas of missing parents and the abandoned child's quest to locate them, and contemplated with humor the cross-racial and class dilemmas that emerge when "a colored waitress in the home of a wealthy white family is permitted to keep a baby girl (presumably her own and fatherless) with her at the place of her service."[49] In this piece, Hopkins once again used her own family history as she crafted the spirited plot; on this occasion, her grandmother appeared, not as the source of a pseudonym but rather as a character. Mrs. Elizabeth Hopkins-Templeton was one of the two sisters who accepted responsibility for raising the abandoned child and seeking for her "a home in a respectable colored family."

The promising serialized novel once again revealed Hopkins's deep interest in family dynamics and events that threaten domesticity, as well as her desire to encourage women to pursue meaningful service to others that could challenge the confining status quo of the day. The well-meaning sisters, the spinster Miss Newbury and her well-to-do sister Mrs. Hopkins-Templeton, represent a new element in the critique of early twentieth-century domesticity and gentility that Hopkins had explored in *Contending Forces*. In many ways, the two women prove to be as essential to the plot of *Topsy Templeton* as Ma Smith and Mrs. Willis were to the proceedings of *Contending Forces*. Despite all their learning and privilege, the sisters are in dire need of real social education. The individual best equipped to provide that transformative education is Topsy, a child whose very name underscores the challenge and the divide—racial and social—between the novella's primary characters. Topsy is only beginning to evolve from the passive and tragic figure of an abandoned mulatto child into a free-spirited and insightful young girl when the *New Era Magazine* ceases publication. In the two installments that she does present, however, Hopkins reveals the characteristic flair that she has for creating memorable dialogue, introduces the most sassy and forthright character she has invented to date, and suggests that the echoes of the antebellum period, captured best by Harriet Beecher Stowe and the little dynamo named Topsy, who must be subdued, humanized, and converted, still affect the modern age.

It may have been demands on Hopkins's time that prompted her to revisit previously successful characters and subplots that appeared in her *Colored American Magazine* days. The pensive figure of Reuel Briggs, for example, re-appears here as Dr. Alwyn, an elusive character who performs on Topsy an act of mesmerism, rather than a traditional act of medical intervention, in order to revive her following a playground brawl. The reference to mesmerism links *Topsy Templeton* to Hopkins's earliest published works, especially the 1900 *Colored American Magazine* story, "Mystery within Us." The protagonist of that scintillating tale was Tom Underwood, a young physician who shares with a friend his story of how the spirit world saved him from committing suicide, righted his precarious financial position, ensured his professional success, and restored his emotional stability. In *Topsy Templeton*, Hopkins seemed ready to develop an intriguing modern conversion narrative, one that would bring Dr. Alwyn, the talented physician and unfortunate racist, to a greater state of caring humanity. The social redemption plot of this novella complemented the articles about racial activism, the persistence of modern-day racism, and the powerful legacies of abolitionist fervor that appeared in the first two issues.

The *New Era Magazine* disappeared from the public reading sphere with little fanfare. It was a disorienting loss that may have been brought on by financial upheaval in the New Era Publishing Company. There also may have been some trouble behind the scenes, although the goodwill emanating from the prospectus and first issues and the rich history that Hopkins and her *New Era Magazine* colleagues shared suggests otherwise. The magazine had long-term plans. There was a marvelous "Easter Number" planned, which was to include pieces by board member Arthur Dunson, two pieces by Hopkins, including one under her pseudonym of S. Shadrach, a biographical profile of a graduate from the Perkins Institute for the Blind, and an article entitled "Higher Education of the Negro—Its Practical Value," by Dr. Horace Bumstead, a former president of Atlanta University.[50] Even the advertisements for the Easter issue hinted at future pieces, such as an article, "The Colored Clerks and Carriers of Greater Boston, Employed in the Postal Service," which was to be "fully illustrated."

The *New Era Magazine* had represented an invaluable opportunity for Hopkins to take her place in the thriving African American periodical culture that marked the onset of the Harlem Renaissance. It may have exacted a high price in ways that never will be known. One of the most chilling signs of compounded loss, though, occurred barely one month after the last issue of the promising periodical was distributed to readers. The events of May 1916 reveal domestic instability and a woman under siege, two subjects about which Hopkins often had written in most compelling ways. Now, though, these issues had become personal, and they represent troubling times and substantial transitions.

On 12 May 1916, Pauline Hopkins appeared before a justice of the peace to sign documents that finalized the sale of her longtime home at 53 Jay Street in Cambridge. At ten minutes past two o'clock on that Tuesday afternoon, Hopkins, identified in the papers as a "singlewoman of Boston," relinquished her claim on "the land in that part of said Cambridge, known as North Cambridge, together with the buildings thereon, being shown as the Southerly ½ lot numbered 256 on a plan of lots on the Old Race Course Land belonging to S. E. Read, situated in North Cambridge, dated 1875." This transaction, however commonplace in its technicalities and legal requirements, represented for Pauline Hopkins her steady and undeserved slide toward the margins of American society.

20

Cambridge Days

(What shall I care, in my quiet room,
For head board or foot board when I am dead)
Better than glory, or honors, or fame,
(Though I am striving for those to-day)
To know that some heart will cherish my name,
And think of me kindly, with blessings, alway.

ELLA WHEELER WILCOX
1870

The summer of 1916 found Pauline Hopkins grappling with one of
the most poignant of life transitions. It had been three years since she
lost her mother, Sarah, in the fall of 1913. The passing of Sarah Hopkins was a major loss to Hopkins, who had shared a home with her mother
and stepfather for almost her entire life. Sarah not only was a woman that
Pauline had cherished, but also a quietly supportive fellow artist with whom
she frequently had collaborated and one of her most trusted allies as she
negotiated her way through the cutthroat world of African American politics and publishing. Earlier in 1916, she had had to oversee the closing of the
promising but costly New Era Publishing Company. Not even the sale of her
family's longtime Clifton Street home in Cambridge, Massachusetts, could
prevent or stave off that professional upheaval. The vision of a sparse and finite
domesticity that Ella Wheeler Wilcox conjured up in her 1870 poem, about
a woman living in a "quiet room," without concern for "a head board or foot
board," and thinking about how much she preferred to "know that some heart
will cherish my name," were sentiments that now summed up the prospects
that Hopkins herself may have been contemplating. Now in her mid-sixties,
Hopkins, like many Americans, was keenly aware of the world war raging in
Europe and the increasing likelihood that the United States would join the
conflict. As Woodrow Wilson delivered his speeches and newspapers kept
Americans abreast of the news from the European fronts, Hopkins listened

and also began to marshal her resources, to prepare as best she could to establish herself in a new and secure home and vocation.

Once she stepped away from the *New Era Magazine*, Hopkins began what would become a fifteen-year-long flirtation with obscurity. This devolution contrasted sharply with historic moments that in many ways promised new opportunities that an accomplished woman like Hopkins had waited a whole lifetime to see. 1920 brought passage of the Nineteenth Amendment, the legislation that finally gave the right to vote to American women. In that year, which also saw the beginning of Prohibition, Hopkins had rather bleak voting choices. The Republican ticket featured Warren Harding and Calvin Coolidge as the presidential and vice presidential nominees. The Democrats put forward James Cox for president and nominated Franklin Delano Roosevelt for the number two position. The nomination of Eugene Debs for the nation's highest office might have appealed to Hopkins's deep-rooted political preference for outspoken and uncompromised candidates; at the time of his nomination, Debs was serving out a harsh ten-year sentence after being convicted of delivering controversial addresses during the World War I era.

Following the loss of her editorship at the *New Era Magazine*, Pauline Hopkins no longer appeared regularly in the Cambridge city directories. For years she had existed behind the entries that identified her stepfather, William, as head of household, and then referred to her mother, Sarah, once William passed away. Since Sarah Hopkins's death, in 1914, Hopkins had been trying to maintain her hold on the family home, but, despite her efforts, or in fact because of them, that became increasingly difficult. In the aftermath of the closing of the New Era Publishing Company and the sale of her Clifton Street property, Hopkins seemed to almost disappear altogether. The 1917 Cambridge city directory included no listing for her, and neither would the editions of 1920 and 1921. She still may have been in the city, but she would have been absorbed into other households or marginalized because she no longer was mistress of her own home. Hopkins began to live a version of the itinerant life that she had created for Sappho Clark, the besieged heroine of *Contending Forces*. She certainly did not have to endure the regular upheaval that she chronicled in her story of Sappho, whose traumatic life and maternal devotion required that she become adept at moving from place to place in short order. She was able to enjoy a relatively lengthy period of stability in the rooms that she took in the Cambridge home of a local African American family.

By 1918, Hopkins had taken rooms at 19 Jay Street, a home in Cambridge owned by a sixty-two-year-old widow named Maria Carter and her forty-four-year-old unmarried son, Leigh. Mrs. Carter, like Hopkins's stepfather, William, was a native of Virginia. She and her son, who was born in Massachusetts in 1878, had a house valued at $7,000, and they regularly boarded adult lodgers, as well as needy wards of the state. In the spring of 1930, during the last months that Hopkins was living on Jay Street, the Carters had taken in three young African American boys: ten-year-old Earl Quick, nine-year-old Edward Jones, and eight-year-old Morris Chase.[1] It may have been the presence of young children in the home or the Carters' desire to allocate more of their home to foster children that prompted Hopkins to seek new lodging. The Cambridge city directory for 1930 indicated that Hopkins now was living at 158 Magazine Street in Cambridge. This may well have been true; however, her death certificate notes that her residence was in fact 19 Jay Street.

During the twelve years in which she boarded at the Carter home on Jay Street, Hopkins was working as a clerk at a still-unidentified location. In 1920, she provided additional information about her employment for the federal Massachusetts census. On this occasion, she continued to repeat the established family account that she was born in 1866, which in 1920 suggested that she was fifty-four rather than sixty-one years old. She also noted that she was working as a proofreader at a "chemical laboratory," a facility that was not identified by name in the census. None of the Cambridge city directories corroborated directly the employment description that was recorded for Hopkins in the 1920 Massachusetts census. Entries in the directories published through the 1920s listed her repeatedly as "stenographer, bds, 19 Jay," or "stenographer, rms, 19 Jay."[2] In 1929, the Cambridge city directory suggested that she had found different work. The entry, which read, "Hopkins, Pauline E. bkpr, r 158 Magazine," indicated that Hopkins now was employed as a bookkeeper. Unfortunately, though, the location of the business or information about her employers continues to prove elusive.

Hopkins lived in the Carter home during World War I, and it was from her rooms on Jay Street that she monitored the news about the influenza epidemics that were killing an estimated twenty to forty million people worldwide. She also kept up with the disturbing images and reports that followed the tumultuous bank robbery, leading to the trials and executions of Nicola Sacco and Bartolomeo Vanzetti for the crime. Their deaths, on 23 August 1927, conjured up the specter of antebellum mobs and lynchings for many, including W. E. B. Du Bois, who "concluded ruefully that 'the social community that mobbed [William Lloyd] Garrison, easily hanged Sacco and Vanzetti.'"[3]

The last fifteen years of Pauline Hopkins's life testified to her industriousness, unrelenting work ethic, and enterprise. In addition, they were an example of the slow creep of anonymity that began to overtake her, the woman formerly celebrated as "Boston's Black Nightingale," who became New England's most accomplished African American woman writer. Hopkins was adapting to substantial changes in the city in which she had come of age, personally and professionally. She and her family had participated in the first decade of the twentieth century in the steady African American exodus out of Beacon Hill and into Roxbury and Dorchester. Now she was witnessing another major migration, this time of European immigrants flocking to Northern urban centers such as Boston. By 1920, the African American population in Boston would number only 45,466 and constitute just over 1 percent of the state's population. European immigrants and their families were thriving; by 1920, immigrants and first-generation children represented 66.8 percent of the Massachusetts population, and only 31.9% of the state identified itself as "native white."[4]

As an only child and as a woman who never married, Hopkins took great comfort from the family history that enveloped her. In the 1920s, she maintained contact with her cousins and was bolstered by the local connection that she shared with the daughters of her loving mentor and uncle, Elijah William Smith Jr., and his wife, Eliza Riley Smith. Hopkins lived in close proximity to Harriet Augusta Smith Burrell and to the family of Anne Elizabeth Smith Simms. Harriet Smith Burrell, born in 1867, affectionately known as "Hattie," was ten years younger than Pauline Hopkins. The two women shared an especially powerful history and were alike in their spirited political inclinations. Harriet worked closely with *Guardian* editor William Monroe Trotter and Maude Monroe Trotter, his sister. One of their most successful collaborations was in their vigorous protest of the incendiary Thomas Dixon film *Birth of a Nation* when it was scheduled to open in Boston in the spring of 1915. It was a moment of enormous collective protest and one that Harriet and her cousin Pauline likely shared and discussed. In the wake of screenings, such as private White House showings for Woodrow Wilson and his family and premieres in New York City and Chicago, African American women and the larger community of color in Boston rallied to protest the inflammatory film. These protests "culminated in Boston, where William Monroe Trotter used the leverage of black votes to pressure Mayor James Michael Curley to consider a ban." After arranging for five of the most controversial scenes to be deleted, Curley then cleared the way for the film to open in a hallowed Boston site, the Tremont Temple. Harriet Burrell may not have been one of the ten protestors that "club-wielding police" arrested at the Tremont Temple, but there is almost no doubt that she and Pauline were in the 2,000-person crowd that Trotter gathered and then led, from Faneuil Hall up to the top of Beacon Hill and the steps of the State House.[5] Harriet Burrell lent her voice to the protest and also penned a poem that expressed further her dismay and resolve.[6] Hopkins could take great pleasure in Harriet's political awareness and the spirited ways in which she used literature to effect social justice.

In the post–World War I era, there were significant socioeconomic differences between Hopkins and her closest kin. The Burrells, for example, were part of the established professional middle-class world. John Madison Burrell, born in the antebellum South in 1861, was a successful attorney. He relocated from Richmond, Virginia, where he was much beloved and honored by his community and clients, to Cambridge, Massachusetts. He and Harriet married in April 1898, and by 1900 the newlyweds had established themselves in a single-family Cambridge home at 9 Clarendon Avenue, where their neighbors were mainly African Americans engaged in an array of occupations that included engineers, messengers, porters, and clerks for auctioneers, and who made sure that their children were enrolled in school.[7] By 1930, the Burrells were a family of four and were still living on Clarendon Avenue, surrounded by neighbors who, like John Burrell, had Southern roots, and who were preserving their hold on steady domesticity. Living with John and Hattie Burrell in 1930 was their niece Edith M. Simms, the daughter of Hattie's sister Anne Smith Simms. In 1930, Edith was thirty-three years of age and working as a clerk in the State House. Her twenty-nine-year-old brother and the Burrell's nephew, Edward Paul Simms, in 1930, had no listed occupation but may well have been in school. Edward Simms graduated with honors from Boston University, became a published poet, and eventually relocated to Norfolk, Virginia, where he began a twenty-one-year tenure as pastor of the First Baptist Church, a congregation founded in 1805.[8] Ed Simms, one of the members of the extended Smith family who came into contact with Hopkins, passed away in 1986; his wife, Tessie Simms, was still living in 1995 and took great comfort in memories of Boston and the sketches of the African Baptist Church on Joy Street that adorned the walls of her room in a Norfolk nursing home.

Hopkins also forged quiet and enduring friendships with women like Florence Walker, one of her Cambridge friends and the person whom she asked to serve as executor of her will. Walker, who was almost twenty years younger than Hopkins, was working in the early 1920s as a dressmaker and living at 29 Hovey Street in Cambridge with Isabelle M. Walker, a relative who may have been a niece and one of the witnesses to the probate documents filed after Pauline Hopkins's death. The 1920 Massachusetts Census includes the 29 Hovey Street home of the Walkers but does not include Florence in this

Cambridge Days

report. The residents of this Cambridge home in 1920 included Rebecca E. Walker, a fifty-seven-year-old mulatto woman and head of household, whose listed occupation is that of matron at a club house. Isabelle M. Walker is identified as the thirty-three-year-old New Hampshire–born daughter of Rebecca. The census reported no occupation for Isabelle Walker.[9] The friendship that Pauline Hopkins forged with the Walkers and the ties that she maintained with the Smith-Burrells helped to ease the difficult last days of her life. These relationships also persisted after her death as her friends and kin attended to the legal details that emerged as a result of Hopkins's death.

Tragedy struck Pauline Hopkins in her rented rooms on Tuesday, 12 August 1930. She was plagued by neuritis and rheumatism, conditions exaggerated by the taxing manual work that she continued to do as a stenographer and bookkeeper. In an effort to reduce her pain, Hopkins soaked some red flannel bandages in liniment and then wrapped them around the limbs that ached. She then turned on an oil stove and began to heat water on it. At some point, she brushed against the flame, and it set the dress that she was wearing on fire. Unable to douse the fire herself, she panicked and ran out into the street, which only increased the flames. Twenty-three-year-old Malcolm Coley of Cambridge, who became a marine fireman before he joined the army in the fall of 1943 and was part of the substantial African American military force fighting in World War II, was, according to news reports, "the first to come to the aged woman's rescue, as she, screaming, ran from her house."[10] Moments later, nineteen-year-old Paul Coley, who lived with his North Carolina–born parents and large family at 178 Western Avenue, and his friend Freddie Morris, came upon the scene.[11] The young men quickly joined Malcolm and "assisted in extinguishing the flame." Despite the heroism of her rescuers, Hopkins survived for barely one day after the accident. On 13 August 1930, she died in the Cambridge Relief Hospital on Prospect Street. Her death certificate, filed with the offices of the Cambridge city clerk, stated that the cause of death was "[e]xtensive burns of entire body."[12]

The friends and next of kin of Hopkins were notified. The news about her horrific accident reached first the Cambridge homes of Harriet and John Burrell and Florence Walker. It then traveled to St. Louis, Missouri, where Hopkins's cousins, Emma Vashon Gossen and George B. Vashon, descendants of Garrisonian abolitionist John B. Vashon and women's club leader Susan Paul Vashon, Elijah and Anne Paul Smith's daughter, were living. Within two weeks, the *Chicago Defender* reported her passing on its front page. The concise article, "Aged Writer Dies of Painful Burns," praised her as a "writer and orator of high recognition" before transporting readers into the awful moment in which Hopkins flung herself out of her house and onto the mercy of men who could help. The wrenching details about Hopkins's desperate last moments embedded in the report defied the article's brevity. It was fitting that her death be recorded for readers in the *Defender*, one of the nation's most influential newspapers, whose founder Robert Abbott once proclaimed as "The World's Greatest Weekly."[13] The *Baltimore Afro-American* also printed a short article about Hopkins's death. "Burns Fatal to Aged Writer," declared the paper in its Saturday, 23 August 1930 issue. The report then provided a graphic account of Hopkins's last moments. The writer acknowledged first that "it is not definitely known how the aged woman's clothing took fire" before describing the horrific scene in which Hopkins became "a human torch": "Her screams attracted the attention of neighbors when she ran screaming from the door of her home, but she was fatally burned before the flames could be extinguished." The article turned abruptly from these awful images to offer readers a solicitous overview of Hopkins's achievements. "Miss Hopkins was a New Englander," announced the writer, an individual "well known as an orator and author, the most popular of her books being 'Contending Forces.'" The account of Hopkins's life concluded on a respectful note, prompted by the revelation that "[i]n spite of her age she was still engaged in research work for the Institute of Technology here."[14]

Hopkins's death resulted in W. E. B. Du Bois offering his long-overdue public acknowledgment of her career. News of her death appeared in the October 1930 issue of the *Crisis*; the delay is perhaps explained by the printing schedule, which may have prevented him from including the announcement in the September issue. The obituary notice was published in a column entitled "East," one of several regional columns in which Du Bois called attention to matters relating to specific areas of the United States. His note, especially in light of the fact that he had more time to gather facts before the October issue of the magazine went to press, was striking for its seemingly deliberate dismissal or suppression of Hopkins's accomplishments. The *Crisis* note read, in full: "Mrs. Pauline Hopkins, 71, authoress and poetess, and a former stenographer at the Massachusetts Institute of Technology, died in Cambridge, Mass., in August."[15] Du Bois's failure to tell Hopkins's story is telling, especially because he knew directly of her efforts to oppose Booker T. Washington, was well familiar with the *Colored American Magazine*, and had moved in some of the same Boston circles. Du Bois, the inveterate researcher and proud historian of the race, could easily have gathered details about Hopkins's literary triumphs, political work, and journalism career. What appeared in the pages of the *Crisis* was a brief notice that contained glaring inaccuracies.

Du Bois did not pay tribute to Hopkins the author, playwright, historian, journalist, and race woman. He instead declared, quite distractingly, that she was a poetess, and also identified her as a married woman.

The "East" column, in which news of Hopkins's passing was shared with the readers of the official journal of the National Association for the Advancement of Colored People, included ten items. The Hopkins obituary notice was sandwiched between articles noting scholarships to Bryn Mawr for the daughter of a prominent Boston dentist and the news that Villa Lewaro, the stately New York mansion of Madam C. J. Walker and her daughter A'Lelia, now was on the market. The obituary was the shortest of all of the entries in this section of the *Crisis*. The longest, which appeared first, was a notice about the Joy Street Church in Boston. Du Bois called attention to the "unique exhibit of historical relics of American Negroes" that Florida Ruffin Ridley had created in collaboration with the Society of the Descendants of Early Negro Families. Ridley, the daughter of Josephine St. Pierre Ruffin and her husband, George, was Hopkins's former colleague in the Boston-based New Era Women's Club and in the National Association for Colored Women. The lengthy description of the exhibition's most intriguing items invoked the Paul family, even though it too did not offer any mention of the church's influential first family. "Among the things exhibited were a selection of books written by New England Negroes," the note read, "a diary of the De Grasse family dating from 1809, and the gold-hilted sword presented to Dr. John De Grasse by Governor Andrew in 1863."[16] The irony here is palpable since this historic site in so many ways tells the story of Pauline Hopkins. In this issue of the *Crisis*, Du Bois managed in the same breath to speak of the Joy Street Church and yet not speak of Pauline Hopkins, a woman for whom that place constituted her history. This juxtaposition was a harbinger of the veil of obscurity that shrouded Pauline Hopkins for more than fifty years after her death.

It remains a tragic irony that Pauline Hopkins, the accomplished and ambitious author for whom the written word was so powerful, died intestate. On 30 August, John M. Burrell, her cousin by marriage, filed the first set of documents that would allow Hopkins's legal affairs to be organized and settled. The courts deemed Florence Walker to be a "competent and suitable person," and she was allowed to become the administratrix and executor of her friend's estate.[17] Just over one week later, the Hopkins estate went into probate and was filed under the name of "Pauline E. N. Hopkins."[18] The initials used here referred to the middle name of Elizabeth and to the surname of Hopkins's biological father, Benjamin Northup. On 8 September 1930, Florence Walker, Isabelle Walker, and the undertaker who attended to Hopkins's final arrangements appeared before Judge Charles N. Harris of the

Middlesex County Probate Court. They all agreed to be "holden and stand firmly bound and obliged" to attend to the probate issues of Hopkins's estate. As the administratrix, Florence Walker pledged to fulfill a set of obligations. These sworn pledges included that Walker would "within three months of her appointment" provide "a true inventory of all the real and personal estate of said deceased," that she would "administer according to law all the personal estate of said deceased which may come to [her] possession," and that she would "render upon oath, a true account of her administration at least once a year, until her trust is fulfilled."[19]

The last narrative to which Pauline Hopkins contributed was a sobering one in every respect and provided wrenching, but long-awaited glimpses, into her private daily life. The probate documents included a detailed evaluation of her estate and specific notes about the final set of expenses incurred as her friends and family laid her to rest alongside her parents and grandparents in the Garden Cemetery in Chelsea, Massachusetts. Her entire estate was valued at $200, and the value of real estate in her possession was noted as "[n]one." Included in the probate file was a "Schedule of Personal Estate in Detail." It reveals that Hopkins had an account at the Home Savings Bank, which, at the time of her death, contained $165.40. "[I]nterest on deposit" was $6.00. She also had in her possession at home a set of uncashed checks that totaled $40.00. Her total personal estate, based on these three amounts, totaled $226.39.[20]

The most evocative accounting of Hopkins's life is contained in Schedule B of the Probate Records housed in the Suffolk County Court House. This document is painfully matter-of-fact in its review of the details pertaining to Hopkins's death and burial. The undertaker hired for the funeral was Thomas M. O'Brien of 800 Main Street in Cambridge. The fees paid to O'Brien and the other charges totaled $232.39 and were allocated in the following manner:

Thomas M. O'Brien, undertaker	180.00
Difference in item as to check	10.00
Difference in item as to household effects	1.99
Underwear	3.00
Carfares, telephones, stamps, cards, etc.	6.15
Funeral notices	5.25
Flowers	5.50
Probate Expenses	5.50
Express	4.00
Nurse	6.00
Minister	5.00[21]

Florence Walker may have collaborated with others to arrange, per her responsibilities as executor and administratrix of Hopkins's estate, a sale of Hopkins's "household effects." The sale brought in $20.99 for unidentified items, and that modest amount was added to Hopkins's meager estate.

John Burrell was steady in his attention to legal matters relating to the affairs of his wife's cousin. He attended promptly and with care in the days after Hopkins's accident and death to the documents that organized her final affairs, even in the absence of a will. He filed the lengthy and involved probate documents and also ensured that the Walkers were kept apprised of their responsibilities. Burrell, from his downtown offices at 10 Tremont Street, also maintained watch of the due dates and filings that had to be made in order to reach closure for Pauline Hopkins and her estate. In accordance with the probate procedures, in September 1930 he began a series of public notices about Hopkins's passing and the condition of her estate. These announcements, which were to be "posted in public places" in Cambridge, informed all who read them of the role that Florence Walker was poised to play in the legal affairs of her friend. "Notice is hereby given that the subscriber has been duly appointed administratrix of the estate of Pauline E. N. Hopkins late of Cambridge in the County of Middlesex, deceased, intestate," the announcements declared, before stating that "[a]ll persons having demands upon the estate of said deceased are required to exhibit the same; and all persons indebted to said estate are called upon to make payment."[22] On 16 November 1931, John Burrell filed the last of the papers relating to the affairs of Pauline Hopkins. Entitled the "Administrator's First and Final Account," the form noted "no tax waiver filed; 1 year expired; No assent of heirs: Harriet A. Burrell, Emma V. Gossen, George B. Vashon," and listed Burrell as the accountant for this last assessment of Hopkins's estate. The Cambridge city directory for 1931 offered the final confirmation that Hopkins had passed on. The entry read simply, "Hopkins, Pauline E., died Aug. 13, 1930."[23]

When Pauline Hopkins spoke in historic Faneuil Hall in December 1905, she used the opportunity to declare, "I am a black daughter of the revolution." She invoked revolutions both historic and symbolic as she conjured up the mighty legacy of her forefathers, men who "poured out their blood" during the Battle at Bunker Hill. On this occasion, a moment when she held forth in public more powerfully than she ever had before or ever would do again, Hopkins also invoked a revolution of intellectual, political, and social dimensions of which she was protective and to which she was indebted. As a daughter of these interrelated uprisings and traditions of resistance, Hopkins was well aware of the need to bring these histories to bear on American society, culture, and memory. Determined to honor the legacies and extend the traditions of literary excellence and political engagement, Hopkins negotiated social divides, political difference, and socioeconomic realities that all too often relegated others to silence.

The histories of race, romance, triumph, and tragedy that infused Hopkins's writings and activism needed vigilant guardians and inspired proponents. The revolution of which she spoke in 1905 and that motivated her throughout her lifetime was as storied as the fight between the British and the Continental soldiers whom she hailed as her forefathers. "You do not recognize black daughters of the Revolution, but we are going to take that right," Hopkins pledged in earnest.[24] When she was laid to rest in her family plot on the Lilac Path in Chelsea's Garden Cemetery, this New England daughter had lived a rich and challenging life of righteous testimony, creative genius, and unwavering activism that, from its inception, had been enriched by awe-inspiring family histories, cherished romances, and bold advocacy for humanity.

Speeches

William Lloyd Garrison Centennial Celebration,
11 December 1905, Faneuil Hall, Boston

COLORED WOMAN MAKES CHIEF ADDRESS

Miss Pauline E. Hopkins spoke in part as follows: I count it, this afternoon, the greatest honor that will ever come to me that I am permitted to stand in this historic hall and say one word for the liberties of my race. I thought to myself how dare I, a weak woman, humble in comparison with these other people. Yesterday I sat in the old Joy street church and you can imagine my emotions as I remembered my great grandfather begged in England the money that helped the Negro cause, that my grandfather on my father's side, signed the papers with Garrison at Philadelphia. I remembered that at Bunker Hill my ancestors on my maternal side poured out their blood. I am a daughter of the Revolution, you do not acknowledge black daughters of the Revolution but we are going to take that right.

The conditions which gave birth to so remarkable a reformer and patriot were peculiar. The entire American Republic had set itself to do evil, and its leading forces, wealth, religion and party, joined the popular side, and threatened the death of Liberty in the Republic. But the darkest hour was but a herald of the dawn. No great reform was ever projected or patronized by any powerful organization or influential individual at the outset. Reformation always begins in the heart of a solitary individual; some humble man or woman unknown to fame is lifted up to the level of the Almighty's heartbeats where is unfolded to him what presently must be done. Thus it was that after the imposition of the colonization scheme, the issuing of Walker's "Appeal," and his own imprisonment at Baltimore, the poor and obscure Newburyport printer's boy, without reputation, social or political influence, or money, inaugurated the greatest reform of the nineteenth century, and within one year of the first issue of the "Liberator," the entire country knew the name of Garrison. God had heard the prayers of suffering humanity. He said "enough." The hour struck on the horologe of Eternity, and the man was there. Side by side with Martin Luther's "Here I take my stand," is the "I will be heard" of William Lloyd Garrison. (Applause.)

In September, 1834, we are told that the Reformer received the greatest individual help that ever came to him during his life, when he married Miss Eliza Benson, daughter of a venerable philanthropist of Rhode Island, and in thereafter woman's subtle, intuitive instinct added another sense to the wonderful powers of this remarkable man. Very shortly after their marriage, this brave woman was called to view the mobbing of her husband by the Boston "Broadcloth Mob." She stepped from a window upon a shed at the moment of his extremest danger, being herself in danger from the rioters.

His hat was lost, and brickbats were rained upon his head while he was hustled along in the direction of the tar-kettle in the next street. The only words that escaped from the white lips of the young wife were: "I think my husband will never deny his principles. I am sure my husband will never deny his principles." The same spirit of encouragement still exists in women. What angers will not a woman dare for the support and comfort of husband, father or brother? Not so long ago, when a Boston young man of color was hustled and beaten and jailed for upholding free speech and independent thought, he was sustained and comforted by the words of a sister: "Remember, this is not disgrace, but honor. It is for principle—it is for principle." (Applause).

Mr. Garrison went about his work against slavery with tremendous moral earnestness. At first he advocated gradual emancipation, but after his baptism of injustice in a Baltimore jail his sentiments changed to the startling doctrine of immediate and unconditional emancipation. Gradual emancipation was a popular and inoffensive doctrine, a safe shore from which to view freedom for the Blacks. It is analogous with the startling propaganda of disenfranchisement or gradual enfranchisement after the Afro-American has proved himself fit for the ballot. We remember that history records the broken promises of freedom given by the southern States to the blacks of Southern regiments in the Revolutionary War. Those men earned their freedom, proved their right to manhood, but at the close of the war were told that, "You have done well, boys, now get home to your masters." The time will never come for the enfranchisement of the black if he depends upon an acknowledgment from the south of his worthiness for the ballot. (Applause.) As if the faithfulness of the black man to this government from the Revolution until this day, the blood freely shed to sustain the Republican principles in every way waged against the Republic, the gentle, patient, docility, with which we have borne every wrong, were not proof of our fitness to enjoy what is right. (Applause.)

Mr. Garrison lived to see his cause triumph in the emancipation of the slave, and died believing that the manhood rights of every citizen of the United States were secured then and forever. But the rise of a younger generation, the influence of an unconquered south, and the acquiescence of an ease-loving north that winks at abuses where commercial relations and manufactures flourish and put money in the purse, have neutralized the effects of the stern policy of these giants of an earlier age.

Great indeed was the battle for the abolition of slavery but greater far will be the battle for manhood rights.

Let us hope that his timely review of the noble words and deeds of Garrison and his followers, may rekindle within our breast the love of liberty. Were Mr. Garrison living in this materialistic age, when the price of manhood is a good dinner, a fine position, a smile of approval and a pat on the back from the man of influence, or a fat endowment again would he cry aloud, "The apathy of the people is enough to make every statue leap from its pedestal, and to hasten the resurrection of the dead."

Here in Faneuil hall, let us vow as the greatest tribute we can pay to Mr. Garrison's memory, to keep alive the sacred flame of universal liberty in the Republic for all races and classes, by every legitimate means, petitions to individuals, to associations, to foreign governments, to legislatures, to congress, print and circulate literature, and let the voice of the agent and lecturer be constantly heard. Let us swear to be "as harsh as truth and as uncompromising as justice." And let us bear in mind the beauty of doing all things for the up building of humanity; persecution and intellectual development have broadened us until we can clearly see that if the blacks are downed in the fight for manhood, no individual or race will be safe within our borders. This government has welded all races into one great nation until now, what is good for the individual member of the body politic is good for all and vice versa. Here where the south and its sympathizers have so strenuously denied the brotherhood of man, by our mixed population. God has proved his declaration, "Of one blood have I made all races of men to dwell upon the whole face of the earth together." This truth Mr. Garrison and his followers freely acknowledged in the beauty and purity of their lives and deeds.

Source: *The Guardian*, 16 December 1905.

Observance of the One Hundredth Anniversary of the Birth of Charles Sumner, 6 January 1911, Park Street Church, Boston

Miss Pauline E. Hopkins of Cambridge, author of *Contending Forces*, who represented the women of the race whom Mr. Sumner championed, said—:

Mr. Chairman, Ladies, and Gentlemen:
There have been a few Americans whose characters we, as a race idealize and whose memories we idolize,—Senator Sumner was one of the few.

Centenary celebrations are good for many things: In the lapse of years the heat of passion passes and calm Reason weighs word and act in the balances of eternal justice[,] and thus we are apt to reach the exact amount of good accomplished under certain conditions. The flight of time has but added laurels to Mr. Sumner's fame in spite of his detractors[,] and the student of sociology is thrilled with enthusiasm over the record of this great life which is today's lesson. This man was an intellectual and moral giant with an added divinity that was almost Godlike: Perfect truth in the midst of hideous error, perfect rectitude in the midst of perjury, violence and fraud, perfect patience while encountering every species of gross provocation. But why try to enumerate his virtues,—we cannot detract from his fame; we can add nothing to his glory. Generations yet unborn shall say of him:

> He is gone;
> Gone; but nothing can bereave him
> Of the force he made his own
> Being here;
> And he wears a truer crown
> Than any wreath that man can weave him.

Mr. Sumner was essentially a reformer—a herald of progress, for his aim was to better existing conditions; he hated evil and adored good. Hence arose the antagonism of a conservative North and South. But conservatism is a fundamental principle in social life. In church, state and society, conservatism is the ruling force and it is the cause of the unrest and turmoil that has ushered in the twentieth century.

Conservatism protects existing conditions and perpetuates them, and dreads and resists the innovations of the reformer.

All heralds of progress—the men who have been of the most benefit in enlightening the world—have encountered the same difficulties from the materialist. Galileo, seeking the law of gravitation, Columbus sailing for the discovery of a New World, Franklin wresting the thunderbolt from the sky and Benjamin Butler transforming black slaves into contrabands of war—all suffered from the animosity of conservatism.

As a reformer Mr. Sumner was aggressive, looking toward the perfection of the future government—a new Republic without the blemish of slavery. But the conflict and the co-operation of these opposing forces has brought about whatever there may be of present harmony of the material with the ideal.

The stupendous energy of the Twentieth Century is sweeping us onward with frightful velocity we know not where. We believe that now is the psychological moment for the forward movement of the dark races upon the world's arena. Not with hostile intent[,] for the white-souled Sumner taught us "there is nothing in hate, nothing in vengeance," but side by side with all other downtrodden people[,] clasp hands in the good fight of all races up and no race down. Thus, and thus alone the Black man shall come into his own. Were Senator Sumner with us today, he would be in the forefront leading the forces engaged in the uplift of all humanity.

Mr. Sumner said when he pleaded for harmony between the races: "Much better will it be when two political parties compete for your vote, each anxious for your support. Only then will that citizenship by which you are entitled to the equal rights of all have its fruits. Only then will there be that harmony which is essential to a true civilization." Events have justified that prophecy.

Life today is the Negro question, Socialism, the Labor question, Woman Suffrage, New Nationalism, Child Labor, White Slavery, The New Thought, Christian Science— life is the loom, mind, and weaver, thought the thread, our good and evil deeds the warp and woof, and the web is the character to posterity as Mr. Sumner bequeathed his to us. Call us then, no longer Negroes, that name so fraught with blood and tears and bitter memories of contemptuous tolerance—but call us Men, mighty factors in the solving of human problems.

The secret of evolution is profound. This American Republic was founded by the Almighty Economist who governs the great seas of progression and retrogression, tossing them hither and thither at his will by unexpected counter currents. Here all races have found a refuge from persecution; here all races were represented among the Abolitionists; here all races are to be participants in the new order of things slowly evolving out of the present unrest.

> Therefore, not unconsoled, I wait in hope
> To see the moment when our righteous cause
> Shall gain defenders zealous and devout
> As they who now oppose us.

Men of the National and New England Leagues, it is a charge of honor given into your hand by Mr. Sumner to be handed down from father to son, not to let the Civil Rights bill fail now or ever.

> Give us the faith to kneel around
> Our country's shrine and swear
> To keep alive the sacred flame
> That Sumner kindled there!

Source: William Monroe Trotter, ed., *The Two Days of Observance of the One Hundredth Anniversary of the Birth of Charles Sumner* (Boston: Boston Sumner Centenary Committee, 1911).

APPENDIX 2
Letters

Cornelia A. Condict to the Colored American Magazine
and Reply from Pauline Hopkins, ca. Spring 1903

We [at the *Colored American Magazine*] are constantly in receipt of letters from our readers in all sections of the country, in fact of the world, and it gives us a great deal of pleasure to note how warm a reception is given our publication among all classes and races. Some friends offer kindly suggestions as to how we can improve and make more helpful "The Colored American Magazine," while others tell of the grand work already accomplished by our periodical. The following letter, recently received from one of our *white* readers, is of more than passing interest to us all:

Dear Sirs:

With Miss Floto I have been taking and reading with interest the COLORED AMERICAN MAGAZINE.

If I found it more helpful to Christian work among your people I would continue to take it.

May I make a comment on the stories, especially those that have been serial. Without exception they have been of love between the coloreds and the whites. Does that mean that your novelists can imagine no love beautiful and sublime within the range of the colored race, for each other? I have seen beautiful home life and love in families altogether of Negro blood.

The stories of these tragic mixed loves will not commend themselves to your white readers and will not elevate the colored readers. I believe your novelists could do with a consecrated imagination and pen, more for the elevation of home life and love, than perhaps any other one class of writers.

What Dickens did for the neglected working class of England, some writer could do for the neglected colored people of America.

For several years I worked (superintended a Sunday school) among a greatly mixed people, by yourselves or others.

My sympathies are with the earnest and spiritual work that is being done for your people, by yourselves or others.

We have kindred who are cultured Christian ladies, who for years have borne the ostracism of the white women of the South for the sake of the colored girls and women of the great South land.

Very respectfully,
CORNELIA A. CONDICT

With regard to your enclosure (letter from Mrs. Condict) [I] will say, it is the same old story. One religion for the whites and another for the blacks. The story of Jesus for us, that carries with it submission to the abuses of our people and blindness to the degrading of our youth. I think Mrs. Condict has a great work to do—greater than she can accomplish, I fear—to carry religion to the Southern whites.

My stories are definitely planned to show the obstacles persistently placed in our paths by a dominant race to subjugate us spiritually. Marriage is made illegal between the races and yet the mulattoes increase. Thus the shadow of corruption falls on the blacks and on the whites, without whose aid the mulattoes would not exist. And then the hue and cry goes abroad of the immorality of the Negro and the disgrace that the mulattoes are to this nation. Amalgamation is an institution designed by God for some wise purpose, and mixed bloods have always exercised a great influence on the progress of human affairs. I sing of the *wrongs* of a race that ignorance of their pitiful condition may be changed to intelligence and must awaken compassion in the hearts of the just.

The home life of Negroes is beautiful in many instances; warm affection is there between husband and wife, and filial and paternal tenderness in them is not surpassed by any other race of the human family. But Dickens wrote not of the joys and beauties of English society; I believe he was the author of "Bleak House" and "David Copperfield." If he had been an American, and with his trenchant pen had exposed the abuses practiced by the Southern whites upon the blacks—had told the true story of how wealth, intelligence and femininity has stooped to choose for a partner in sin, the degraded(?) Negro whom they affect to despise, Dickens would have been advised t[o] shut up or get out. I believe Jesus Christ when on earth rebuked the Pharisees in this wise: "Ye hypocrites, ye expect to be heard for your much speaking"; "O wicked and adulterous(?) nation, how can ye escape the damnation of hell?" He didn't go about patting those old sinners on the back and saying, "All right, boys, fix me up and the Jews will get there all right. Money talks. Di[v]vy [up] the money you take in the exchange business of the synagogue, and it'll be all right with God." Jesus told the thing as it was and the Jews crucified him! I am glad to receive this criticism for it shows more clearly than ever that white people don't understand *what pleases Negroes*. You are between Scylla and Charybdis. If you please the author of this letter and your white clientele, you will lose your Negro patronage. If you cater to the *demands* of the Negro trade, away goes Mrs. ——. I have sold to many whites and have received great praise for the work I am doing in exposing the social life of the Southerners and the wickedness of their caste prejudice.

Let the good work go on. Opposition is the life of an enterprise; criticism tells you that you are doing something.

Respect.,

PAULINE E. HOPKINS

Source: *Colored American Magazine*, March 1903.

Mrs. Robert Mitchell Floyd to Pauline Hopkins, 8 February 1904

Hotel Carlton, Boston, Feb. 8. 1904.

My Dear Miss Hopkins—

Through our friend, Mr. John C. Freund, of New York, we have heard of your work on your magazine. If quite agreeable to you, I would like to call, with my friend Miss Snelling, and have the pleasure of meeting you personally. Send magazines to

Mrs. Robert M. Floyd, Hotel Carlton, Boston, Mass.
Miss Caroline Snelling, 1078 Boylston St., Boston, Mass.
Mr. W. H. Johnson, 18 Summer St., Cambridge, Mass.
Mr. Wm. McIntosh, care Buffalo Evening News, Buffalo, N.Y.
Mrs. Elvira Floyd Froemcke, Montreal, Canada.

Very sincerely yours,
Mrs. Robert Mitchell Floyd.

Source: Letter to Pauline E. Hopkins from Mrs. Robert Mitchell Floyd, *Colored American Magazine*, May 1904.

Isabella Beecher Hooker to Pauline Hopkins, 20 March 1904

Hartford, Conn., March 20, 1904.

Pauline E. Hopkins:

Dear Friend—Permit me to congratulate you on the March issue of your magazine. To begin with, the cover is admirable and the contents match the cover.

In Mr. Freund you have discovered a noble champion, a trustworthy leader in the cause of humanity. Please send me his address that I may thank him for every word of his late utterance at your dinner. The problem is to get people to read this number of your magazine and subscribe for it. Somebody ought to get Governor Vardaman to do this, and every decent newspaper in the land ought to lend a hand in its circulation.

I am already a subscriber, but if you will send me some extra copies wrapped for mailing, I will try to add to your list. If I had a thousand dollars to spare, I would spend it in this way.

I am faithfully yours,
Isabella Beecher Hooker.

Source: "Testimonials of Friendship from Influential People of All Sections," *Colored American Magazine*, May 1904, 379–80.
Note: There is no copy of a response from Hopkins in the Hooker Family Papers, Harriet Beecher Stowe Center, Hartford, Conn.

A. Kirkland Soga to Pauline Hopkins, ca. July 1904

IZWI LABANTU Office
East London, Cape Colony

MY DEAR MISS HOPKINS:

Your last letter appointing me a member of the Colored American League is far and beyond anything that I could reasonably desire or expect in the way of appreciation. I shall have to return to the subject again as I have only just taken a first glance at the proceedings at the Revere House, which inaugurated the formation of this notable, and I trust, epoch-making body. I have already remarked in speaking of this honor conferred on me in the columns of IZWI, that no title or insignia which could be conferred now or hereafter can give me more satisfaction than the simple little button in red, white and blue, with its sufficing motto, "For Humanity." Not for white, mark you, nor yet for black alone, or yellow, but for all mankind. Surely this is a creed the very noblest that could be held by man or woman in the pursuit of a common brotherhood in Christ—but the accomplishment, ah! how hard. The ideal, however, being what it is, there is nothing else required but to push on toward the prize of our high calling and to bring such material weapons as we can into service toward that great objective. I am therefore distributing your magazine at different points in South Africa among intelligent native friends, and in due course will be able to submit you the names of men and women, who, by taking your excellent magazine, will bring its gifts to the doors of our people, who, if they appreciate it as well as I do as a mine of information of the most valuable character on those questions germane to the black and colored races who are being gradually, if skillfully, welded and brought into unity by unseen forces, will be bound to keep taking it, once they have given it a trial. I shall ask them to act as agents in their several districts and submit their names to you. After that you can deal direct with the parties concerned. I shall also call attention in our columns to the League, and trust that in one way and another, the noble work begun at the Revere House will fully justify in course of time (and oh! may it be soon) the great expectations of its honored patron, John C. Freund, and the other men and women patriots who graced the inauguration ceremony with their presence and patronage.

Yours faithfully,

A. KIRKLAND SOGA, Editor IZWI
East London, South Africa

Source: *Colored American Magazine*, August 1904.

53 Clifton St., No. Cambridge, Mass.,
April 16, '05

Mr. W. M. Trotter,
Boston, Mass.

My dear Mr. Trotter: —

Herewith I send you a detailed account of my experiences with the *Colored American Magazine* as its editor and, incidentally, with Mr. Booker T. Washington in the taking over of the magazine to New York by his agents. It is necessarily long and perhaps tedious at the outset, but I trust that you will peruse it to the end. I have held these facts for a year, but as my rights are ignored in my own property, and I am persistently hedged about by the revengeful tactics of Mr. Washington's men, I feel that I must ask the advice of some one who will give me a respectful hearing and judgment as to the best way to deal with this complicated case. I hope that you will do what you can for me.

In May 1903, *The Colored American Magazine*, a well-known and powerful Negro organ, was sold by its creditors to the highest bidders, — Messrs. W. H. Dupree, Wm. O. West, and Jesse Watkins of Boston, and I was engaged as literary editor because I was well-known as a race writer, had gained the confidence of my people, and also because there seemed to be at that time, no one else as well qualified to fill the position, for as yet the editing of a high-class magazine was puzzling work even to our best scholars.

From the start it was a struggle for us to keep our heads above water because of the financial crisis just passed and the strain that had been placed upon the confidence and purses of our people. I received a salary of $7 per week and the type-writer $3, while the owners, of course, received nothing. Mr. Dupree made up a deficit each month and becoming discouraged he notified me in August that he would close up the business as he was running behind and could not stand the strain. Mr. Watkins, however, protested, and his brother James H. Watkins[,] thinking that under his more experienced business management matters could be improved, offered to take the business and keep us going for what he might make out of it until March 11, 1904. The firm accepted his proposition, discharged the type-writer, raised my salary to $8 per week, I doing her work of correspondence and my own editorial work, and we jogged along until November.

In November, the "Announcements" were due for the ensuing year and I began to look about me for material from writers of prominence and influence. There was no money to pay contributors so I planned a circular which I knew would touch the people in a kindly vein asking for articles on "INDUSTRIAL EDUCATION; WILL IT SOLVE THE NEGRO PROBLEM?" These articles were to be contributed without charge. I also asked for any other matter that writers were willing to give us. A copy of this letter was sent to Hon. William Lloyd Garrison, Rev. Edward A. Horton, Mrs. Ella Wheeler Wilcox, Mrs. John A. Logan, Prof. W. E. B. Du Bois, Prof. B. T. Washington, Editor T. Thomas Fortune, Roscoe Conkling Bruce, Prof. Kelly Miller, Editor A. Kirkland Soga

(East London, South Africa), and a number of other writers of prominence. Every one approached responded with a free contribution except Prof. Miller who charged $5. (See accompanying copy of magazine, December 1903.)

Mr. Dupree was greatly pleased with my success and told me that he thought he could help too by soliciting Mr. John C. Freund, Editor of *The Music Trades*, New York, for permission to reproduce his series of articles and[,] finding them exceptionally interesting and instructive, urged Mr. Dupree to secure them if possible. This he accomplished through the intervention of Mr. Barker of the Boston General Post Office. For full account see Mr. Dupree's own narrative in accompany[ing] marked March number, 1904. In November, 1903, Mr. Dupree received a letter from Mr. Freund promising us the articles on the Island of Jamaica in these words:—"It will give me sincere pleasure to prepare them for your magazine, and also to accompany them with such cuts as may be desirable." (See accompanying letter marked "1.")

Previous to this event, in the last of October, we had received a call and a proposition from Mr. Peter Smith, founder of *The Boston Colored Citizen*, an employee and intimate friend of Mr. B. T. Washington, asking us to allow him to remove his plant to our office at 82 West Concord St. as his quarters on Charles St. were too cramped. This we refused him in a very few words for we mistrusted his intentions knowing the man.

Our correspondence with Mr. Freund was of the most satisfactory kind. He gave us the articles, furnished cuts of a size suitable for our magazine and gave us $15 per month toward defraying the expense of manufacturing the same. So genial, so kind, so disinterested did he appear that he soon won our entire confidence. (He repeatedly assured us that "I have no axe to grind.") No mention was made of Mr. B. T. Washington to me and I thought it a case of pure philanthropy, one of those rare cases which are sometimes found among wealthy, generous and eccentric white men. About January 1, 1904, he wrote us that he would entertain 20 leading ladies and gentlemen, including our staff, at any hotel in Boston that Mr. Dupree might select at a cost of $2 per place, in order to meet us all and become better acquainted than we could by letter, and also, to further the interest of the magazine by personal effort thinking that the knowledge that an influential white man was interested in our enterprise would tend to stimulate the colored people themselves to greater effort. We were greatly surprised[,] not to say overwhelmed at the honor thrust upon us, but Mr. Dupree set about working up the dinner in a style worthy of the giver, and he succeeded admirably. (For full account see accompanying March, 1904 number.)

The dinner was given at the Revere House, Boston, and some interesting things which were said and done there have never been recorded. Among them was the opposition of Commander Wolff, Commander Massachusetts Department, G. A. R., who spoke decidedly against our accepting any overtures leading to a removal to New York before the close of the Presidential campaign, and he concluded by predicting that such a move would involve a loss of the magazine. I was called upon to offset the speech made by Mr. Wolff by detailing our hardships and financial difficulties. I learned that Mr. Freund was greatly incensed over Mr. Wolff's remarks; I could not understand his enmity but have concluded since that Mr. Wolff was on the right track in his prediction. On Monday morning following the dinner, Mr. Dupree asking me what I thought of it all and I said "it is a political move, but if you can get back your money why, we can say nothing as long as we keep the magazine afloat." The others agreed with me.

Mr. Freund took hold of our business ostensibly to correct our errors made in ignorance of the needs of a successful publication. We had been late in the month in getting out and he strove hard to have us out on time. He criticised our work harshly and nothing we did would please him, but we cared not for that as we were bent on keeping his friendship and profiting by his experience and ripe judgement. He proposed that the March number should be a great boom, sensational in character, forming the diners of January 24th into a society for the support of the magazine and having branches of the same in all sections of the country, and taking for its motto, "For humanity." The badge of the order was to be a red, white and blue button with those words on the margin. This was to be given to each subscriber together with a receipt printed in three colors. 5,000 buttons were ordered and 2,500 receipts. The price of the magazine was changed, and single copies sold at 10 cents per copy instead of the former price 15 cents; yearly subscriptions fell from $1.50 to $1. All this was for the good of the cause, but made a marked shortage in our receipts which he generously made up from his private purse. (See accompanying letters marked 2, 2a, 3a, and 4 which I enclose in order to show you more clearly Mr. Freunds mode of action, and to give you a slight idea of the amount of money he expended.)

Early in February, 1904, Mr. Freund sent me a bouquet of Russian violets by his Boston representative, Mr. Albert Loomis; the book *Self-Help* by Smiles, an expensive set of furs, a $25-check and a book *Eternalism*. I had seemed to be a favorite with our benefactor and these special attentions made my position in the office very uncomfortable. As I am not a woman who attracts the attention of the opposite sex in any way, Mr. Freund's philanthropy with regard to myself puzzled me, but knowing that he was aware of my burdens at home, I thought that he was trying to help me in his way. I was so dense that I did not for a moment suspect that I was being politely bribed to give up my race work and principles and adopt the plans of the South for the domination of the Blacks.

Mr. Freund had interviewed our creditors, examined our books, knew our weakest as well as our strongest points, and held with each one of us the patriarchal relation of ancient days. He was spoken of by us in our conversations together as "Papa Freund." The following extract shows how familiar he was with my business:—

The *Colored American Magazine*, No. 82 West Concord St., Boston, is a good periodical for the price—a dollar a year; ten cents a copy—as good as any except the *Strand*, of London. It contains interesting articles and stories and is brightly illustrated. The editress is a colored woman; a company of colored men are the publishers. John C. Freund, of *Music Trades*, is enthusiastic about their work. "What do you think," he writes me, "of a colored editress, whose salary is eight dollars a week when she gets it—with a bedridden mother to support? What do you think of a backer of the magazine, a coalblack Negro, who has put the savings of his life, from day's labor, to help it along, because he thinks it may give people a better idea of his race? What do you think of a grizzled veteran, who came out of the War an emancipated slave, unable to read or write, but has educated himself until he is the superintendent of the second largest branch of the Boston postoffice?" It is a far cry for Mr. Freund of Oxford University and the society of distinguished authors, actors and musicians to the association with Negroes, but he throws his whole heart into every philanthropic mission.

Stephen Fiske, in "Sports of the Times," New York

Mr. Freund caused my salary to be raised. (See accompanying letter marked 4.) Little by little he opened his views to me and I found that he was curtailing my work from the broad field of <u>international</u> union and <u>uplift</u> for the Blacks in all quarters of the globe, to the narrow confines of the question as affecting solely the Afro-American. (See accompanying letter marked 5.)

In February another dinner was given the staff at the Revere House, Boston. Plans were laid for storming Boston by giving a grand reception in the name of the magazine, to Mr. Freund on March 19th at which 200 guests would be entertained. He seemed pleased with the fact that the league was doing good work for us and said:—

There will be three Leagues in the field—
1. <u>The Business League</u> with <u>Booker Washington</u> at the head
2. <u>The Colored American League</u> with <u>Col. W. H. Dupree</u> at the head
3. <u>The Political League</u> with <u>Fortune</u> at the head.
(See letters marked 6 and 7.)

Mr. Freund's letter contained many compliments on my editorial ability. (See letter marked 8.) But sometimes there was a note of alarm which puzzled me. He told me that there must not be a word on lynching, no mention of our wrongs as a race, nothing that would be offensive to the South. He wrote:—"If you are going to take up the wrongs of your race, then you must depend for support absolutely upon your own race. For the colored man today to attempt to stand up to fight would be like a canary bird to face a bulldog, and an angry one at that. The whole line of work must be conciliatory, constructive, and that is where Booker Washington is showing himself to be such a giant."

None of our efforts as a force pleased our patron; the manufacturing of the magazine he treated with contempt, and constantly bewailed the fact that he had not removed the magazine to New York where he could have supervised it personally. This, however, Mr. Dupree had flatly refused to allow until his interests were fully protected. Mr. Freund gracefully waived the point. (See letters marked 9, 10, 11, 12.) (Also programme of reception.) Mr. Dupree's confidence did not extend to allowing Mr. Freund to take the magazine to New York without the passing of legal papers which he attempted to do.

After the reception Mr. Freund began to show little by little, his true errand; he began a Washington campaign as shown by letter dated "March 24th," where he says:—

The work itself is to me so exhilarating that if I have any regret it is that my face is not black and that with such education and force as I have, I cannot go right out into the open and battle for justice alongside Booker T. Washington.

Colonel Dupree has an excellent idea—that the magazine will soon be able to get some ads from the various colored universities and high schools. I agree with him thoroughly. I shall personally go to Tuskegee after I have met Booker Washington, and give him a write-up that will make his hair stand on end. <u>You need his support</u>.

(See letter marked 13.)

The next day I received a telegram. (See copy marked 13a.) In this telegram I was asked to write a letter of introduction; I was to introduce <u>Mr. Freund to Mr. Washington!</u> Mr. Dupree and the staff requested me to comply strictly with Mr. Freund's request, so, although I had no personal acquaintance with mr. washington, I wrote a letter to him detailing our situation, recounting Mr. Freund's kind acts and craving Mr. Washington's good offices as a race man in our favor. I regret that I did not preserve a copy of this letter which to say the least was unique in its character and mission. (See letter marked 14.)

Received letter marked 15 stating that mr. washington would call upon him. (See letter marked 15.)

Received another letter dated "March 31," stating that mr. washington had called upon him. (See letter marked 16a.)

Mr. Dupree received one dated "March 31," which we call "the washington letter," and which is especially interesting as it details Mr. Washington's opinions regarding the magazine and its work. (See letter marked 16.)

Mr. Dupree received a letter dated "April 6," which threw a firebrand into the office and made my position unbearable. (See letter marked 17.) In this letter we note the following:—

There is, however, one rock squarely ahead of us. That is the persistence with which matter is put into the magazine, which has no live interest, and furthermore, is likely to alienate the very few friends who might help us. Now, I have spoken on the subject already more than I care to. Either Miss Hopkins will follow our suggestion in this matter and put live matter into the magazine, eliminating anything which may create offense; stop talking about wrongs and a proscribed race, or you must count me out absolutely from this day forth. I will neither personally endorse nor help a business proposition which my common sense tells me is foredoomed to failure. Every person that I have spoken to on the subject is with me. it is mr. booker washington's idea.

If you people, therefore, want to get out a literary magazine, with article[s] on the filipino, I refuse to work one minute longer with you. That is my ultimatum and I shall say no more on the subject.

To explain my position I will refer the reader to the fact that I had begged for help from many noted people, and had announced the articles which would appear during the year. Our subscribers would hold us to our promises and expect the articles offered them as inducements for their subscriptions. Among these writers were Hon. Wm. Lloyd Garrison, Rev. Edward A. Horton, Editor A. K. Soga, and a paid contributor, Prof. Hamedoe.

Prof. Hamedoe is a colored linguist who has mastered seven modern languages and thirteen Chinese dialects. He is a man well-versed in history, a traveler who has visited every corner of the globe; his work is instructive and greatly admired by colored readers.

I could not cut the articles contributed by these authors without giving great offense and alienating true friends, some of whom had gone to great expense to get matter for and to me from a distance; all were chivalrous in their desires to help the woman editor maintain her unique position with credit to the race.

A "literary magazine" applied to the articles of Editor Soga who was the corner stone of my "international policy," and whose "glittering generalities" were shown in the gracefulness of his diction and the power of his thought on race matters. He is a friend and correspondent of Editor Morales of *The West African Mail.* "Proscribed race," was a hit at my book *Contending Forces* and my serial story *Hagar's Daughter*[,] both of which had aroused the ire of the white South, male and female, against me [and] many of whom had paid me their compliments in newspaper squibs and insulting personal letters sent to the old management of the magazine. But Mr. Garrison's article on "Industrial Education," and Prof. Hamedoe's on "El Sr. Jose Rizal" the Filipino martyr were the arousers of our patron's ire and of Mr. Washington's wrath because they not only offended the South, but, also, seemingly reflected upon President Roosevelt's Philippine policy. (See accompanying April magazine for the articles of Mr. Garrison, Mr. Soga, and Prof. Hamedoe.)

Messrs. Dupree, West, and Watkins were influenced by Mr. Freund's threat of withdrawal, and matters grew unbearable for me at the office; I was absent for a number of days. During this absence I wrote to Mr. Freund outlining to him some of the difficulties I was encountering not knowing that they were caused by him. (See letter marked 18.)

In letter 19 he virtually gives up the enterprise and tells me of the unflattering comments made upon my work (the work so recently eulogized by himself) by Boston people. (See letters marked 19 and 20.)

My Boston critics were all men working for and under Mr. Washington. $150 promised us by Mr. Freund was given right after the reception to Mr. Charles Alexander, Editor of the *Boston Colored Citizen*[,] a paper publicly believed to have been born at Mr. Washington's suggestion for the express purpose of putting *The Boston Guardian* out of business.

About the last of April or the first of May, 1904, negotiations were opened with Mr. Dupree by Mr. Fred Moore, National Organizer of the Business League, looking to the purchase of the *Colored American Magazine*. It was planned to remove this plant to New York and have T. Thomas Fortune as the Editor and Pauline E. Hopkins as Associate Editor. It was understood by the force that Mr. Moore represented and <u>covered</u> Mr. B. T. Washington. I was offered $12 per week[,] which I decided to accept having determined that I would accept the situation as I found it, succumb to the powers that were, and do all I could to keep the magazine alive unless they asked me to publicly renounce the rights of my people. They held, also, the plates of my book *Contending Forces*, and 500 bound and unbound copies of the same. The book had been sold to the former management on the monthly installment plan, and when the company failed they still owed me $175. So, being a creditor and a shareholder and a member of the Board of Directors, I had a deep interest in the business of the corporation.

After I was settled in New York, Mr. Freund wrote me a letter congratulating me on my earnest and faithful work for the purchaser of the magazine. Many promises were made me, but I soon found that I was being "frozen out" for Mr. Roscoe Conkling SIMMONS a nephew of MRS. B. T. WASHINGTON who now holds the position which I was forced to resign last September.

I learned much in New York. I learned that to gain full control of the *New York Age*, Mr. Peterson had received the consulship to Venezuela. I learned from the lips of Mr. and Mrs. Fortune that Mr. Fortune wrote *Up From Slavery* and the famous Atlanta speech "separate as the fingers of the hand"; Mr. Fortune complains that he writes many of Mr. Washington's magazine articles at a great sacrifice to himself, financially, as to do this he has had to give up his work on white organs that netted him a good monthly income. Dr. Wheatland, of Newport, R.I., I am told on good authority, was told by Dr. Fortune that he (Fortune) wrote *Up From Slavery*.

I learned that the first mortgage on Mr. Fortune's home at Red Bank, N. Jersey, is held by the Afro-American Investment Company, 14 Douglass St., Brooklyn, N. Y., Mr. Fred R. Moore, President, and that Mr. Fortune owes Mr. B. T. Washington $2500. This money was borrowed by Mr. Fortune, I am told, to help him out on his trip to the Philippines he (Fortune) intending to repay the same upon receipt of his salary for that work. He has never received a cent (or had not up to last September)[,] his salary being held up at Washington, D. C. by the government.

In dictating a letter to me for Mr. Washington, Mr. Moore said,—

"I was more fortunate than you for I got my $400 from Fortune, but you have not yet received a dollar."

All of these facts go to show that the *New York Age* is a subsidized sheet for its editor [and] is under money obligations to Mr. Washington, and a man so situated is not a free agent by any means. Mr. R. L. Stokes[,] formerly Mr. Washington's secretary at Tuskegee[,] was placed in the *Age* office last September to assist Mr. Fortune.

Mr. Washington's active agents and trusted allies are Mr. Wilford H. Smith, Counsellor-at-law, 115 Broadway, New York; Mr. Charles Anderson, recently appointed inspector Port of New York; Mr. T. Thomas Fortune, editor of the *New York Age*; Mr. Fred R. Moore, National Organizer of the Business League. Meetings are held frequently at the Stevens House, Broadway, New York, and after one of these meetings one may look out for startling occurrences. Plans are laid for "downing" opposing Negroes, wires are pulled for paying political jobs, and "ward-heeling" schemes are constantly resorted to.

Stranger than all is the fact that these men do not represent the majority of the best Negroes in the city, but are representative of the sporting Negroes alone. None of these men affiliate with the church; they are decidedly in the minority, but they are all Mr. Washington's intimate friends.

A new magazine has been started since the *Colored American* became defunct, so to speak—*The Voice of the Negro*, published at Atlanta, Georgia. This organ has offended Mr. Washington deeply by adopting an independent course. The *Voice* has caught the New York trade and Mr. Moore is swearing vengeance. He is planning to drive the

Voice out of the field by closing the doors of the convention hall of the Negro Business League which meets in New York in August, against the representatives of the *Voice*[,] thus placing them publicly under the ban of Mr. Washington's displeasure.

Formerly the agents of the *Colored American Magazine* sold from 800–1500 copies of the magazine in New York each month[;] now its sale averages 200 a month. Agents are urging Mr. Washington to come out in the open and acknowledge that he is the real owner of the magazine as that would make their work lighter in selling the *Colored American*. These facts were given me by a trusted agent.

RECAPITULATION

The *Colored American Magazine* was the strongest Negro organ put upon the market since the days of Frederick Douglass. It caught and held the attention of the colored reading public because of its strong essays on race matters and its race serial stories. Pauline E. Hopkins was a leading writer, and considered a mischievous person by the South.

The policy of the South is non-agitation of the Negro question.

Messrs. Freund and Washington are men with large business interests in the South, and, naturally are dominated by Southern opinion.

The financial disasters which overtook the magazine were sufficient to kill the enterprise if no helping hand were extended. The white creditors approached Mr. Washington, Mr. R. C. Bruce, Mr. J. H. Lewis of Boston, and prayed them to buy the magazine. All of these men said, — "No, let it die." Mr. Dupree then stepped into the gap moved by the tears and entreaties of Jesse W. Watkins, one of the founders, and myself.

It was unexpected and unpleasant news to the opposition when they learned that the magazine was once more being issued at Boston.

The new management maintained a respectful and conservative attitude towards Mr. Washington's policy, but held firmly to race fealty. The articles referred to on "Industrial Education" created consternation in the ranks of the Southern supporters because they were written by writers of so high a standing in the literary world as to prove that the policy of industrial education solely for the Negro was not popular, and was doomed to failure in the end. Then it must have been that the plot was formed to get possession of the magazine and turn its course into the desired channel.

We needed money. Mr. Freund assumed the character of the disinterested philanthropist with "no axe to grind." Dissensions entered into the little business family. The editor and writer was maligned and "turned down." The rest was easy.

The great question is, — Did Mr. Freund intend to help the enterprise when he took it up at the beginning and was he turned from his purpose by the influence of Mr. Washington's expressed views and desires, or was it a mutual understanding between these gentlemen from the beginning?

The letter of introduction was a curiosity. Was it possible that Mr. Freund had not met Mr. Washington? Why, if so, did he not avail himself of the help of many mutual influential white acquaintances among the white business men of great New York, anyone of whom would have performed the necessary social requirement gladly?

Another incident is the fact that he would write to Mr. Dupree and me on the same day; the letter to me would be conciliatory and complimentary to a degree; the letter to Mr. Dupree would condemn me and my methods wholesale, and its tone would be threatening in character.

It is interesting to note, after the passage of one year, that Mr. Freund's policy of "not a word of complain[t]," no "literary" efforts, "not talk of wrongs," or of "a proscribed race," no "glittering generalities," no "international aspect" of the Negro question, no talk of "Filipinos," has been in full swing under the rule of the purchasers who took the magazine over to New York.

What was the result? A rain of dollars into the treasury? Far from it.

The agents in the city have complained bitterly of the change of policy; it has hurt their sales; many of them have given the book up. In New York city we sold from 800 to 1500 per month; under the new policy the sales have shrunk to <u>200</u> per month and the magazine would be out of business were it not for the fact that it is supported from Mr. Washington's private purse. Nor did the whites rally to the support of the pitiful rag issued each month which was but a shadow of its former self[.] Numbers of agents, in disgust, have taken up the sale of the *Voice of the Negro*, the new colored organ published at Atlanta, Ga.

It is curious to note that with his usual ease, Mr. Washington has changed his tactics as to the magazine's old policy and is creeping back, gradually to the position of the old management in Boston. His men are, also, planning the overthrow of the *Voice*, which has refused to adopt partisan lines.

Witnesses to the truth of these facts I have laid down in these pages are the following gentlemen:—

Mr. Wm. H. Dupree, Superintendent Station A, Boston.
Jesse W. Watkins, 439 W. 35th St., New York City.
Wm. O. West, 528 Columbus Ave., Boston, Mass.
Mrs. Jesse W. Watkins, New York City.

Mr. Dupree, of course knows more of the facts than I do, and I have no doubt would be willing to tell all that he knows if he were guaranteed protection from the malice of Mr. Washington's friends.

With the knowledge which we possess, can we be expected to worship Mr. Washington as a pure and noble soul?

Can we be expected to join in paeans of praise to his spotless character and high principles?

One cannot help a feeling of honest indignation and contempt for a man who would be a party to defraud a helpless race of an organ of free speech, a band of men of their legal property and a woman of her means of earning a living.

Sincerely yours,
Pauline E. Hopkins

N. B. This is necessarily personal in its character as I was forced to detail events just a they occurred.

Source: Pauline Hopkins Papers, Franklin Library Special Collections, Fisk University, Nashville, Tenn.

53 Clifton St.,
No. Camb., Mass.
April 18, 1905

Mr. J. Max Barber,
Editor "Voice of the Negro."
Atlanta, Ga.

Dear Sir:—

Your favor at hand and contents duly noted. I wish you would kindly forward me what you can for my work as I need it for immediate use in meeting a bill. Will you also, let me know if you wish the last number of the series or not so that I may not spend my time in needless labor if it is not wanted. By doing this you will greatly oblige me.

With regard to the future of the Voice let me say, I believe that the same forces are at work that crushed the C.A.M. into the pitiful rag that it is at present. Perhaps you do not know that Mr. Booker T. Washington is the real owner of the C.A.M. Mr. Moore, really, I believe, only covers Mr. Washington's ownership. The taking over of the C.A.M. to New York was a dastardly trick and they are about to play the same tactics on you unless you go under.

Last May I went to New York to continue my work on the magazine under the new management. In some way it was learned that your firm has made advances towards buying the C.A.M. This fact enraged Mo[o]re and Fortune. Fortune said to me then, "Wait, and you will see us put the Voice out of business; It will take a little time but it will come." I wrote this to Dodson after I left the office and told him to forward to you that information for your protection. I do not know if he did as requested.

Mo[o]re's plan is, as far as I could learn, to get back all the old force that he can— writers, agents, etc., get the best matter and infuse new life into the book; then, he will work to drive you out of the field. Some of the Agents are asking Mr. Washington to make the fact known that he is the owner of the magazine[,] and in this way their work will become easier in regaining old subscribers. The League will bar you and your representatives from the convention and advise the people to buy the other book. Mr. Dodson was expecting to have a call from Mr. Washington at any time. He says that the commission is too low for him to make any money without working hard as he has to allow the agents under him so large a percentage. Mr. Moore has been after Dodson for some weeks, and has offered him large concessions to give you up. Mr. Washington is so powerful among white men in New York that if he works against Dodson in the firm where he is employed, it will settle it. But aside from that fact, Dodson wants to get into the Office of the AGE to work, as he feels that it will advance him a step in literary work, and he is willing to meet Moore ~~than~~ more than half way.

Here is an illustration of the way they are working: Roscoe Simmons has been to the Y.M.C.A., Brooklyn, where your book has been placed in the reading rooms by

Dodson, and has spoken there two Sundays in succession and has offered a prize of $5 to the men for the one who brings in the greatest number of the new members before their anniversa[r]y in May. Mr. Moore follows him in speaking for the C.A.M. Such tactics will naturally win with the men even before M. Washington addresses them in May, Mr. Peabody, chairman of the meeting.

I suppose your write up of Tuskegee is given to illustrate your impartiality. I hope so at any rate.

So far as advice is concerned, —I can notnnn-advise you. But I can do what I can to help you to a stick to break your enemy's head. There will be, in a short time, material for you to make a stinging editorial against the C.A.M. without seeming to go out of your way to do it in malice. I can and will help you in ways you knknow not of.

I intend to advertise in your book, and I have a friend who will want space shortly. The reason I could not do so at once is that Mr. Moore holds my matter in the shape of 500 copies of my book "Contending Forces" along with my plates. In this way I had nothing to advertise.

Let me know how you come on. Don't give up, and don't go over to your enemy any farther than you can help to keep living. I will keep you posted on all that I hear or can learn of how matters look up this way.

Fraternally yours,
[signed] Pauline E. Hopkins.

Source: Pauline Hopkins to J. Max Barber, "Editor 'Voice of the Negro,'" 18 April 1905, W. E. B. Du Bois Papers, Special Collections, Du Bois Library, University of Massachusetts, Amherst, Mass.

Jesse Max Barber to W. E. B. Du Bois regarding
Pauline Hopkins, 27 April 1905

Professor W. E. B. DuBois,
Atlanta University
Atlanta, Ga.

My Dear Sir:-

I am sending you in this letter the information for which you asked when I was at the University last Saturday. You will observe that I have made copies of all of these letters for the originals have been sent to our Mr. Hertel at Chicago.

I have pinned together my letter to Rev. D. J. Jenkins, his letter to me and the clipping from his paper, The Messenger, which caused the correspondence in question. The clipping is a statement of the facts that I furnished Mr. Jenkins when in Charleston last Christmas. It appeared in the Messenger in March more than two months after my visit to Charleston. You will observe, according to this letter from Mr. Jenkins, that as soon as this editorial appeared, Mr. Washington opened correspondence and finally succeeded in having the editor make a statement in his paper in the editorial columns to the effect that he had made a mistake in the previous editorial and he now apologized to Mr. Scott for the same.

I am sending you a letter from Miss Pauline Hopkins of Boston. The letter speaks for itself. You will find enclosed, also, a letter from Mr. N. B. Dodson, the agent to whom Miss Hopkins refers. Mr. Dodson is at present our general agent in New York City. It is perfectly evident from these two letters that the Business League machinery is being mustered against The Voice of the Negro.

If you can use these facts in any way to help the cause of decent journalism and fair play, you are perfectly welcome, not only to the facts, but to use my name in sending these letters to the Editor of the Post. Please ask him not to make the facts public, for the reason that if Mr. Washington finds out that we are aware of his plans, he can easily switch off between now and August and resort to some other plan. We have got to protect ourselves in this matter, you will understand, and at the same time, if possible, catch this man in the very act of using the Business League to do a dirty deed.

I should be pleased to know what the editor of the Post has to say after he has seen these letters.

Yours, truly,
[signed] J. Max Barber

Source: Letter from J. Max Barber to W. E. B. Du Bois, 27 April 1905, W. E. B. Du Bois Papers, Special Collections, Du Bois Library, University of Massachusetts, Amherst, Mass.

Pauline Hopkins to John E. Bruce, 8 April 1906

53 Clifton St., No. Camb., Mass.,
April 8, '06

Mr. John E. Bruce
Yonkers, N. Y.

Dear Sir:—

I wish to thank you for the excellent and instructive article which appeared in this last issue of the "Guardian" in "New York News Notes."

Mr. Wallace's remarks were those of an astute, intelligent, progressive man of business who might have sprung from any trade in the world. Your comments were pertinent and bristling with "hits." Between you two gentlemen you have managed to present food for thought to our leading men and women if they are not too greatly wrapped up in self to be willing to acknowledge the pertinence and timeliness of your arguments. I have argued the union of the Negro with labor for a number of years, but being only a woman have received very small notice; however, it matters not who moves the sun as long as we are convinced that "she do move." In other words, let us progress at any cost under any right leadership. With best wishes for more power to your arm and pen. I am,

Respectfully yours,
Pauline E. Hopkins

Source: Letter from Pauline Hopkins to J. E. Bruce, 8 April 1906, John E. Bruce Papers, Schomburg Center for Research in Black Culture, The New York Public Library, New York, N.Y.

Review of *Contending Forces*

Review by Addie Hamilton Jewell of Contending Forces,
5 December 1899

Review of the so styled "Humorous Chapter["] of the book entitled
"Contending Forces" by Miss Pauline Hopkins of Boston

In reviewing the Chapter styled "Humorous" in the book Contending Forces soon to
be published by the Authoress Miss Pauline Hopkins.

I make no attack upon it as a literary effort. I have neither the inclination or ability
so to do.

But in the light of a possible injury to the race, in its influence upon intelligent
readers of the Caucasian race; who are ever on the lookout for flaws in our character,
to justify them in treating us as inferior people.

My reason for criticizing the chapter is due to the belief that our situation in the
country to-day is born of the contempt felt for us by the majority of our white fellow
citizens. And I feel that any effort that is calculated to strengthen instead of lessening
contempt for us, is a wrong done the race, and a hindrance to the cause of Justice.

I believe that the situation of the black man in this country is so critical to-day that
it calls for earnest sincere effort and untiring energy upon the part of every member of
the race.

I believe that every deed should be first careful[ly] considered [and] every word
weighed,—each one so <u>acting</u> will hasten the time when we shall gain the respect of
our white neighbors, our elevations in the eyes of the world and equality before the
law.

Being numbered with the masses[,] it becomes my duty to inquire into every accusation which tends to place them upon a lower scale them that which through poverty
and prejudice they now occupy.

Being present at the meeting of the Col. Nat. League of Boston on the evening of
December the 5th, I listened with interest to the reading of the selected chapters by the
authoress, and to the words of a lady who told us that the Book "Contending Forces"
was written in the hope of aiding in putting down lynch law; and that the book would
be to the Anti Lynching cause what Harriet Beecher Stowe's "Uncle Tom's Cabin" had
been to the Anti Slavery Cause.

I fully realized what such a work would be to the cause. How Grand an opportunity for one of the race so gifted—so inspired to give to the people of another race an
impetus to act against the butchery and murder of our people in this the era of mob
law and bloodshed in the South.

How noble it would be for one of our race whose mind was full of the Justness of our cause—whose heart thrilled with love for the race—whose charity was boundless and whose motive was unimpeachable; how encouraging it would be to the race to own such a champion! one who would show to the world the wrong done the race by first forcing them into servitude[,] then closing the avenues of wealth and comfort to them by the accursed barrier of prejudice to color.

I knew what a stern but sacred duty hers would be to lay bare the life of many a parent whose ambition and aspiration have been blighted by the deadly breath of prejudice.

How self[-]sacrifice for the improved condition of her children have made many a martyr mother.

I felt [that] could the world know of our inward struggles—know the same feelings activated us as those of other races—that were the longings of the spirit—painted as clearly as were those of mind and needs of the body,—it would soften the hearts of many who now look upon us as something scarcely human because of the color of our skin.

So thinking and feeling[,] I listened until the readings of the so called "Humorous" chapter. I found it filled [with] coarse slang [and] the spirit of meanness and envy. A chapter calculated to fill the mind with scorn and contempt for the subject.

It tells the story of preparation for a church "fair" where others than the members have been invited to assist.

The outsiders are supposed members of the "four hundred[,]" their purity of purpose being doubted by members of the committees; their agreeing to aid gives rise to a strong display [of] ignorance and uncharitableness[;] one member says "They only come among for their own interest—[.]" Another says I hope none of the four-hundred will get that piano. I want it for my daughter. Another one says—I don't like these whiteish coloured people no how.

If that was all that was faulty in the chapter we might only ask how much power such a chapter contained to aid the work of bringing law and order in the parts of the country where violence and blood-shed obtains, but the Authoress concludes her ~~remark~~ chapter with this remark.

"This chapter is given to illustrate a feeling that exists among some of our people in opposition to those who live upon a higher plane[.]"

If the concluding remark had been withheld we might recognize the feeling as existing among people not of our race; [a] feeling existing in other organizations as well as in church associations, among persons who are jealous of every opportunity to make themselves conspicuous, who aim to be the great I in all gatherings.

Best written for the purpose of showing ~~of~~ our opposition ~~for~~ to that which is elevating[,] I am forced [to] condemn it and protest against it as calculated to retard the work which the author aims to hasten viz the securing [of] our rights as "American Citizens and the protection of the Law."

If the chapter ~~was~~ had been written simply to provoke laughter it would be out [of] place in a work of so serious a nature—but if it lessens respect for the race then it is malicious as well as useless.

I shall quote from an eminent writer—Henry Home/Howe? of Thames. One of the Senators of the College of Justice and one of the Lords Commissioners of Justiciary of Scotland, in his work "Thames? of Criticism," Chapter 7. Page 230. Objects that cause lag laughter may be distinguished into two kinds:

"They are either visible or ridiculous. A visible object is mirthful only. A ridiculous object is both mirthful and contemptable.

The first raises an emotion of laughter which is altogether pleasant—

The pleasant emotion of laughter raised by the other is blended with the painful emotion of contempt."

A chapter devoted to ridicule then is injurious to the cause and we suffer hourly from these ridiculous attacks upon us as a race.

The chapter calls for a sequel which shall illustrate the life of those on the so called higher plane. Without out the illustration[,] the remark of the Author is an unsupported assertion.

The effort to bring about law and order in our land is a laudable one—and one of vast importance to us as a race, to the country, and to the world at large. To us, because when the question of our right to the protection of the government is secured, our advancement and elevation is assured.

To the country as it concerns the rightful settlement of a question which would remove the dark blot that makes this boasted land of liberty and justice[,] in reality[,] the home of oppression and injustice.

To the World as an educational factor, teaching all mankind that the departure from truth and honor—be it in individuals or Nations, leads to retrogression, demoralization and dishonor.

A subject then which embraces so much of value to mankind in general should be treated with befitting seriousness.

If the work is to be a narrative of the wrongs and suffering of the race, then according to "Home, page 241, Chapter 21[,]" [e]very useless circumstance ought to be suppressed; because every such circumstance loads the narration.

If it is intended to unfold the human heart causing it to beat with sympathy for us in our upward journey then it should be written with truthfulness and care[.] Home asks what other science is of great importance to human beings than the heart unfoldment?

I maintain that whatever way we examine the chapter[,] it is useless to the cause the Author professes to serve[—]"the cause of Justice" and hurtful to the race.

The writer concludes the chapters as though it was perfectly natural for a feeling of opposition to exist among us against those who live upon a higher plane.

I hold that the feeling is an unnatural one and that a sequel to the chapter to is necessary that we may know the cause of this unnatural state of feeling.

That those upon this so called higher plane are always truthful, always honest, always courteous, always charitable, always respectful in their manner when dealing with those they consider their inferiors. These are the characteristics of those on the higher plane of life.

Selfishness is overcome.

These characters live for the good they can do and thus elevate themselves above the selfish majority. A class of persons opposing spiritual elevation are monstrosities who never can command the respect of thinking people black or white. A class of people who oppose social, mental, and moral elevation are beyond redemption.

~~Standing~~ Foremost in the ranks of our white fellow citizens who assert the impossibility of our elevation stands Senator Morgan to day who says "To force political and social equality upon the Negro is to clog the progress of all mankind."

Shall one agree with him in even the smallest particular!

Shall we by word or deed add to the burdens we already bear!

Rather let us work for our elevation believing in ourselves.

Believing that he who would set wrong aright in another must first himself be right.

I remain yours for Justice[,]
Addie Hamilton Jewell
Cambridge, Mass
Jan 13, 1900

Source: Review by Addie Hamilton Jewell, John E. Bruce Papers, Schomburg Center for Research in Black Culture, The New York Public Library, New York, N.Y.

Notes

ABBREVIATIONS

BTW *Papers*
The Booker T. Washington Papers (Urbana: University of Illinois Press, 1974–84).
Du Bois Papers
W. E. B. Du Bois Papers, Special Collections, Du Bois Library, University of Massachusetts, Amherst, Mass.
Hopkins Papers
Pauline Hopkins Papers, Franklin Library Special Collections, Fisk University, Nashville, Tenn.
Ruffin Papers
George L. Ruffin Collection and Ruffin Family Papers, Moorland-Spingarn Research Center, Howard University, Washington, D.C.

INTRODUCTION

1. Gwendolyn Brooks, "Afterword," 406.

CHAPTER ONE

1. The Faneuil family, like many others in New England, had businesses that linked them to the Atlantic slave trade, and their extensive charitable giving was facilitated by profits from that trade (Greene, *Negro in Colonial New England*, 29). Peter Faneuil (1703–43), who provided the funds to build Faneuil Hall, which was completed in 1742 just one year before his death, was well known among slave traders because of the 1742 attack by Portuguese and Africans off the coast of Guinea on his slave ship, the *Jolly Bachelor*. For more details about the Faneuils and slavery, see ibid. For details about Faneuil Hall, see Drake, *Old Landmarks and Historic Personages of Boston*.

2. Hopkins, "William Lloyd Garrison Centennial Speech."

3. See Zorn, "New England Anti-Slavery Society"; Horton and Horton, *Black Bostonians*; and *Annual Report: Massachusetts Anti-Slavery Society*.

4. Anne Catherine Paul and Elijah Smith were married in 1824 by Anne's uncle, the Reverend Benjamin Paul. Their four children were Susan Paul Smith, who later married educator and poet George Boyer Vashon; Elijah Smith Jr., a lifelong Bostonian who married Eliza Riley; Thomas Paul Smith; and George Boyer Smith. When Anne Paul Smith died tragically in 1835, at age twenty-seven of lung fever, many mourned her, including William Lloyd Garrison. Her *Liberator* obituary referred to her as one who "like a tree shall thrive, / With waters near the root / Fresh as the leaf her name shall live— / Her works are heavenly fruit" (*The Liberator*, 27 June 1835, 103).

5. For information about the Roberts family, the 1849 school segregation suit, and the nineteenth-century Boston Equal School Rights movement that featured Paul family members, see Jacobs, "The Nineteenth Century Struggle over Segregated Education"; White, "Antebellum School Reform in Boston"; Levy and Philips, "The Roberts Case"; Mabee,

"A Negro Boycott to Integrate Boston Schools"; and Kendrick and Kendrick, *Sarah's Long Walk*.

6. "Obituary of Thomas Paul."

7. Public records, local New Hampshire histories, Baptist church records, and census returns indicate that Caesar and Lovey Paul had at least three sons and two daughters: Thomas, Nathaniel, Benjamin, Ann (Nancy), and Dorothy. There are several competing accounts, however, of the number and identities of children born to Caesar and Lovey Paul. Most sources reference only the Paul brothers and do not mention any of their sisters. In addition, those that refer to the Paul sons most often only cite Thomas, Nathaniel, and Benjamin by name. Pauline Hopkins, in her *Colored American Magazine* article on Elijah Smith, asserts that there were five Paul sons and only one daughter, Ann, whom she refers to as the ancestor of James Whitfield ("Elijah William Smith," 97). Sources such as C. Peter Ripley et al.'s *Black Abolitionist Papers* (1:42) and the 1973 *Old-Time New England* Paul family biographical profile by J. Marcus Mitchell ("The Paul Family," 73–77), for example, note that there were six Paul sons and do not refer to any Paul daughters. Entries on Nathaniel and Thomas Paul in Rayford Logan and Michael Winston's *Dictionary of American Negro Biography* (481–82) refer to a Paul son named Shadrach but do not mention any sisters. James Horton and Lois Horton in *Black Bostonians* report incorrectly that Nathaniel Paul was a son of Thomas Paul (43).

8. Levesque, "Inherent Reformers—Inherited Orthodoxy," 494.

9. Ibid., 513, 507.

10. Nell, *Colored Patriots of the American Revolution*, 362–63, cited in ibid., 503.

11. Bentley, *Diary of William Bentley*, 4:523.

12. Rev. Thomas Paul stepped down as pastor in 1829, two years before he succumbed to tuberculosis. His resignation was linked to health reasons, but it is clear that there also were difficulties in the church community. Some members left and founded a new congregation, the Twelfth Baptist Church, and selected the Reverend Leonard Grimes to serve as their minister. Historians continue to speculate about the issues that may have prompted the rifts in the church. See Levesque's compelling history of the African Baptist Church, "Inherent Reformers—Inherited Orthodoxy."

13. The Paul family ancestors to whom Hopkins alluded in her Garrison Centennial speech were the Reverend Thomas Paul (1776–1831), the church's first minister, whose leadership in the black community facilitated Garrison's efforts to organize interracial abolitionist organizations; Susan Paul (1809–41), the youngest daughter of Rev. Thomas Paul and Catherine Paul and a well-known Boston schoolteacher, abolitionist, and Garrisonian; and the Reverend Nathaniel Paul (17??–1839), an ardent abolitionist who traveled throughout England with Garrison in the 1830s on successful antislavery fund-raising tours.

14. Hopkins, "William Lloyd Garrison Centennial Speech."

15. Anonymous, "Pauline E. Hopkins, Author," 218.

16. Lindee, "American Career of Jane Marcet's Conversations," 23.

17. Wright, "Marcella O'Grady Boveri," 629. Boveri went on to teach at Albertus Magnus College. Her daughter, Margret, was a lover of pioneering biologist and legendary Howard University professor Ernest Everett Just. See also Manning, *Black Apollo of Science*.

18. For details about Joan Imogen Howard, see Hopkins, "Famous Women of the Negro Race. VIII: Educators." See also Hopkins, "Mrs. Jane E. Sharp's School for African Girls," 181–84. For information about Girls' High School of Boston, see the Girls' High School Association Papers, Schlesinger Library, Radcliffe College, Cambridge, Mass.

19. Exeter Historical Society Files, Folder A, 4, Exeter, N.H.

20. Berlin, "Time, Space, and the Evolution of Afro-American Society," 52.

21. Cunningham, "The First Blacks of Portsmouth," 189.

22. Bell, *History of the Town of Exeter*, 423.

23. *Exeter News-Letter*, 11 December 1911, 1.

24. Ibid., 5 April 1847, 3–6.

25. Hammond, "Letter to the Editor," 62–65.

26. Bell, *History of the Town of Exeter*, 88.

27. American Independence Museum, "Ladd-Gilman House." The enslaved Bob lived in the Ladd-Gilman house, the site that served as the state treasury during the American Revolution and, in the late eighteenth and early nineteenth centuries, as the governor's mansion.

28. Greene, *Negro in Colonial New England*, 78. Exeter's pre–Revolutionary War black population in 1775 amounted to only .02 percent of the town's population. In Portsmouth, forty miles to the east of Exeter, the majority of the state's business and slave trading occurred and there was a higher concentration of people of African descent. In 1767, people of color made up 33 percent of the total population of the colony. Notable Portsmouth residents included Prince Whipple, a former African prince enslaved to William Whipple, a future signer of the Declaration of Independence. Portsmouth natives lodged several notable petitions for freedom, including the 1779 suit filed by self-described "natives of Africa forcibly detained in slavery" (Hammond, "Letter to the Editor," 63).

29. Lacy, *Meaning of the American Revolution*, 76.

30. Bell, *History of Exeter*, 467.

31. Gilman, *Old Logg House by the Bridge*, 11.

32. Bell, *History of Exeter*, 236–37.

33. Chidsey, *French and Indian War*, 81.

34. Parkman, *Montcalm and Wolfe*, 293.

35. Cooper, *Last of the Mohicans*, 226.

36. Steele, *Betrayal*, 117.

37. Parkman, *Montcalm and Wolfe*, 559.

38. *New Hampshire Gazette*, 9 September 1757, 1.

39. Bell, *History of Exeter*, 236.

40. Ibid., 237.

41. Bouton, *Provincial Papers*, 6:765.

42. Buckner, "The Peopling of Canada," 49. Buckner estimates that between 1608 and 1760, the year in which Caesar Paul returned to New Hampshire and Montreal fell to the British, there were "3,300 soldiers, 1,800 Acadians, 1,500 French women, 1,200 indentured workers, 900 slaves, 600 British subjects (most taken captive during the wars with the British), 500 male clergy, 250 self-financed migrants, and 200 deported prisoners."

43. Ibid.

44. The date and the circumstances surrounding Caesar Paul's transition from enslavement to freedom remain elusive. It is not clear, for instance, whether Gilman's 1761 request for reimbursement was motivated by some measure of compassion and a means for securing indirectly some compensation for Caesar. Slaves and indentured servants who did military service, by state law, were ineligible for government compensation. Unfortunately, Gilman, who committed suicide by drowning, appears to have left no will or other papers that might have shed light on the nature of his relationship with Caesar Paul.

45. First Census of the United States, 1790, New Hampshire.

46. Peixotto, *A Revolutionary Pilgrimage*, 41.

47. Holbrook, *Massachusetts Vital Records, Boston 1630–1849; Deaths Index, 1801–1848.* The Paul family suffered a series of devastating losses in the 1830s. Thomas Paul died in April 1831, his mother, Lovey, passed in April 1832, and Thomas's oldest daughter, Anne Paul Smith, died in 1835.

48. Oedel, "Slavery in Colonial Portsmouth," 3.

49. Hammond, "Letter to the Editor," 62.

50. Greene, *Negro in Colonial New England,* 77; Carmer and Hill, *Yankee Kingdom,* 181. To date, colonial historiography has devoted more attention to southern New England states such as Massachusetts and Rhode Island. Documentation of African Americans in northern regions such as New Hampshire before and after the American Revolution is sparse. Details may be found, however, in works such as Nell, *Colored Patriots of the American Revolution;* Zilversmit, *First Emancipation;* and Piersen, *Black Yankees.*

51. Zilversmit, *First Emancipation,* 117.

52. Fordham, *Major Themes in Northern Black Religious Thought.* It is fitting that the Free-will Baptists, the New England denomination that ran the New Hampshire academy where Susan Paul's father, Thomas, prepared for the ministry, officially declared slavery sinful in 1835, the same year in which Susan Paul published *Memoir of James Jackson, the Attentive and Obedient Scholar.*

53. Yellin, *Women and Sisters.*

54. *The Liberator,* 21 April 1837, 67.

55. Zorn, "New England Anti-Slavery Society," 176.

56. New England Anti-Slavery Society, *First Annual Report, 1833,* 1:22.

CHAPTER TWO

1. References to Northup Hopkins, a man who does not exist in the life or genealogy of Pauline Hopkins, have appeared in many biographical profiles, critical essays, and writings on Hopkins. The confusion arises because Hopkins's death certificate lists her father as "Northup Hopkins."

2. The 1844 *Providence City Directory* includes a tantalizing entry for a man identified as "Hopkins, William A.," a machinist at Cupola Furnace, who resided at 273 North Main. This man, however, is not the person who eventually married Sarah Allen; William Hopkins of Virginia was born in 1835 and so could not be this man.

3. The Seventh Census of the United States, 1850, Rhode Island, for Providence contains an entry for Cato Northup and his family. Every member of the family is listed as mulatto and as having been born in Rhode Island. The family includes Cato Northup, age forty-eight; Alice Northup, age forty-two; and their seven children: Edward, twenty-five; Mary, twenty-four; James, twenty; Benjamin, eighteen; Charles, sixteen; Mary, twelve; and David, ten.

4. McLoughlin, *Rhode Island,* 106.

5. Historian Robert Cottrol asserts that African American communities, severely constrained and relegated to specific kinds of employment, often regarded the successes and enterprise of the manual laborer as emblematic of their highest aspirations. See Cottrol, *The Afro-Yankees,* 131.

6. Ibid., 124–25.

7. McLoughlin, *Rhode Island,* 132.

8. Providence city directories for 1832, 1836, 1838, and 1841 contain the following listings for Cato Northup: 1832: "Northup, Cato, laborer, Cushing"; 1836: "Northup, Cato,

laborer, Planet"; 1838: "Northup, Cato, laborer, Federal Hill"; 1841: "Northup, Cato, laborer, near Westminster."

9. See McLoughlin, *Rhode Island*; Leslie, "The Gaspee Affair"; and Maier, "Popular Uprisings and Civil Authority in Eighteenth-Century America."

10. *History of the State of Rhode Island with Illustrations*, 253–59.

11. Cottrol and Diamond, "The Second Amendment." Cottrol and Diamond discuss the de facto exclusion of African Americans from state-sponsored militias, the options for African Americans to form private militias for self-protection, and the 1821 formation of the African Greys of Providence.

12. McPherson, "Should Americans Support IRA Disarmament." McPherson refers to race riots and mob attacks in Boston, Providence, and Pittsburg in his discussion of the nineteenth-century effort that prompted the formation of groups like the African Greys in Providence and efforts to establish similar protective forces in Boston.

13. Brown, *Life of William J. Brown*, 120.

14. Gilkeson, *Middle-Class Providence*, 12.

15. Cottrol, *The Afro-Yankees*, 69. Original citation is Brown, *Life of William J. Brown*, 86.

16. William Lloyd Garrison to Henry Benson, 29 August 1831, in Merrill, *Letters of William Lloyd Garrison*, 1:128.

17. William Lloyd Garrison to Harriet Minot, 9 April 1831, in ibid., 1:218.

18. William Lloyd Garrison to *The Liberator*, 13 September 1832, in ibid., 1:171.

19. In 1830, the Reverend Sebastian Streeter was pastor of the Universalist Church located on North Bennett Street. His name and church affiliation are noted in the list "Churches and Ministers" published in the 1830 *Boston City Directory*.

20. The Eighth Census of the United States, 1860, Rhode Island, contains an entry for a Benjamin Northup, a twenty-six-year-old Rhode Island native and a mariner living in the North Kingstown home of sixty-seven-year-old Margaret Pierce. He is listed with another resident in the home, thirty-year-old Robert Northup, a mariner whose surname suggests that the two men may have been kin. The race of Benjamin Northup is not specified; since the other entries in this portion of the census do identify individuals who are mulatto and black, Northup may have been a white man (ibid., North Kingstown, Washington County, R.I.: Roll M653, 297). A thirty-year-old mariner named Benjamin Northup also is listed as a head of household in North Kingstown, R.I., in the 1860 census. The owner of real estate valued at $800 and with a personal estate valued at $100, he lived with his nineteen-year-old wife Besy and his one-year-old daughter Mary J. (ibid., 298). Other Benjamin Northups include a white thirty-four-year-old cooper living with his wife, Rachel W. Northup, in Richmond, R.I. (ibid., 344).

21. The Rhode Island Veterans' Census contains two entries for men named "Benjamin R. Northup" (*Special Schedules of the Eleventh Census*, 1890, Rhode Island, Roll 92, 3). Listed on the same page, one after the other, neither appears to be the Northup who is the father of Pauline Hopkins. In addition, Civil War databases for African American veterans, such as the Civil War Soldiers and Sailors System that ultimately will include information from 6.3 million National Archives records, do not include any conclusive information about Benjamin Northup.

22. The 1860 *Boston City Directory* entry for Paul Willard notes that he is a "counsellor" with offices located at 22 Tremont Row and a residence in Charlestown.

23. "Sarah Allen Northup vs. Benjamin Northup," Suffolk County, Supreme Judicial

Court, 1864 April Term, Case Number 384, Judicial Archives, Massachusetts State Archives, Boston.

24. Glenda Riley, in *Divorce*, states that between 1860 and 1864 the number of marriages ending in divorce rose from 1.2 to 1.8 per thousand (78).

25. For a discussion of African American divorce patterns, see ibid.; Gutman, *The Black Family in Slavery and Freedom*; White, *Ar'n't I a Woman?*; and Manfra and Dykstra, "Serial Marriage and the Origins of the Black Stepfamily."

26. Carlier, *Marriage in the United States*, 114–15, cited in Riley, *Divorce*, 78.

27. "Sarah Allen Northup vs. Benjamin Northup," Suffolk County, Supreme Judicial Court, 1864 April Term, Case Number 384, Judicial Archives, Massachusetts State Archives, Boston.

28. Ibid.

29. "Colored Voters, Boston—1864: 1st List after Emancipation, New and Old Voters," Ruffin Papers, Box 37-1, Folder 34. There is no date of compilation included in the handwritten list of male voters, so this item, although valuable because it places Benjamin Northup in Boston, does not confirm conclusively when he was documented as living at this Russell Street address.

30. The Seventh Census of the United States, 1850, Massachusetts, reveals that Henry Cummings was born in Maine in 1811. By 1860, Cummings was living in Boston's Ward 1 with his thirty-six-year-old wife, Harriet, their three-year-old daughter, Harriet, their four-month-old daughter, Ellen, and Harriet's eighty-one-year-old mother, Ellen Robinson.

31. "Sarah Allen Northup vs. Benjamin Northup," Suffolk County, Supreme Judicial Court, 1864 April Term, Case Number 384, Judicial Archives, Massachusetts State Archives, Boston.

32. Hopkins, "Elijah William Smith," 96.

33. Levesque, "Inherent Reformers—Inherited Orthodoxy," 517. By 1870, the Twelfth Street Baptist Church, with its 700-plus members, was the largest Baptist congregation in its Northeastern federation. Attendees included some of Boston's most well-known and inspiring citizens—men such as Shadrach Minkins, Dr. John Rock, and Lewis Hayden, the formerly enslaved man and "Boston's most daring and committed Underground Railroad activist" (Grover and da Silva, *Historic Resource Study*, 106). He rallied many to the abolitionist cause by his defiant stands against slave catchers, such as those who came to his home determined to recapture William and Ellen Craft in 1850. For more information about Grimes and about the Twelfth Street Baptist Church, see Horton and Horton, *Black Bostonians*.

CHAPTER THREE

1. "Return of a Death: William A. Hopkins," City of Cambridge and the Commonwealth of Massachusetts. The death certificate of William Hopkins lists the names of his parents and the states in which they were born. This document gives the maiden name of his mother, Catherine, as "Vaughn," but other references to William Hopkins's kin suggest that this may be a misspelling of "Waugh," the documented family surname.

2. Cassius Lee, the son of Sara and Edmund Jennings Lee, was part of an established white slave-owning family. In 1833, Cassius, then a widowed father of seven, took Hannah Phillipa Ludwell Hopkins, a distant descendant of King Edward I of England, as his second wife. Before her death in 1844, Hannah Lee bore five children. See Alexander, *Stratford Hall and the Lees*.

3. "Alexandria—Past and Present."

4. Ibid.

5. The decision to re-cede Alexandria and the lands on the north side of the Potomac River was prompted by several factors. Historian H. Paul Caemmerer writes: "The action of Congress and the President was based upon petitions of the people of the town and county of Alexandria. The chief reasons were two: First, that the United States did not need Alexandria County for the purpose of the seat of government; the public buildings were all erected on the north side of the river, as required by law—none on the south side—and it was declared that so far as it could be foreseen the United States would never need that part of the District of Columbia for the purpose of the seat of government. Secondly, the petitioners said that the people of Alexandria had failed to derive or share in the benefits which had been enjoyed by the residents of the Maryland portion of the District of Columbia in the disbursements for public improvements, etc., while on the other hand they were deprived of those political rights incident to citizenship in a State." See Caemmerer, *Washington: The National Capital*, 51.

6. Goddard, "Henceforth and Forever Free," 44.

7. Goddard notes that "slave dealers not only made the District their headquarters but also 'used the federal jails freely to house their chattel in transit'" (ibid., 44). Goddard cites Green, *Washington: A History of the Capital*.

8. Federal Writers' Project, *Washington: City and Capital*, 69.

9. Ibid.

10. *African American Mosaic*; Federal Writers' Project, *Washington: City and Capital*, 69. In his "Chronology on the History of Slavery and Racism," Eddie Becker notes that the 1830 census for Alexandria included lists of individuals held at slave pens or prisons such as the Armfield and Franklin site.

11. Both Franklin and Armfield and the Bruin Negro Jail were in business until the Civil War. Union troops eventually occupied the Franklin and Armfield site, and it was used "as a jail for captured Confederate soldiers and rowdy Union soldiers, as well as housing and a hospital for 'contraband,' escaped or freed slaves" (Alexandria Convention and Visitor's Association, "A Remarkable and Courageous Journey," 6). The walls of the slave pens finally were demolished in 1870. According to local historians of Alexandria, Bruin attempted to escape the city when Union troops occupied Alexandria in 1861. In addition to having his property confiscated, Bruin was captured and imprisoned for six weeks before being released. For additional history and images of the sites, see Pacheco, *Failed Escape on the Potomac*; and Ricks, *Escape on the Pearl*.

12. Alexandria Convention and Visitor's Association, "A Remarkable and Courageous Journey," 5.

13. Goddard, "Henceforth and Forever Free," 51.

14. Federal Writers' Project, *Washington: City and Capital*, 71. For additional information about the *Pearl* and the fugitive slaves whose plight gained national attention as well as the interest of Harriet Beecher Stowe, see Painter, "Fugitives of the Pearl."

15. Goddard, "Henceforth and Forever Free," 51.

16. Federal Writers' Project, *Washington: City and Capital*, 71.

17. Goddard, "Henceforth and Forever Free," 38. Original citation, Du Bois, *Black Reconstruction in America*, 562.

18. The Compromise of 1850, brokered in large part by Senator Henry Clay, included eight resolutions. In addition to outlawing the slave trade and maintaining slavery in the District of Columbia, the bill admitted California as a free state, refrained from outlawing

slavery or maintaining freedom in the former Mexican lands obtained during the Mexican-American War, attended to the boundaries of New Mexico and of Texas, strengthened the Fugitive Slave Act of 1793, and absolved Congress of legal responsibility for issues relating to slave trading among the states. For more information about the Compromise of 1850, see Foner, *History of Black Americans*; and Rozwenc, *Compromise of 1850*.

19. Goddard, "Henceforth and Forever Free," 38.

20. Douglass, "Address by Hon. Frederick Douglass," 13.

21. See Brown and Lewis, *Washington from Banneker to Douglass*, for an overview of tensions in the city.

22. Snethen, *The Black Code*, 55. See Brown and Lewis, *Washington from Banneker to Douglass*, for an overview of African American education in the city.

23. Nicholas Franklin, Moses Liverpool, and George Beall were the three men who founded the school. See Brown and Lewis, *Washington from Banneker to Douglass*, for additional information about the effort.

24. Goddard, "Henceforth and Forever Free," 42. See also Green, *Washington* and *The Secret City*, for more details about African American schools in Washington, D.C.

25. Jones, "Their Chains Shall Fall Off," 22.

26. Alexandria Convention and Visitor's Association, "A Remarkable and Courageous Journey," 1.

27. Jones, "Their Chains Shall Fall Off," 23. Jones cites a membership register for 1830 that "lists several Mount Zion members with the status of 'gone away,'" a phrase that she interprets as a sure indication that "these enslaved members of the congregation had escaped to freedom on the Underground Railroad."

28. Stanley Harrold refers to the antislavery District of Columbia community as a "subversive community." Harrold, *Subversives*, 12.

29. Alexandria Convention and Visitor's Association, "A Remarkable and Courageous Journey," 10.

30. The identities and successes of these Underground Railroad organizations have been obscured both because of historical oversight and because the organizations required anonymity in order to be effective. The Society for the Abolition of Slavery based in Washington, D.C., was but one of many groups there that protested slavery and worked to ease the burdens of those in bondage.

31. *Vital Statistics of Deaths Registered in Providence, Rhode Island*, 8:302. The death record for John A. Waugh includes a reference to "John G. Hopkins" in the column provided for additional comments. The family relationship between the Waughs and the Hopkinses does suggest initially that this may be a reference to a relative. However, Providence city directories suggest otherwise. John G. Hopkins is listed in the 1850 and 1852–53 Providence city directories as a cabinetmaker in the city. It is most likely that Hopkins, who was a white man, was the undertaker and perhaps also the craftsman of the casket that the Waughs purchased for their son.

32. *Births Recorded in Providence*, 583. The Waughs' second-born son, Daniel, was born four years later in 1853.

33. The case of Sarah Roberts in 1849 led to the first desegregation of Boston's public schools. Although many think that the city's contentious battle over school desegregation and busing in the 1960s was the first time that the city had confronted the issue, Bostonians, in fact, had been lobbying for equal education rights and desegregated classrooms since the early 1800s. The Roberts case in 1849, brought by the printer and race activist Benjamin F. Roberts on behalf of his six-year-old daughter, Sarah, was the first case to

reach the Massachusetts courts. Roberts was represented by white Bostonian and U.S. senator Charles Sumner and by the first African American admitted to the Massachusetts bar, Robert Morris. The *Roberts* case both mobilized and polarized Boston's African American community. Thomas Paul Jr., the son of the Reverend Thomas Paul and the brother of highly successful teacher Susan Paul, was installed as the principal of the school shortly before the case went to trial. Paul Jr., perhaps because of his position and his family's long commitment to the education of African Americans, advocated that the Smith School be maintained. Others, most notably William Cooper Nell, a Smith School alumnus, advocated that school desegregation was paramount and that the Smith School, no matter its history, was an emblem of the separate and unequal doctrine that undermined all people of color in the United States. For more on the Smith School and the *Roberts* case, see Kendrick and Kendrick, *Sarah's Long Walk*.

34. Abbot, "Fourteenth Regiment, Rhode Island Heavy Artillery."

35. *Anglo-African*, 6 August 1859, 2–3.

36. *The Liberator*, 19 August 1859, 132, and 28 August 1859, 136, cited in Wesley and Uzelac, *William Cooper Nell*, 570.

37. *Anglo-African*, 5 May 1860, 3.

38. "General Affidavit of Mark DeMortie," William A. Hopkins Pension File, Library of Congress, Washington, D.C. The 1855 State Census, Massachusetts, returns for Mark De Mortie reveal that he and his mother, Francis, both of whom were identified as mulattos, were Virginia natives (New England Historical Genealogical Society, *People of Color in the Massachusetts State Census, 1855–1865*). For its rich biographical profile of De Mortie, the dearest friend of Hopkins's stepfather, the *New Era Magazine*, which Hopkins launched in 1916, drew heavily from the 1913 entry on De Mortie included in *The African Abroad* by William Ferris.

39. For more information about African American societies such as the Histrionic Society, see Horton and Horton, *Black Bostonians*.

40. *The Liberator*, 23 April 1858, 67, cited in Wesley and Uzelac, *William Cooper Nell*, 35. Music and theater historian Bernard Peterson, who has assembled the most complete profile of the group to date, notes that this group was "one of the earliest amateur [African American] theatre groups of record." See Peterson, *African American Theatre Directory*, 96.

41. Peterson, *African American Theatre Directory*, 96.

42. *The Liberator*, 23 April 1858, 67.

43. Brown, *The Black Man*, 240.

44. For additional information about Ruffin, see Dorman, *Twenty Families of Color in Massachusetts*.

45. Library of Congress, <http://memory.loc.gov/ammem/rbpehtml/rbpebibTitles41 .html>. The December 1858 debate about the condition of enslaved people featured "Mr. Charles D. O'Reilly, for the affirmative, and Mr. John F. Wright, for the negative."

46. *The Liberator*, 23 April 1858, 67, cited in Wesley and Uzelac, *William Cooper Nell*, 36.

47. Ibid.

48. The play *Honey Moon* was a popular choice of other nineteenth-century American theater troupes as well. In mid-October 1858, *Honey Moon* was the first play staged in Thalian Hall in Wilmington, North Carolina, an impressive 1,000-seat theater designed by John Montague Trimble, one of the premier nineteenth-century theater architects, which now is the "longest continuously operated theatre in North Carolina" (<http://www.thalianhall

.com/map.htm>). Thalian Hall offered audiences the chance to see some of the era's most celebrated performers, including John Philip Sousa and Buffalo Bill Cody.

49. Rafroidi, *Irish Literature in English*, 2:46. For additional information about James Kenney and his works, see Cooke, *Dublin Book of Irish Verse*.

50. Peterson, *African American Theatre Directory*, 96.

51. Ibid.

52. *The Liberator*, 6 April 1833, 55.

53. Ibid., 27 April 1833, 67.

54. "William A. Hopkins: Pension Questionnaire," Can 684, Bundle 1, 1, Library of Congress, Washington, D.C.

55. *Massachusetts Soldiers, Sailors, and Marines in the Civil War*, 188.

56. "William A. Hopkins: Pension Questionnaire."

57. Gregory, "Marauders of the Sea."

58. Morris and Morris, *Encyclopedia of American History*.

59. National Park Service, "A Forgotten Milestone"; Clark-Lewis, *First Freed*, 19.

60. William Hopkins's change in rank and duties reflected the kinds of opportunities for men of color to which naval historians often point.

61. Naval Historical Center, "U.S.S. *Niagara*."

62. Gould, *Diary of a Contraband*, 145.

63. George Steers, the fourth of thirteen children, was exposed to shipbuilding while still a child. His father, Henry, a Devonshire, England, native, emigrated to the United States and established a shipyard in New York City on East Tenth Street. George Steers, who began designing boats when he was ten years old, built a variety of ships, including racing vessels such as the *America*, schooners, steamers that traversed the Great Lakes, pleasure boats, and at least one ship, *Sunny South*, that became a slaver. For additional information on George Steers, see *Dictionary of American Biography*.

64. Gould, *Diary of a Contraband*, 145.

65. Naval Historical Center, "U.S.S. *Niagara*"; *Dictionary of American Biography*.

66. History Central.com, "Civil War Naval History: May 1861." The USS *Niagara* was one of the most active and well-armed ships in the Union fleet, and its exploits continued after William Hopkins's term of enlistment expired. William J. Gould, an African American sailor who also served on the *Niagara* during the Civil War, kept logs of the events that occurred during his time aboard. See Gould, *Diary of a Contraband*, for one of the most detailed accounts of life aboard the ship and the experiences of African American sailors published to date. In 1865, the ship was involved in a tense confrontation with the CSS *Stonewall*, an ironclad vessel with much less firepower, off the coast of Spain. Gould was aboard at the time and witnessed firsthand the decision to allow the Confederate vessel to go free. For additional information about the confrontation between the *Niagara* and the *Stonewall*, see Gregory, "Marauders of the Sea."

67. W. W. McKean to H. H. Adams, 28 May 1861, cited in *Official Records of the Union and Confederate Navies in the War of the Rebellion*, 133.

68. Naval Historical Center, "U.S.S. *Niagara*."

69. "West Gulf Blockading Squadron—United States Navy."

70. Naval Historical Center, "U.S.S. *Niagara*."

71. Department of the Navy records state that the *Niagara* reentered the Civil War in June 1864, after a lengthy stay in the drydock that involved the dismantling of much of the newly installed weaponry that was found to be overloading the ship. The ship was assigned to "European waters," and it engaged in the capture of the Confederate raider *Georgia* and

in a controversial encounter with the ironclad ship *Stonewall* that it should have fired upon but did not. The *Niagara* returned to Boston after its European tour, and "for nearly two decades she was laid up at the Boston Navy Yard, while proposals to rebuild her as an armored warship were considered but not implemented." The ship was "sold for scrapping" in 1885 (Naval Historical Center, "U.S.S. *Niagara*").

72. Brown and Tager, *Massachusetts*, 214.

73. Grover and Da Silva, *Historic Resource Study*, 71; *Boston City Directory*, 1865.

74. *Boston City Directory*, 1846, 590, 592.

75. Horton, *Free People of Color*, 35.

76. Ibid.

77. Ibid., 36.

78. *Boston Business City Directory*, 1868.

79. Ninth Census of the United States, 1870, Massachusetts, Ward 3, Boston, Suffolk County, 281. The racial identity of all residents in the Hopkins home is given as mulatto.

80. The *Boston City Directory* for 1870 includes an entry for William Hopkins but lists only his place of residence. The 1872 issue notes his occupation as dermatologist. City directories for the mid- to late 1870s include entries for two men named William A. Hopkins. In the 1878 directory, one of these individuals is in fact the husband of Sarah Allen. The other man is employed as a clerk in offices located at 156 Oliver and boards in West Dedham during the years that Sarah's husband, William, is maintaining his home at State Street and later on Chambers Street.

81. Whitehill and Kotker, *Massachusetts*, 233.

82. Wiencek, *Smithsonian Guide to Historic America*, 44.

83. Ibid., 36.

84. *Boston City Directory*, 1891. Entries for William Hopkins in the city directories of the 1880s confirm his post–Civil War stability. Information about De Mortie appears in the 1893 *Boston Almanac and Business Directory*, where he is listed in the "Clothes Cleaners" section as having his business at 7 Alden (345).

CHAPTER FOUR

1. James P. Kraft, in "Artists as Workers," suggests that Elijah Smith's Progressive Musical Union was an African American music union, one that was part of a growing national trend to create unions that protected performers of color and that "maintained loose contacts with their white counterparts but had their own meeting halls, officials, and arrangements with proprietors." The organization that Kraft should reference is the Union Progressive Association, founded by William Cooper Nell in 1861, which organized political rallies at sites such as Tremont Temple and coordinated labor arrangements for African American men in the city. Mark De Mortie was an active member of the Union Progressive Association. See chapter 19, as well as Wesley and Uzelac, *William Cooper Nell*, and Quarles, *Lincoln and the Negro*, for more details about the group. There does not appear to be much evidence that Smith used the organization as a labor union.

2. Paul's accomplishments also included the 1835 publication of *Memoir of James Jackson, the Attentive and Obedient Scholar*, a pioneering biography of one of her most gifted students and the earliest known published prose narrative by a black woman in the United States. For more information about Susan Paul, her antislavery work, and her musical accomplishments, see also Brown, "Out of the Mouths of Babes."

3. Trotter, *Music and Some Highly Musical People*, 174.

4. *Boston Globe*, 24 June 1872, 8.

5. Bacon, *Boston: A Guide Book*, 25.

6. Trotter, *Music and Some Highly Musical People*, 175.

7. Thompkins, *History of the Boston Theatre*, 8.

8. Trotter, *Music and Some Highly Musical People*, 174.

9. Hopkins, "Famous Women of the Negro Race. I: Phenomenal Vocalists," 48.

10. In 1850, Pendell was living in Boston with Sally Pendell, an African American woman born in New Hampshire. This may have been his first wife or a relative.

11. Hopkins, "Famous Women of the Negro Race. I: Phenomenal Vocalists," 49.

12. In 1862, Wyzeman Marshall was the "sole lessee and manager" of the Howard Athenaeum. He booked Menken, characterized on Howard Athenaeum broadsides as "the celebrated poetess, actress, danseuse & pantomimist," to perform at the venue in July 1862. A promotional broadside for this event that includes a wood-engraved portrait of Menken is held in the collection of the Hay Harris Library, Brown University.

13. Hopkins, "Famous Women of the Negro Race. I: Phenomenal Vocalists," 45.

14. Ibid., 46.

15. Ibid.

16. "Daughters of Hawaii."

17. De Abajian, *Blacks in Selected Newspapers*.

18. *Anglo-African*, 31 December 1859, 3.

19. Hopkins, "Famous Women of the Negro Race. I: Phenomenal Vocalists," 46.

20. Ibid.

21. McCallum, "Norma, Opera Australia."

22. *Anglo-African*, 3 December 1859, 3.

23. Pindell's contemporaries included Elizabeth Taylor Greenfield, whose Quaker mistress, Mrs. Holliday Greenfield, manumitted Elizabeth's parents from their enslavement on her Natchez, Mississippi, plantation and sent them to Liberia before she relocated to Philadelphia with their daughter. In 1849, Greenfield, who had received support for her vocal talents from her former mistress, drew widespread attention as she moved from private concerts hosted by potential benefactors to public performances in Boston, New York City, and Toronto. For additional details about Greenfield, see Thompson, "Greenfield, Elizabeth Taylor."

24. *Anglo-African*, 26 February 1859, 3.

25. *Boston Globe*, 10 March 1875, 4.

26. The song "On Mossy Banks" is credited to Gilbert in the Progressive Musical Union program. A song with this title is listed in the *Complete Catalogue of Sheet Music and Musical Works* (New York: Da Capo, 1973) but is credited to Schubert, not Gilbert.

27. Trotter, *Music and Some Highly Musical People*, 297. Trotter provides a few facts about the Auber Quartet, but there is much yet to be learned about its founding and concert schedule and reviews it received. That Elijah Smith established a musical group with this name testifies to his knowledge and appreciation of classical European music. Auber (1782–1871), the director of the Paris Conservatoire from 1842 to 1870, is regarded as the best-known composer of opéra comique. For more information about Auber, see Sadie, *New Grove Dictionary of Music and Musicians*, 1:680–81.

28. Gustav Reichardt's "The Image of the Rose" (1862) included a tenor solo and chorus. *Dictionary Catalogue of the Music Collection: Boston Public Library*, 626.

29. James Monroe Trotter notes that Oswell became "deservedly popular as an organizer of musical entertainments . . . and as a promoter of a regard for good music by the people.

He is quite well known in St. John, N.B., Portland . . . and in Boston, in which places he has frequently appeared at public concerts; and has been often complimented by the press." See Trotter, *Music and Some Highly Musical People*, 300.

30. In 1837, Susan Paul's Juvenile Choir so impressed a reviewer that he declared the children's music more powerful than any production staged by the city's Handel and Haydn Society. For the full text of the highly complimentary review, see *The Liberator*, 12 May 1837, 79.

31. The evening's program identified the composer of "Angel of Peace" as Keller. This citation may have referred to Matthias Keller, but music catalogs do not include any listing that matches. The person identified in reference sources as Keller is credited for composing "The Angel of Dream" (1865), a ballad for alto or baritone with pianoforte accompaniment. This may be the song performed at the concert but incorrectly listed in the program.

32. *Boston Globe*, 10 March 1875, 4.

33. Ibid.

34. For more information about the Fisk Jubilee Singers, see Ward, *Dark Midnight When I Rise*; Cooper, *Slave Spirituals and the Jubilee Singers*; and Lotz, "The Black Troubadours."

35. The antebellum Adelphic Union Library had provided a welcome intellectual forum for African Americans in Boston. Entertainment groups such as William Cooper Nell's Histrionic Club, of which Pauline's future stepfather, William, was a member, provided memorable performances during the 1840s, many of them based on Nell's own writings. For a history of Boston's early arts initiatives, see Porter, "Organized Educational Activities of Negro Literary Societies"; and Brown, "Out of the Mouths of Babes." For additional details about antebellum African American literary societies and reading practices, see Horton and Horton, *Black Bostonians*; McHenry, "Rereading Literary Legacy"; and McHenry, *Forgotten Readers*.

36. "Elijah W. Smith," 2, Special Collections and Archives Division, Boston Public Library, Boston.

37. To date, no roll of students from Susan Paul's public school classes or Juvenile Choir rosters have been unearthed. Unfortunately, while newspaper reviews such as those that appeared in *The Liberator* did highlight the acclaimed performances of individual children, the articles often only mentioned children by their first names.

38. Trotter, *Music and Some Highly Musical People*, 307.

39. Elijah W. Smith Sr. married Anne Catherine Paul in 1824. Following his wife's death in 1835, Smith Sr. moved to New Orleans and left his children in the care of their maternal relatives. In "The Paul Family," J. Marcus Mitchell reports that Elijah Smith Sr. and his wife were "active abolitionists" (75). Smith Jr., a grandson of the Reverend Thomas Paul and his wife Catherine, was raised by his maternal aunt Susan after his mother's untimely death in the summer of 1835. As a child living in the Paul household and participating in the public school and Baptist Sabbath school systems in which she was a teacher, Elijah Smith Jr. witnessed firsthand Paul's acts of political intervention and racial uplift. As a student in the segregated Abiel Smith School, which opened in 1835 and was adjacent to his grandfather's African Baptist Church, Smith would have participated in one of the African American juvenile choirs that Susan Paul and her fellow teachers organized.

40. Hopkins, "Elijah William Smith," 98. Hopkins cites Brown's *Rising Son* in her 1902 *Colored American Magazine* profile of her cousin.

41. Trotter, *Music and Some Highly Musical People*, 295–96. Trotter includes a facsimile copy of the program for the Progressive Musical Union concert on 9 March 1875.

42. Hopkins, "Elijah William Smith," 97. Elijah Smith Jr. was eight years old when his

aunt, Susan Paul, died of tuberculosis in 1841. He and his siblings were spared additional domestic upheaval because for the time being they were able to continue living with their maternal grandmother, Catherine Paul, at her Beacon Hill home at 3 Grove Street. In 1842, however, Smith and his family moved from there to 3 Fruit Street Place, the home of Thomas Paul Jr., their maternal uncle and a newly minted Dartmouth College graduate and educator. Despite the care that they received from their mother's family, their limited financial means and the hardships that they faced as orphans may have curtailed the Smith children's dreams of higher education. Elijah followed in the footsteps of his uncle, Thomas Jr., when he began a printer's apprenticeship at *The Liberator*. He mastered the trade, but when health issues forced him to leave that work, he became a waiter on steamships before returning to Boston and beginning a career as a head steward at Young's Hotel in the city.

43. Ibid.

44. Ibid., 98. The poem was also published on the front page of the Washington-based newspaper, *New National Era*, 18 April 1870, 1.

45. *Boston Globe*, 8 October 1895, 8.

46. Hopkins, "Elijah William Smith," 97.

47. Ibid., 99.

48. *Boston City Directory* listings for 1876 list William's employment as janitor. His home and place of work are listed as being in the same place, 15 State Street.

49. For more details about Susan Paul, see Paul, *Memoir of James Jackson*; and Brown, "Out of the Mouths of Babes."

50. British abolitionist George Thompson was scheduled to address the Boston Female Anti-Slavery Society October meeting, but when he was unable to do so, Garrison took his place. Paul, the first African American member and a former officer in the society, which often held its meetings in the lecture hall across from the *Liberator* office, was one of the members escorted out of the building moments before the mob invaded the building. Just after Paul and the society's ladies exited, the angry crowd descended upon the place in search of Garrison. He fled for his life and barely escaped lynching.

51. Notices about the appearance of the Reverend Josiah Henson, the former slave upon whom Harriet Beecher Stowe based her character Uncle Tom, appeared in the *Boston Globe*, 23 March 1875, 1. Edwin Booth appeared as Othello during 1875. See the *Boston Globe*, 16 March 1875. In an effort to assist the West Boston Relief Society in its efforts to establish a temporary home for Boston's destitute children of color, the Alexander Dumas Association organized a charity concert at the Tremont Temple. See the *Boston Globe*, 29 March 1875, 1.

52. Scrapbook, Hopkins Papers.

53. Booth's roles and appearances are listed in *Boston Globe* advertisements published on 16 March and 17 March 1875.

54. In the years preceding and immediately following the publication of *Pauline; or, The Belle of Saratoga*, George Cooper was better known for his secular and religious compositions. These included *Picnic* (1869); *The Chaplet of Original Hymns and Songs: Christmas and Easter Carols, Concert Exercises, & c.* (1873); and *Little Red Riding-Hood: An Operetta for Juveniles* (ca. 1876). By the late 1880s, however, he was composing lyrics for songs that perpetuated the myth of the happy Negro slave, the pastoral plantation South, and other stereotypes advanced in minstrel productions. These titles included "Hustle Children: Plantation Song" (ca. 1894); "Aunt Jemima's Lullaby" (ca. 1896); and "Don't You Remember Me Mass; or, The Slaves Return" (ca. 1899). The canon of Hart Pease Danks, composer of the music for *Pauline; or, The Belle of Saratoga*, also included religious compositions and

plantation songs. He composed works suitable for churches, including *Choral Anthems: A Collection of Anthems, Sentences, Motets, Etc. for Church and Home Use* (1877) and *Christmas Chimes: A Children's Service for the Christmas Festival*. He provided music for the lyrics of such plantation songs as "Come Back to de Ole Plantation" by Arthur French and composed the music for at least one more operetta, *Zanie, An Operetta*, with a libretto by Fanny Crosby.

55. *Boston Saturday Evening Gazette*, 7 March 1875, 3; *Boston Courier*, 25 March 1877, 2.

56. *Boston Courier*, 25 March 1877, 2.

57. *Pauline; or, The Belle of Saratoga* program, Hopkins Papers.

58. According to the Ninth Census of the United States, 1870, Massachusetts, City of Cambridge, Ward 2, 66, thirty-eight-year-old James Henry and his thirty-nine-year-old wife, Georgiana, were both Virginians. He worked as a laborer; his wife's occupation was given as "keeping house."

59. By 1900, William Walker and his family were living at 79 Phillips Court, in close proximity to Elijah Smith, whose family had been longtime residents at 1 Phillips Court. Walker, who in 1900 worked as a beef carrier, was widowed. His three children lived with him at home. William, his twenty-three-year-old son, was employed as a clerk; his twenty-one-year-old daughter, Mary, worked as a domestic; and his fourteen-year-old daughter, Gertrude, attended school. Twelfth Census of the United States, 1900, Massachusetts, Boston: Suffolk County, Ward 11, Roll T623, 7A.

60. In 1870, fourteen-year-old Parker Bailey, the fifth of six children, was living with his large family in Suffolk County, Boston. His father, John, a Maryland native, worked as a sparring teacher and owned real estate valued at $5,000; his mother kept house. His older siblings, who ranged in age from nineteen to twenty-eight, all of whom were born in Maryland, worked as dressmakers, printers, and waiters. Parker and his younger brother, Peter, were the only children in the family born in Massachusetts. Ninth Census of the United States, 1870, Massachusetts, Suffolk County, Ward 3, Boston, Roll 593, 307.

61. Trotter, *Music and Some Highly Musical People*, 294. Trotter also notes that Mrs. Boston is better known by her maiden name, Cecilia Thompson.

62. It has not yet been possible to identify conclusively Florence J. Smith, the woman who played the role of Clara Rivers, or Addie J. Smith, the chorus director. The play's program refers to a twenty-five-person chorus but does not identify by name any of the members.

63. Cooper, *Pauline; or, The Belle of Saratoga*, act II.

64. Ibid., act I, 3.

65. Ibid.

66. Ibid., act II, 7.

67. Ibid., act II, 6.

68. Ibid.

69. Ibid., act II, 8.

70. The official disbanding of the Ku Klux Klan in 1869 did not bring an end to racial terror in the South. For histories of the group and accounts of vigilante raids and attacks on African Americans after the end of the federally mandated Reconstruction, see Randel, *Ku Klux Klan*; Horn, *Invisible Empire*; Katz, *Invisible Empire*; and Chalmers, *Hooded Americanism*.

71. Garnet, "An Address to the Slaves," 87.

72. There is at least one historical account of a mulatto slave who was able to convince Mexican War recruitment officers that he was white. His master subsequently reclaimed

him and he was remanded back into slavery. For details, see May, "Invisible Men." For more information about African Americans and the Mexican War, see Robert E. May, "African Americans," in Frazier, *United States and Mexico at War*, 3–4.

73. May, "Invisible Men," 465.

74. There were a number of slaves attached to the Missouri First Regiment of Mounted Volunteers led by Colonel Alexander Doniphan. During the Battle of Sacramento, a number of armed slaves, led by the slave of Lieutenant Duncan, opened fire on attacking Mexican lancers and succeeded in driving them back. See Dawson, *Doniphan's Epic March*, for more details about the regiment, the slaves accompanying it, and the Battle of Sacramento skirmish.

75. *The Liberator*, letter dated 29 June 1847, 106.

76. Castel, "And Shed American Blood," 37.

77. *Genius of Universal Emancipation*, August 1836, 159.

78. Castel, "And Shed American Blood," 43.

79. *Genius of Universal Emancipation*, August 1836, 163.

80. Finkelman, "Slavery," 387.

81. *Genius of Universal Emancipation*, August 1836, 131.

82. Finkelman, "Slavery," 387.

83. Christy, *Jim Crow Polka*; M'Carty, *National Songs, Ballads, and Other Patriotic Poetry*; Patten, "Episodes of the Mexican War." Other creative works based on the Mexican War include Small, "Guadaloupe; Ballentine, *Autobiography of an English Soldier*; and such historical novels as Halyard, *Heroine of Tampico*.

84. Cited in Mahar, "Black English in Early Black Face Minstrelsy," 263. For extended and foundational critiques of dialect, see Gates, *Figures in Black*.

85. Gottschild, *Digging the Africanist Presence in American Performance*, 12.

86. Almost exactly one month after Pauline Allen's debut with the Progressive Musical Union, the *Boston Herald* announced that the nationally known "Hick's Georgia Minstrels" were enjoying their third week of sold-out shows (15 April 1875, 5).

87. Wittke, *Tambo and Bones*, 70. For additional discussions of blackface minstrelsy and its representations of African Americans, see Lott, *Love and Theft*; Toll, *Blacking Up*; and Mahar, *Behind the Burnt Cork Mask*.

88. Wittke, *Tambo and Bones*, 70.

89. Sampson, *The Ghost Walks*, 25.

90. Ibid., 5.

91. Saxton, *Rise and Fall of the White Republic*, 4.

92. Watkins, *On the Real Side*, 103.

93. Cooper, *Pauline; or, The Belle of Saratoga*, act I.

94. *The Liberator*, 22 January 1847, 14.

95. Ibid.

96. Ibid.

97. Cooper, *Pauline; or, The Belle of Saratoga*, act II.

98. Ibid., act II.

99. Ibid., act II, 7 (emphasis mine).

100. Ibid., act II, 8.

101. Hopkins's first drama, copyrighted under the title of *Aristocracy—A Musical Drama in 3 Acts* and renamed *Colored Aristocracy*, was performed publicly and, most likely, staged well beyond Boston. *Aristocracy* was performed by the Hyers Sisters Combination, the gifted sisters Anna Madah and Emma Louise Hyers whom Hopkins met in Boston during

the early 1870s and with whom she worked closely on her most successful play, *Peculiar Sam; or, The Underground Railroad*. For information about the Hyers Sisters, see Southern, *African American Theater*; Southern, *Biographical Dictionary of Afro-American and African Musicians*, 191–92; Smith, *Notable Black American Women*, 550–52; Hine, Brown, and Terborg-Penn, *Black Women in America*, 1:272–74; and Hill, "The Hyers Sisters."

CHAPTER FIVE

1. Listings of name changes that were filed in Massachusetts courts do not include any entries for Pauline Allen. It was possible to change one's name without filing formal legal documents. In the family's first Massachusetts state census entry in 1865 and their first federal census entry in 1870, Pauline was not identified specifically as Pauline Allen or as Pauline Hopkins. She was listed simply as a member of the household headed by William Hopkins. It is her school papers and the materials related to her performances with the Progressive Musical Union, for instance, that reveal her use of the name Pauline Allen until 1875. See chapter 3 for a discussion of the Hopkins family census returns.

2. For more details about Lucas and his triumphs on the stage and on the minstrel circuit, see Southern, *The Music of Black Americans*, 240; Hill and Hatch, *A History of African American Theatre*, 112–13; and Peterson, *A Century of Musicals in Black and White*.

3. *Minneapolis Tribune*, 28 March 1879, 5.

4. *Milwaukee Sentinel*, 1 April 1879, 4.

5. *Minneapolis Sentinel*, 23 April 1879, 3.

6. Ibid.

7. *Minneapolis Tribune*, 19 April 1879, 2–3; Wright, "*Das Negertrio* Jiminez in Europe," 161. For additional information on de Salas, see Reed, "Distinguished Negroes of the West Indies."

8. Hill, "The Hyers Sisters," 115–30.

9. Southern, *African American Theater*, 18. Southern's groundbreaking research on the Hyers Sisters and her republication of the plays and songs in which the sisters performed have had a great impact on scholarship on nineteenth-century African American drama and theater history. See also Southern, *Biographical Dictionary of Afro-American and African Musicians*; and Hill, "The Hyers Sisters."

10. *Milwaukee Sentinel*, 31 March 1879, 4.

11. Poggi, *Theater in America*, 6.

12. *Minneapolis Tribune*, 18 April 1879, 4.

13. *Boston Herald*, 21 August 1877, 3.

14. The Redpath Lyceum Bureau was founded in 1868 by James C. Redpath, a Scottish immigrant printer, writer, and *New York Tribune* journalist who worked with Horace Greeley. He also worked closely with African Americans in considering a colonization movement in Haiti during the 1850s. The Redpath Bureau contributed significantly to the Lyceum movement, was a major booking agency, and had offices in cities such as Boston, Chicago, Kansas City, Missouri, and White Plains, New York. See Records of the Redpath Chautauqua Collection at the University of Iowa, Iowa City; Boyd, "James Redpath and American Negro Colonization in Haiti"; and Scott, "The Popular Lecture and the Creation of a Public in Mid-Nineteenth-Century America."

15. *Minneapolis Theater History Notes*, 1.

16. *Milwaukee Sentinel*, 28 March 1879, 5.

17. Carvajal, "German-American Theatre," 184.

18. *Milwaukee Sentinel*, 1 April 1879, 4.

19. Ibid., 21 February 1879, 5.

20. Ibid., 11 February 1879, 8.

21. Ibid., 31 March 1879, 4; 1 April 1879, 4.

22. Ibid., 1 April 1879, 4.

23. *Minneapolis Tribune*, 21 April 1879, 4.

24. Ibid., 18 April 1879, 4.

25. Ibid., 19 April 1879, 4.

26. Ibid.

27. Ibid., 23 April 1879, 4.

28. Ibid.

29. Ibid., 28 April 1879, 2.

30. *Boston Herald*, 19 August 1877, 3.

31. Ibid., 21 August 1877, 3.

32. Hopkins, *Peculiar Sam*, in Southern, *African American Theater*, 121.

33. Ibid.

34. Ibid., 122.

35. Ibid., 124.

36. Ibid.

37. Zanger, "The Tragic Octoroon in Pre–Civil War Fiction," 64.

38. White, *Ar'n't I a Woman*, 58.

39. Hopkins, *Peculiar Sam*, in Southern, *African American Theater*, 120.

40. In addition to the work of Deborah Gray White, see Jewell, *From Mammy to Miss America and Beyond*.

41. Hopkins, *Peculiar Sam*, in Southern, *African American Theater*, 123.

42. Ibid., 123-24.

43. Ibid.

44. Ibid., 124.

45. Huggins, *Harlem Renaissance*, 255.

46. Lott, *Love and Theft*, 18.

47. Hopkins, *Peculiar Sam*, in Southern, *African American Theater*, 124.

48. Ibid., 123.

49. Ibid., 126.

50. Ibid.

51. Ibid.

52. Ibid., 130.

53. Ibid., 131.

54. William J. Mahar, in his instructive writings on minstrelsy, remarks on the way that dialect embodies the "American delight in self-parody." See Mahar, "Black English in Early Black Face Minstrelsy"; and *Behind the Burnt Cork Mask*.

55. Hopkins, *Peculiar Sam*, in Southern, *African American Theater*, 131-32.

56. Ibid., 140.

57. Ibid.

58. Ibid.

59. Ibid., 128.

60. Dunbar, "The Deserted Plantation," in *The Complete Poems of Paul Laurence Dunbar*, 67-68.

61. Hopkins, *Peculiar Sam*, in Southern, *African American Theater*, 141.

62. Ibid., 141–42.

63. Ibid., 142.

64. Ibid., 142–43.

65. Ibid., 143.

66. Ibid., 144.

CHAPTER SIX

1. Twain and Warner, *Gilded Age*, xi.

2. Ibid.

3. Hopkins, "The Latest Phases of the Race Problem in America," 245.

4. In *Race and Reunion*, David Blight documents and analyzes the marginalization of African American history and memory in the deliberate, elaborate, and increasingly staged events that commemorated the Civil War, honored veterans, and revisited American history in the effort to promote unity. Blight's considerations of cultural and political conceptions of national healing and justice, in the aftermath of the bloody and costly Civil War, are invaluable to considerations of the political and sociocultural interventions that Hopkins was making in *Peculiar Sam* and in its supplementary performances.

5. *King's Hand Book of Boston*, 237.

6. *Boston Herald*, 24 June 1883, 11.

7. Ibid., 4 July 1880, 9.

8. Ibid.; ibid., 7 July 1880, 3.

9. Ibid., 7 July 1880, 3.

10. Peterson, *Doers of the Word*, 197.

11. *King's Hand Book of Boston*, 237.

12. *Boston Herald*, 20 June 1880, 3.

13. Ibid.

14. Ibid., 24 June 1883, 11.

15. Ibid.

16. Ibid.

17. Ibid., 8 July 1880, 1.

18. Ibid., 25 July 1880, 4.

19. Ibid., 11 July 1880, 9. The "other dramatic pieces" mentioned in the *Herald* included the play *Aristocracy*, in which the Hyers Sisters performed regularly in the 1880s. The *Boston Herald* biographical note also makes tantalizing references to additional Hopkins's plays. Advertisements for Boston's summer theaters and entertainment venues, however, contain no references to additional Hopkins plays that were performed in Boston venues during the 1880s.

20. Ibid., 3.

21. Ibid., 18 July 1880, 3.

22. The 1880 *Boston City Directory* entry identifies William Hopkins's business partner as David Walker. Hopkins and Walker appear to have maintained the clothes cleaning business for two years. In 1881, they moved their business to 29 Doane. See *Boston City Directory*, 1880, 1881.

23. *Boston Herald*, 1 August 1880, 3.

24. *Boston Daily Globe*, 8 August 1880, 8.

25. Pauline Hopkins Scrapbook, 9, Hopkins Papers.

26. Ibid.

27. *King's Hand Book of Boston*, 251. The GAR ended in 1956 upon the death of its last Union veteran. For more information about the organization, see Beath, *History of the Grand Army of the Republic*; Dearing, *Veterans in Politics*; and McConnell, *Glorious Contentment*. Salvatore, *We All Got History*, includes a fascinating account of the GAR in Worcester, Massachusetts, and the activities of Webber, an African American Civil War veteran.

28. For more information about the African American Civil War regiments of Massachusetts, see Cornish, *The Sable Arm*; Burchard, *One Gallant Rush*; Emilio, *A Brave Black Regiment*; and O'Connor, *Civil War Boston*.

29. *Boston Herald*, 21 September 1880, 3. A mentally unstable postal worker who claimed to be an ardent supporter of Chester Arthur shot President Garfield on 2 July 1881. Arthur, the defeated Democratic presidential nominee, was vice president and succeeded Garfield upon his death.

30. *Boston Globe*, 30 September 1881, 3.

31. *Boston Herald*, 30 September 1880, 4. Like Fred Lewis, the orchestra conductor, Alden worked with Sam Lucas when he performed in Boston during the next few years. In 1883, she appeared at the Grand Sacred Concert featuring Lucas and Pauline Hopkins at the Park Square Pavilion. She also performed in duets with Pauline Hopkins when both appeared as members of the Original Savannah Jubilee Singers. In the fall of 1884, she was the "pianista" who accompanied Sam Lucas's Jubilee Concert Company during their Tremont Temple concert. Information about Alden is gleaned from advertisements in the *Boston Herald*. See *Boston Herald*, 27 May 1883, 11.

32. Shortly after his fall 1880 appearance with the Hopkins Colored Troubadours, Lewis provided accompaniment for the "devout melodies" that Lucas and the Hyers Sisters performed during their own "[g]rand sacred concerts" in Boston. In June 1883, Lewis was the accompanist at the Boston Theatre performance of the Callendar's Consolidated Companies, a group that included the Hyers Sisters and Sam Lucas.

33. *Boston Herald*, 30 September 1881, 4.

34. Ibid.

35. *Boston Daily Globe*, 30 September 1881, 3.

36. Ibid.

37. *Boston Herald*, 29 July 1882, 3.

38. Ibid., 31 July 1880, 3.

39. Ibid., 29 July 1882, 3.

40. Pauline Hopkins Scrapbook, Hopkins Papers.

41. Ibid.

42. *Boston Herald*, 27 May 1883, 11.

43. Pauline Hopkins Scrapbook, Hopkins Papers.

44. Ibid.

45. Ibid.

46. In addition to the Hopkins family members and Alden, the other members of the Original Savannah Jubilee Singers identified in the 27 May *Boston Herald* advertisement were George Morris, Mr. Freeman, Mr. Tolliver, and Mr. Tinsley.

47. *Boston Herald*, 3 June 1883, 15.

48. For additional information about class hierarchies and Boston's black elite, see Hill, *The Other Brahmins*.

49. "Grand Masters of the Most Worshipful Prince Hall." The Lews traced their Massachusetts roots back to the mid-1700s, and one of their best-known American ancestors was Barzillai Lew, a Revolutionary War fifer. In his comprehensive study of Boston's African

American community, John Daniels also notes that "tradition has it that about a dozen members of the Lew family, which appears to have combined valor, musical ability, and thrift, formed themselves into a guerrilla fighting organization known as 'Lew's Band'" (Daniels, *In Freedom's Birthplace*, 14).

50. *Boston Sunday Herald*, 24 August 1884, 11.

51. For detailed genealogical information about the Lews, see Dorman, *Twenty Families of Color in Massachusetts*.

52. *Boston Herald*, 24 August 1884, 11.

53. Dorman, *Twenty Families of Color in Massachusetts*, 304. William Edward Lew's accomplishments in the years following 1884 include his selection as "principal tenor at St. Peter's Church in Cambridge" (304) and election as chairman of the music departments at Lane College in Jackson, Tennessee, and Miles Memorial College in Birmingham, Alabama (304). Edward Lew flourished during his years of intensive musical training with leading teachers in Massachusetts and at the New England Conservatory of Music. At the advanced age of seventy-eight, he joined the Merchant Marines and worked as a cook (304).

54. *Boston Herald*, 5 August 1883, 11.

55. Ibid., 3 August 1884, 11.

CHAPTER SEVEN

1. Anonymous, "Pauline Hopkins," *Colored American Magazine* (January 1901): 218.

2. Ibid., 219.

3. Lewis, *W. E. B. Du Bois*, 108. In his reference to Du Bois's lecture, Lewis refers to the group as the National Colored League. The terms may have been interchangeable, but the group identified itself as the Colored National League. In January 1904, Hopkins was a founding member of the Colored American League, a group that was inspired by the Colored National League. Unlike that organization, which was open only to African American men, the Colored American League included men and women on its membership rolls.

4. Anonymous, "Pauline Hopkins," 219.

5. Ibid. The son of Hopkins's employer, Henry Parkman Jr. had an active Republican political life in the early 1900s. In 1933, he ran for mayor of Boston, and in 1940, he ran for a seat in the U.S. Senate. For more information about Parkman and Homans, see "The Political Graveyard," a website at <http://www.politicalgraveyard.com>. In 1889, *Boston Almanac and Directory* included an entry for Parkman Sr. His law office was located at 209 Washington Street (370). The 1906 *Boston Social Register* (New York: Social Register Association, 1906) also includes an entry for Parkman and his family. An entry for Alpheus Sanford also appears in the lawyers section of the 1889 *Boston Almanac and Directory* (Boston: Sampson, Murdock, 1889). In that year his law practice was located at 70 Kilby, Room 51, in Boston (372).

6. See Smith, "The Grand Army of the Republic and Kindred Societies," and historic Boston guide books, such as *Bacon's Dictionary of Boston* (1886), for information about the city's GAR posts, their locations, and their meeting times.

7. Hayden's membership in the Robert A. Bell Post made him the first African American member of the GAR. See Robboy and Robboy, "Lewis Hayden."

8. Brundage, *Lynching in the New South*, 7. Lynching, a documented pandemic in the South, was not confined to that region of the country. Brundage and other historians of lynching note that mob violence and vigilantism plagued the Northeast, Midwest, and West.

According to Brundage, between 1880 and 1930, there were 9 lynching deaths in the Northeast, 260 deaths in the Midwest, and some 485 in the Far West. Tragically, however, these numbers were far "overshadowed by the estimated 723 whites and 3,220 blacks lynched in the South between 1880 and 1930" (ibid., 8).

9. Ibid., 9.

10. For more information about the Charles Street AME Church, which is thriving today in Roxbury, Massachusetts, see "Charles Street Meeting House."

11. Anonymous, "Pauline E. Hopkins."

12. *Boston Globe*, 1 June 1892, 4.

13. Ibid.

14. Ibid.

15. The Bureau of Statistics of Labor became the Bureau of Statistics in 1909, ten years after Hopkins left her position there. See Drown, "Massachusetts Bureau of Statistics."

16. Deutsch, *Women and the City*, 111.

17. Drown, "Massachusetts Bureau of Statistics," 134.

18. Fitzpatrick, "Leading American Statisticians in the Nineteenth Century," 314. For additional information about the Massachusetts Bureau of Statistics of Labor and its chiefs, or commissioners, see also Porter, *Women of the Commonwealth*.

19. Gettemy, *Massachusetts Bureau of Statistics*, 39–40.

20. Hill, *The Other Brahmins*, 49.

21. For more information about Boston's African American political accomplishments and majority in postbellum nineteenth-century America, see ibid.

22. Branham and Foner, *Lift Every Voice*, 680.

23. Once Dupree became part of the *Colored American Magazine* board of directors, the journal published an informative biographical profile about him and his impressive career. He and his wife became key supporters of Hopkins and the magazine editorial board. See "Col. William Dupree," *Colored American Magazine* (July 1901): 228–32.

24. "Death Of The Foremost Colored Lawyer in New England."

25. Pauline Hopkins to U.S. Pension Office, 27 April 1906, 1, United States Navy Files, "Pension Record of Hopkins, William A.," Pension Number Navy WC 17-916, National Archives and Records Administration, College Park, Md.

26. Ruffin, "A Charge to Be Refuted," 10.

27. Matthews, "New York," 3.

28. Logan, *We Are Coming*, 132–33.

29. Matthews, "New York," 3.

30. Florence Balgarnie to Mrs. Florida Ruffin Ridley, 19 July 1895, in *The Woman's Era* (August 1895): 12.

31. Matthews, "New York," 3.

32. Minutes from the meeting and published newspaper articles about the event reveal that an additional day of "business" (9) was added to the conference. Attendees met to "finish business Thursday morning, at 10 A.M., in Charles St. Church to complete organization." On Thursday, 1 August, "devotional exercises" began the meeting, followed by the reading and approval of minutes, a statement by Ruffin about a "false statement made in the *Boston Journal*" (9), and lengthy discussion of the conference resolutions, a national role for the Boston New Era Club, and the manner in which the Conference might work "toward a union" (10) with the Colored Women's National League. For more details, see the published minutes included in National Association of Colored Women, *A History of*

the Club Movement. See also Giddings, *When and Where I Enter*; and Jones, "Mary Church Terrell."

33. National Association of Colored Women, *A History of the Club Movement*, 3.

34. Ibid., 5.

35. Harriet Smith, one of Elijah Smith's daughters and the woman who would marry Pauline Hopkins's attorney, John Burrell, in 1898, served with L. C. Carter, the second secretary of the convention.

36. Smith and Carter, "Minutes of the First National Conference Of Colored Women," 2.

37. *Boston Herald*, 30 July 1895, 10.

38. Ibid., 10 July 1895, 10.

39. Ibid.

40. Ibid., 31 July 1895, 10. The recently wed Wells-Barnett was invited to speak but declined to attend the meeting.

41. I. Garland Penn, a highly regarded editor, influential officer in the Methodist Episcopal Church organization, and author of *The Afro-American Press and Its Writers* (1891), declared that Matthews was "the most popular woman journalist among her peers" (Logan, *We Are Coming*, 131). Matthews was one of nine children born to Caroline Smith, an enslaved woman in Fort Valley, Georgia. Smith, who became a self-emancipated woman when she escaped from her master, eventually returned to the area to reclaim her children. Tragically, she could locate only four of her nine children. She initiated legal proceedings that enabled her to retrieve two of them, Victoria and Anna, from the home of their white slave-owner father. Matthews, her mother, and three siblings relocated to New York City, the place in which Matthews would marry her love of writing with her keen desire to provide for needy mothers, young women, and children. Matthews also was well known for the memorable testimonial celebration that she organized in honor of Ida B. Wells. Held in New York City's Lyric Hall, the event drew some 250 women and succeeded in raising $700 to support Wells and her tireless antilynching efforts. In 1897, Matthews established the White Rose Industrial Association, a New York City mission that provided accommodations and services for African American women newly arrived in the North. For more information about Matthews and her work, see Cash, "Victoria Earle Matthews"; Lerner, "Early Community work of Black Club Women"; Gautier, "African American Women's Writings"; and Matthews, "The Value of Race Literature."

42. Cash, "Victoria Earle Matthews," 760.

43. Matthews, "The Value of Race Literature," 83.

44. Ibid., 10.

45. Ibid.

46. Ibid.

47. Hopkins, *Contending Forces*, 13.

48. Matthews, "The Value of Race Literature," 10.

49. Hopkins, *Contending Forces*, 13–14.

50. As Claudia Tate notes in her seminal study of late nineteenth-century black women writers, "[m]any of the black women writers of the post-Reconstruction period complemented their literary interventionism with activism in specific reform movements (temperance, women's suffrage, the nullification of segregation laws, the reform of convict-lease systems, and anti-lynching legislation), activism that was an expression of conviction in the ultimate power of Christian virtue to advance human society" (11). See Tate, *Domestic*

Allegories of Black Political Desire, for an extended and informative explication of African American women's literary activism.

51. Harlan, Smock, and Kraft, *BTW Papers*, 5:19.

52. Ibid., 8.

53. Ibid., 94.

54. *Boston Herald*, 25 April 1899, 2.

55. Ibid., 7.

56. Ibid.

57. *Boston Globe*, 20 May 1899, 12.

58. For more information on Maria Louise Baldwin (1856–1922), see Wesley, "Maria Louise Baldwin."

59. According to the 20 May 1899 *Boston Globe* article on the conference, the group of white women who addressed the audience in Chickering Hall included Mrs. Edwin D. Mead, Mrs. Mary Clement Leavitt, and Mrs. Alice Freeman Palmer.

60. *Boston Globe*, 20 May 1899, 12.

61. Ibid.

62. Ibid.

63. Ibid.

64. Ibid.

65. "Mrs. M. F. Pitts, Mrs. M. E. Williams, and Eliza Gardner to Miss Catherine Impey, 30 July 1895," *The Woman's Era* (August 1895): 4.

66. Northen, a descendant of seventeenth-century English immigrants to Virginia, was raised in Jones County, Georgia, and educated at Mercer University, where his father taught. Northen left his teaching career in Sparta to join the Civil War and was assigned to the Confederate Army company that his father commanded. After the Civil War, Northen pursued teaching, farming, and politics. See "William Jonathan Northen" and his profile on the National Governor's Association website, <http://www.nga.org> (May 2007).

67. Benjamin Arnett Jr. was born in Brownsville, Pennsylvania, and, like his father, was deeply involved in the AME Church. Arnett, whose multiracial background included African American, Scottish, Native American, and Irish ancestors, became a beloved and inspired bishop of the AME Church. He was active in the Republican Party and was a visible contributor at the state conventions, where in 1880 and 1896 he served as chaplain of the state and national conventions, respectively. See Van Tine and Pierce, *Builders of Ohio*; "Benjamin William Arnett," in Logan and Winston, *Dictionary of American Negro Biography*, 17–18; and the Benjamin William Arnett Papers at Carnegie Library, Wilberforce University, Wilberforce, Ohio.

68. *Congregational Club Manual for 1899*.

69. *Boston Herald*, 23 May 1899, 12; *Boston Globe*, 23 May 1899, 1.

70. *Boston Herald*, 23 May 1899, 12.

71. One of the four signatories was Mrs. W. H. Grady, widow of Henry Woodfin Grady, *Atlanta Constitution* editor and an ardent supporter of white supremacy, who was known among his contemporaries as the "spokesman of the New South." Another signatory was Mrs. Gordon, wife of General Gordon, the acknowledged head of the Georgia Ku Klux Klan and the U.S. senator who played a leading role in the creation of the Compromise of 1877, which hastened the end of Reconstruction in the South. The last two women who collaborated on the message for the Congregational Club audience were Mrs. F. P. Gale, manager of the Kindergarten League, and Mrs. Candler, wife of the then-presiding Georgia governor Allen Daniel Candler, a former Confederate colonel and promoter of a white-only

state Democratic primary. In 1899, Candler refused the requests of African Americans in the state that he veto an extension of the bill that maintained racial segregation in the Pullman railroad cars. The deceptively accommodationist rhetoric of the telegram was undone by the women's identities and the public campaigns with which their husbands were so well associated. To those who knew more about the Atlanta women, it may have been no surprise to hear the traditional blend of white complaint and challenge that marked Northen's speech.

72. *Boston Globe*, 23 May 1899, 2.

73. Ibid.

74. Ibid.

75. Ibid., 1.

76. Ibid., 2.

77. Ibid.

78. Ibid., 1.

79. Ibid.

80. *Boston Herald*, 23 May 1899, 2.

81. *Boston Globe*, 23 May 1899, 2.

82. Aptheker, *A Documentary History of the Negro People*, 2:775, cited in Wolfenstein, "On the Road Not Taken." Du Bois, who was on the faculty at Atlanta University at the time, was en route to the *Atlanta Constitution* offices with an editorial article on the "facts" as he knew them but turned back when he heard that the lynching had occurred and that Wilkes's knuckles were on display in a nearby Atlanta grocery shop.

83. *Boston Globe*, 23 May 1899, 2.

84. Ibid.

CHAPTER EIGHT

1. *Colored American Magazine* (September 1900): 196.

2. Addie Hamilton Jewell, "Review of the So Styled Humorous Chapter of the Book Entitled 'Contending Forces' by Miss Pauline Hopkins of Boston," 13 January 1900, 1, Reel 1, Manuscript 237, John E. Bruce Papers, Schomburg Center for Research in Black Culture, New York Public Library, New York, N.Y.

3. *Colored American Magazine* (September 1900): 196.

4. Judge George Ruffin's decline was monitored in several issues of the *Boston Advocate*, and details about his career, sickness, and death also are found in Boston newspapers such as the *Boston Transcript*. See also Hill, *The Other Brahmins*; and Dorman, *Twenty Families of Color in Massachusetts*.

5. Hopkins, *Contending Forces*, 391.

6. Detiege, *Henriette Delille*, 35.

7. Ibid., 18.

8. Ibid., 23.

9. Before forming the Sisters of the Holy Family in 1842, Delille and eight other African American women founded the Sisters of the Presentation in 1836. Their motto was "'to be of one heart and one soul' as they cared for the sick, helped the poor and instructed the ignorant" (ibid., 26). The social and religious precedents they set in their ministry to people of all races and their membership of sanctified colored women were ended by a legislative act meant to preserve the rigid class and race structure of nineteenth-century Louisiana. The law classified the sisters' work as disruptive social behavior and forced them to disband.

10. Ibid., 15.

11. Ibid., 27.

12. Ibid., 40.

13. In *Roads to Rome*, Penny Franchot asserts that all "nineteenth-century American nuns adhered to the rule of enclosure" (126). But the Sisters of the Holy Family did not; they emphatically rejected cloistered life. Their active participation in the public sphere contrasts with the traditional enclosure, withdrawal, and regulated private "social work" of white orders. The sisters' example invites more comparative study of Catholic practices of nineteenth-century orders, especially the racially motivated social policies and justification of visible roles in the community.

14. The first female religious to arrive in the Louisiana colony were French Ursuline nuns. Used initially to staff the local hospital, they also were contracted to educate the young girls in the colony. As Emily Clark and other historians have noted, the Ursuline sisters were instrumental in beginning effective outreach to Native American girls and girls of African descent. See Clark, "By All the Conduct of Their Lives."

15. Detiege, *Henriette Delille*, 47.

16. Clark, *"The Greatest Gift of All,"* 116.

17. Ibid.

18. Alphonse's fictional genealogy, which is tied to his mother's traumatic adolescent sexual assault by her white half-uncle, calls attention to another potential autobiographical lapse on Hopkins's part. Does the graphic tale in the novel in any way echo the real life circumstances of Alphonse Allen, the youngest child in the Chelsea home of her maternal grandparents, Jesse and Elizabeth Allen? Boston city records suggest that the child, also identified as Alphonso, was born to Elizabeth Allen at the couple's Belmont Street home in 1848. Alphonse/Alphonso Allen was in his fifties when *Contending Forces* appeared in 1900. Although she may have wanted to honor her uncle by invoking his name in the novel, Hopkins's decision hardly seems to be a tribute, given the sobering experiences of the character that she creates.

19. Hopkins, *Contending Forces*, 89.

20. Ibid., 98.

21. Ibid., 89.

22. Ibid., 98.

23. Ibid.

24. Giddings, *When and Where I Enter*, 83.

25. Hopkins, *Contending Forces*, 99–100.

26. Ibid., 100.

27. Ibid. In this exchange between Sappho Clark and Dora Smith, Hopkins cites lines from Elizabeth Doten's "I Still Live," a work published in *Poems from the Inner Life* (Boston, 1864) and reportedly "[g]iven under the inspiration of Miss A. W. Sprague, at the conclusion of a lecture in Philadelphia, October 25, 1863" (ibid., 80). Doten (1829–?), was a native of Plymouth, Massachusetts, who claimed that her poems were dictated to her by spirits, most notably the departed spirit of Edgar Allan Poe. Her *Poems from the Inner Life* included several compositions that she attributed to Poe. The Poe-inspired works, such as "Streets of Baltimore," which clearly invoked "The Raven," often were updated revisions of original Poe writings. In addition to *Poems from the Inner Life*, Doten published *Poems of Progress* (1871) and lectured throughout New England during the 1860s and 1870s.

28. Hopkins, *Contending Forces*, 100.

29. Ibid., 101.

30. Ibid., 100.

31. Milton, *Paradise Lost*, Book XI, l. 108.

32. Hopkins, *Contending Forces*, 101.

33. Ibid., 100 (emphasis mine).

34. Ibid., 129.

35. Daniels, *In Freedom's Birthplace*, 213, cited in Deutsch, *Women and the City*, 301.

36. The home was an actual asylum established for elderly African American women in the Boston community. Dora and Sappho visited the home at its second location, 27 Myrtle Street. Founded in 1860 to meet the needs of destitute African American women who were denied sanctuary in local private asylums, the home was always located in the heart of the African American Beacon Hill community. It served women of the community for eighty-three years before being closed. There is little information about the home in social histories of Boston. For more information about it and its history, see MacCarthy, "Home for Aged Colored Women"; and Shoenfeld, "Applications for Admission to the Home for Aged Colored Women." For information on Leonard Grimes, see Hopkins, "Men of Vision. II: Rev. Leonard A. Grimes," and Levesque, "Inherent Reformers." For information on Rebecca Parker, see Clarke, *Autobiography, Diary, and Correspondence*.

37. *Boston Globe*, 16 December 1905, 1.

38. Ibid.

39. Hopkins, *Contending Forces*, 144.

40. Ibid., 14-15.

41. Ibid., 146.

42. Ibid., 147.

43. Ibid.

44. Ibid.

45. Ibid., 148.

46. Shadrach, "Furnace Blasts: I, The Growth of the Social Evil," 259.

47. Hopkins, *Contending Forces*, 142-43.

48. Ibid., 148.

49. Ibid.

50. Ibid., 149.

51. Ibid. (emphasis in original).

52. Ibid., 156.

53. Ibid., 149-50.

54. *New Catholic Encyclopedia*, 14:703. For additional discussion of the Catholic conception of virginity, see the *New Catholic Encyclopedia* entry for virginity (14:544-48).

55. Ibid. I owe my use of this particular aspect of the Catholic stance on virginity to McFeely, "This Day My Sister Should the Cloister Enter."

56. Hopkins, *Contending Forces*, 155.

57. Ibid., 148.

58. Foucault, *History of Sexuality*, 61.

59. Ibid., 63.

60. Ibid., 62.

61. Elizabeth Ammons's description of Sappho as a "model of the silenced female artist" is useful to consider in this context as well. Ammons focuses on Sappho's victimization and proposes that her silencing is a sobering metaphor for Hopkins's own trying experiences as an artist. See chapter 5 in Ammons, *Conflicting Stories*.

62. Hopkins, *Contending Forces*, 155.

63. Ibid., 156.

64. Ibid.

65. Foucault, *History of Sexuality*, 61.

66. Ibid., 63.

67. Gunning, *Race, Rape, and Lynching*, 103.

68. Tate, *Domestic Allegories of Political Desire*, 174.

69. Hopkins, *Contending Forces*, 344.

70. Ibid., 345.

71. In *Domestic Allegories*, Tate suggests that Sappho's "heroic self-transformation" occurs when she changes her name from Mabelle Beaubean to Sappho Clark. In *The Coupling Convention*, Ann duCille suggests that this name change is, in fact, not heroic since the "signal name change . . . is not from Mabelle Beaubean to Sappho Clark but from Sappho Clark to Mrs. Will Smith" (43).

72. Hopkins, *Contending Forces*, 346.

73. Ibid., 307.

74. Ibid., 346.

75. Brooks, "New Women, Fallen Women," 107.

76. Hopkins, *Contending Forces*, 348. Between 1880 and 1904, the Sisters of the Holy Family instituted a schedule of solicitation: "Cash donations were solicited each week and pay-day from the laborers on the Docks, and monthly room the employees at the city Hall, Court House, and Custom House[.] The Railroad pay stations were solicited both weekly and monthly. Prior to 1904 an orphan accompanied the Sisters on these rounds." Hopkins decided to place just one nun at the station in her fictional account of Sappho's reunion with the nuns and seems to have decided against using a heavy-handed image of Sappho and Alphonse meeting their Southern mirror images.

77. Detiege, *Henriette Delille*, 6.

78. Ibid., 47.

79. Hart, *Violets in the King's Garden*, 35.

80. Ibid., 36.

81. Sister Mary Catherine, "Origin and the Development of the Welfare Activities," 38.

82. Ibid.

83. Hopkins, *Contending Forces*, 349.

84. Franchot, *Roads to Rome*, 126.

85. Hopkins, *Contending Forces*, 349.

86. Ibid., 350.

87. Ibid.

88. Ibid.

89. Ibid.

90. Hopkins, *Contending Forces*, 350–51.

91. Ibid., 349.

92. Ibid., 398.

93. Ibid., 391.

94. Ibid., 392.

95. Ibid., 385.

96. Brown, "Defensive Postures," 65.

97. Hopkins, *Contending Forces*, 386–87.

98. Giles, *American Catholic Arts and Fictions*, 107.

99. Brooks, "New Women, Fallen Women," 91.

100. Hopkins, *Contending Forces*, 386.

101. Ibid., 347.

102. Ibid., 401.

103. Terrell, "Report to President, Officers, and Members of the NACW," 307.

CHAPTER NINE

1. Hopkins, *Contending Forces*, 31.

2. Ibid., 79.

3. Ibid., 21.

4. Ibid., 40.

5. Ibid., 78.

6. Ibid.

7. Ibid., 78, 79.

8. Ibid., 384.

9. Ibid., 370, 371.

10. Ibid., 374, 375.

11. Ibid., 14.

12. There appear to be two men named Jesse Allen living in Boston during the period in which Hopkins's grandfather Jesse Allen is in New England. The 1830 directory includes a listing for "Allen, Jesse, coach maker, Ivers," in the section of individuals who are not relegated to the "Africans" section. But this individual does not appear to be the grandfather of Pauline Hopkins, since, by this time, that man is living in Exeter, New Hampshire, and, according to the Third Census of the United States, 1830, Massachusetts, is established there with his family.

13. Bell, *History of the Town of Exeter*, 62.

14. Kessler-Harris, *Out to Work*, 17.

15. Exeter Historical Society Files, 4, Exeter, N.H.

16. Reference to the shooting death of the Whitfields' second son is made in the Exeter Historical Society Files, 11, Exeter, N.H.

17. Swasey, *History of the Baptist Church, Exeter, New Hampshire*, 101.

18. Exeter Historical Society Files, 11, Exeter, N.H.

19. Chipman, *New England Vital Records from the Exeter News-Letter*.

20. *The Liberator*, 14 March 1839, 47.

21. Ibid., 16 March 1838, 43.

22. *Frederick Douglass' Paper*, 22 April 1853.

23. In the Sixth Census of the United States, 1840, Massachusetts, Suffolk County, Ward 6, Boston, Roll 197, the Allens were counted as free people of color and their Suffolk County household was listed as including two adults and seven children: four were girls under the age of ten years and three were girls between ten years and twenty-four years.

24. *Anglo-African*, 17 December 1859, 5.

25. Ibid.

26. Ibid.

27. Ninth Census of the United States, 1870, New York, Tompkins County, City of Ithaca, Roll M593, 196.

28. The company, which began publishing in the 1830s, also published works by Stephen Foster and other leading musical figures of the nineteenth century, including the British baritone Henry Russell. The company maintained a commitment to publish works by African

American artists. During the 1850s and 1860s, the Ditson Company was working with such talented musicians as Henry Williams, a gifted and "extremely versatile musician, proficient in many styles from dance music to the classics," who provided musical scores for prominent bands such as those led by Patrick S. Gilmore and Frank Johnson. Its commitment to African American artists continued through the twentieth century and led to publications of arrangements by prominent artists such as J. Rosamond Johnson, brother of James Weldon Johnson, the accomplished NAACP officer and diplomat and author of *Autobiography of an Ex-Coloured Man.*

29. Hopkins, "Famous Women of the Negro Race. I: Phenomenal Vocalists," 49. The firm of Oliver Ditson and Company grew out of a business relationship between Oliver Ditson and his employer Samuel Parker, who owned a bookstore in which Ditson worked. The pair began publishing music as early as the 1830s. Following Parker's departure from the company in the mid-1840s, Charles Ditson, son of Oliver, and John C. Haynes, joined the enterprise. Pindell's works were followed later by other Ditson publications of African American composers, including Samuel Coleridge-Taylor, whose *Twenty-Four Negro Melodies: Transcribed for the Piano*, an important 1905 collection of spirituals by the respected musician that included a foreword by Booker T. Washington. Additional information about Ditson can be found on the website of the McCain Library and Archives at the University of Southern Mississippi (<http://www.lib.usm.edu/archives/m361.htm>).

30. De Abajian, *Blacks in Selected Newspapers*. The circumstances that led to the decline of the Allen-Pindell marriage remain a mystery, but the same issue of the San Francisco–based *Pacific Appeal* that printed the couple's divorce notice also reported that Joseph Pindell had married a woman by the name of Mary H. T. Coffey. Annie Pauline Pindell did not return to the East to live once her performance career came to a close and her marriage ended. Instead, she became self-employed and stayed in San Francisco where she maintained herself as a "teacher of music, needle work and hair works" and advertised for clients and students in local papers such as the African American–owned *San Francisco Elevator*. She did accept local invitations to perform in the years to come, appearing at additional benefit concerts for the Zion African Methodist Episcopal Church in the city, for example. In 1866, she engineered a renaissance and, as the newly renamed "Nightingale of the Pacific," began to hold concerts. In 1889, she returned to Boston while ailing from an unidentified condition but sometime later returned to California. In 1901, she passed away while living in Los Angeles.

31. Cook, *Massachusetts*, 206–7.

32. Bermuda Genealogy and History, "A Survey of Inhabitants."

33. "Bermuda Worship."

34. Ibid.

35. Ship passenger lists were not required for all ships before 1820, with two exceptions. Lists were compiled routinely for ships entering the ports in New Orleans and in Philadelphia.

36. Williamson, *History of North Carolina*, 211.

37. Gilpatrick, *Jeffersonian Democracy in North Carolina*, 14.

38. Lainhart, *1865 Massachusetts State Census, Charlestown, Ward 2*, 319.

39. *Edenton District, Loose Estates Papers*, 2:92.

40. Ibid.

41. Greene and Harrington, *American Population before the Federal Census of 1790*, 170.

42. "Lawson, John," 27549.

43. For details about the early settlement of New Bern, the first populations and the terms

under which they took up residence, see Hawks, *Embracing the Period of the Government, from 1663 to 1729.*

44. Brock, *Scotus Americanus,* 37.

45. Carter, *Colonial and Revolutionary Periods,* 186. Pollock also owned Harkers Island, a 2,400-acre island also known as Craney Island and Crane Island, located in the Core Sound.

46. Ibid., 187.

47. Robinson, *North Carolina Guide,* 184.

48. Winborne, *Vaughan Family of Hertford County, N.C.,* 49.

49. Vass, *History of the Presbyterian Church in New Bern, N.C.,* 135.

50. Ibid.

51. "Historic Homes of Bertie County."

52. Ibid.

53. Vass, *History of the Presbyterian Church in New Bern, N.C.,* 136.

54. Urquhart, "Devereux, Runiroi, Uniroy, Runiroy Plantation."

55. Winborne, *Vaughan Family of Hertford County, N.C.,* 49.

56. Calhoun, "A Troubled Culture," 78.

57. Trenholme, *Ratification of the Federal Constitution in North Carolina,* 17.

58. Aptheker, *American Negro Slave Revolts,* 213. Aptheker also notes documents that reveal that in 1830 New Bern and other cities were "considerably excited, with the anticipation of insurrectional movements among their slaves" and that "the inhabitants of Newbern being advised of the assemblage of sixty armed slaves in a swamp in their vicinity, the military were called out, and surrounding the swamp killed the whole number" (290).

59. Calhoun, "A Troubled Culture," 76.

60. Ibid., 81.

61. Hopkins, *Contending Forces,* 32.

62. Bryant, "The Antiquity of Freedom," 198–99.

63. Ibid., 199.

64. Ibid.

65. Ibid., 200.

66. Bigelow, *William Cullen Bryant,* 80.

67. Menschel, "Abolition without Deliverance," 191.

68. Bigelow, *William Cullen Bryant,* 81.

69. Ibid., 80–81.

70. Hopkins, *Contending Forces,* 22.

71. Prince, *History of Mary Prince,* 62.

72. Hopkins, *Contending Forces,* 22.

73. Prince, *History of Mary Prince,* 93.

74. Ibid., 93–94.

75. Wilkinson, *Bermuda from Sail to Steam,* 1:210.

76. Ibid., 1:212.

77. Ibid., 1:210.

78. Ibid., 1:230.

79. Ibid.

80. Ibid., 1:228.

81. Quarles, *Black Abolitionists,* 130–31.

82. *Freedom's Journal,* 20 April 1827, 22; ibid., 20 July 1828, 74.

83. Ibid., 20 April 1827, 22.

84. James, *Religious Life of Fugitive Slaves*, 133.

85. In 1840, Adey was one of the attendees at the historic World Anti-Slavery Society Convention in London and was included in the well-known Benjamin Haydon portrait of the convention participants, which also included William Wilberforce.

86. Paul's American abolitionist community learned of the marriage when it was announced in the 31 August 1833 *Liberator*. A few months later, Garrison contemplated the implications of such a match in his formal *Report to the Managers of the New-England Anti-Slavery Society*. He began by noting the encouraging and widespread freedoms with which persons of color could move in Europe. "I found that colored persons were as readily admitted into the coaches as white persons," he reflected. "I met [persons of color] in circles of refinement and gentility—at the tables of opulent and reputable individuals—on the platforms in public meeting with the peers of the realm—as spectators in the House of Commons and in the House of Lords—arm-in-arm with gentlemen in the streets &c. &c." "Nay, while I was in London," he concluded with great relish, "a colored American (the Rev. Nathaniel Paul) was united in wedlock to a white lady of respectability, talent and piety. What an uproar such an occurrence would create in this country! Even in Massachusetts, the marriage would by law be null and void, and the clergyman performing it would be fined £50" (New England Anti-Slavery Society, *Appendix of Second Annual Report*, 34).

87. *The Liberator*, 15 October 1841, 167.

88. Ibid.

89. William Lloyd Garrison to George W. Benson, 25 June 1844, in Merrill, *Letters of William Lloyd Garrison*, 3:258–60.

90. In the years following her husband's death, Ann Adey Paul came to rely increasingly on the beneficence of white abolitionists for support. William Lloyd Garrison, who was devoted to the Paul family, took a special interest in helping the woman whom he regarded as "a martyr all the while she remained on these shores" (*The Liberator*, 15 October 1841, 167). He was instrumental in negotiating her board with Thankful and Joseph Southwick, the ardent Quaker abolitionists of Boston known for offering "hospitality [that] was generous to an extreme." The Southwicks "entertained her for so long a time," but eventually they became "naturally desirous . . . that she should find some retreat that she can call or regard as her home" (William Lloyd Garrison to George W. Benson, 25 June 1844, in Merrill, *Letters of William Lloyd Garrison*, 3:258). Ann Paul's time with the Southwicks, who were part of the city's elite white abolitionist circles, placed her within reach of leading abolitionists and prominent New Englanders such as John G. Whittier, Nathaniel Hawthorne, Abby Kelley, Theodore Parker, the Chapman sisters, and Ralph Waldo Emerson. Ann Paul's time with the Southwicks also coincided with Elizabeth Cady Stanton's arrival in the city in 1843, and the two women, whose paths likely crossed, shared a deep appreciation for the Southwicks. Paul eventually left the Southwicks for Northampton, but, although they pledged financial support to her, her situation was hardly secure. In 1844, Garrison did his best to secure a place for Ann Paul at the Northampton Association of Education and Industry, a utopian community whose membership of just over 200 owned nearly 500 acres of land near the city of Northampton that included residences, "timberland, a saw mill, and a silk factory" (Merrill, *Letters of William Lloyd Garrison*, 3:95). In June 1844, Garrison was beseeching George W. Benson, his brother-in-law and a resident at the Northampton Association, to take Ann Paul "under [his] sheltering care for a year." The *Liberator* editor tried earnestly to broker a deal, noting that Benson would be "guaranteed a dollar a week for her board (which I suppose will cover the cost of it,) or if that be not sufficient, one dollar and a half." The Southwicks would provide "half of her board," and Garrison would unabashedly "beg

the other half from other friends, if necessary." "She will need little or no clothing during the year, as she has a sufficient quantity to carry her through," he noted, and insisted that "[s]he has also a mattress and bed clothes, which she can carry with her" (ibid., 3:258–60). He assured Benson that, as Paul's much-needed patron, he would be able to reap the profits from "all that she can earn during the year." "Mrs. Southwick says she will be able to do much," insisted Garrison, "either with her needle, in the silk department, or in some other kinds of labor—and she will not be backward in trying to do whatever lies in her power" (ibid., 3:259).

Garrison's correspondence does not reveal the final arrangements that he was able to make on Ann Adey Paul's behalf. Later letters of his do reveal, however, that Paul had relocated to Northampton. By 1848, she was "boarding with an old lady" and hoping desperately to gain access to the home of the Bridgeman family. When Garrison visited her there in July, he found her "slowly improving" from a malady that may have necessitated her taking the water cure (ibid., 3:572). Three months later, in October, he thoughtfully arrived with "a large bundle of newspapers . . . for her perusal" and walked some four miles to find her. In a note to his wife, Helen, he mused that Ann Paul's life "is one of peculiar uncertainty, no doubt" (ibid., 3:597).

91. *The Liberator*, 15 October 1841, 167.

92. Nell, *Colored Patriots*, 156.

93. *North Star*, 7 September 1849, 2.

94. *Anti-Slavery Bugle*, 24 August 1850, 1, cited in Sherman, "James Monroe Whitfield," 175.

95. *Frederick Douglass' Paper*, 15 July 1853, 3.

96. Ibid., 1. Also serving on the committee were the Reverend A. N. Freeman and H. O. Wagoner.

97. Hopkins, *Contending Forces*, 13.

98. LaCapra, *History and Memory after Auschwitz*, 20.

99. Ibid., 11.

100. Hopkins, *Contending Forces*, 16.

101. Ibid., 13.

CHAPTER TEN

1. The Museum of Afro-American History in Boston acquired the African Baptist Church property in 1972. One of the key historic sites that the museum owns, the African Meeting House as it is known now, has been restored to its 1854 design. In December 1998, First Lady Hillary Clinton visited the church and officially designated the church as one of America's National Treasures. She described it as "a place that holds [meaning] not only for African Americans and their enduring struggle for justice, but for all of us who believe that learning about our past will guide and inspire us for a better future" (<clinton4.nara .gov/WH/EOP/First_Lady/html/generalspeeches/1998>). For more information about the church and the museum, see the Museum of Afro-American History's official website, <www.afroammuseum.org>.

2. *Grants of Suffolk County, Massachusetts*, 197; Sarah A. Hopkins to Commissioner of Pensions, 27 April 1906, "Pension Record of Hopkins, William A.," Pension Number Navy WC17-916, National Archives and Records Administration, College Park, Md. Hopkins outlined the circumstances related to the purchase of the house in the papers that she and her mother and stepfather filed in order to secure his military pension.

3. Sarah A. Hopkins to United States Navy and Bureau of Pensions, 27 April 1906, 1, "Pension Record of Hopkins, William A.," Pension Number Navy WC17-916, National Archives and Records Administration, College Park, Md.

4. Michael H. Burchett notes that many African Americans in the South were "entrenched at the bottom of a racial caste system maintained by brute force and increasingly, as the century drew to a close, by the validation of law" ("Promise and Prejudice," 312). For additional information about the Great Migration, see Gregory, *Southern Diaspora*; Lemann, *The Great Black Migration and How It Changed America*; Sernett, *Bound for the Promised Land*; and Arnesen, *Black Protest and the Great Migration*.

5. Braithewaite, *Negro Digest*, 1947, 21–26. In 1901, the prolific Boston-born poet and *Colored American Magazine* book review editor William Stanley Braithwaite, in his recollection of Walter Wallace, described the periodical in this way.

6. Gatewood, *Black Americans and the White Man's Burden*, 222.

7. Historian Willard Gatewood Jr. suggests that "nothing created more anxiety among black Americans than the outbreak of violence which threatened their personal security." He cites the *Cleveland Gazette*, 18 March 1899; and the Washington, D.C., newspaper, the *Colored American*, 10 February 1900. See Gatewood, *Black Americans and the White Man's Burden*, 224.

8. Gatewood, *Black Americans and the White Man's Burden*, 224.

9. Ibid.

10. *Colored American Magazine* (May 1900): 1.

11. In addition to Wallace and Fortune, the three other lodgers included James Hardaway, a forty-six-year-old hotel waiter who was born in Massachusetts to Southern parents.

12. "History of Boydton." Randolph-Macon College relocated to Ashland, Virginia, after the Civil War.

13. The Twelfth Census of the United States, 1900, Massachusetts, lists Wallace's birth as June 1874; his May 1901 *Colored American Magazine* profile gives his year of birth as 1873. The Ninth Census of the United States, 1870, Virginia, identified M. R. Wallace as a twenty-four-year-old student living with his parents.

14. General Samuel Armstrong, who received support for Hampton Institute from the American Missionary Association, envisioned the school as a multiracial institution for Native Americans and African Americans. In 1878, Armstrong enrolled some thirty former prisoners of war who had been held for three years at Fort Marion in St. Augustine, Florida. The program grew substantially and became what scholars W. Roger Buffalohead and Paulette Fairbanks Molin have referred to as a highly regulated biracial school whose staff was determined that its Native American students absorb and adopt white American cultural traditions. According to historian Virginia Lantz Denton, nearly 1,400 American Indian students enrolled at Hampton during a forty-five-year period (*Booker T. Washington and the Adult Education Movement*, 77). See Buffalohead and Molin, "A Nucleus of Civilization." For additional information about Hampton's American Indian students and curriculum, see Fear-Segal, "Use the Club of White Man's Wisdom."

15. Elliott, "The Story of Our Magazine," 45, 69; Ninth Census of the United States, 1870, Virginia, Powhatan Township, James City County, Roll M593-1657, 333.

16. For more information about Fort Marion, known now as Castillo de San Marcos, see <http://www.nps.gov/casa>.

17. Anderson, *Education of Blacks in the South*, 33.

18. Engs, *Educating the Disenfranchised and Disinherited*, 152.

19. Denton, *Booker T. Washington and the Adult Education Movement*, 70.

20. Ibid., 82.

21. Anderson, *Education of Blacks in the South*, 34.

22. Denton, *Booker T. Washington and the Adult Education Movement*, 63.

23. Elliott, "The Story of Our Magazine."

24. Ibid.

25. "Walter N. Wallace," in Culp, *Twentieth Century Negro Literature*, 348.

26. Semmes, *Racism, Health, and Post-Industrialism*, 114. According to David Cecelski and Timothy Tyson, Leonard Medical College was severely criticized in a 1910 evaluation by a Carnegie Foundation reviewer. They note that Abraham Flexner, a white man, "effectively maligned the quality" of the Leonard Medical College at Shaw University. In his 1910 report, Flexner concluded that "Flint at New Orleans, Leonard at Raleigh, the Knoxville, Memphis, and Louisville school are ineffectual . . . sending out undisciplined men, whose lack of real training is covered up by the imposing M.D.," and he recommended that they be closed (198). The medical school did rally but closed in 1918 when the president insisted that all professional programs at Shaw be disbanded. See Cecelski and Tyson, *Democracy Betrayed*. For additional information about African American medical schools and physicians, see Johnson, "History of the Education of Negro Physicians"; Morais, *The History of the Negro in Medicine*; Bousfield, "An Account of Physicians of Color in the United States."

27. Ibid.; Elliott, "The Story of Our Magazine," 45.

28. The original entry in the Twelfth Census of the United States, 1900, Massachusetts, for Fortune lists his first name incorrectly, as "Harker" rather than as "Harper."

29. Elliott, "The Story of Our Magazine," 46.

30. On the eve of his spring 1898 marriage to Harriet Smith, Burrell, who had been living in Richmond, Virginia, was feted by his colleagues and business associates. "Among the many presents which he received," reported the *Richmond Planet*, "was a purse of $115 in gold, given by the trade union of white and colored citizens. We hope him a bright and happy future" (*Richmond Planet*, 23 April 1898, 4). In 1900, Burrell and Hattie, the affectionate name by which his wife of two years was known to friends and family, were living in the house that they owned at 9 Clarendon Avenue. Their neighbors primarily were African American families whose primary wage earners worked in a range of professions that included positions as engineers, janitors, messengers, and porters.

31. *Colored American Magazine* (May 1901): 46–47.

32. Elliott, "The Story of Our Magazine," 47.

33. Ibid., 46.

34. *Colored American Magazine* (May 1900): 63.

35. Elliott, "The Story of Our Magazine," 47.

36. Ibid., 46.

37. William Budd, thirty-eight, and his twenty-nine-year-old wife, Gabrielle, lived with Budd's sixteen-year-old sister. Like six of the lodgers in his home, the thirty-eight-year-old Budd was a waiter, and the other three men who rented from him also worked in the service industry. Thirty-two-year-old Harry Anderson was a waiter, twenty-five-year-old John Baskerville was a bellman, and twenty-three-year-old James Jackson was a porter. All of the residents at the Budd home, including Budd's twenty-nine-year-old wife and sixteen-year-old sister, identified themselves as literate.

38. Elliott, "The Story of Our Magazine," 47.

39. "History of Blyden Branch Library." Norfolk Mission College closed in 1916; see "Norfolk Mission College Site."

40. Elliott, "The Story of Our Magazine," 47.

41. Ibid.

42. During the early 1700s when Thomas Jefferson Jr. lived in the region, it was part of Henrico County and lay in the area of the James River falls. See Risjord, *Chesapeake Politics*, 48; Peterson, *Thomas Jefferson and the New Nation*, 4; and Horn, *Petersburg Campaign*, 35.

43. Elliott, "The Story of Our Magazine," 45.

44. Ibid., 46.

45. The group, whose ages ranged from early twenties to thirty-one, included one married couple, James and Mary Shannonhouse, who had family ties to Virginia and to British Canada, respectively. Watkins worked as a janitor. The other men in the house worked as waiters, day laborers, porters, and messengers. Women often are listed as "keeping house," but Cora Watkins is listed as having a job as a waiter also; the occupation line for Mary Shannonhouse, the only other woman on the premises, is blank, a traditional way of signaling her domestic work at home.

46. Elliott, "The Story of Our Magazine," 45.

47. Ibid.

48. Ibid., 46.

49. Ibid.

50. Skocpol and Oser, "Organization despite Adversity," 385.

51. Ibid., 387.

52. Ibid., 385.

53. Palmer, "Negro Secret Societies," *Social Forces* 23 (December 1944): 210, cited in ibid., 397.

54. Ibid., 367.

55. The *Colored American Magazine* promoted the Grand United Order of True Reformers, and, in October 1902, its "Here and There" column characterized the society as "undoubtedly the strongest race organization known." The magazine also noted that it was proud to accept the "aid of the Grand Worthy Secretary Wm. P. Burrell," with whom the magazine would collaborate to "give its readers a general synopsis of the Order and the many branches of its good work in uplifting, inculcating character and instilling unity." Readers also were reminded of the Order's bold plans to support racial solidarity and entrepreneurship across the nation, its "capacity and facilities" that made it "unsurpassed for the handling of large conventions," like a recent 300-member Negro Business League conference in Richmond.

56. See Johnson and Johnson, *Propaganda and Aesthetics*.

57. "Editorial and Publishers' Announcements," *Colored American Magazine* (May 1900): 60.

58. In June 1900, Wallace was residing in his parents' Richmond, Virginia, home and participated in the census there also. His occupation was listed as "journalist." Twelfth Census of the United States, 1900, Virginia, Henrico County, Richmond City, Roll T623, 16B.

59. Schneider, "Boston's Pro–Civil Rights Bookerites," 159.

60. "The Home of the Colored American Magazine." In March 1904, during Hopkins's tenure as editor, the offices moved again, to 82 West Concord Street in Boston.

61. Walter Wallace to Booker T. Washington, 6 August 1901, in Harlan, Smock, and Kraft, *BTW Papers*, 6:184.

62. "The Home of the Colored American Magazine."

63. Ibid.

64. "Editorial and Publishers' Announcements," *Colored American Magazine* (May 1900): 61.

65. Ibid.

66. Du Bois, "A Proposed Negro Journal," 78–79.

67. Ibid., 78.

68. Ibid., 79.

69. "Editorial and Publishers' Announcements," *Colored American Magazine* (January–February 1902): 254.

70. *Colored American Magazine* (May 1900): 62.

71. "From Our Friends in the Far East," 145.

72. "Editorial and Publishers' Announcements," *Colored American Magazine* (May 1900): 60.

73. Ibid.

74. Ibid.

75. Carby, Introduction to *Contending Forces*, xxiii. Carby suggests that the illiteracy rates translated into "historical limitations to what could be achieved" by the *Colored American Magazine*.

76. Barber, "The Morning Cometh," 38.

77. *Colored American Magazine* (May 1901): 43.

78. Elliott, "The Story of Our Magazine," 77.

79. Ibid.

80. Ibid., 66.

81. "Constitutional Rights Association of the United States," 311.

82. Washington, *Up from Slavery*, 221–22.

83. Advertisement, *Colored American Magazine* (March 1904).

84. Hutton, *Early Black Press in America*, 3.

85. *Colored American Magazine* (May 1900): 63–64.

86. Elliott, "The Story of Our Magazine," 47; Washington, *An Autobiography*, 313.

87. Smith, who was some fifteen years younger than Hopkins, was one of the first students to attend the Chicago school that opened in 1893, established with funds provided by Philip Danforth Armour, who made his fortune in the meatpacking and grain businesses. Smith graduated from the Armour Institute of Technology in 1894, having had the opportunity to pursue a broad range of studies, from chemistry to library science, architecture to engineering. In 1940, Armour Institute merged with Lewis Institute, a Chicago institution that focused primarily on science and engineering courses, and the two became known as the Illinois Institute of Technology. See "History of IIT."

88. Born in 1869 to parents who both had African American and Montauk Indian ancestry, Ward was an emerging poet on the eve of the twentieth century. Her volume, *Original Poems*, published in 1899, received high praise from well-known writers such as Paul Laurence Dunbar. For additional biographical information about Bush Banks, see the scholarly volume prepared by her great-granddaughter, Bernice F. Guillaume, *Olivia Ward Bush-Banks*; and Bolden, "Olivia Ward Bush."

89. Elliott, "The Story of Our Magazine."

90. "Editorial and Publishers' Announcements," *Colored American Magazine* (October 1901): 479.

91. Ibid.

92. Ibid.

93. "Editorial and Publishers' Announcements," *Colored American Magazine* (December 1901): 101.

94. *Colored American Magazine* (September 1900): 262.

95. *Colored American Magazine* (October 1900): 333.

96. *Colored American Magazine* (May 1901): 79.

97. Hopkins to J. Max Barber, 27 April 1905, 2, Du Bois Papers.

98. *Colored American Magazine* (October 1900): 333.

99. Braithwaite, "The House under Arcturus," 188, cited in Johnson and Johnson, *Propaganda and Aesthetics*, 207.

100. Carter, "The Opening Century," 309.

101. *Colored American Magazine* (October 1901): 479.

102. Elliott, "The Story of Our Magazine," 44.

103. Walter N. Wallace to Booker T. Washington, 6 August 1901, in Harlan, Smock, and Kraft, *BTW Papers*, 6:184.

104. Historian Mark Schneider suggests that announcements like those that Wallace made in the first *Colored American Magazine* issues identify the magazine as a "nominally pro–Booker Washington" publication, one of two produced in Boston in the early 1900s. The other pro-Washington Boston journal was *Alexander's Magazine*, founded in 1905 and organized first by Washington as an alternative to *The Guardian*, a weekly newspaper founded and edited by William Monroe Trotter.

105. Walter N. Wallace to Booker T. Washington, 6 August 1901, in Harlan, Smock, and Kraft, *BTW Papers*, 6:184.

106. Ibid.

107. Ibid., 185.

108. Ibid.

109. Ibid.

110. Booker T. Washington to Francis Jackson Garrison, 17 May 1905, in Harlan, Smock, and McTigue, *BTW Papers*, 8:281.

111. Baker and Womack, *A Companion to the Victorian Novel*, 17.

112. Langbauer, *Novels of Everyday Life*, 10.

113. In *Hired Pens*, Ronald Weber considers how the profession of authorship evolved in direct relation to the literary marketplaces of the nineteenth century. He focuses specifically on the "class of full-time independent professional writers who came into existence once there was a market for their wares and who managed to live more or less exclusively by the pen" (2). The careers of these individuals, notes Weber, were affected greatly by the postbellum boom in the worlds of publishing and print culture.

114. Hopkins to William Monroe Trotter, 16 April 1905, 1, Hopkins Papers.

115. Ibid.

CHAPTER ELEVEN

1. *Colored American Magazine* (May 1900): 1.

2. Du Bois's "Men of Mark" series in the *Crisis* focused primarily on contemporary figures, and the articles were much more brief than those that Hopkins published in the *Colored American Magazine* or in the *New Era Magazine*.

3. Schomburg, "The Negro Digs Up His Past," 670.

4. Chesnutt, *Frederick Douglass*, ix.

5. John Ernest makes a compelling case for "liberation historiography," works that aimed

not only to interpret the dominant white historical record but also to intervene there when necessary. If the act of writing history is indeed "an act of moral imagination," as Ernest proposes so persuasively, the work of antebellum American historians of color such as James T. Holly, William Cooper Nell, James Pennington, and William Still constitutes major scholarly and cultural reconstruction and an effort to write the race into the national record. See Ernest, "Liberation Historiography."

6. Franklin, cited in Dagbovie, "Black Women Historians," 241–61; Franklin and Collier-Thomas, "Biography, Race Vindication, and African-American Intellectuals," 1.

7. Hopkins, "Famous Women of the Negro Race. III: Harriet Tubman," 210.

8. Still, *The Underground Railroad*, 4, cited in Hopkins, "Famous Women of the Negro Race. III: Harriet Tubman," 211.

9. Ibid.

10. Ernest, "Liberation Historiography," 418.

11. Schomburg, "The Negro Digs Up His Past," 671.

12. Howe, "Editorial Statement," 142.

13. Ibid.

14. Grimké's first published work, *William Lloyd Garrison: The Abolitionist* (1891), was published by the white mainstream New York City press Funk and Wagnalls. *Charles Sumner, the Scholar in Politics* (1892) was a substantive history of the white Boston abolitionist, resourceful lawyer, and influential senator who survived a vicious attack by Representative Preston Brooks and led key legal fights for equal rights in Boston.

15. When Chesnutt published the biography, the Beacon Biographies series included ten works. The lone female author was Mrs. James T. Field, who had produced the biography of Nathaniel Hawthorne. The remaining works were on Douglass, John Brown, Phillips Brooks, Aaron Burr, David Glasgow Farragut, Robert E. Lee, James Russell Lowell, Thomas Paine, and Daniel Webster. Additional works listed as being "in preparation" included volumes on John James Audubon, Edwin Booth, James Fenimore Cooper, Benjamin Franklin, and Sam Houston.

16. Stanford, *Tragedy of the Negro in America*, 4.

17. Chesnutt, *Frederick Douglass*, ix.

18. Ibid., x.

19. Dagbovie, "Black Women Historians," 241–61.

20. Doreski, "Inherited Rhetoric and Authentic History," 72.

21. Edmund Wilson, *Axel's Castle: A Study in the Imaginative Literature of 1870-1930* (New York: Scribner's, 1969), 122–23, cited in Doreski, "Inherited Rhetoric and Authentic History."

22. Dagbovie, "Black Women Historians," 241.

23. Hopkins, "Famous Men of the Negro Race. III: "William Wells Brown," 234; Brown, *The Black Man*, 26.

24. Hopkins, "Famous Women of the Negro Race. I: Phenomenal Vocalists," 50.

25. The image of L'Ouverture that accompanies Hopkins's November 1900 *Colored American Magazine* article on the Haitian leader most closely resembles the image of L'Ouverture that the engraver Francois Bonneville created in 1802. Bonneville's image was published in *Portraits des hommes celebres de la Revolution* (1802). The fate of the Hopkins-owned portrait is not known.

26. "Editor's and Publisher's Announcements," *Colored American Magazine* (August 1900): 191.

27. Hopkins, "Famous Men of the Negro Race. XI: Robert Morris," 337.

28. Hopkins, "Famous Men of the Negro Race. IX: John Mercer Langston," 177.

29. Hartsock, *History of American Literary Journalism*, 39.

30. Ibid.

31. "Editorial and Publishers' Announcements," *Colored American Magazine* (May 1900): 60.

32. Hopkins, "Famous Men of the Negro Race. XI: Robert Morris," 337.

33. Hopkins, "Famous Men of the Negro Race. IV: Robert Browne Elliott," 294.

34. Elliott, "The Story of Our Magazine," 43.

35. Ibid.

36. Hopkins, "Famous Men of the Negro Race. I: Toussaint L'Ouverture," 9.

37. Holly, "The Negro Race, Self-Government, and the Haitian Revolution."

38. Hopkins, "Famous Men of the Negro Race. I: Toussaint L'Ouverture," 9.

39. Ibid., 14.

40. Saunders first delivered the text of the *Haytian Papers* as an address at the historic Bethel African Methodist Episcopal Church that ministers Richard Allen and Absalom Jones had founded in 1794 in Philadelphia. See Dixon, *African Americans and Haiti*, 33. For additional information about Saunders, see White, "Prince Saunders."

41. Hopkins, "Famous Men of the Negro Race. I: Toussaint L'Ouverture," 23.

42. Martineau, *Harriet Martineau's Autobiography*, 334.

43. Webb, *Harriet Martineau*, 191.

44. Thomas Carlyle to Mrs. Emerson, 21 February 1841, *Carlyle-Emerson Letters*, 317–18, cited in ibid.

45. Ibid., 192.

46. Harriet Martineau, *Hour and the Man*, cited in Hopkins, "Famous Men of the Negro Race. I: Toussaint L'Ouverture," 19.

47. Hopkins, "Famous Men of the Negro Race. I: Toussaint L'Ouverture," 19. Hopkins's considerable investment in the political symbolism of Haiti and L'Ouverture modifies what Srinivas Aravamudan recently has identified as a tendency toward tropicopolitan iconography, images that protest French rule but at the same time are "resoundingly stated in vocabulary that the colonial power can understand, admire, and regret" (Aravamudan, *Tropicopolitans: Colonialism and Agency, 1688-1804*, 303). Hopkins's insistent focus on L'Ouverture relegated French colonial history to the background in her tribute to self-determination and black manhood.

48. "Hayti," 225.

49. Dowling, "Sketches of New-York Baptists," 295.

50. Dixon, *African Americans and Haiti*, 28. Vesey, who actively solicited the Haitian government for aid for American campaigns to overthrow slavery, had ties to Haiti that predated his purchase by slave owner Captain Joseph Vesey.

51. "Hayti: Appointment of Mr. Paul."

52. Daniel Sharp to the Reverend Thomas Paul, 13 April 1823, cited in *American Baptist Magazine, and Missionary Intelligencer* 4, no. 6 (November 1823): 225.

53. *American Baptist Magazine, and Missionary Intelligencer* 4, no. 3 (May 1823): 134–36.

54. Hopkins, "Famous Men of the Negro Race. I: Toussaint L'Ouverture," 11–12.

55. Doreski, "Inherited Rhetoric and Authentic History," 74.

56. Hopkins, "Famous Men of the Negro Race. VII: Charles Lenox Remond," 34.

57. This term refers to the Americas, Africa, and the Caribbean, the three sites among which rum, sugar, and slaves were traded.

58. Hopkins, "Famous Men of the Negro Race. VII: Charles Lenox Remond," 35.

59. Hopkins, "Famous Men of the Negro Race. IX: John Mercer Langston," 177.

60. Ibid., 183.

61. Schomburg, "The Negro Digs Up His Past," 671.

62. Ibid.

63. Hopkins, "Famous Men of the Negro Race. III: William Wells Brown," 232.

64. Hopkins, "Famous Men of the Negro Race. IV: Robert Browne Elliott," 295.

65. Hopkins, "Famous Men of the Negro Race. XI: Robert Morris," 337.

66. Mossell, *Work of Afro-American Women*, 99.

67. Hopkins, "Famous Women of the Negro Race. II: Sojourner Truth," 124.

68. Nell, *Colored Patriots of the American Revolution*, 124.

69. Hopkins, "Famous Women of the Negro Race. II: Sojourner Truth," 125.

70. Ibid., 124.

71. Hopkins, "Famous Women of the Negro Race. III: Harriet Tubman," 211.

72. Ibid., 212.

73. Hopkins, "Famous Women of the Negro Race. IV: Some Literary Workers," 278.

74. Ibid., 277.

75. Ibid.

76. Ibid., 278.

77. Hopkins, "Famous Women of the Negro Race. V: Literary Workers," 369, 366.

78. Ibid., 367.

79. Ibid.

80. Ibid., 371.

81. Hopkins, "Famous Men of the Negro Race. III: William Wells Brown," 236.

82. Hopkins, "Famous Women of the Negro Race. III: Harriet Tubman," 210.

83. Hopkins, "Famous Women of the Negro Race. I: Phenomenal Vocalists," 47.

84. Hopkins, "Famous Women of the Negro Race. XII: Higher Education of Colored Women," 450.

85. Hopkins, "Famous Women of the Negro Race. V: Literary Workers," 371.

86. Ibid.

87. Hopkins, "Famous Women of the Negro Race. I: Phenomenal Vocalists," 46.

88. Hopkins, "Women's Department," 122.

89. Hopkins, "Famous Women of the Negro Race. IV: Some Literary Workers," 277.

90. See Tate, *Domestic Allegories of Political Desire*, for a discussion of African American women's strategic cultural critiques.

91. Hopkins, "Famous Women of the Negro Race. IX: Club Life among Colored Women," 276.

92. Washington, "Introduction," in Lewis A. Scruggs's *Women of Distinction*, cited in Tate, *Domestic Allegories of Political Desire*, 150.

93. Hopkins, "Famous Women of the Negro Race. IX: Club Life among Colored Women," 277.

94. Ibid.

95. Hopkins, "Famous Women of the Negro Race. XII: Higher Education of Colored Women," 445.

96. Ibid.

97. Ibid., 446.

98. Ibid., 447.

99. Ibid., 448.

100. Hopkins notes that Harriet Allen taught penmanship at the seminary for some time before leaving for Canada. It is not entirely clear when, where, or for how long Harriet H. Allen was in Canada. The 1860 Massachusetts census returns for Charlestown reveal that she was a student and that she was living at home. According to the regional return included in the 1865 State Census, Massachusetts, City of Charlestown, twenty-three-year-old Harriet was living at home with her parents, her older sister, Mary, and her five-year-old niece, E. M. F. A. Johnson, whose mother, Frances Allen Johnson, had passed away. The Ninth Census of the United States, 1870, Massachusetts, indicates that two years after the death of her father, Jesse, in 1868, twenty-eight-year-old Harriet was single, working as a dressmaker, and living at home in Charlestown. For the 1860 family census return, see Eighth Census of the United States, Massachusetts, Charlestown, Middlesex County, Roll M653, 248. For the 1865 Charlestown census return for the Allens, see Lainhart, *1865 Massachusetts State Census, Charlestown, Ward 2*, 319.

101. Hopkins, "Famous Women of the Negro Race. XII: Higher Education of Colored Women," 447.

102. Ibid., 448.

103. Ibid., 449.

104. Ibid., 450.

105. Ibid.

106. Whittier, "A Word for the Hour," 191.

107. Ibid.

108. Hopkins, "Whittier, the Friend of the Negro," 324.

109. Ibid., 325.

110. Ibid., 327.

111. Ibid.

112. Ibid., 330.

113. Hopkins, "Munroe Rogers," 20.

114. Ibid., 25.

115. Ibid., 26.

116. See Ernest, "Liberation Historiography," for a discussion of "artful *untellings*" as characteristic of African American historian biographies and discussions of their work.

CHAPTER TWELVE

1. Advertisement, *Colored American Magazine* (January 1901).

2. Ibid.

3. Hopkins, *Hagar's Daughter*, 79. The Bowen home, with all of its high finery and tasteful displays of Bowen's wealth, recalls details reported in turn-of-the-century accounts of capital life, such as those that Ellen Maury Slayden, wife of a Texas senator, created during her husband's political career. The Slaydens benefited from the work of "Aunt Frances," an ebullient woman whom Mrs. Slayden had hired in Texas and brought with them as the cook for their Washington, D.C., townhouse. Like the family working relationships that Aunt Henny experiences in *Hagar's Daughter*, the Aunt Frances who works for the Slaydens sees her daughter Maggie, whom Slayden described as "a black but comely damsel," hired to work as "maid." See Slayden, *Washington Wife*.

4. *Colored American Magazine* (January 1901): 237.

5. William Dean Howells to Charles Chesnutt, 25 October 1900, cited in Andrews, "William Dean Howells and Charles W. Chesnutt," 331. Andrews notes that Howells's

requests of Chesnutt, extended on behalf of the publisher Harper and Brothers, reveal the carefully manicured African American realism that Howells and other white readers believed to be palatable and appealing.

6. Andrews, "William Dean Howells and Charles W. Chesnutt," 332.

7. The intertextuality that Hopkins deploys in *Hagar's Daughter* answers one of the key questions that contemporary scholars have raised about the challenges facing early twentieth-century African American writers: how could Hopkins and her contemporaries gain access to white American markets and how might they encourage white consumption of African American writing? William Andrews, speaking to these very questions in his discussion of Chesnutt's interactions with Howells, suggests that the interactions between Chesnutt and Howells, for example, revealed "a central problem" for turn-of-the-century African American writers: "How to get a hearing for an increasingly vigorous expression of protest from a white reading audience, which, if listening at all, was already attuned to the more soothing message of Booker T. Washington" (328). Andrews calls attention to the double-sided nature of Washington's accommodationism with which Hopkins and other of her peers like Chesnutt had to contend. This predicament also highlights the real constraints that the palatable and indulgent tenets of Washington's accommodationism placed on hands that sought to do work other than that which he described so memorably in his "Atlanta Compromise" address at the 1895 Cotton States Exposition. See Andrews, "William Dean Howells and Charles W. Chesnutt."

8. Hopkins, *Hagar's Daughter*, 3.

9. For more information about Brown's attendance at the Second General Peace Congress and his interactions with American and European figures, including antislavery supporters, see the copies of Brown's letters about the events in Ripley et al., *British Isles*.

10. McCarthy, *America Revisited*, cited in Tocqueville, *Democracy in America*, 317.

11. Tocqueville, *Democracy in America*, 317.

12. Ibid.

13. Ibid.

14. Ibid.

15. See Foreman, "The Spoken and the Silenced," for a full demonstration of Foreman's insightful thesis of "the undertell."

16. For a discussion of Ona Staines, the self-emancipated woman from Mount Vernon, see Gerson, "Ona Judge Staines"; and McCully, *The Escape of Oney Judge*.

17. Hopkins, *Hagar's Daughter*, 3.

18. Ibid., 7.

19. Sinha, *Counterrevolution of Slavery*, 221.

20. Hopkins, *Hagar's Daughter*, 3.

21. Stein, *Answerable Style*, 18.

22. Milton, *Paradise Lost*, Book I, 490–92.

23. Eckenrode, *Jefferson Davis*, 92.

24. Gomez, *Exchanging Our Country Marks*, 1.

25. Holland, *A Refutation of the Calumnies*, 61, cited in Aptheker, *American Negro Slave Revolts*, 15.

26. Johnson and Roark, *No Chariot Let Down*, 7–8.

27. Ibid., 8.

28. Ibid. In their riveting edition of the recently unearthed correspondence of the Ellisons, one of the city's most prosperous free families of color, scholars Michael Johnson and James Roark call attention to the racial and class distinctions that shaped the free population of

color and note that in and beyond Charleston, "freedom was associated with light skin." In South Carolina, individuals identified as mulattoes constituted only 5 percent of those enslaved in the state. In sharp contrast, mulattoes represented some 75 percent of the state's 9,914 free people of color. The "brown aristocrats," as Johnson and Roark refer to them, were "a working aristocracy" and well established as extremely skilled tradesmen. Although less than 25 percent of the free people of color in Charleston owned property, those who did could count an enslaved person or real estate valued at or above $2,000.

29. Hine, "Black Politicians in Reconstruction Charleston, South Carolina," 556.

30. Rucker, "I Will Gather All Nations," 133. For an excellent overview of Charleston's antebellum economy, see Lander, "Charleston: Manufacturing Center of the Old South."

31. Allen, Jewett, and Wakelyn, *Slavery in the South*, 206.

32. Bancroft, *Slave Trading in the Old South*, 165.

33. Johnson and Roark, *No Chariot Let Down*, 19.

34. "Notes and News," 420.

35. Bancroft, *Slave Trading in the Old South*, 166.

36. Hine, "Black Politicians in Reconstruction Charleston, South Carolina," 557.

37. The collective history of the group reflected well-known and often suppressed Southern racial realities. Charlestonian Francis Louis Cardozo, who was educated at the University of Edinburgh, was a prominent light-skinned man whose father Isaac Nunez Cardozo was a wealthy Jewish merchant. Democrat Benjamin Kinlock was a light-skinned man descended from one of the most prominent Scottish families in Charleston (ibid., 559).

38. Ibid., 561.

39. Boritt, *Jefferson Davis's Generals*, 56, 55.

40. Bancroft, *Slave Trading in the Old South*, 165.

41. Wright, *South Carolina*, 100.

42. Bancroft, *Slave Trading in the Old South*, 165.

43. Petty, *Growth and Distribution of Population in South Carolina*, 65, cited in Hine, "Black Politicians in Reconstruction Charleston, South Carolina," 556.

44. Wallace, *South Carolina*, 525.

45. Ibid., 529.

46. Ibid. James Henry Hammond (1807–64) was a South Carolina native who, after becoming a lawyer, went on to serve the state in the House of Representatives for one term, 1835 through 1836. He was elected governor in 1842 and served through 1844. He represented the state in the U.S. Senate from 1857 through 1860. He died on 13 November 1864 and was buried in the Beech Island Cemetery on Beech Island, South Carolina. Hammond did regret his post-Lincoln election resignation from the Senate. As historian Harold Schultz notes, Hammond in his correspondence referred to others who resigned as "great asses for resigning" and characterized the political response as "an epidemic and very foolish" (Schultz, *Nationalism and Sectionalism in South Carolina*, 227). See also Hamilton, "James Henry Hammond."

47. Lander, "Charleston: Manufacturing Center of the Old South," 330.

48. Sinha, *Counterrevolution of Slavery*, 244.

49. Schultz, *Nationalism and Sectionalism in South Carolina*, 230.

50. *Carolina Spartan*, 3 January 1860, cited in ibid., 230.

51. Eckenrode, *Jefferson Davis*, 92.

52. Hopkins, *Hagar's Daughter*, 13.

53. Ibid.

54. Milton, *Paradise Lost*, Book I, 679–80, 680–84.

55. Ibid., 688, 670–71, 689–90.

56. Ibid., 722, 724, 726–30.

57. Ibid., 733–35.

58. Ibid.

59. Hopkins, *Hagar's Daughter*, 13–14.

60. Milton, *Paradise Lost*, Book I, 77.

61. Ibid., 127, 79–80.

62. Ibid., 392, 412–14, 440–41, 447–48, 462–63, 470.

63. Hopkins, *Hagar's Daughter*, 14.

64. Freehling and Simpson, *Secession Debated*, 31.

65. Varina Howell Davis, *Jefferson Davis*, 1:409–12, cited in Allen, *Jefferson Davis, Unconquerable Heart*, 270–71.

66. Allen, *Jefferson Davis, Unconquerable Heart*, 292.

67. Ibid., 250.

68. Rable, *Confederate Republic*; Allen, *Jefferson Davis, Unconquerable Heart*, 271.

69. Allen, *Jefferson Davis, Unconquerable Heart*, 271.

70. Ibid.

71. Hopkins, *Hagar's Daughter*, 14.

72. Ibid.

73. Freehling and Simpson, *Secession Debated*, 32.

74. Ibid., 32–33.

75. Perman, *Road to Redemption*, 7.

76. Freehling and Simpson, *Secession Debated*, 51. See Schott, *Alexander H. Stephens of Georgia*, for comprehensive information about Stephens; see also nineteenth-century texts such as Johnston and Browne, *Life of Alexander H. Stephens*.

77. Rable, *Confederate Republic*, 67.

78. Freehling and Simpson, *Secession Debated*, 32.

79. Ibid.

80. Ibid., 54.

81. Douglass, *Life and Times of Frederick Douglass*, 327, 326.

82. Crofts, *Reluctant Confederates*, 10.

83. For discussions of Stephen Douglas and his political positions on slavery, see Crofts, *Reluctant Confederates*; and also Forgie, *Patricide in the House Divided*; and Crofts, *Reluctant Confederates*, 10.

84. Douglass, *Life and Times of Frederick Douglass*, 327.

85. Ibid., 326.

86. Hopkins, *Hagar's Daughter*, 15.

87. Ibid.

88. Allen, *Jefferson Davis, Unconquerable Heart*, 92.

89. Boritt, *Jefferson Davis's Generals*, xiii, 55.

90. Hopkins, *Hagar's Daughter*, 16.

91. Ibid., 15.

92. Ibid., 18.

93. Ibid.

94. Ibid., 8.

95. Ibid.

96. Ibid., 9.

97. Moore, *Memoirs of Doctor Brown*, cited in Hopkins, "Famous Men of the Negro Race. III: William Wells Brown," 236.

98. Hazel Carby was the first to note Hopkins's use of Brown's writing.

99. Hopkins, *Hagar's Daughter*, 8.

100. Brown, *Biography of an American Bondman*, 25.

101. Hopkins, *Hagar's Daughter*, 8 (emphasis mine).

102. Brown, *Biography of an American Bondman*, 26; Hopkins, *Hagar's Daughter*, 8.

103. Moore, *Memoirs of Doctor Brown*, cited in Hopkins, "Famous Men of the Negro Race. III: William Wells Brown," 236.

104. Brown, *Narrative of William Wells Brown*, 38; Brown, *Biography of an American Bondman*, 26.

105. Brown, *Narrative of William Wells Brown*, 41.

106. Brown, *Clotel*, 12.

107. Brown, *Biography of an American Bondman*, 26.

108. Brown, *Clotel*, 12.

109. Hopkins, *Hagar's Daughter*, 9.

110. Ibid.

111. Brown, *Clotel*, 12.

112. Ibid., 13.

113. Ibid., 17–18.

114. Hopkins, *Hagar's Daughter*, 12.

115. Brown, *Clotel*, 17.

116. Ibid., 14.

117. Ibid., 16.

118. Ibid.

119. Hopkins, *Hagar's Daughter*, 24.

120. For more information about Smalls, see Miller, *Gullah Statesman*; Uya, *From Slavery to Public Service*; and Sterling, *Captain of the Planter*.

121. Hopkins, *Hagar's Daughter*, 24.

122. Ibid., 64.

123. Ibid.

124. Ibid., 64–65.

125. Ibid., 256.

126. Milton, *Paradise Lost*, Book IV, ll. 132, 134–36.

127. Ibid., ll. 141, 143.

128. Hopkins, *Hagar's Daughter*, 30.

129. Gayley, *The Classic Myths in English Literature and in Art*, 27.

130. Lehner and Lehner, *Folklore and Symbolism of Flowers, Plants and Trees*, 112.

131. Ibid., 120.

132. Hopkins, *Hagar's Daughter*, 33.

133. Tennyson, "Milton," ll. 10–11, in Hill, *Tennyson's Poetry*.

134. Hopkins, *Hagar's Daughter*, 36.

135. Ibid., 37.

136. Ibid., 46.

137. Ibid., 31.

138. Ibid., 214.

139. Beer, *Darwin's Plots*, 118, cited in Fischler, "Love in the Garden," 764.

140. Noble, *Eternal Adam and the New World Garden*, 101.

141. Hopkins, *Hagar's Daughter*, 67.

142. Ibid.

143. Marshall, *A Tennyson Handbook*, 129.

144. Tennyson, "Maud," Part 1, l. 352, in Hill, *Tennyson's Poetry*.

145. Schulman, "Mourning and Voice in *Maud*," 633.

146. Marshall, *A Tennyson Handbook*, 127.

147. Ibid.

148. Tennyson, "Maud," Part 1, ll. 1–4, in Hill, *Tennyson's Poetry*.

149. Ibid., l. 5.

150. Ibid., ll. 9–11.

151. Hopkins, *Hagar's Daughter*, 35.

152. Ibid., 210.

153. Tennyson, "Maud," Part 11, Section XXII, ll. 901–6, in Hill, *Tennyson's Poetry*.

154. Ibid., ll. 887–92 (emphasis mine).

155. Hopkins, *Hagar's Daughter*, 130.

156. Ibid., 91. For information about Modjeska, see Coleman, *Fair Rosalind*; and Collins, *The Story of Helen Modjeska*.

157. Lehner and Lehner, *Folklore and Symbolism of Flowers, Plants, and Trees*, 33.

158. Schulman, "Mourning and Voice in *Maud*," 637.

159. Ibid., 636.

160. Hopkins, *Hagar's Daughter*, 80.

161. Ibid., 120.

162. Ibid.

163. Ibid., 123.

164. Ibid., 124.

165. Ibid.

166. Klein, *A Time to Be Born*, 143.

167. Hopkins, *Hagar's Daughter*, 91, 93, 92.

168. Bronner, *From Eve to Esther*, 34.

169. Chesnutt, *House behind the Cedars*, 146–47.

170. Schwartz, *Reimagining the Bible*, 58–59.

171. See also Jones, "This Dainty Woman's Hand."

172. Soitos, *Blues Detective*, 60.

173. See "Anna Katherine Green and the Gilded Age," in Nickerson, *Web of Inquiry*.

174. See also Rohrbach, "To Be Continued: Double Identity, Multiplicity and Anti-genealogy."

CHAPTER THIRTEEN

1. Hopkins, "Winona," act I, 1, Hopkins Papers.

2. Ibid., act V, 3.

3. In Longfellow's poem, Nokomis, the future grandmother of Hiawatha, suffers at the hands of a jealous rival, who cuts a grapevine swing and causes Nokomis to fall: "From the full moon fell . . . / Fell the beautiful Nokomis, / She a wife, but not a mother" (Longfellow, *Hiawatha*, III, ll. 4–6). Although Hopkins declines to attribute any romantic history to the Nokomis in *Winona*, she does borrow from Longfellow's poem the native woman's eloquent explanations of the natural world and her role as a tender teacher of the gifted

warrior Hiawatha. The love that White Eagle's daughter develops for nature recalls that which Hiawatha so enjoys in his early childhood.

4. Hopkins, "Famous Men of the Negro Race. I: Toussaint L'Ouverture," 13.

5. Sanborn, *Recollections of Seventy Years*, 84.

6. Ibid.

7. See Patterson, "Kin' o' Rough Justice fer a Parson," for additional considerations of Hopkins's incorporations of violent antislavery events.

8. Hopkins, *Winona*, 288.

9. Whitfield and his family enjoyed domestic stability during his twenty years in Buffalo. By 1848 he had moved to 194 South Division Street, their longtime home.

10. Yensan, *The History of Grand Island*, 2.

11. Ibid., 6.

12. See Sarna, *Jacksonian Jew*.

13. Hopkins, *Winona*, 288–89.

14. Ibid., 289.

15. Ibid., 294.

16. Augusta Rohrbach also considers this point. See "To Be Continued: Double Identity, Multiplicity and Antigenealogy."

17. For information about Black Hawk, see Jackson, *Black Hawk, An Autobiography*; and Nichols, *Black Hawk and the Warrior's Path*. For attentive analyses of the Black Hawk memoir and discussions of the politics of memoir, see Walker, *Indian Nation: Native American Literature and Nineteenth-Century Nationalisms*; and Schmitz, "Captive Utterance."

18. "Chichester Parkinson-Fortescue, 1st Baron Carlingford." See Hammond, *Gladstone and the Irish Nation*, for information about the political work of Chichester Parkinson-Fortescue.

19. McCordick, *Scottish Literature*, 925. Scholars have favorably compared Oliphant's *Chronicles of Carlingford* to the Barsetshire novels of Anthony Trollope. Oliphant admitted that the series "*almost* made me one of the popularities of literature. *Almost*, never quite" (Oliphant, *Autobiography*, 70).

20. Hopkins, *Winona*, 290. Both works feature characters named Thomson.

21. Oliphant, "The Executor," 599.

22. Ibid.

23. Battle Creek Health System, "Native American Names and Meanings"; 21st Century Learning Initiative, "What's New."

24. In "Kin o' Rough Justice fer a Parson," Patterson suggests that Hopkins hesitated to "appl[y] a . . . code of violent resistance to a full-blooded African character" (451).

25. II Kings 15:9–10.

26. Claudia Tate refers to this interconnection. See Tate, "Pauline Hopkins," 60–61.

27. Shadrach, "Furnace Blasts: II, Black or White," 348 (emphasis in original).

28. Hopkins, *Winona*, 303.

29. Ibid., 290.

30. Ibid., 375.

31. Ibid., 375–76.

32. Ibid., 376.

33. Ibid., 417, 435.

34. Ibid., 435.

35. Bell, *Afro-American Novel*, 18.

36. Tate, *Domestic Allegories*, 201.

37. Hopkins, *Winona*, 356.

38. Ibid., 418.

39. Ibid.

40. *Oxford English Dictionary*.

41. Ibid.

42. Hopkins, *Winona*, 418.

43. Redpath, *Public Life of Capt. John Brown*, 25. In his preface to this volume, Redpath notes that he refused to accept the invitation from a New York publisher who asked him to write a biography that could be used as a "Republican campaign document." Redpath did accept with great humility and earnestness, however, the invitation of his Boston publishers, who "believed in John Brown . . . wished to do him justice; and they desired to assist his destitute family" (8).

44. Hopkins, *Winona*, 289, 435.

45. Ibid., 436.

46. Brown, *My Southern Home*, 154.

47. Hopkins, *Winona*, 436.

48. Ibid.

49. Brown, *My Southern Home*, 156.

50. Hopkins, *Winona*, 437.

CHAPTER FOURTEEN

1. Shadrach, "Mrs. Jane E. Sharp's School for African Girls," 181. Sharp, who was known before her marriage as Jennie Davis, was a Missouri native who grew up in Boston. AME bishop Henry McNeal Turner was familiar with Sharp and her husband, Jesse, a successful coffee planter and business man, and noted during his early 1890s journal accounts of his own African tour that she had "responded to the call of Dr. Blyden in 1882 for teachers" to work at Liberia College and that Sharp "went to work, not even waiting to be acclimated, and[,] using the material she had, organized the school, and has continued teaching ever since, with marvelous success" (Turner, *Miscellaneous Letters*, 493). Hopkins, writing under the pseudonym of J. Shirley Shadrach, advocated for Sharp's continued Liberian educational outreach in her essay, "Mrs. Jane E. Sharp's School for African Girls."

2. Hopkins, *Primer of Facts*, 12.

3. *Columbia Encyclopedia, Sixth Edition*, 8289, 43405.

4. Davidson, *Lost Cities of Africa*, 36.

5. Burstein, "The Kingdom of Meroe," 135.

6. Ibid., 132. As Burstein notes, Pliny the Elder made deliberate references to "six men who visited Meroe, most probably in the third century B.C.E., including a certain Dalion who lived in the city for six years and published accounts of their experiences" (132). Historian Bruce Tigger confirms the steady intensification of Meroitic scholarship, noting that by 1969, "Meroe seems well on its way to being regarded as the hearth of sub-Saharan African civilization and a principal transmitter to the rest of the continent of traits coming from the north" (25). See Tigger, "Myth of Meroe and the African Iron Age."

7. Burstein, "The Kingdom of Meroe," 134.

8. Ibid.

9. Hopkins, *Of One Blood*, 442.

10. Ibid., 441, 445, 441.

11. Ibid., 561.

12. London *Times*, 8 August 1854, cited in Schapera, *Livingstone's African Journal*, ix.

13. Schapera, *Livingstone's African Journal*, ix.

14. Hawthorne, *Blithedale Romance*, 9, cited in Coale, *Mesmerism and Hawthorne*, 1.

15. Luciano, "Passing Shadows," 150.

16. See Horvitz, "Hysteria and Trauma in Pauline Hopkins' *Of One Blood*," for a thorough overview of the scholarly and medical debates about trauma, hysteria, and the role of mesmerism that may have influenced Hopkins's novel.

17. James, "Hidden Self," 371.

18. Hopkins, *Of One Blood*, 442.

19. James's "Hidden Self" reviewed recent works by the French philosopher M. Pierre Janet and also considered the experiments and positions of Bernheim, Pitres, Edmund Gurney, and Alfred Benet.

20. Ibid., 373.

21. Hopkins, *Of One Blood*, 445.

22. Ibid.

23. Ibid.

24. Ibid.

25. Ibid., 446.

26. In 1999, Bartman's remains were "safely tucked away in Paris's Musée de l'Homme" (Sharpley-Whiting, *Black Venus*, 27); in 2002, they finally were returned to South Africa for burial in the Eastern Cape region where she was born. See Arnfred, *Re-thinking Sexualities in Africa*, 7–34, and 59–78.

27. Sharpley-Whiting, *Black Venus*, 27.

28. Ibid., 28.

29. Hopkins, *Of One Blood*, 608.

30. Ibid.

31. Ibid., 603.

32. For more information about Piatt, see Bennett, *Poets in the Public Sphere*.

33. Hopkins cited all but one line of the first two stanzas from Piatt's 1872 poem, which praises the stoic beauty of an enslaved woman, a princess who "wore a precious smile, so rare / That at her side the whitest queen / Were dark—her darkness was so fair." Hopkins was taken by Piatt's biographical poem, a deceptively simple and crafted work that, through the subtitle that declared it a "true fable," challenged the veracity and genre of the authentic story that she proposed to be recalling. Hopkins incorporated portions of the eleven-stanza poem into two of her most memorable accounts of mystical women, Aunt Frances in *Contending Forces* and Aunt Henny in *Of One Blood*.

34. Hopkins, *Of One Blood*, 614.

35. Ibid., 614–15.

36. Ibid., 615.

37. Ibid., 616.

38. Esedebe, *Pan-Africanism*, 40. See also Noble, *Chicago Congress on Africa*.

39. "Edward Wilmot Blyden," 1.

40. For information about the Atlanta meeting organized by Gammon Theological Seminary and the Steward Missionary Foundation, see Bowen, *Africa and the American Negro*.

41. Esedebe, *Pan-Africanism*, 40, 39.

42. Ibid., 42.

43. Ibid., 40–41.

44. Adi and Sherwood, *Pan-African History*, 48.

45. Bandele, "Pan African Conference," 1.

46. Mossell, *Work of African-American Women*, 67.

47. The cover of *Primer of Facts* cites Hopkins as "Author of 'Contending Forces,' 'Hagar's Daughter,' 'Winona,' 'Talma Gordon,' 'Famous Men of the Negro Race,' 'Famous Women of the Negro Race,' Etc." That there is no reference to *Of One Blood* invites speculations about the pamphlet's date of creation, Hopkins's evaluation of *Of One Blood*, and her assessments of other works that complement the educational and political agendas of the *Primer of Facts*.

48. Hopkins, *Primer of Facts*, title page.

49. King James Bible, Acts 17:26.

50. Hopkins, *Primer of Facts*, 11.

51. See Gruesser's discussion of Hopkins and Africa in *Black on Black*, 20–49.

52. Hopkins, *Primer of Facts*, 18. The first name of Rev. Agbebi is misspelled as Majola in the article.

53. Ibid.

54. For details about Charles Parkhurst and his indictments of corruption, see Gilfoyle, "Moral Origins of Political Surveillance"; and Wilson, "Stephen Crane and the Police."

55. Hopkins, *Primer of Facts*, 20.

56. Ibid., 26.

57. Ibid., 31.

CHAPTER FIFTEEN

1. Hopkins to William Monroe Trotter, 16 April 1905, 8, Hopkins Papers.

2. Ibid., 1.

3. Ibid.

4. Harlan, *Booker T. Washington*, 35.

5. Fox, *Guardian of Boston*, 28.

6. Article II, Boston Literary and Historical Association By-Laws, cited in DeVaughn, "The Boston Literary and Historical Association," 12.

7. Two of the six Boston Literary and Historical Association officers for 1902–1903 were women. Harriet L. Smith was the association secretary, and Hannah Smith served as assistant secretary. The Twelfth Census of the United States, 1900, Massachusetts, includes a listing for a Hannah Smith of African American descent. In 1900, Smith is listed as the forty-five-year-old Canadian-born wife of James Smith, a fifty-year-old Ohio native. The couple, married for twenty-three years, have no children, and James Smith, listed as the primary breadwinner, is employed and his occupation is given as superintendent. The actual notation relating to his employment is difficult to read; it appears to read "Supt. Color," but the last word may refer to something else. Historian Sarah Deutsch, in her study of Boston (*Women and the City*), refers to Hattie Smith and notes that Smith's father had been "prominent in state politics" (368 [n. 232]).

Two of the seven executive board members were women. Maria L. Baldwin (1856–1922), a highly respected teacher, mentor, community educator, and pioneering principal, who, in 1916, when she was promoted to master of the Agassiz School in Cambridge, became the first woman of color in New England to hold that position. Maria Baldwin also was connected to local Boston politics through Louis F. Baldwin, her brother and a former local councilman. For more information on Baldwin, see Brown, *Homespun Heroines and Other Women of Distinction*; and Wesley, "Maria Louise Baldwin."

In 1904–5, Addie Hamilton Jewell served as vice president of the organization. The executive board included Eliza J. Benjamin and Maude A. Trotter, sister-in-law to Geraldine Pindell Trotter and sister of *Guardian* editor William Monroe Trotter.

8. McHenry suggests that the Boston Literary and Historical Association was "[c]onvinced that the underlying objective behind industrial education was the maintenance of a hierarchical society in which blacks would remain subservient" and that members were "vehemently opposed to spreading this 'social gospel' throughout the black population" (144). See McHenry, *Forgotten Readers*.

9. Hart, an 1880 Harvard College graduate and 1883 Ph.D. from the University of Freiburg in Germany, became full professor at the school in 1897. His prodigious publication record included influential texts in American history, including a biography of Salmon Portland Chase, a study entitled *Foundations of American Foreign Policy* (1901), and a volume entitled *Slavery and Abolition* (1906) that was part of his highly regarded American Nation series.

10. McHenry, *Forgotten Readers*, 182. Additional Boston Literary and Historical Association sessions in January and February 1903 included addresses by the Reverend H. Astley Parris and the Rabbi Charles Fleischer.

11. "Ovation to Prof. Du Bois," *The Guardian*, 10 January 1903, 1, cited in McHenry, *Forgotten Readers*, 182–83.

12. Luker, *Social Gospel in Black and White*, 217.

13. McHenry, *Forgotten Readers*, 144.

14. "Boston Literary and Historical Society Program, 1902–03—Second Half Year," *Guardian of Boston* Collection, Special Collections, Mugar Library, Boston University.

15. In May 1897, for example, Hart queried Washington about his availability to "meet Professor Woodrow Wilson at dinner at the Colonial Club in Cambridge, at half past six on Wednesday, June second" (Harlan, Kaufman, Kraft, and Smock, *BTW Papers*, 4:289). Hart penned several notes to Washington over the years and did not hesitate to share his thoughts about the collaborations that he thought would be of great benefit to African Americans. "I am quite anxious to see you," he confessed in a June 1897 note in which he also revealed his hope that their next conversation would accommodate "an especial reference to Professor DuBois, who it seems to me ought naturally to find his field of labor associated with you" (Harlan, Kaufman, Kraft, and Smock, *BTW Papers*, 4:299). In 1899, Hart, impressed by Du Bois's stirring address as part of a fund-raising campaign for Harvard, endeavored once again to secure for his talented student a position. "Practically no member of his race in America has had so thorough and so well qualified opportunities for the highest education," insisted Hart. "It is worth a great deal for your cause to have such an example of a man of excellent abilities, thoroughly trained and at the same time modest and sensible. He is a standing refutation of some of the hardest things said about the negro race" (Harlan, Smock, and Kraft, *BTW Papers*, 5:127). For more information about Hart's overtures to Washington, see the notes appended to the 27 July 1894 note from Du Bois to Washington included in Harlan, Kaufman, and Smock, *BTW Papers*, 3:459.

16. Harlan, *Booker T. Washington*, 17.

17. Hill, *The Other Brahmins*, 82.

18. Roses, "The Black Church."

19. Hopkins to Trotter, 16 April 1905, 1, Hopkins Papers.

20. Ibid., 2.

21. Both William Dupree and James Trotter married Isaacs women, daughters of

Elizabeth-Ann Fossett Isaacs, a member of the Hemings family, of which Sally Hemings, the longtime companion of Thomas Jefferson, was a part. Elizabeth Fossett Isaacs was the daughter of the Monticello blacksmith shop foreman who was enslaved on the Monticello plantation. She and members of her immediate family were sold in 1827 after the president's death, and she ultimately was freed when her father, Joseph Fossett, endeavored heroically to purchase his wife and some of their eight children. Dupree's and Trotter's connection to the Isaacs family was forged in Ohio. It was there that Elizabeth-Ann Fossett Isaacs of Monticello moved with Tucker Isaacs, her free mulatto husband, after he was charged in Albemarle County in 1850 with forging free papers. For more information about the Isaacs and the Trotter and Dupree connection, see "For Love of Liberty."

22. "Editorial and Publishers' Announcements," *Colored American Magazine* (July 1901): 239.

23. "Col. William H. Dupree," 231.

24. The Dupree profile is infused with Hopkins's characteristic rich prose and inspired literary invocations and concludes with a quote drawn from a poetical work by John Greenleaf Whittier, to whom Hopkins often turned as she concluded her *Colored American Magazine* articles.

25. Dupree's prominence in Boston also was demonstrated when he chaired the committee "in charge of the dedication ceremonies attending the unveiling of the Crispus Attucks monument on Boston common," a statue of great importance to Boston's African American community. The history of Attucks was continually marginalized or overlooked in white accounts of the Revolution, even though many regarded Attucks's actions as the definitive and earliest act of black martyrdom in America. Dupree also played central roles in the events preceding the much-heralded unveiling of the St. Gauden's Shaw Memorial sculpture, placed directly opposite the golden-domed Boston State House. The sculpture continues to draw thousands of visitors today. Dupree served as "secretary of the committee which brought the veterans from all over the country together to be present at the unveiling of this sacred and historical memorial to Colonel Shaw and his brave black followers." His wife, Maria Elizabeth, known as Lizzie, was a "beautiful and accomplished lady" from a prominent Chillicothe, Ohio, family. Lizzie Dupree, just one generation removed from slavery on the Monticello plantation of Thomas Jefferson, became a beloved member of Boston's black Brahmin society. She "aided her husband materially in all his efforts" and, like Sarah and Pauline Hopkins, was active in the Women's Relief Corps. Her sister Virginia married James Monroe Trotter, and their son William excelled at Harvard, became an "implacable foe of the gradualist policies of Booker T. Washington," and embodied his grandfather Tucker Isaacs's relentlessly enterprising spirit to achieve freedom, in all its aspects, for those who lived without it.

26. "Col. William H. Dupree," 229.

27. Ibid.

28. Ibid., 231.

29. Hopkins, "How a New York Newspaper Man," 152.

30. Hopkins to Trotter, 16 April 1905, 2, Hopkins Papers.

31. Hopkins, "How a New York Newspaper Man," 152.

32. The 16 April 1905 letter from Hopkins to William Trotter is part of the modest collection of her papers housed at Fisk University that, otherwise, is painfully devoid of correspondence. It is notable that the letter from Hopkins to Trotter is not part of the Trotter Papers housed at Boston University.

33. Hopkins to Trotter, 16 April 1905, 2, Hopkins Papers.

34. *Bay State Monthly: A Massachusetts Magazine* 1, no. 6 (June 1884): 55; Howells, *A Modern Instance*, 111.

35. "Twelve Missing in Boston Fire," *New York Times*, 1; *Harvard University Letters* 1, no. 7 (November 2004): 1.

36. Hopkins, "How a New York Newspaper Man," 152.

37. Ibid., 158.

38. "John C. Freund, Founder and Editor of Musical America, Dies after Long Illness," 21.

39. "Real Music and Art Rising Out of a Sea of Fake."

40. "John C. Freund, Owner of Musical America, Dies in New York," 10.

41. "Real Music and Art Rising Out of a Sea of Fake."

42. Hopkins, "How a New York Newspaper Man," 153.

43. Ibid.

44. For access to the contemporary music-related website that grew out of Freund's 1898 *Musical America* weekly, see <http://www.MusicalAmerica.com>.

45. "About Us," MusicalAmerica.com.

46. "John Christian Freund."

47. Macleod, *Women Performing Music*, 44, cited in Hunt, "Musical Women in England," 224.

48. By 1913, when interviewed for an article published in the *New York Times*, Freund shared altogether different perspectives on women's abilities and creative freedom: "Our women really are thinking," he stated, and "[i]t is they who will be responsible for the coming uplift in music, art, and drama in this country. They have helped us gain the lead which we already hold in literature. It is the women who are [the] back of our Philharmonic Society, our Volpe Orchestra, our Schola Cantorum in New York: there are few towns in the United States who have not women's clubs for the cultivation of music and literature" ("Real Music and Art Rising Out of a Sea of Fake").

49. Hopkins, "How a New York Newspaper Man," 152.

50. Ibid., 153.

51. Ibid., 155.

52. Hopkins to Trotter, 16 April 1905, 2, Hopkins Papers.

53. "Why Mr. Freund Left the City," 8.

54. Ibid.

55. Ibid.

56. Ibid. Financial troubles for the Freund family continued even after the editor's death in 1924. The Freunds were featured prominently in New York newspapers in stories about the scandalous embezzlement of his estate perpetrated by James Gallagher, his erstwhile son-in-law. According to reports, the forty-three-year-old lawyer, Gallagher, was accused by the Westchester County District Attorney of having "converted $36,000 of the Freund estate to his own use, and the total of $113,000 had been reduced by January 1939 to $2.85." Gallagher, a coexecutor of the will, with Freund's widow, "frequently bought Liberty bonds for the estate, but almost immediately in each instance," reported the *New York Times*, "sold them again and converted the money to his own use." The jury, which heard unintentional but nonetheless incriminating testimony from the widowed Mrs. Anastasia Freund and Gallagher's wife, Annette, deliberated less than two hours before returning a decisive verdict of guilty. Gallagher and his wife had a young child together, and by trial's end, both mother and child were reported to be "ill at their home." This sad news did not

help to reduce the penalty imposed. He was sentenced to serve two and a half years at Sing Sing. See "Lawyer Convicted of Looting Estate," *New York Times*, 14 December 1940, 12; and "Lawyer Sentenced for Looting Estate," *New York Times*, 22 January 1941, 15.

57. Hopkins to Trotter, 16 April 1905, 3, Hopkins Papers.

58. Ibid., 4. In 1904, sixty-four-year-old Stephen Fiske was the dramatic editor of the *Sports of the Times*, the nation's first sporting journal, which journalist William Trotter Porter had founded in December 1831. The periodical had been known by other names, such as *Spirit of the Times*, during its history of mergers and acquisitions and had done much to raise the profile of American sports and athletes. Like Freund and Hopkins, he had been active in theater during the 1870s. Fiske's professional life in the theater included a stint in 1874 as manager of the Fifth Avenue Theatre, during which time he oversaw the American debut of Madame Helena Modjeska (1840-1909), the acclaimed Polish actress whom many in America came to regard as the most influential Shakespearean actress of her time ("Stephen Fiske Seriously Ill," *New York Times*, 3 February 1904). For information about Fiske, see his *New York Times* obituary, "Stephen Fiske"; Hornblow, *A History of the Theatre in America*; and Rothschild, *Lincoln, Master of Men*. For information about William Trotter Porter and the *Sports of the Times*, see Hudson, *Humor of the Deep South*; and a biographical profile, "William Trotter Porter."

59. Hopkins to Trotter, 16 April 1905, 4, Hopkins Papers.

60. Ibid.

61. Ibid., 3.

62. Hopkins, "How a New York Newspaper Man," 155.

63. Ibid.

64. Ibid., 154.

65. Hopkins to Trotter, 16 April 1905, 3, Hopkins Papers.

66. Ibid., 2.

67. "Supplement to the Colored American Magazine."

68. Hopkins, "How a New York Newspaper Man," 155.

69. Hopkins to Trotter, 16 April 1905, 3, Hopkins Papers.

70. Ibid.

71. Hopkins, "How a New York Newspaper Man," 153.

72. Hopkins to Trotter, 16 April 1905, 3, Hopkins Papers.

73. Ibid.

74. "Publishers' Announcements," *Colored American Magazine* (March 1904): 223.

75. Hopkins to Trotter, 16 April 1905, 3, Hopkins Papers.

76. Baldwin, *Henry Ford and the Jews*, 17.

77. Ibid.

78. "Samuel Smiles"; Smiles, *Self-Help*, 2.

79. Hopkins to Trotter, 16 April 1905, 3, Hopkins Papers.

80. Ibid., 4.

81. For more information about Soga and the context of his relationship with Pauline Hopkins and the *Colored American Magazine*, see chapter 15. For biographical information about Soga, see Sarah A. Allen, "A. Kirkland Soga," *Colored American Magazine* (February 1904): 114-16; and "Allan Kirkland Soga," at <pzadmin.pitzer.edu/masilela/newafrre/asoga/asogaS.htm>.

82. Hopkins to Trotter, 16 April 1905, 4, Hopkins Papers.

83. Smiles, *Self-Help*.

84. Luthin and Nevins, *American Demagogues*, 12. For additional evaluations of Varda-

man and his political career, see Holmes, *White Chief*; Kirwan, *Revolt of the Rednecks*; and Krane and Shaffer, *Mississippi Government and Politics*.

85. Sansing, "James Kimble Vardaman," 2.

86. Hopkins, "How a New York Newspaper Man," 159.

87. Ibid., 160.

88. Ibid., 159.

89. Ibid., 160.

90. *Colored American Magazine* (May 1904): 380.

91. Booker T. Washington to Francis Jackson Garrison, 22 February 1904, in Harlan and Smock, *BTW Papers*, 7:446.

92. Hopkins to Trotter, 16 April 1905, 5, Hopkins Papers.

93. "Publishers' Announcements," *Colored American Magazine* (March 1904): 223.

94. Ibid.

95. Hopkins to Trotter, 16 April 1905, 5, Hopkins Papers.

96. Ibid., 5–6.

97. Ibid., 6–7.

98. Bradley Gilman to Booker T. Washington, 31 December 1904, in Harlan, Smock, Valenza, and Harlan, *BTW Papers*, 13:512. Gilman became editor of the *Christian Register* in 1915 and later relocated from Massachusetts to Palo Alto, California.

99. Harlan, *Booker T. Washington*, 59.

100. The first issues of the *Colored Citizen* appeared in 1903, the last year in which the *Colored American Magazine* was an autonomous entity. During its publication years, Washington participated directly in its production. He instructed Emmett Scott, his personal secretary at Tuskegee and ghostwriter, to "have editorial and other notes written out for the paper" whenever "anyone in the office has time to do it" (Harlan, *Booker T. Washington*, 59). Such methods for producing "news" sharply contrasted with the active solicitation of potential domestic and international contributors in which Hopkins was engaged. The first editors that Washington installed at the Boston-based *Colored Citizen* were Peter Smith and J. Will Cole. Harlan describes Smith as "an inept journalist" who "pleaded with Washington for a direct subsidy, saying: 'All the editor wants is the kind of encouragement that greases the wheels of the machinery in a substantial way so as to have them run along smoothly'" (59). See Harlan, *Booker T. Washington*, for additional accounts of Smith's unabashed solicitation of funds and complete disregard for his professional responsibilities as editor.

101. Allen, "Mr. Alan Kirkland Soga," 114.

102. Trapido, "African Divisional Politics in the Colony," 97.

103. For more information about Rubusana, see "Walter Rubusana: Clergyman, Humanist, Politician" (<http://www.knowledge4africa.co.za/eastlondon/rubusana.htm>); and Jordan, "Zemk' Inkomo Magawalandini."

104. Soga served as Convener of the Queen Victoria Memorial "for the erection of a national tribute (scholastic and educational) in honor of Queen Victoria, The Good, whose high character as a sovereign contributed not a little to ameliorate the condition of her Black subjects in South Africa during her reign" (Allen, "Mr. Alan Kirkland Soga," 116).

105. Ibid. Soga and his colleague, F. Z. S. Peregrino, an African nationalist, founder of the South African Native Press Association, and the managing editor of the *South African Spectator*, were greatly impressed by Tuskegee's institutional plan and mission and sought "to introduce the Tuskegee educational system into South Africa and to send students to Tuskegee" (Smock, *Booker T. Washington in Perspective*, 87). Soga wrote directly to Washington in 1903 and, according to historian Manning Marable, received from Washington

in return a portrait and information about the school that he was invited to reprint in *Izwi Labantu*. The exchange between the two men, as historian George Shepperson notes, was part of a growing correspondence and interaction between South Africans and African Americans. The exchange between Soga and Washington was promising but limited. See Louis R. Harlan, in Smock, *Booker T. Washington in Perspective*; and Marable, "Booker T. Washington and African Nationalism," 398–406.

106. Hopkins to Trotter, 16 April 1905, 6, Hopkins Papers. Hamedoe's *Colored American Magazine* essays included "Major-General Antonio Maceo: The Idol of Cuba and the Cuban Insurgents" (November 1900); "Menelik, Emperor of Abyssinia" (December 1900); and an essay on the Filipino patriot José Protacio Rizal, whose execution in 1896 elevated him to the status of martyr and fueled the Filipino fight for independence from Spain. Hamedoe's dynamic and timely profiles complemented the American biographies that Hopkins was producing and would publish during the magazine's first two years.

107. Nelson, *Colonialism in the Congo Basis*, 79. See also Zwick, "Reforming the Heart of Darkness." The Congo Reform Association disbanded in 1913 when Morel became convinced that proposed new reforms would effect long-overdue change in the region.

108. Crawford, *Argument and Change*, 201.

109. "Editorial and Publishers' Announcements," *Colored American Magazine* (May 1900): 63.

110. Harlan and Smock, *BTW Papers*, 7:509.

111. Frederick Randolph Moore to Booker T. Washington, 20 May 1904, in Harlan and Smock, *BTW Papers*, 7:509.

112. Lewis, *W. E. B. Du Bois*, 230.

113. Booker T. Washington to T. Thomas Fortune, 9 June 1904, in Harlan, Smock, Valenza, and Harlan, *BTW Papers*, 13:510.

114. Walker, *Encyclopedia of African American Business History*, 418. Estimates of National Negro Business League memberships varied wildly—Walker suggests that by 1915 the organization had anywhere from 5,000 to 40,000 members (417).

115. Ibid., 416.

116. Washington, "A Speech before the National Negro Business League," in Harlan, Smock, and Kraft, *BTW Papers*, 5:601.

117. "Publishers' Announcements," *Colored American Magazine* (June 1904): 458.

118. Ibid. Moore took the unusual step of signing his name after two of the announcements included in this section. He signed himself "Publisher and Manager" for this specific note. In an address to "our friends and public" that offered shares of stock and touted the value of the investment in the magazine, he signed himself "Fred R. Moore, General Manager."

119. The 3 March 1943 *New York Times* obituary for Moore ("F. R. Moore, Editor, Harlem Leader, 85") states that he accepted the diplomatic posting to Liberia but "resigned several months later without having gone to that post" (24).

120. Ibid.

121. Editor's Note, Timothy Thomas Fortune to Booker T. Washington, 25 January 1899, in Harlan, Smock, and Kraft, *BTW Papers*, 5:19.

122. John Freund to Frederick Moore, *Colored American Magazine* (June 1904): 453–54.

123. Hopkins to Trotter, 16 April 1905, 7, Hopkins Papers.

124. Ibid.

125. Ibid.

CHAPTER SIXTEEN

1. Still, *Mirror for Gotham*, 257. James's citation is from *American Scene* (1907).

2. Still, *Mirror for Gotham*, 257, 260.

3. "Times Square"; "The Up-Town Building of the New York Times," 6.

4. Still, *Mirror for Gotham*, 260.

5. *New York Times*, 27 May 1904, 6.

6. Child, *Letters from New York*, "Letter X: October 21, 1841," 68.

7. R. S. Elliott, "The Story of Our Magazine," 68.

8. Ibid.

9. Ibid.

10. Fourteenth Census of the United States, 1920, New York, Kings County, Borough of Brooklyn, Roll T625, 10A; Elliott, "The Story of Our Magazine," 68.

11. Elliott, "The Story of Our Magazine," 65.

12. Barbara Owen suggests that the "proud but poor family" had "its roots still stuck deep into the Southern soil" (Lewis, "Review: James V. Hatch," 688).

By June 1900, the Dodsons were living at 162 Prince Street in an integrated neighborhood, although many of their immediate neighbors on Prince Street were primarily native New Yorkers or first generation Americans whose parents had come from Ireland or England. They did have African American neighbors next door, and further down the street there was a cluster of homes occupied by African Americans, who, like them, hailed from Virginia as well as North Carolina. At 160 Prince Street, just next door to the Dodsons, were the Moles, an African American family made up of a mother, daughter, and aunt from Maryland. Sarah Dodson, like her neighbors, sixty-year-old Sarah Moles, fifty-seven-year-old Susan Weeks, and a few other white women on Prince Street, earned a living as a laundress (Twelfth Census of the United States, 1900, New York, Brooklyn, Ward 11, Roll T623, 19B).

13. The 1910 census does not list any occupation for Sarah Dodson, who at that time had five children ranging in age from five months to eleven years. See Thirteenth Census of the United States, 1910, New York, Brooklyn, Ward 26, Roll T624, 4A.

14. Elliott, "The Story of Our Magazine," 66.

15. See the chapter on Owen Dodson in Bloom, *Modern Black American Poets and Dramatists*.

16. Sarah Dodson suffered a stroke shortly after bearing Owen, her last child, and he "always bore tremendous guilt" for his mother's suffering (Grant, "Extending the Ladder," 640). Owen had the most celebrated career of all the Dodson children. He became a Yale University–educated poet, award-winning dramatist, and teacher at prestigious and historically black institutions such as Spelman College and Hampton Institute. Harold Bloom, who has written about the literary triumphs of the Dodsons' youngest son, notes that Sarah was a "social worker and devout churchgoer" whose faith and humanist perspectives shaped her children and especially her son Owen, for whom she was the source of "a religious sensitivity that would infuse both his life and his work" (Bloom, *Modern Black American Poets*, 78). For more information about playwright Owen Dodson, see also Hatch, *Sorrow Is the Only Faithful One*.

17. Elliott, "The Story of Our Magazine," 66.

18. Ibid.

19. Ibid.

20. Ibid.

21. Lincoln and Mamiya, *Black Church in the African-American Experience*, 176. In his contemporary assessment of Concord Baptist Church, Raymond Billingsley refers to it as a "megachurch," whose community influence was manifested in its significant set of businesses and community organizations, including its own private elementary school, nursing home, senior citizen apartment complex, and credit union, with assets valued at $1.5 million. See Billingsley, *Mighty Like a River*, 146.

22. Charles William Anderson to Booker T. Washington, 20 July 1907, in Harlan, Smock, and McTigue, *BTW Papers*, 8:24. Gilbert (1862–1917) presided at Mt. Olivet Baptist Church from 1904 to 1910 (25).

23. "Notes," 346.

24. Woodson, "Proceedings of the Annual Meeting," 1.

25. "A Pioneer and Wise Counsellor," chapter 12.

26. See Simmons's *Men of Mark* for an especially noteworthy and enthusiastic biography of Dixon and for more details about his growth in the Baptist Church. Dixon died in 1909.

27. *Brooklyn Daily Standard Union*, 13 December 1894, cited in Elliott, "The Story of Our Magazine," *Colored American Magazine* (May 1901): 66.

28. Dodson was in correspondence with J. Max Barber, the *Voice of the Negro* editor and the man targeted ruthlessly by Washington following his unpopular criticism of the Tuskegee president. Barber wrote to W. E. B. Du Bois in 1905 asking for help as he and his agents, like Dodson, sought to sustain the *Voice* in the face of attacks and undermining from pro-Washington groups like the National Negro Business League. See J. Max Barber to W. E. B. Du Bois, 27 April 1905, Du Bois Papers.

29. Federal Writers' Project (N.Y.), *New York City Guide*, 67.

30. Overmyer, *America's First Hamlet*, 29.

31. Earle, *Stage-Coach and Tavern Days*, 184. Archivist Charles L. Blockson proposes that Fraunces "probably spent more time with George Washington than any of the Founding Fathers." Fraunces, who "dominated the culinary profession," also had a reputation as a "well-liked, bon vivant, jovial, and urbane" man, and by 1761 he had become "one of colonial New York's premier innkeepers." Fraunces's service to Washington and to the country was steady and generous, as was that of his family. His daughter Phoebe even foiled an extremely well-planned plot concocted by the British general Tryon and implemented by an enterprising Irish man named Thomas Hickey. Tragically, Fraunces was and still is relegated to an unmarked grave in the downtown Philadelphia St. Peter's Cemetery. For more information about Fraunces, his interactions with and letters from George Washington, and the Queen's Head Tavern, see Blockson, "Black Samuel Fraunces"; Marvin and Lowenthal, *This Was New York*; Earle, *Stage-Coach and Tavern Days*; Walker, *Encyclopedia of African American Business History*; Dunshee, *As You Pass By*; Fitzpatrick, *The Writings of George Washington from the Original Manuscript Sources*; and Little, *George Washington*.

32. Albion and Pope, *Rise of New York Port*, 280.

33. Geisst, *Wall Street: A History*, 109. In 1882, eighty-five New York City buildings that had been wired to use electrical lights were illuminated with power generated by the city's first central station, located on Pearl Street (Kirkland, *A History of American Economic Life*, 393).

34. Silverberg, *Light for the World*, 172.

35. For more information about Edison and particularly the work that he completed and

oversaw from the Pearl Street location in New York City, see Dyer and Martin, *Edison*; and Silverberg, *Light for the World*.

36. "Say He Hired Acid Throwers," 12.

37. "Telegraph to Move Nov. 15.," 19; "Bankruptcy Notices," 14.

38. McMurry, *To Keep the Waters Troubled*, 111.

39. Ibid.

40. Hopkins to William Monroe Trotter, 16 April 1905, 7, Hopkins Papers.

41. Ibid., 8.

42. Hopkins to J. Max Barber, 18 April 1905, 1, Du Bois Papers.

43. Nathaniel Dodson to *Voice of the Negro*, 22 April 1905, 1, Du Bois Papers.

44. Ibid.

45. Hopkins to J. Max Barber, 18 April 1905, 2, Du Bois Papers.

46. Ibid.

47. Austin N. Jenkins to Emmett Jay Scott, 5 August 1904, in Harlan, Smock, and McTigue, *BTW Papers*, 8:39 (emphasis in original).

48. Booker T. Washington to Doubleday, Page and Company, 9 August 1904, in ibid., 43.

49. Meier, "Booker T. Washington and the Negro Press," 70.

50. Emmett Jay Scott to Austin N. Jenkins, 9 August 1904, in Harlan, Smock, and McTigue, *BTW Papers*, 8:44.

51. Booker T. Washington to Emmett Jay Scott, 9 August 1904, in ibid., 41.

52. "Publisher's Announcements," *Colored American Magazine* (September 1904): 606. A number of Washington scholars have concluded that the Tuskegee president closely scrutinized the African American press and that he did in fact purchase the *Colored American Magazine*. Louis Harlan and Raymond Smock note that in 1904 Washington "bought the Boston-based *Colored American Magazine* and made Moore editor" (Harlan, Smock, and Kraft, *BTW Papers*, 5:18–19). August Meier, in his study of Washington's subsidies of the African American press in general and of the *Colored American Magazine* in particular, indicates that the magazine was one of "at least five or six periodicals which Washington aided by sustained cash contributions," and he also concludes that Washington "partly owned" the New York *Age* and the *Colored American Magazine* (Meier, "Booker T. Washington and the Negro Press," 68).

53. T. Thomas Fortune to Frederick Moore, 25 May 1904, in *Colored American Magazine* (June 1904): 454.

54. Booker T. Washington to Roscoe Conkling Simmons, 13 May 1905, in Harlan, Smock, and McTigue, *BTW Papers*, 8:276.

55. "Publisher's Announcements," *Colored American Magazine* (November 1904).

56. Margaret Murray Washington also served as director of the Girls Institute at Tuskegee and was president of the National Federation of Afro-American Women. See Thompson, "Washington, Margaret Murray."

57. By 1906, Simmons was editor of the African American weekly paper, *National Review*. A diehard Republican, he at one point in his career was reported as saying that he would "rather vote for a dog on the Republican ticket than the best Democrat who ever lived" and that "any black man who votes for a Democrat is placing a curse on the soul of Abraham Lincoln" (Keneally, "Republicans during the New Deal," 123). He became known to many as "the Colonel," ran unsuccessfully for Congress in 1932, and became a "social chameleon" who was "on familiar terms with black America's most powerful businessmen and editors, entertainers and mobsters, but equally comfortable among the working men and women

with whom he gossiped in barber shops and at church picnics" (Kaye, "Colonel Roscoe Conkling Simmons"). See also Moon, *Balance of Power*.

58. Hopkins to Trotter, 16 April 1905, 10, Hopkins Papers.

59. Ibid., 9.

60. Ibid., 10.

61. Ibid.

CHAPTER SEVENTEEN

1. Pickens, "Jesse Max Barber," 485.

2. Ibid. Pickens, a distinguished graduate of several schools, including Fisk, Yale, and Wiley, was a professor of foreign languages, chair of the Greek and sociology departments, and active member and officer of the NAACP. Hopkins, writing under the pseudonym of J. Shirley Shadrach, published "William Pickens, Yale University," in the July 1903 *Colored American Magazine*. She sought to ameliorate the "unpopular opinions" that Pickens had advanced in some musings about African American suffrage and about the need to abandon black governance in Haiti in his prizewinning Ten Eyck oration. Writings by and about Pickens include Andrews, *Bursting Bonds*; and Hughes, "Hate Only Hate, Fear Only Cowardice."

3. Eighth Census of the United States, 1880, South Carolina, Chester County, Blackstock, Roll T9, 115.

4. Pickens, "Jesse Max Barber," 485.

5. Ibid.

6. Anderson, *Education of Blacks in the South*, 70.

7. Pickens, "Jesse Max Barber," 485.

8. Ibid.

9. Ibid., 486.

10. Shadrach, "William Pickens, Yale University," 517.

11. Booker T. Washington to John Hopkins, 2 November 1903, cited in Harlan, "Booker T. Washington and the *Voice of the Negro*," 46.

12. Booker T. Washington to Emmett Jay Scott, 4 November 1903, in Harlan and Smock, *BTW Papers*, 7:328–29.

13. Lewis, *W. E. B. Du Bois*, 63.

14. For more information about the First Congregational Church and Proctor's influential ministry, see the church website, <http://www.1stchurchatlanta.com/history.html>, January 2006.

15. Lewis, *W. E. B. Du Bois*, 75.

16. Gaines, *Uplifting the Race*, 60. Gaines also notes that Proctor worked to prevent African American disenfranchisement in Georgia.

17. Editorial, *Voice of the Negro*, January 1904, 33.

18. Harlan, "Booker T. Washington and the *Voice of the Negro*," 48.

19. Emmett Scott to Hertel, Jenkins and Company, 4 August 1904, cited in ibid., 49.

20. Jesse Max Barber to Philip A. Payton, 5 January 1905, cited in ibid., 51.

21. Emmett Scott to Wilford H. Smith, 25 January 1905, cited in ibid.

22. Advertisement, *Voice of the Negro*, January 1904, 2.

23. Ibid., November 1904.

24. Ibid.

25. Toll, *Resurgence of Race*, 133, 123.

26. Advertisement, *Voice of the Negro*, November 1904.

27. Kevin Gaines has characterized the *Voice of the Negro* as "the voice of Atlanta's black leadership" (*Uplifting the Race*, 60).

28. "Voice of the Negro for 1905."

29. In *Uplifting the Race*, Gaines provides an insightful analysis of Barber's journalistic work and politics. Gaines puts the circulation of the *Voice of the Negro* at a high of 15,000 issues in 1906. That number represented a 500 percent increase from the 3,000 subscribers that the magazine obtained in its first year of publication. Gaines also notes that the *Voice of the Negro* had great appeal to other publications, and it became a valuable resource for "the press of both races" (60).

30. "Voice of the Negro for 1905."

31. For more information about Mary Church Terrell, see her autobiography, *Colored Woman in a White World*; Jones, "Mary Church Terrell"; Jones, *Quest for Equality*; and Aptheker, *Woman's Legacy*. For more information about Fannie Barrier Williams, see Hedricks, "Fannie Barrier Williams."

32. "Voice of the Negro for 1905."

33. Hopkins to J. Max Barber, 18 April 1905, 1, Du Bois Papers.

34. "Voice of the Negro for 1905."

35. Ibid.

36. "Inside with the Editor," *Voice of the Negro* (October 1905): n.p.

37. Floyd, who was born in 1869 and passed away in 1923, wrote the *Voice of the Negro*'s highly popular "Wayside" column. In 1920, former *Voice of the Negro* publisher Austin Jenkins published Floyd's *Short Stories for Colored People Both Old and Young*, a volume that also included an African American etiquette manual entitled *National Capitol Code of Etiquette*, by Edward S. Green. For more information about Silas Xavier Floyd, see the notes about him that preface his 1902 biography, *Life of Charles T. Walker, D.D., "The Black Spurgeon," Pastor, Mt. Olivet Baptist Church, New York City* (Nashville: National Baptist Publishing Board, 1902).

38. Hopkins, "New York Subway," 605.

39. Ibid., 608.

40. Ibid.

41. Emerson, "Address Delivered in Concord."

42. Some editorial confusion and mislabeling of the final article suggested that there were six articles in the series, but Hopkins only published five pieces. The June 1905 essay, "Part IV: Africa," is followed in July 1905 by one numbered and titled "VI: The North American Indian.—Conclusion."

43. Hopkins, "Dark Races of the Twentieth Century. VI: The North American Indian.—Conclusion," 461.

44. There are few extant copies of Barber's *Negro of the Earlier World*. It is part of the Charles Henry Boone Papers, held at the Tennessee State Library in Nashville. Boone (1870–1953) was an AME minister and teacher who worked throughout the Midwest and in the Upper South.

45. Barber, *Negro of the Earlier World*, cited in Gaines, *Uplifting the Race*, 109.

46. Ibid.

47. Hopkins, "Dark Races of the Twentieth Century. I: Oceanica," 108.

48. Ibid.

49. Shakespeare, *Merchant of Venice*, act II, 1, ll. 1–2.

50. For biographies and assessments of Ira Aldridge, see Hill, *Shakespeare in Sable*; Lind-

fors, "Nothing Extenuate, Nor Set Down Aught in Malice"; Lindfors, "Mislike Me Not for My Complexion"; Shalom, "The Ira Aldridge Troupe"; Dewberry, "The African Grove Theatre and Company"; and Warner, "A Soliloquy 'Lately Spoken at the African Theatre.'"

51. Hopkins, "Dark Races of the Twentieth Century. I: Oceanica," 108.

52. For more information about Delany, see Levine, *Martin Delany, Frederick Douglass, and the Politics of Representative Identity.*

53. Hopkins, "Dark Races of the Twentieth Century. I: Oceanica," 108.

54. Ibid., 109. In his essay, "Black Americans' Racial Uplift Ideology," Gaines also discusses Hopkins's "staunchly religious worldview" and its manifestations in her *Voice of the Negro* writings.

55. Hopkins, "Dark Races of the Twentieth Century. I: Oceanica."

56. Ibid., 110.

57. Ibid., 111.

58. Ibid., 113.

59. Hopkins, "Dark Races of the Twentieth Century. II: The Malay Peninsula," 188.

60. Hopkins, "Dark Races of the Twentieth Century. VI: The North American Indian.—Conclusion," 459.

61. Hopkins, "Dark Races of the Twentieth Century. IV: Africa," 415.

62. Ibid.

63. Gaines, "Black Americans' Racial Uplift Ideology," 444.

64. Reed, *Negritos of Zambales.*

65. Martin, *Thomas Jefferson: Scientist*, 132, 131; Hopkins, "Dark Races of the Twentieth Century. II: The Malay Peninsula," 191. For more information about Buffon, see works such as Mayr, *Growth of Biological Thought*; and Benjamin, *A Question of Identity.*

66. Fiske, *The Unseen World*, 59.

67. Ibid.

68. Hopkins, "Dark Races of the Twentieth Century. II: The Malay Peninsula," 191.

69. Gilbert, *Selected Writings of John Edward Bruce*, 23, 24.

70. Esedebe, *Pan-Africanism*, 21, 22.

71. Hopkins, "The Dark Races of the Twentieth Century. IV: Africa," 462, 463.

72. Hopkins, "The Dark Races of the Twentieth Century. VI: The North American Indian.—Conclusion," 460.

73. Ibid., 461.

74. Ibid., 463.

75. Ibid.

76. Boamah-Wiafe, "Dr. James Emman Kwegyir Aggrey of Achimota," 182. Aggrey, who was born in 1875, died suddenly in 1927 when he was struck down by pneumococcus meningitis while in New York City. He had been scheduled to lecture at Columbia University and to help raise funds for his alma mater, Livingstone College. For more information about Aggrey, his family, his work as an educator, his friendship with prominent African Americans such as John E. Bruce, and his efforts with the Phelps-Stokes Foundation and American Baptist Foreign Missionary Society, see Smith, *Aggrey of Africa*; Jacobs, "James Emman Kwegyir Aggrey"; King, "James E. K. Aggrey"; Frederickson, *Black Liberation*; and Boamah-Wiafe, "Dr. James Emman Kwegyir Aggrey of Achimota."

77. Jacobs, "James Emman Kwegyir Aggrey," 47.

78. Boamah-Wiafe, "Dr. James Emman Kwegyir Aggrey of Achimota," 184.

79. Lewis, *W. E. B. Du Bois*, 417. Lewis refers to Aggrey as a student at Livingstone College in 1913, the year in which Aggrey "sent a worshipful letter . . . begging Du Bois to

take him on as a summer intern at *The Crisis* (though this appears not to have occurred)" (417). According to Boamah-Wiafe, Aggrey graduated from Livingstone College in 1902 and completed his master's degree there in 1912.

80. Jacobs, "James Emman Kwegyir Aggrey," 47.

81. Hopkins to Barber, 18 April 1905, 2, Du Bois Papers.

82. Johnson and Johnson, *Propaganda and Aesthetics*, 17.

83. Garrison, "Announcement," 1.

84. Hopkins to Barber, 18 April 1905, 1, Du Bois Papers.

85. Ibid.

86. Ibid., 1–2.

87. Ibid., 2.

88. Barber to Du Bois, 27 April 1905, 1, 2, Du Bois Papers. Although Barber encouraged Du Bois to be in touch with Villard, it was not likely that Du Bois would follow that route. He and the descendant of William Lloyd Garrison, who insisted that Du Bois provided him with evidence of these acts, had been in a heated tussle that concluded with Du Bois issuing a response that biographer David Levering Lewis characterizes as "tantamount to a rebuke" (Lewis, *W. E. B. Du Bois*, 315).

89. Toll, *Resurgence of Race*, 124.

90. William Toll proposes that the Du Bois essay offered a major boost to Barber and the *Voice*, as it "not only reiterated Du Bois's criticism of Washington as stated in *The Souls of Black Folk*, but also showed how effectively Barber and Bowen had resisted Washington's designs on their journal" (ibid., 124).

CHAPTER EIGHTEEN

1. *Alexander's Magazine*, 15 August 1905, 42.

2. *Boston Globe*, 31 May 1905.

3. *Alexander's Magazine*, 15 August 1905, 21–26.

4. *Journal of Negro History*, 1922. See citation for Concord Baptist Church. Unfortunately, the text of Hopkins's Dorcas Society lecture is not part of the Fisk collection of her papers, and it does not appear to have been reprinted in any other contemporary sources.

5. Taylor, *Black Churches of Brooklyn*, 173–74.

6. Bordin, *Frances Willard*, 71.

7. *History of Black Baptist Women*.

8. Pauline Allen, "The Evils of Intemperance and Their Remedies," 1, ca. 1870s, Hopkins Papers.

9. *Alexander's Magazine*, 15 July 1905, 21.

10. Toll, *Resurgence of Race*, 122.

11. Ibid., 99.

12. Ibid., 128.

13. *The Guardian*, 16 December 1905, 1.

14. Booker T. Washington to Editor of the *New York Times*, *New York Times*, 16 October 1905, 7.

15. The *New York Times* lead article on the city's Garrison anniversary events, "Negroes Honor Memory of William L. Garrison," was relegated to page 8. In New York at the Bethel Methodist Episcopal Church, Washington used the occasion to insist that "[i]t is for us of the black race to show in our daily life and conduct that we are a people worthy of the birthright of American citizenship."

16. "Tribute at Cooper Union."

17. Harlan and Smock, *BTW Papers*, 12:12.

18. For more information about Cuney Hare, see Grider and Rodenberger, *Texas Women Writers*.

19. Dorman, *Twenty Families of Color in Massachusetts*, 409–10.

20. Brown, *Homespun Heroines*, 183.

21. Just two years before, on 30 July 1903, Maude had been shoulder to shoulder with her brother William and 2,000 others who gathered both to hear and to protest Booker T. Washington's speech at the AME Zion Church on Columbus Avenue in Boston. Maude became part of the spirited melee and was arrested on charges that she had used her hat pin to stab one of the eleven police officers on duty at the event. See Harlan, *Booker T. Washington*, 44.

22. Daniels, *In Freedom's Birthplace*, 456. Imani Perry cites the installation of an African American Heritage Trail marker at 30 Parker Street in Cambridge, Morris's former home. Perry gives Morris's occupations as "druggist, porter, and stationary steam engineer." Although he had no college education, Morris "amassed an anti-slavery library so impressive that Harvard professors reportedly sent their students to research his collection. He was both an everyman and an intellectual," Perry concludes. See Perry, "There Goes the Neighborhood."

23. "Son of Garrison Speaks at Smith Court Church."

24. Hopkins, "Elijah William Smith," 96.

25. "Son of Garrison Speaks at Smith Court Church."

26. Ibid.

27. "Greater Boston's Two Days' Garrison Centennial."

28. "Son of Garrison Speaks at Smith Court Church."

29. Ibid.

30. Ibid.

31. "Several Hundred Brave Storm at Statue."

32. Ibid.

33. Hopkins, *Contending Forces*, 129.

34. "Touching Service by Colored Women at Homestead," 1.

35. The death certificate for William Hopkins indicates that his physician, George A. Miles, had his office at 249 Elm Street in West Somerville.

36. *The Guardian*, 14 January 1911, 4.

37. Brown and Tager, *Massachusetts*, 252.

38. As early as 1914, the *Cambridge City Directory* corroborated Hopkins's efforts, listing her now as "Hopkins, Pauline E. stenographer, bds. 53 Clifton," just above the entry that informed the public about Sarah's death: "Hopkins, Sarah A. (53 Clifton) died Sept. 24, 1913." See *Cambridge City Directory*, 1914.

CHAPTER NINETEEN

1. Harlan, *Booker T. Washington*, 454.

2. *Announcement and Prospectus of the New Era Magazine*, 1.

3. The *Messenger*, launched in 1917, became the official publication of the Brotherhood of Sleeping Car Porters, the nation's first African American union and an organization that prevailed in spite of fierce opposition from employers such as the Pullman Company and objections within the race, namely from Booker T. Washington and his supporters. For

additional information about the *Messenger* and its editors, see Kornweibel, *No Crystal Stair*; and Kersten, *A. Philip Randolph*.

4. W. E. B. Du Bois, "Editorial," *Crisis* 5 (November 1912): 28, cited in Johnson and Johnson, *Propaganda and Aesthetics*, 31.

5. Advertisement, *New Era Magazine* (April 1916): n.p.

6. Hopkins to J. Max Barber, 18 April 1905, 2, Du Bois Papers.

7. "Editorial and Publisher's Announcements," *New Era Magazine* (April 1916): 124.

8. Ibid.

9. Ibid.

10. Ibid.

11. *Announcement and Prospectus of the New Era Magazine*, 1 (emphasis in original).

12. Despite James Blackwell's darker coloring and pronounced African ancestry, the Fourteenth Census of the United States, 1920, Massachusetts, listed him as white. The entire Blackwell family experienced this racial transformation in the 1920 census, one that suggests the unreliability of the reporting on occasion. Both James and his wife, Mazie, now were listed as white; the information about their parentage and James's occupation as a hotel waiter confirms that the 1920 entry is for the same individual given as mulatto in the 1910 census. By 1920, the Blackwells had relocated to 52 Forest Street in Boston, and the family had grown to include two more children: Charlotte, age three years, and James H. Jr., age three months.

13. Fourteenth Census of the United States, 1920, Massachusetts, City of Cambridge, Ward 7, Middlesex County, Mass., Roll T625, 2B. The census entries for the Cromwells identified them both as mulattos. Gertrude was born in Massachusetts to parents from Canada; her fifty-nine-year-old husband, William, was born in Wisconsin to a New York–born father and English mother. He worked as a banker at State Capitol in Boston.

14. *Announcement and Prospectus of the New Era Magazine*, 1.

15. Ibid.

16. *New Era Magazine* (February 1916): 5.

17. Prospectus, *New Era Magazine*, 2.

18. Ibid.

19. Lewis, *Trader Horn*, 25. Wolo's Liberian home was on the Atlantic coast approximately 200 miles south of the capital city of Monrovia. In 1916, he was living a world away from the "Boys of Grand Cess," whom explorer Alfred Aloysius Horn had deemed "the finest body of men I ever saw in any country, muscular and well-built and splendid workers" (ibid.). Wolo, who served in the cabinet of President Edwin Barclay during the 1930s, met Charles S. Johnson, Fisk University professor and former *Opportunity* editor, when Johnson came to Liberia on behalf of the League of Nations to investigate claims that "the country was an object of propaganda" (Young, *Liberia Rediscovered*, 75). Unfortunately, Johnson regarded Wolo as an obstruction to his mission, which ultimately found that Liberian natives "as a whole have no voice in the Government" and that many "captives taken in wars between tribes made up a numerous group held in bondage" that constituted modern-day enslavement (ibid.). Johnson characterized Wolo as "an overrated Harvard product," who possessed "intelligence but lack[ed] energy" ("Seasons in Hell," 197–98). The lofty prose of Wolo's debut article, "The 'Colored' Peoples and the War," published in the second volume of the *New Era Magazine*, hints at the characteristics that so maddened Johnson.

20. Dunn, "The Challenge of Our National Purpose and Agenda," 1.

21. Pérez e Gonzìlez, *Puerto Ricans in the United States*, 30.

22. Garcia, "Dr. Pedro Albizu Campos," 1. When Campos returned from fighting in

World War I, he began graduate studies in law at Harvard and resumed his connection with the Cosmopolitan Club. In 1930, the year that Pauline Hopkins died, Campos was elected president of the Puerto Rican Nationalist Party and began a fearless career of exposing white American predation on Puerto Rican nationals and maintaining the illegality of American claims on the island. He was jailed several times and served more than twenty-five years in prison. During that time, he was subjected to illegal medical experiments, including trials that exposed him to radiation. Campos died in 1965, more than a decade after his last and highly tumultuous confrontation with police. For more information about Campos, see Natal, *Pedro Albizu Campos*; Schultz et al., *Encyclopedia of Minorities in American Politics*; Correa, *The Shadow of Don Pedro*; Aoki, Haynie, and McCulloch, *Encyclopedia of Minorities*, 416; Poitevin, "Political Surveillance, State Repression," 89–100; and Pérez e Gonzìlez, *Puerto Ricans in the United States.*

23. Aldrich, *Crowding Memories*, 49.

24. In December 1862, Phoebe Garnaut married George Washington Smalley, a Civil War army correspondent, *New York Tribune* reporter, and, later, reporter on staff at the London *Times*, who came to be regarded by many as America's leading foreign correspondent. Wendell Phillips was instrumental in arranging Smalley's employment at the *Tribune*, the newspaper in which Smalley would publish his acclaimed Civil War reports. The couple had five children together before they separated in 1898. Garnaut passed away in 1923. For more information about Phoebe Garnaut Phillips Smalley, see Sherwin, *Prophet of Liberty*; and Bartlett, *Wendell Phillips, Brahmin Radical*. For details about Smalley and his career, see Aldrich, *Crowding Memories*; and Slide, *Lois Weber*.

25. "Abraham Lincoln," 7.

26. "Lincoln's Rules for Living," 6.

27. Hopkins, "Men of Vision. I: Mark Réne De Mortie," 35.

28. Ibid.

29. Ibid.

30. Ibid., 37.

31. Ibid., 38.

32. Ibid.

33. Ibid., 35.

34. Ibid., 37.

35. Ibid.

36. Ibid.

37. Ibid., 35.

38. Pendleton, *Narrative of the Negro*, 171.

39. *Announcement and the Prospectus of the New Era Magazine*, 6.

40. Ibid.

41. Ibid.

42. Gardiner, "Reminiscences of Early Days," 49.

43. Ibid.

44. "The Bosfield Case," 120.

45. Ibid., 119.

46. Ibid., 120.

47. "Question of Segregation," 90.

48. Prospectus, *New Era Magazine*, 2.

49. Ibid.

50. "Announcement," *New Era Magazine* (April 1916): 127.

CHAPTER TWENTY

1. Fourteenth Census of the United States, 1920, Massachusetts, Middlesex County, City of Cambridge, Mass., Roll T625, 7A. Maria Carter also is included in Cambridge city directories and listed in the 1913 and 1923 editions as living at 19 Jay Street, Cambridge.

2. *Cambridge City Directory*, 1922; *Cambridge City Directory*, 1923, 531.

3. Brown and Tager, *Massachusetts*, 258.

4. Tager, *Boston Riots*, 244.

5. Jordan, *Black Newspapers and America's War for Democracy*, 52.

6. Mitchell, "The Paul Family," 76–77.

7. Twelfth Census of the United States, 1900, Massachusetts, Middlesex County, City of Cambridge, Mass., Ward 5, Roll T623, 8B.

8. Mitchell, "The Paul Family," 76; "First Baptist Church of Norfolk."

9. The Massachusetts census and the Cambridge city directories have different spellings of the name of Florence Walker's younger relative. In the Fourteenth Census of the United States, 1920, Massachusetts, Walker's name is spelled "Isabel"; in the 1923 *Cambridge City Directory*, she is identified as "Isabelle" (810).

10. "Aged Writer Dies of Painful Burns," *Chicago Defender*, 23 August 1930, 1. Some thirteen years after his heroic response to Pauline Hopkins, Malcolm Coley was working as a marine fireman and file clerk. He became part of the massive African American enlistment for World War II when he enlisted in Boston on 15 September 1943. His military record confirms that his enlistment was for "the duration of the War or other emergency, plus six months, subject to the discretion of the President or otherwise according to law" (World War II Army Enlistment Records, 1938–46, National Archives and Records Administration, College Park, Md.).

11. The 1920 Massachusetts census reveals that the Coley family was headed by fifty-two-year-old Richard, a porter at an electronics factory, and his fifty-year-old wife, Beadie, whom the census reported as working at home. The Coleys were living on Western Avenue in Cambridge with their three daughters and three sons, as well as their son-in-law James Cole and granddaughter Frances (Cambridge, Ward 7, Middlesex, Massachusetts, Roll T625, 8B).

12. Pauline E. Hopkins, Record of Death, City of Cambridge.

13. Lowery and Marszalek, *Encyclopedia of African-American Civil Rights*, 98.

14. "Burns Fatal to Aged Writer," *Baltimore Afro-American*, 23 August 1930, 19.

15. "East."

16. Ibid.

17. "Pauline Hopkins," 8 September 1930, Middlesex County Probate Records, Suffolk County Court House, Cambridge, Mass.

18. Record Book 1139, Case number 179889, 370, Middlesex County Probate Records, Suffolk County Court House, Cambridge, Mass.

19. "Pauline Hopkins," 8 September 1930, Middlesex County Probate Records, Suffolk County Court House, Cambridge, Mass.

20. "Pauline E. N. Hopkins," Schedule A, Middlesex County Probate Records, Suffolk County Court House, Cambridge, Mass.

21. Ibid.

22. Ibid.

23. *Cambridge City Directory*, 1931.

24. "Colored Woman Makes Chief Address."

Bibliography

ARCHIVAL SOURCES

Amherst, Mass.
  Special Collections, Du Bois Library, University of Massachusetts
    W. E. B. Du Bois Papers
Boston, Mass.
  Massachusetts State Archives
    Judicial Archives
  Special Collections, Mugar Library, Boston University
    Guardian of Boston Collection
Cambridge, Mass.
  Schlesinger Library, Radcliffe College
    Girls' High School Association Papers
College Park, Md.
  National Archives and Records Administration
    Civil War Pension Records
    World War II Army Enlistment Records, 1938–46, Record Group 64
Exeter, N.H.
  Exeter Historical Society
    Exeter Historical Society Files, Nancy Merrill, comp.
Iowa City, Iowa
  University of Iowa Library
    Records of the Redpath Chautauqua Collection
Nashville, Tennessee
  Franklin Library Special Collections, Fisk University
    Pauline Hopkins Papers
  Tennessee State Library
    Charles Henry Boone Papers
New York, N.Y.
  Schomburg Center for Research in Black Culture, The New York Public Library
    John E. Bruce Papers
Washington, D.C.
  Moorland-Spingarn Research Center, Howard University
    George L. Ruffin Collection and Ruffin Family Papers
Wilberforce, Ohio
  Carnegie Library, Wilberforce University
    Benjamin William Arnett Papers

GOVERNMENT DOCUMENTS

First Census of the United States, 1790: New Hampshire
Third Census of the United States, 1830: Massachusetts
Sixth Census of the United States, 1840: Massachusetts

Seventh Census of the United States, 1850: Massachusetts
Seventh Census of the United States, 1850: Rhode Island
1855 State Census, Massachusetts: City of Charlestown, Mass.
Eighth Census of the United States, 1860: Rhode Island
1865 State Census, Massachusetts: City of Charlestown, Mass.
Ninth Census of the United States, 1870: Massachusetts
Ninth Census of the United States, 1870: New York
Ninth Census of the United States, 1870: Virginia
Tenth Census of the United States, 1880: South Carolina
Special Schedules of the Eleventh Census Enumerating Union Veterans and Widows of Union Veterans of the Civil War, 1890: Rhode Island
Twelfth Census of the United States, 1900: Massachusetts
Twelfth Census of the United States, 1900: New York
Twelfth Census of the United States, 1900: Virginia
Thirteenth Census of the United States, 1910: New York
Fourteenth Census of the United States, 1920: Maine
Fourteenth Census of the United States, 1920: Massachusetts
Fourteenth Census of the United States, 1920: New York
Grants of Suffolk County, Massachusetts
Middlesex County Probate Records, Suffolk County Court House, Cambridge, Mass.
Office of the City Clerk, Cambridge, Mass.
Official Records of the Union and Confederate Navies in the War of the Rebellion. Edited by Richard Rush and Robert H. Woods. Washington, D.C.: Government Printing Office, 1896.

ANNUAL REPORTS AND MINUTES

Annual Report: Massachusetts Anti-Slavery Society. Vols. 1–10, 1833–42. Westport, Conn.: Negro Universities Press, 1970.
New England Anti-Slavery Society. *First Annual Report, 1833.*
———. *Annual Report: Massachusetts Anti-Slavery Society.* Vols. 1–10, *1833–1842.* Westport, Conn.: Negro Universities Press, 1970.
———. *Appendix of Second Annual Report.*

CITY DIRECTORIES

Boston Almanac and Business Directory. 1893.
Boston City Directory. 1813, 1816, 1830, 1846, 1860, 1865, 1870, 1872, 1875, 1876, 1877, 1880, 1881, 1882, 1885, 1889, 1891.
Boston Social Register. 1906.
Cambridge City Directory. 1914, 1922, 1923, 1931.
Providence City Directory. 1832, 1836, 1838, 1841, 1844, 1850, 1852–53.

NEWSPAPERS AND PERIODICALS

Alexander's Magazine. Boston, Mass.
American Baptist Magazine, and Missionary Intelligencer. Boston, Mass. American Antiquarian Society, Worcester, Mass.
Anglo-African. New York, N.Y.

Baltimore Afro-American

Bay State Monthly: A Massachusetts Magazine. Boston, Mass.

Boston Courier

Boston Globe

Boston Herald

Boston Saturday Evening Gazette

Brooklyn Daily Standard Union

Carolina Spartan. Spartanburg, S.C.

Chicago Defender

Colored American Magazine. Boston, Mass.

Frederick Douglass' Paper. Rochester, N.Y.

Genius of Universal Emancipation. New York, N.Y.

The Guardian. Boston, Mass.

The Liberator. Boston, Mass.

Milwaukee Sentinel

Minneapolis Sentinel

Minneapolis Tribune

New Era Magazine. Boston, Mass. Moorland-Spingarn Research Center, Howard
    University, Washington, D.C.

New Hampshire Gazette. Portsmouth, N.H.

New National Era. Washington, D.C.

New York Times

The North Star. Rochester, N.Y.

Richmond Planet

WORKS BY PAULINE HOPKINS

Allen, Sarah A. (pseudonym). "Converting Fanny." *New Era Magazine* (February 1916):
    33–34.

———. *Hagar's Daughter: A Story of Southern Caste Prejudice. Colored American
    Magazine* (March 1901–March 1902).

———. "Latest Phases of the Race Problem in America." *Colored American Magazine*
    (February 1903): 244–51.

———. "Mr. Alan Kirkland Soga." *Colored American Magazine* (February 1904): 114–16.

———. "Mr. M. Hamilton Hodges." *Colored American Magazine* (March 1904): 167–69.

———. "A New Profession: The First Colored Graduate of the Y.M.C.A. Training
    School, Springfield, Mass." *Colored American Magazine* (September 1903): 661–63.

———. "The Test of Manhood: A Christmas Story." *Colored American Magazine*
    (December 1902): 113–19.

Hopkins, Pauline. "As the Lord Lives, He Is One of Our Mother's Children." *Colored
    American Magazine* (November 1903): 795–801.

———. "Bra's Abram Jim Son's Wedding: A Christmas Story." *Colored American
    Magazine* (December 1901): 103–12.

———. "Charles Sumner Centenary Speech." In *The Two Days of Observance of the One
    Hundredth Anniversary of the Birth of Charles Sumner*, edited by William Monroe
    Trotter, 48–49. Boston: Boston Sumner Centenary Committee of the New England
    Suffrage League and the Massachusetts Branch of the National Independent Political
    League, 1911.

————. *Contending Forces: A Romance Illustrative of Negro Life North and South*. Boston: Colored Co-operative Publishing Company, 1900.

————. "The Dark Races of the Twentieth Century. I: Oceanica: The Dark-Hued Inhabitants of New Guinea, the Bismarck Archipelago, New Hebrides, Solomon Islands, Fiji Islands, Polynesia, Samoa, and Hawaii." *Voice of the Negro* (February 1905): 108–15.

————. "The Dark Races of the Twentieth Century. II: The Malay Peninsula: Borneo, Java, Sumatra, and the Philippines." *Voice of the Negro* (March 1905): 187–91.

————. "The Dark Races of the Twentieth Century. III: The Yellow Race: Siam, China, Japan, Korea, Thibet." *Voice of the Negro* (May 1905): 330–35.

————. "The Dark Races of the Twentieth Century. IV: Africa: Abyssinians, Egyptians, Nilotic Class, Berbers, Kaffirs, Hottentots, Africans of Northern Tropics (including Negroes of Central, Eastern, and Western Africa), Negroes of the United States." *Voice of the Negro* (June 1905): 415–18.

————. "The Dark Races of the Twentieth Century. VI: The North American Indian— Conclusion." *Voice of the Negro* (July 1905): 459–63.

————. "A Dash for Liberty." *Colored American Magazine* (August 1901): 243–47.

————. "Echoes from the Annual Convention of Northeastern Federation of Colored Women's Clubs." *Colored American Magazine* (October 1903): 709–13.

————. "Elijah William Smith: A Poet of Early Days." *Colored American Magazine* (December 1902): 96–100.

————. "Famous Men of the Negro Race. I: Toussaint L'Ouverture." *Colored American Magazine* (November 1900): 9–24.

————. "Famous Men of the Negro Race. II: Hon. Frederick Douglass." *Colored American Magazine* (December 1900): 121–32.

————. "Famous Men of the Negro Race. III: William Wells Brown." *Colored American Magazine* (January 1901): 232–36.

————. "Famous Men of the Negro Race. IV: Robert Browne Elliott." *Colored American Magazine* (February 1901): 294–301.

————. "Famous Men of the Negro Race. V: Edwin Garrison Walker." *Colored American Magazine* (March 1901): 358–66.

————. "Famous Men of the Negro Race. VI: Lewis Hayden." *Colored American Magazine* (April 1901): 473–77.

————. "Famous Men of the Negro Race. VII: Charles Lenox Remond." *Colored American Magazine* (May 1901): 34–39.

————. "Famous Men of the Negro Race. VIII: Sergeant William H. Carney." *Colored American Magazine* (June 1901): 84–89.

————. "Famous Men of the Negro Race. IX: John Mercer Langston." *Colored American Magazine* (July 1901): 177–84.

————. "Famous Men of the Negro Race. X: Senator Blanche K. Bruce." *Colored American Magazine* (August 1901): 257–61.

————. "Famous Men of the Negro Race. XI: Robert Morris." *Colored American Magazine* (September 1901): 337–42.

————. "Famous Men of the Negro Race. XII: Booker T. Washington." *Colored American Magazine* (October 1901): 436–42.

————. "Famous Women of the Negro Race. I: Phenomenal Vocalists." *Colored American Magazine* (November 1901): 45–53.

———. "Famous Women of the Negro Race. II: Sojourner Truth." *Colored American Magazine* (December 1901): 124-32.

———. "Famous Women of the Negro Race. III: Harriet Tubman ('Moses')." *Colored American Magazine* (January-February 1902): 210-23.

———. "Famous Women of the Negro Race. IV: Some Literary Workers." *Colored American Magazine* (March 1902): 276-80.

———. "Famous Women of the Negro Race. V: Literary Workers." *Colored American Magazine* (April 1902): 366-71.

———. "Famous Women of the Negro Race. VI: Educators." *Colored American Magazine* (May 1902): 41-46.

———. "Famous Women of the Negro Race. VII: Educators (Continued)." *Colored American Magazine* (June 1902): 125-30.

———. "Famous Women of the Negro Race. VIII: Educators (Concluded)." *Colored American Magazine* (July 1902): 206-13.

———. "Famous Women of the Negro Race. IX: Club Life among Colored Women." *Colored American Magazine* (August 1902): 273-77.

———. "Famous Women of the Negro Race. X: Artists." *Colored American Magazine* (September 1902): 362-67.

———. "Famous Women of the Negro Race. XII: Higher Education of Colored Women in White Schools and Colleges." *Colored American Magazine* (October 1902): 445-50.

———. "General Washington: A Christmas Story." *Colored American Magazine* (December 1900): 95-104.

———. "Heroes and Heroines in Black. I: Neil Johnson, America Woodfolk, Robert Small, et al." *Colored American Magazine* (January 1903): 206-11.

———. "How a New York Newspaper Man Entertained a Number of Colored Ladies and Gentlemen at Dinner in the Revere House, Boston, and How the Colored American League Was Started." *Colored American Magazine* (March 1904): 151-60.

———. "Men of Vision. I: Mark Réne De Mortie." *New Era Magazine* (February 1916): 35-39.

———. "Men of Vision. II: Rev. Leonard A. Grimes." *New Era Magazine* (March 1916): 99-105.

———. "Munroe Rogers." *Colored American Magazine* (November 1902): 20-26.

———. "The Mystery within Us." *Colored American Magazine* (May 1900): 14-18.

———. "The New York Subway." *Voice of the Negro* (December 1904): 605, 608-12.

———. *Of One Blood; or, The Hidden Self.* Colored American Magazine (November 1902-November 1903).

———. *A Primer of Facts Pertaining to the Early Greatness of the African Race and the Possibility of Restoration by Its Descendants.* Cambridge, Mass.: P. E. Hopkins, 1905.

———. "Reminiscences of the Life and Times of Lydia Maria Child." *Colored American Magazine* (February 1903): 279-84; (March 1903): 353-57; (May-June 1903): 454-59.

———. "A Retrospect of the Past." *Colored American Magazine* (November 1900): 64-72.

———. "Talma Gordon." *Colored American Magazine* (October 1900): 271-90.

———. *Topsy Templeton.* New Era Magazine (February 1916): 9-20, 48; (March 1916): 75-84.

———. "Whittier, the Friend of the Negro." *Colored American Magazine* (September 1901): 324-30.

———. "William Lloyd Garrison Centennial Speech." Boston, Mass., 16 December 1905. Reprinted in *The Guardian*, 16 December 1905, 1.

———. *Winona: A Tale of Negro Life in the South and Southwest. Colored American Magazine* (May 1902–October 1902).

———, ed. "Women's Department." *Colored American Magazine* (June 1900): 118–23.

Shadrach, J. Shirley (pseudonym). "Charles Winter Wood; or, From Bootblack to Professor." *Colored American Magazine* (September 1902): 345–48.

———. "Furnace Blasts. I: The Growth of the Social Evil among All Classes and Races in America." *Colored American Magazine* (February 1903): 259–63.

———. "Furnace Blasts. II: Black or White—Which Should Be the Young Afro-American's Choice in Marriage." *Colored American Magazine* (March 1903): 348–52.

———. "Mrs. Jane E. Sharp's School for African Girls." *Colored American Magazine* (March 1904): 181–84.

———. "Rev. John Henry Dorsey." *Colored American Magazine* (October 1902): 411–17.

———. "William Pickens, Yale University." *Colored American Magazine* (July 1903): 517–21.

BOOKS, ARTICLES, DISSERTATIONS, AND WEBSITES

Abbot, Joel Commodore. Camp No. 21. "Fourteenth Regiment, Rhode Island Heavy Artillery," <http:suvcwricamp21.tripod.com/Artillery/14artmain.htm>, January 2006.

"About Us," MusicalAmerica.com, <http://MusicalAmerica.com>, May 2007.

"Abraham Lincoln." *New Era Magazine* (February 1916): 7.

Adi, Hakim, and Marika Sherwood. *Pan-African History: Political Figures from Africa and the Diaspora since 1787*. New York: Routledge, 2003.

African American Mosaic, <http://www.loc.gov/exhibits/african/afam005.html>, January 2006.

"Aged Writer Dies of Painful Burns." *Chicago Defender*, 23 August 1930, 1.

Albion, Robert Greenhalgh, and Jennie Barnes Pope. *The Rise of New York Port, 1815–1860*. New York: Charles Scribner's, 1939.

Aldrich, Mrs. Thomas Bailey. *Crowding Memories*. Boston: Houghton Mifflin, 1920.

Alexander, Frederick W., comp. and ed. *Stratford Hall and the Lees Connected with Its History*. Oak Grove, Va.: F. W. Alexander, 1912.

Alexandria Convention and Visitor's Association. "A Remarkable and Courageous Journey: A Guide to Alexandria's African American History." Alexandria: Alexandria Convention and Visitor's Association, 2001.

"Alexandria—Past and Present," <http://alexandriava.gov/city/kyc/past_present.html>, May 2007.

Allen, Felicity. *Jefferson Davis, Unconquerable Heart*. Columbia: University of Missouri Press, 1999.

Allen, John O., Clayton E. Jewett, Jon L. Wakelyn, eds. *Slavery in the South: A State-by-State History*. Westport, Conn.: Greenwood Press, 2004.

Allred, Randal. "Catharsis, Revision, and Re-enactment: Negotiating the Meaning of the American Civil War." *Journal of American Culture* 19 (Winter 1996): 1–13.

American Independence Museum. "Ladd-Gilman House: Its History," <http://www.independencemuseum.org/aim_lghx.htm>, January 2006.

Ammons, Elizabeth. *Conflicting Stories: American Women Writers at the Turn into the Twentieth Century*. New York: Oxford University Press, 1992.

Anderson, James D. *The Education of Blacks in the South, 1860-1935.* Chapel Hill: University of North Carolina Press, 1988.

Andrews, William. *Bursting Bonds: The Autobiography of a New Negro.* Notre Dame, Ind.: University of Notre Dame Press, 2005.

————. "William Dean Howells and Charles W. Chesnutt: Criticism and Race Fiction in the Age of Booker T. Washington." *American Literature* 48, no. 3 (November 1976): 327–39.

Anonymous. "Pauline E. Hopkins, Author of 'Contending Forces,' 'Talma Gordon,' 'General Washington,' Etc." *Colored American Magazine* (January 1901): 218.

Aoki, Andrew L., Kerry L. Haynie, and Anne M. McCulloch, eds. *Encyclopedia of Minorities in American Politics.* Phoenix, Ariz.: Oryx Press, 2000.

Aptheker, Bettina. *Woman's Legacy: Essays on Race, Sex, and Class in American History.* Amherst: University of Massachusetts Press, 1982.

Aptheker, Herbert, ed. *Against Racism: Unpublished Essays, Papers, Addresses, 1887-1961.* Amherst: University of Massachusetts Press, 1985.

————. *American Negro Slave Revolts.* New York: International Publishers, 1993.

————, ed. *A Documentary History of the Negro People in the United States.* Vol. 2. New York: Citadel Press, 1970.

Arac, Jonathan. *Critical Genealogies: Historical Situations for Postmodern Literary Studies.* New York: Columbia University Press, 1987.

Aravamudan, Srinivas. *Tropicopolitants: Colonialism and Agency, 1688-1804.* Durham, N.C.: Duke University Press, 1999.

Arnesen, Eric. *Black Protest and the Great Migration: A Brief History with Documents.* Boston: Bedford/St. Martins, 2002.

Arnfred, Signe, ed. *Re-thinking Sexualities in Africa.* Uppsala, Sweden: Nordic African Institute, 2004.

Bacon, Edwin M. *Bacon's Dictionary of Boston.* Boston: Houghton Mifflin, 1886.

————. *Boston: A Guide Book.* Boston: Ginn, 1903.

Baker, William, and Kenneth Womack. *A Companion to the Victorian Novel.* Westport, Conn.: Greenwood Press, 2002.

Baldwin, Neil. *Henry Ford and the Jews: The Mass Production of Hate.* New York: Public Affairs, 2001.

Ballentine, George. *Autobiography of an English Soldier in the United States Army: Comprising Observations and Adventures in the States and Mexico.* New York: Stringer and Townsend, 1853.

Bancroft, *Slave Trading in the Old South.* Baltimore: J. H. Furst, 1931.

Bandele, Ramla. "Pan-African Conference for Global Black Unity." *Global Mappings,* <http://diaspora.northwestern.edu/mbin/WebObjects/DiasporaX.woa/wa/display Article?atomid=461>, January 2006.

"Bankruptcy Notices." *New York Times,* 11 June 1904, 14.

Barber, J. Max. "The Morning Cometh," *Voice of the Negro* (January 1904): 38.

————. *The Negro of the Earlier World: An Excursion into Ancient Negro History.* Philadelphia: AME Concern, n.d.

Bartlett, Irving H. *Wendell Phillips, Brahmin Radical.* Boston: Beacon Press, 1961.

Battle Creek Health System. "Native American Names and Meanings," <http://www.bchealth.com/services/birthcenter/nativeambabynames.shtml>, January 2006.

Beath, Robert Burns. *History of the Grand Army of the Republic.* New York: Bryan, Taylor, 1889.

Becker, Eddie. "Chronology on the History of Slavery and Racism 1830–the End," <http://www.innercity.org/holt/chron_1830_end.html>, January 2006.

Beer, Gillian. *Darwin's Plots: Evolutionary Narrative in Darwin, George Eliot, and Nineteenth-Century Fiction*. Cambridge: Cambridge University Press, 2000.

Bell, Bernard W. *The Afro-American Novel and Its Tradition*. Amherst: University of Massachusetts Press, 1989.

Bell, Charles H. *History of the Town of Exeter, New Hampshire* (1888). Bowie, Md.: Heritage Books, 1990.

Benjamin, Marina. *A Question of Identity: Women, Science, and Literature*. New Brunswick, N.J.: Rutgers University Press, 1993.

"Benjamin William Arnett." *Notable Black American Men*. Gale Research, 1998.

"Benjamin W. Arnett, Jr., DD (1838–1906)." In "Ohio's African American State Legislators," <http://www.georgewashingtonwilliams.org>, May 2007.

Bentley, William. *Diary of William Bentley, D.D., Pastor of the East Church, Salem, Massachusetts*. Vol. 4. Salem, Mass.: Essex Institute, 1914.

Berlin, Ira. "Time, Space, and the Evolution of Afro-American Society on British Mainland North America." *American Historical Review* 85, no. 1 (February 1980): 44–78.

Bermuda Genealogy and History. "A Survey of Inhabitants, c. 1789," <http://www.rootsweb.com/~bmuwgw/survey1.html)>, January 2006.

"Bermuda Worship," <http://www.insiders.com/bermuda/main-worship.htm>, January 2006.

Bernhard, Virginia. "Beyond the Chesapeake: The Contrasting Status of Blacks in Bermuda, 1616–1663." *Journal of Southern History* 54 (November 1988): 545–64.

———. *Slaves and Slaveholders in Bermuda, 1616–1782*. Columbia: University of Missouri Press, 1999.

Bennett, Paula Bernat. *Poets in the Public Sphere: The Emancipatory Project of American Women's Poetry, 1800–1900*. Princeton, N.J.: Princeton University Press, 2003.

Bhan, Esme, and Charles Lemert. *The Voice of Anna Julia Cooper: Including a Voice from the South and Other Important Essays*. Lanham, Md.: Rowman and Littlefield, 1998.

Bigelow, John. *William Cullen Bryant*. Boston: Houghton Mifflin, 1890.

Billingsley, Raymond. *Mighty Like A River: The Black Church and Social Reform*. New York: Oxford University Press, 1999.

Blight, David. *Race and Reunion: The Civil War in American Memory*. Cambridge: Belknap Press of Harvard University, 2001.

Blockson, Charles L. "Black Samuel Fraunces, Patriot, White House Steward and Restaurateur Par Excellence," <http://www.library.temple.edu/collections/blockson/Fraunces.htm>, January 2006.

Bloom, Harold. *Modern Black American Poets and Dramatists*. New York: Chelsea House, 1995.

Boamah-Wiafe, Daniel. "Dr. James Emman Kwegyir Aggrey of Achimota: Preacher, Scholar, Teacher, and Gentleman." In *Black Lives: Essays in African American Biography*, edited by James L. Conyers, 182–96. Armonk, N.Y.: M. E. Sharpe, 1999.

Bolden, Tonya. "Olivia Ward Bush," <http:www.digital.nypl.org/schomburg/writers_aa19/bio2.html>, January 2006.

Bordin, Ruth B. A. *Frances Willard: A Biography*. Chapel Hill: University of North Carolina Press, 1986.

Boritt, Gabor S. *Jefferson Davis's Generals*. New York: Oxford University Press, 1999.

"The Bosfield Case." *New Era Magazine* (April 1916): 119–20.

Bousfield, M. O. "An Account of Physicians of Color in the United States." *Bulletin of the History of Medicine* 17, no. 1 (January 1945): 61–84.

Bouton, Nathaniel, ed. *Provincial Papers: Documents and Records relating to the Province of New-Hampshire, from 1749–1763.* Vols. 1–7. Manchester: James M. Campbell, 1872.

Bowen, J. W. E., ed. *Africa and the American Negro: Addresses and Proceedings of the Congress on Africa.* Atlanta, Ga., 1896.

Boyd, Willis D. "James Redpath and American Negro Colonization in Haiti, 1860–1862." *The Americas* 12, no. 2 (October 1955): 169–82.

Branham, Robert James, and Philip S. Foner. *Lift Every Voice: African American Oratory, 1787–1900.* Tuscaloosa: University of Alabama Press, 1998.

"Brief History of Brownsville, Pa.," <http://www.hhs.net/itforce/flatiron/hist.html>, January 2006.

Briére, Jean-François. "Abbé Grégoire and Haitian Independence." *Research in African Literatures* 35, no. 2 (2004): 34–39.

Brock, William R. *Scotus Americanus: A Survey of the Sources for Links between Scotland and America in the Eighteenth Century.* Edinburgh: Edinburgh University Press, 1982.

Bronner, Leila Leah. *From Eve to Esther: Rabbinic Reconstructions of Biblical Women.* Louisville, Ky.: Westminster/John Knox, 1994.

"Brooklyn." *New York Times*, 27 September 1851, 1.

Brooks, Gwendolyn. "Afterword." In *Contending Forces: A Romance Illustrative of Negro Life North and South*, 403–9. Carbondale: Southern Illinois University Press, 1978.

Brooks, Kristina. "New Women, Fallen Women: The Crisis of Reputation in Turn of the Century Novels by Pauline Hopkins and Edith Wharton." *Legacy* 13, no. 2 (1996): 91–112.

Brown, Hallie Quinn. *Homespun Heroines and Other Women of Distinction.* 1926. New York: Oxford University Press, 1992.

Brown, Josephine. *Biography of an American Bondman, by His Daughter.* Boston: R. F. Wallcut, 1856. In *Digital Schomburg: African American Women Writers of the 19th Century*, <http://digital.nypl.org/schomburg/writers_aa19>, January 2006.

Brown, Letitia W., and Elsie M. Lewis. *Washington from Banneker to Douglass, 1791–1870.* Washington, D.C.: Smithsonian Institution, 1971.

Brown, Lois. "Defensive Postures in Pauline Hopkins's *Contending Forces*." In *The Unruly Voice: Rediscovering Pauline Elizabeth Hopkins*, edited by John Gruesser, 50–70. Urbana: University of Illinois Press, 1996.

———, ed. *Memoir of James Jackson, the Attentive and Obedient Scholar, Who Died in Boston, October 31, 1833, Aged Six Years and Eleven Months, by His Teacher Miss Susan Paul.* Cambridge: Harvard University Press, 2000.

———. "Out of the Mouths of Babes: Susan Paul and the Abolitionist Campaign of the Colored Juvenile Choir." *New England Quarterly* (March 2002): 52–79.

Brown, Richard, and Jack Tager. *Massachusetts: A Concise History.* Amherst: University of Massachusetts Press, 2000.

Brown, William J. *The Life of William J. Brown, of Providence, R.I., with Personal Recollections of Incidents in Rhode Island.* Providence, R.I.: Angell, 1883.

Brown, William Wells. *The Black Man, His Antecedents, His Genius, and His Achievements.* Boston: R. F. Wallcutt, 1863.

———. *Narrative of William Wells Brown, an American Slave, Written by Himself.* 1847. London: Charles Gilpin, BishopGate-St. Without, 1849. Electronic text available at

Documenting the American South, <http://docsouth.unc.edu/brownw/brown.html>, January 2006.

————. *The Rising Son; or, The Antecedents and Advancement of the Colored Race*. 1874. Boston: A. G. Brown, 1876.

————. *My Southern Home; or, The South and Its People*. Boston: A. G. Brown, 1880.

Brundage, W. Fitzhugh. *Lynching in the New South: Georgia and Virginia, 1880–1930*. Urbana: University of Illinois Press, 1993.

Bryant, William Cullen. "The Antiquity of Freedom," in *Poetical Works of William Cullen Bryant*, 198–99. New York: D. Appleton, 1899.

Buckner, Phillip. "The Peopling of Canada." *History Today* 43, no. 1 (November 1993): 48–54.

Budick, Emily Miller. *Engendering Romance: Women Writers and the Hawthorne Tradition, 1850–1990*. New Haven: Yale University Press, 1994.

Buffalohead, W. Roger, and Paulette Fairbanks Molin. "'A Nucleus of Civilization': American Indian Families at Hampton Institute in the Late Nineteenth Century." *Journal of American Indian Education* 35, no. 3 (Spring 1996): 59–94.

Burchard, Peter. *One Gallant Rush: Robert Gould Shaw and His Brave Black Regiment*. New York: St. Martin's, 1965.

Burchett, Michael H. "Promise and Prejudice: Wise County, Virginia, and the Great Migration, 1910–1920." *Journal of Negro History* 82, no. 3 (1997): 312–27.

Burstein, Stanley M. "The Kingdom of Meroe." In *Africa and Africans in Antiquity*, edited by Edwin M. Yamauchi, 132–58. East Lansing: Michigan State University, 2001.

Caemmerer, H. Paul. *Washington: The National Capital*. Washington, D.C.: Government Printing Office, 1932.

Calhoun, Robert. "A Troubled Culture: North Carolina in the New Nation, 1790–1834." In *Writing North Carolina History*, edited by Jeffrey Crow and Larry Tise, 76–110. Chapel Hill: University of North Carolina Press, 1979, 76–110.

Carby, Hazel. Introduction to *Contending Forces: A Romance Illustrative of Negro Life North and South*. 1900. New York: Oxford University Press, 1988.

Carlier, Auguste. *Marriage in the United States*. 1867. Salem, N.H.: Ayer Company, 1972.

Carmer, Carl, and Ralph Nading Hill. *Yankee Kingdom: Vermont and New Hampshire*. New York: Harper and Row, 1960.

Carter, R. D. W. *The Colonial and Revolutionary Periods, 1584–1783*. Vol. 1 of *History of North Carolina*. Chicago: Lewis Publishing Company, 1919.

Carter, Robert W. "The Opening Century." *Colored American Magazine* (February 1901): 309.

Carvajal, Christa. "German-American Theatre." In *Ethnic Theatre in the United States*, edited by Maxine Schwartz Seller, 175–89. Westport, Conn.: Greenwood Press, 1983.

Cash, Floris Barnett. "Matthews, Victoria Earle." In *Black Women in America: An Historical Encyclopedia*, edited by Darlene Clark Hine, Elsa Barkley Brown, and Rosalyn Terborg-Penn, 2:760. Bloomington: Indiana University Press, 1993.

Castel, Albert. "'And Shed American Blood upon American Soil': A Look at How the Mexican War Came About." *American History Illustrated* 3, no. 3 (June 1968): 36–43.

Cecelski, David, and Timothy Tyson. *Democracy Betrayed: The Wilmington Race Riot of 1898 and Its Legacy*. Chapel Hill: University of North Carolina Press, 1998.

Chalmers, David. *Hooded Americanism: The History of the Ku Klux Klan*. Chicago: Quadrangle Books, 1968.

Chesnutt, Charles Waddell. *Frederick Douglass*. Boston: Small, Maynard, 1899.

———. *The House behind the Cedars.* Edited by William Andrews. Athens: University of
  Georgia Press, 1988.

"Chichester Parkinson-Fortescue, 1st Baron Carlingford," <http://www.wikipedia.org/
  wiki/Chichester_Parkinson-Fortescue_1st_Baron_Carlingford>, January 2006.

Chidsey, Donald B. *The French and Indian War.* New York: Crown Publishers, 1969.

Child, Lydia Maria. *Letters from New York.* New York: C. S. Francis, 1843.

Chipman, Scott Lee, ed. *New England Vital Records from the Exeter News-Letter, 1831–
  1840.* Vol. 1. Camden, Maine: Picton Press, 1993.

Christy, E. P. *Jim Crow Polka.* New York: Horace Waters, 1847.

Clark, Emily. "'By All the Conduct of Their Lives': A Laywomen's Confraternity in New
  Orleans, 1730–1744." *William and Mary Quarterly* 54, no. 4 (October 1997): 769–94.

Clark, Peter W., ed. *"The Greatest Gift of All": A Pictorial Biography of Mother Henriette
  Delille, Foundress of the Sisters of the Holy Family, Nov. 21, 1842.* New Orleans:
  Heritage of America Foundation Press, 1992.

Clark-Lewis, Elizabeth, ed. *First Freed: Washington, D.C., in the Emancipation Era.*
  Washington, D.C.: Howard University Press, 2002.

Clarke, James Freeman. *Autobiography, Diary, and Correspondence.* Boston, 1891.

Coale, James Freeman. *Mesmerism and Hawthorne: Mediums of American Romance.*
  Tuscaloosa: University of Alabama Press, 1998.

Coleman, Marion Moore. *Fair Rosalind: The American Career of Helena Modjeska.*
  Cheshire, Conn.: Cherry Hill Books, 1969.

Collins, Mabel. *The Story of Helena Modjeska.* London: W. H. Allen, 1883.

"Colored Woman Makes Chief Address." *The Guardian,* 16 December 1905, 1.

Columbia Encyclopedia, Sixth Edition. New York: Columbia University Press, 2004.

"Col. William H. Dupree." *Colored American Magazine* (July 1901): 228–31.

Congregational Club Manual for 1899. N.p., n.d.

"Constitutional Rights Association of the United States." *Colored American Magazine*
  (October 1900): 311.

Conyers, James L. *Black Lives: Essays in African American Biography.* Armonk, N.Y.:
  M. E. Sharpe, 1999.

Cook, Frederic W. *Massachusetts: A Guide to Its Places and People.* Federal Writers'
  Project of the Works Progress Administration of Massachusetts. Boston: Houghton
  Mifflin, 1937.

Cooke, John, ed. *Dublin Book of Irish Verse, 1728–1909.* Dublin: Hodges, Figgis, 1909.

Cooper, Anna Julia. "The Ethics of the Negro Question (1902)." In *The Voice of Anna
  Julia Cooper: Including a Voice from the South and Other Important Essays,* edited by
  Esme Bhan and Charles Lemert, 206–15. Lanham, Md.: Rowman and Littlefield, 1998.

Cooper, George. *Pauline; or, The Belle of Saratoga. An Operetta in Two Acts.* New York:
  J. L. Peters, 1873.

Cooper, James Fenimore. *The Last of the Mohicans: A Narrative of 1757.* Edited by James
  Daugherty. Cleveland: World Publishing, 1957.

Cooper, Michael. *Slave Spirituals and the Jubilee Singers.* New York: Houghton Mifflin,
  2001.

Correa, R. R. Rivera. *The Shadow of Don Pedro.* New York: Vantage Press, 1970.

Cornish, Dudley. *The Sable Arm: Negro Troops in the Union Army.* New York, 1956.

Cott, Nancy, ed. *Women Together: Organizational Life.* Munich: K. G. Saur, 1993.

Cottrol, Robert J. *The Afro-Yankees: Providence's Black Community in the Antebellum Era.*
  Westport, Conn.: Greenwood Press, 1982.

Cottrol, Robert J., and Raymond Diamond. "The Second Amendment: Toward an Afro-Americanist Reconsideration," <http://www.saf.org/journal/7_toward.html>, January 2006.

Craven, Wesley Frank. "An Introduction to the History of Bermuda." *William and Mary College Quarterly Historical Magazine*, 2d ser., 17, no. 2 (April 1937): 176–215.

Crawford, Neta. *Argument and Change in World Politics: Ethics, Decolonization, and Humanitarian Intervention.* Cambridge: Cambridge University Press, 2002.

Crofts, Daniel. *Reluctant Confederates: Upper South Unionists in the Secession Crisis.* Chapel Hill: University of North Carolina Press, 1989.

Crow, Jeffrey, and Larry Tise, eds. *Writing North Carolina History.* Chapel Hill: University of North Carolina Press, 1979.

Culp, Daniel Wallace, ed. *Twentieth Century Negro Literature: Or, a Cyclopedia of Thought on the Vital Topics relating to the American Negro by One Hundred of America's Greatest Negroes.* Naperville, Ill.: J. L. Nichols, 1902.

Cunningham, Valerie. "The First Blacks of Portsmouth." *Historical New Hampshire* 44 (Winter 1999): 181–201.

Dagbovie, Pero Gaglo. "Black Women Historians from the Late 19th Century to the Dawning of the Civil Rights Movement." *Journal of African American History* 89 (2004): 241–61.

"Dahomey on Broadway." *New York Times*, 19 February 1903, 9.

Daniels, John. *In Freedom's Birthplace: A Study of the Boston Negroes.* New York: Negro Universities Press, 1968.

"Daughters of Hawaii," <http://www.daughtersofhawaii.org/hanaiakamalama/index.shtml>, January 2006.

Davidson, Basil. *The Lost Cities of Africa.* Boston: Little, Brown, 1959.

Davis, Varina Howell Jefferson. *Jefferson Davis, Ex-President of the Confederate States of America: A Memoir by His Wife.* 2 vols. New York: Belford, 1890.

Dawson, Joseph G., III. *Doniphan's Epic March: The 1st Missouri Volunteers in the Mexican War.* Lawrence: University Press of Kansas, 1999.

De Abajian, James T. *Blacks in Selected Newspapers, Censuses, and Other Sources: An Index to Names and Subjects.* Vol. 3, P–Z. Boston: G. K. Hall, 1977.

Dearing, Mary. *Veterans in Politics: The Story of the G.A.R.* Baton Rouge: Louisiana State University Press, 1952.

"Death of the Foremost Colored Lawyer in New England." *Colored American Magazine* (February 1901): 291.

Denton, Virginia Lantz. *Booker T. Washington and the Adult Education Movement.* Gainesville: University Press of Florida, 1993.

Department of City Planning, City of Norfolk, Va. "Norfolk Mission College Site," <http://www.historicnorfolk.org/A19.html>, January 2006.

Detiege, Sister Audrey Marie. *Henriette Delille, Free Woman of Color.* New Orleans: Sisters of the Holy Family, 1976.

Deutsch, Sarah. *Women and the City: Gender, Space, and Power in Boston, 1870–1940.* New York: Oxford University Press, 2000.

DeVaughn, Booker T. "The Boston Literary and Historical Association: An Early 20th Century Example of Adult Education as Conducted by a Black Voluntary Association." *Lifelong Learning: An Omnibus of Practice and Research* 9, no. 4 (January 1986): 11–16.

Dewberry, Jonathan. "The African Grove Theatre and Company." *Black American Literature Forum* 16, no. 4 (Winter 1982): 128–31.

Dictionary Catalogue of the Music Collection: Boston Public Library. Vol. 15. Boston: G. K. Hall, 1972.

Dixon, Chris. *African Americans and Haiti: Emigration and Black Nationalism in the Nineteenth Century.* Westport, Conn.: Greenwood Press, 2000.

Doreski, Carol. "Inherited Rhetoric and Authentic History." In *The Unruly Voice: Rediscovering Pauline Elizabeth Hopkins,* edited by John Gruesser, 71–97. Urbana: University of Illinois Press, 1996.

Dorman, Franklin A. *Twenty Families of Color in Massachusetts, 1742–1998.* Boston: New England Historic Genealogical Society, 1988.

Douglass, Frederick. "Address by Hon. Frederick Douglass, Delivered in the Congregational Church, Washington, D.C., April 16, 1883: On the Twenty-first Anniversary of Emancipation in the District of Columbia." In *African American Perspectives: Pamphlets from the Daniel A. P. Murray Collection, 1818–1907,* 13, <http://memory.loc.gov>, January 2006.

———. *Life and Times of Frederick Douglass: His Early Life as a Slave, His Escape from Bondage, and His Complete History.* 1892. Reprint with an introduction by Rayford Logan, New York: Collier Books, 1962.

———. *Life and Times of Frederick Douglass, Written by Himself, . . . With an introduction by George L. Ruffin, of Boston.* Boston: De Wolfe and Fiske, 1892.

Dowling, John. "Sketches of New-York Baptists. IV: Rev. Thos. Paul and the Colored Baptist Churches." In *Baptist Memorial and Monthly Record: Devoted to the History, Biography, Literature and Statistics of the Denomination,* vol. 8, edited by Rev. Enoch Hutchinson and Rev. Stephen Remington. New York: Z. P. Hatch, 1849.

Drake, Samuel Adams. *Old Landmarks and Historic Personages of Boston.* Boston: Little, Brown, 1906.

Drown, Frank S. "The Massachusetts Bureau of Statistics." *Annals of the American Academy of Political and Social Science* 35, (suppl., March 1910): 134–36.

Du Bois, William Edward Burghardt. *Black Reconstruction in America, 1860–1880.* 1935. New York: Athenaeum, 1992.

———. "A Proposed Negro Journal." In *Against Racism: Unpublished Essays, Papers, Addresses, 1887–1961,* edited by Herbert Aptheker. Amherst: University of Massachusetts Press, 1985.

———. "To the Nations of the World." 1900. In *The Oxford W. E. B. Du Bois Reader,* edited by Eric J. Sundquist, 625–27. New York: Oxford University Press, 1996.

duCille, Ann. *The Coupling Convention: Sex, Text, and Tradition in Black Women's Fiction.* New York: Oxford University Press, 1993.

Dunbar, Paul Laurence. *The Complete Poems of Paul Laurence Dunbar.* New York: Dodd, Mead, 1913.

Dunn, D. Elwood. "Speech to the Liberian Association of Metropolitan Atlanta," 29 July 2000, <http://www.theperspective.org/dunn.html>, January 2006.

Dunshee, Kenneth Holcomb. *As You Pass By.* New York: Hastings House, 1952.

Dyer, Frank Lewis, and Thomas Commerford Martin. *Edison: His Life and Inventions.* Vol. 1. New York: Harper and Brothers, 1910.

Earle, Alice Morse. *Stage-Coach and Tavern Days.* New York: B. Blom, 1969.

"East." *Crisis* (October 1930): 344.

Eckenrode, H. J. *Jefferson Davis: President of the South.* New York: Macmillan, 1923.

Edenton District, Loose Estates Papers, 1756–1806. Vol. 2, *Gillikin-Niel.* Abstracted by Stephen E. Bradley Jr. Raleigh, N.C.: State Library of North Carolina, 1995.

"Edward Wilmot Blyden," <http://www.africawithin.com/bios/edward_blyden.htm>, January 2006.

Elliott, R. S. "The Story of Our Magazine." *Colored American Magazine* (May 1901): 42–77.

Emerson, Ralph Waldo. "Address Delivered in Concord on the Anniversary of the Emancipation of the Negroes, in the British West Indies, August 1, 1844." In *Miscellanies (1884)*, vol. 11 of *The Complete Works of Ralph Waldo Emerson*, <RWE.org>, January 2006.

Emilio, Luis F. *A Brave Black Regiment: History of the Fifty-fourth Regiment of Massachusetts Volunteer Infantry, 1863–1865*. Boston: Boston Book Company, 1894.

Engle, Ron, and Tice L. Miller, eds. *The American Stage: Social and Economic Issues from the Colonial Period to the Present*. Cambridge: Cambridge University Press, 1993.

Engs, Robert Francis. *Educating the Disenfranchised and Disinherited: Samuel Chapman Armstrong and Hampton Institute, 1839–1893*. Knoxville: University of Tennessee Press, 1999.

Ernest, John. "Liberation Historiography: African American Historians before the Civil War." *American Literary History* 14, no. 3 (2002): 413–43.

Esedebe, P. Olisanwuche. *Pan-Africanism: The Idea and Movement, 1776–1991*. Washington, D.C.: Howard University Press, 1994.

Fear-Segal, Jacqueline. "'Use the Club of White Man's Wisdom in Defence of Our Customs': White Schools and Native Agendas." *American Studies International* 40 (2002): 6–32.

Federal Writers' Project. *Washington: City and Capital*. Washington, D.C.: Government Printing Office, 1937.

Federal Writers' Project (N.Y.). *New York City Guide: A Comprehensive Guide to the Five Boroughs of the Metropolis Manhattan, Brooklyn, the Bronx, Queens, and Richmond*. New York: Random House, 1939.

Ferris, William H. *The African Abroad, Or, His Evolution in Western Civilization, Tracing His Development under Caucasian Milieu*. New Haven: Tuttle, Morehouse, & Taylor Press, 1913.

Finkelman, Paul. "Slavery." In *The United States and Mexico at War: Nineteenth-Century Expansionism and Conflict*, edited by Donald S. Frazier, 387–88. New York: Macmillan Reference USA, 1998.

"First Baptist Church of Norfolk," <"www.firstnorfolk.org">, January 2006.

Fiske, John. *The Unseen World, and Other Essays*. Boston: Houghton Mifflin, 1904.

Fitzpatrick, John C., ed. *The Writings of George Washington from the Original Manuscript Sources, 1745–1799*. Vol. 28. Washington, D.C.: Government Printing Office, 1931.

Fitzpatrick, Paul J. "Leading American Statisticians in the Nineteenth Century." *Journal of the American Statistical Association* 52, no. 279 (September 1957): 301–21.

Foner, Eric. *History of Black Americans: From the Compromise of 1850 to the End of the Civil War*. Westport, Conn.: Greenwood Press, 1983.

Foner, Philip S., ed. *The Voice of Black America: Major Speeches by Negroes in the United States, 1797–1971*. New York: Simon and Schuster, 1972.

Fordham, Monroe. *Major Themes in Northern Black Religious Thought, 1800–1860*. Hicksville, N.Y.: Exposition Press, 1975.

Foreman, P. Gabrielle. "The Spoken and the Silenced in *Incidents in the Life of a Slave Girl* and *Our Nig*." *Callaloo* 13, no. 2 (Spring 1990): 313–24.

Forgie, George B. *Patricide in the House Divided: A Psychological Interpretation of Lincoln and His Age*. New York: W. W. Norton, 1979.

"For Love of Liberty," <http://www.monticello.org/gettingword/GWties1.html>, January 2006.

Fortune, T. Thomas. "Industrial Education: I." *Colored American Magazine* (January 1904): 17.

Foucault, Michel. *The History of Sexuality: An Introduction*. Vol. 1. 1976. New York: Vintage Books, 1990.

Fox, Stephen. *The Guardian of Boston: William Monroe Trotter*. New York: Athenaeum, 1970.

Franchot, Penny. *Roads to Rome: The Antebellum Protestant Encounter with Catholicism*. Berkeley: University of California Press, 1994.

Franklin, V. P., and Bettye Collier-Thomas. "Biography, Race Vindication, and African-American Intellectuals: Introductory Essay." *Journal of Negro History* 81, no. 4 (Winter 1996): 1–16.

Frazier, Donald S., ed. *The United States and Mexico at War: Nineteenth-Century Expansionism and Conflict*. New York: Macmillan Reference USA, 1998.

Frederickson, George M. *Black Liberation: A Comparative History of Black Ideologies in the United States and South Africa*. New York: Oxford University Press, 1995.

Freehling, William W., and Craig M. Simpson. *Secession Debated: Georgia's Showdown in 1860*. New York: Oxford University Press, 1992.

"F. R. Moore, Editor, Harlem Leader, 85." *New York Times*, 3 March 1943, 24.

"From Our Friends in the Far East." *Colored American Magazine* (August 1900): 145.

Fultz, Michael. "'The Morning Cometh': African American Periodicals, Education, and the Black Middle Class, 1900–1930." *Journal of Negro History* 80, no. 3 (Summer 1995): 97–112.

Gaines, Kevin. "Black Americans' Racial Uplift Ideology as 'Civilizing Mission': Pauline E. Hopkins on Race and Imperialism." In *Cultures of United States Imperialism*, edited by Amy Kaplan and Donald E. Pease, 433–55. Durham, N.C.: Duke University Press, 1993.

———. *Uplifting the Race: Black Leadership, Politics, and Culture in the Twentieth Century*. Chapel Hill: University of North Carolina Press, 1996.

Garcia, Marvin. "Dr. Pedro Albizu Campos, 1891–1965," <http://www.nl.edu/academics/cas/ace/resources/campos.cfm>, January 2006.

Gardiner, Eliza. "Reminiscences of Early Days." *New Era Magazine* (February 1916): 49–53.

Garnet, Henry Highland. "An Address to the Slaves of United States of America." 1843. In *The Voice of Black America: Major Speeches by Negroes in the United States, 1797–1971*, edited by Philip S. Foner, 87. New York: Simon and Schuster, 1972.

Garrison, William Lloyd. "Announcement." *The Liberator*, 1 January 1831, 1.

Gates, Henry Louis, Jr., *Figures in Black: Words, Signs and the Racial Self*. New York: Oxford University Press, 1987.

Gatewood, Willard B., Jr. *Black Americans and the White Man's Burden, 1898–1903*. Urbana: University of Illinois Press, 1975.

Gautier, Amina. "African American Women's Writings in the Woman's Building Library." *Libraries and Culture* 41, no. 1 (2006): 55–81.

Gayley, Charles Mills. *The Classic Myths in English Literature and in Art Based Originally*

on Bulfinch's "Age of Fable" (1855) Accompanied by an Interpretative and Illustrative
Commentary. Boston: Ginn, 1911.

Geisst, Charles R. Wall Street: A History. New York: Oxford University Press, 1999.

Gerson, Evelyn. "Ona Judge Staines: Escape from Washington," <http://www
.seacoastnh.com/blackhistory/ona.html>, January 2006.

Gettemy, Charles F. The Massachusetts Bureau of Statistics, 1869-1915: A Sketch of
Its History, Organization and Functions, Together with a List of Its Publications and
Illustrative Charts. Boston: Wright and Potter, 1915.

Giddings, Paula. When and Where I Enter: The Impact of Black Women on Race and Sex in
America. New York: Morrow, 1984.

Gilbert, Peter, ed. The Selected Writings of John Edward Bruce: Militant Black Journalist.
New York: Arno Press, 1971.

Giles, Paul. American Catholic Arts and Fictions: Culture, Ideology, Aesthetics. Cambridge:
Cambridge University Press, 1992.

Gilfoyle, Timothy J. "The Moral Origins of Political Surveillance: The Preventive Society
in New York City, 1867-1918." American Quarterly 28, no. 4 (Autumn 1986): 637-52.

Gilkeson, John. Middle-Class Providence, 1820-1870. Princeton, N.J.: Princeton
University Press, 1986.

Gilman, Robbins Paxson. The Old Logg House by the Bridge. Portsmouth, N.H.: Peter E.
Randall, 1985.

Gilpatrick, Delbert Harold. Jeffersonian Democracy in North Carolina, 1789-1816. New
York: Columbia University Press, 1931.

Goddard, Richlyn. "Henceforth and Forever Free: The African American Press and
Emancipation in the District of Columbia." In First Freed: Washington D.C. in the
Emancipation Era, edited by Elizabeth Clark-Lewis, 38-68. Washington, D.C.: Howard
University Press, 2002.

Gomez, Michael A. Exchanging Our Country Marks: The Transformation of African
Identities in the Colonial and Antebellum South. Chapel Hill: University of North
Carolina Press, 1998.

Gottschild, Brenda Dixon. Digging the Africanist Presence in American Performance.
Westport, Conn.: Greenwood Press, 1996.

Gould, William B., IV, ed. Diary of a Contraband: The Civil War Passage of a Black Sailor.
Stanford, Calif.: Stanford University Press, 2002.

"Grand Masters of the Most Worshipful Prince Hall Grand Lodge Free and Accepted
Masons of Massachusetts," <http://www.princehall.org>, January 2006.

Grant, Nathan L. "Extending the Ladder: A Remembrance of Owen Dodson." Callaloo 2,
no. 3 (1998): 640-45.

"Greater Boston's Two Days' Garrison Centennial an Unprecedented Success." Boston
Guardian, 16 December 1905, 1.

Green, Constance McLaughlin. The Secret City: A History of Race Relations in the
Nation's Capital. Princeton, N.J.: Princeton University Press, 1967.

———. Washington: A History of the Capital, 1800-1950. New York: Garland, 1993.

Greene, Evarts B., and Virginia D. Harrington. American Population before the Federal
Census of 1790. New York: Columbia University Council for Research in the Social
Sciences/Columbia University Press, 1932.

Greene, Lorenzo Johnston. The Negro in Colonial New England. New York: Athenaeum,
1969.

Gregory, James N. The Southern Diaspora: How the Great Migrations of Black and White

Southerners Transformed America. Chapel Hill: University of North Carolina Press, 2005.

Gregory, Mackenzie. "Marauders of the Sea, Confederate Merchant Raiders during the American Civil War: *CSS Stonewall*. 1865. Captain T. J. Page," <http://www.ahoy .tk-jk.net/MaraudersCivilWar/CSSStonewall.html>, January 2006.

Grem, Darren. "Henry W. Grady, 1850–1889," in *The New Georgia Encyclopedia*, <http:// www.georgiaencyclopedia.org>, January 2006.

Grider, Sylvia Ann, and Lou Halsell Rodenberger, eds. *Texas Women Writers: A Tradition of Their Own*. College Station: Texas A&M Press, 1997.

Grover, Katherine, and Janine V. da Silva. *Historic Resource Study: Boston African American National Historic Site*. Boston, 2002.

Gruesser, John. *Black on Black: Twentieth-Century African American Writings about Africa*. Lexington: University Press of Kentucky, 2000.

———, ed. *The Unruly Voice: Rediscovering Pauline Elizabeth Hopkins*. Urbana: University of Illinois Press, 1996.

Guillaume, Bernice F., ed. *Olivia Ward Bush-Banks: The Collected Works of Olivia Ward Bush-Banks*. New York: Oxford University Press, 1991.

Gunning, Sandra. *Race, Rape, and Lynching: The Red Record of American Literature, 1890–1912*. New York: Oxford University Press, 1996.

Gutman, Herbert G. *The Black Family in Slavery and Freedom, 1750–1925*. New York: Vintage Books, 1976.

Haley, James T. *Afro-American Encyclopaedia; or, The Thoughts, Doings, and Sayings of the Race, Embracing Lectures, Biographical Sketches, Sermons, Poems, Names of Universities, Colleges, Seminaries, Newspapers, Books, and a History of the Denominations, Giving the Numerical Strength of Each. In Fact, It Teaches Every Subject of Interest to the Colored People, as Discussed by More Than One Hundred of Their Wisest and Best Men and Women*. Nashville: Haley and Florida, 1895.

Hall, Dennis. "Civil War Reenactors and the Postmodern Sense of History." *Journal of American Culture* 17 (Fall 1994): 4–5.

Hall, Thalian. <http://www.thalianhall.com>, January 2006.

Halyard, Harry. *The Heroine of Tampico; or, Wildfire the Wanderer: A Tale of the Mexican War*. Boston: F. Gleason, 1847.

Hamedoe, S. E. F. C. C. "Menelik, Emperor of Abyssinia." *Colored American Magazine* (December 1900): 140–53.

Hamilton, J. G. de Roulhac. "James Henry Hammond, 1807–1864." *Dictionary of American Biography*. Vol. 9. New York: Scribner's Sons, 1928.

Hammond, Isaac W. "Letter to the Editor: Slavery in New Hampshire." *Magazine of American History* 21, no. 1 (January 1889): 62–65.

Hammond, J. L. *Gladstone and the Irish Nation*. London: Longmans, 1938.

Harlan, Louis R. *Booker T. Washington: The Wizard of Tuskegee, 1901–1915*. New York: Oxford University Press, 1983.

———. "Booker T. Washington and the *Voice of the Negro*, 1904–1907." *Journal of Southern History* 45, no. 1 (February 1979): 45–62.

Harlan, Louis R., Stuart Kaufman, Barbara Kraft, and Raymond Smock, eds. *1895–1898*. Vol. 4 of *The Booker T. Washington Papers*. Urbana: University of Illinois Press, 1975.

Harlan, Louis R., Stuart Kaufman, and Raymond Smock, eds. *1889–1895*. Vol. 3 of *The Booker T. Washington Papers*. Urbana: University of Illinois Press, 1974.

Harlan, Louis R., Raymond W. Smock, and Barbara S. Kraft, eds. *1899-1900*. Vol. 5 of
The Booker T. Washington Papers. Urbana: University of Illinois Press, 1977.
———, eds. *1901-1902*. Vol. 6 of *The Booker T. Washington Papers*. Urbana: University of
Illinois Press, 1977.
Harlan, Louis R., and Raymond W. Smock, eds. *1903-1904*. Vol. 7 of *The Booker T.
Washington Papers*. Urbana: University of Illinois Press, 1977.
Harlan, Louis R., Raymond Smock, and Geraldine McTigue, eds. *1904-1906*. Vol. 8 of
The Booker T. Washington Papers. Urbana: University of Illinois Press, 1979.
Harlan, Louis R., and Raymond W. Smock. *1912-1914*. Vol. 12 of *The Booker T.
Washington Papers*. Urbana: University of Illinois Press, 1982.
Harlan, Louis R., Raymond Smock, Susan Valenza, and Sadie M. Harlan, eds. *1914-15*.
Vol. 13 of *The Booker T. Washington Papers*. Urbana: University of Illinois Press, 1984.
Harrold, Stanley. *Subversives: Antislavery Community in Washington, D.C., 1828-1865*.
Baton Rouge: Louisiana State University Press, 2003.
Hart, Sister Mary Frances Borgia. *Violets in the King's Garden: A History of the Sisters of
the Holy Family of New Orleans*. New Orleans, 1976.
Hartsock, John. *A History of American Literary Journalism: The Emergence of a Modern
Narrative Form*. Amherst: University of Massachusetts Press, 2000.
Hatch, James V. *Sorrow Is the Only Faithful One: The Life of Owen Dodson*. Urbana:
University of Illinois Press, 1993.
Hawks, Francis. *Embracing the Period of the Government, from 1663 to 1729*. Vol. 2 of
History of North Carolina: With Maps and Illustrations. Fayetteville, N.C.: E. J. Hale,
1858.
"Hayti." In "Report of the Baptist Missionary Society in Massachusetts," *American
Baptist Magazine, and Missionary Intelligencer* 4, no. 3 (May 1823): 102-3.
"Hayti: Appointment of Mr. Paul." *American Baptist Magazine, and Missionary
Intelligencer* 4, no. 3 (May 1823): 134-36.
Hedricks, Wanda. "Fannie Barrier Williams." In *Black Women in America: An Historical
Encyclopedia*, edited by Darlene Clark Hine, Elsa Barkley Brown, and Rosalyn
Terborg-Penn, 2:1259-61. Bloomington: Indiana University Press, 1993.
"Here and There." *Colored American Magazine* (October 1902): 459.
Hill, Adelaide Cromwell. *The Other Brahmins: Boston's Black Upper Class, 1750-1950*.
Fayetteville: University of Arkansas Press, 1994.
Hill, Errol. "The Hyers Sisters: Pioneers in Black Musical Comedy." In *The American
Stage: Social and Economic Issues from the Colonial Period to the Present*, edited by Ron
Engle and Tice L. Miller, 115-30. Cambridge: Cambridge University Press, 1993.
———. *Shakespeare in Sable: A History of Black Shakespearean Actors*. Amherst:
University of Massachusetts Press, 1984.
Hill, Errol, and James V. Hatch. *A History of African American Theatre*. Cambridge:
Cambridge University Press, 2003.
Hill, Robert W., Jr., ed. *Tennyson's Poetry*. New York: W. W. Norton, 1999.
Hine, Darlene Clark, Elsa Barkley Brown, and Rosalyn Terborg-Penn, eds. *Black Women
in America: An Historical Encyclopedia*. Vols. 1-2. Bloomington: Indiana University
Press, 1993.
Hine, William C. "Black Politicians in Reconstruction Charleston, South Carolina:
A Collective Study." *Journal of Southern History* (November 1983): 555-84.
"Historic Homes of Bertie County," at "Bertie County—NCGenWeb Project Page,"
<http:www.rootsweb.com/~ncbertie/homes.htm#ashland>, January 2006.

HistoryCentral.com. "Civil War Naval History: May 1861," <http://www.multied.com/
Navy/cwnavalhistory/May 1861.html>, January 2006.
"History of Blyden Branch Library," <http://www.npl.lib.va.us/branches/blyden/blyden_
history.html>, January 2006.
"History of Boydton," <http://www.boydton.org/history.htm>, January 2006.
"History of IIT," <http://www.iit.edu/about/history.html>, January 2006.
History of the State of Rhode Island with Illustrations. Philadelphia: Hong, Wade, 1878.
Holbrook, Jay Mack, comp. *Massachusetts Vital Records: Boston, 1630-1849. Boston
Marriages: 1849-1860, Marriages 1857.* Oxford, Mass.: Holbrook Research Institute,
1985.
Holbrook, Paul. *Massachusetts Vital Records, Boston 1630-1849; Deaths Index, 1801-1848,
Volume N-S.* Oxford, Mass.: Holbrook Research Institute, 1985.
Holland, E. C. *A Refutation of the Calumnies Circulated against the Southern and Western
States Respecting the Institution and Existence of Slavery among Them,* 61. Cited in
Herbert Aptheker, *American Negro Slave Revolts.* 1943. New York: International
Publishers, 1993.
Holly, James T. "The Negro Race, Self-Government, and the Haitian Revolution." In *Lift
Every Voice: African American Oratory, 1787-1900,* edited by Robert James Branham
and Philip S. Foner, 290. Tuscaloosa: University of Alabama Press, 1998.
Holmes, William F. *The White Chief: James Kimble Vardaman.* Baton Rouge: Louisiana
State University Press, 1970.
"The Home of the Colored American Magazine." *Colored American Magazine* (January-
February 1902): 253.
Hone, Philip. *The Diary of Phillip Hone.* Edited by Allan Nevins. New York: Dodd,
Mead, 1927.
Horn, John. *The Petersburg Campaign: June 1864-April 1865.* Conshohocken, Pa.:
Combined Publishing, 1999.
Horn, Stanley. *Invisible Empire: The Story of the Ku Klux Klan.* Boston: Houghton
Mifflin, 1939.
Hornblow, Arthur. *A History of the Theatre in America from Its Beginnings to the Present
Time.* Vol. 2. New York: J. B. Lippincott, 1919.
Horton, James. *Free People of Color: Inside the African American Community.* Washington,
D.C.: Smithsonian Institution Press, 1993.
Horton, James, and Lois Horton. *Black Bostonians: Family Life and Community Struggle in
the Antebellum North.* New York: Holmes and Meier, 1979.
Horvitz, Deborah. "Hysteria and Trauma in Pauline Hopkins' *Of One Blood; or, The
Hidden Self.*" *African American Review* 33, no. 2 (Summer 1999): 245-60.
Howe, M. A. De Wolfe. "Editorial Statement." In Charles Chesnutt, *Frederick Douglass,*
142. Boston: Small, Maynard, 1899.
Howells, William Dean. *A Modern Instance.* Boston: James R. Osgood, 1882.
————. *Years of My Youth.* New York: Harper and Brothers, 1916.
Hudson, Arthur Palmer, ed. *Humor of the Deep South.* New York: Macmillan, 1936.
Huggins, Nathan. *Harlem Renaissance.* New York: Oxford University Press, 1971.
Hughes, C. Alvin. "Hate Only Hate, Fear Only Cowardice: William Pickens, a
Philosopher of Activism, an Advocate for Democracy." *Griot* 17 (1998): 11-20.
Hunt, Tamara L. "Musical Women in England, 1870-1914: 'Encroaching on All Man's
Privileges' and Women Performing Music: The Emergence of American Women as

Classical Instrumentalists and Conductors." *Journal of Social History* 36, no. 1 (Fall 2002): 223–27.

Hutchinson, Rev. Enoch, and Rev. Stephen Remington, eds. *Baptist Memorial and Monthly Record: Devoted to the History, Biography, Literature and Statistics of the Denomination.* Vol. 8. New York: Z. P. Hatch, 1849–50.

Hutton, Frankie. *The Early Black Press in America, 1827–1860.* Westport, Conn.: Greenwood Press, 1993.

Jackson, Donald. *Black Hawk: An Autobiography.* Urbana: University of Illinois Press, 1955, 1990.

Jacobs, Donald M. "The Nineteenth Century Struggle over Segregated Education in the Boston Schools." *Journal of Negro Education* 39, no. 1 (Winter 1970): 76–85.

Jacobs, Sylvia M. "James Emman Kwegyir Aggrey: An African Intellectual in the United States." *Journal of Negro History* 81, no. 1/4 (Winter/Autumn 1966): 47–61.

James, Lewis K. *Religious Life of Fugitive Slaves and Rise of Coloured Baptist Churches, 1820–1865, in What Is Now Known as Ontario.* New York: Arno Press, 1980.

James, William. "The Hidden Self." *Scribner's* 7, no. 3 (March 1890): 361–74.

"James Kenney," <http://www.pgileirdata.org/html/pgil_datasets/ authors/k/ Kenney,J(d.1849)/life.htm>, January 2006.

Jewell, K. Sue. *From Mammy to Miss America and Beyond: Cultural Images and the Shaping of U.S. Social Policy.* London: Routledge, 1993.

"John C. Freund, Founder and Editor of Musical America, Dies after Long Illness." *New York Times*, 4 June 1924, 21.

"John C. Freund, Owner of Musical America, Dies in New York." *Chicago Daily Tribune*, 4 June 1924, 10.

"John Christian Freund." In *Baker's Biographical Dictionary of Musicians*, 766. New York: Schirmer, 2001.

Johnson, Abby Arthur, and Ronald Maberry Johnson. *Propaganda and Aesthetics: The Literary Politics of African-American Magazines in the Twentieth Century.* Amherst: University of Massachusetts Press, 1979, 1991.

Johnson, Leonard W. "History of the Education of Negro Physicians." *Journal of the National Medical Association* 42 (1967): 439–46.

Johnson, Michael P., and James L. Roark, eds. *No Chariot Let Down: Charleston's Free People of Color on the Eve of the Civil War.* Chapel Hill: University of North Carolina Press, 1984.

Johnson, Phillip James. "Seasons in Hell: Charles S. Johnson and the 1930 Liberian Labor Crisis." Ph.D. diss., Louisiana State University and Agricultural and Mechanical College, 2004.

Johnston, Richard M., and William H. Browne. *Life of Alexander H. Stephens.* Philadelphia: J. B. Lippincott, 1878.

Jones, Beverly. "Mary Church Terrell and the National Association of Colored Women, 1896 to 1901." In *Women Together: Organizational Life*, edited by Nancy Cott, 307–20. Munich: K. G. Saur, 1993.

———. *Quest for Equality: The Life and Writings of Mary Church Terrell, 1863–1954.* Brooklyn, N.Y.: Carlson, 1990.

Jones, Ida E. "Their Chains Shall Fall Off: The Activism of Mt. Zion United Methodist Church." In *First Freed: Washington, D.C., in the Emancipation Era*, edited by Elizabeth Clark-Lewis, 21–37. Washington, D.C.: Howard University Press, 2002.

Jones, Paul Christian. "'This Dainty Woman's Hand . . . Red with Blood': E. D. E. N.

Southworth's the Hidden Hand as Abolitionist Narrative." *American Transcendental Quarterly* 15, no. 1 (2001): 59–80.

Jordan, Pallo. "Zemk' Inkomo Magawalandini: The Life and Times of W. B. Rubusana (1858–1936)," <http://www.sahistory.org.za/pages/people/rubusana-wb.htm>, April 2007.

Jordan, William G. *Black Newspapers and America's War for Democracy, 1914–1920.* Chapel Hill: University of North Carolina Press, 2001.

Kaplan, Amy, and Donald Pease. *Cultures of United States Imperialism.* Durham, N.C.: Duke University Press, 1993.

Karcher, Carolyn, ed. *A Lydia Maria Child Reader.* Durham, N.C.: Duke University Press, 1997.

Katz, William Loren. *The Invisible Empire: The Ku Klux Klan Impact on History.* Washington, D.C.: Open Hand Publishers, 1986.

Kaye, Andrew M. "Colonel Roscoe Conkling Simmons and the Mechanics of Black Leadership." *Journal of American Studies* 37, no. 1 (April 2003): 79–98.

Kendrick, Stephen, and Paul Kendrick. *Sarah's Long Walk: The Free Blacks of Boston and How Their Struggle for Equality Changed America.* Boston: Beacon Press, 2004.

Keneally, James J. "Black Republicans during the New Deal: The Role of Joseph W. Martin, Jr." *Review of Politics* 55, no. 1 (Winter 1993): 117–39.

Kennedy, Sister Jean de Chantal. *Biography of a Colonial Town: Hamilton-Bermuda, 1790–1897.* Hamilton: Bermuda Book Stores, 1961.

Kersten, Andrew. *A. Philip Randolph: A Life in the Vanguard.* Lanham, Md.: Rowman and Littlefield, 2007.

Kessler-Harris, Alice. *Out to Work: A History of Wage-Earning Women in the United States.* New York: Oxford University Press, 1982.

King, Kenneth. "James E. K. Aggrey: Collaborator, Nationalist, Pan African." *Canadian Journal of African Studies* 3, no. 3 (Autumn 1969): 511–30.

King's Hand Book of Boston. Cambridge, Mass.: Moses King, 1883.

Kirkland, Edward C. *A History of American Economic Life.* New York: Appleton-Century-Crofts, 1951.

Kirwan, Albert. *Revolt of the Rednecks: Mississippi Politics, 1876–1925.* New York: Harper and Row, 1965.

Klein, Michele. *A Time to Be Born: Customs and Folklore of Jewish Birth.* Philadelphia: Jewish Publication Society, 1998.

Kornweibel, Theodore. *No Crystal Stair: Black Life and the Messenger, 1917–1928.* Westport, Conn.: Greenwood Press, 1975.

Kraft, James P. "Artists as Workers: Musicians and Trade Unionism in America, 1880–1917." *Musical Quarterly* 79, no. 3 (Autumn 1995): 512–43.

Krane, Dale, and Stephen Shaffer. *Mississippi Government and Politics: Modernizers versus Traditionalists.* Lincoln: University of Nebraska Press, 1992.

Kroessler, Jeffrey A. *New York Year by Year: A Chronology of the Great Metropolis.* New York: New York University Press, 2002.

LaCapra, Dominick. *History and Memory after Auschwitz.* Ithaca, N.Y.: Cornell University Press, 1998.

Lacy, Dan. *The Meaning of the American Revolution.* New York: Mentor Books, 1966.

Lainhart, Ann, comp. *1865 Massachusetts State Census. Charlestown, Ward 2.* Boston: A. S. Lainhart, 1992.

Lander, Ernest M., Jr. "Charleston: Manufacturing Center of the Old South." *Journal of Southern History* (August 1960): 330–51.

Langbauer, Laurie. *Novels of Everyday Life: The Series in English Fiction, 1850–1930.* Ithaca, N.Y.: Cornell University Press, 1999.

"Lawson, John." In *The Columbia Encyclopedia, Sixth Edition.* New York: Columbia University Press, 2004, 27549.

Leamon, James S. *Revolution Downeast: The War for American Independence in Maine.* Amherst: University of Massachusetts Press, 1993.

Lehner, Ernst, and Johanna Lehner. *Folklore and Symbolism of Flowers, Plants, and Trees.* New York: Tudor, 1960.

Lemann, Nicholas. *The Great Black Migration and How It Changed America.* New York: Knopf, 1992.

Lemus, Rienzi B. "The Third Annual Meeting of the National Negro Business League." *Colored American Magazine* (October 1902): 459.

Lerner, Gerda. "Early Community Work of Black Club Women." *Journal of Negro History* 59, no. 2 (April 1974): 158–67.

Leslie, William. "The Gaspee Affair: A Study of Its Constitutional Significance." *Mississippi Valley Historical Review* 39, no. 2 (September 1952): 233–56.

Levesque, George. "Inherent Reformers—Inherited Orthodoxy: Black Baptists in Boston, 1800–1873." *Journal of Negro History* 60, no. 4 (October 1975): 491–525.

Levine, Robert S. *Martin Delany, Frederick Douglass, and the Politics of Representative Identity.* Chapel Hill: University of North Carolina Press, 1997.

Levy, Leonard W., and Harlan B. Philips. "The Roberts Case: Source of the 'Separate but Equal' Doctrine." *American Historical Review* 56, no. 3 (April 1951): 510–18.

Lewis, Barbara. "Review: James V. Hatch, *Sorrow Is the Only Faithful One: The Life of Owen Dodson.*" *African American Review* 29, no. 4 (1995): 687–90.

Lewis, David Levering. *W. E. B. Du Bois: Biography of a Race, 1868–1919.* New York: Henry Holt, 1993.

Lewis, Ethelreda. *Trader Horn: Being the Life and Works of Alfred Aloysius Horn.* New York: Simon and Schuster, 1927.

Lincoln, C. Eric, and Lawrence H. Mamiya. *The Black Church in the African-American Experience.* Durham, N.C.: Duke University Press, 1990.

"Lincoln's Rules for Living." *New Era Magazine* (February 1916): 6.

Lindee, M. Susan. "The American Career of Jane Marcet's Conversations on Chemistry, 1806–1853," *Isis* 82, no. 1 (March 1991): 8–23.

Lindfors, Bernth. "'Mislike Me Not for My Complexion . . .': Ira Aldridge in Whiteface." *African American Review* 33, no. 2 (Summer 1999): 347–54.

———. "'Nothing Extenuate, Nor Set Down Aught in Malice': New Biographical Information on Ira Aldridge." *African American Review* 28, no. 3 (Autumn 1994): 457–72.

Little, Shelby. *George Washington.* New York: Minton, Balch, 1929.

Logan, Rayford Whittingham, and Michael R. Winston. *Dictionary of American Negro Biography.* New York: W. W. Norton, 1982.

Logan, Shirley Wilson. *We Are Coming: The Persuasive Discourse of Nineteenth-Century Black Women.* Carbondale: Southern Illinois University Press, 1999.

Longfellow, Henry Wadsworth. *The Complete Poetical Works of Henry Wadsworth Longfellow.* Boston: Houghton, Mifflin, 1883, 1893.

Lott, Eric. *Love and Theft: Blackface Minstrelsy and the American Working Class*. New York: Oxford University Press, 1993.

Lotz, Rainer E. "The Black Troubadours: Black Entertainers in Europe, 1896–1915." *Black Music Research Journal* 10, no. 2 (Autumn 1990): 253–73.

Lowery, Charles D., and John F. Marszalek, eds. *Encyclopedia of African-American Civil Rights: From Emancipation to the Present*. New York: Greenwood Press, 1992.

Luciano, Dana. "Passing Shadows: Melancholic Nationality and Black Critical Publicity in Pauline E. Hopkins's *Of One Blood*." In *Loss: The Politics of Mourning*, edited by David Eng and David Kazanjian, 148–87. Berkeley: University of California Press, 2003.

Luker, Ralph E. *The Social Gospel in Black and White: American Racial Reform, 1885–1912*. Chapel Hill: University of North Carolina Press, 1991.

Luthin, Reinhard, and Allan Nevins. *American Demagogues: Twentieth Century*. Boston: Beacon, 1954.

Mabee, Carleton. "A Negro Boycott to Integrate Boston Schools." *New England Quarterly* 41, no. 3 (September 1968): 341–61.

MacCarthy, Esther. "The Home for Aged Colored Women, 1861–1944." *Historical Journal of Massachusetts* (Winter 1993): 55–73.

Macleod, Beth Abelson. *Women Performing Music: The Emergence of American Women as Instrumentalists and Conductors*. Jefferson, N.C.: McFarland, 2001.

Mahar, William J. *Behind the Burnt Cork Mask: Early Blackface Minstrelsy and Antebellum American Popular Culture*. Urbana: University of Illinois Press, 1999.

———. "Black English in Early Black Face Minstrelsy: A New Interpretation of the Sources of Minstrel Show Dialect." *American Quarterly* 37, no. 2 (Summer 1985): 260–85.

Maier, Pauline. "Popular Uprisings and Civil Authority in Eighteenth-Century America." *William and Mary Quarterly* 27, no. 1 (January 1970): 3–35.

Maine: A Guide Down East. Boston: Houghton Mifflin, 1937.

Manfra, Jo Ann, and Robert R. Dykstra. "Serial Marriage and the Origins of the Black Stepfamily: The Rowanty Evidence." *Journal of American History* 72 (June 1985): 18–44.

Manning, Keith. *Black Apollo of Science: The Life of Ernest Everett Just*. New York: Oxford University Press, 1993.

Marable, W. Manning. "Booker T. Washington and African Nationalism." *Phylon* 35, no. 4 (1974): 398–406.

Marshall, George O., Jr. *A Tennyson Handbook*. New York: Twayne, 1963.

Martin, Edwin T. *Thomas Jefferson: Scientist*. New York: Collier, 1961.

Martineau, Harriet. *The Hour and the Man*. Cited in Pauline Hopkins, "Toussaint L'Ouverture." *Colored American Magazine* 2, no. 1 (November 1900): 19.

———. *Harriet Martineau's Autobiography*. London: Virago, 1983.

Marvin, Frank, and Monaghan Lowenthal. *This Was New York: The Nation's Capital in 1789*. New York: Doubleday, Doran, 1943.

Mary Catherine, Sister. "The Origin and the Development of the Welfare Activities of the Sisters of the Holy Family." B.A. thesis, Xavier University, New Orleans, 1933.

Marzoff, Marion. *Up from the Footnote: A History of Women Journalists*. New York: Hastings House, 1977.

Massachusetts Adjutant General's Office. *Massachusetts Soldiers, Sailors, and Marines in the Civil War*. Vol. 8. Brookline, Mass.: Riverdale, 1935.

Matthews, Victoria Earle. "New York." *The Woman's Era* (July 1895): 3.

———. "The Value of Race Literature." *Boston Herald*, 31 July 1895, 10.

May, Robert E. "'Invisible Men': Blacks and the U.S. Army in the Mexican War." *Historian* 49, no. 4 (August 1987): 463–77.

Mayr, Ernst. *The Growth of Biological Thought; Diversity, Evolution, and Inheritance.* Cambridge: Belknap Press of Harvard University Press, 1982.

M'Carty, William. *National Songs, Ballads, and Other Patriotic Poetry, Chiefly Relating to the War of 1846.* Philadelphia: W. M'Carty, 1846.

McCallum, Peter. "Norma, Opera Australia," 28 June 2004, <http://www.smh.com .au/articles/2004/06/27/1088274623952.html?from=storyrhs&oneclick=tru>, January 2006.

McCarthy, Eugene J. *America Revisited: 150 Years after Tocqueville.* Garden City, N.Y.: Doubleday, 1978.

McConnell, Stuart. *Glorious Contentment: The Grand Army of the Republic, 1865–1900.* Chapel Hill: University of North Carolina, 1992.

McCordick, David, ed. *Scottish Literature: An Anthology.* New York: Peter Lang, 1996.

McCully, Emily. *The Escape of Oney Judge: Martha Washington's Slave Finds Freedom.* New York: Farrar, 2007.

McFeely, Maureen. "'This Day My Sister Should the Cloister Enter': The Convent as Refuge in *Measure for Measure.*" In *Subjects on the World's Stage: Essays on British Literature of the Middle Ages and the Renaissance*, edited by David Allen and Robert White, 200–216. Newark: University of Delaware Press, 1995.

McHenry, Elizabeth. *Forgotten Readers: Recovering the Lost History of African American Literary Societies.* Durham, N.C.: Duke University Press, 2002.

———. "Rereading Literary Legacy: New Considerations of the 19th-Century African-American Reader and Writer." *Callaloo* 22 (1999): 477–82.

McKivigan, John. *The War against Proslavery Religion: Abolitionism and the Northern Churches, 1830–1865.* Ithaca, N.Y.: Cornell University Press, 1984.

McLoughlin, William E. *Rhode Island: A Bicentennial History.* New York: W. W. Norton, 1978.

McMurry, Linda O. *To Keep the Waters Troubled: The Life of Ida B. Wells.* New York: Oxford University Press, 1998.

McPherson, Scott. "Should Americans Support IRA Disarmament?" <http://www .lewrockwell.com/orig3/mcpherson1.html>, January 2006.

Meier, August. "Booker T. Washington and the Negro Press: With Special Reference to the Colored American Magazine." *Journal of Negro History* 38, no. 1 (January 1953): 67–90.

Menschel, David. "Abolition without Deliverance: The Law of Connecticut Slavery, 1784–1848." *Yale Law Journal* 111, no. 1 (October 2001): 183–222.

Merrill, Walter, ed. *1822–1835.* Vol. 1 of *The Letters of William Lloyd Garrison.* Cambridge: Belknap Press of Harvard University Press, 1971.

———. *No Union with Slave-Holders, 1841–1849.* Vol. 3 of *The Letters of William Lloyd Garrison.* Cambridge: Belknap Press of Harvard University Press, 1973.

Miller, Alice. "To the Woman's Era Club." *The Woman's Era* (August 1895): 15.

Miller, Edward. *Gullah Statesman: Robert Smalls from Slavery to Congress, 1839–1915.* Columbia: University of South Carolina Press, 1995.

Milton, John. *Paradise Lost* (1674). In *John Milton: The Complete Poems*, edited by John Leonard. New York: Penguin Books, 1998.

"Mission to Hayti." *American Baptist Magazine, and Missionary Intelligencer* 4, no. 8 (May 1824): 305.

Mitchell, J. Marcus. "The Paul Family." *Old-Time New England* (1973): 73–77.

Moon, Henry Lee. *The Balance of Power: The Negro Vote*. Garden City, N.Y.: Doubleday, 1948.

Morais, Herbert M. *The History of the Negro in Medicine*. New York: Publishers Co., 1967.

Morris, Jeffrey B., and Richard B. Morris, eds. *Encyclopedia of American History*. New York: HarperCollins, 1996.

Mossell, Mrs. N. F. *The Work of Afro-American Women*. 1894. Philadelphia: Geo. S. Ferguson, 1908.

Natal, Carmelo Rosario. *Pedro Albizu Campos, Estudiante de Ponce: Nuevas Revelaciones*. San Juan, Puerto Rico: Selecciones HistUricas, 2003.

National Association of Colored Women. *A History of the Club Movement among the Colored Women of the United States of America, as Contained in the Minutes of the Conventions, Held in Boston, July 29, 30, 31, 1895, and of the National Federation of Afro-American Women, Held in Washington, D.C., July 20, 21, 22, 1896*. Washington, D.C.: National Association of Colored Women, 1902.

National Park Service. "Charles Street Meeting House," <http://www.nps.gov/boaf/historyculture/charles-street-meeting-house.htm>, May 2007.

———. "A Forgotten Milestone: Blacks in the U.S. Navy," <http://www.nps.gov/vick/vicstr/sitebln/a_forgot.htm>, January 2006.

Naval Historical Center. "U.S.S. *Niagara* (1857–1885)," <http://www.history.navy.mil/photos/sh-usn/usnsh-n/niagara2.htm>, January 2006.

"Negroes Honor Memory of William L. Garrison." *New York Times*, 11 December 1905, 8.

Nell, William Cooper. *The Colored Patriots of the American Revolution, with Sketches of Several Distinguished Colored Persons: To Which Is Added a Brief Survey of the Condition and Prospects of Colored Americans*. 1855. New York: Arno Press, 1968.

Nelson, Samuel H. *Colonialism in the Congo Basin, 1880–1940*. Athens: Ohio Center for International Studies, 1994.

New Catholic Encyclopedia. Vol. 14. New York: McGraw Hill Book Company, 1967.

New England Historical Genealogical Society. *People of Color in the Massachusetts State Census, 1855–1865*, <http://www.newenglandancestors.org>, January 2006.

"New York City below Forty-second Street, Part 1." *Historic Texts*, 1936, <http://www.nyc-architecture.com/ARCH/Notes-1930_below42nd.htm>, January 2006.

Nichols, Roger. *Black Hawk and the Warrior's Path*. Arlington Heights, Ill.: Harlan Davidson, 1992.

Nickerson, Catherine Ross. *The Web of Inquiry: Early Detective Fiction by American Women*. Durham, N.C.: Duke University Press, 1998.

Noble, David W. *The Eternal Adam and the New World Garden: The Central Myth in the American Novel since 1830*. New York: Braziller, 1968.

Noble, Frederic Perry. *The Chicago Congress on Africa, 1894*. Chicago: 1894.

"Norfolk Mission College Site." Department of City Planning, City of Norfolk, Va., <http://www.historicnorfolk.org/A19.html>, January 2006.

"Notes." *Journal of Negro History* 7, no. 3 (July 1922): 346–47.

"Notes and News." *American Historical Review* 5, no. 2 (December 1899): 406–22.

"Obituary of Thomas Paul." *Genius of Universal Emancipation* (April 1831): 197.

O'Connor, Thomas H. *Civil War Boston: Home Front and Battlefield*. Boston: Northeastern University Press, 1997.

O'Donoghue, D. J. *The Poets of Ireland: A Biographical Dictionary*. Dublin: Hodges Figgis, 1912.

Oedel, Howard T. "Slavery in Colonial Portsmouth." *Historical New Hampshire* 26, no. 3 (Autumn 1966): 3–11.

Oliphant, Margaret. *The Autobiography of Mrs. Oliphant*. Edited by Harry Coghill. Chicago: University of Chicago Press, 1988.

———. "The Executor." *Blackwood's Edinburgh Magazine* 89, no. 547 (May 1861): 595–614.

Overmyer, Grace. *America's First Hamlet*. New York: New York University Press, 1957.

Ovid. *Metamorphoses, Book XI*. Translated by A. D. Melville and with an introduction and notes by E. J. Kenney. New York: Oxford University Press, 1998.

Pacheco, Josephine. *A Failed Escape on the Potomac*. Chapel Hill: University of North Carolina Press, 2005.

Painter, John H. "The Fugitives of the Pearl." *Journal of Negro History* 1, no. 3 (June 1916): 243–64.

Parkman, Henry, Jr. *Montcalm and Wolfe*. Boston: Little, Brown, 1902.

Parsons, Elsie Clews. "Bermuda Folklore." *Journal of American Folklore* 38, no. 148 (April–June 1925): 42–64.

Patten, George W. "Episodes of the Mexican War: A Poem Delivered before the New York Associated Veterans of the Mexican War, at the Lexington Avenue Opera House, New York City, on the Thirty-first Anniversary of the Capture of the City of Mexico." New York: Brentano's Literary Emporium, 1878.

Patterson, Martha. "'Kin o' Rough Justice fer a Parson': Pauline Hopkins's Winona and the Politics of Reconstructing History." *African American Review* 32, no. 3 (Autumn 1998): 445–60.

Paul, Susan. *Memoir of James Jackson, the Attentive and Obedient Scholar, Who Died in Boston, October 31, 1833, Aged Six Years and Eleven Months, by His Teacher Miss Susan Paul*. Edited by Lois Brown. Cambridge: Harvard University Press, 2000.

Paul, Rev. Thomas. "To Massachusetts Baptist Missionary Society." *American Baptist Magazine, and Missionary Intelligencer* 4, no. 6 (November 1823): 225–27.

"Pauline E. Hopkins." *Colored American Magazine* (January 1901): 219.

Peixotto, Ernest. *A Revolutionary Pilgrimage: Being an Account of a Series of Visits to Battlegrounds and Other Places Made Memorable by the War of the Revolution*. New York: Charles Scribner's, 1917.

Pérez e Gonzìlez, Marie E. *Puerto Ricans in the United States*. Westport, Conn.: Greenwood Press, 2000.

Perman, Michael. *The Road to Redemption: Southern Politics, 1869–1879*. Chapel Hill: University of North Carolina Press, 1984.

Perry, Imani. "There Goes the Neighborhood." *02138*, <http://www.02138mag.com/magazine/article/1206.html>, May 2007.

Peterson, Bernard. *The African American Theatre Directory, 1816–1960: A Comprehensive Guide to Early Black Theatre Organizations, Companies, Theatres, and Performing Groups*. Westport, Conn.: Greenwood Press, 1997.

———. *A Century of Musicals in Black and White: An Encyclopedia of Musical Works by, about, or involving African Americans*. Westport, Conn.: Greenwood Press, 1993.

Peterson, Carla. *"Doers of the Word": African-American Women Speakers and Writers in the North, 1830–1880*. New York: Oxford University Press, 1995.

Peterson, Merrill D. *Thomas Jefferson and the New Nation: A Biography*. New York: Oxford University Press, 1975.

Petty, Julian J. *The Growth and Distribution of Population in South Carolina*. Columbia, S.C.: State Council for Defense, Industrial Development Committee, 1943.

Piatt, Sarah Morgan Bryant. "The Black Princess (A True Fable of My Old Kentucky Nurse)." In *Nineteenth-Century American Women Poets: An Anthology*, edited by Paula Bernat Bennett, 244–46. Malden, Mass.: Blackwell, 1998.

Pickens, William. "Jesse Max Barber." *Voice of the Negro* (November 1906): 483–88.

Piersen, William. *Black Yankees: The Development of an Afro-American Subculture in Eighteenth-Century New England*. Amherst: University of Massachusetts Press, 1988.

"A Pioneer and Wise Counsellor." In *The Reformed Reader*, <http://www.reformedreader .org/history/pius/chapter12.htm>, May 2007.

Poggi, Jack. *Theater in America: The Impact of Economic Forces, 1870–1967*. Ithaca, N.Y.: Cornell University Press, 1968.

Poitevin, Rene Francisco. "Political Surveillance, State Repression, and Class Resistance: The Puerto Rican Experience." *Social Justice* 27, no. 3 (2000): 89–100.

Porter, Dorothy B. "The Organized Educational Activities of Negro Literary Societies, 1828–1846." *Journal of Negro Education* 5, no. 4 (October 1936): 555–76.

Porter, Susan L. *Women of the Commonwealth: Work, Family, and Social Change in Nineteenth-Century Massachusetts*. Amherst: University of Massachusetts Press, 1996.

Preston, Harriet Waters. "Men and Letters: Mrs. Oliphant." *Atlantic Monthly*, August 1897, 424–27.

Prince, Mary. *The History of Mary Prince, A West Indian Slave, Related by Herself*. Edited by Moira Ferguson. Ann Arbor: University of Michigan Press, 1997.

"Prince Saunders." "Virtual American Biographies," <http://www.famousamericans.net/ princesaunders>, January 2006.

Putzi, Jennifer. "'Raising the Stigma': Black Womanhood and the Marked Body in Pauline Hopkins's *Contending Forces*." *College Literature* 31, no. 2 (2004): 1–21.

Quarles, Benjamin. *Black Abolitionists*. New York: Oxford University Press, 1969.

———. *Lincoln and the Negro*. New York: Oxford University Press, 1962.

"The Question of Segregation." *New Era Magazine* (April 1916): 90.

Rable, George. *The Confederate Republic: A Revolution against Politics*. Chapel Hill: University of North Carolina Press, 1994.

Rafroidi, Patrick. *Irish Literature in English: The Romantic Period, 1789–1850*. Vol. 2. Gerrards Cross, Buckinghamshire, England: Colin Smythe, 1980.

Randel, William Peirce. *The Ku Klux Klan: A Century of Infamy*. New York: Chilton, 1965.

Rashidi, Runoko. "Pauline Elizabeth Hopkins: Dean of African-American Women Writers. In *The Global African Presence*, <http://www.cwo.com/~lucumi/dean.html>, January 2006.

"Real Music and Art Rising Out of a Sea of Fake." *New York Times*, 9 March 1913, 60.

Redpath, James. *The Public Life of Capt. John Brown*. Boston: Thayer and Eldridge, 1860.

Reed, Gladys Jones. "Distinguished Negroes of the West Indies." *Negro History Bulletin* (January 1941): 79.

Reed, William Allan. *Negritos of Zambales*. Manila: Bureau of Public Printing, 1904.

Rice, Anne P., ed. *Witnessing Lynching: American Writers Respond*. New Brunswick, N.J.: Rutgers University Press, 2003.

Ricks, Mary Kay. *Escape on the Pearl: The Heroic Bid for Freedom on the Underground Railroad*. New York: William Morrow, 2007.

Riley, Glenda. *Divorce: An American Tradition*. Lincoln: University of Nebraska Press, 1991.

Ripley, C. Peter, Jeffery Rossbach, Roy E. Finkenbine, Fiona Spiers, and Debra Susie, eds. *The British Isles, 1830-1865*. Vol. 1 of *The Black Abolitionist Papers*. Chapel Hill: University of North Carolina Press, 1985.

Ripley, Peter, Roy E. Finkenbine, Michael F. Hembree, and Donald Yacovone, eds. *Witness for Freedom: African American Voices on Race, Slavery, and Emancipation*. Chapel Hill: University of North Carolina Press, 1993.

Risjord, Norman K. *Chesapeake Politics, 1781-1800*. New York: Columbia University Press, 1978.

Roach, Joseph. "Culture and Performance in the Circum-Atlantic World." In *Performativity and Performance*, edited by Andrew Parker and Eve Kosofsky Sedgwick, 45-63. New York: Routledge, 1995.

Robboy, Stanley J., and Anita W. Robboy. "Lewis Hayden: From Fugitive Slave to Statesman." *New England Quarterly* 46, no. 4 (December 1973): 591-613.

Robinson, Blackwell P., ed. *The North Carolina Guide*. Chapel Hill: University of North Carolina Press, 1955.

Rohrbach, Augusta. "To Be Continued: Double Identity, Multiplicity and Antigenealogy as Narrative Strategies in Pauline Hopkins's Magazine Fiction." *Callaloo* 22, no. 2 (1999): 483-98.

Roses, Lorraine Elena. "The Black Church," <http://www.bostonblackhistory.org/history/church.html>, January 2006.

Rothschild, Alonzo. *Lincoln, Master of Men: A Study in Character*. Boston: Houghton Mifflin, 1906.

Rozwenc, Edwin. *The Compromise of 1850*. Washington, D.C.: Heath, 1957.

Rucker, Walter C. "'I Will Gather All Nations': Resistance, Culture, and Pan-African Collaboration in Denmark Vesey's South Carolina." *Journal of Negro History* 86, no. 2 (Spring 2001): 132-47.

Ruffin, George. Introduction to *Life and Times of Frederick Douglass, Written by Himself*. . . . *With an introduction by George L. Ruffin, of Boston*. Boston: De Wolfe and Fiske, 1892.

Ruffin, Josephine St. Pierre. "A Charge to Be Refuted." *The Woman's Era* (June 1895): 9.

Sadie, Stanley, ed. *The New Grove Dictionary of Music and Musicians*. Vol. 1. London: Macmillan, 1980.

Salvatore, Nick. *We All Got History: The Memory Books of Amos Webber*. New York: Times Books, 1996.

Sampson, Henry T. *The Ghost Walks: A Chronological History of Blacks in Show Business, 1865-1910*. Metuchen, N.J.: Scarecrow Press, 1988.

"Samuel Smiles." *The Gazetteer for Scotland, 1995-2005*, <www.geo.ed.ac.scotgaz/people/famousfirst363.html>, January 2006.

Sansing, David G. "James Kimble Vardaman, Thirty-sixth Governor of Mississippi: 1904-1908." *Mississippi History Now* (January 2004): 2.

Sarna, Jonathan D. *Jacksonian Jew: The Two Worlds of Mordecai Noah*. New York: Holmes and Meier, 1981.

Saxton, Alexander. *Rise and Fall of the White Republic*. New York: Verso, 1990.

"Say He Hired Acid Throwers." *New York Times*, 1 February 1904, 12.

Schapera, I. *Livingstone's African Journal, 1853-1856*. Vol. 1. Berkeley: University of California Press, 1963.

Schechter, Patricia A. *Ida B. Wells-Barnett and American Reform, 1880-1930*. Chapel Hill: University of North Carolina Press, 2001.

Schmitz, Neil. "Captive Utterance: Black Hawk and Indian Irony." *Arizona Quarterly* 48 (1992): 1-18.

Schneider, Mark. "Boston's Pro-Civil Rights Bookerites." *Journal of Negro History* 80, no. 4 (Autumn 1995): 157-69.

———. *"The Colored American* and *Alexander's*: Boston's Pro-Civil Rights Bookerites." *Journal of Negro History* 80, no. 4 (Autumn 1995): 157-69.

Schomburg, Arthur A. "The Negro Digs Up His Past." *Survey Graphic* (March 1925): 671.

Schott, Thomas E. *Alexander H. Stephens of Georgia: A Biography*. Baton Rouge: Louisiana State University Press, 1988.

Schulman, Samuel E. "Mourning and Voice in *Maud.*" *Studies in English Literature, 1500-1900* 23, no. 4 (Autumn 1983): 633-46.

Schultz, Harold S. *Nationalism and Sectionalism in South Carolina, 1852-1860: A Study of the Movement for Southern Independence*. Durham, N.C.: Duke University Press, 1950.

Schultz, Jeffrey, Kerry L. Haynie, Anne M. McCulloch, Andrew L. Aoki, eds. *Encyclopedia of Minorities in American Politics*. Vol. 2. Phoenix: Oryx, 2000.

Schwartz, Howard. *Reimagining the Bible: The Storytelling of the Rabbis*. New York: Oxford University Press, 1998.

Schwartz, Richard I. *Well-Known Soloists from All Walks of Life, T-Z*, <http://www.angelfire.com/music2/thecornetcompendium/new_page_4.html>, January 2006.

Scott, Donald. "The Popular Lecture and the Creation of a Public in Mid-Nineteenth-Century America." *Journal of American History* 66, no. 4 (March 1980): 791-809.

Scruggs, Lewis A. *Women of Distinction: Remarkable in Works and Invincible in Character*. Raleigh, N.C.: L. A. Scruggs, 1893.

Seller, Maxine Schwartz, ed. *Ethnic Theatre in the United States*. Westport, Conn.: Greenwood Press, 1983.

Semmes, Clovis E. *Racism, Health, and Post-industrialism: A Theory of African American Health*. Westport, Conn.: Praeger, 1996.

Sernett, Milton. *Bound for the Promised Land: African American Religion and the Great Migration*. Durham, N.C.: Duke University Press, 1997.

"Several Hundred Brave Storm at Statue." *Boston Guardian*, 16 December 1905, 1.

Shakespeare, William. *The Merchant of Venice*. Edited by Jay Halio. New York: Oxford University Press, 1998.

Shalom, Jack. "The Ira Aldridge Troupe: Early Black Minstrelsy in Philadelphia." *African American Review* 28, no. 4 (Winter 1994): 653-58.

Sharpley-Whiting, T. Denean. *Black Venus: Sexualized Savages, Primal Fears, and Primitive Narratives in French*. Durham, N.C.: Duke University Press, 1999.

Sherman, Joan. "James Monroe Whitfield, Poet and Emigrationist: A Voice of Protest and Despair." *Journal of Negro History* 57, no. 2 (April 1972): 169-76.

Sherwin, Oscar. *Prophet of Liberty: The Life and Times of Wendell Phillips*. New York: Bookman Associates, 1958.

Shoenfeld, Sarah. "Applications for Admission to the Home for Aged Colored Women,

1860-1887." *New England Historical and Genealogical Register* 155 (July 2001): 251–72; 156 (October 2001): 397–413.

Silverberg, Robert. *Light for the World: Edison and the Power Industry*. Princeton, N.J.: D. Van Nostrand, 1967.

Simmons, William J. *Men of Mark: Eminent, Progressive, Rising*. 1887. New York: Arno Press, 1968.

Sinha, Manisha. *The Counterrevolution of Slavery: Politics and Ideology in Antebellum South Carolina*. Chapel Hill: University of North Carolina Press, 2000.

Skocpol, Theda, and Jennifer Lynn Oser. "Organization despite Adversity: The Origins and Development of African American Fraternal Organizations." *Social Science History* 28, no. 3 (2004): 367–437.

Slayden, Ellen Maury. *Washington Wife: Journal of Ellen Maury Slayden from 1897-1919*. New York: Harper and Row, 1963.

Slide, Anthony. *Lois Weber: The Director Who Lost Her Way in History*. Westport, Conn.: Greenwood Press, 1996.

Small, William F. "Guadaloupe: A Tale of Love and War: By One Who Served in the Campaign of 1846-7, in the Late War with Mexico." Philadelphia: J. B. Smith: 1860.

Smiles, Samuel. *Self-Help; With Illustrations of Character and Content*. Boston: Fields, Osgood, 1870.

Smith, Albert E. "The Grand Army of the Republic and Kindred Societies," Library of Congress, <http://www.loc.gov/rr/main/gar/garhome.html>, January 2006.

Smith, Edwin. *Aggrey of Africa: A Study in Black and White*. London: Garden City Press, 1929.

Smith, Harriet, and L. C. Carter. "Minutes of the First National Conference Of Colored Women." *The Woman's Era* (August 1895): 2.

Smith, Jessie Carney, ed. *Notable Black American Women*. Detroit: Gale Research, 1992.

Smock, Raymond W., ed. *Booker T. Washington in Perspective: Essays of Louis R. Harlan*. Jackson: University Press of Mississippi, 1988.

Snethen, Worthington G. *The Black Code of the District of Columbia, in Force, September 1st, 1848*. New York: William Harned, 1848.

Snow, Edwin M. *Alphabetical Index to Births Recorded in Providence from 1851-1870*. Providence, R.I.: Sidney S. Rider, 1879.

Soitos, Stephen F. *The Blues Detective: A Study of African American Detective Fiction*. Amherst: University of Massachusetts Press, 1996.

"Son of Garrison Speaks at Smith Court Church." *Boston Guardian*, 16 December 1905, 9.

Southern, Eileen. *Biographical Dictionary of Afro-American and African Musicians*. Westport, Conn.: Greenwood Press, 1982.

———. *The Music of Black Americans: A History*. New York: W. W. Norton, 1997.

———, ed. *African American Theater: Out of Bondage (1876), and Peculiar Sam; or The Underground Railroad (1879)*. Vol. 9 of *Nineteenth-Century American Musical Theatre*. New York: Garland, 1994.

Stanford, Peter Thomas. *The Tragedy of the Negro in America: A Condensed History of the Enslavement, Sufferings, Emancipation, Present Condition and Progress of the Negro Race in the United States of America*. Boston: Charles A. Wasto, 1897.

Stanton, Elizabeth Cady. *Eighty Years and More: Reminiscences of Elizabeth Cady Stanton (1815-1897)*. London: T. Fisher Unwin, 1898.

Steele, Ian. *Betrayal: Fort William Henry and the "Massacre."* New York: Oxford University Press, 1991.

Stein, Arnold. *Answerable Style: Essays on Paradise Lost*. Minneapolis: University of Minnesota Press, 1953.

"Stephen Fiske" (obituary). *New York Times*, 28 April 1916, 11.

Sterling, Dorothy. *Captain of the Planter: The Story of Robert Smalls*. Garden City, N.Y.: Doubleday, 1958.

Still, Bayrd. *Mirror for Gotham: New York as Seen by Contemporaries from Dutch Days to the Present*. New York: New York University Press, 1956.

Still, William. *The Underground Railroad*. Philadelphia: 1872.

Streitmatter, Rodger. "Josephine St. Pierre Ruffin: A Nineteenth-Century Journalist of Boston's Black Elite Class." In *Women of the Commonwealth: Work, Family, and Social Change in Nineteenth-Century Massachusetts*, edited by Susan L. Porter, 147–63. Amherst: University of Massachusetts Press, 1996.

"Supplement to the Colored American Magazine, March 1904: The Founders of the Colored American League." *Colored American Magazine* (March 1904).

Swasey, Benjamin F. *History of the Baptist Church, Exeter, New Hampshire, 1800–1900*. Exeter, N.H.: Exeter News-Letter Press, 1901.

Tager, Jack. *Boston Riots: Three Centuries of Social Violence*. Boston: Northeastern University Press, 2001.

Tate, Claudia. *Domestic Allegories of Political Desire: The Black Heroine's Text at the Turn of the Century*. New York: Oxford University Press, 1996.

———. "Pauline Hopkins: Our Literary Foremother." In *Conjuring: Black Women, Fiction and Literary Tradition*, edited by Marjorie Pryse and Hortense Spillers, 53–66. Bloomington: Indiana University Press, 1985.

Taylor, Clarence. *The Black Churches of Brooklyn*. New York: Columbia University Press, 1994.

"Telegraph to Move Nov. 15." *New York Times*, 2 November 1931, 19.

Terrell, Mary Church. *Colored Woman in a White World*. Washington, D.C.: Ransdell, 1940.

———. "Report to President, Officers, and Members of the NACW from Tuskegee Women's Club, September 15, 1901." Cited in Beverly Jones, "Mary Church Terrell and the National Association of Colored Women, 1896 to 1901." In *Women Together: Organizational Life*, edited by Nancy Cott. Munich: K. G. Saur, 1993.

Thompkins, Eugene. *The History of the Boston Theatre, 1854–1901*. Boston: Houghton Mifflin, 1908.

Thompson, Kathleen. "Greenfield, Elizabeth Taylor." In *Black Women in America: An Historical Encyclopedia*, edited by Darlene Clark Hine, Elsa Barkley Brown, and Rosalyn Terborg-Penn, 1:499–501. Bloomington: Indiana University Press, 1993.

———. "Washington, Margaret Murray." In *Black Women in America: An Historical Encyclopedia*, edited by Darlene Clark Hine, Elsa Barkley Brown, and Rosalyn Terborg-Penn, 2:1233–35. Bloomington: Indiana University Press, 1993.

Thornbrough, Emma Lou. "American Negro Newspapers, 1880–1914." *Business History Review* 40, no. 4 (Winter 1966): 467–90.

Tigger, Bruce G. "The Myth of Meroe and the African Iron Age." *African Historical Studies* 2, no. 1 (1969): 23–50.

"Times Square." *New York Times*, 27 April 1904, 8. Reprint from *Utica Press*.

Tocqueville, Alexis de. *Democracy in America*. Translated by Arthur Goldhammer. New York: Library of America, 2004.

Toll, Robert. *Blacking Up: The Minstrel Show in Nineteenth-Century America*. New York: Oxford University Press, 1974.

Toll, William. *The Resurgence of Race: Black Social Theory from Reconstruction to the Pan-African Conferences*. Philadelphia: Temple University Press, 1979.

"Touching Service by Colored Women at Homestead." *Boston Guardian*, 16 December 1905, 1.

Trapido, Stanley. "African Divisional Politics in the Colony, 1884 to 1910." *Journal of African History* 9, no. 1 (1968): 79–98.

Trenholme, Louise Irby. *The Ratification of the Federal Constitution in North Carolina*. New York: Columbia University Press, 1932.

"Tribute at Cooper Union." *New York Times*, 11 December 1905, 8.

Trotter, James Monroe. *Music and Some Highly Musical People: Containing Brief Chapters on I. A Description of Music. II. The Music of Nature. III. A Glance at the History of Music. IV. The Power, Beauty, and Uses of Music. Following Which Are Given Sketches of the Lives of Remarkable Musicians of the Colored Race. With Portraits, and an Appendix Containing Copies of Music Composed by Colored Men*. 1881. New York: Johnson Reprint Corporation, 1968.

Trowbridge, J. T. *My Own Story with Recollections of Noted Persons*. Cambridge: Riverside Press, 1904.

Twain, Mark, and Charles Dudley Warner. *The Gilded Age: A Tale of Today*. Vol. 1. 1873. New York: P. F. Collier, 1922.

"Twelve Missing in Boston Fire; Blaze Starts in Old Revere House and Spreads to Nearby Buildings." *New York Times*, 16 January 1912, 1.

21st Century Learning Initiative. "What's New," <http://www.21learn.org/acti/winona.html>, January 2006.

"The Up-Town Building of the New York Times." *New York Times*, 11 August 1902, 6.

Urquhart, Molly, contributor. "Devereux, Runiroi, Uniroy, Runiroy Plantation," in "Historic Homes of Bertie County," at "Bertie County-NCGenWeb Project Page," <http:www.rootsweb.com/~ncbertie/homes.htm#ashland>, January 2006.

Uya, Okon Edet. *From Slavery to Public Service: Robert Smalls, 1839-1915*. New York: Oxford University Press, 1971.

Van Tine, Warren R., and Michael Pierce. *Builders of Ohio: A Biographical History*. Columbus: Ohio State University Press, 2003.

Vass, L. C. *History of the Presbyterian Church in New Bern, N.C., with a Resumé of Early Ecclesiastical Affairs in Eastern North Carolina, and Sketch of the Early Days of New Bern, N.C.* Richmond, Va.: Whittet and Shepperson, 1886.

Vital Statistics of Deaths Registered in Providence, Rhode Island. Vol. 8. Providence, R.I., 1898.

"The Voice of the Negro for March." *Voice of the Negro* (March 1905): n.p.

"The Voice of the Negro for 1905." *Voice of the Negro* (January 1905): n.p.

Walker, Cheryl. *Indian Nation: Native American Literature and Nineteenth-Century Nationalisms*. Durham, N.C.: Duke University Press, 1997.

Walker, Juliet E. K. *Encyclopedia of African American Business History*. Westport, Conn.: Greenwood Press, 1999.

Wallace, David Duncan. *South Carolina: A Short History, 1520-1948*. Columbia: University of South Carolina Press, 1961.

Ward, Andrew. *Dark Midnight When I Rise: The Story of the Fisk Jubilee Singers Who Introduced the World to the Black Music of America*. New York: Farrar, Straus, and Giroux, 2000.

Warner, Michael. *An Autobiography: The Story of My Life and Work*. Atlanta, Ga.: J. L. Nichols, 1901.

———. "A Soliloquy 'Lately Spoken at the African Theatre': Race and the Public Sphere in New York City." *American Literature* 73, no. 1 (March 2001): 1–46.

———. *Up from Slavery: An Autobiography*. New York: A. L. Burt, 1901.

Watkins, Mel. *On the Real Side: Laughing, Lying, and Signifying: African American Humor That Transformed American Culture, from Slavery to Richard Pryor*. New York: Simon and Schuster, 1994.

Webb, R. K. *Harriet Martineau: A Radical Victorian*. London: Heineman U.S., 1960.

Weber, Ronald. *Hired Pens: Professional Writers in America's Golden Age of Print*. Athens: Ohio University Press, 1997.

Wertenbaker, Thomas J. *The Golden Age of Colonial Culture*. New York: New York University Press, 1942.

Wesley, Dorothy Porter. "Maria Louise Baldwin." In *Black Women in America: An Historical Encyclopedia*, edited by Darlene Clark Hine, Elsa Barkley Brown, and Rosalyn Terborg-Penn, 1:79–80. Bloomington: Indiana University Press, 1993.

Wesley, Dorothy Porter, and Constance Porter Uzelac, eds. *William Cooper Nell: Selected Writings, 1832–1874*. Baltimore: Black Classic Press, 2002.

"West Gulf Blockading Squadron—United States Navy," <http://www.geocities.com/usshartford/West_Gulf_Blockading_Squadron_1.html>, January 2006.

White, Arthur O. "Antebellum School Reform in Boston: Integrationists and Separatists." *Phylon* 34, no. 2 (1973): 203–17.

———. "Prince Saunders: An Instance of Social Mobility among Antebellum New England Blacks." *Journal of Negro History* 60, no. 4 (October 1975): 526–35.

White, Deborah Gray. *Ar'n't I a Woman: Female Slaves in the Plantation South*. New York: W. W. Norton, 1985.

Whitehill, Walter Muir, and Norman Kotker. *Massachusetts: A Pictorial History*. New York: Charles Scribner's, 1976.

Whittier, John Greenleaf. "A Word for the Hour." In *The Complete Poetical Works of John Greenleaf Whittier*, 191. Boston: Houghton Mifflin, 1884.

"Why Mr. Freund Left the City." *New York Times*, 15 January 1880, 8.

Wiencek, Henry. *The Smithsonian Guide to Historic America: Southern New England*. New York: Stewart, Tabori, and Chang, 1989.

Wilcox, Ella Wheeler. *Poetical works of Ella Wheeler Wilcox*. Edinburgh: W. P. Nimmo, Hay, and Mitchell, 1917.

———. *Shells*. Milwaukee: Hauser and Storey, 1873.

Wilkinson, Henry C. *Bermuda from Sail to Steam: The History of the Island from 1784 to 1901*. 2 vols. London: Oxford University Press, 1973.

"William Jonathan Northen (1835–1913)." *Dictionary of American Biography*, <http://galenet.galegroup.com.proxy.mtholyoke.edu>, January 2006.

Williamson, Hugh. *The History of North Carolina*. Vol. 2. Philadelphia: Thomas Dobson, 1812.

"William Trotter Porter." <www.famousamericans.net/williamtrotterporter>, January 2006.

Wilson, Christopher P. "Stephen Crane and the Police." *American Quarterly* 48, no. 2 (June 1996): 273–315.

Winborne, Benjamin. *The Vaughan Family of Hertford County, N.C.* 1909.

Wittke, Carl. *Tambo and Bones: A History of the American Minstrel Stage.* Durham, N.C.: Duke University Press, 1930.

Wolfenstein, Victor. "On the Road Not Taken: 'Revolt and Revenge' in W. E. B. Du Bois's *The Souls of Black Folk.*" *Journal for the Psychoanalysis of Culture and Society* 5 (2000): 121–32.

Woodson, Carter G. "Proceedings of the Annual Meeting of the Association for the Study of Negro Life and History Held in New York City, November 8–12, 1931." *Journal of Negro History* 17, no. 1 (January 1932): 1–7.

Wright, Josephine. "*Das Negertrio* Jiminez in Europe." *Black Perspective in Music* 9, no. 2 (Autumn 1981): 161–76.

Wright, Louis B. *South Carolina: A Bicentennial History.* New York: Norton, 1976.

Wright, Margaret R. "Marcella O'Grady Boveri (1863–1950): Her Three Careers in Biology." *Isis* 88, no. 4 (December 1997): 627–52.

Wright, W. D. *Black History and Black Identity: A Call for a New Historiography.* Westport, Conn.: Praeger, 2002.

Yellin, Jean Fagan. *Women and Sisters: The Antislavery Feminists in American Culture.* New Haven, Conn.: Yale University Press, 1989.

Yensan, Frances M. *The History of Grand Island,* <http:/isledegrande.com/gihist.htm>, January 2006.

Young, James C. *Liberia Rediscovered.* Garden City, N.Y.: Doubleday, Doran, 1934.

Zanger, Jules. "The Tragic Octoroon in Pre–Civil War Fiction." *American Quarterly* 18, no. 1 (Spring 1966): 63–70.

Zilversmit, Arthur. *The First Emancipation: The Abolition of Slavery in the North.* Chicago: University of Chicago Press, 1967.

Zorn, Roman J. "The New England Anti-Slavery Society: Pioneer Abolition Organization." *Journal of Negro History* 42, no. 3 (1957): 157–76.

Zwick, Jim, ed. "Reforming the Heart of Darkness: The Congo Reform Movement in England and the United States," <http://www.boondocksnet.com/congo/index.html>, January 2006.

Index

Allen, Pauline Elizabeth, 43, 60, 69, 70, 74, 75–76, 81, 82, 83, 86, 87, 91, 99, 100, 101, 102, 105, 106, 107, 491, 579 (n. 1). *See also* Hopkins, Pauline

Allen family: Alphonse, 229; Angelina Grimké, 227, 228; Anne (Annie) Pauline, 168, 227 (*see also* Pindell, Annie Pauline); Caroline A., 228; Charles H., 228; Elizabeth, 43, 79, 201, 223, 227, 228, 230–31, 501, 591 (n. 23); Frances E., 227, 229; George J. M. B., 228; Grace, 225, 232, 243; Harriet H., 228, 231, 311–12, 604 (n. 100); Jesse, 60, 201, 221–52, 311, 501, 591 (nn. 12, 23); Mary E., 227; Nelson, 225, 231–33, 243; Sarah A., 34, 41, 42–45, 56, 60, 64–69, 227, 311, 364, 469, 513 (*see also* Hopkins, Sarah A.)

Allied Forces, 503

Allston, Mass., 155, 521

Amalgamation, 542, 543

Amateur Society (Boston, Mass.), 60

America and Other Poems, 249

American Baptist Home Mission Society, 461

American Bible Society, 296

American Colonization Society, 245

American Colored League, 212

American Historical Review, 335

American Missionary Association, 261

American Revolution, 237, 293, 335

American Sabbath School Union, 31

Amesbury, Mass., 314

Amherst College, 312

Anderson, Charles, 448, 552

André, John, 21

Andrew, John A., 150, 517

Anglican Church (Bermuda), 232

Anglo-African, 80, 229

Anshi Lubavitch congregation (Boston, Mass.), 254, 497. *See also* African Baptist Church

Anson County, N.C., 233–34

Antilynching movement, 2, 165–66, 170, 172, 175, 179–89, 190, 193, 194, 319, 423, 516, 558

Antislavery movement, 7, 9, 13, 14, 18, 29–32, 38–41, 45, 53–54, 55, 72, 86–87,

96, 116, 169, 242–45, 252, 306, 345, 368, 380, 495, 498, 558

Appleton's Popular Science Monthly, 405

Arcanum Hall (Allston, Mass.), 155

Arkell, A. H., 389

Armfield, John, 48

Armfield and Franklin, 48, 569 (n. 11)

Armstrong, Samuel, 257, 596 (n. 14)

Arnett, Benjamin W., Jr., 183–89, 586 (n. 67)

Arnold, Benedict, 21

Artist, Guitar, and Mandolin Club (Boston, Mass.), 259

Association for the Study of Negro Life and History, 448, 490

Asylum of the Children of the Holy Family (New Orleans, La.), 196

Atlanta, Ga., 185, 272, 400, 438, 452, 457, 460, 463, 464, 465, 487, 552, 556

Atlanta Constitution, 188, 586–87 (n. 71), 587 (n. 82)

Atlanta Exposition, 179, 452, 552

Atlanta Riot, 463

Atlanta University, 409, 468, 470, 486, 525, 556, 587 (n. 82)

Atlantic Monthly, 278, 282, 292, 325, 415

Attucks, Crispus, 521, 615 (n. 25)

Auber, Daniel-François-Esprit, 80

Auber Quartet, 81–82, 87, 91, 574 (n. 27)

Auburn, N.Y., 303, 489

August 1 anniversary, 149, 471

Augustine, St., 205

Australia, 81, 156

Ayer, Mass., 150

Bahamas, 521

Bailey, Parker, 91, 577 (n. 60)

Baker, Elizabeth, 312

Bakwena peoples, 481

Baldwin, Maria, 181, 306, 496, 613 (n. 7)

Balgarnie, Florence, 170

Baltimore, Md., 76, 235, 319, 352, 537

Baltimore Afro-American, 532

Banneker, Benjamin, 304

Bannister, Edward, 59

Bannister family, 57

Baptist Church (Exeter, N.H.), 227

Barber, Jesse, 460

Cambridge Latin School, 521
Cambridge Relief Hospital, 531
Camp Dexter (Providence, R.I.), 55
Campos, Pedro Albizu, 512, 513, 519, 628-29 (n. 22)
Canaan, N.H., 94
Canada, 25-26, 53, 55, 109, 110, 134, 135, 311, 371, 379, 507, 544
Candace, 388, 399
Canton, Mass., 432
Cape Colony, 545
Caribbean, 432. *See also* West Indies
Carlier, Auguste, 43
Carlisle, James H., 336
Carlyle, Thomas, 294-95, 417
Carnegie, Andrew, 487
Carolina Spartan, 336
Carter, Leigh, 528
Carter, Maria, 528
Carter, Robert W., 278-79
Cary, Charles C., 111
Cary, Mary Ann Shadd, 306, 308, 519
Catholicism, 193, 194-96, 199, 200, 205-7, 213-16, 218
Central America, 250
Central Square (Cambridge, Mass.), 254
Century Magazine, 405
Channing, William Ellery, 294
Chapelle, Lillian, 497
Chapman, Ida, 508
Chapman, Mary Weston, 88
Chapman Hall (Boston, Mass.), 58
Charles, Josephine, 195
Charles River, 65, 390
Charles II (England), 235
Charles Street African Methodist Episcopal Church (Boston, Mass.), 165, 172
Charleston, S.C., 63, 296, 325, 332, 333-37, 339, 343, 350, 365, 462, 556
Charlestown, Mass., 68, 229, 230, 231, 311
Charlestown Navy Yard, 64
Charlestown Seminary (Charlestown, Mass.), 312
Chase, Morris, 528
Chehaw, Ala., 503
Chelsea, Mass., 230-31, 290, 500, 501, 534
Cheney, Ednah Dow, 181, 182
Chesapeake Bay, 353

Chesnutt, Charles, 278, 285-86, 288, 325, 326, 362, 409, 489, 491
Chester County, S.C., 460
Chesterfield County, Va., 261
Cheves, James M., 37
Chicago, Ill., 111, 112, 279, 400, 402, 516, 527, 556
Chicago Advance, 400
Chicago Conference on Africa (1893), 399-402
Chicago Defender, 521
Chicago Tribune, 417
Chickering Hall (Boston, Mass.), 180, 181, 182, 184
Child, Lydia Maria, 169, 285, 294, 306, 314, 372, 442, 444
Chowan, N.C., 235
Christian Science, 540
Christie, Agatha, 364
Christy, E. P., 97
Christy Minstrels, 97
Chronicles of Carlingford, The, 374-75
Church, Mary. *See* Terrell, Mary Church
Church of England, 222
Cincinnati, 136
Civil Rights Act (1875), 480, 541
Civil War, 5, 14, 42, 96, 109, 110, 134, 137, 230, 231, 250, 260, 261, 314, 326, 327, 330, 333, 335, 343, 356, 365, 404, 420, 469, 475, 489, 495, 519; African American soldiers and, 6, 62, 102, 150, 257, 308, 413, 423, 489, 517-18
Clarkson, Thomas, 245
Clark University, 468
Clay, Henry, 236
Clement, Edward H., 180
Cleveland, Grover, 165, 439
Cleveland Gazette, 255
Clipper, The, 101
Coenties Slip (New York, N.Y.), 449
Cole, Bob, 117
Cole, Thomas, 498
Colenso, Bishop, 400
Coleridge, Samuel, 59
Coley, Malcolm, 531, 630 (nn. 10, 11)
Coley, Paul, 531, 630 (n. 11)
College of Justice (Scotland), 559
Collins, Wilkie, 91

Crane, Stephen, 354
Crane, Winthrop Murray, 316
Cranford, Alfred, 188
Cranford, Mrs., 188
Crawford, J. H., 111, 116
Crimean War, 356
Crisis, The, 109, 285, 412, 433, 484, 496,
    503, 504, 532-33
Crittenden, John J., 342
Cromwell, Gertrude, 511-12
Cromwell, William, L., 512
Crummell, Alexander, 174, 400
Cuba, 111, 180, 181, 432, 433, 434, 456
Cuggo, Canada, 25
Cullen, Countee, 412
Cullen, Thomas, 235
Cummings, Henry, 43, 568 (n. 30)
Curaçao, 296
Curley, James Michael, 529
Cush, Kingdom of, 388
Cushman, Charlotte, 75
Cutler family: Dorothy Paul, 498; John B.,
    498; Tobias, 60, 498
Cuvier, Georges, 396
C. W. Durant Sugar Refinery (New York,
    N.Y.), 450

Dallas Express, 455
Danehy, Timothy T. A., 500
Danks, Hart Pease, 89, 576-77 (n. 54)
Dark Blue, 417
Darling, Grace, 303
Dartmouth College, 13, 339
Darwin, Charles, 354
David, 399
Davis, Jefferson, 61, 337, 339-40, 341,
    343-44
Davis, Varina, 340
Dawes, Henry, 368
Dawes Act, 368-69
Dawsey, Elizabeth, 65
Day, August, 521
Deamus, George, 151
De Bériot, Charles, 114, 115
Debs, Eugene, 527
Declaration of Independence, 66, 330
De Courcy, Mr., 79
Deep Creek, Va., 260

De Gromes, Mr., 79, 80
Delany, Martin, 335, 389, 402, 475
Delille, Henriette, 195, 210, 218, 587 (n. 9)
Democracy in America, 327
Democratic Party, 102, 106, 335, 339, 342,
    520
De Mortie family: Cordelia, 56, 516;
    Louise, 519; Mark, 56, 66, 495, 515-19
De Salas, Claudio José Domingo Brindis,
    111, 140
Detiege, Sister, 212
Devereaux, Frances Edwards Pollock, 236
Devereaux, John, 236
DeWolfe family, 36
Dialect, 126-30, 133, 138
Dickens, Charles, 75, 281, 542, 543
District of Columbia, 47, 48-54
Divorce, 42-44
Dixon, Thomas, 529
Dixon, William T., 448
Dodson, Lillian, 446
Dodson family: Nathaniel, 447; Nathaniel
    Barnett, 444-49, 452-53, 486, 487,
    555, 557, 620 (n. 12); Owen, 447, 620
    (n. 16); Sarah Elizabeth Goode, 444-49,
    490, 620 (nn. 12, 16)
Domesticity, 119, 124-25, 134, 202, 258,
    307, 322, 523
Dominican Republic, 496
Donizetti, Gaetano, 80
Dorcas Home Missionary Society, 490,
    491
Dorchester, Mass., 529
D'Ormy, Josephine, 72
Doten, Lizzie, 199, 393, 588 (n. 27)
Doubleday and Page, 453,
Douglas, Stephen A., 339, 342
Douglass, Charles, 489
Douglass, Frederick, 18, 51, 62, 87, 174,
    241, 249, 250, 279, 285, 288, 300, 306,
    316, 324, 342, 370, 381, 489, 494, 553
Douglass, Margaret, 260
Douglass Street (Brooklyn, N.Y.), 552
Dover, N.H., 22
Downing, George T., 56
Dred Scott, 96
Dreiser, Theodore, 354
Drury Lane, 59

Mecklenburg County, N.J., 258
Medfield State Hospital (Medfield, Mass.),
521–22
Melancholia, 313, 327, 380, 387, 390, 393,
394, 397, 482
Melville, Herman, 450
Memoir of James Jackson, 31, 32, 398. *See
also* Paul family: Susan
Memorial Day, 164, 165, 489–90
Memphis, Tenn., 219, 411
Mencken, H. L., 412
Mendelssohn, Felix, 85
Menelik, 388, 434
Menken, Adah Isaacs, 76, 574 (n. 12)
Men of Mark, 504
Merchant of Venice, 88, 385, 474
Mermaid Club (Cambridge, Mass.), 415
Meroe, 387–89, 391, 397, 398, 611 (n. 6)
Merrimac, 21, 260
Merritt, Emma F. G., 483
Mesmerism, 264, 393
Messenger, The, 503, 556, 627–28 (n. 3)
Metropolitan Theater (Milwaukee, Wis.),
113
Mexican Republic, 97
Mexican War, 89, 92, 94–98, 102, 103,
104, 382, 577–78 (n. 72)
Mexico, 94, 95, 96, 105, 503
Mexico City, 98
Michigan, 112
Middle Passage, 216, 300, 382, 392
Migration, 253, 254, 273, 448. *See also*
Great Migration
Miles, George, 500
Millard, Harrison, 82
Miller, Kelly, 255, 409, 413, 466, 468, 491,
546, 547
Milton, John, 326, 332, 338–39, 352, 353
Milwaukee, Wis., 111, 113–14, 115
Milwaukee Sentinel, 114
Milwaukee Theater, 113
Mingall, Georgeanna, 66
Mink, Alice, 111
Minneapolis, Minn., 111, 114, 115–16
Minneapolis Tribune, 113, 115, 116
Minnesota, 112
Minot, Harriet, 40

Minstrelsy, 99–102, 111, 114, 116, 117,
119, 129, 142, 143, 145
Miscegenation, 75, 185
Mississippi, 127, 135, 307, 428
Mississippi River, 128, 142, 350
Missouri, 51, 112, 113, 344, 368, 531
Missouri Compromise, 97, 369
Missouri Press Association, 170
Mitchell, Charles, 423
Mitchell, Nellie B., 423–24, 499
Mobile, Ala., 63
Mob rule, 142, 162, 192, 272, 280, 330
Mob violence, 38, 40, 164–65, 174, 180,
185–86, 219, 255, 267, 324, 585–86 (n. 8)
Modern Instance, A, 415
Modjeska, Helena, 358, 617 (n. 58)
Mohawk tribe (French), 22
Monroe, James, 52
Monrovia, Liberia, 387
Montcalm, Louis-Joseph de, 23–24
Montfort, Joseph, 233
Monticello, 413, 614–15 (n. 21)
Montreal, 544
Moore, Alonzo, 345
Moore, Frederick Randolph, 426, 435–41,
444, 452, 453, 454, 456, 460, 465, 466–
67, 468, 485, 486, 551, 552–53, 555–56,
619 (nn. 118, 119)
Moore, Thomas, 48
Morales, Mr., 551
Morehead, J. I., 513
Morel, Edmund Dené, 434
Morgan, Clement G., 179, 316, 408, 496
Morgan, Mrs. Clement G., 496
Morgan, John Pierpont, 450
Morning Telegraph (New York, N.Y.), 450
Morris, Cummono, 300
Morris, Elizabeth, 508
Morris, Emery T., 179, 496, 507–8, 513,
627 (n. 22)
Morris, Freddie, 531
Morris, George, 156
Morris, Robert, 65, 291, 292, 300, 500,
507
Morris, William, 417
Morris Brown College, 470
Morris-Gordon, Emery T., 511–12

Shadrach, J. Shirley, 203, 376, 469, 524.
  See also Hopkins, Pauline
Shakespeare, William, 385, 473, 474–75
Sharp, Daniel, 296
Sharp, Jane E., 19, 387, 611 (n. 1)
Shaw, Robert Gould, 187, 443, 489, 517
Shaw University, 259, 597 (n. 26)
Shaw Veteran Association (Boston, Mass.),
  489
Sherman, William Tecumseh, 443
Sherry's Restaurant (New York, N.Y.),
  471
Short View of Great Questions, 426
Sierra Leone, 481
Sierra Leone News, 400
Simmons, Roscoe Conklin, 441, 455–56,
  486, 552, 555–56, 622–23 (n. 57)
Simms, Anne Elizabeth Smith, 529, 530
Simms, Edith, 530
Simms, Edward Paul, 530
Simms, Tessie, 530
Simonds, George, 151, 152
Sisters of St. Margaret (Boston, Mass.),
  200
Sisters of the Holy Family (New Orleans,
  La.), 194–96, 210–16, 218, 590 (n. 76)
16 and L Street School (Washington,
  D.C.), 365
Skeete, Alexander, 324
Slater Fund for Negro Education, 184
Slavery, 27, 42–43, 45, 47–51, 52, 53, 58,
  61, 95–97, 131, 179, 220, 263, 298, 306,
  315, 327, 345–50, 368–70, 481, 520;
  abolition of, 110, 515; artistic and literary critiques of, 31, 79, 95–97, 102–4,
  127, 152; Bermuda and, 242–43, 244–
  45; British abolition of, 149, 222, 471;
  Canada and, 25; concubinage and, 122,
  204–5; District of Columbia and, 48–54;
  history of, 142; Hopkins family and, 45,
  46–47, 69, 146, 252; mammy figure in,
  124–25; marriage and, 110–11, 118–19,
  120–23, 126–28, 137, 151, 232; Mexican War and expansion of, 94, 97, 104;
  New England and, 7, 20–22, 26; New
  Hampshire and, 20–22, 27–28, 302,
  329; North Carolina and, 236–38, 240–
  42; Northup family and, 35–36; Paul

family and, 20–21, 25, 31, 291; Pauline
  Hopkins on, 2, 4, 19, 109–38, 139, 142,
  144–45, 150–51, 160, 162, 163, 192–93,
  196, 219, 221–23, 231–32, 243–45, 291,
  298–300, 302–4, 306, 310, 321–22,
  327–50, 367–70, 379, 382, 388, 392–
  93, 540; plays about, 75, 110, 117–18;
  postbellum representations of, 142–44;
  Rhode Island and, 35–36, 38–39, 240,
  302; slave trade, 2, 7, 14, 20–21, 28,
  47–49, 50, 97, 104, 121, 185, 234, 240,
  244–45, 248, 298, 302, 344, 345–50,
  563 (n. 1); South Carolina and, 334, 336,
  460; Underground Railroad and, 110;
  in United States, 2, 163; Virginia and,
  47–49
Small, Maynard, and Company, 287, 288
Smalls, Robert, 350
Smiles, Samuel, 426, 428, 470, 548
Smith, Albreta Moore, 275, 279, 599
  (n. 87)
Smith, Gerrit, 87
Smith, Howard H., 429
Smith, Jennie, 111
Smith, John J., 65, 179
Smith, Orlando, 426
Smith, Peter, 432, 547, 618 (n. 100)
Smith, Wilford, 465, 552
Smith Court Church (Boston, Mass.), 498.
  See also African Baptist Church
Smith family: Anne Catherine Paul, 83,
  201, 531, 563 (n. 4) (*see also* Paul family:
  Anne Catherine); Elijah Sr., 60, 79,
  84, 201, 563 (n. 4); Elijah Jr., 9, 45, 60,
  70, 71, 81–88, 89–91, 95, 98, 102, 103,
  106–7, 141, 146, 159, 167, 172, 179,
  181, 193, 201, 228, 250–51, 285, 289,
  501, 507, 531, 563 (n. 4), 574 (n. 27), 575
  (n. 39), 575–76 (n. 42); Eliza Riley, 172,
  529, 563 (n. 4) (*see also* Smith family:
  Elijah Jr.); George Boyer, 563 (n. 4);
  Hannah, 315, 496; Harriet, 172, 259,
  496, 597 (n. 30); Susan Paul, 250, 563
  (n. 4); Thomas Paul, 563 (n. 4)
Snelling, Caroline, 429, 544
Snowden, Rev. Samuel, 13
Snow Town riot, 38
Socialism, 540

White House, 492, 529

White Nile, 389

White Rose Mission (New York, N.Y.),
176

Whitfield family: Dorothy (Dolly), 15, 19;
Elizabeth, 223, 226, 227, 248-49; James
Monroe, 17, 18, 125, 227, 248, 249, 289,
290, 370, 402, 475, 494, 610 (n. 9);
Joseph Sr., 192-93, 224, 226-27, 370;
Joseph Jr., 227, 517-18; Nancy Paul, 370

Whittier, John Greenleaf, 285, 313, 314-15

Wilberforce Settlement, 245

Wilberforce University, 432, 468

Wilcox, Ella Wheeler, 413, 521, 526, 546

Wilder, David, 285

Wilkes, Sam, 188, 587 (n. 82)

Willard, John D., 499

Willard, Judge, 43

Willard, Paul, 42, 567 (n. 22)

William Lloyd Garrison Memorial Church
(Roxbury, Mass.), 412

William Lloyd Garrison Society (Boston,
Mass.), 165

Williams, Bert, 117

Williams, Captain, 180

Williams, Fannie Barrier, 467, 468

Williams, Fred, 162

Williams, George Washington, 389, 403

Williams, Henry Sylvester, 400

Williams, Lillie, 111

Williams, Marie Selika, 76

Williams, S., 151, 152

Williams College, 257

Wilmington, N.C., 233

Wilson, Butler R., 179, 408, 429, 497

Wilson, Mrs. Butler, 180, 181, 182, 423

Wilson, Mrs. D., 82

Wilson, Harriet, 303

Wilson, Henry, 50

Wilson, Woodrow, 411, 503, 526, 529

Winnisimet. *See* Chelsea, Mass.

Winterbotham, W., 232

Winters, Mrs. S. J., 444

Wisconsin, 512

Wolff, James H., 423, 424, 496, 547

Wolff, Mary, 424

Wolo, Plenyono Gbe, 401, 512, 513, 519,
521, 628 (n. 19)

Woman's Era, The, 170, 181, 274

Woman's Era Club (Boston, Mass.), 181,
194, 275, 309, 314

Woman's Journal, 8

Women of Distinction, 309

Women's Christian Temperance Union,
490

Women's club movement, 3, 5, 6, 15, 19,
169-77, 178, 194, 201-16, 304, 512

Women's Relief Corps, 15, 150, 164, 178

Worcester, Mass., 82

Wordsworth, William, 59, 294, 474

Work of the Afro-American Woman, The,
402. *See also* Mossell, Gertrude Bustill

World Peace Jubilee, 72, 75, 81

World War I, 513, 527, 528, 530

World War II, 531, 630 (n. 10)

Wright, Carroll Davidson, 166

Yakima War (1855), 371

Yale Divinity School, 464

Yale University, 92, 462

Yates, Josephine Silone, 467

Yeaton, William, 47

YMCA Training School (Springfield,
Mass.), 285

Yonkers, N.Y., 429

Young Men's Christian Association
(Brooklyn, N.Y.), 453, 486, 555-56

Young's Hotel (Boston, Mass.), 179, 507